SEARCHING FOR PEACE
IN CENTRAL AND SOUTH ASIA

A project of the European Centre for Conflict Prevention
(Utrecht, the Netherlands) in cooperation with the
Center for Conflict Management (Almaty, Kazakhstan),
the Institute for Peace and Conflict Studies (New Delhi, India),
and the International Center for Peace Initiatives (New Delhi, India).

Financially supported by the Ministries of Foreign Affairs
of the Netherlands, Austria, and Canada, the
Department for International Development of the United Kingdom,
and the Sasakawa Peace Foundation (Tokyo, Japan).

SEARCHING FOR PEACE IN CENTRAL AND SOUTH ASIA

An Overview of Conflict Prevention and Peacebuilding Activities

edited by
Monique Mekenkamp, Paul van Tongeren,
and Hans van de Veen

LYNNE
RIENNER
PUBLISHERS

BOULDER
LONDON

Published in the United States of America in 2002 by
Lynne Rienner Publishers, Inc.
1800 30th Street, Boulder, Colorado 80301
www.rienner.com

and in the United Kingdom by
Lynne Rienner Publishers, Inc.
3 Henrietta Street, Covent Garden, London WC2E 8LU

Library of Congress Cataloging-in-Publication Data
Mekenkamp, Monique.
    Searching for peace in Central and South Asia : an overview of conflict
    prevention and peacebuilding activities / Monique Mekenkamp, Paul
    van Tongeren, and Hans van de Veen.
    Includes bibliographical references and index.
    ISBN 1-58826-096-8 (hc : alk. paper) — ISBN 1-58826-072-0 (pbk. : alk. paper)
    1. Pacific settlement of international disputes. 2. Peaceful change (International
relations) 3. Confidence and security building measures (International relations)
4. Reconciliation. 5. Conflict management. 6. Asia, Central—Politics and government.
7. South Asia—Politics and government. I. Mekenkamp, Monique. II. Tongeren,
Paul van. III. Veen, Hans van de.
JZ5597 .S43 2002
327.1'72—dc21   2002017882

British Cataloguing in Publication Data
A Cataloguing in Publication record for this book
is available from the British Library.

Printed and bound in the United States of America

        The paper used in this publication meets the requirements
    ∞ of the American National Standard for Permanence of
        Paper for Printed Library Materials Z39.48-1984.

    5 4 3 2 1

Contents

Foreword, Barnett R. Rubin   ix
Acknowledgments   xi

Introduction, *Monique Mekenkamp, Paul van Tongeren,*
    and Hans van de Veen   1

Part I Reflections
1   Making Our Way Back to Humanity: Beyond 11 September   9
     John Paul Lederach
2   Mapping the Dimensions of Contemporary Conflicts
     and Human Rights Violations   17
     Berto J. Jongman
3   Calling for a Broad Approach to Conflict Resolution   29
     Hugh Miall, Oliver Ramsbotham, and Tom Woodhouse
4   Positive Vibrations: Successes Large and Small   35
     Jim Wake
5   Lessons Learned from Ten Years of Experience
     in Conflict Prevention   47
     Jos Havermans

Part 2 Surveys of Conflict Prevention and
        Peacebuilding Activities
6   Central Asia   65
    6.1   Regional Introduction: A Host of Preventable Conflicts,
         John Schoeberlein   66
    6.2   Policy Recommendations: Some Strategies for Stability,
         Anara Tabyshalieva   76
    6.3   Bones of Contention: Conflicts over Resources,
         John Schoeberlein   85
    6.4   Islamic Militancy: Religion and Conflict, *Olivier Roy*   97
    6.5   Afghanistan: The Challenge of "Winning the Peace,"
         Mohammed Haneef Atmar and Jonathan Goodhand   109

6.6   The Ferghana Valley: In the Midst of a Host of Crises,
        Randa M. Slim   141
6.7   Tajikistan: From Civil War to Peacebuilding,
        Randa M. Slim and Faredun Hodizoda   168
6.8   Uzbekistan: Authoritarianism and Conflict, *David Lewis*   188

7   South Asia   209
7.1   Forging New Solidarities: Nonofficial Dialogues,
        Navnita Chadha Behera   210
7.2   The Need for Confidence-Building Measures, *P. R. Chari*   237
7.3   Border Conflicts and Regional Disputes, *Sushil K. Pillai* 249
7.4   Protecting the Victims of Forced Migration:
        Mixed Flows and Massive Flows, *Ranabir Samadar*   267
7.5   Water-Related Conflicts: Factors, Aspects, Issues,
        Ramaswamy R. Iyer   277
7.6   Understanding Religious Conflicts, *Rajmohan Gandhi*   291
7.7   Bangladesh: Indigenous Struggle in the Chittagong Hill
        Tracts, *Jenneke Arens and Kirti Nishan Chakma*   304
7.8   India   325
        7.8.1   Multiculturalism in India: Diverse Dots in a
                 Multiple Mosaic, *N. Manoharan* 326
        7.8.2   Religious Conflict: A Brief Survey of the
                 Hindu-Muslim Problem, *Asghar Ali Engineer* 336
        7.8.3   Demands for Autonomy: Internal Weaknesses of a
                 Multiethnic, Multicultural, and Multinational State,
                 Ashok Behuria 345
        7.8.4   The Background to the Violent Conflicts in India,
                 Kristoffel Lieten 357
        7.8.5   Jammu and Kashmir: Half a Century of Conflict,
                 Kristoffel Lieten 362
        7.8.6   The Naxalite Movement, *Suba Chandran and
                 Mallika Joseph* 382
        7.8.7   Caste Violence and Class in Bihar: The Ranvir Sena,
                 Suba Chandran and Alok Kumar Gupta 395
        7.8.8   Multiple Conflicts in Northeast India,
                 Kristoffel Lieten 407
7.9   Nepal: Maoist Insurgency Against Lopsided
        Development, *Kristoffel Lieten*   433
7.10   Pakistan   447
        7.10.1   An Introduction to Pakistan's Ethnic and Religious
                 Conflicts, *Farhan Hanif Siddiqi* 448
        7.10.2   The Sindhi-Mohajir Conflict, *Moonis Ahmar* 452
        7.10.3   Fratricidal Conflict Between Pakistan's Shias and
                 Sunnis, *Karan R. Sawhny and Nidhi Narain* 465
7.11   Sri Lanka: Finding a Negotiated End to Twenty-Five
        Years of Violence, *Nick Lewer and Joe William*   483

Part 3 Directory

Introduction to the Directory   505
Australia 507
Austria 509
Bangladesh 509
Belgium 515
Canada 516
Denmark 517
France 517
Hong Kong 518
India 518
Indonesia 540
Japan 541
Kazakhstan 543
Kyrgyzstan 546
Malaysia 552
Nepal 552
The Netherlands 562
Pakistan 565
Sri Lanka 576
Sweden 587
Switzerland 588
Tajikistan 591
Thailand 599
United Kingdom 600
United States 608
Uzbekistan 617

Internet Resources   619
Selected Bibliography   629
Subject Index   639
Index of Organizations   657
About the Searching for Peace Program   663
About the Book   665

Foreword

Barnett R. Rubin

With its previous guides to global resources on the prevention of violent conflict and its unique, in-depth handbooks on Africa and Europe and Eurasia, the European Centre for Conflict Prevention has already established itself as one of the world's most important and reliable sources of usable knowledge for conflict prevention.

Those earlier efforts dealt with the regions most familiar to students and practitioners of post–Cold War conflict prevention and preventive diplomacy: sub-Saharan Africa and the postcommunist states of Europe. With a timeliness its editors and authors could not have foreseen, this new volume adds to those earlier indispensable ones with contributions on the region that the events of 11 September 2001 and their aftermath have catapulted to the center of global attention.

Before that time, Central and South Asia still seemed marginal to most actors preoccupied with the big issues of the global arena. But the experience with conflict analysis and early warning of those scholars and practitioners represented in this work led them to focus on problems whose neglect turned out to be far more costly than even the most insistent of warnings ever anticipated.

One of the principal lessons of these recent events is familiar to specialists in conflict prevention: in a world where networks of communication, exchange, and travel are ever more extensive and closely knit, even small conflicts can expand in unpredictable ways. Who would have predicted that the long-standing conflict in Afghanistan, a seemingly humanitarian problem without major strategic importance, would interact with conflicts in the Persian Gulf, Israel-Palestine, Kashmir, and Central Asia in such a way as to lead to the most violent attack ever on U.S. soil, threaten nuclear war on the subcontinent, and transform the strategic map of much of the world?

For years, however, conflict analysts have been mapping out the networks through which these interactions occur. *Searching for Peace in Africa* and its sequel on Europe and Eurasia showed how both continents contained subregions, such as the Horn of Africa, the Great Lakes, West Africa, the Balkans, and the Caucasus, where sets of conflicts interacted with and reinforced each other. The work on resource flows in both of these books—on diamonds, oil, and small arms in particular—showed how these regional networks were in turn linked to global ones. The current volume shows again how conflicts over resources, identity, and competing notions of justice can cross borders to destabilize whole regions and threaten the lives and livelihoods of millions of people. That the conflicts in this region ultimately killed even people living far away in the world's most powerful and best-defended state shows only that these regional conflict formations are parts of global networks of violence.

But the European Centre is dedicated above all not to documenting and explaining violence, but to preventing it. In publications such as *People Building Peace* and in its conferences and consultations, this organization has demonstrated that global citizens acting together can use knowledge such as that communicated in works like this both to prevent the escalation of violence and to transform the conditions that sometimes make violence nearly ineluctable.

As the European Centre and its partners have shown, the formation of strategic alliances among groups in different parts of the globe is key to effective preventive action. Actors and organizations with different sources of knowledge, relationships with different groups involved in actual or potential conflict, and influence over different centers of power can form networks of cooperation. The information that the centre's publications provide about both grassroots and elite-based organizations in each region it studies has proved an indispensable resource for those working to form and strengthen these networks, even as the analytical chapters help provoke dialogues about strategy and tactics among partners with different perspectives and priorities.

Searching for Peace in Central and South Asia arrived too late to help prevent the events of 11 September 2001, and all the suffering and violence that preceded and followed them. But as international actors seek to move beyond war in Afghanistan to genuine peacebuilding, as they struggle to assure that the struggle against terrorism addresses the sources of violence rather than endorsing further repression, the lessons, analyses, and resources contained in this work are likely to prove even more widely needed than its publishers could have anticipated.

Barnett R. Rubin, director of studies at the Center on International Cooperation, New York University (www.cic.nyu.edu), was formerly director of the Center for Preventive Action, Council on Foreign Relations.

Acknowledgments

This publication is an outcome of the Searching for Peace in Asia and the Pacific project of the European Centre for Conflict Prevention. It results from the contributions of many people from Asia, Europe, and the United States who provided advice and support in developing the project, participated in seminars, gave feedback on the draft texts, and contributed chapters to the book. Without their help, the publication would not have been possible. Here we would like to express our gratitude for this constructive cooperation.

We are indebted to the Ministries of Foreign Affairs of Austria, Canada, and the Netherlands, the Department for International Development of the United Kingdom, and the Sasakawa Peace Foundation, Japan, for providing the financial support for this project.

Searching for Peace in Asia and the Pacific is part of a continuous effort of the European Centre to produce overviews of conflict prevention and peacebuilding initiatives in the main conflict areas in the world. The Asia and Pacific project started in January 2000 with preliminary research done by the staff of the European Centre.

A seminar on the "Role of NGOs in Conflict Prevention" organized by the Japan Institute for International Affairs (JIIA) and the Japan Centre for Preventive Diplomacy (JCPD) in June 2000 in Tokyo helped us in further shaping the Asia and Pacific project, and some critical decisions for additional developments were made. Cooperation was discussed and developed with many participants. During the seminar we consolidated partnerships with two organizations that are based in New Delhi, India: the Institute for Peace and Conflict Studies and the International Centre for Peace Initiatives. We also developed a further partnership with the Japanese NGOs, JIIA and JCPD. We would like to thank the participants for their input: Kamarulzaman Askander, Sathivale Balakrishnan, Ashok Behuria, Maureen Belen-Loste, Somri Berger, Therese Bouchard, P. R. Chari, Kevin Clements, Tyrol Ferdinands, Owen Green, Chira Hongladarom, Esmeraldo B. Lampauog, Sandra Melone, Ben Reilly, Elena Sadovskaya, Ajai Sahni, and Karan Sawhny.

We decided to divide the Asia and Pacific project into several regions, first focusing on Central and South Asia, followed by Southeast and East Asia and the Pacific. The Southeast and East Asia and the Pacific project is planned for completion in mid-2003.

The chapters and surveys are written by practitioners and scholars with long-term expertise on the specific conflict or issue. Some of them write on conflicts in the area where they live, others write on conflicts and issues in which they have gained extensive experience from working and/or researching them. We greatly appreciate the authors' outstanding efforts in presenting a balanced view of conflicts in which they are sometimes, inevitably, involved. We hope their analysis will help a wide audience to better understand the situation. All authors had their draft texts reviewed by a broadly composed group of experts and practitioners. In particular we would like to thank the following people for comments and suggestions: Sunila Abeysekera, Imtiaz Ahmed, Naeem Ahmed, Sathivale Balakrishnan, Sunil Bastian, Paul Beersmans, Nayana Bose, Brian Cloughley, Mohammed EhsanZia, Alexander Evans, Shiva Hari Dahal, Dipak Gupta, Meghna Guhathakurta, Dipak Gyawali, Mukul Hazarika, Sanjoy Hazarika, Maya John Ingty, Peter Kuperus, Luingam Luithui, William Maley, Rita Manchanda, Amena Mohsin, Joseph Montville, M. A. Raina, Ahmed Rashid, Devasish Roy, Barnett Rubin, Ajit Rupasinghe, Teresita Schaffer, Willem van Schendel, Susanne Schmeidel, Farhan Hanif Siddiqi, Kingsley de Silva, Marcel Smits, Father Timm, Michael Walt van Praag, Frans Welman, Elizabeth Winter, and Iftekhar Zaman.

We are very grateful for the willingness and flexibility shown by all authors in revising and updating their texts in a short time frame. When, in the course of the process, we concluded that some additional texts were needed and some surveys needed to be rewritten, Kristoffel Lieten from the Asia Studies Department at Amsterdam University helped produce these texts. We are very thankful to him.

In addition to sending the drafts to many resource persons, we also organized several meetings bringing together practitioners, scholars, and experts to discuss the draft texts. The purpose was to ensure the accuracy and objectivity of the analysis in the surveys, and the meetings proved to be very useful. Local input was further ensured by this consultative process.

Together with the Institute of Peace and Conflict Studies (IPCS), we organized a three-day seminar in New Delhi in 2001 to discuss the draft texts of the surveys and issue-based articles on India. Valuable input was given and we gained many more insights in the issues and conflicts in India. We are thankful for your input and comments: Asghar Ali Engineer, Kanti Bajpaj, Ashok Behuria, Navnita Chadha Behera, P. R. Chari, Suba Chandran, Meenakshi Gopinath, Ramaswamy R. Iyer, Mallika Joseph, Ravi Kant, Alok Kumar Gupta, Arun Kumar, Pramod Kumar, N. Manoharan, Amitabh Matoo, Riyaz Punjabi, Ajai Sahni, Karan Sawhny, Dilip Simeon, and Kamal Singh. We are extremely grateful to the staff of the IPCS, P. R. Chari, Suba Chandran, and Mallika Joseph, for their efforts in coorganizing this meeting. Following the seminar in Delhi, we also had a similar three-day event in Colombo, Sri Lanka, where we discussed drafts of the other conflict surveys on South Asia. Many of the authors were present at this seminar, which was coorganized by the Inter-Religious Peace Foundation. Freddy de Alwis was extremely helpful in setting up and managing this seminar. We greatly appreciate the feedback, input, and presentations of the participants and authors: Moonis Ahmar, Ariyaratne, Mustafa Aziz, S. Balakrishnan, Sunil Bastian, Tapan K. Bose, Suba Chandran, Rev. Freddy de Alwis, Rev. Prince Devanandan, Tyrol Ferdinands, Fr. Oswald B. Firth, Abdur Rob Khan, Nick Lewer, I. A. Rehman, Victor Robinson, Ajit Rupashinghe, Karan Sawhny, Gopal Siwakoti Chintan, Ven Madampegama Assaji Nayake Thero, Joe William, and Sherine Xavier.

At the end of November 2001, we organized a regional seminar in Almaty, Kazakhstan, bringing together almost thirty participants from the five Central Asian republics to discuss the potential role of NGOs in peacebuilding and conflict prevention. We are grateful for the beneficial input from the participants on the texts dealing with Central Asia. The lively discussions ensured an actual input from the region and an up-to-date view of the situation. Among the many to whom our gratitude is due, we would particularly like to give thanks for their useful input to Mavlyuda Abduhalimova, Atirkul Alicheva, Akmal Gafurov, Gulnoz Hidoyatova, Abdudjabor Hotamov, Raya Kadyrova, Alla Kuvatova, Mariya Lisizina, Ahmet Muradov, Rano Kuldasheva, Madina Najimova, Parviz Mullodjanov, Azizi Rahimulla, Dodarbek Saidaliev, Igor Savin, John Schoeberlein, Olga Sosnina, Elena Voronina, Evgeni Zhovtis, and Tatyana Zlobina. We are very grateful to Svetlana Bekmambetova, Elena Sadovskaya, and Lada Zimina for the excellent coorganizing of this event.

We want to express our sincere gratitude to the Center for Conflict Management in Kazakhstan, in particular Lada Zimina and Elena Sadovskaya, for working extremely methodically to compile the directory of organizations for Central Asia. Without their invaluable collaboration it would not have been possible to provide profiles of organizations of this region that are not well known internationally. The directory profiles of South Asia were excellently compiled and arranged by Iris Wielders, based on continuous research and questionnaires. Her contribution has been crucial to the final product. The final profiles were written by Esther Bakker, Bas Jongerius, and Wang Hsu Oe.

The cooperation with the Bureau M&O–Environment and Development Productions in Amsterdam was fruitful and enjoyable. It again proved the key to success of the process and publication. Several journalists at the bureau provided an invaluable service in editing the chapters and surveys. We thank Bram Posthumus, Niall Martin, and Jim Wake. Karel Meyer of MMS Grafisch Werk developed all the maps.

Finally, this publication has been made possible only by the input of several of the staff members of the European Centre. Juliette Verhoeven, the project coordinator for the Europe and Eurasia project, also worked on the Central Asia section of this publication. Mats Lundstrom coordinated the development of articles and research into East Asian conflicts and issues. Furthermore, a number of interns have been constructive in research, assistance in organizing seminars, and support for the project and organization in general: Guidita Scordino, Peter Oehmen, Shiva Hari Dahal, Renske Heemskerk, Joost Janmaat, and Chikako Minei. From April until August 2001, Emmy Toonen put all her efforts and energy into assisting the project, followed by Iris Wielders from September until December. We are extremely grateful for their positive spirit and help during a difficult phase of the project. In the last phase of the making of this book, Pieter Schultz and Nicci Simmonds provided very useful support. Further we express our gratitude to Annelies Heijmans for her instrumental assistance in the final editing of this publication.

While thankful for all the support they have received, the editors assume full responsibility for this publication.

—*The Editors*

Introduction

Monique Mekenkamp, Paul van Tongeren & Hans van de Veen

Large parts of Central and South Asia are affected by wars and violent conflicts. Many of these conflicts have been analyzed thoroughly and much is known about their causes and the reasons for their escalation and violence. However, one of the main problems confronting people and organizations working for peace is the lack of information about the many initiatives that have been and are currently being undertaken. Nor is sufficient information available about the people and institutions that have gained expertise in specific conflicts or subregions. Furthermore, there is a rising tide of complaints about the flagrant lack of communication and coordination between organizations that in one way or another are involved in conflict prevention, conflict management, and/or peacebuilding—local and international, governmental and nongovernmental.

Searching for Peace in Central and South Asia is meant to meet these challenges. The main purpose of this publication is to fill the gaps in information, communication, and coordination. The ultimate aim is to contribute to a peaceful transformation of violent wars and conflicts in Central and South Asia.

At the start of the program in January 2000, several experts predicted a growth in conflicts in Asia, or at least in the intensity of the conflicts. Regrettably, this has been the case. Examples are the outbreak of violence during elections in Sri Lanka and the growing political dissent and armed conflict in Nepal between the government and the Maoists. The terrorist attack on New York City and the Pentagon on 11 September 2001, the war in Afghanistan, and the present unstable situation that followed have far-reaching consequences and impacts on Central Asia, as well as South Asia. This enormous area, with its many pressing problems, is certain to remain a focus of attention of the international community. There is a chance now that this will lead to positive developments of increased development aid, postwar reconstruction, and economic progress. To make this happen, today, more than ever, there is a need for increased efforts to prevent the escalation of existing conflicts, initiatives to manage and resolve conflicts, and efforts to build peace and stimulate reconciliation.

I

Worldwide attention focuses on those conflicts in the region that have immediate effects on the international situation and even threaten world peace: Afghanistan and Kashmir especially. The "war on terrorism" has also turned the spotlights on Central Asia; however, the focus is almost completely limited to the question of religious extremism. This publication not only deals at length with the root causes of present problems in Afghanistan, Pakistan, or Uzbekistan, but it also deals with much less well-known violent conflicts in India's Northeast, Bangladesh, and Nepal, to name just a few others. It also provides a wealth of information on transnational issues such as migration or conflicts over natural resources.

Internal conflicts aimed at political participation, autonomy, or straightforward separation of a specific region and its population are predominant. Many of those conflicts are the result of clashes between dominant ethnic majorities and underprivileged minorities: urban, rural, and "tribal." The emergence of religious fundamentalism in Central Asia as well as in large parts of South Asia is only one of the many threats to present and future communal relations.

Compared to other regions in the world, until 11 September 2001 there was not much interference from outside "peace seekers" in both Asian regions, be it on the (supra)national or the NGO level. Undoubtedly, this lack of international involvement in conflict prevention and conflict management was largely due to the characteristics of the many conflicts that were seen as largely "internal" affairs, resulting in a general lack of knowledge about the conflicts in the rest of the world. Furthermore, people in the region are very sensitive toward outside involvement—which is quite understandable in the light of their long and traumatic period of colonial occupation. However, these feelings could also be exploited by authoritarian regimes or opposition movements, allowing them to act as they liked.

Yet, it is civil society that is positioned to play an increasingly important role in this field. In many conflict situations, civil groups and institutions such as churches and women's groups have shown their ability to bring about conflict resolution and reconciliation at the community level. Business groups and scholarly institutions within civil society have also been actively studying and disseminating knowledge about ways to de-escalate violent conflicts. In several cases they have been supported by international NGOs that focus on conflict resolution. The role of nongovernmental organizations and local capacities for peace should therefore be strengthened and more attention should be put into these efforts.

Many more civilian actors, both inside and outside of the conflict zones, could be stimulated to engage themselves in the field of conflict prevention. By virtue of their nongovernmental and nonmilitary approaches, these actors from civil society are comparatively well placed to contribute to the resolution of violent conflicts vis-à-vis more formal and state-based institutions. But while the nevertheless essential contributions by states and multilateral agencies are discussed and coordinated in many networks and fora, the activities of

NGOs in this field are still much less systematically linked to each other and lack effective structures of mutual support.

This publication includes thirteen so-called Surveys of Conflict Prevention and Management Activities, which provide brief background analysis of the main violent conflicts in the region, an overview of the activities of key local and international actors to manage and transform the violent conflicts, and present prospects and recommendations. Service information, such as web sites, resource persons, literature, etc., will give the reader a further guide into the conflict issues. There is also a directory of 187 organizations involved in conflict prevention and peacebuilding activities in Central and South Asia.

This publication has been compiled by the European Centre for Conflict Prevention, an independent NGO with an overall objective of contributing to prevention and/or resolution of violent conflicts in the international arena. The Centre also acts as the secretariat of the European Platform for Conflict Prevention and Transformation and initiates, coordinates, and implements its activities. The European Platform for Conflict Prevention and Transformation was founded in 1997, and is currently an open network of more than 150 key organizations working in the field of prevention and resolution of violent conflicts in the international arena. Its mission is to facilitate the exchange of information and experience among participating organizations, as well as to stimulate cooperation and synergy.

The European Centre's main objectives are:

- To raise awareness of the importance and possibilities of conflict prevention and resolution through publications and media productions for a broad audience, and lobby activities aimed at governments and the European Union
- To raise knowledge of and insight into conflicts by producing surveys that describe the background and dynamics of conflicts and provide an overview per conflict of organizations active in the field of conflict prevention and resolution, and their activities
- To facilitate contacts, networking, and information exchange between organizations active in the field of conflict prevention and resolution in Europe and other parts of the world (information clearinghouse)

The Searching for Peace program, a multiannual regional program on prevention, management, and peacebuilding activities in violent conflicts, was designed to facilitate the sharing of knowledge and experience between organizations and to identify the main actors, experts, publications, and events in the relevant areas. The program had its first publication in October 1999 with *Searching for Peace in Africa—An Overview of Conflict Prevention and Management Activities.* February 2002 saw the launch of *Searching for Peace in Europe and Eurasia.* This publication, *Searching for Peace in Central and South Asia,* will shortly be followed by *Searching for Peace in Southeast and*

East Asia and the Pacific. Activities to compile this publication are in full swing.

The Searching for Peace program has a unique formula combining several objectives and results. It provides basic information on who does what and practical information about important publications, resource contacts, web sites, and data bases. It also offers insight into the varying approaches used in conflict prevention and management in different situations. This may help organizations to better attune and harmonize their activities, and work together in order to develop a more effective and fine-tuned policy. More importantly, it gives a voice to local/regional NGOs by working in cooperation with and drawing upon the expertise of local people. The directory, containing short profiles of the organizations working in this field, helps to expose less widely known local groups, not only to the international community but also to the local and regional NGOs. Furthermore, it promotes the development of often much-needed regional networks. The program moreover acts as a bridge between NGOs, networks, academic institutions, and resource persons, facilitates exchanges between these different actors, and brings them closer together. Finally, the policy seminars that are organized as a follow-up to the programs provide an opportunity to discuss efforts for effective conflict transformation and to develop concrete policy recommendations.

The program is coordinated by the European Centre. However, contributions, input, suggestions, and feedback are given by many people and institutions from all over the world. The Searching for Peace in Central and South Asia program should really be seen as a concerted effort of the European Centre, regional partner organizations, academic centers, and other institutes and NGOs in both regions.

The final selection of conflicts to be reported on, issues for more general articles, and suggestions for local and regional experts to guide us through the process of compiling the information were discussed at several preparatory meetings. Many of the conflict-prevention surveys and chapters were written by those regional experts, most of them working for universities, research institutes, or NGOs. Draft versions of the surveys and chapters were sent to, and commented upon by, many more resource persons and regional advisors. Furthermore, in May 2001 in Delhi, India, and Colombo, Sri Lanka, many of the authors and advisors gathered to discuss the draft texts. Following this meeting, the authors incorporated the relevant comments and suggestions in a final version. It was a sometimes difficult and challenging endeavor, but a rewarding one. We feel the result makes the effort more than worthwhile.

We would not have started this immense task without the sincere belief that there is a clear need for this kind of information. We sincerely hope that this project can act as a bridge between intergovernmental organizations, governments, NGOs, academic institutions, networks, and resource persons and serve the final objective of facilitating exchanges between these different groups and bringing them closer together, hopefully thereby contributing to lasting peace in many conflict-affected areas.

Monique Mekenkamp is coordinator of the Asia Program of the European Centre for Conflict Prevention (ECCP), based in Utrecht, the Netherlands. Paul van Tongeren is founder and executive director of ECCP. Hans van de Veen is senior journalist and coordinator of an independent network of journalists, Environment and Development Productions, based in Amsterdam.

PART I

Reflections

1

Making Our Way Back to Humanity: Beyond 11 September

John Paul Lederach

Our global community, with the events of 11 September 2001, has been challenged in ways not imagined only a few months earlier. Following are a few reflections on where we stand in this field of peacebuilding as we think about these current situations, locally and globally. I can speak to what I see and feel from the context of my home, recently affected so directly and massively by an act of violence unprecedented on our soils, and I can speak from what I learn from my travels with peacebuilders in various parts of the globe.

It seems to me that the events of 11 September 2001 shattered a number of important myths by which many in my homeland have guided their sense of daily order and security. A myth, it should be remembered, is composed of both truth and fiction that takes on a life of its own, passed on from one generation to another, creating an invisible, unspoken, but often powerful shared meaning and view of reality. There are times, however, when things happen that push the myth from invisibility to the center stage of explicit attention. We have come to see some of what we have believed in a new light, and we find ourselves suspending what we have taken for granted and believed without much further thought to be true. This can be a scary and very disconcerting notion, but it can also potentially be a rich experience of discovery and exploration. In the aftermath of 11 September, I believe many people are seeking explanations for what is going on. What happened to the world we knew? Was it actually the world we thought it was? The moment becomes pregnant with possibilities of new births, new understandings, and the ever-present possibility that we revert simply to a more rigid grasp of our existing worldview. Let us examine for a moment what myths might be under exploration and new discovery.

Core Myths Reconsidered

As we stand in the first decade of a new century the events of 11 September 2001 loom as a defining moment in history. The catastrophic violence, so visible and "live on our televisions," shattered a security that we in the North, particularly citizens of the United States, took for granted. At the writing of this chapter, just months after those events, I have found the views shifting. I cannot speak for peoples across the globe. I can only attest to observations emerging in the North American perception. While it is far too early to know whether these actually represent significant and lasting changes, I believe we have witnessed important shifts of perception, new levels of questions, or at least the initial stages of questions that accompany those shifts. Several come to mind. Let me frame them as "core myths reconsidered."

1. *The problems of the world are out there, not in here and certainly not at home.* If 11 September destroyed anything it was the sense that the difficulties and violence we witnessed on the news, the stories of wars and terror, were essentially problems located in other places. It had little to do with us, and there was little we could do about it, since it was "out there" and "not our problem." In a day that myth fell with a nearly palpable gasp: we are connected to the global community and the global community is connected to us in ways we never knew. This was perhaps something that went well beyond New York and the U.S. borders, a global community that saw itself as interdependent. How we choose to define that interdependence remains before us, but now more than ever we know we are connected.

2. *Security is related to protecting national borders.* Historically, with the rise of the modern nation-state our understandings of security have been tied primarily to the idea of protecting and defending national borders. Accompanying this image is a notion that the "enemy" is out there and protecting ourselves is a matter of defending our borders against visible, invading armies. Suddenly, in the aftermath of 11 September, it became clear that national borders are not much more than a social construction of human imagination and that security, no matter how well conceived and built, is not primarily lodged in protecting a border. The greatest threat came from within our borders, with the simplicity of using the availability of the system against itself. Our notions of security are shifting; in what direction and how radically remains to be seen. It appears in the early days that we are reverting to old views and approaches to face new challenges.

3. *Security is best protected by more and larger weapon systems.* Another of the shifts has been the remarkable lack of discussion of the missile defense systems so prominent just prior to 11 September. We have traditionally expended our greatest economic and sociopolitical investments into the fundamental idea that bigger, faster, and more powerful weapons create greater security. This myth has collapsed around us. Perhaps for the first time in multiple centuries of nation-state building, the idea that more and bigger weapons create greater security is under revision, for there was not one weapon that could have prevented or stopped the events of 11 September, though we had researched and purchased nearly every weapon imaginable to humankind. Security, that elusive human value and need, was no longer tied to weapons.

And the search has begun that addresses the question, "What exactly does increase our security?" How far we go in rethinking our understanding remains to be seen.

4. *Suffering, poverty, and political marginalization of people and their cries for respect and inclusion are not our problem.* This issue takes time, for in the immediate aftermath of the outrageous violence against civilians as was witnessed in New York, it is not easy to raise questions about the roots of such rage, or why people are this angry with us. Yet over the ensuing months exploration and conversations were initiated. If security is not linked primarily to the size and quantity of our weapons, then it may be linked to something else, such as, for example, the quality of our government's relationships with other people, how they view us, and how we care for each others' needs. For the first time we are hearing much more explicit statements that our security is connected to the inclusion of people in gaining a voice and access to the basic resources necessary for a healthy global community. Social, political, and economic exclusion of people are the soils where insecurity is bred and are directly connected to the responsibility of the global community, particularly those who are wealthy.

5. *We can solve these problems on our own.* Finally, though we may agree or disagree with the "war on terrorism" as it is currently being played out in Afghanistan, one thing remains clear. The events of 11 September have seriously eroded the American myth that "we can do it alone." The tendencies of isolationism, present throughout U.S. history, coupled with our self-definition that we must do things "our way" and "on our own," have met the new realities of a global community. We are on the fast track of discovery of what many have known for decades, i.e., that we are mutually dependent. Seeking solutions and addressing human security will require cooperation, mutual understanding, and respect. The myth of the lone cowboy fighting evil may be alive in Hollywood, but it has crumbled in the face of the global challenges of this century.

New Horizon: Interdependence

Looking at these shifts in how we see the world, we are engaged with a new and different horizon to guide our sense of order, direction, and relationships. I believe this horizon is best summed up as a new and fuller understanding of *interdependence*. Each of the above myths can be seen taking new shapes as the light of interdependence is cast upon our global community.

1. *We are linked.* Relationships and the quality of our relationships become central, not peripheral, to understanding security at home and abroad. This begins with a simple recognition: what affects one of us, affects us all. As a story from Liberia went during the war, Rat's trap is not just for Rat. It's about how things are connected. More specifically, it suggests that the fate and well-being of one group affects the rest, even if the rest act as if this is not their problem. It says, in an intriguing way, "watch carefully what traps you

Afghanistan: fighters of the Northern Alliance at the front line; a soldier praying next to his tank.

set, listen carefully to cries for help, for while you may think you are ridding yourself of one problem, the way you do it may circle back to catch you in the trap."

2. *New alliances are possible.* This is true at the highest level of political relationships. To address the challenge of terrorism, leaders and countries who would not normally interact have begun the process of recognizing their need to cooperate and each others' needs, views, and resources. But it is equally true at the level of citizens. We are witnessing the globalization of community and citizenship, a sense of shared responsibility that requires us to move beyond the structures that have traditionally governed our global community, to move beyond politics and economics controlled by political elites, to find our way to each other at the level of people and citizens. The ultimate strength of the political alliances will rely more now than ever on the strength of people-to-people relationships.

3. There is growing recognition that the globalization of cconomics has shown itself to be unresponsive and oppressive to human need and equity of participation. Interdependence suggests that *security is connected to new ways of relating in our global community* based on inclusion, participation, and access to meeting basic needs. This is more possible now than ever.

4. Finally, we are faced with the singularly greatest challenge of this century: we must make our way back to humanity. We must develop lenses to see people again. Just recently I received a report that summed this up from the West African Network for Peacebuilding (WANEP), Accra, Ghana. It was titled

"Statistics Do Not Bleed. People Do." This recognition is one of our biggest challenges in peacebuilding. So often we work with peace programs, institution building, and peace processes, but we too easily lose sight of people. Making our way back to understanding that people and relationships are at the core of our work, and at the core of building peace, remains the key to sustainability.

Conclusion

What I find particularly engaging about these past months is the insight that the lessons we are slowly but surely learning in the aftermath of 11 September are precisely the lessons hard won from the soils and by the peoples of Africa, Latin America, the Middle East, and Asia. Perhaps the most important is the simple idea that when we lose sight of people, when we ignore the voices of those who feel left at the margins and excluded, our actions come back to haunt us. The lesson is this: we are connected. Life is about being part of a community. And ultimately, our security is linked to the quality of our global relationships, not the quantity or size of our weapons.

John Paul Lederach is professor of International Peacebuilding at the Joan B. Kroc Institute for International Peace Studies, University of Notre Dame, and Distinguished Scholar at the Conflict Transformation Program, Eastern Mennonite University.

Voices from Central Asia on the Impact of 11 September

"1. The most militant groups of Islamic extremists of Central Asian origin (such as the Islamic Movement of Uzbekistan) based in Northern Afghanistan are destroyed, due to the anti-Taliban forces offensive. This fact is stabilizing the positions of the ruling regimes in the majority of the Central Asia republics.

2. The stabilization of local regimes has a flip side: some of the local rulers are feeling more confident to violate human-rights standards, suppress the opposition, the mass media, etc. In the case of Tajikistan, that would be a violation of some of the terms of the Peace Treaty.

3. The geopolitical situation around Tajikistan has changed essentially as well. Russian influence in the region is decreasing, while the influence of the United States and NATO in contrast is increasing."

—Parviz Mullodjanov,
Center for Civic Education, Dushanbe, Tajikistan

"Successful actions against terrorists in Afghanistan helped to destroy the aggressive Taliban regime and gave a chance to the Afghan people to begin a new life. For Tajikistan it means to have a more peaceful neighbor without drugs and military attacks. September 11, in that sense, helped the world to look to our country as well and changed its image, because of the hundreds of journalists that came here to get into Afghanistan. New agreements were signed and it will facilitate Tajikistan's development and cooperation."

—Alla Kuvatova, Traditions and Modernity, Dushanbe, Tajikistan

"Our president, government and parliament have condemned terrorism and supported the USA and other countries in fighting against international terrorists. Kyrgyzstan has granted its two biggest airports for the transfer of humanitarian aid. This presence of the coalition's military forces is met with opposite views. Some assume that this is beneficial for the republic, both from the economic and political sides (the country's image will be improved; Muslim troops will cease to terrorize the country's Southern frontiers). Others suspect the USA of building long-term geographical strategic goals (excellent position between Russia and China). The population is unhappy with the fact that all information regarding the arrival of the American military forces to Kyrgyzstan is not made public, or at best is disseminated in parts. In connection with the changed conditions in the world and our region, it is necessary to inform the population of the political situation, Kyrgyz official position, and consequences of the terrorist acts and bombing of Afghanistan. The Foundation for Tolerance International is trying to fill up the information vacuum in South Kyrgyzstan, especially in the Batken province, and having found the possibility, will direct its groups comprised of authoritative persons and competent specialists to these zones."

—Raya Kadyrova,
Foundation for Tolerance International, Bishkek, Kyrgyzstan

"In Kazakhstan we have been observing a kind of "ostrich" attitude—when the military campaign in Afghanistan started, the main question in peoples' minds was to what extent it was going to touch upon their lives. The government of course assured that Kazakhstan is under no threat, and since that time the interest has considerably fallen down. People are too preoccupied with their daily problems to care about somebody else. Personally, I have the impression that in the future historians will probably mark the "September 11" as the start of the Third World War. I don't believe that the current military campaign can create space for further reconstruction and peacebuilding—there is too much ill will behind it."

—Lada Zimina,
Centre for Conflict Management, Almaty, Kazakhstan

Voices from South Asia on the Impact of 11 September

"Look out over the political landscape of South Asia, and you find governments all too willing to try and finish the 'terrorist' problem once and for all."

—Himalmag commentary South Asia,
"SAARC Sans Terrorism,"21 December 2001

"For a number of people he symbolizes the hatred of the US which, as a superpower, has demonstrated much arrogance and its imperialist policies have turned people away. That's why some people rally around Osama."

—"Dawn: The World Today Is Divided Between Dictating Powers
and Subject Countries," interview with Dr. Syed Jaffar Ahmed, Pakistan
Study Centre, Karachi University, 21 December 2001

"Undoubtedly, a primary reason for the attack on Afghanistan is the installation of a regime that will oversee an American-owned pipeline bringing oil and gas from the Caspian Basin."

—John Pilger, "There Is No War on Terrorism,"
Akhbar: A Window on South Asia, *21 November 2001*

"Modern civilisation, Gandhi wrote in his Hind Swaraj, is 'not an incur-
able disease.' Today when the U.S. has started a war to protect modernity,
it must be reminded that others too have the right to define modernity.
Can we say this at the risk of aggravating America's present mood?"

—Krishna Kumar,
"Structural Adjustment: Helping New, Unexpected Clients,"
The Times of India, *1 November 2001*

"Even as reports of hunger and death come in from Afghanistan, and the
people of South Asia steel themselves to bear the brunt of U.S.-led
NATO's imperialist war against the third world, the governments and
media in the region continue to present this offensive as the 'civilised'
world's fight to surmount terrorism. In Pakistan, General Musharaf seems
delighted he can combine his service to 'civilisation' with postponing
elections and return to democracy."

—"Propaganda of the Empire: Governments and Media in South Asia
Fall in Line," Akhbar: A Window on South Asia, *21 November 2001*

"The only real solution is a political one. It requires removing the causes
that create the discontent. It is despair that feeds fanaticism and it is a
result of Washington's policies in the Middle East and elsewhere."

—Tariq Ali,
"A Political, Not a Military Solution Is Required," 21 November 2001

"President Bush can no more rid the world of 'evil-doers' than he can
stock it with saints. It's absurd for the U.S. government to even toy with
the notion that it can stamp out terrorism with more violence and oppression. Terrorism is the symptom, not the disease.
    "Terrorism as a phenomenon may never go away. But if it is to be
contained, the first step is for America to at least acknowledge that it
shares the planet with other nations, with other human beings who, even
if they are not on TV, have loves and griefs and stories and songs and sor-
rows and, for heaven's sake, rights.
    "The September 11 attacks were a monstrous calling card from a
world gone horribly wrong. The message may have been written by Bin
Laden (who knows?) and delivered by his couriers, but it could well have
been signed by the victims of America's old wars."

—Arundhati Roy, "The Algebra of Infinite Justice,"
The Guardian *(London), 21 November 2001*

2

Mapping the Dimensions of Contemporary Conflicts and Human Rights Violations

Berto J. Jongman

Today, no walls can separate humanitarian or human rights crises in one part of the world from national security crises in another. What begins with the failure to uphold the dignity of one life, all too often ends with a calamity for entire nations.
—UN Secretary-General Kofi Annan, 2001

Human rights violations are precursor events to violent conflicts and military hostilities. On the other hand, gross human rights violations and large-scale humanitarian emergencies are a consequence of armed conflict. It makes sense, then, to map both human rights abuses and conflicts together. The PIOOM Conflict and Human Rights Map provides a visualization of the global situation in mid-2001. In this chapter the section on Asia is excerpted from this map. A number of developments related to the first war of the new millennium are highlighted.

For some years PIOOM—the Interdisciplinary Research Programme on Causes of Human Rights Violations—has been registering manifestations of political violence and armed conflict. Part of its findings are published annually in a map format. The present map covers the period mid-2000 to mid-2001, focusing chiefly on upper levels of violent and armed conflicts. Part of the information comes from PIOOM's own data bank; other facts and figures are derived from scientific literature, reports, and other publications from international organizations, NGOs, and governments. The data are based on a comparison of diverse sources, partisan and nonpartisan, and usually reflect low estimates.

In an attempt to compare PIOOM's findings with the results of other armed-conflict registers, information is included on how the others have listed specific cases. The table can be found at the end of this chapter. As PIOOM casts its net a bit wider than others, there are a number of differences. PIOOM

17

not only registers wars, but also warlike high-intensity conflicts (more than 1,000 conflict-related fatalities in a year). PIOOM's next category covers LICs—low-intensity conflicts (between 100 and 1,000 fatalities in a year). The next lowest category covers VPCs—violent political conflicts (less than 100 deaths in a year but usually more than 25 fatalities). While some registrars of "war" or "major armed conflict" include only those conflicts in which a government is one of the parties, PIOOM also focuses on specific intercommunal conflicts. An effort is made to disaggregate these individual violent communal conflicts, listing them separately.

Due to more thorough monitoring, based on a daily coding of multiple sources of information, including media reports, government reports, NGO accounts, and academic literature, PIOOM feels it is able to present a comprehensive concise overview of contemporary political conflict in the open literature. Completeness, however, is not claimed. As conflicts are less intense and therefore less visible, they can escape the eye of the distant observer for quite some time. The current map also excludes massacres and campaigns of violence by criminal actors, except in those cases where these have clear political or terrorist overtones. Despite the care with which the data have been checked, many of the findings are only estimates of magnitudes rather than exact numbers. They will require correction once the full proportions of conflicts become visible when the fog of war and censorship has cleared. It is likely that a number of cases should have been placed in a higher category of conflict. However, PIOOM would rather err on the side of caution than exaggeration.

Table 2.1 Stage of Conflict with Crises Thresholds

Stage I: Peaceful Stable Situation
- High degree of social stability and regime legitimacy

Stage II: Political Tension Situation
- Growing levels of systemic strain
- Increasing social and political cleavages, often along factional lines

POLITICAL CRISIS

Stage III: Violent Political Conflict
- Erosion of the government's political legitimacy
- Rising acceptance of factional politics

Stage IV: Low-Intensity Conflict
- Open hostility and armed conflict among factional groups
- Regime repression
- Insurgency

HUMANITARIAN CRISIS

Stage V: High-Intensity Conflict
- Organized combat between rival groups
- Mass killings
- Displacement of sectors of the civilian population

World Conflict and Human Rights Map 2001/2002: Asia by PIOOM

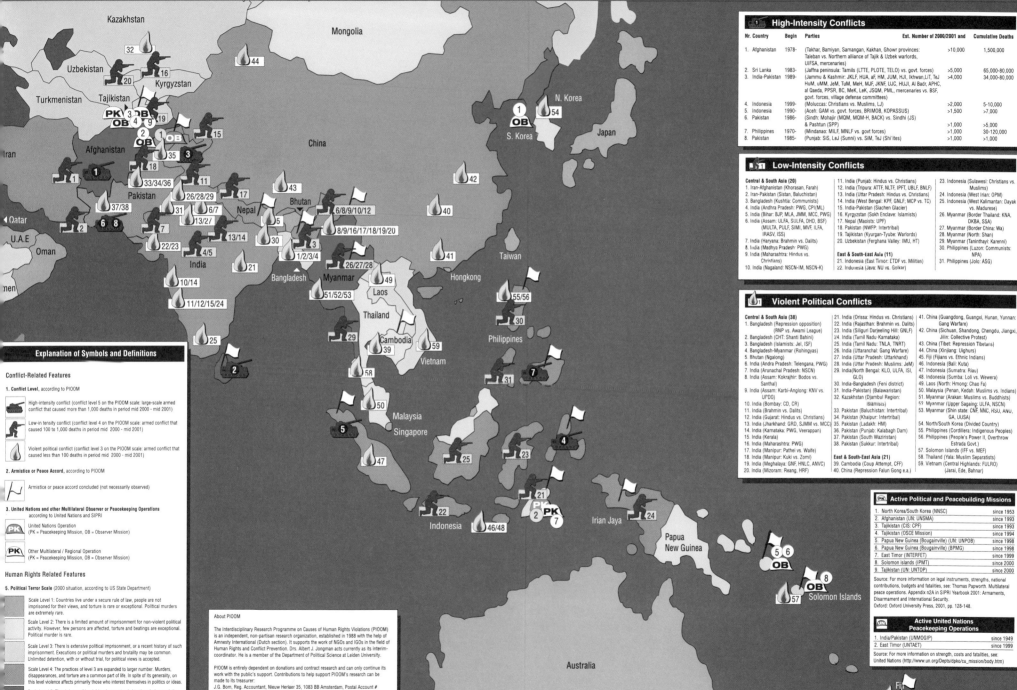

High-Intensity Conflicts

Nr.	Country	Begin	Parties	Est. Number of 2000/2001 and	Cumulative Deaths
1.	Afghanistan	1978-	(Takhar, Bamiyan, Samangan, Kakhan, Ghowr provinces: Taleban vs. Northern alliance of Tajik & Uzbek warlords, UIFSA, mercenaries)	>10,000	1,500,000
2.	Sri Lanka	1983-	(Jaffna peninsula: Tamils (LTTE, PLOTE, TELO) vs. govt. forces)	>5,000	65,000-80,000
3.	India-Pakistan	1989-	(Jammu & Kashmir: JKLF, HUA, aF, HM, JUM, HJI, Ikhwan,LIT, TeJ HuM, uMM, JeM, TuM, MeH, MJF, JKNF, UJC, HUJI, Al Badr, APHC, al Qaeda, PPSR, BC, MeK, LeK, JSQM, PML, mercenaries vs. BSF, govt. forces, village defense committees)	>4,000	34,000-80,000
4.	Indonesia	1999-	(Moluccas: Christians vs. Muslims, LJ)	>2,000	5-10,000
5.	Indonesia	1990-	(Aceh: GAM vs. govt. forces, BRIMOB, KOPASSUS)	>1,500	>7,000
6.	Pakistan	1986-	(Sindh: Mohajir (MQM, MQM-H, BACK) vs. Sindhi (JS) & Pashtun (SPP)	>1,000	>5,000
7.	Philippines	1970-	(Mindanao: MILF, MNLF vs. govt forces)	>1,000	30-120,000
8.	Pakistan	1985-	(Punjab: SIS, LsJ (Sunni) vs. SiM, TsJ (Shi'ites)	>1,000	>1,000

Low-Intensity Conflicts

Central & South Asia (20)
1. Iran-Afghanistan (Khorasan, Farah)
2. Iran-Pakistan (Sistan, Baluchistan)
3. Bangladesh (Kushtia: Communists)
4. India (Andhra Pradesh: PWG, CPI(ML))
5. India (Bihar: BJP, MLA, JMM, MCC, PWG)
6. India (Assam: ULFA, SULFA, DHD, BSF) (MULTA: PULF, SIMI, MVF, ILFA, IRASV, ISS)
7. India (Haryana: Brahmin vs. Dalits)
8. India (Madhya Pradesh: PWG)
9. India (Maharashtra: Hindus vs. Christians)
10. India (Nagaland: NSCN-IM, NSCN-K)
11. India (Punjab: Hindus vs. Christians)
12. India (Tripura: ATTF, NLTF, IPFT, UBLF, BNLF)
13. India (Uttar Pradesh: Hindus vs. Christians)
14. India (West Bengal: KPF, GNLF, MCP vs. TC)
15. India-Pakistan (Siachen Glacier)
16. Kyrgyzstan (Sokh Enclave: Islamists)
17. Nepal (Maoists: UPF)
18. Pakistan (NWFP: Intertribal)
19. Tajikistan (Kyurgan-Tyube: Warlords)
20. Uzbekistan (Ferghana Valley: IMU, HT)

East & South-East Asia (11)
21. Indonesia (East Timor: ETDF vs. Militias)
22. Indonesia (Java: NU vs. Golkar)
23. Indonesia (Sulawesi: Christians vs. Muslims)
24. Indonesia (West Irian: OPM)
25. Indonesia (West Kalimantan: Dayak vs. Madurese)
26. Myanmar (Border Thailand: KNA, DKBA, SSA)
27. Myanmar (Border China: Wa)
28. Myanmar (North: Shan)
29. Myanmar (Taninthayi: Karenni)
30. Philippines (Luzon: Communists: NPA)
31. Philippines (Jolo: ASG)

Violent Political Conflicts

Central & South Asia (38)
1. Bangladesh (Repression opposition) (RNP vs. Awami League)
2. Bangladesh (CHT: Shanti Bahini)
3. Bangladesh (Islamists: JeI, ISF)
4. Bangladesh-Myanmar (Rohingyas)
5. Bhutan (Ngalong)
6. India (Andra Pradesh: Telengana, PWG)
7. India (Arunachal Pradesh: NSCN)
8. India (Assam: Kokrajhir: Bodos vs. Santhal)
9. India (Assam: Karbi-Anglong: KNV vs. UPDO)
10. India (Bombay: CD, CR)
11. India (Brahmin vs. Dalits)
12. India (Gujarat: Hindus vs. Christians)
13. India (Jharkhand: GRD, SJMM vs. MCC)
14. India (Karnataka: PWG, Veerappan)
15. India (Kerala)
16. India (Maharashtra: PWG)
17. India (Manipur: Pathei vs. Waife)
18. India (Manipur: Kuki vs. Zomi)
19. India (Meghalaya: GNF, HNLC, ANVC)
20. India (Mizoram: Reang, HRF)
21. India (Orissa: Hindus vs. Christians)
22. India (Rajasthan: Brahmin vs. Dalits)
23. India (Siliguri Darjeeling Hill: GNLF)
24. India (Tamil Nadu-Karnataka)
25. India (Tamil Nadu: TNLA, TNRT)
26. India (Uttaranchal: Gang Warfare)
27. India (Uttar Pradesh: Uttarkhand)
28. India (Uttar Pradesh: Muslims: JeM)
29. India(North Bengal: KLO, ULFA, ISI, GLO)
30. India-Bangladesh (Feni district)
31. India-Pakistan (Balawaristan)
32. Kazakhstan (Djambul Region: Islamists)
33. Pakistan (Baluchistan: Intertribal)
34. Pakistan (Khaipur: Intertribal)
35. Pakistan (Ladakh: HM)
36. Pakistan (Punjab: Kalabagh Dam)
37. Pakistan (South Waziristan)
38. Pakistan (Sukkur: Intertribal)

41. China (Guangdong, Guangxi, Hunan, Yunnan: Gang Warfare)
42. China (Sichuan, Shandong, Chengdu, Jiangxi, Jilin: Collective Protest)
43. China (Tibet: Repression Tibetans)
44. China (Xinjiang: Uighurs)
45. Fiji (Fijians vs. Ethnic Indians)
46. Indonesia (Bali: Kuta)
47. Indonesia (Sumatra: Riau)
48. Indonesia (Sumba: Loli vs. Wewera)
49. Laos (North: Hmong: Chao Fa)
50. Malaysia (Penan, Kedah: Muslims vs. Indians)
51. Myanmar (Arakan: Muslims vs. Buddhists)
52. Myanmar (Upper Sagaing: ULFA, NSCN)
53. Myanmar (Shin state: CNF, NNC, KSU, ANU, GA, UUSA)
54. North/South Korea (Divided Country)
55. Philippines (Cordillera: Indigenous Peoples)
56. Philippines (People's Power II, Overthrow Estrada Govt.)
57. Solomon Islands (IFF vs. MEF)
58. Thailand (Yala: Muslim Separatists)
59. Vietnam (Central Highlands: FULRO) (Jarai, Ede, Bahnar)

East & South-East Asia (21)
39. Cambodia (Coup Attempt, CFF)
40. China (Repression Falun Gong e.a.)

Active Political and Peacebuilding Missions

1.	North Korea/South Korea (NNSC)	since 1953
2.	Afghanistan (UN: UNSMA)	since 1993
3.	Tajikistan (CIS: CPF)	since 1993
4.	Tajikistan (OSCE Mission)	since 1994
5.	Papua New Guinea (Bougainville) (UN: UNPOB)	since 1998
6.	Papua New Guinea (Bougainville) (BPMG)	since 1998
7.	East Timor (INTERFET)	since 1999
8.	Solomon islands (IPMT)	since 2000
9.	Tajikistan (UN: UNTOP)	since 2000

Source: For more information on legal instruments, strengths, national contributions, budgets and fatalities, see: Thomas Papworth. Multilateral peace operations. Appendix n2A in SIPRI Yearbook 2001: Armaments, Disarmament and International Security. Oxford: Oxford University Press, 2001, pp. 128-148.

Active United Nations Peacekeeping Operations

1.	India/Pakistan (UNMOGIP)	since 1949
2.	East Timor (UNTAET)	since 1999

Source: For more information on strength, costs and fatalities, see: United Nations (http://www.un.org/Depts/dpko/cu_mission/body.htm)

Explanation of Symbols and Definitions

Conflict-Related Features

1. Conflict Level, according to PIOOM

High-intensity conflict (conflict level 5 on the PIOOM scale: large-scale armed conflict that caused more than 1,000 deaths in period mid 2000 - mid 2001)

Low-in tensity conflict (conflict level 4 on the PIOOM scale: armed conflict that caused 100 to 1,000 deaths in period mid 2000 - mid 2001)

Violent political conflict (conflict level 3 on the PIOOM scale: armed conflict that caused less than 100 deaths in period mid 2000 - mid 2001)

2. Armistice or Peace Accord, according to PIOOM

Armistice or peace accord concluded (not necessarily observed)

3. United Nations and other Multilateral Observer or Peacekeeping Operations according to United Nations and SIPRI

United Nations Operation (PK = Peacekeeping Mission, OB = Observer Mission)

Other Multilateral / Regional Operation (PK = Peacekeeping Mission, OB = Observer Mission)

Human Rights Related Features

5. Political Terror Scale (2000 situation, according to US State Department)

Scale Level 1: Countries live under a secure rule of law, people are not imprisoned for their views, and torture is rare or exceptional. Political murders are extremely rare.

Scale Level 2: There is a limited amount of imprisonment for non-violent political activity. However, few persons are affected, torture and beatings are exceptional. Political murder is rare.

Scale Level 3: There is extensive political imprisonment, or a recent history of such imprisonment. Executions or political murders and brutality may be common. Unlimited detention, with or without trial, for political views is accepted.

Scale Level 4: The practices of level 3 are expanded to larger number. Murders, disappearances, and torture are a common part of life. In spite of its generality, on this level violence affects primarily those who interest themselves in politics or ideas.

Scale Level 5: The violence of level 4 has been extended to the whole population. The leaders of these societies place no limits on the means or thoroughness with which they pursue personal or ideological goals.

About PIOOM

The Interdisciplinary Research Programme on Causes of Human Rights Violations (PIOOM) is an independent, non-partisan research organization, established in 1988 with the help of Amnesty International (Dutch section). It supports the work of NGOs and IGOs in the field of Human Rights and Conflict Prevention. Drs. Albert J. Jongman acts currently as its interim-coordinator. He is a member of the Department of Political Science at Leiden University.

PIOOM is entirely dependent on donations and contract research and can only continue its work with the public's support. Contributions to help support PIOOM's research can be made to its treasurer:
J.G. Born, Reg. Accountant, Nieuw Herlaer 35, 1083 BB Amsterdam, Postal Account # 431304, Amsterdam, The Netherlands.

© Albert J. Jongman

Map and graphics by Kasemir Publicity & Design, Groningen, The Netherlands.

General Overview of Conflicts in Central and South Asia

Covering the year from summer 2000 to summer 2001, the total number of HICs (high-intensity conflicts) on the PIOOM list decreased from twenty-six to twenty-three. The war against terrorism, however, might result in a further escalation of conflict in Chechnya, the Middle East, Pakistan, Kashmir, the Philippines, and Indonesia. Eight of the twenty-three HICs are located in the Asian region, which caused over the years the death of at least 25,000 people. The total death toll of the eight conflicts in the Asian region amounts to 1,647,000 people.

The number of LICs increased by one during the year. Africa and Central Asia remain the most conflict-prone regions. In Central and South Asia the number of LICs decreased by one. The majority are located in India, where almost every federal state has its own guerrilla war or severe communal conflict.

A total of 59 (out of 175) VPCs are located in the Asian region, 38 of those in Central and South Asia. Almost every Indian state has its own conflict. Also Bangladesh and Pakistan have multiple VPCs. The "jihad factor" plays an important role. In the coming years, developments in the five Central Asian republics will be crucial. They have joined the international coalition against international terrorism in the hope that they will be supported in the struggle with their own domestic Islamist terrorist movements. Whether these movements will gain popular support and become important political factors will largely depend on the reaction of these autocracies and their willingness to reform.

Of the 334 tension situations registered by PIOOM during the year, 80 were located in the Asian region, 30 of which were in Central and South Asia. The majority of the tension situations are related to the negative impact of modernization and development on the way of life of indigenous peoples. The current conflict potential underlines the importance of conflict prevention.

First War of the New Millennium

In the first big war of the new millennium, the United States and Great Britain launched "Operation Enduring Freedom" on 7 October 2001 by attacking Afghanistan with air strikes. The attack was triggered by the 11 September 2001 multiple terrorist attack on the most visible symbols of U.S. power, the World Trade Center in New York and the Pentagon in Washington, by using hijacked civilian airplanes and crashing them into the targets. In the devastating attacks an estimated three thousand people were killed, which makes it the most lethal international terrorist incident in human history. As those responsible for the attacks showed no moral restraint in killing innocent human beings, the danger of the use of weapons of mass destruction has increased. Intelligence information indicates that the Al-Qaida organization that is held responsible for the "9-11" attacks has been involved in attempts to acquire weapons of mass destruction that it may use in a possible next stage of its holy war against the "infidels" (especially the United States and Israel).

Immediately after the "9-11" attacks, the U.S. government mobilized an international coalition to fight international terrorism. NATO members perceived the attacks as an attack on the alliance and by activating Article 51, NATO supported the United States in fighting its new war against international terrorism. The United States formulated a war plan that consisted of three missions: prevent any further attacks against U.S. assets by Al-Qaida; kill its leader Osama bin Laden and destroy Al-Qaida and all of its linked organizations on a worldwide basis; and punish all countries that have supported Al-Qaida, beginning with Afghanistan.

In less than two months the United States succeeded in overthrowing the Taliban regime and disrupting the Afghan infrastructure of the Al-Qaida network. On 22 December 2001, a new interim administration was installed under the leadership of Hamid Karzai and the first units deployed of the International Security Assistance Force sanctioned by the United Nations. The force will number about 4,500 soldiers. The interim government has a six-month mandate. A grand council (*loya jirga*) will meet in that time to set up a two-year transitional authority after which elections will be held. A successful reconstruction of the country will be dependent on continuing world attention. International donors met in January 2002 in Tokyo to discuss commitments to Afghanistan's reconstruction. Total costs are estimated as high as $15 billion for the coming ten years.

While the United States shouldered a heavy burden in leading the military campaign, it expects other countries, led by Germany and Japan, to take the lead in reconstruction. The cost of the war for the United States is estimated at $2 billion per month. The United States will spend large parts of its earmarked money for Afghanistan on rebuilding its embassy and a major antidrug program. The Taliban ban on opium production boosted production in Thailand and Myanmar. With a totally destroyed agricultural system, Afghan farmers often have no other choice than to grow poppies. The delivery of unprecedented amounts of food to Afghanistan in December 2001 averted a predicted major famine. However, continued warlord activity prevents relief organizations from reaching all the people in need.

The hide-and-wait strategy pursued by the Taliban and Al-Qaida failed. They lacked the antiaircraft weapons to pose a dissuasive threat against high-flying U.S. warplanes equipped with the latest electronic countermeasures. U.S. Special Forces, operating with the Afghan opposition militia groups on the ground, were able to guide the precision munitions to their targets. The devastating U.S. bombing forced retreats or negotiated surrenders. There were very few decisive encounters on the ground. A total death toll is not available yet. Media reports indicate that more than 3,700 Afghan civilians were killed. It can be assumed that almost double that number of Taliban and Al-Qaida fighters died in the bombing raids and battles. An estimated 7,000 Taliban and Al-Qaida fighters have been taken prisoner. Thousands of others escaped via well-organized escape routes to neighboring countries, including probably the most important culprits Osama bin Laden and Mullah Omar Mohammed.

Crucial in the success against the Taliban and Al-Qaida has been the role of Afghanistan's neighbors. Pakistan made several bases available for U.S.

forces and equipment. To the north, Uzbekistan and Tajikistan also made facilities available and, on the west, even Iran was not an obstacle. It is however
doubtful whether the United States has accomplished its war aims. Although
several leading commanders of the Taliban and Al-Qaida have died in the military operations, the most important leaders have escaped and their fate is not
known. Many Taliban officials and soldiers remain unharmed and could try to
mount guerrilla attacks on the new government and international peacekeep-
ers. Regional warlords such as Rashid Dostum in the north, Gul Agha in Kandahar, Ismail Khan around Herat, and Haji Abdul Qadir in Jalalabad, continue
with their activities and are focused on the maintenance of their own power.
The lack of central control has created widespread lawlessness that has slowed
food aid and has created dangers for international soldiers. It has yet to be
seen whether the call for an integrated Afghan army will contribute to an improvement of the security situation.

It is expected that the United States will expand its struggle against international terrorism to other countries and regions. To a large extent, the new
war will be fought behind the scenes. The United States will encourage a number of governments to cooperate in fighting terrorists by providing weapons,
training, and information, while local forces will do the dirty work. In exchange for this cooperation, the countries will receive financial and economic
support. Some observers have suggested that voluntary measures alone will be
insufficient to mobilize actions against terrorist networks. David L. Philips, director of the Center for Preventive Action of the Council on Foreign Relations,
has suggested that a covenant binding states to counter terrorism would be an
effective instrument in the war on terror. It would provide an operational
framework lending coherence to the coalition, and it would help to focus the
next phase of the global campaign.

The new war against terrorism was a continuation of a covert CIA operation that had already been initiated during the Clinton regime following the
terrorist attacks against the U.S. embassies in Kenya and Tanzania in 1998.
Part of this program was the establishment of a team of Afghans who were assigned to track Osama bin Laden and report on a daily basis to a special CIA
unit. Translating this information into action was a key problem. President
Clinton missed at least three chances to seize Osama bin Laden. The Bush administration appeared to be more committed and considered an even more ambitious plan to destroy Osama bin Laden and his Al-Qaida network. In the
summer of 2001, the National Security Council drafted a proposal with two
important aims: the destabilization of the Taliban regime in Afghanistan and
the worldwide destruction of Al-Qaida cells. Since the 11 September attacks,
President Bush has authorized a much more sweeping and lethal CIA program
against Osama bin Laden, with a budget of more than $1 billion.

The 11 September 2001 terrorist attacks immediately triggered a worldwide debate on the effectiveness of counterterrorist measures. Currently, the
military approach is being emphasized. However, the toolbox of counterterrorism contains a wide variety of tools that can be applied in different areas.

Psychological, educational, and communications aspects should not be forgotten. By countering the political propaganda of terrorist organizations, it is possible to prevent them from gaining new recruits and keeping their constituencies committed to their cause. The war against terrorism has to be fought on many fronts, including: counterproliferation, international cooperation, diplomacy, intelligence, image, police, development assistance, military power, and emergency planning. Dysfunctional societies and "failed states" are an important root cause of terrorism.

A long-term strategy should focus on shrinking the zones of chaos around the world where terrorist organizations have found sanctuaries by improving the social and economic conditions. A short-term strategy should focus on changing conditions in areas that have offered safe haven to terrorist organizations and in areas of concern for the future. Closing down terrorist bases and expelling known terrorists have become essential preconditions for positive relations with the United States. Continued tolerance of terrorist activity will involve a high and continuing cost. By gradually promoting democracy and economic development, several war-torn nations have to be rebuilt, not only for humanitarian reasons but also for reasons of collective defense. Some observers conclude that we now have a global confrontation between hierarchical/state actors and networked/nonstate actors. It is very likely that the Al-Qaida network has the design of a spider's web, with multiple centers and peripheries. This design allows it to attack from multiple directions by dispersed small units. Following a swarmlike doctrine, it attacks in campaigns of episodic, pulsing attacks by various nodes of the network at locations sprawled across global space and time. This mode of operation makes the Al-Qaida network very hard to defeat. Success is only possible if similar swarming tactics are developed, meaning an ability to create ad hoc patterns of activity among widely distributed cells. Cooperation between intelligence and police services will play a critical role in organizing a sustained assault on the broader network.

Impact on Asia

The "9-11" attacks and the military response set in motion a chain of events that could result in new wars and might increase the level of insecurity in the world, including the Asian region. The military operations may result in the collapse or a severe destabilization of several governments, including that in Pakistan.

Immediately after the U.S. air campaign in Afghanistan, tensions escalated between India and Pakistan over Kashmir. The military buildup was triggered by suicide attacks on the local legislature in Kashmir on 1 October 2001 and on the Indian parliament in New Delhi on 13 December 2001, in which a total of fifty-two people were killed. India blamed Islamist terrorist groups fighting to drive Indian forces from Kashmir and accused the Pakistani government of supporting the attackers. Both countries mobilized their military forces and concentrated troops along the Line of Control. Civilian casualties from nightly skirmishes mounted. Standing eyeball to eyeball, even a minor incident can lead to an uncontrolled chain reaction. A peaceful resolution rests on both nations stepping back from their rigid positions, something neither has shown much of a willingness to do in the past. Both countries were put under severe international pressure to avoid a new war. For India, Kashmir is a symbol of national unity. There are genuine fears that independence for Kashmir would be a first step in the breakup of the Indian union into various ethnic and linguistic entities. The United States has tried to reframe the conflict as a battle over terrorism, not territory. If Pakistani president General Pervez Musharraf makes the wrong move, he runs the risk that elements of the armed forces and large sections of the Islamic clergy will turn against him. It will take time before he will be able to get complete control over rogue elements within his military intelligence agency ISI, which dealt with the armed groups in Kashmir. Musharraf appointed a new director-general for the agency that has been described as a state within a state. At the same time India has yet to recognize that it cannot use force alone to crush the aspirations for independence or even greater self-government. Under the assumption that the conflict can be defused, some kind of arms-control framework will be necessary to assure the world that a firefight over the Line of Control does not risk rapid escalation into a nuclear exchange.

During the seven-year regime of President Chandrika Kumaratunga in Sri Lanka, an increasingly hard line was followed against the Tamil Tigers. The new government of prime minister Ranil Wickremesinghe, which came to power in December 2001, immediately made new moves to end the long-running civil war. A cease-fire between the Tigers and the government forces was brokered by Norway. It is still unclear when negotiations will begin or whether a political settlement to end the ethnic conflict can be reached. Liberation Tigers of Tamil Eelam (LTTE) leader Velupillai Prabhakaran has indicated for the first time that the LTTE would consider settling for less than a separate nation in Sri Lanka's north and east. Ranil Wickremesinghe's new government is hopeful that the changed international climate toward terrorism will put added pressure on the Tamil Tigers to settle. Public opinion is in favor of an honorable, negotiated settlement within the framework of an undivided Sri Lanka.

In Nepal, the military is engaged in an offensive that began in November 2001 in response to an upsurge in attacks on government targets by Maoist guerrillas. Prime Minister Sher Bahadur Deuba has said that the offensive will continue until the guerrillas surrender or until they are disarmed. The guerrilla struggle began in 1986 and has already claimed the lives of several thousand people. The intensification of the conflict followed the murder of the royal family by crown prince Dipendra in June 2001. As the guerrilla movement tried to exploit the situation of a political vacuum, the new king agreed to the deployment of the armed forces against the Maoists.

In India's northeast, the United Liberation Front of Assam (ULFA) is fighting a separatist guerrilla war against the Indian government. ULFA operates from camps on the border with Bhutan and its leader, Paresh Barua, has said that it will not enter talks until the government agrees to discuss Assam's sovereignty. In the new war against international terrorism, Bhutan has indicated its willingness to close the ULFA camps. The struggle in Assam is just one of more than a dozen armed uprisings across India intended to break existing states into smaller ones that better suit the ethnic and economic demands of the inhabitants. India has a total of twenty-eight states. Soon after independence in 1947, sixteen states were created along linguistic lines. More were added in the 1960s and 1970s. In 2000, Uttaranchal, Jharkhand, and Chattisgarh were created in response to the demands from local people. In at least ten areas across India, groups are asking for new states on the basis of their ethnic identity, economic neglect, and underdevelopment. Examples are Telengana in Andhra Pradesh and Harit Pradesh in Uttar Pradesh. In some cases it is questionable whether the newly formed state can be self-sufficient. In other cases, the creation of a new state replicates the old model of neglect and top-down governance on a smaller scale.

The former Soviet republics in Central Asia have developed into consolidated autocracies and static economies and belong to the least-advanced cluster, according to Freedom House. In its annual report, twenty-seven postcommunist states are monitored with respect to political and economic developments. Freedom House found significant declines in democratization indicators in Kazakhstan and Kyrgyz Republic. Only Tajikistan registered progress and climbed to the rank of a transitional country. In Turkmenistan and Uzbekistan the situation remained static. All five Central Asian states suffered from deeply flawed electoral processes or are de facto one-party dictatorships or dominant party states in which the opposition has had no reasonable chance of taking power, has been repressed, or has been virtually nonexistent. In the Central Asian republics, presidential power is either absolute or predominant. Cronyism and nepotism are major features of the division of economic power. While depicting a bleak landscape, Freedom House concludes that there are forces that can be mobilized to promote political openings and to strengthen pro-reform currents.

We can expect the Central Asian republics to become increasingly vulnerable to externally and internally generated shocks. Several of the Central Asian republics face radical Islamist groups. Geostrategically, the region has become more important for the exploitation of natural resources and major transport routes. Several republics also play critical roles in the transit of narcotics from Afghanistan to Western Europe. Several observers expect an armed struggle for control over the strategic Ferghana Valley. Currently, the United States is upgrading a number of military air bases in Central Asian republics and will step up its military presence. In exchange, the republics will receive substantial economic aid.

A Comparison of Seven Major Data Projects

In the following tables, seven major data projects, of which PIOOM is one, are compared. The current PIOOM conflict list is used, and it is indicated whether the cases on the PIOOM list are covered by six other projects. The table lists all the HICs and LICs to indicate overlap and lacunae. VPCs were included only if they were covered by at least one of the other six projects. The legend explains the acronyms used in the table.

The following databases are all used in the selection of the conflicts for inclusion in this publication's conflict surveys:

- PIOOM (Interdisciplinary Research Project into the Root Causes of Gross Human Rights Violations, Leiden, the Netherlands)
- AKUF (Working Group on the Causes of War, Hamburg, Germany)
- CIDCM (Center for International Development and Conflict Management, Maryland, United States)
- DPCR (Department of Peace and Conflict Research, Uppsala, Sweden)
- HIIK (Heidelberg Institute for International Conflict Research, Heidelberg, Germany)
- SIPRI (Stockholm International Peace Research Institute, Stockholm, Sweden)
- SOWAP (State of War and Peace Atlas, International Peace Research Institute, Oslo, Norway)

Table 2.2 Comparison of Seven Database Evaluations of Conflicts in Central and South Asia

	PIOOM	AKUF	CIDCM	DPCR	HIIK	SIPRI	SOWAP
High-Intensity Conflicts (HICs)							
Central and South Asia							
1. Afghanistan (NA, UIFSA)	HIC A2	War/ Ongo	E/M7/	War	War	War	War
2. India-Pakistan (Kashmir)	HIC B1	War/ Ongo	E/M3	War	War	War	War
(2a.) India (Kashmir)		AC		War		War	War
3. Pakistan (Punjab: SSP vs. TJP)	HIC						
4. Pakistan (Sindh: MQM)	HIC	AC Repr	E/M1/		SCR		
5. Sri Lanka (Jaffna: LTTE)	HIC A2	War/ Ongo	E/M7/	War	War	War	War
Low-Intensity Conflicts (LIC)							
Central & South Asia							
1. Bangladesh (Kushtia: communists)	LIC	Susp	E/M2/				
2. India (Andhra Pradesh: PWG/, a.o.)	LIC	War/ A2		MAC			War
3. India (Bihar: MLA, JMM, MCC, PWG)	LIC						
4. India (Assam: ULFA, SULFA, a.o.)	LIC	War/ B2	E/M2/ Spor	IAC	SCR	War	War
5. India (Haryana: Brahmin vs. Dalits)	LIC						
6. India (Madhya Pradesh: PWG)							
7. India (Maharashtra: Hd. vs. Chr.)							
8. India (Nagaland: NSCN-IM, NSCN-K)	LIC	AC					

(continues)

Table 2.2 contd.

	PIOOM	AKUF	CIDCM	DPCR	HIIK	SIPRI	SOWAP
9. India (Punjab: Hind. vs. Christ.)	LIC						
10. India (Tripura: ATTF, NLTF, a.o.)	LIC	War/ B2		MAC			War
11. India (Uttar Pradesh: Hd. vs. Chr.)	LIC						
12. India (West Bengal: KPF, GNLF, a.o.)	LIC						
13. India-Pakistan (Siachen Gl.)	LIC						
14. Kyrgyzstan (Sokh Enclave)	LIC				SCR		
15. Nepal (Maoists: UPF)	LIC	War/ A2	P/M1/ Ongo	MAC	SCR		War
16. Pakistan (NWFP: Intertribal)	LIC						
17. Tajikistan (Kyurgan-Tyube)	LIC	AC	P/M3/ Susp		CRI		
18. Uzbekistan (Ferghana Valley)	LIC	War/ AE1		MAC	SCR		War

Violent Political Conflicts (VPC)
Central and South Asia

	PIOOM	AKUF	CIDCM	DPCR	HIIK	SIPRI	SOWAP
1. Bangladesh (BNP vs. Awami League)	VPC				CRI		
2. Bangladesh-Myanmar (Rohingyas)	VPC				CRI		
3. India (Manipur: Pathei vs. Waife)	VPC						
4. India (Manipur: Kuki vs. Zomi)	VPC			MAC			War
5. India (Kokrajhir: Bodos)	VPC	War/ B2					
6. India-Bangladesh (Feni dist.)	VPC				CRI		

Legend: PIOOM: HIC: High-intensity conflict; LIC: Low-intensity conflict; VPC: Violent political conflict.

AKUF: WAR: War; AC: Armed conflict (AKUF makes distinction between the following types of war: A: Anti-regime war; B: War for autonomy or secessionist war; C: Interstate war; D: Decolonization war; E: Other intrastate war; 1: War with direct foreign intervention; 2: War without direct foreign intervention).

CIDCM: Conflicts characterized: C: Communal; E: Ethnic; I: International; P: Political (Conflicts ranked according to magnitude based on a scale for the number of deaths: M1-10: Magnitude of conflict on a scale from 1 [low damage and limited scope] to 10 [total destruction]; Status of the conflict as of 7 November 2000: Ongo: Ongoing [active, coordinated military operations]; Spor: Sporadic [occasional militant clashes or terrorist incidents, without evidence of sustained challenges]; Repr: Repressed [sufficient armed force has been deployed to contain serious challenges by the opposition despite the fact that the underlying source of the conflict remains serious and unresolved]; Susp: Suspended [conflict has been suspended for a substantial period due to stalemate, cease-fire, or peace settlement).

DPCR: Three categories of conflict: WAR: Major armed conflict; IAC: Intermediate armed conflict; and MAC: Minor armed conflict.

HIIK: Four categories of conflict of which only the first two are violent: WAR: War; SCR: Serious crisis; CRI: Crisis; LCR: Latent crisis;

SIPRI: Identifies only the major wars, which largely coincide with DPCR's major armed conflicts. WAR: War

SOWAP: The Atlas lists armed conflict during the 1990–2000 period. The table lists the conflicts with an ongoing combat states during the year 2000. WAR: War

Resources

Reports

AKUF (Working Group on the Causes of War, Hamburg, Germany), *Das Kriegs-geschehen 2000. Daten und Tendenzen der Kriege und bewaffneten Konflikte,* edited by Thomas Rabehl and Wolfgang Schreiber. Opladen, Leske+Budrich, 2001.

CIDCM (Center for International Development and Conflict Management, Maryland, United States), *Peace and Conflict 2001. A Global Survey of Armed Conflicts, Self-Determination Movements, and Democracy,* by Ted Robert Gurr, Monty G. Marshall, and Deepa Khosla. University of Maryland, College Park, 2001.

DPCR (Department of Peace and Conflict Research, Uppsala, Sweden), *Armed Conflict, 1989–2000,* by Peter Wallensteen and Margareta Sollenberg. *Journal of Peace Research,* 38(5), 2001.

HIIK (Heidelberg Institute for International Conflict Research, Heidelberg, Germany), *Konfliktbarometer 2000. Krisen, Kriege, Putsche, Verhandlungen, Vermittlung, Friedensschlüsse. 9. Jährliche Konfliktanalyse.* Heidelberg: Heidelberger Institut für Internationale Konfliktforschung e.V, 2001.

PIOOM (Project Interdisciplinary Research into the Root Causes of Gross Human Rights Violations, Leiden, the Netherlands), *Annual Conflict and Human Rights Map*

SIPRI (Stockholm International Peace Research Institute, Stockholm, Sweden), *SIPRI Yearbook 2001. Armaments, Disarmament and International Security.* Oxford: Oxford University Press, 2001.

SOWAP (State of War and Peace Atlas, International Peace Research Institute, Oslo, Norway), *Counting Wars: The Research Implications of Definitional Decisions,* by Dan Smith. Paper presented at the Uppsala Conflict Data Conference, Department of Peace and Conflict Research, Uppsala, 8–9 June 2001. (The data presented in this paper will be published in the 2002 edition of the *State of War and Peace Atlas.*)

Selected Internet Sites

AKUF: http://www.sozialwiss.uni-hamburg.de/Ipw/Akuf/kriege00_txt.htm
CIDCM: http://www.bsos.umd.edu/cidcm; http://members.aol.com/cspmgm/warlist.htm
DPCR: http://www.pcr.uu.se
Freedom House: http://freedomhouse.org
HIIK: http://www.HIIK.de
SIPRI: http://www.sipri.se

Berto J. Jongman worked at the Polemological Institute of the University of Groningen, the Netherlands, from 1982 to 1987. A cooperation with Alex P. Schmid resulted in the reference work Political Terrorism: A New Guide to Actors, Authors, Concepts, Data Bases, Theories, and Literature *(1988). Since then, Jongman worked with the PIOOM Foundation, an interdisciplinary research organization analyzing the root causes of gross violations of human rights. In February 2002, PIOOM's research secretariat in Leiden was closed. Currently, Jongman works as a political strategic analyst at the Dutch Ministry of Defense. The annual PIOOM World Conflict and Human Rights Map has appeared since 1997.*

3

Calling for a Broad Approach to Conflict Resolution[1]

Hugh Miall, Oliver Ramsbotham & Tom Woodhouse

A broad conflict-resolution approach requires prevention, manage-ment, and transformation of deadly conflicts. Interventions across in-ternational frontiers are valuable, but the key goal should be strengthening the conflict-resolution capacity of societies and com-munities within conflict areas.

Conflict resolution as a defined specialist field has come of age in the post–Cold War era. The development of the field started to accelerate in the 1950s and 1960s, at the height of the Cold War, when the development of nuclear weapons and the conflict between the superpowers seemed to threaten human survival. A handful of people in North America and Europe began to establish research groups to develop new ideas, part of which de-rived from experience with conflict management in industrial relations and from community mediations. These people's efforts were not taken very se-riously, but nevertheless, the new ideas attracted interest. The field began to grow and spread. Scholarly journals in conflict resolution were created. In-stitutions to study the field were established. By the 1980s, conflict-resolu-tion ideas were also increasingly making a difference in existing conflicts, such as in Northern Ireland, where groups inspired by the new ideas had set up community-relations initiatives that were reaching across community divides.

By the closing years of the Cold War, the climate for conflict resolution was changing radically, which had a huge impact on the field. As a result of improved relations between the superpowers and a sharp rise in the number of ethnic and other types of internal conflicts, a climate arose in which the at-tention of scholars of international relations and comparative politics turned to exactly the type of conflict that had preoccupied the conflict-resolution thinkers for many years. A richer cross-fertilization of ideas developed be-tween conflict resolution and the traditional fields.

A Wider View

One of the most outspoken new developments that surfaced in the post–Cold War era has been the shift of focus from international wars to internal conflicts. In response there has been a differentiation and broadening in the scope of third-party intervention. Whereas classical conflict resolution was mainly concerned with entry into the conflict itself and with how to enable parties in violent conflict to resolve the issues between them in nonviolent ways, the contemporary approach is to take a wider view of the timing of intervention. It suggests that efforts to resolve conflict should begin before armed conflict has started. They should be maintained even in the heat of battle and are applicable to peacekeeping and humanitarian intervention. Efforts also include assisting parties to settle violent conflicts. And conflict-resolution approaches continue to be relevant into the postsettlement phase, when peacebuilding must address the continuing issues in conflict.

More Attempts

As the concept of conflict resolution has gained currency, many more conflict-resolution attempts are being made. They involve different kinds of agencies, address different groups, and vary in form, duration, and purpose. Although the primary responsibility for responding to contemporary conflicts no doubt lies within the affected state, outsiders are inevitably involved as they often are part of the cause of a conflict or are affected by it. A large part of the outsiders'

Howard Davies/Panos Pictures

1998: Refugees from Chinese occupied Tibet wait with their ID cards, to be registered by UNHCR in Kathmandu, Nepal. After walking for three weeks to flee from their homeland, they will continue on to Dharamsala, the exiled home of the Dalai Lama in India.

involvement in conflicts concerns third-party mediation by governmental actors, including the UN. It is ironic, however, that contemporary conflicts that, in an overwhelming amount of cases, reflect a weakening of state structures, the collapse of sovereignty, and a local breakdown in the state system, primarily rely on involvement of international institutions that are still based on precisely the system of sovereignty and noninterference that the new conflicts undermine. It is not surprising that the international community struggles to find effective means of response.

The United Nations has made several efforts to increase its role as a prime instrument through which the international community attempts to defuse crises and de-escalate conflicts, but the post–Cold War experience has been mixed, with notable successes (Namibia, Cambodia, El Salvador, and Mozambique) alongside dismal failures (Somalia, Bosnia, and Rwanda). The vital factor distinguishing success from failure has usually been not so much the UN institutions, but rather the policies of the major powers on the Security Council and the intractability of the conflicts themselves.

The UN's Agenda for Peace, issued in 1992, proposed that the UN should be involved in peacekeeping, peacemaking, and peacebuilding from the earliest stage of conflict prevention to the stage of postconflict reconstruction. The scope of UN action has certainly enlarged and, for all its weaknesses, the UN remains the only institutional expression of the international community as a whole in its conflict-resolution capacity. Regional organizations make up a second tier of external agents in contemporary conflict resolution. The member states of the Organization for Security and Cooperation in Europe have gone farthest in accepting a role for their regional organization in reviewing the human-rights and security practices of member states. The charter of the Organization of African Unity (OAU) precludes interference in the affairs of member states and has therefore been reluctant to involve itself in internal conflicts. However, in 1993 it set up the OAU Mechanism for Conflict Prevention, Management and Resolution (MCPMR) to provide assistance to states affected by war.

Indigenous Traditions

It is an undisputed fact that there are gaps in the coverage of internal conflicts by the official arms of the international community. This leaves space for humanitarian agencies and nongovernmental organizations to play a larger role. Agencies such as the International Committee of the Red Cross have taken on an enhanced profile in internal conflicts. NGOs have also become more important. The number of NGOs involved with conflict resolution increased rapidly in the 1980s, as development agencies, aid donors, and governments became willing to fund their activities.

Whatever the constraints on individual NGOs, as a whole, given their multiplicity and variety, they have the advantage of flexibility and adaptability. They are able to work with local protagonists without the worry of thereby conferring official recognition, and can operate at the grass roots as well as at some higher levels. NGOs have played a significant role in a number of peace-making breakthroughs, although in individual cases the appropriateness and effectiveness of particular NGO initiatives have been criticized.

The current trend in NGO interventions is moving away from entering into the conflict situations by outsiders, and toward training people inside the society in conflict in the skills of conflict resolution, and combining these with indigenous traditions.

Criticism

An increased presence and visibility of the conflict-resolution field over the past decade, along with a greater degree of impact, has also brought greater scrutiny on the theoretical level. Realists criticized conflict resolution as soft-headed and unrealistic. From a different angle, neo-Marxists and radical thinkers from development studies saw the conflict-resolution enterprise as misconceived, since it attempted to reconcile interests that should not be reconciled and failed to take sides in unequal and unjust struggles. Other critics were skeptical of overblown claims made for the field by conflict-resolution proponents. This latter group also questioned whether the models of conflict resolution that were developed during the Cold War still had application to post–Cold War conflicts.

This last criticism is the most challenging. Are we witnessing a fundamentally new kind of conflict, to which previous ideas do not apply? If modern conflicts are becoming neomedieval struggles between warlords, drug barons, mercenaries, and militias who benefit from war and have made it their only means of making a living, of what value will be efforts to resolve conflicts between them peacefully? Can conflict resolution apply in situations such as those that have prevailed in Bosnia, where ethno-nationalist leaders whipped up ethnic hatred and courted war in order to serve their own political purposes?

Appreciating the Role of Internal Parties

These questions led to new discussions and the taking of new positions in the field. We argue that the developing tradition of thinking about conflict and conflict resolution is all the more relevant as the fixed structures of sovereignty and governance break down. All over the world, societies are facing burdens from population growth, structural change in the world economy, migration into cities, environmental degradation, and rapid social change. Societies with institutions, rules, or norms for managing conflict, and well-established traditions of governance are generally better able to accommodate peacefully to change; those with weaker governance, fragile social bonds, and little consensus on values or traditions are more likely to buckle. Strengthening the capacity of conflict resolution within societies and political institutions, especially preventively, is a vital part of the response to the phenomena of warlordism and ethnonationalism.

We approve of a shift from seeing third-party intervention as the primary responsibility of external agencies toward appreciating the role of internal third parties or indigenous peacemakers. Instead of outsiders offering the forums for addressing conflicts in one-shot mediation efforts, the emphasis should be on the need to build constituencies and capacity within societies and to learn from domestic cultures how to manage conflicts in a sustained way over time. This implies supporting domestic peace constituencies, developing domestic institutions, and eliciting from those in conflict what approaches are socially and culturally acceptable.

Behind all this lies an increased sensitivity to the culture question in general and the hope that if the conflict-resolution field has in the past been too narrowly Western, it may in the future become the truly cooperative cross-cultural venture that its founders conceived it to be. We emphatically argue that although the theories and practices of conflict resolution we deal with spring from Western roots, every culture and society has its own version of what is, after all, a general social and political need. The point is not to abandon conflict resolution because it is Western, but to find ways to enrich Western and non-Western traditions through their mutual encounter. It is in the encounter with local traditions that important lessons about conflict resolution are being learned, particularly about the limitations of the dominantly Euro-American model. In his study of the Arab Middle East, for instance, Salem has noted a "rich tradition of tribal conflict management [that] has thousands of years of experience and wisdom behind it."[2] Such perspectives are now beginning to emerge in current understandings and practices of conflict resolution.

A Broad Approach

We also argue for a broad understanding of conflict resolution. It would be wise to include not only mediation between the parties but also efforts to address the wider context in which international actors, domestic constituencies, and intra-party relationships sustain violent conflicts. The implication of this broadening of scope and applicability of conflict-resolution approaches has been to see the need for a complementary range of third-party interventions. They should be multitrack instead of just Track I (governmental) or Track II (NGOs, churches, civil society, etc.), and address both elites and the grassroots.

A broad view of conflict transformation is necessary to correct the misperception that conflict resolution rests on an assumption of harmony of interests between actors, and that third-party mediators can settle conflict by appealing to the reason or underlying humanity of the parties. On the contrary, conflict transformation requires real changes in parties' interests, goals, or self-definitions. These may be forced by the conflict itself, or may come about because of intraparty changes, shifts in the constituencies of the parties, or changes in the context in which the conflict is situated. Changes in the context in which a conflict is embedded may sometimes have even more dramatic effects than changes within the parties or in their relationships. The end of the Cold War—to give an example—is the prime recent context transformation that has shown to unlock protracted conflicts in South Africa, Central America, and elsewhere.

Robust Interventions

In line with the necessity of a broad view, conflict resolution should concern itself not only with the issues that divide the main parties, but also with the social, psychological, and political changes that are necessary to address root causes, the intraparty conflicts that may inhibit acceptance of a settlement, the context that affects the incentives of the parties, and the social and institutional capacity that determines whether a settlement can be made acceptable and workable. In other words, a multitrack approach is necessary, relying on interventions by different actors at different levels.

Looking back on recent history, one can safely say that some interventions and negotiated settlements are more robust than others. Although generalization is treacherous, successful settlements are thought to have the following characteristics: first, they should include the affected parties. The parties are more likely to accept a settlement if they have been involved in the process that reaches it; this argues for inclusiveness and against imposed settlements. Second, settlements need to be well crafted and precise, especially as regards details over transitional arrangements—for example, demobilization assembly points, cease-fire details, and voting rules. Third, they should offer a balance between clear commitments and flexibility. Fourth, they should offer incentives for parties to sustain the process and to participate in politics, for example through power sharing rather than winner-take-all elections. Fifth, they should provide for dispute settlement, mediation and, if necessary, renegotiation in case of disagreement. And sixth, they should deal with the core issues of the conflict and bring about a real transformation, incorporating norms and principles to which the parties subscribe, such as equity and democracy, while at the same time creating political space for further negotiations and political accommodation.

Hugh Miall is lecturer at the Richardson Institute of Peace Studies, Department of Politics and International Relations, University of Lancaster. Oliver Ramsbotham is senior lecturer in Peace Studies, University of Bradford. Tom Woodhouse is codirector of the Centre for Peace Studies, also at the University of Bradford.

Notes

1. This is an authorized summary of *Contemporary Conflict Resolution* by Hugh Miall, Oliver Ramsbotham, and Tom Woodhouse, Oxford: Polity Press/Blackwell Publishers, 1999.

2. Paul Salem (ed.), *Conflict Resolution in the Arab World: Selected Essays.* New York: American University of Beirut, 1997, p. 95.

4

Positive Vibrations: Successes Large and Small

Jim Wake

Headlines, in general, are reserved for assassins, torturers, warlords, and fanatics—the sorts of disreputable character who happen to be in plentiful supply in the unsettled political climate of Central Asia, where Soviet-imposed order once prevailed; the mountains of Afghanistan echoing with the reverberations of more than two decades of war; and South Asia, where domestic tranquility remains as much a hope as a reality fifty-plus years after the end of British rule. But there is also good news to report, even in those difficult circumstances—of brave and committed people pursuing their dreams and their visions to bring people together, to encourage understanding and tolerance, to replace warfare with dialogue, and ignorance with knowledge.

Meaningful peacebuilding activities in the region take many forms and operate at many levels, from the street to the highest levels of society, addressing everyday local conflicts such as disputes over access to water resources and local markets, as well as cross-border disputes with serious international ramifications. In some cases, those involved may see incremental progress, in a few, a major breakthrough, but often all that drives them is their conviction that individuals can make a difference. These particular stories focus on three areas where notable successes have been achieved: nonofficial dialogue, interreligious dialogue, and peacebuilding by and for women. It should be stressed that these stories, and the specific areas here receiving attention, are merely exemplary; other successes in other fields of endeavor are every bit as inspiring and impressive. Here, then, are some of the stories that haven't made the headlines.

Nonofficial Dialogue

The Inter-Tajik Dialogue[1]
In Tajikistan, the collapse of the Soviet Union led not just to independence, but to political instability, and eventually to a fiercely fought civil war. Even

during the 1980s, as *perestroika* brought some degree of political freedom throughout the Soviet Union, opposition groups had begun to organize themselves to contest the stranglehold on power held by the long-ruling Tajiks from the northern region around Kojand. These movements forged a coalition and backed a single candidate for the presidency in the first postindependence election, held in November 1991. But the election was rigged, most observers concluded, and the coalition candidate was defeated. In the months following, the government became increasingly repressive, and in May 1992, hostilities broke out. By September 1992, fighting was widespread.

With the outbreak of a full-scale civil war, the United Nations became involved in efforts to restore peace and stability in Tajikistan. In April 1994, government and opposition representatives met in Moscow for three rounds of UN-sponsored negotiations, and agreed to a cease-fire. Finally, in June 1997, most of the parties to the conflict signed the General Agreement on the Establishment of Peace and National Accord in Tajikistan.

What is unusual about this process is that, more than a year before the two sides met to engage in "official" negotiations, informal discussions had already begun in Moscow under the auspices of the Dartmouth Conference Regional Conflicts Task Force, a forum for U.S.-Soviet (and later U.S.-Russian) discussions dating back to 1960. The Inter-Tajik Dialogue brought together a small group—ten citizens—divided between pro-government and pro-opposition delegates, to examine the causes of the conflict and, according to Task Force co-chair Harold Saunders, "to see whether a group [could] be formed from within the civil conflict to design a peace process for their own country." Saunders, a former U.S. assistant secretary of state, employed a methodology he had developed called "Sustained Dialogue," which creates a "safe political space"[2] for dialogue and allows for slow, steady, but meaningful progress toward a sustainable peace. Saunders identified five stages in this process:

1. Deciding to engage
2. Mapping the relationship together
3. Probing the dynamics
4. Experiencing the relationship by thinking together
5. Acting together

The idea behind this process is that these unofficial discussions can "focus on relationship issues such as dehumanization, fear, identity, and historical roots that are beyond the scope of mediation and negotiation, by 'reaching toward the heart of the relationship where enemies are made, where reconciliation takes place, and where fundamental change can produce working relationships capable of post-conflict peacebuilding.'"[3]

During the early meetings, which continued until August 1993, the participants at first spoke to each other about their own feelings about the war, and then addressed the conditions that would be necessary to start actual negotiations. In January 1994, opposition groups, united under the banner of the Coordination

Centre of Democratic Forces of Tajikistan, presented a set of proposals regarding a settlement to the pro-government participants. For two days, the two parties discussed this platform. Pro-government participants were convinced that the proposals were serious and could serve as a basis for a negotiations. They took this message to the Tajik government, and shortly thereafter the government informed the UN special envoy that it would participate in a UN-sponsored peace process.

The participants met again in March 1994 and prepared the first of many memoranda that helped to provide guidance to participants at the official peace negotiations. And so, finally, in April 1994, the actual UN-sponsored talks began. They would continue over several years, finally leading to the General Agreement. Once the peace talks began, the Inter-Tajik Dialogue continued to meet in a more "consultative" role, with the aim of "designing a political process of national reconciliation for the country." Several participants also participated in the official negotiations.

It is impossible to know if some other channel for peace talks might have been established had the Inter-Tajik Dialogue not existed, but it is clear that in 1993, the dialogue was the only channel for communication across the political divide, and one high Tajik official observed that "after six meetings of the dialogue, it was no longer possible to argue credibly that negotiation between the government and the opposition was impossible." A number of proposals developed by the dialogue, such as a staged transition to a more inclusive political system and the establishment of a coordinating council responsible for implementing agreements, were taken up during negotiations and helped shape

Jon Spaull/Panos

Meeting of social workers, Khatlan province, Tajikistan.

the General Agreement, which provided for a Commission on National Reconciliation quite similar in function to the Coordinating Council.

Participants in the dialogue themselves say that they came to understand the roots of the conflict by taking part, and through a better understanding they were more willing to moderate their positions and to consider compromises. At present, Tajikistan still has a long way to go before peace, prosperity, and stability is assured. But thanks in part to those individuals who came together in the Inter-Tajik Dialogue, there is now hope for the future, and relative peace on the ground.

Pakistan-India People's Forum for Peace and Democracy

"At a time when the governments of India and Pakistan are intensifying mutual confrontation, with government and political leaders openly talking about the inevitability of a conflict and stockpiling of nuclear weapons, the situation in the sub-continent is on the brink of war. In a climate of hysteria forces of bigotry and religious intolerance threaten the fabric of civil society on the sub-continent. In such a bellicose atmosphere democratic rights of the people are imperiled. There is therefore an urgent need for saner voices to prevail."[4]

So began the very first public statement of the Pakistan-India People's Forum for Peace and Democracy, issued in September 1994 following a series of meetings among people on both sides of the India-Pakistan border. They were representatives of NGOs and trade unions, artists and journalists, academics and human-rights activists—twenty-five concerned citizens who had, as their statement said, "come to the conclusion that the crisis in their relations was being deliberately maintained by the ruling elites in utter disregard of the common interest and aspirations of the people of the two countries."

In view of subsequent developments—the political instability and military coup in Pakistan, guerrilla war, terrorist attacks, and border clashes in Kashmir, and the detonation of nuclear warheads by both India and Pakistan—the 1994 statement was without a doubt prophetic. That first statement also outlined in general terms the general principles that should guide relationships between Indian and Pakistan—that the politics of confrontation between India and Pakistan had failed to achieve benefits of any kind for the people of either country, the people of both countries increasingly wanted genuine peace and friendship and wanted their respective governments to honor their wishes. The statement asserted that peace between the two countries would help to reduce communal and ethnic tension in the subcontinent and stimulate economic and social progress in the South Asian region, and that a democratic solution to the Kashmir dispute was essential for promoting peace in the subcontinent. It urged the governments of Pakistan and India to agree to an unconditional no-war pact.

In November 1994, the group met again, this time in Delhi, to sketch out a program that included the exchange of information on activities promoting peace and democracy; public education activities on a wide range of relevant peace and justice issues; and cultural, scientific, and technological exchanges.

At the time, the forum also agreed to organize a convention in New Delhi for February of the following year.

That convention, attended by over two hundred people, was viewed as a breakthrough, the first-ever people-to-people dialogue on such a scale between the citizens of Pakistan and India. In addition to discussions on the political conflict, the convention also included cultural programs, discussions on economic and scientific cooperation, and planning for future steps to strengthen and expand the peacebuilding efforts.

Since those early days, and despite the ongoing conflict and heightened tensions, the forum has continued to meet, to address the issues that it first addressed in 1994 and 1995, and to actively engage in a wide variety of activities to build peace and understanding. In April 2000, the fifth convention of the forum was held in Bangalore. The forum itself acknowledges that in many ways, the situation on the subcontinent is worse now than it was when they first initiated a cross-border dialogue. But in an environment where dialogue has barely existed, where even sporting events are canceled because of political conflict, and where it has often been easier for Pakistanis and Indians to travel thousands of miles to meet in Europe than to visit each other in their own homes, the Pakistan-India People's Forum for Peace and Democracy is proof that it still is possible for sensible and sensitive people to bridge the divide and talk to each other about ways to build a safer and saner world.

Ajoka Theatre Group[5]

Yet another form of people-to-people peacebuilding, truly at the grassroots level, occurs through culture, and through cultural exchange. The Ajoka Theatre Group, for example, works with relatively limited resources to bring a message of religious tolerance, nonviolence, and respect for civil and human rights to ordinary folk. The artistic director of the group, Madeeha Gauhar, was a well-known actress on Pakistani television, but for more than fifteen years her primary focus has been Ajoka.

The group presented its first play in the yard of a private home in 1984, when General Zia-ul-Haq was Pakistan's military ruler, free expression was a risky enterprise, and all forms of political or opposition activity were prohibited. Since then, Ajoka has continued to present thought-provoking, socially relevant theater in Pakistan, and outside the Pakistani borders as well. Ajoka is committed to using theater as a means of contributing to the struggle for a just, humane egalitarian Pakistan. And in fact, the example of Ajoka has inspired numerous other similar theater groups throughout Pakistan.

Though Gauhar has stated that the continued existence of the group is itself an achievement, it is probably even more notable that Ajoka has managed to develop relationships with theater groups in India, and to perform there on a fairly regular basis. In an interview with an Indian newspaper in Chandigarh, where she was conducting an Indian-Pakistani workshop in 2001, Gauhar noted that with the increase in religious intolerance, cultural exchange through theater is one way to help India, Pakistan, and Bangladesh to rise above political differences and come together.

Interreligious Dialogue

Inter-Religious Peace Foundation in Sri Lanka

In Sri Lanka, a brutal civil war has been raging since the early 1980s, pitting the Hindu Tamils who live in the north of the country against Buddhist Sinhalese, who predominate on the rest of the island. For centuries, the various ethnic and religious groups inhabiting Sri Lanka, which include Muslims and Christians as well as Tamils and Sinhalese, had lived in relative harmony, but following independence from Britain in 1947, the Sinhalese attained a dominant position in the political structures of what was originally called Ceylon, and after 1972, Sri Lanka. The Tamil community was increasingly marginalized, with the Sinhalese language designated as the official state language in 1956 and Buddhism accorded the "foremost place" in the 1972 Constitution—even as that same constitution guaranteed freedom of religion.

Political and intercommunal violence increased throughout the 1970s and full-scale war broke out in 1983, with the government fighting the Liberation Tigers of Tamil Eelam (LTTE), commonly known as the Tamil Tigers. Despite repeated attempts to end the war, cease-fire agreements, and external intervention, the war continues to this day. And while it is clear that the adversaries in this war are Hindus and Buddhists, the conflict is not, essentially, about religion, but about self-determination for a population that feels its rights have been denied.

Building trust and encouraging dialogue in the tortured environment of Sri Lanka is a nearly impossible challenge, but three Sri Lankan clergymen have, nonetheless, created a space where people from the various Sri Lankan communities are able to come together for the purposes of fostering fellowship and harmony among the conflicting communities, promoting a culture of peace, and developing a democratic state and social order based on principles of equality, solidarity, dignity, autonomy, security, and freedom. This "space" takes the form of the Inter-Religious Peace Foundation (IRPF), which developed out of a series of meetings in the early 1990s between an Anglican minister, Reverend Rienzi Perera; a Catholic priest, Father Oswald Firth; and a Buddhist monk, Venerable Pandit Madampagama Assaji Thero. During those meetings, they came to understand that, with no dialogue at all between the government and the Tamil Tigers, it was important to create an interreligious, community-based approach to peacebuilding.

The underlying belief of IRPF is that "religiosity" can act as a unifying factor in peacebuilding work because it is, in and of itself, not tied to any particular set of beliefs, and that differences do not necessarily have to lead to division and exclusion. Religious beliefs, even when they differ, can indeed be a binding element and can thus provide common ground for peaceful dialogue.

IRPF activities take many different forms. The groups organizes symposia for religious leaders, for example, where representatives of all of Sri Lanka's communities come together to discuss issues related to religion and peace. These meetings have given the participants a feeling of empowerment, providing them with an all-too-infrequent opportunity to reflect on the conflict. By providing the space for moderate religious leaders to come together, the symposia have helped to marginalize the extremist voices that had previously been so dominant.

IRPF has also been involved in peace education activities in local schools in nearly every school district in the country, offering the notion of a culture of peace as an alternative to a culture of polarization and confrontation. And IRPF has engaged in information and advocacy activities, such as poster campaigns spreading messages of peace and tolerance, and the publication in both Tamil and Sinhalese of a newsletter called "Hundred Petals."

Although it is always difficult to gauge the impact of activities where the primary outcome is dialogue, IRPF has clearly brought individuals together who would have almost certainly not otherwise had any opportunity for meaningful exchange. And these exchanges have altered the participants' perceptions of those they've met, and of the possibilities for resolving conflict. That these individuals can take this message back to others in their communities opens up opportunities for increased understanding that would not have been possible without the existence of IRPF.

The Assam Hill People: Moral Re-Armament Instead of Violent Conflict[6]

Ever since India gained its independence, it has been engaged in constant struggle—often violent—to hold the disparate elements together. In northeast India, in Assam State, the Naga people launched a violent struggle in the 1950s for independence and the establishment of a greater Naga nation, which ultimately led to the establishment of Nagaland as a state within the Indian nation in 1963. Meanwhile, in 1960, when the Indian government decreed that Assamese would be the official language in the Assam State, other peoples living in the hill area of Assam also began to campaign for statehood. As the rhetoric heated up, a very real fear grew that the language dispute would lead to another violent independence struggle, and to conflict between the hill people and those people living in the plains of Assam.

That this did not occur is due in large part to the efforts of Stanley Nichols-Roy, the general secretary of the All-Party Hill Leaders Conference, who had been introduced in 1967 to the idea of "moral re-armament." Nichols-Roy attended a dinner organized by members of Moral Re-Armament (MRA), a movement launched in the 1920s by U.S. Lutheran pastor Frank Buchman in response to what he saw as a need for a "moral and spiritual awakening." According to the tenets of MRA, individuals should work toward a "hate-free, fear-free, greed-free world," and social change can only be achieved through personal transformation. Individuals need to search, through times of silence that connect them to God, for spiritual growth and a clear sense of direction. MRA's approach to conflict resolution is to "engender a heightened spiritual sensitivity in both parties and to thereby induce them to enter into a genuine and deep dialogue marked by a reciprocal sense of moral obligation." At the end of World War II, the precepts of Moral Re-Armament were applied in Europe as part of the efforts to achieve reconciliation between France and Germany.

Nichols-Roy heard of this work that first evening, and was both impressed and inspired. "My visit . . . convinced me that MRA is the ideology to bring sanity and peace to India's troubled Northeast, and to help it play its rightful part in Asia and the world," he later recalled. He himself went through a personal transformation, a transformation not lost on B. P. Chaliha, the first minister of Assam State. Chaliha saw the possibility to work with Nichols-Roy to find a way to reach a settlement and avoid violence—and an important part of the process became an outreach campaign, embracing the ideas of MRA, which included films and plays that were based on true stories of tolerance, personal transformation, and nonviolent conflict resolution. The campaign had a profound impact on the many thousands of ordinary people, soldiers, and political figures who saw the films, helping to defuse a highly volatile situation. And so, in the end, the Assamese hill people achieved their dream, with the establishment of the new state of Mehalaya, meaning "Abode of the Clouds," on 2 April 1970, which was, subsequently followed in the 1970s and 1980s by the establishment of the states of Manipur, Tripura, Caghar, and Mizoram in other parts of the territory of Assam State. B. P. Chaliha affirmed the importance of MRA, saying "MRA has transformed the climate of Assam."

Women Working for Peace and Justice

Women Take the Initiative to Help Themselves in Tajikistan[7]
Following the civil war of the 1992–1993, Tajiks are now engaged in the slow process of rebuilding their social and political structures, and creating space for public discourse in a civil society. The active role that women have played in this process has been quite remarkable. Between 1995 and 1998, for example, the number of women's organizations increased from three to fifty-four. Women in rural areas have taken the initiative to organize small enterprises supported by microcredit programs, and to market their handicrafts. In the cities, they have organized crisis centers for women and have been involved in a variety of educational projects.

One organization that has made important contributions to these efforts is Traditions and Modernity, an NGO established by Tajik women in 1996 with the goal of improving the status of women by disseminating information to help women understand their rights, and by encouraging increased participation of women in the political process. Traditions and Modernity also carries out sociological studies on gender issues, investigates cases of mental and physical violence in Tajik families, and provides counseling and rehabilitation to victims of violence.

One of the most notable projects in which it has been involved has been the School of Political Leadership for Women, which it helped to organize in 1998, in cooperation with the Union of Tajikistan Women and other NGOs.

With support from the Tajik government, the United Nations, and other international organizations, the school has conducted training sessions in six Tajik cities. Its objectives are to promote women's civic initiatives, to change gender stereotypes regarding participation in politics, and to promote a culture of democratic discourse.

Nearly two hundred women have participated in these sessions, and potential candidates for the Tajik parliament and other political offices have emerged. Tradition and Modernity has worked with these women to provide them with the knowledge they need on such matters as election law and political campaigning. Although Tajikistan remains a traditional society, and women face an uphill struggle to be treated as equals, they have made significant gains since Traditions and Modernity, and the School for Political Leadership for Women, first started their work; in the parliamentary elections of 2000, the number of women elected to the parliament increased from three to eight.

Dalit Women Begin to Assert Themselves[8]

The Dalit population of Indian—better know in the West as the "Untouchables"—has suffered poverty and humiliation for centuries, and not surprisingly, Dalit women suffer particularly severe indignities. Few are permitted even basic education, and stories of horrible violence and abuse are distressingly common. In Indian society, they are at the very bottom of the heap, viewed as barely human by the higher castes, and relegated to a subservient role by the tradition of male domination within the Dalit culture. But very slowly Dalit women are beginning to organize themselves, to stand up for their rights, and with the experience of such severe oppression, for the rights of abused, exploited, and oppressed people in general. It started in the 1970s, with the establishment of the All India Progressive Women's Organisation by Kumudtai Pawde, herself a Dalit woman, and gained momentum with the establishment of an organization to promote the welfare of agricultural workers in the early 1990s. In 1995, the National Federation for Dalit Women was established.

Dalit women face particularly difficult challenges in asserting their rights, in part because the male-dominated Dalit leadership is preoccupied with the more general issue of Dalit rights, to the exclusion of women's concerns, and because when the women's movement in India has pushed for better treatment of women, it has rarely done so in the context of India's caste system.

But Teesta Setalvad, writing in the Indian magazine *Communalism Combat,* sees important progress. "Increasingly, Dalit women activists and groups are creating their own distinct spaces to identify and articulate the sources of what they see as distinct patriarchal biases within the men of their own community even while standing side by side with Dalit men when it comes to demanding that the world recognize caste crimes against Dalits as a crime against humanity and caste itself as an organized system of hidden apartheid."

And slowly, writes Setalvad, advocates for the poor, for other minority women, and for women's rights are joining forces with Dalit women to forge alliances to oppose the exploitation and marginalization of all Indian women.

The effects of these activities may barely have registered to date, but the Dalit women's movement is a movement destined to grow, as consciousness grows and more and more women—from within the Dalit community and outside the community as well—seek to redress generations of injustice.

RAWA: Courage Behind the Veil[9]

Over the past twenty-five years, as the shadow of war, repression and intolerance has cast a pall over Afghanistan, one group, the Revolutionary Association of the Women of Afghanistan (RAWA), has provided a glimmer of hope—though at times it may have been difficult to discern. RAWA was established in 1977 by Meena Keshwar Kamal, a young woman who left her university studies to devote herself to the cause of social activism. In the early days of the organization, Meena organized opposition to the Soviet occupation, established a magazine called *Payam-e-Zan* (Women's Message), organized programs to assist refugees, and spoke out against Islamic fundamentalism. In February 1987, she was assassinated in Pakistan by agents of the KGB in collaboration with Islamic fundamentalists, but RAWA continued to pursue her goals of secular democracy and equal rights for women.

RAWA, unlike so many of the organizations described in this chapter, has recently gained some international prominence as its courageous activities under the harsh regime of the Taliban have come to the attention of the public. With women banned from schools and the workplace, shrouded in the burka, and executed for the crime of adultery, RAWA braved severe repercussions by organizing secret home-based schools for Afghan girls and boys, and clandestine literacy classes for and women. At considerable risk, they allowed cameras into one of those schools and smuggled the film to the outside world to show that even under the Taliban, women were still intent on educating themselves.

Thousands of RAWA members have provided health care, both inside Afghanistan and in the sprawling refugee camps in Pakistan, and trained women in first aid and health care. RAWA members have delivered babies, brought war-injured Afghans to hospitals in Pakistan, and participated in a large-scale polio vaccination program. RAWA also provides economic assistance and advice to women engaged in farming and business activities.

When women join RAWA, they agree, as a condition of membership, to act as witnesses and record what is going on inside Afghanistan. RAWA members have, accordingly, provided some of the most important information to international organizations on human-rights violations, including the secretly filmed public execution of a woman in the Kabul football stadium—vividly exposing the brutal nature of the Taliban regime. Ironically, this and other activities of RAWA were only possible because the women of RAWA are able to conceal their activities and hide their identities "behind the veil." Beyond information on human-rights violations, they've also provided support to women traumatized by such violations and the ongoing war.

Their activities in support of the rights of women, and of human rights and democracy in general, remain risky. In December 2000, RAWA members demonstrating in Pakistan against the Taliban government in Afghanistan were attacked, and several were injured. "We face a lot of security problems, not only from the Taliban and fundamentalist forces, but also from the government of Pakistan," RAWA activist Sahar Saba said in a radio interview in March 2001. "There can be no doubt that in the long term we face problems, but for us that's not important. For us it's important that the world can hear our words on behalf of the women and the people of Afghanistan."

Afghan women have regained some of their dignity and their human rights with the fall of the Taliban at the end of 2001, but RAWA's work is certain to continue. The word "revolutionary" in its name is no accident; the organization seeks to radically alter the balance of power between men and women in Afghanistan, and that struggle will go on for many years. RAWA has, in the past, been harshly critical of the Northern Alliance, which it accuses of human-rights violations and mistreatment of women. As Afghanistan embarks on a new phase in its development, RAWA can continue to play a constructive role.

Exemplary but Not Exclusive

As noted at the outset, the stories that have been told in this chapter are exemplary but not exclusive—there are many others that might have been chosen, mostly of people working quietly, out of the glare of cameras, frequently squeezed for resources and often in the face of adversity. Beyond their vision, these people should be admired for their pluck, for continuing to believe when around them chaos reigns, and for refusing to give in to frustration. They may not make the headlines, but they do make a difference to the many thousands of people whom they touch.

Jim Wake is a U.S. free-lance journalist based in the Netherlands.

Notes

1. Much of the information in this section is drawn from "Politics of Compromise: The Tajikistan Peace Process," Kamoludin Abdullaev and Catherine Barnes, editors, Conciliation Resources, 2001 (available online at www.c-r.org/accord10/index.htm); and "Tajikistan: From Civil War to Peace Building," by Randa M. Slim and Faredun Hodizoda, which appears in *Searching for Peace in Europe and Eurasia: An Overview of Conflict Prevention and Peacebuilding Activities*, a joint publication of Lynne Rienner Publishers and the European Centre for Conflict Prevention, 2002. See in particular "The Inter-Tajik Dialogue," pp. 44–47 (www.c-r.org/accord10/inter.htm) in "The Politics of Compromise."

2. Gennady I. Chufrin and Harold H. Saunders, "A Public Peace Process," *Negotiation Journal* 9(3), April 1993, pp. 155–177. The citation is drawn from a summary, available on the internet at www.colorado.edu/conflict/peace/example/chuf7416.htm, prepared by Tanya Glaser of the Conflict Research Consortium at the University of Colorado.

3. Ibid.

4. Information for this section is drawn in large part from the following websites: www.mnet.fr/aiindex/PIF/ and www.pucl.org/reports/National/indopak.htm.

5. See: www.pakistanlink.com/community/2001/Aug/03/12.html and www.mnet.fr/aiindex/i_aii/ajoka.html.

6. Much of the material in this section is drawn from "War Prevention Works: 50 Stories of People Resolving Conflict," published by the Oxford Research Group, 2001.

7. Information in this section is drawn from an article on the web site of the Initiative for Social Action and Renewal in Eurasia, available at www.isar.org/isar/archive/GT/GT8kuvatova.html.

8. The primary source for the information in this section comes from Teesta Setalvad, "Thrice Oppressed," *Communalism Combat,* May 2001. Available online at: http://sabrang.com/cc/archive/2001/may01/cover.htm.

9. For information on RAWA, see http://rawa.fancymarketing.net/index.html, http://rawa.false.net/rawa.html, and http://news.bbc.co.uk/hi/english/world/south_asia/newsid_1562000/1562596.stm.

5

Lessons Learned from Ten Years of Experience in Conflict Prevention

Jos Havermans

There are no overall recipes for ending or preventing conflicts, because every conflict is unique. But there are general conclusions to be drawn, and communal lessons to be learned, from ten years of experience with conflict prevention. The international project Lessons Learned in Conflict Interventions and Peacebuilding, initiated by the European Centre for Conflict Prevention, took up the challenge to address the need for more and better reflection methodologies and frames in order to enhance the learning capacity of practitioners and policymakers in the field. The project's aim is not only to collect lessons but also to disseminate them in such a way that organizations and actors involved in violent and nonviolent situations could learn from each other's experiences. This chapter summarizes the main findings of the project.[1]

Practitioners of peacebuilding have learned a remarkable variety of lessons from their experience with stopping or preventing conflicts over the past years. In this rich variety, some lessons stick out. When asked what major lesson they learned from their peace work, the most frequent answer practitioners give is that there is no blueprint for building peace, that every conflict is different and, as a consequence, that what may work in one situation may not in another. This may come as a cold shower for those looking for common denominators and references to go by when embarking on peace efforts. At the same time, it gives evidence to the adventurous nature of peace work. Values such as inspiration and risk taking seem to be as relevant as the more academic, rational notions underlying efforts to build peace.

Most practitioners and organizations use the lessons they learn within the scope of their own activities. An organization, for instance, that focuses on working with grassroots groups on the village level, will learn from its mistakes and successes in the past in adapting its design of new projects in similar settings. Applicability will not be an issue in these circumstances. But it is clear that the lessons learned by such an organization may be the complete opposite of those learned by another organization working on a different level. The Institute for Multi-Track Diplomacy (IMTD), for instance, said that it has learned from efforts to set up a dialogue between opposing groups in Cyprus that transparency is of crucial importance. Being totally open about what is being discussed at community meetings, and literally keeping the door open to all citizens to attend, has turned out to be of crucial importance for building trust between the local communities, the IMTD found. Yet, it is obvious that this kind of transparency and openness to the general public would have been counterproductive in many other instances, especially for peace initiatives on the official level. When it comes to brokering peace between political leaders, confidentiality is usually an indispensable requirement for success. The need for confidentiality is an important "lesson learned" from the Oslo talks on the Middle East conflict. Had it not been for the absolute seclusion and confidentiality of the first overtures, this process might have irreparably stalled in the very early stages.

Despite the irreconcilability of some lessons learned and a good amount of contradiction or paradoxes among them, it makes sense to look for common lessons. A need is felt to assess where we are currently standing in the field of conflict prevention. What has been learned so far, in the most concrete terms? Where do we look in order to find clues to improve peacemaking practices?

Increasing awareness about the kind of lessons learned is expected to contribute to improving the practice and profession of peacebuilding. Knowing what approaches and lessons other practitioners found most compelling can make peacemakers feel more confident about the approaches they choose in areas and other conflicts new to them.

Many projects, conferences, and seminars held over the past few years on the subject of conflict prevention and peacebuilding have resulted in lists of lessons learned, but few efforts have been made so far to add them all up and identify the most recurrent conclusions and observations. One of the exceptions is "Mapping Approaches to Lesson Learning" developed by Michael Lund.[2] Lund tried to classify several types of lessons, derived from activities at different levels, in varying regions of the world, into one framework that can be helpful in choosing an approach to drawing conclusions from peace efforts. One of the characteristics of Lund's efforts is that he seeks to take into account who the target audiences for lessons learned are and what purpose the lessons and conclusions are supposed to serve.

In this chapter, a number of lessons are discussed that have been mentioned most frequently by professionals in the field of conflict resolution. There is, no doubt, a good degree of incongruity among them. Awareness of the diverse background and context in which lessons were drawn is, therefore, of essential importance. Lessons are drawn from engagement in peace work by widely varying categories such as women's groups, grassroots initiatives, government undertakings, religious communities, or even the military. In addition, the lessons these actors brought forward may each be connected to different stages of a conflict, such as the pre- or postconflict stages. Then there are different qualities of involvement playing a role: early warning, prevention, mediation, or reconciliation.

Another factor that needs to be mentioned here is that the lessons that have been drawn over the years are coming from different sources. The most significant difference here is that some are drawn from academic analysis done by scholars, others from day-to-day experiences that peace workers have gone through. These practitioners may have been local volunteers, totally immersed in the conflict themselves, or professional outsiders working for NGOs or governments. All this accounts for the undoubtedly highly subjective quality of the lessons discussed. Yet, when the hundreds of lessons drawn over the past decade are sifted, a number of larger, recurring lessons emerge. They may be helpful, informative, and instructive for both experienced peace workers and newcomers in the field of conflict prevention and resolution.[3]

Lessons Learned

The terrorist attacks on New York and Washington on 11 September 2001 seem to have had a big impact on people working in the field of peacebuilding. Some professionals, such as a staffer of Search for Common Ground working in Macedonia, expressed disillusionment. Acknowledging he now felt doubt about the relevance of conflict prevention, Search for Common Ground's Eran Fraenkel said: "What sense does it make for me to get up every morning and work for peace if a few individuals are able to come in and destroy everything."

No one in the field, however, seems to have turned their back on the goals and ways of conflict prevention because of what happened on 11 September. Most people, including Mr. Fraenkel, seem to believe the attacks and their aftermath are all the more reason to reflect on where the field should be heading. They want to try to improve practices of peacemaking. A remarkable lot of peacemakers since "9-11" called on their colleagues to be more imaginative in developing ideas and strategies that can make nonviolent conflict resolution more effective.

Dozens, if not hundreds, of lessons can be drawn from ten years of experience with conflict prevention. Many are related exclusively to a specific situation, at a specific time. But there is a lot of similarity among a number of the lessons learned. Experiences with seeking peace in totally different conflicts, spread far apart over the world, seem to have led to similar conclusions. The lessons discussed below have been retrieved from a wide variety of conference reports and seminars as well as findings and conclusions brought forward by attendees of conferences, including the latest and biggest meeting on the subject, "Toward Better Peace Building Practice," held in Soesterberg, the Netherlands, in October 2001.

There Are No Blueprints

The most marked conclusion drawn from years of experience with conflict prevention is that there are no overall recipes for ending conflicts. "There are no blueprints" was the lesson listed number one on a pile of twelve presented by Kevin Clements, secretary-general of International Alert. Clements stressed that "the uniqueness of all conflicts" needs to be kept in mind all the time. "There are no overall recipes for solutions. However, I believe we do need a code of conduct and shared values," he said.

The working group on early warning at the same conference said it bluntly as well: there is no blueprint for early warning. All methods that have been developed may work everywhere, provided they be adapted to the needs of end-users and the specific context of the countries or region involved.

People who are active in setting up networks of organizations working toward peace also came up with the message: there is not one ultimate, omnipotent model. The shape of a network would have to vary according to certain national or regional circumstances, they say. For NGOs in Sweden, for example, it may be very acceptable to include government agencies in a network aimed at propagating reconciliation in a foreign conflict. But in conflict regions themselves, NGOs are often seen by the government as dangerous opposition forces. Networking with the government may be the last thing these NGOs would want to do.

Conflict Prevention Works

Based on case studies, a group of scholars contributing to a Carnegie Commission study, *Opportunities Missed, Opportunities Seized: Preventive Diplomacy in the Post–Cold War,* concluded that conflict prevention is a realistic, viable strategy. It "can be done," as the scholars put it.

"Preventive diplomacy is not just a noble idea, but is a viable real world strategy," Bruce Jentleson, who edited the study, concluded.[4] The study also pointed out that despite the fact that many conflicts may have deep historical roots, they are not inevitable, or predestined to happen. They are much more the consequence of conscious calculations than historical determinism, giving room to influencing the course of events.

Even people living in a conflict area who come in touch with foreign peacemakers believe preventing conflicts or reducing tension by nonviolent means is viable, despite their initial skepticism about what outsiders could do to prevent further escalation of "their" conflict. "Although we feel that we are more experienced experts on what war entails than many of the people coming to our region to support reconciliation, we do believe that programs offered by peacebuilders make sense," said Slavica Slavnic, representative of a multiethnic civic organization in the Republika Srbrsca. "The ethnic groups should talk to each other as much as possible and we welcome efforts that help facilitate this."

Avoid Becoming a Pretext for Inactivity

NGOs should try to keep their role in peacemaking from becoming a pretext for governments not to do anything. The effectiveness of NGO work in the field of peacemaking has increased dramatically, but it should not become a replacement for government action. A multi-track approach can often be more effective than either a government or NGO on its own. The successful intervention of the Roman Catholic Italian Sant'Egidio in Mozambique in the early 1990s proves a case in point. Sant'Egidio closely cooperated with the Italian ministry of Foreign Affairs in getting the Mozambican government and rebel movement Renamo to talk to each other.

Be Aware of the Limitations of Conflict Prevention

There is a need for a sense of proportionality of what outsiders can do, many professional peace workers say. There are limitations, some of which are of a practical character, as Kevin Clements pointed out. "The U.S. in the fall of 2001 earmarked forty billion dollars for the fight against terrorism," he explained. "There will undoubtedly be less money for us now, while the needs are enormous for cure and prevention," he said.

To a certain extent, peace workers say, preventive activities may show their effectiveness only in the long term. This is another notion of modesty peace workers should keep in mind: a quick reward is unlikely. Sometimes, results of peace work seem very limited. "We didn't stop the war, but we did get our message across," a professional working on the production of what is called "interethnic programming" in Macedonia reported. "For us, making someone stop in their tracks to think about what they are doing was a positive outcome," she added.

Awareness of the limitations of conflict prevention is an opening to acknowledging that even limited successes can make preventive efforts worthwhile. As Bruce Jentleson noted in the acclaimed study *Opportunities Missed, Opportunities Seized:* in some cases the success of conflict prevention may not be a total resolution of the dispute, but the prevention of a conflict escalating into mass killings. Jentleson also points out that some successes may prove to be transitory. Some conflicts, such as in Congo, finally developed into war, despite efforts to defuse tension that were in themselves successful at the time. "However," Jentleson says, "unless it is demonstrated that the principal reasons for eventual failure were integral to the initial success of prevention, as an analytic matter such an eventuality would not totally negate the earlier success."[5]

Jonathan Freedland, a reporter for *The Guardian* newspaper, made the point that even peace talks that seem to have failed, in most cases save lives. "For all its flaws, the Northern Ireland effort can claim to have saved nearly six hundred lives," he wrote in summer 2001, when the Northern Irish peace process was going through another setback. "Until the IRA cessation in 1994, approximately one hundred people were killed per year. . . . With more than hundred dead since 1994, that leaves close to six hundred saved in seven years," he wrote. Freedland also mentioned that the collapse of the Middle East peace process in 1999 resulted in about seven hundred deaths until late 2001, strengthening him in his belief that "talk saves lives" and that "whatever else happens, peace processes have to keep on." "Don't stop" is Freedland's simple and clear recommendation.[6]

Make Sure to Take Enough Time for Dealing with a Conflict

It seems too obvious an advisory, but early-warners in particular often find they have to do too much in too little time. Michael Lund, for instance, was commissioned to assess the potential for conflict in Zimbabwe and a few other African countries. "I did not have enough time to gather information on covert diamond trading the elite is supposed to be involved in certain countries. Some subjects are hard to get into, even though they are essential for understanding politics," Lund said.

Long-Term Commitment

Peacebuilding and reconciliation should be seen as a process, rather than a goal with a clear-cut ending in time. Peace can only be built up over a long period of time. Preferably, long-term relationships are built across the dividing lines of conflict in a society. Sustainability of interventions is therefore of essential importance. When interventions of outsiders are over, their action should, ideally, have left behind the capacity for continued interventions in the conflict by local actors.

Early warning experts stress that for early warning to be successful, it is necessary to link quick "go and look" efforts to structures and organizations that are engaged in continual, ongoing monitoring. These monitors could provide timely information to the experts making the final early warning assessments on which to act. "Early warning cannot be practiced ad hoc," one says.

A slow steady process of trust building is often necessary before official negotiations can start. Successful examples of this approach are the activities of the Lutheran World Federation in Guatemala or the Lebanon Conflict Resolution Network. It took years of incubation before these groups entered a concrete process of conflict resolution and reconciliation.

Many practitioners believe that NGOs are very well positioned to guarantee the kind of long-term commitment required. "NGOs may be better equipped for long-term engagement than governments who tend to take a short term view, for instance because they need to be re-elected every four years," Susan Collin Marks of Search for Common Ground said. According to Freedland, trying to reach finality in a peace process could even be detrimental. "Do not seek finality," he wrote in the article in *The Guardian* referred to earlier. He pointed out that Israeli prime minister Ehud Barak during peace talks in 2000 wanted PLO leader Yasser Arafat to declare an end to the Palestinian-Israeli conflict for their deal to be comprehensive. "Such a goal is laudable, but incompatible with the pragmatic, piecemeal business that is peacemaking," Freedland commented.[7]

Pay More Attention to Conflict Dynamics

More attention should be paid to conflict dynamics. How do conflicts change over time? Practitioners should try to discern changes over time in order to see when a certain type of intervention is needed. Early warning experts came to the same conclusion: "It is important to be aware of the changing nature of conflict when doing early warning analyses," was one of their major conclusions.

Build a Theory

Many practitioners and academics believe it is necessary to build a new theory of peace to work with.

"What is our theory? What vision do we have? We need a vision of a just world. Answers to questions such as how to find space to exchange visions, aspirations, dreams without doing harm to the dreams and aspirations of others. I believe we need to be more explicit of what we do and want," Kevin Clements says. Clements is among practitioners who want to design a wide-ranging theory on which to build their approach to make peace. He believes conflict resolution is a new political philosophy that should be defined in more detail. Clements: "I am in favor of developing a new political philosophy, geared toward a more collaborative way of policy making and some reduction of military solutions."

Norbert Ropers supports Clements's view. "It is important to improve the capacities of our fields to reduce the suffering of those drawn into conflicts. But is it enough?" he stated. "I believe that we should not just be a service-providing movement. We should also be a political movement. Let's not limit ourselves to just doing social work on a global level. We also want to transform the world. Where is the agenda of our field? I believe that we should connect to political movements who discuss these issues."

Building a theory underlying the work of conflict prevention touches on sensitive political questions, says Simon Fisher of the British organization Responding to Conflict. Fisher suggested that people working in the realm of conflict prevention may have to decide what their priority is: peace and stability, or justice. "We need to make a choice: who are we working for?" Fisher said at a conflict prevention seminar in Londonderry in February 2001. "Are we in the conflict resolution field acting as unwitting accomplices of inequality—protecting the rich but thinking we're doing the opposite? Are we helping the non-violent transformation of the world in the direction of more disparities?"

Roberto Ricigliano, an American scholar who formerly worked for the Conflict Management Group, thinks practitioners should reflect on their work more often at the outset. Ricigliano proposes working with other fields in order to become engaged with people who think differently; differently, that is, from workers in the field of conflict prevention. "I want to work on developing an integrated approach. Let's not isolate ourselves in our field," he says.

Some experts working in the field of early warning put the relevance of a new theory in perspective: "It is necessary to use theory as a guide for analyses, but let's not get bogged down in frameworks that are too strict and may cloud knowledge gained from new experiences," said one practitioner.

In direct response to the wish to develop a theory and world vision as a fundament for conflict prevention, many practitioners say that there must also be room for imagination and intuition. Sue Williams said that in assessing the factors and events that are responsible for a possible escalation of a specific conflict, theories do not always work. "Sometimes it is your gut feeling that tells you where things will go," she said.

Cultural Understanding

Given that there are no blueprints for solving conflicts, it makes sense to gain insight into the uniqueness of any individual conflict. This includes, experienced peace makers say, creating sensitivity to cultural heritages. "What works positively in one setting can be totally ineffective in another. It is important to have good understanding of cultures," concluded women working in gender projects varying from Sudan to Macedonia and Nepal.

Awareness of cultural and traditional customs may result in realizing new openings in a peace process. Tapping into traditional means of dealing with conflict especially can be very meaningful. Peace workers in West Africa explicitly recommend seeking intervention programs tailored to traditional approaches embedded in the local culture. The West African Network for Peacebuilding in particular believes that there is still a lot to gain from paying more attention to traditional peacebuilding practices. It called for a study into African traditional peacebuilding methods in order to enable outsiders to build on what has been developed over decades in conflict regions themselves.

Cultural differences should also be taken into account among peace organizations working together. Different cultures and procedures of government agencies and NGOs and among NGOs themselves should be taken into account if alliances or networks are forged to work on a specific conflict.

Keep the Regional Scope in Mind

Most early warning activity still focuses one-sidedly on conflict within the boundaries of a state. There should be more and better account taken of

Judge at People's Court session in a village in Rangpur, India.

regional dimensions, say practitioners and academics. Keeping an eye on regional conditions makes sense also because research has shown that the likelihood of concerted efforts to preventive diplomacy is higher in cases in which a potential regional impact is clearly demonstrated, Jentleson has said.

The field should think more about the relationships between conflicts instead of treating them individually. The conflicts in Burundi and Congo, for instance, were clearly interconnected. Practitioners therefore should think in terms of "systems of conflicts."

Put Effort into Mobilizing Local Actors

Engaging local actors is of crucial importance in order to create local capacity in peacebuilding and early warning. "Capacity building is extremely important," people gathered in an early warning working group said, "because even if people may say they want to work with you, the question remains: will they do it? Sometimes it is lack of capacity building that keeps them from taking initiatives."

"We should stand alongside local peacemakers," International Alert's Clements said. "Provide a safe place for dialogue. We should accompany peacemakers and show solidarity with the poor and oppressed. If you feel you come in with a solution, you probably bring deception."

Strengthening local capacities for peace may take many forms, including education and training, nurturing the volunteer spirit in society, and highlighting the work of local peace workers in the media. Focus on local capacities may also result in tapping into traditional peacemaking processes effectively. Identifying what local traditions could do for making peace, along with respect for certain cultural traditions, will enhance the chance of success. Somali people, for example, place high value on poetry, which in nomadic society is as important as radio or television. Traditional elders, who became engaged in efforts to defuse tensions in the country in the late 1990s, therefore brought in poets as well as religious leaders to reconcile warring clans, with good results.

Early warning specialists also stressed that more attention should be paid to giving the general public access to early warnings. In doing so, a lot of energy might be unleashed that will be directed toward politicians, aimed at putting pressure on them to take measures that defuse tension. "Mobilizing the general population in order to put pressure in policy makers is not fully used yet," the early warning working group at the Soesterberg conference concluded.

Acknowledge the Importance of Irrational Factors

Getting warlords or villagers to change their attitudes from hatred and an inclination to violence to attitudes of reconciliation and openness to dialogue is, apart from instances of cool calculation, about changing people's hearts. No matter how vague these processes may seem, they are mentioned as an essential part of many successful cases of conflict prevention or conflict resolution. It is, therefore, crucial to develop and maintain heightened sensitivity to the direction people's attitudes are heading and to the places where people may find inspiration for a change of heart. The Oxford Research Group said it was surprised to find that nearly half of the interventions it studied were carried out by people with some spiritual basis for their activities. The most important factor named by participants engaged in peacemaking was a sense of direction inspired "by some connection with a source of strength greater than their own ego."[8]

The importance of emotions and inspiration is also mentioned frequently in connection with working through women's groups to make peace. Women have frequently been found to offer the ingredients essential to making peace, particularly in addressing the feelings involved. Examples in this regard are the Mothers of the Plaza del Mayo and the Wajir Peace Group. "Most of what was accomplished was done by people with a heart for peace, rather than training in conflict resolution," Dekha Ibrahim Abdi, member of the Wajir group, said.[9]

John McDonald, a former diplomat active in the field of conflict prevention (see Resources below), confirmed that irrational factors are of crucial importance, but official institutions often find them hard to grasp.

> You cannot change the way people think about their enemy without touching their hearts, but this is difficult to accept for institutions such as the World Bank or the State Department. I once spoke to an economist of the World Bank who told me his institution had built three hundred houses for displaced people in Bosnia but was appalled that they were not being used. I told him it was out of fear that people had not returned to these villages. He had never worried about fear, he tended to think in measurable things like numbers of houses or roads built. But you have to think about emotions like fear.

A Holistic Approach Suits Best

Practitioners in the field of conflict prevention stress that effective prevention is derived from a variety of activities, addressing all aspects of society and all relevant actors. Working to just bridge ethnic gaps or defuse socioeconomic tension is usually not enough. The whole scale of human activities and dimension should ideally be engaged in the process. Clements, of International Alert, says, "We need a holistic view, encompassing conflict resolution, development and democratization. There will be no peace without justice, democracy and development. We need to include this in mechanisms for dealing with conflicts non-violently."

"No one group—be it a government, a group of citizens or an international NGO—can bring peace alone. That is the lesson, I think, we've got to learn," John McDonald, founder and chairman of The Institute for Multi-Track Diplomacy, said. The need for what it called a "multidisciplinary approach" was put forward independently by the West African Network for Peacebuilding, based on its experience with peace work in West Africa, as well as by many other organizations and individual peace workers.

Efforts to include a broad scale of approaches require networking, because it is clear that not all individual organizations are able to develop knowledge and capacity in all relevant fields. "We have to work together in order to be able to do justice to the complexity of the issue at stake," professionals reflecting on the need of national, regional, and global conflict prevention networks said. A well-functioning network of conflict prevention organizations can give assurance that a wide range of possible approaches is looked at when trying to keep a specific conflict in check. However, bringing different NGO sectors together in a network has been identified as one of the major hurdles toward establishing a holistic approach. "Reservations and barriers between various NGO sectors and milieus is one of the main problems to be overcome," said network members. The main driving forces in the field of conflict prevention are often conflict resolution, research, and human-rights organizations, while NGOs working in the fields of development and humanitarian assistance often hesitate to join, not least because they fear they might lose part of their funding from government budgets to conflict-resolution newcomers.

A holistic approach could also entail combining official and nonofficial forces to work for peace. Multi-track efforts, as these approaches are usually called, can only be effective if the exchange of information between official and nonofficial actors occurs frequently and for the long term, a condition that is not often met.

Build a Network
"Networking is critical for coordinating peace-building efforts," peacemakers in West Africa and other conflict regions concluded. Be it a formal network, supported by a secretariat and regular meetings, or a loose set of contacts, using the knowledge, information, and insight of a larger number of people is enriching and improves the quality of peacemaking efforts. A network often provides a data base of experts and practitioners who can be contacted.

Look Actively for Chances for Peace
In early warning activities most attention appears to be devoted to trying to assess what developments contribute to the escalation of conflict. There is little analysis and data collection about available capacities and chances to stop conflict, or prevent it from escalating. "The early warning industry is really at risk making mistakes because it always tends to look at factors that may cause conflict, but it does not focus on the capacity for peace," Michael Lund said. "This may lead to unbalanced assessments. Early warning people tend to ignore informal mechanisms regulating conflicts, for instance. You look at the ability of actors to make trouble, much less on their ability to make things change for the better," he pointed out.

Give Both Sides Something to Lose
If moves toward peace and reconciliation are rewarded with economic help or other valuable gains, then there is less chance of a backlash in the peace process. As soon as people feel they have something to lose from returning to violence they are less likely to do so. This point has been raised most strongly by *The Guardian* journalist Jonathan Freedland, as he compared the peace

processes in Northern Ireland and the Middle East. "The most glaring difference between the Middle East and Northern Irish peace processes is economic. Huge investment has flown into the province . . . ensuring the next generation has an interest in maintaining tranquility. [But] Palestinians' standard of living has declined since Oslo, leading to abject poverty in Gaza and soaring unemployment in the West Bank. Young Palestinian men might as well take up violence; they have nothing to lose."[10]

Coordinate Development and Peacebuilding Programs

As many conflicts occur in developing countries and are often perceived as being at least partly rooted in poverty, paying attention to the relationship between conflict resolution and development is a must. First, the field of conflict prevention has been calling on governments and other professionals in the developing aid area to assess whether aid programs may negatively affect stability in a society. Second, building up trust between groups engaged in a conflict is much easier when moves are made toward improving the socioeconomic conditions for all. Therefore, development issues are very relevant for peace and reconciliation, especially in the postconflict stages. This is why the West African Network for Peacebuilding, to give one example, has urged NGOs and governments to integrate development programs into peacebuilding.

Become More Media Savvy

NGOs working in the field of conflict prevention need to acquire skills about how to give their cause publicity. Some practitioners feel that peace workers are being surpassed in being media conscious by warmongers and others betting on violence. "Even terrorists have very good PR these days. They develop smart publicity campaigns, create media events and are good to the media," an NGO representative observed. "As a civil society organization you have to have people who know how media work."

Peace organizations should acquire basic skills such as how to organize a press conference and write a press release (at the minimum), practitioners in the field say. Other practitioners remarked that media savvy is increasingly important as it is becoming harder and harder to get stories from peacemakers into the mainstream media. Many required skills seem very accessible, such as writing concise reports on an organization's activities. "Uniform structured reports help end-users to locate information. The concise nature of reports makes sure that the most important information reaches the end-user and does not get lost in lengthy and cumbersome write-ups. No one reads long, tedious reports," a practitioner active in early warning said.

Conflict Prevention Needs Good Public Relations

There is a need to improve the image of working for peace among the general public and politicians, many practitioners believe. Some observers, such as Luc Reychler, professor at Leuven University, Belgium, stated that "there is a real need for marketing people" to help peace workers boost the status of their work. "Peace has a bad name," Reychler said. "It should be presented as something enticing and positive." Professionals feel that it is important to communicate "best practices" and "success stories" of conflict-prevention initiatives. Good PR and providing accessible information on activities is essential in order to gain support from a wider audience and funding institutions. It may also boost morale among people already active in the field.

In this regard, the use of "the bookkeeping argument" was recommended: more focus could be put on cost analysis in order to push actors to realize that prevention is cheaper than humanitarian assistance after a conflict. It is important to always keep in mind the answers to simple, and legitimate, questions put forward to practitioners of conflict prevention, many experts say. Such questions as "Why should Western countries give money to contain a conflict in a remote area on the other side of the world?" should immediately bring to mind such answers as: "To enhance security in the globalizing world and to prevent economic disruption."

Another suggested argument is what Bruce Jentleson has called the "Humpty Dumpty Problem." Putting severely shattered societies back together again is enormously difficult, hugely expensive, very risky, and in some cases just not possible. This should make a strong point for embarking on preventive initiatives.

There are several studies that provide figures that could accompany these arguments. The Oxford Research Group has pointed out that the maximum costs of bringing representatives of warring factions together amounts to several dozens of millions of dollars. In one case, in Sierra Leone, a conflict resolution initiative brought peace in a region of the country, probably saving dozens of lives, for just $2,700. NATO's bombing of Serbia in 1999 cost approximately $4 billion, in addition to more than $30 billion needed for postwar reparations.

In addition to being aware of the way the media can respond to conflict, it is of great importance to realize that the media can also be used as a direct tool for peace. Organizations producing television and radio shows spreading a message of reconciliation and peace say their work has shown that the contribution of media can be effective. Media can help change the attitude of a community. For instance, an evaluation of a television show run in Macedonia by Search for Common Ground showed 60 percent of children who watched the first eight editions said they would invite kids from other ethnic groups to their homes. This figure went up progressively during the course of the series. The powerful role of media is being acknowledged by most practitioners.

Evaluate

Lastly, and perhaps most importantly, look back on what you did and reflect on what could have been done better or what went wrong. Many professionals in the field, as well as academics, feel that peacemakers tend to neglect reflection on specific activities. In many cases they may not even have the time to write down a report on what they've tried in a specific conflict. Reflection

John McDonald: "Put Your Ego Behind You."

A former U.S. diplomat, John McDonald, director of the Institute for Multi-Track Diplomacy in Washington, D.C., went through more than a decade of "alternative" efforts to boost peace and reconciliation. Being a good listener and putting your ego behind you are among the most important lessons he says he learned during his years as a peacemaker.

McDonald: "One of the major personal lessons I've learned is that people embarking on peace processes, especially diplomats, should be much better listeners than they usually are. I have remarked earlier that American diplomats were the most arrogant in the world, the poorest listeners and the most impatient people in the world. If you put all three together—arrogance, impatience, poor listening—you're not going to be a very good diplomat, not a good representative of your country and not a peace builder. I am absolutely convinced that these characteristics haven't changed since I retired as a diplomat. But at least they are all correctable. And if you would correct them, you would become more effective when you work in other parts of the world.

"The other thing that I learned is that you have to put your ego behind you, and not in front of you. Every diplomat, every politician, almost every leader puts his ego out in front and says 'Here I am and I'm here to make a difference.' But when you relate to people who are in pain and suffering, you have to put your ego behind you and don't worry about that image. And you never take credit for what happened. You always let somebody else have the credit. Your goal is to build a peace process, not to build your ego.

"One of the surprises for me is what we learned during the upheaval of 1989 and afterward: that an individual can make a difference. This is a powerful lesson. Most of the developing world waits for the government to act or not act, and the people there don't realize that they can act themselves. This has now changed, because people have shown that it is possible to change the system by raising their voices to demonstrate, activities that we call peace activism. Look what happened in Jakarta where students managed to change the system. Look what happened in Yugoslavia. For five years the West had been trying to get rid of Milosevic. But it was the people of Belgrade and surroundings, who marched against the flaw of elections, who finally made the difference. That's fantastic. Most governments and most people underestimate people power. I believe this is a whole new area that we have to recognize. There can come a point when people get fed up and they will risk their lives to express their anger and frustration. It happened in Ivory Coast and happened in other countries. It will continue to happen because governments don't hear, they don't listen."

is of essential importance to maintaining the professional level and effectiveness of peacemaking interventions.

Jos Havermans is a free-lance journalist based in the Netherlands.

Resources

Other Publications
Opportunities Missed, Opportunities Seized. Preventive Diplomacy in the Post–Cold War World, edited by Bruce W. Jentleson, Carnegie Commission on Preventing

Deadly Conflict, Carnegie Corporation of New York. New York: Rowman & Little-field Publishers, 2000.

Reaching for Peace: Lessons Learned from Mott's Foundation's Conflict Resolution Grantmaking, 1989–1998. Flint, MI: Charles Stewart Mott Foundation, 1999.

Towards Better Peacebuilding Practice. Working Document for International Conference "Towards Better Peace Building Practice," Soesterberg, Netherlands, 24–26 October 2001. European Centre for Conflict Prevention, Utrecht, 2001.

Towards Better Peacebuilding Practice: On Lessons Learned, Evaluations Practices and Aid and Conflict, by Anneke Galama and Paul van Tongeren. Utrecht: European Centre for Conflict Prevention, 2002.

War Prevention Works: 50 Stories of People Resolving Conflict, by Dylan Matthews. Oxford: Oxford Research Group, 2001.

Notes

1. This chapter is a slightly adapted version of the author's article under the same title that appeared in Anneke Galama and Paul van Tongeren, eds., *Towards Better Peacebuilding Practice: On Lessons Learned, Evaluations Practices and Aid and Conflict,* Utrecht: European Centre for Conflict Prevention, 2002, pp. 123–141.

2. See Michael Lund, "Mapping Approaches to Lesson Learning," in *Towards Better Peacebuilding Practice: On Lessons Learned, Evaluation Practices and Aid and Conflict,* Utrecht: European Centre for Confict Prevention, 2002, pp. 89–94.

3. Unless otherwise noted, quotations included in the following part of this chapter were derived from personal communication with individuals attending the international conference "Towards Better Peace Building Practice" in Soesterberg, the Netherlands, in October 2001. This conference was organized by the European Platform for Conflict Prevention and Transformation, in close cooperation with Cordaid, and hosted by Kontakt der Kontinenten.

4. See Bruce W. Jentleson, *Opportunities Missed, Opportunities Seized: Preventive Diplomacy in the Post–Cold War World,* Carnegie Commission on Preventing Deadly Conflict, Carnegie Corporation of New York, New York: Rowman & Littlefield Publishers, 2000, p. 319. The concluding chapter of this book was published in *Towards a Better Peacebuilding Practice: On Lessons Learned, Evaluation Practices and Aid and Conflict,* Utrecht: European Centre for Conflict Prevention, 2002, pp. 203–212.

5. See Jentleson, *Opportunities Missed, Opportunities Seized,* p. 322.

6. Also see Freedland, "Ten Steps to Peace," *The Guardian,* 8 August 2001, in *Towards Better Peacebuilding Practice: On Lessons Learned, Evaluation Practices, and Aid and Conflict,* Utrecht: European Centre for Conflict Prevention, 2002, pp. 143–146.

7. Ibid.

8. Also see Mathews, "What Lessons Can Be Learned?" in Dylan Matthews, *War Prevention Works: 50 Stories of People Resolving Conflict,* Oxford: Oxford Research Group, 2001.

9. Ibid.

10. Freedland, "Ten Steps to Peace."

PART 2

Surveys of Conflict Prevention and Peacebuilding Activities

6

CENTRAL ASIA

6.1

Regional Introduction: A Host of Preventable Conflicts

John Schoeberlein

Following the collapse of the Soviet Union a decade ago, observers within Central Asia and abroad predicted that numerous conflicts would break out in the region between irreconcilable forces that had been held in check under Soviet rule. Conflict arising from ethnic tensions, Islamist militancy, or social upheaval has not proven to be as inevitable as many supposed. Apart from a devastating but relatively short civil war in Tajikistan, a decade of independence in the region has largely been characterized by peace. However, many signs now point to rising conflicts both within and between states—conflicts that are in no way inevitable, but rather arise from the regional leadership's policies, which have failed to address points of tension and in many cases have instead exacerbated them. More farsighted leadership and engagement from the international community will be required to avert the increasing tensions and the outbreak of proliferating regional conflict and chaos.

The demise of the Soviet Union in 1991 resulted in the softening of once virtually hermetic boundaries that separated Central Asia from Iran, Afghanistan, and China. At the same time, the emergence of five independent states now outside of Russia's direct control has resulted in the appearance of increasingly sharp lines of fragmentation, both between the Central Asian states and within each one. Soviet Central Asia had been relatively seamless, with virtually no significant tensions between the Soviet republics and few apparent internal political and social rifts. The Soviet system, for all its inefficiencies and injustices, did not foster ethnic clashes, while it did further the formation of a stable equilibrium of regional power elites. It also established a form of authority that was almost universally considered legitimate despite a distinct social hierarchy of access to privilege and power. Contrary to the predictions of some, the Soviet Union did not retreat from Central Asia due to radical discontent or violent resistance.

Independence came to the Central Asians peaceably, almost without their even trying for it. If there was much less violence than some expected in the early years of independence, the region has nevertheless been extremely unstable. Potential causes of violent conflict are very present and threaten to increase. Though in 1997 Tajikistan achieved a peace accord ending its five-year civil war, the country is still very much under the sway of the military commanders and factions that emerged during the war. Also, the wartime fighting forces have yet to be fully demilitarized, and military clashes and frequent assassinations remain a feature of life in the country. Much worse is the situation in Afghanistan, which has suffered nearly a quarter century of continuous civil war. Here, in the five years of fighting since the emergence of the Taliban movement with Pakistan's support, the Northern Alliance was defeated in all but a tiny fraction of the country's territory, saved only by the support they received from Russia, Iran, and others. The intervention of the U.S.-led coalition at the end of 2001 has dramatically reversed the balance between the Northern Alliance and the Taliban, and while it is too early to tell whether a stable new government will emerge to unite disparate elements within Afghanistan, it is clear that many years and considerable foreign assistance will be required in the best-case scenario to reestablish the institutions of government in a country devastated by a quarter century of continuous war. In the absence of stability over the near term, the threat of spreading violence, corrupting contraband trade, and refugees will continue to emanate from Afghanistan for a long time to come. Developments in western China (Xinjiang, or Eastern Turkistan) also pose a threat to Central Asia as an aggrieved Uyghur population there conducts a militant insurgency supported by a network that extends into Central Asia and Afghanistan. Like other discontented groups in the region that have been driven underground by lack of democratic avenues for pursuing their interests, Uyghur activists who see their homeland being overrun numerically and economically by Han Chinese are building links across borders that provide an economic base for insurgency, and provide weapons and training for antigovernment activities.

In spite of this regional instability, during the first years of independence there was relatively limited conflict in and between the other four Central Asian states—Uzbekistan, Turkmenistan, Kyrgyzstan, and Kazakhstan. As compared with the Caucasus, which emerged from Soviet domination with a series of devastating wars and has since undergone periodic changes of government, in these four Central Asian countries the same heads of state that came to power in the last years of the Soviet Union have remained. They have presided over remarkably peaceful development. In the *perestroika* period that culminated in the collapse of the USSR, there had been numerous incidents of intercommunal violence across the region. The worst of these included a pogrom in 1989 carried out against Meskhetian Turks in Uzbekistan, which resulted in hundreds of deaths and the exodus of 100,000 Meskhetians from the region. In summer 1990, even more severe violence broke out in southern Kyrgyzstan in clashes between the Uzbek and Kyrgyz communities, which resulted in perhaps a thousand deaths (the official figures are generally considered unreliable, but some confidential sources within the security apparatus put the number of deaths as high as 6,000). By contrast, no incident even remotely comparable has occurred since 1991 apart from the civil war in Tajikistan, and for a number of years it appeared that Central Asia could undergo the transition to independence with remarkably little turmoil.

The last several years have seen a sharp change in the prospects for peace in the region. This change traces to failures in leadership—largely avoidable—in two key areas: governance and the economy. In governance, the leaders have opted for authoritarianism, carrying out systematic efforts to eliminate all means for the popular will to be expressed through institutionalized political pluralism. In the economy, the leaders have pursued somewhat different paths, but in every case they have failed to establish a legal regime that would protect market development—foreign investment, entrepreneurship in the productive economy, or small-time local trader—from predatory government officials and stifling corruption. Instead, the leaders themselves all appear to be tightly enmeshed in a patronage system that favors cronies and powerful families, first and foremost their own. The rampant unemployment and deepening poverty, combined with a pervasive sense of resentment toward a narrow, rapacious, and self-absorbed elite, together with the absence of legitimate means to mobilize opposition, is prompting a growing segment of the population to support radical and violent means to oust the current regimes. The number of people ready to use violence remains comparatively small. However, there is a growing danger that the element of violence could severely disrupt the delicate balance that exists in the society and, as in Tajikistan, bring about an irreversible chain of events with devastating ramifications.

In addition to fostering internal tensions, the leaders in some of the countries have adopted a confrontational stance and aggressive policies toward their neighbors that could turn existing interstate conflicts over such vital issues as access to water and transportation corridors into confrontations and possibly even war. There have been a series of very serious incidents already between Uzbekistan and Tajikistan involving armed incursions from the territory of one country into the other. For example, in 1998, insurgents led by Mahmud Khudayberdiev entered Tajikistan from Uzbekistan, seeking to wrest the northern part of the country from government control. In 1999 and the following years, there have been annual campaigns by the Islamic Movement of Uzbekistan emanating from the territory of Tajikistan. In every case, the country where the insurgents originate denies supporting them, but the country victimized by these incursions considers that their neighbor's support is undeniable. These and other tensions have led to an increasing militarization of the borders and military buildup in general, and there are growing fears that insurgencies, water disputes, internal disorder, or disputes over borders could lead to escalating armed clashes between the Central Asian states.

Other aspects of the postindependence social and political environment have the potential for fostering social tensions and conflict as well. A critical factor is the decline of education, which was at a relatively high level during Soviet times. Now many children and youth are no longer getting access to education on all levels, with declining literacy and ensuing consequences for the economy and for interethnic communication. There have been considerable setbacks also for women, who were extensively engaged in the economy and the public sphere during Soviet times. Now there has been a resurgence of "conservative" values on the official and popular levels that press for women to withdraw from these spheres, and the genereal economic decline has driven women out of many aspects of the economy. At the same time, in many communities, there has been an increasing need to rely on women despite these trends, since their contributions to the household economy have grown more vital as resources become strained and men grow increasingly scarcer due to migration.

The development of civil society varies greatly among the Central Asian countries, with some governments—notably Kyrgyzstan and Kazakhstan—allowing considerable latitude for the activity of NGOs while others often view them as antigovernment by nature—especially Turkmenistan and Uzbekistan. In all cases, however, there is a great need for an expanded role for nongovernmental actors as the governments show themselves as increasingly unable to fill social-welfare functions that the state fulfilled during Soviet times. Nongovernmental actors have the potential to play an important role in conflict prevention and mitigation, but so far there is only limited NGO capacity, not only because of governmental interference in many countries, but also because of their weak institutional development, weak links with popular constituencies, and lack of ability to mobilize resources apart from sources in international aid organizations.

A key problem for all countries in Central Asia is the lack of strong linkages between the population and their governments. Weakly developed democratic institutions mean that people have few means of influencing the policies of their governments. The widespread corruption undermines the people's trust and diminishes the sense of loyalty that is vital if all are to work together to overcome social tensions and other challenges facing the region. Unfortunately, where popular support is lacking, the governments have often sought to force the populations' cooperation by coercive means, much as they did during Soviet times. The risk is that such coercive control cannot be effective in the current globalizing environment, and popular discontent will increasingly be channeled into radical and underground movements.

Five Different Paths Toward the Same Place?

Each of the Central Asia countries has followed a somewhat different path of development since independence, due to differing circumstances, cultures, and proclivities of the leaders. Two countries—Kyrgyzstan and Tajikistan—are constrained by extremely poor resources, even including agricultural land due to their mountainous terrain. Kazakhstan is blessed with some of the world's richest oil resources, Turkmenistan has an abundance of natural gas, and Uzbekistan is able to gain considerable export earnings from gold and cotton.

Yet despite their resources, none of these richer countries have committed needed resources to bring the poorest segment of the population out of severe poverty. Kazakhstan has been very progressive in introducing market reforms, whereas governments in Turkmenistan and Uzbekistan retain tight controls over the economy, and Kyrgyzstan and Tajikistan have very little indeed to export. In all five countries, the general perception is that only a narrow elite is benefiting from economic independence and many people long for Soviet times, characterized by substantially greater prosperity and generous state social services.

Turkmenistan is the quietest—and possibly the most explosive—of the Central Asian countries. President Saparmurat Niyazov has pursued a policy of "neutrality," avoiding military or other alignments with other countries, but in effect, this has amounted to keeping the country under an iron hand and sealed off from the world at large. He has promoted a Stalinesque personality cult and has provided virtually no latitude for the development of civil society and none for political pluralism. The discontents of the poor and of large ethnic minorities such as the Uzbeks are effectively suppressed by fear and repression. The country consists of a series of enclave or oasis populations distributed around the Qara-Qum Desert, which occupies the country's heart— enclaves inhabited by diverse clan and ethnic groups. Niyazov maintains control of these by handpicking the leadership and demanding absolute loyalty. There is much anticipation of the struggle for control of the country after Niyazov's term of office, which he has made a lifetime presidency, comes to an end. Since power is personalized, there are no institutionalized mechanisms for mediating the struggle for power, and it is probable that the succession struggle will be violent. Niyazov's policy of neutrality and isolation has indeed led to generally peaceable relations with Turkmenistan's neighbors. Some significant tensions have nevertheless arisen on the border with Uzbekistan as both countries have engaged in unilateral actions to determine where the border should run. Some parts of this border are inhabited on both sides by Uzbek communities, which once had intensive interactions and now are perceived as a security threat and subjected to persecution by the Turkmenistan government. Still Niyazov, for all his megalomania in relation to his own country, does not appear to have ambitions for a role of regional domination, and the greatest threat of conflict comes from tensions within the country— temporarily thoroughly suppressed, but it is impossible to know for how long.

In Uzbekistan, the situation is much more complex. While the government of President Islam Karimov shows not much more affinity for political pluralism, the country by its nature has more diverse bases for power and opposition. Uzbekistan consists of a series of regions, represented by elites whose power was balanced in a careful equilibrium through Soviet times. These regions include, notably, the Ferghana Valley, the country's most populous and agriculturally rich region; Tashkent, the capital; and Samarqand, from where Karimov originates. After Karimov came to power, he steadily consolidated his control in a struggle especially with the Tashkent elite, and through careful manipulation of patronage and alliances, he gradually marginalized competing regions and achieved overwhelming dominance. In this "success," meanwhile, lie tremendous tensions whereby such groups as the powerful Ferghana Valley elite see their interests as severely eroded.

The tensions have greatly worsened since the mid-1990s, when the government began a campaign to eliminate Islamic groups and organizations that were not directly under its control. Islam, which had flourished as an organizational force following the lifting of Soviet-era controls under Gorbachev, was increasingly perceived as the only viable institutional basis for opposition to the regime. It indeed became so following Karimov's banning and suppression immediately after independence of all of the secular opposition groups that had emerged in the *perestroika* era. These campaigns against "unofficial" Islam have led to thousands of arrests and widespread police abuse of elements of the population that were not previously politicized, but rather were focused on religious observance. Religious activity itself has been treated as a marker of disloyalty to the regime, and these efforts at suppression have gone far to politicize religion and to antagonize the population against the regime. While militants remain very few in number, they are gaining in force and popular support. Some of those fleeing possible arrest in Uzbekistan are joining the Islamic Movement of Uzbekistan (IMU). For the past three years, IMU has made its ambition of toppling the Karimov regime known through clashes each summer with security forces and guards on the borders of Kyrgyzstan and Uzbekistan.

These very limited skirmishes, involving a couple of thousand guerilla fighters, will not threaten broader stability in the region, despite the significant though limited support they have received from outside Islamist forces, including the Taliban. With the Taliban virtually routed now, some of the Islamist forces targeting other parts of Central Asia have undoubtedly been dealt a setback, but it is quite probable that Islamists will continue to find support among former *mujahedeen* groups in Afghanistan. Support from outside is not the most important factor, meanwhile, and the internal discontent that has fueled support for militancy is likely to grow stronger, adding support to militants operating out of Afghanistan and elsewhere. Of much greater significance meanwhile are the underground Islamist movements within Uzbekistan—most notably the Hizb ut-Tahrir, or "Party of Liberation." Though they espouse nonviolence, Hizb ut-Tahrir is equally bent on ousting the *faqir* ("nonbeliever") regime of Karimov, and their rapidly growing popularity, fed mainly by the government repression, makes this ambition increasingly credible. Perhaps the greatest danger of violent conflict comes from the possibility that discontented elite elements who have been marginalized by Karimov's consolidation of power could form an alliance of convenience with Islamist forces in making a bid for power. It is possible that such an alliance indeed lies behind the massive car bombings that shook Tashkent in February 1999, severely damaging a number of monuments to the prestige of the current regime.

The government of Uzbekistan has raised the alarm, pointing to threats of instability coming from outside forces and international Islamist networks and thereby evoking some resonance from states such as Russia and the United States, who see themselves as sharing this enemy. However, the key sources for the growing potential for violent conflict actually come from within the country and even within the regime.

In Tajikistan, large-scale violent conflict is already a feature of the post-Soviet experience. Independence came to Tajikistan at a time when the communist leadership was weak and the opposition had gained considerable organizational strength and popular support. Therefore, unlike in any of the other Central Asian countries, there was a threat to the continuity of power of the communists. The opposition received a strong impetus from the backlash against hard-liners following the attempted coup against Gorbachev in August 1991. Mass demonstrations led to the replacement of the Tajik Communist Party first secretary and president, Qahhar Mahkamov, who had made the mistake of aligning himself with the coup plotters. Though the opposition failed to elect its candidate in the presidential election later that year, the standoff, which persisted through spring 1992, led ultimately to the formation of armed groups. The decisive moment came when the new president, Rahman Nabiev, distributed weapons to a crowd of his supporters, creating the Presidential Guard that eventually was to grow into the fighting force that came victorious out of the civil war.

Many factors contributed to the escalation of fighting. A decisive factor was the flow of weapons from the Russian army through illegal sales, probably to both sides, as the result of the chaos and lack of discipline that affected the army at the time of the collapse of the Soviet Union. Another was the previous existence of tensions between regional groups, which became the sides in the conflict as it progressed—chiefly, the Kölabi who eventually won the war and the Gharmi who formed the core of the militant opposition, though a number of other groups were also important. For example, Pamiris, who differ from the main Tajik population by language, religion (they are predominantly Ismaili Shiites), and physical appearance, became the victims of ethnic cleansing as the Kölabi fighters took control of the capital Dushanbe. Within the space of a few weeks, what had been mild antagonisms turned into mortal opposition as entire villages were destroyed thanks to effective demagoguery and the availability of firepower. Within half a year, about 50,000 people were killed and roughly a fifth of the country's population was displaced. The next five years saw ongoing battles in the region near Afghanistan where the opposition forces took refuge and learned much about guerilla warfare from the Afghan *mujahedeen.*

Ultimately, a power-sharing agreement was concluded in 1997 that resulted in a divvying up of portfolios and economic assets between the combatants of the war. The country remains under the control of commanders from both sides, though increasingly President Emamali Rahmanov has consolidated power on the model of other Central Asian authoritarian leaders. The current tensions in Tajikistan are far greater than before the war, though the war-weariness of the population may provide some insurance against any widespread outbreak of violence. Despite the direct experience with war, the prospects for new conflict may be as great in Tajikistan as anywhere in Central Asia. The rise to power of the Kölabi fighters has meant that other regions have been subject to widespread appropriation of assets at gunpoint and a patronage system like elsewhere in Central Asia but here enforced by violence and frequent assassinations, thus stifling economic development and generating strong resentments among other groups. A particularly volatile element of the population is the former fighters, many of whom retain their weapons, for whom peace has meant no jobs and the end of profitable pillaging. One consequence of the peace accord was the emergence of the only pluralist political system in Central Asia, where even the groups that the government likes the least have been allowed to participate. However, as Rahmanov consolidates his power, he and his supporters are working to reduce pluralism. In fact, though the opposition were assured 30 percent of government positions in the peace agreement, that promise was never fulfilled and a number of those who did get positions have been turning up dead.

Kyrgyzstan, in the early years of independence, seemed to be following a distinctly democratic path with wide latitude given for the development of opposition parties, independent media, nongovernmental organizations, and generally the features of a burgeoning civil society. The leaders of neighboring countries argued that democracy led to chaos, and insisted that a measure of authoritarianism was essential to avoid developments as in Tajikistan. President Askar Akaev of Kyrgyzstan, meanwhile, insisted that his people in fact were politically mature enough to implement democracy, and events bore this out in that tensions and violence in Kyrgyzstan were no greater than in any neighboring country. Yet at the same time as it was proceeding quickly with market reforms, Kyrgyzstan has supported flourishing corruption and has become the most highly stratified country in the former Soviet Union, with two-thirds of the population living in poverty while a narrow elite enjoys conspicuous wealth. Flagrant corruption on the part of those close to the president and increasing criticisms from independent voices of Akaev's record have prompted him to cope with growing opposition by stripping the judiciary and parliament of their powers and by assuming increasingly authoritarian control. Where previously a flourishing party system allowed for relatively effective popular participation, now the leaders of the strongest opposition parties are regularly faced with criminal charges or thrown in jail in order to prevent their winning elections. All of the media outlets that have been most critical of the government have been shut down, and leaders of some of the most influential NGOs have been intimidated or beaten up by people widely presumed to be members of the security services. The government works in many ways to restrict the activities of Islamic groups, as in Uzbekistan and elsewhere (though less actively), and the consequences are to increase the feeling of persecution among devoted Muslims and the support that groups such as Hizb ut-Tahrir receive in Kyrgyzstan as well.

Kyrgyzstan, like its neighboring countries, is heavily divided by regionalism, ethnic tensions, politicized Islam, and elite privilege and cronyism. Many of these issues coalesce in the Ferghana Valley region of southern Kyrgyzstan, where there is a very large Uzbek minority who have been systematically excluded from power and experience and fallen under the scrutiny of the security services particularly intensely because of their greater devotion to Islam. Uzbeks are generally outside of the patronage networks that allow one to get a job in law enforcement or the judiciary. Meanwhile, they do well for themselves in agricultural production and the markets, which has sometimes led to resentment from less well-to-do Kyrgyz. The narrowing of effective political participation and growing alienation from what is seen as a highly privileged, corrupt, and unjust regime has resulted in increasingly militant views among a segment of the population, including Kyrgyz as well as Uzbeks. Here as elsewhere, authoritarianism is pursued in order for the current leader to hold onto power, but it has the effect of increasing the likelihood of conflict. This potentiality has begun to manifest itself increasingly in confrontation with the government, usually in demonstrations in response to economic hardship, arrests of religious activists, and actions against opposition leaders.

In Kazakhstan, too, there has been increasing tension toward authoritarianism on the backdrop of some greater leeway for the development of markets and civil society. There is some hope that with its tremendous oil resources, the government will have the capacity to ensure the well-being of its broader population, though there is little sign of sharing the wealth so far. Kazakhstan, like its neighbors, is very regionally divided, with some western regions holding most of the oil resources, southern regions being very poor and oriented more strongly toward Islam, and the north having an overwhelmingly Russian population.

In the country as a whole, Kazaks make up the largest group by a slim margin. Kazakhstan was previously seen as relatively immune to the influences of radical Islam since observance of the religion had widely diminished or disappeared in much of the country, yet here too it is increasingly forming the foundation for underground mobilization. While the presence of large numbers of Russians makes the country potentially vulnerable to pressures and interference from Russia, President Nazarbaev has successfully pursued a policy of inclusion, at least on the level of state ideology. On the level of everyday life, meanwhile, many Russians see no future in a country where Kazaks are actively promoted over other nationalities. Those with the youth and skills required to resettle and find employment in Russia have left Kazakhstan in large numbers, severely damaging the country's economy but releasing some of the internal pressures, at least temporarily. With rampant corruption and growing perceptions of inequity, Kazakhstan is also not immune to the tensions that have the potential of tearing the region apart.

Prospects

The comparison with Iran prior to the revolution is very pertinent to Central Asia. Iran descended into violence and revolution, not because of a lack of resources, but rather because of the perception of inequity linked to authoritarian rule, increasing social stratification, resentment of the West's support for the dictator, and the regime's suppression of forms of Islam that it saw as potentially threatening. All of these conditions exist increasingly in Central Asia. Nevertheless, the leadership everywhere seems to find hope in shoring up their position by increasing repression, and many in the West seem determined to make the same mistake as they made in Iran, supporting undemocratic rule, and ultimately sowing distrust of Western involvement among the wider population.

There is a broad array of factors that could lead to the sparks that provoke wider conflict: ethnic tensions, regional imbalances, interstate disputes over resources and borders, and the state-driven radicalization of Islam, among others. Each of these issues must be addressed to avoid increasing tensions and the eventuality of widespread violent conflict. None of these issues can be resolved if the underlying problems of economics and governance are not adequately addressed. Without effective democratic institutions, the governing elite will be unresponsive to the needs and interests of the wider population. Without curtailing patronage, corruption, and cronyism, even the resource-rich countries will remain highly stratified and unreliable for investment, and in the poorer countries the broad population will grow increasingly desperate and angry.

The increased interest that the West now shows in Central Asia in connection with the war in Afghanistan represents both challenges and opportunities. There is ground for hope that there will be the commitment that is required to build stronger economies and democratic systems. Yet there is also the risk that Western engagement will be led by the kind of security support to undemocratic regimes that has increased polarization and radicalization and promoted anti-Westernism in other countries such as Iran, Egypt, Palestine, and Algeria. Western military leaders have found it convenient to pursue close relations with the government of Uzbekistan, for example, which could lead to a closer dialogue and greater influence on economic and political reform processes, but could also have the effect of reducing the pressure to democratize and could even intensify the tensions that have existed between Uzbekistan and its neighbors, with Western support unwittingly encouraging aspirations for a regionally dominant role. International calls for the kinds of reforms that are essential in order to reduce the chances of tensions and conflict have already become weaker as leaders focus on tightening regional security through military and other similar means.

John Schoeberlein is a political anthropologist and director of the Forum for Central Asian Studies at Harvard University (since 1993). He also heads the International Crisis Group's Central Asia Project (since 2000), serves as president of the Central Eurasian Studies Society, and led the United Nations Ferghana Valley Development Programme focusing on regional conflict prevention (1998–1999). His research focuses on issues of identity, including nationalism, Islam, ethnicity, community organization, and conflict.

6.2

Policy Recommendations: Some Strategies for Stability

Anara Tabyshalieva

The five nations of Central Asia have had a difficult time since gaining independence in 1991. They have been plagued by violence, political instability, and economic hardship, and despite some progress toward the development of democratic institutions, and despite enormous potential from the exploitation of natural resources, the risks of continued political instability, ethnic violence, and even interstate conflict remain. Complicating factors are the burgeoning drug trade and the threat posed by religious extremists. The events of 11 September 2001 and the U.S. antiterrorist action in Afghanistan seriously changed the security situation in post-Soviet Central Asia. Internally, democratic institutions and civil society need to be further developed. External actors can contribute by addressing the severe poverty in the region, and by working with governmental and nongovernmental actors to build conflict-prevention and conflict-resolution structures.

In the Soviet era, unrest in Central Asia (Uzbekistan, Kazakhstan, Tajikistan, Kyrgyzstan, and Turkmenistan) was managed and held in check through the highly centralized political structure. Although the Kremlin's propaganda of proletarian internationalism played a somewhat positive role in achieving rapprochement among ethnic groups, it did not provide any mechanism, free from paternalist ideology, guardianship, and strict control from the center, for natural cooperation based on mutual economic interests and horizontal links. The Central Asian states entered the postcommunist era suffering from sharp economic decline and experiencing ethnic and political divisions, a legacy of ethnic and religious violence and Soviet border demarcation.

The five relatively homogeneous states of Central Asia have been unable to prevent conflict in the region. Experts argue that the Central Asian region is sitting on a time bomb that could explode at any moment. International terrorism, violent religious extremism, organized crime, poverty, and drug trafficking represent increasing challenges to the security of Central Asia. Underdevelopment and deprivation, poor governance, overpopulation, scarcity of water, and environmental stress greatly contribute to underlying sources of conflict in Central Asia. The essential differences with regard to cultural backgrounds, level of political and economic development, and degree of transformation and democratization in the five Central Asian states will increase. There are also different perceptions with respect to a conflict-prevention agenda in Central Asia among governments, international organizations, nongovernmental organizations, and scholars. In some cases conflict-prevention measures are perceived by Central Asian governments as a challenge to a state's sovereignty and an opportunity to muzzle any opposition within the country.

Preventing Religious Extremism and Terrorism

Events of 11 September 2001 and the actions of the antiterrorist alliance in Afghanistan opened a new chapter on the security and geopolitical balance of power in the Central Asian region. All five states expressed a readiness to help the alliance; Uzbekistan offered military bases for the U.S. armed forces against Afghanistan. In response, the Taliban leaders declared a *jihad* against Uzbekistan authorities. Soon after, the Taliban regime crumbled but there is still the risk of retaliation by the Islamic Movement of Uzbekistan (IMU) or former Taliban fighters in Central Asian states. One of the most serious fears is that the man-made water reservoirs could be a target of terrorist attacks. All Central Asian countries unprepared for refugee influx have different policies toward refugees. Moreover, Uzbekistan and Turkmenistan have closed their borders to them and stay away from regional cooperation on this issue. Afghan refugees become a Central Asian issue and can be resolved only at a regional level.

Other religious extremists of Hizb ut-Tahrir intend to boost their activities aimed at overthrowing the constitutional order in the Central Asian states. The influence of radical and militant Islam in the Central Asian states and their neighbors poses a number of structural challenges to the region's stability. The emergence of such groups should certainly be viewed in the broader context of global trends, such as the rise of international terrorism and increasing poverty in the region. Meanwhile, Central Asian governments may use the "war against terrorism" as an excuse to further undermine respect for human rights and religious freedom.

There is an alarming tendency to equate Islam with extremism just because a small group of young people are motivated by religion to engage in activities fomenting social unrest, and use religion to justify their terrorist activities. Anti-Islamic propaganda and the oversimplification of the current religious situation in Central Asia may lead to flawed decisionmaking. One evidence of that is the increasing deportation of citizens of neighboring states, mainly traders, and the tightening passport and visa regime that restricts people's movement within Central Asia. Although all Central Asian leaders declare common goals and concerns over terrorism, each country has its own agenda and is engaged in rivalry with its neighbors. The Washington-Tashkent alliance is changing the role of Uzbekistan in the region. For Uzbekistan, it might be a slippery slope not only in the form of further repression of zealous Muslims and other religious believers, but in continuing land-mining and a hurried demarcation of borders with weaker countries such as Tajikistan and Kyrgyzstan. The U.S. engagement in Central Asia is also a serious test for Russian influence in the region.

It is clear that in the Central Asian security arena, small and poor countries are more affected than others; Tajikistan and Kyrgyzstan could strengthen their independence. International and local experts suggest consultations and negotiation with the external opposition in Uzbekistan. Local actors such as governments, NGOs, or regional organizations may be able to deal with small-scale crises with mediation, conciliation, and assistance with negotiations. Central Asian states should encourage joint actions involving the international community focusing on conflict resolution in Afghanistan. The West may also support intervention to end conflict at whatever stages of development such conflicts have reached.

Development of Civil Society

There is an urgent need to enhance the capacity and expertise of NGOs in long-term conflict prevention. All governments in Central Asia are still suspicious of nonstate actors. Therefore they are reluctant to grant a monitoring or "intelligence" function to NGOs working together in a network, even though such a network could provide an effective early warning service and might also serve to direct attention to emerging issues. NGOs in Central Asia can also play important roles in actually intervening in conflict situations to ease tensions, and to provide mediation and facilitation functions. Increasing regional cooperation among state officials and NGOs would be extremely beneficial in progressive political and democratic reforms, including the strengthening of the rule of law, good governance, and respect for human rights.

Joint programs between Central Asian and Western grassroots organizations are of particular value. It is important to cooperate in the area of conflict prevention and human rights. It is only by embracing the idea of universal human rights that ethnic or subethnic group interests can be transcended in the region. The donors and international organizations could use their influence to encourage improvements in legislative procedures and to facilitate moves toward truly law-abiding civic societies that would replace autocratic governmental structures headed by territorial-based clans or families. The work of NGOs in intervening to resolve disputes should be improved, as well as their capacities to provide policy-relevant information and analysis.

There is a real need for effective monitoring and systematic research in the Ferghana Valley, shared by three states. Monitoring, in and of itself, acts as a stabilizing factor in Central Asia. It allows ethnic and social interests to be manifested and leads to reduced tension. The participation and attention of external parties would induce more responsible attitudes from stakeholders on conflict-related issues. To prevent the recurrence of violent conflict in Central

Asia, more research on the causes of such conflicts needs to be conducted, and the necessary theoretical models need to be created to help analyze future eventualities.

The open-minded and well-educated people in nongovernmental and governmental sectors are eager to participate in critical discussions on the problems of democratization and conflict prevention. They may monitor conflict and provide early warning and insight into situations in Tajikistan, the Ferghana Valley, and other areas; provide a neutral forum where key stakeholders can discuss factors contributing to destabilization of the social, ethnic, and religious situation; initiate mediation between conflicting parties (for example, between the IMU and the government of Uzbekistan); initiate education and training for conflict resolution and conflict prevention; advocate press freedom and initiate media activities; monitor elections and prevent electoral violence; and warn of potentially violent situations.

More effective participation of women in the male-dominated decision-making and security processes in Central Asia is essential. Protection, assistance, and training for refugee women, internally displaced women, and children in need of international protection must be articulated and advocated. The gender aspect in the conflict-prevention agenda should not be neglected.

Responding to Poverty

The burden of unresolved economic problems is increasing ethnic and social tension, and could lead to open clashes. Many believe that economic development will reduce interethnic and religious tension. But without radical improvements in the socioeconomic situation, which are highly unlikely in the near future, there is little reason for optimism. Such change is dependent on the manifestation of political will in the Central Asian states. In the light of recent Afghanistan crises and U.S. engagement in Central Asia, the governments of the region must redirect their meagre funds from social needs to defense and security issues. Unemployment and cross-border trade are primary issues to be addressed. The top priority for a policy toward Central Asia should be job-creation programs. Active microcredit programs to small and medium-size farms are one effective way to respond to unemployment and social tension. A majority of the unemployed are young people; a family-planning policy could also lead to stabilization in population numbers and stop uncontrolled growth. The concept of ethnic cleansing remains embedded in the collective consciousness of some groups, and could become a grim reality if the economic and social situation in the region deteriorates. The threat of separatist and ethnic violence exists in all the Central Asian states; the monoethnic upper echelon must learn to listen to the voices of national minorities to prevent both discrimination based on ethnicity and actual ethnic conflict.

Fostering Regional Cooperation for Conflict Prevention

The end of Soviet rule has given new impetus to changing relationships within and among Central Asian states. In this new situation, as these republics deal with each other for the first time without strict control from Moscow, they must invent a way to live next to each other. The development of new horizontal relations has been uneven and incoherent. Regional efforts to cooperate for the sustainable development of Central Asia are often fragile and not adequate to combat a process of disintegration. Despite the geographic and economic interdependency of the Ferghana Valley states, this tendency toward continuing disintegration continues to plague the region.

Interstate frictions over trade, custom fees, borders, water and energy distribution, old debts, and different levels of democratic and economic reforms may only increase. The Central Asian states have failed to make their national currencies mutually convertible, using U.S. dollars in trade. The problems of resources, especially the shortage of water, seem to be the most serious issues confronting this huge area. Other problems include the absence of developed economic concepts of cooperation, lack of cooperation in food security, and inadequate mechanisms to implement the numerous agreements among the Central Asian states. Despite numerous meetings and declarations of the Central Asian politicians, a cold war over custom fees with both an economic and political character is assuming new unpredictable forms.

There are many sites subject to dispute along the borders of the Central Asian states. Experts believe with further deterioration of the irrigation systems and mismanagement of the water distribution systems, the number of local conflicts will increase. Environmental problems are also a serious threat to stability in Central Asia. The leaders of the five Central Asian republics still have a unique opportunity to develop truly effective (cooperative as opposed to competitive) regional organizations centered on the management and use of regional water supplies. Conflict over natural resources, especially water and land, is, in addition, complicated by different styles of political leadership in the post-Soviet era and different levels of economic development in each country. In such a conflict-prone environment, it is clear that entirely new forms of regional cooperation are required to avoid the kind of flare-ups that have occurred in the Ferghana Valley and in Tajikistan. It is vitally important to build the capacity of regional governmental and nongovernmental organizations to deal with conflict prevention at various levels.

The emergence of intergovernmental organizations such as the Central Asian Economic Union (CAEU) provides a positive example of cooperation. Security, water and energy management, transport and communication, customs checkpoints, and mutual payments will all be addressed by the CAEU. The conflict management role of the CAEU could be strengthened. The Central Asian states should create a mechanism for making common decisions, focusing on common ecological and environmental problems. Obvious common interests such as road construction and drug control will remain the most potentially fruitful avenues for regional coordination in Central Asia. For example, all Central Asian countries could benefit if these landlocked states were to establish a consortium for the creation of transcontinental connections.

Attacking Narco-Trafficking

The total value of the drug trade in Central Asia is not known, but probably now constitutes the largest national income stream in Tajikistan and is close to that in Kyrgyzstan. Both opposition and official branches of the Tajik government receive money from the drug trade, as do some law enforcement officers, customs officials, and military officers in other countries, according to local informants. It is not primarily an urban phenomenon, but occurs mostly in the mountainous rural areas where other economic alternatives are scarce. The drug trade is fueled by the poverty prevailing in the most neglected regions. The Ferghana Valley is a center of such activity.

Presently, large numbers of people all across Central Asia are involved in the production and trafficking of narcotics, and state structures seem powerless to prevent this kind of "regional cooperation" and "ethnic accord." During severe downturns in the regional economies, more and more people turn to growing opium poppies and cannabis. The growing power of the "Mafia network" means that criminals will increase their influence in political and economic decisionmaking throughout the region. The accumulation of revenue and weapons from the operation of these criminal networks could be a serious threat to ethnic stability in the Ferghana Valley, the site of considerable narcotics transshipment. If the Central Asian states and international community are serious about eliminating drug trafficking and drug use, they must address the economic issues that have resulted in the mass involvement of unemployed people in this business. In affected regions, local governmental and nongovernmental stakeholders, and international actors should work together to attack the worldwide network of the narco-mafia.

Reinforcing the Peace Process in Tajikistan

The war in Tajikistan, one of the world's poorest countries, was the most destructive in the region. Tajikistan's government is still unable to assert control over parts of its territory, with private paramilitary groups operating within some parts of Tajikistan or from across the borders with Kyrgyzstan and Uzbekistan. The peace process in Tajikistan is an encouraging example of how to overcome a military conflict involving divergent interests within one society, and to gradually establish a culture of peaceful political cooperation. Tajik society still needs to recover from the consequences of the civil war, and to now address with determination the issue of the postconflict reconstruction and rehabilitation processes in order to provide a basis for stable reforms. Job-creating programs in Tajikistan can contribute to stabilization of the situation and the integration of military men into postconflict reconstruction. The uncontrolled presence of small arms and light weapons, inherited from the civil war in Tajikistan, hampers security in the country as well as in the neighboring states of Kyrgyzstan and Uzbekistan. Tajikistan should disarm and integrate the paramilitary groups in order to prevent the proliferation of small arms and light weapons. It is clear that because of the weakness of the government and economy, Tajikistan is not able, on its own, to tackle the consequences of the war, such as the illegal paramilitary groups, the accumulation of arms, drug trafficking, a porous Afghan-Tajik border, and many other problems that should be resolved by appropriate collective measures. The international community should provide assistance in designing appropriate collective measures to address these problems.

Anticipating Militarization of the Caspian Subregion
The interest of the Western countries in the oil and gas resources of the Caspian Basin is great, and the natural resources in Central Asia are also bound to become increasingly important to China and India. One can expect growing competition among regional as well as several extraregional players for access to the vast oil and gas reserves thought to be in the Caspian Sea Basin. Among the major obstacles to the use of the Caspian oil and gas resources is a dispute over the existing Caspian Sea legal regime and the divergent approaches to its resolution supported by the various Caspian Sea states (Azerbaijan, Iran, Kazakhstan, Russia, and Turkmenistan).

Transportation of oil and gas from the Caspian Basin to outside consumers passing through Russia is another problem. An inevitable conflict of interests among the littoral states is developing, spurred in part by growing involvement of the United States, Russia, and some European and Asian countries. Moreover, the security of oil and gas transportation routes passing across or located close to zones of local conflict is increasingly dependent on the resolution of these conflicts.

Some experts predict an increase in the militarization of the Caspian Basin countries, which would lead to further interstate tensions in the subregion. The profits from the oil industry could benefit a small, privileged elite. Those oil dollars could also lead to further arms proliferation, and nobody excludes the possibility that new conflicts among the Caspian Basin states could develop. Clearly, the completion of pipelines in the future will result in a very different political and economic situation, as well as a new security climate in the whole Central Asian region.

Increasing External Aid and International Intervention
The millions of dollars invested by the West in technical assistance and building democratic institutions in Central Asia have not been wasted. All five states are full-fledged members of the Organization for Security and Cooperation in Europe (OSCE). They have adopted the OSCE commitments and the region is an integral part of the OSCE space. Although Central Asian governments have failed to implement many of the recommendations with respect to fair elections that have been offered by the OSCE and other international organizations, the nations of Central Asia have made some slow progress in the field of democratic reform in the last ten years.

Recent conflicts in the region indicate that the United Nations, the OSCE organizations, and other international actors need to be better equipped to practice conflict-prevention activities in the Central Asian region. At the same time, in the context of conflict prevention, the OSCE needs to cooperate with other multilateral institutions. International and regional organizations can help in building the institutional framework for electoral systems, party systems, legislative structures, government, and NGOs. However, institutional competition between international organizations, and a lack of cooperation or coordination among these organizations, are important impediments to conflict prevention in the region. The governments of the Central Asian states should stimulate donor activity on conflict prevention in the region.

The UN, Bretton Woods Institution, OSCE, and other international organizations should deal more systematically with the regional dimension of the conflict-prevention agenda in Central Asia, fostering economic and political reforms. The painful lessons in Tajikistan, Afghanistan, and the Ferghana Valley have brought the structural deficiencies of the international organization to light. To prevent conflict in Central Asia, the international community should give more priority to a conflict-prevention agenda and set up a coalition of key actors, to include governmental and nongovernmental actors, scholars, religious leaders, and other prominent persons. The international and local communities should learn more from recent experience and reinforce their awareness, build coalitions, and design their agenda within a broader regional context of conflict prevention. The international organizations and donor countries could provide robust support for conflict prevention, contributing more to regional cooperation in Central Asia among governmental and nongovernmental actors. Conditionality could be more widely used to encourage adherence to democratic and economic reforms, respect for human rights, religious freedom, protection of minority rights, and the encouragement of regional cooperation.

It is likely that Russia, the United States, China, and Japan will remain engaged in Central Asian conflict prevention. Still, there is no outside power sufficiently interested in the region to make major investments in its security. Their interests are often very limited, focusing on the potential of this region to cause instability in "more important" areas through the drug trade or the spread of Islamist radicalism.

The effectiveness of conflict-prevention efforts depends to a large extent on the actions undertaken by many key actors on their own and in collaboration with other key actors. But it would be wrong to embrace a one-size-fits-all approach to conflict prevention in Central Asia. Of course no single measure can completely eliminate tensions in the region and prevent conflict, but it is possible to counteract and drift toward destabilization, to minimize the risk of ethnic cleansing, and in so doing, to save the lives of potential victims. However, compared to the level of instability and economic hardship, the current efforts of the various stakeholders to improve the situation and prevent conflict are woefully inadequate. The Central Asian region can serve as an incubator for a more peaceful future if proper efforts are made, or it can become a place of disaster for the millions of people who live there.

Anara Tabyshalieva is director of the Institute for Regional Studies (an NGO in Kyrgyzstan). She was a senior fellow at the United States Institute of Peace, a visiting scholar at the UN University in Tokyo, and Dorothy Cadberry fellow at Selly Oak College in Birmingham. She has a number of publications, including The Challenge of Regional Cooperation in Central Asia: Preventing Ethnic Conflict in the Ferghana Valley *(1999) and* Faith in Turkestan *(1993).*

6.3

Bones of Contention:
Conflicts over Resources

John Schoeberlein

In the divergent accounts of the reasons for the civil war in Tajikistan, one often encounters two diametrically opposed explanations for the conflict. Some hold that there were conflicting agendas for how society and politics should be transformed in the wake of the collapse of Soviet rule, as indeed some of the key actors in the conflict maintained. Others dismiss all high-minded aspirations and contend that it was simply a scramble for control of resources. This chapter explores the role of resources in conflict in Central Asia.

Resources come into play in many conflict situations in two ways. In the onset of conflict, one of the key issues is often control over resources. And once violent conflict develops, resources are essential to both sides in order to maintain the capacity to continue fighting. Recent scholarship on some African cases has shown that when major resources are available to the combatants, such as diamonds in western and southern Africa, the struggle over control of resources becomes the driving force in civil war.[1] Central Asia's recent experience of conflict does not offer cases where substantial wealth-generating resources are at stake, and there appear to be no cases analogous to those in Africa, where the tremendous resources involved make it very difficult to bring an end to the fighting.

It is notoriously difficult to assess, in the murkiness of conflict situations, what the true motivating factors are and where combatants are obtaining their material support. The roles played by resources in Central Asia in cases of tensions and strife are various. The shortage of key resources is a major factor in stimulating popular discontent. Differential access to resources has prompted tensions between ethnic and other communities. Resources that are contested between states across borders, such as irrigation water and mineral resources, have threatened to be one of the most explosive issues in prompting interstate conflict. During and after the outbreak of war in Tajikistan, the leaders of military factions have engaged in violent struggle over control of pieces of the country's productive economy. And it appears that the region's massive illicit drug trade is one of the key sources of financing for the military leaders in various Central Asian conflicts. Thus, whether or not resources are a primary cause, they certainly play a role in shaping the development of violent conflicts in the region.[2]

It is difficult to generalize from the diverse cases that the five former Soviet states of Central Asia represent, yet nevertheless they offer a useful comparative frame. For the most part, civil war in this region is more of a potentiality than an actuality. Only in Tajikistan has there been full-scale civil war. Violent conflict otherwise has taken the form of occasional clashes between state security forces and their underground opponents, sporadic acts of violence by underground groups of various kinds, and on several occasions relatively large-scale incursions of militant groups from the territory of one Central Asian country into another. At the same time, former Soviet Central Asia is surrounded on several sides by regions that have experienced severe tensions and conflict in the past decade or so—in western China, Afghanistan, and the Caucasus—and there is a distinct threat of increasing conflict both within and between Central Asian states.

The following analysis begins by laying out some of the common features and dynamics of tensions and conflicts across the region, which must be understood if efforts to prevent conflict are to be successful. It then characterizes each of the major areas of conflict in the region and the impact of resources in their origins and development.

Because many of the issues that can lead to conflict are common across the region, and because there are links between underlying conditions and radical underground networks, the potential for conflict beginning in one area and spreading across the region is considerable. The following are some of the key developments that increase the possibilities for wider regional conflict.

• Underground Islamist movements. Throughout southern Central Asia there are growing Islamist movements operating in the underground because they are everywhere illegal, regardless of whether they espouse violence. In Uzbekistan in particular, such movements as Hizb ut-Tahrir provide one of the few available avenues to respond to discontent, given the general exclusion of real popular participation in politics. The severe government crackdown on anyone suspected of sympathizing with such groups, including thousands of arrests and widespread police harassment, has given additional impetus to the movements, mainly in Uzbekistan, but in all of the other Central Asian countries as well. The most widely supported underground groups are not militant, though as discontent grows, this could change rapidly.

• Ethnic tensions. The greatest tensions exist around groups that represent ethnic enclaves of groups which are also the titular nationality in neighboring states—such as Russians in Kazakhstan, Tajiks in Uzbekistan, and Uzbeks in all of the states that surround Uzbekistan—because ethnic tensions are generally linked with interstate politics. Tensions most often emerge when disparities of access to resources occur along ethnic lines.

• Regional elite politics. Considerable tensions exist in each country within the ruling elite circles over the role of regions in the dominance of national politics, and efforts in the center to control regional elites. Most often these conflicts are played out in backroom politics, but there is often a tendency to mobilize popular constituencies to exert pressure in this political arena, with the result of wider civil conflict. Most often, tensions revolve around the control of resources, which is a point of struggle between central authorities and regional elites. This was an important element in the Tajik civil war, and also looms as a prospect in all of the other countries.

• Tensions between a discontented population and the government. There is growing unrest connected with feelings of inequity and injustice, in response to arbitrary and authoritarian rule, corruption of officials and oligarchic elites, and economic policies that are dramatically worsening the well-being of the wider population.

Regional Context: The War in Afghanistan and Uyghur Nationalist Insurgency in Xinjiang

Though the decades-long war in Afghanistan is outside the scope of this chapter, it has had many implications for former Soviet Central Asia, such as feeding the drug-trafficking economy, providing bases and support for combatants in Central Asian conflicts, and creating flows of refugees. The U.S.-led intervention in Afghanistan is likely to have a mixed impact on Central Asia. With the end of the Taliban regime, there is also an end on their policy to ban poppy cultivation, and preliminary reports indicate that there may already be an increase in trafficking of opiates from Afghanistan through Central Asia. This has the potential to foster corruption in the region, and while the influx of profits from this trade can boost local employment, the drug trade is also accompanied by increased drug abuse and concomitant spread of diseases such as HIV/AIDS, which have a devastating effect on the economy over the longer term. Drug-eradication programs could follow on the stabilization of Afghanistan, if this is achieved, and those Northern Alliance leaders now in power who have had a vested interest in the drug trade can be persuaded of this need.

Also flowing out of the recent U.S.-led intervention in Afghanistan is the prospect for increased aid to Central Asia, partly as a quid pro quo for U.S. basing rights in Central Asian countries, and partly as a result of the increased attention to the region and the need to stem potential instability there. Major increases in resources in the form of aid can have mixed consequences, however. There is a risk that these resources could also become a bone of contention if they enter the system in a way that fosters corruption or a sense of inequity. Differential assistance to one country, such as Uzbekistan, could further tip the balance in power relations between Central Asian states and strengthen policies that have led to resource tensions over recent years.

The steady development of the Uyghur nationalist insurgency in the Xinjiang-Uyghur Autonomous Province of western China also has an important impact on neighboring Central Asia. Uyghur separatists for the past decade have been conducting a low-level terrorist campaign and sporadic demonstrations, which have evoked large numbers of arrests and killings by the authorities. The networks supporting the separatists have links in former Soviet Central Asia and can play into the development of insurgency outside of China. Though good information is scarce about the shadowy networks that link insurgent groups across the region, it is clear that militants and their supporters are able to move personnel and arms across this difficult-to-control border. This plays an important role in sustaining the insurgency in China, and Chinese authorities have put considerable pressure on the leadership of Kazakhstan and Kyrgyzstan to crack down on insurgents and sympathizers operating out of their territory. It appears that much of the arms trade across the border is linked closely with the burgeoning consumer-goods trade networks that supply cheap goods to Central Asian markets and are operated in large part by Uyghurs from Xinjiang. Just as the governments make common cause against the insurgents, there appears to be a network of mutual support among discontented elements at various levels of the society in Xinjiang, Kazakhstan, and Kyrgyzstan. Meanwhile, in the absence of good information, we can probably surmise that the strength and prevalence of this network is exaggerated by the authorities, who use such claims without substantiation to justify authoritarian crackdowns.

The Tajik Civil War

Officially extending from 1992 to 1997, the civil war in Tajikistan emerged from the upheaval of the demise of the USSR. It resulted in about 50,000 people killed, the great majority of deaths occurring during the first eight months of the conflict. A peace agreement was concluded in 1997, but violence continues, if on a more limited scale, including occasional outbreaks of insurgency by groups that were not yet fully integrated with Tajikistan or operate from the territory of Uzbekistan, and assassinations against members of the opposing sides continue as a regular feature of Tajik political life.

The key grievances that led to the outbreak of war in Tajikistan included regional imbalances in economic development and investments. Throughout most of the Soviet period, the elite of the northern province of Tajikistan, Leninabad, predominated in the national government of the republic. Correspondingly, a disproportionate share of investments in development of industry and other aspects of the economy went into this province—so much so that over half of the country's economy at the onset of the civil war was concentrated in this one province. At the same time, representatives of other provinces felt that their regions were being exploited for their mineral or agricultural wealth, in a kind of internal colonialism.

This was most sharply articulated in the case of Badakhshan, Tajikistan's southeastern province, where economic grievances combined with cultural distinctiveness to prompt the coalescing of a movement for enhanced regional autonomy, called Lali Badakhshan. Badakhshan had, since Tajikistan's creation as a republic in the 1920s, been assigned a nominal status as the Mountain

Badakhshan Autonomous Province, based on the predominance among the region's population of speakers of Pamiri languages (only rather distantly related to Tajik) and adherents to Ismaili Islam (as distinct from Tajikistan's overwhelmingly Sunni population). Though this autonomy movement had never led to serious attempts at separatism, there was strong support in the region for the political alliance that opposed the communist government, and both migrants from this region as well as the region itself were subject to retribution as the conflict progressed.

Severe interregional tensions were also expressed in relations between the southern province of Kölab, whose elite eventually came out victorious in the civil war. In the years prior to the war, the Kölab elite had made attempts to dominate and even annex the neighboring province of Qörghanteppa, and after several previous attempts, this annexation was completed during the civil war with the formation of Khatlan Province, which subsumed the two. Prior to the civil war, the Kölab elite had functioned as junior partners to the dominant group in the Communist Party and government—the Leninabad elite—from which they derived some marginal economic benefits for their region. During the civil war, however, the relations of domination between these two provinces were inverted and subsequently the Kölab elite have sought to take control of the economic assets of the northern province as well.

Once conflict broke out in Tajikistan in 1992, the economy of war with destruction of life and property on a massive scale required considerable inputs of resources. Few concrete data are available regarding the sources of support for the military factions in the early, most destructive part of the war. Anecdotal information indicates that the Soviet (later Russian) army played a role in arming the military faction leaders on both sides. Unsubstantiated claims also suggest that Iran intervened to support the opposition. Yet apart from outside support, it appears that locally mobilized resources were crucial in arming the sides. Though not systematically documented, it is widely claimed that the Russian arms that made their way into the hands of the combatants on both sides were not given away as part of a central policy of intervention, but rather were sold by commanders locally who may have sought to supplement their dwindling budgets or enrich themselves by such sales.

In any case, the crucial question is from where Tajik military leaders derived the resources needed to supply their supporters with weapons and pay. One key source was certainly the plundering of the nation's economy. During the early period of the civil war, many factories and other enterprises were stripped of anything that could be sold. Later, military faction leaders took control of some economic assets and sought to maintain a level of productive capacity to support their particular faction.

Though it is impossible to document adequately, another very important factor for both sides in the civil war was drug trafficking. During this period, trade from Afghanistan and through Tajikistan came to provide the great majority of the opiates available on the European market. On the Afghanistan side, much of this trade was maintained by the *mujahedeen* factions belonging to the Northern Alliance, which controlled poppy-growing areas and trade routes in the northeast part of the country. On the Tajikistan side, opposition forces that continued to control territory in the southeast until the peace accord, as well as the government forces and even the Russian military that have been stationed on the border, have all been implicated as participants in the trade. The details of this trade are far from clear, but it appears to be the case that it played a critical role in financing the militaries, and eventually a dimension of the regional conflict was also the critical matter of control over this trade, leading to fighting not only between the government and opposition sides but occasional among the factions on either side.

In the aftermath of the civil war, tensions over resources in Tajikistan remain more acute than ever. The winning side in the war, which is largely identified with factions stemming from Kölab Province, have taken control of virtually all economic resources in the country, though military faction leaders often make poor managers of enterprises. Even the northern part of the country, which largely escaped hostilities during the war and functioned somewhat autonomously until after the peace accord in 1997, has been subjected to increasing appropriation of positions in government and control of the economy as the Kölab faction in the capital has consolidated its authority. There have been some instances of open resistance to this trend, but for the most part the population has been patient in its desire to avoid repetition of the civil-war violence. Many local analysts, meanwhile, anticipate limits to this patience and the potential for tensions to erupt into violent reactions.

Islamic Movement of Uzbekistan

The cross-border insurgencies initiated by the Islamic Movement of Uzbekistan (IMU), which began in August 1999, would not meet the usual criteria for a civil war. So far, though they are targeted at the government of Uzbekistan, they have occurred mainly in Kyrgyzstan against Kyrgyz troops. Fatalities have numbered in the hundreds, and the civilian population has not been targeted, except by the governments of Uzbekistan and Kyrgyzstan in the form of forced relocation of people who are seen as potentially sympathetic to the rebels.

The IMU is a rebel military force, estimated to have 2,000–3,000 fighters—at least prior to the U.S.-led intervention in Afghanistan. The original incursions were conducted from clandestine bases in Tajikistan. The core of the IMU was constituted by dissident elements from Uzbekistan who had been forced into exile by Uzbek government crackdowns on opposition in the early to mid-1990s. Quite probably the bases in Tajikistan were established with the knowledge of at least some elements within the government of Tajikistan. Some key elements of the IMU had collaborated with the Tajik opposition during Tajikistan's civil war. Quite possibly, the IMU was also engaged with the drug trade and gained crucial material resources from there. After Tajikistan officially moved to expel the IMU, the Uzbek rebels relocated to Afghanistan, where they were developing increasingly close relations with the Taliban and

Al-Qaida forces, which by then had advanced to take control of near-bordering areas of Afghanistan.

As in the lead-up to the war in Tajikistan, the grievances that have fed support to the IMU have included issues of access to resources both between and within Uzbekistan's regions. Much of the IMU's limited popular support comes from the Ferghana Valley region of Uzbekistan, where an array of problems have led to deteriorating living conditions and an increasing sense of resentment toward the government. The Ferghana Valley encompasses nearly half of Uzbekistan's population on 4 percent of its territory. It contains some of the most productive agricultural land as well as several of the largest cities. Meanwhile, the rural economy has suffered from an unreformed command economy that requires farms to produce cotton for sale to government-controlled entities at a fraction of its market value. As a result, the rural economy has been drained of resources, unemployment has reached high levels (though no reliable official figures are published), and the cities have also been unable to absorb the increasingly desperate population. At the same time, the Ferghana Valley elite has largely been marginalized in national politics, with the steady increase of centralized control over regional resources, creating discontent on all levels of society.

The policy of sustained centralized control of the economy has led to tensions and discontent in other parts of Uzbekistan as well. For example, the western territories of Karakalpakistan (a nominally autonomous territory within Uzbekistan) and Khorezm have fared poorly under existing conditions. Karakalpakistan, which surrounds the southern part of the Aral Sea, has been devastated by the catastrophic desiccation of that water body. Due to an excess of irrigation use of the water upstream, the Amu Darya and Sir Darya rivers now carry a tiny fraction of their former flow to the Aral. The concentration of agricultural chemicals and salts in the dried-up seabed has so poisoned the environment that not only is agriculture no longer possible in many areas even if granted a water supply, but it is also life-threatening to nearby inhabitants. The prioritization of irrigation to upstream areas has fostered deep resentment and desperation among a growing segment of the Karakalpakistan population, many of whom are forced to flee the region for their survival. In neighboring Khorezm, the population suffers from increasingly restricted borders, which are a consequence of the central government's monetary policy and desire to limit trade that might circumvent official exchange-rate controls and monopolistic concessions. Thus, a lively cross-border trade economy that would otherwise flourish—as indeed it did during the early post-Soviet years before restrictions were imposed—has been in decline. The central government has invested the surpluses gained from tightly controlled cotton trade (the country's chief foreign currency earner) and other exports into monumental infrastructure projects that predominantly benefit the capital. Meanwhile, rural residents who may be drawn to the capital seeking the opportunities that are lacking in their home villages are subjected to arbitrary arrests and harassment from Tashkent law enforcement officials.

The wider population of Uzbekistan has shown great patience in hardship, and is generally inclined to put its trust in the top leadership, if not in the local authorities whose self-enrichment and arbitrary rule may be more apparent to average citizens. Yet there are some signs that the population is growing more discontented. There have been sporadic demonstrations, despite harsh responses by the authorities. And there is increasing support for underground Islamist movements, such as Hizb ut-Tahrir, whose political agenda is to overthrow the current regime, albeit avowedly by peaceful means. Hizb ut-Tahrir and other similar movements represent more than just a reaction to the economic situation, and importantly entail an orientation toward spiritual renewal and a return to conservative "Islamic" values. Yet resentments about corruption and claims that the current leadership are selling off the country's wealth for their personal gain are prominent among the reasons people cite for supporting these radical movements.

Growing Tensions Elsewhere in Central Asia

Though tensions have only rarely erupted into open violent conflict in other parts of Central Asia, there are many areas where tensions are sufficiently severe as to make outbreaks of conflict possible and even likely, at least on a local scale. In southern Kyrgyzstan, for example, there are grounds to fear a repetition of violence in 1990 that led to hundreds of deaths in clashes between the Kyrgyz and Uzbek populations of Osh, Uzgen, and other towns. The chief catalyst of that conflict was a sense of grievance over differential access to essential resources. Arable land in the region had traditionally been occupied by Uzbeks, though the once nomadic Kyrgyz inhabitants were increasingly moving into these areas. With Kyrgyz officials dominating positions of authority, Uzbeks feared that land was increasingly reallocated to Kyrgyz residents. Though there is a common determination to avoid new outbreaks of violence, the issues remain, with land growing increasingly scarce for the rapidly growing population of these areas and little progress in the government's avowed intention of ensuring more inclusion of Uzbeks in positions of authority.

Similarly, severe tensions leading to open conflict have occurred in communities on the Tajikistan-Kyrgyzstan border in the southern Ferghana Valley. The main issue here has been access to scarce water on watercourses that flow across boundaries between the two counties. Recent growth of Kyrgyz communities in areas where the water supply is insufficient has prompted some to seek to "reclaim" water sources that were controlled by Tajik communities.

Access to transportation corridors is another increasingly prevalent form of resource-based conflict. The government of Uzbekistan in particular has sought to tighten control on cross-border movement, partly in response to militant insurgencies of the IMU, and partly in order to control trade and currency exchange as necessitated by its artificial official exchange rate. As a result, the transportation corridors that formerly united the region have now become sometimes minutely dissected by border control posts and often closed borders. This has separated many people from their former sources of livelihood, increased the opportunities for corrupt officials to extract bribes at border crossings, and sometimes led to violence and even deaths in spontaneous outbursts of resentment against the officials. Some of the most severe incidents of border violence have occurred on the border between Kazakhstan and Uzbekistan, where Uzbek official are building border fortifications around territories in dispute, where the inhabitants often do not wish to end up under what is seen as more authoritarian and arbitrary rule in Uzbekistan.

Cross-border resource disputes have the potential to evoke conflict not only between citizens but also between governments. In southern Kyrgyzstan territory, for example, there are natural-gas fields that are exploited by facilities that were built in neighboring Uzbekistan under the unified Soviet system. Kyrgyz authorities have claimed that, since independence, Uzbekistan has continued to exploit this resource without providing compensation to Kyrgyzstan. At moments when tensions between the two countries have been at a peak over various issues, there have been threats that Kyrgyzstan could reclaim this resource through unilateral action. Similarly, since most of the water that supplies irrigation to the Uzbekistan part of the Ferghana Valley flows from Kyrgyzstan, Kyrgyz authorities have sought to claim compensation from Uzbekistan for the maintenance of irrigation infrastructure on their territory as well as the diminished hydroelectric capacity that is necessitated by agricultural use of the water. Kyrgyz authorities could seek to reclaim territory that was reallocated to Uzbekistan for a reservoir during Soviet times—a temporary arrangement, as the Kyrgyz authorities see it. To counter this possibility, Uzbek authorities have positioned military facilities around the reservoir. The issue of transport corridors has also heightened tensions between states and even between government and population. There was popular outcry in Kyrgyzstan, for example, when it appeared that the government could bow to Uzbek pressure to cede territory that would provide a link to isolated Uzbek territories, but at the same time impose a break in transportation links between parts of Kyrgyzstan.

Though Kazakhstan has been relatively free of open conflict in the post-Soviet period, there are grounds for concern here as well. Unlike many of its neighbors, Kazakhstan has the capacity to build a flourishing economy due to its tremendous wealth in oil, provided it avoids the pitfalls of resource-based, regionally imbalanced economic development. Virtually all of Kazakhstan's oil resources are concentrated in a few western provinces of the country, and control of these resources is in the hands of a very narrow elite. The country's leadership has developed a reputation as among the most corrupt in the world, and many believe that the majority of export earnings are deposited in the personal accounts of a few top officials. The extent of the accuracy of such claims may never be known, but the perception of inequity severely undermines the legitimacy of the government. There is also a risk that great regional disparities in the resources at the disposal of local authorities could lead to tensions over cutbacks in pensions, social services, and capital investments in disadvantaged regions. The potential for problems is particularly acute in southern

Kazakhstan, where the economy is weak, there is a large Uzbek minority population, and there is growing attraction among both Uzbeks and Kazakhs to radical Islamist movements that capitalize on these disparities and discontent.

Pervasive Themes

The economic dimensions of conflict include unemployment and poverty, the criminal networks and wealth created by the trade in drugs and other contraband, the sharply growing stratification of societies (which sometimes has ethnic dimensions), and issues of reform and government control of the economies. It is essential to understand these issues in order to develop effective strategies in conflict prevention.

Unemployment, Poverty, and Stratification

Unemployment and poverty were already quite high in Central Asia during Soviet times, but have risen sharply throughout the region as a result of the collapse of the integrated Soviet economy, market reforms, and the predatory role of the elites in plundering their countries' economic infrastructure and natural resources under privatization. As a result, in some areas unemployment is estimated to exceed 80 percent and the large majority of the population is in severe poverty.

It is apparent that severe stratification and even sharp increases in unemployment and poverty do not necessarily lead to violent conflict and civil war. However, in the Central Asian context, perceptions of a moral social order play an important role. If the community accepts that their lot is "as it should be," then they are very patient. If they perceive serious injustice, then some people become ready to mobilize, even to use violence. We see this in the wide-scale attacks on Meskhetian Turks in 1989 when many hundreds of people were killed and 100,000 Meskhetians were forced to flee Uzbekistan; the underlying motivation for most of the killers was the perception that they were suffering as a result of the Meskhetians' strong position in the local agricultural markets. Likewise, the major motivator of the conflict in Osh in 1990 between Uzbeks and Kyrgyz was the perception that scarce land resources were being unfairly allocated. Similar grievances are currently rife, and are often perceived along ethnic lines, though not always. There is sharply growing resentment toward the national elites, who are increasingly seen as flourishing while most people are suffering.

The unemployment issue has a special dimension in Tajikistan where there is a major problem of employment of former combatants, many of whom reside in the most underdeveloped regions and who often know few other avenues to obtain a livelihood aside from being the client of a military faction leader. At the same time, affirmative action for former combatants has the potential to seriously compromise the interests of other groups, as the participants in combat from both sides become the winners and those who did not fight are "punished."

Illegal Trade

The primary commodity for illegal trade is the opium produced in Afghanistan and traded through Central Asia to Russia and Europe. This has created a resource-rich network between these countries with strong links both to insurgent movements and to state structures. In some areas there are other forms of illegal trade, including weapons trade and trafficking in women. There are also some commodities that are currently under the control of governments and the narrow elites associated with them which could become bones of contention in civil conflict, such as gold in Uzbekistan and cotton exports from Tajikistan, Kyrgyzstan, and Uzbekistan.

The impact of the trade in such commodities is generally quite local and does not characterize the country as a whole in terms of propensity for conflict, but rather are factors that operate on the local level. The impact of drug trafficking, for example, is not uniform: on the one hand, income from work as couriers in the drug trade alleviates pressures caused by unemployment, while the trade also fosters corruption and associated problems of governance and economic development.

The country where illegal trade plays the most important role is in Tajikistan, where a "warlord economy" emerged from the peace agreement that essentially divided the spoils of the country's wealth and productive capacity, and there are an array of actors who are not interested in the development of a normal, market-based national economy.

Economic Policy

In the case of former Soviet Central Asia, the issue of economy revolves around the degree of state control and the question of how much the social protections that were provided under the Soviet system are eroded by reorientation of the benefits of the system toward the elite, whether this is through privatization or continued direct state control.

Economic reforms or the lack of them can both be conflict-generating factors. In the case of agricultural-sector reforms in Kyrgyzstan, for example, decollectivization resulted in the collapse of the rural economy with resulting flight to the cities and other disastrous consequences. The rural population was essentially left without its resource base. In Uzbekistan, by comparison, the failure to reform and the retention of the Soviet planned economy in the cotton sector has resulted in severe impoverishment of the rural population as this sector has been used to subsidize elite prosperity and government's priority investments.

To conclude, several points should be made regarding the possibilities for generalizing about the role of economic resources in conflict:

1. While an economic base may be decisive in maintaining conflict, it is often not decisive in initiating it. In the Tajik civil war, 50,000 people were killed in a burst of violence that entailed only very limited resource outlays

over a short time, and that short episode has determined the development of the country for decades.

2. In many Central Asian cases, the economic stakes are actually rather small, due to scarcity of resources, and do not offer a significant resource base for prolonged conflict. Yet conflicts themselves generate their own economic base through the nexus with drugs and other contraband.

3. The economic considerations entailed in negotiating peace, where the goal is sharing power among combatants, are very different from those entailed in preventing conflict, which must take into consideration the interests of a much wider and diverse array of actors and stakeholders.

4. The units of analysis are critical. The economic factors that could spark conflict can be quite local in their effect. A national-level analysis might miss these factors.

5. There can be no broad recipe for how to formulate economic policies that will address the problems that can spark conflict. Policy approaches must be tailored to the specificity of particular situations on the subnational level.

6. Cultural factors, also often quite local, can be decisive in determining whether people with grievances choose to seek to address them through violence.

7. International aid providers must make a careful assessment of each aid project to anticipate where its impact could increase tensions that can lead to conflict.

John Schoeberlein is a political anthropologist and director of the Forum for Central Asian Studies at Harvard University (since 1993). He also heads the International Crisis Group's Central Asia Project (since 2000), serves as president of the Central Eurasian Studies Society, and led the United Nations Fergana Valley Development Programme focusing on regional conflict prevention (1998–1999). His research focuses on issues of identity, including nationalism, Islam, ethnicity, community organization, and conflict.

Notes

1. See, for example, Guy Lamb, "A Literature Review on the Current Relationship Between War and Economic Agendas in Africa," Staff Papers, Centre for Conflict Resolution, Cape Town, South Africa, December 2000; Paul Collier, "Economic Causes of Civil Conflict and Their Implications for Policy," Washington, DC: World Bank, 2000; Ibrahim Elbadawi and Nicholas Sambanis, "Why Are There So Many Civil Wars in Africa? Understanding and Preventing Violent Conflict," *Journal of African Economies* 9(3), 2000, pp. 244–269.

2. Analogous situations have been observed in some of the other key conflict zones on the territory of the former Soviet Union; see Charles King, "The Benefits of Ethnic War: Understanding Eurasia's Unrecognized States," *World Politics* 53(4), July 2001.

6.4

Islamic Militancy:
Religion and Conflict in Central Asia

Olivier Roy

In post-Soviet Central Asia, Tajikistan and Uzbekistan have both seen periods of armed conflict. In each case, Islamic militants played an active role. In Tajikistan, the Islamist movement, in the form of the Islamic Renaissance Party, was characterized by an important Tajik nationalist dimension in addition to the religious dimension. Tajik Islamists joined forces early on with the Tajik democratic opposition and reformers, and have now entered the mainstream of Tajik political life. In Uzbekistan, a more radical Islamist movement, the Islamic Movement of Uzbekistan, has been closely identified with the Taliban in Afghanistan and with the al-Qaida network, and has been involved in ongoing armed conflict. This movement, less expressly nationalist, has accordingly changed its name to the Islamic Movement of Turkestan. It has, however, suffered serious setback as a result of the war in Afghanistan and the fall of the Taliban, and may no longer be an effective force or threat to the Uzbek government. In recent years, a third, less expressly political form of Islamic militancy has gained in importance, the Hizb ut-Tahrir. This movement, which cuts across national lines, embraces radical Islamic rhetoric, seeking, for example, to revive the caliphate, but to date, it has rejected armed struggle and eschewed mainstream political activities.

In Central Asia, anti-Russian and anti-Soviet upheavals have historically had a religious dimension, including, for example, the Andijan uprising in 1898, and the Basmachi movement against Soviet rule from 1920 to 1931. Postindependence events seem to confirm the importance of the Islamic religious dimension in antigovernment upheavals. Only two armed conflicts have taken place in Central Asia since the Central Asian states achieved independence, and in both cases Islamist militancy played a role. The civil war in Tajikistan (1992–1997) pitched "Islamists" against "neo-communists," and the forays made from Afghanistan through Kyrgyzstan in the direction of Uzbekistan by the Islamic

Movement of Uzbekistan (August 1999 and August 2000) were aimed at toppling the Uzbek regime to replace it with an Islamic state.[1]

In contrast to what happened in colonial Russian and Soviet times, however, these conflicts have not pitted Muslims against non-Muslims. They have instead been the more visible dimension of a larger phenomenon of militant Islam that is contesting the Islamic credentials of the postindependence regimes. The recent emergence in Uzbekistan of the Hizb ut-Tahrir, or Liberation Party, is a case in point; the party, although nonviolent, dismisses all the existing regimes as religiously illegitimate. Still, it is worth noting that Islam-related insurgency never challenged the Christian (that is, Russian) presence in the south. In fact all Islam-related violence was aimed at other fellow Muslims, who were accused of being either bad or non-Muslims (*kafir*). Even the social and ethnic unrest occurring between 1989 and 1991 was never directed at non-Muslims: the targets were the Meskhetian Turks in Ferghana in 1989 and the Uzbeks and Kyrghyzes in Osh 1990. On occasion, evangelical Protestant Christian efforts to convert local Muslims have been met with strong opposition from governments (in Turkmenistan, for example), but were unopposed by local Muslim clerics, or even, for that matter, by activists. Indeed, there hasn't been a single report of a church being attacked by a Muslim mob anywhere in Central Asia. Given the fact that Christians have been, up to the present day, identified with Russians (or, to be more precise, with Europeans), it is clear that the main fault line in Central Asia does not divide the Muslim population from the non-Muslim population, but creates, rather, a deep schism within the Muslim population.[2]

Given this fact, how should the role of religion in the postindependence conflicts be assessed? There are clearly two factors that come into play: first, the avowed motivation for much of the unrest is ideological, and second, the underlying rationale for much of the conflict has been, until recently, regional factionalism. Two armed movements aiming at toppling established governments and taking political power have been active: the Tajik Islamic Renaissance Party (IRP) and the Islamic Movement of Uzbekistan (IMU). Both are rooted in a previously united, pan-Soviet IRP, which split in the early 1990s into national branches. The present IMU, however, also includes leaders and militants who left the IRP because they did not share the IRP's enthusiasm for entering normal politics and participating in elections. Between 1992 and 1997, links between Tajik IRP and IMU remained very close: the IMU militants, expelled from Uzbekistan, joined the IRP-led guerilla movement, which had been established in the upper valleys of the Gharm area in southern Tajikistan and in Afghanistan. Two events split this alliance: the takeover of Kabul by the Taliban in September 1996, and the Moscow agreement on a coalition government in Dushanbe in June 1997. IMU chose armed struggle and the Taliban, while IRP allied itself with Afghan Northern Alliance leader Masoud and pursued negotiations. The IRP has since become a "normal" Tajik political party, and its ideological dimension has faded away. The IMU, on the other hand, has been so closely associated with the Taliban that many of its fighters have been killed during the allied offensive against the Taliban in Afghanistan and it has been placed on the list of terrorist organizations by the U.S. government.

Political Islam, as it existed at the beginning of the 1990s, has thus almost disappeared, either through integration or through military defeat. But this does not mean that radical Islam no longer plays a role in regional politics. A new trend of Islamic radicalization seems to have appeared in the wake of the failure of the armed opposition groups. This trend is linked more to a social and generational gap, and is oriented more toward changing society through religious proselytizing than through political mobilization aimed at gaining political power through armed struggle. This trend is embodied in the Hizb ut-Tahrir movement.

In the following sections, those ideological Islamist movements that have put their marks on the first decade of independence are discussed, followed by a discussion of the growing influence of other groups.

The Ideological Dimension
of the Islamic Opposition: The IRP

The all-union Islamic Renaissance Party was founded in Astrakhan, Russia, in June 1990. At that time, the party was explicitly pan-Soviet and was not in favor of independence for the Soviet republics. The elected chairman was Ahmed Qadi Akhtayev, an Avar from Daghestan and a physician by profession, and the deputy chairman was Valiahmed Sadur, a Tatar scholar whose field of study is Indonesian. The founding fathers were mainly Tatars or came from the Northern Caucasus, like Abbas Kebedov (from Kyzil Yurt) and Mohammad Bahauddin. Some Tajiks, however, including Dawlat Osman, future deputy chairman of the Tajik branch, were also present. The party had two main publications: *Al Wahdat* (Unity) in Russian and *Hedayat* (Guidance) in Persian. While the Russian section had no difficulty registering as a political party, problems and pressures arose for the Central Asian groups. Laws were passed in almost all Central Asian republics to ban political activities made in the name of Islam, and the party was banned from the outset in Uzbekistan, Turkmenistan, and Tajikistan.

Nevertheless, the IRP did take root in Central Asia, though its influence was mostly restricted to Tajikistan and Uzbekistan. The Tajik section, the largest, was founded on 6 October 1990 at an underground meeting.[3] It was officially recognized in November 1991, in the wake of the crisis of the post-communist regime. The Uzbek section gathered in Tashkent in January 1991, but the meeting was broken up by the police. In Kazakhstan, the IRP has been supplanted by another Islamist organization, Alash Orda, probably because the primary constituency of the IRP, in this republic, was among non-Kazakh Muslims, Uzbeks, and Uyghurs.[4] The same thing happened in Kyrgyzstan, where the few IRP members seem to have been Uzbeks from Osh. In Turkmenistan, the IRP does not appear to have any significant membership. In fact, the IRP took roots in areas where conservative Islam has traditionally been strong, and not in the tribal and more superficially Islamized populations (Turkmens, Kazakhs, and Kyrgyzes). But even in Uzbekistan and Tajikistan, the party's constituency roughly coincided with regional identities: people originating from Ferghana for the former and from the Gharm valley for the latter. This regionalism would become an obstacle for the extension of the party in both countries.

The IRP, through its ideology and constituency, is clearly very close to the mainstream Middle Eastern and South Asian Sunni Islamist movements, such as the Egyptian Muslim Brethren and the Pakistani Jama'at-i Islami. In interviews with Tajik leaders, only scarce reference has been made to the Iranian revolution. The official IRP program, released in July 1990, rejected terrorism. The aim of the party, according to its statutes, was to "unify the Muslims on all the Soviet territory."[5] It opposed ethnic conflicts and nationalism, and pledged to respect the Soviet constitution and not to oppose the existence of the USSR. Nevertheless, its discourse and terminology were close to the Islamist vulgate. The party claimed to be a "social and political organization" (*ijtemâ'i wa syâssi*). It stressed the need for predication (*dawat*) among Muslims as well as Christians. It criticized the official clergy for its lack of militancy, and appealed for the building of a high-level Muslim educational network. It advocated "Islamic social justice" based on *zakat* and *sadaqat*. In brief, its slogans and programs, as well as terminology, were identical to that of all Sunni Islamist movements, with no visible Iranian influence.

The organizational structure of the party was also a combination of two models: the Muslim Brethren and the Communist Party. The party's congress (*anjoman*), made of deputies (*vâkil*) of primary cells (*tashkilat-i ibtida'i*), elects a Council of Ulama (fifteen members), which in turn puts forward to the congress the candidacy of the amir, who, once elected, appoints a coordinating committee (*koordinatsya*). One of the distinguishing features of the IRP, when compared with the Egyptian Muslim Brethren and the Pakistani Jama'at-i Islami, is that the priestly group (*ulama*) are supposed to have the upper hand in the party's final decisions (they can dismiss the amir without calling the congress). The paradox is that, at the time of its foundation, there was no real *ulama* in the party. The party stresses therefore the role of the "intellectuals" (*alimân*), who, although not being *ulama*, might base their analyses on Koran and Sunna. Clearly, the reference to "*ulama*" is wishful thinking, while the "intellectuals" with a secular background are the real social basis of the IRP, as they are in the other parts of the Sunni Muslim world.[6] This organizational model is a good indication of the ideological leaning of the IRP, but was never really implemented, because the party split along national lines.

The recruitment of the IRP cadres is close to that of the Egyptian Muslim Brethren or the Pakistani Jama'at: relatively young (born in the 1950s) and educated people, mainly in sciences (note, for example, two important leaders: Mullah Nuri, an engineer in geodesics, and Mullah Himmatzadeh, a mechanical engineer). But many of these intellectuals were also "parallel" teachers (*mullahs*). This double identity is specially strong in predominantly rural

Tajikistan, where there is no real urban elite: while the bulk of the local parallel *mullahs* were officially working as *kolkhozians*, some members of the intelligentsia who received secular training at state universities and institutes became parallel *mullahs* in their own native districts. They received relatively extensive religious education (for Soviet standards) by participating in clandestine educational networks. Nuri and Himmatzadeh attended the courses of Hajji Mohammad Rustamov, alias Mawlawi Qari Hindoustani, an Uzbek who was educated in the traditional *madrassa* of Deoband in India before World War II. In fact the IRP was joined by militants who had already entered into Islamic militancy during the 1980s on a very local basis. The sudden liberalization of 1988 gave an opportunity to militants from different areas to merge into one Islamic party.

But this coalescence of loose networks of militants did not survive independence: the IRP was caught up in and split by rivalries among national identities, while representatives of foreign religious groups rushed toward the USSR in order to sponsor and develop the Islamic revival. The split with the Tajik branch occurred in December 1991, after a pledge of support by the federal IRP for the candidacy of president Nabiev, the former head of the Tajik Communist Party, in the presidential elections of November, while the Tajik IRP endorsed the candidacy of Davlat Khudonazarov (himself a democrat and an Ismaili, which means that his Islamic credentials were rather weak from an Islamist point of view). As a result, the democratic and nationalist opposition forces were united in support of a complete split with Russia and a reorientation of the Tajik foreign policy toward Afghanistan and Iran. The Tajik branch was strongly criticized by the Moscow headquarters, and subsequently the party decided to break its ties with the federal IRP and operate independently.

The IRP in Tajikistan:
From Islamism to Nationalism, Through Regionalism
Three factors gave the Tajik IRP a higher profile than in other areas: its alliance with the head of the official clergy, its strong popular basis among one of the local regionalist factions (the Gharmis), and the building of a coalition with the nationalist and democratic forces. In Tajikistan, the official representative of the Soviet clergy, the Qazi Akbar Turajanzade, although not a member of the party, advocated its registration by the government in October 1991, a rare instance of collaboration between the IRP and official clergy. That the IRP could take root within a significant faction of the population was a consequence of the highly politicized regional factionalism in Tajikistan. Of the four main regional factions, two were identified with the communist elites (the Leninabadis and the Kölabis). One, very secular-minded and active in the early sovietization of the republic (the Pamiris), was pushed out of official positions in early 1992. The fourth, the Gharmis (people originating from the Gharm valley, even if many of them live now in the Kurgan-Tepe Province), were never associated with power sharing, remained very tradition-minded, and underwent a process of radicalization paired with Islamic fundamentalism

during the late 1970s and the 1980s. The Qazi was a Gharmi, like Mullahs Nuri and Himmatzadeh.

The alliance of the IRP with the Democratic Party, the nationalist Rastakhiz movement, and the Pamiris was not only a coalition of those excluded from the power. It also had a common basis, which made it a rather lasting alliance. This basis was a common Tajik nationalism. All these parties conceived the Tajik identity as the inheritance and a last expression of the Persian culture that had profoundly influenced all of Central Asia since the end of the first millennium. Such a nationalism is part of a broader cultural identity, and not just the expression of a narrow ethnic nationalism, as it is in Uzbekistan. Without understanding the connection between Islamic and national identity in Tajikistan, it is not possible to understand the political positions embraced by the IRP. This connection helps to explain why Tajikistan is one of the few places in the Muslim world where a lasting common front has been established between an Islamist movement and nationalist or democratic parties. Islam is seen as a pillar of a national identity that has been endangered both by the Soviet system and by the reach and influence of Turkic culture. Such a synthesis has been supported by the Qazi Turajanzade himself.[7]

This endeavor to coalesce Islam and nationalism, reminiscent of what had been achieved in the Iranian revolution, and the call for the restoration of an "Islamic Persian identity" inevitably brought the IRP closer to Iran, but it soon became evident that each side understood Islam and nationalism in a different way: Sunni and anti-Uzbek for the Tajiks, Shi'a and based on a regional strategy for Iran. And as a result, the Tajiks and the Iranians have been unable to forge a common strategy from their common cultural heritage.

The evolution of the Tajik IRP shows that it is more an "islamo-nationalist" movement than an internationalist one. In September 1996, the Taliban took Kabul and pledged support for the Central Asian Islamist parties based in northern Afghanistan. But the Tajik IRP, which spearheaded the United Tajik Opposition (UTO), stayed in the area controlled by Ahmad Shah Masoud of the Northern Alliance opposition. In June 1997, it signed an agreement with the government of Dushanbe, under the auspices of Russia and Iran. Mullah Nuri left Mashhad in Iran to participate in the coalition government, but then his plane was forced to land in Taliban-held territory. The Taliban tried unsuccessfully to convince him to cancel the agreement and to stay with them, but Nuri refused. Hence the UTO had opted for ethnic solidarity (by remaining with Masoud, a Tajik, and opposing the Pashtun Taliban) and for national solidarity rather than ideology. Despite many ups and downs, the coalition government was able to stay in charge, united by a common distrust of Uzbek hegemonism in Central Asia. All the former ideological coalitions split and were transformed into ethnic ones. The ethnic Uzbek but Tajik citizen, Mahmud Khodaberdaiev, a local warlord and staunch ally of Tajik president Rahmanov in his campaign against the Islamists in 1992, changed loyalties after the agreement of 1997, and, with the hidden support of Tashkent, launched a failed offensive to destabilize the Tajik coalition government in November

1998. On the other hand, Masoud was allowed to use Tajikistan as his rear base, with the support of Russia and Iran. All of these strategic alignments could be interpreted in ethnic and national terms rather than ideological terms. The linkage between Islam and Tajik nationalism (with its relationship to the Persian heritage) is often clearly expressed by leaders such as Qazi Turajanzade.[8]

The history of the IRP after 1997 is that of "normalization," which has brought with it some negative consequences. The leaders entered the government as a sort of junior partner, which allowed them, for example, to enjoy certain "perks"; Qazi Akbar Turajanzade, for instance, gained control of a cotton mill in Kafirnehan. IRP armed militias have been partly integrated into the Tajik armed forces. One of the main UTO commanders, Mirza Ziayev, has been appointed head of the Ministry for Emergencies, where he has command of some armed forces. Many commanders have used their local power to make money, while maintaining links with their former Uzbek brothers in arms, helping them in 1999 and 2000 to cross the Kyrgyz borders for attacks on Uzbekistan. Nevertheless, the remote areas still under IRP control do not manifest any Islamist influence. In fact ideology does not play any role in the IRP. A new IRP generation, whose representative is Mohiddin Kabiri (in charge of the party's external relations), too young to have been involved in the civil war, is trying to transform the IRP into an all-Tajik political movement, breaking with the Gharmi regionalist identity. Even if this move was not reflected in the January 2000 legislative elections (the IRP received less than 8 percent of the vote), which were openly rigged, it seems that the party has extended its constituency all over Tajikistan, including the Ismaili Gorno-Badakhshan. The IRP, as well as the Tajik Communist Party, are seen as the only credible political opposition to the government of President Rahmanov: both are attracting more and more voters, who are more interested in protesting corruption and clientism than they are in any ideological agenda.

If one also takes into consideration the fact that Islamization has pervaded all social strata in Tajikistan, taking the form of social conservatism (polygamy is now openly practiced by many people, including many officials), Islam as such is no longer a determinative political factor in Tajikistan. The IRP has approved the U.S. military campaign in Afghanistan, which ended with the victory of its Afghan allies, the Northern Alliance.

The Islamic Movement of Uzbekistan: From Islamization to Armed Struggle

In 1991, the Uzbek IRP branch, led by Abdullah Utaev, split from the all-Soviet IRP; like its Tajik counterpart. But, in Uzbekistan, the IRP did not succeed in becoming a significant player for two reasons: competition and repression. Repression was very harsh: Utaev was arrested in December 1992 and disappeared in jail, as did Sheykh Abdoul Vali, *imam* of the Andijan Jami mosque, in August 1995. The Uzbek IRP had to go underground. The Uzbek government undertook to cut the local IRP from its foreign contacts by restricting the availability of visas, especially for Pakistanis, from 1992 onwards.

It also extended its grip on the *muftiyya,* by sacking Mohammad Yussuf in spring 1993. The government also cleverly exploited less politicized Muslim networks, such as the *naqshbandi* brotherhood. On the other hand, the IRP did not have a monopoly within the Islamist political opposition. The main opposition party, Birlik, although officially secular, also stressed the Islamic component of the Uzbek identity, while some young militants left the IRP to create their own organization.

In Ferghana, local movements endeavored to create "Islamic territories," as for example in Namangan. In 1991, disturbances erupted in this city. Two young men in their twenties, Tahir Yoldashev and Joma Khojaiev "Namangani" (a former Soviet soldier in Afghanistan, where he became a "born again" Muslim out of admiration for the Afghan *mujahedeen*) took over a local mosque and endeavored to Islamize the city, enforcing the veil for women, establishing *shariah* courts to deal with petty crimes, and setting up a local militia to enforce law and order. They originally were members of the IRP but soon broke with a party they considered too legalist. They established the *adalat* movement and the Islam Lashkari militias ("Islam's Army"). Other movements were established locally, including *tawba* (repentance). In fact, most of these movements had a constituency around a local mosque and a *mahalla* (neighborhood). Unlike the IRP, these militants were critical of the official clergy (headed by the mufti Mohammed ·Yussuf, although he later was, like Turajanzade, close to the Muslim Brethren). From the beginning, Uzbek Islamists seemed to have been more radical than their Tajik counterparts.

In April 1992 the government cracked down on these autonomous "Islamic territories." Tahir Yoldashev and Joma Namangani fled to Tajikistan, where they fought alongside the IRP, which they followed into Afghanistan. Namangani organized the Uzbek refugees around Mazar and Kunduz, while Yoldashev went to Peshawar to find support and to recruit among Uzbek students who had gone to Pakistani *madrassa* to study. They, along with Mullah Nuri, then head of the UTO, were linked with the informal networks of Pakistani radical religious movements centered around Lahore, training militants in Pakistani *madrassa* for their religious education and in Afghanistan for military training. The Afghan training camps, which had actually existed since 1988 (established with the help of the Pakistani intelligence services) came under the control of the Taliban after their victory against Masoud in September 1996. In 1997, the Taliban decided to give to Osama bin Laden control over all the non-Pakistani foreign volunteers—mostly Arabs, but also including Uzbeks—who were entering Afghanistan. As we saw, the Tajik IRP refused to follow the move and left for Tajikistan. The Uzbek IMU, however, became more and more associated with Al-Qaida, the militant and internationalist movement headed by bin Laden.

From 1999 onwards the IMU launched military forays into Kyrgyzstan, with the probable aim of seizing the Uzbek mountainous enclave of Sukh and establishing a permanent guerrilla base to threaten Ferghana. Although two campaigns, August 1999 and August 2000, failed to achieve this goal, such

Teun Voeten/Panos

Religious meeting in
city park in Peshawar, Pakistan

attacks had a tremendous impact in the area, fueling insecurity and instability. Meanwhile, the February 1999 assassination attempt on President Karimov was attributed to the IMU, although the actual perpetrators have never been identified with any certainty. A general crackdown on any form of opposition sent hundreds of militants to Afghanistan. Uzbekistan entered the Shanghai Five cooperation organization (created in 1996 and including Russia, China, Tajikistan, Kyrgyzstan, and Kazakhstan), in order to strengthen what was extremely weak regional security cooperation. But one of the negative side effects of the stress on security was the closure of many points on the border, new visa requirements, and increasing tensions between Uzbekistan and Kyrgyzstan over control of the border. In a word, the perceived Islamic threat had increased regional tensions between states and contributed to the deterioration of the economic situation, fueling popular resentment.

In Afghanistan, Namangani established an Uzbek battalion of some 3,000–5,000 soldiers, who were, for the first time, engaged against Masoud in June 2001, indicating that Namangani no longer had a purely Uzbek agenda but had identified himself totally with the Taliban and with bin Laden's strategy, that is to say, pursuing international solidarity above national interests. There have been indications, although not confirmed, of a merging between the Taliban's leadership, Al-Qaida, and IMU. In spring 2001, IMU changed its name, becoming the Islamic Movement of Turkestan, thus indicating its willingness not to be identified as an Uzbek nationalist movement. But the merging of IMU and Al-Qaida has also been the death warrant for IMU; after the 11 September 2001 terrorist attacks, IMU was placed on the list of the terrorist groups by the U.S. government and its troops in northern Afghanistan, which sided with the Taliban, were targets of U.S. bombing missions. Hundreds of IMU fighters died during the fightings around Kunduz in November 2001, including its leader Namangani. Whatever the resiliency of the movement, the IMU seems, at least for the medium term, to have been maneuvered out of the Central Asian political scene.

The Hizb ut-Tahrir and the New Generation: Toward New Sources of Armed Conflict or Political Integration?

The armed Islamic movements that led the struggle in Tajikistan and Uzbekistan are either integrated or running out of steam. But this does not mean that militant Islam is dead. Since 1996, a new movement, the Hizb ut-Tahrir, has emerged in Uzbekistan. It had been spreading for years among ethnic Uzbeks in Uzbekistan, as well as northern Tajikistan and Kyrgyzstan, but it now seems to be extending its influence to ethnic Tajiks and Kyrghyzes. The Hizb ut-Tahrir is new on the regional scene, and has apparently no contact with the militant Islamic networks based in Afghanistan and Pakistan (there is a Pakistani section of Hizb ut-Tahrir, but it was established after the Uzbek section). It presents a strange case of a former islamo-nationalist movement (Palestinian) that has become a supranational movement, now based in London. The Hizb ut-Tahrir was founded in 1953 in Amman, Jordan, as a splinter group of the Muslim Brothers. Its founder, Sheikh Nabhani, criticized the lack of support from the Muslim Brothers for the Palestinian struggle for national liberation: it was probably the first "Islamo-nationalist" party. The party migrated to Beirut and then in the late 1970s to London, where it underwent a transformation. In London, it has recruited primarily among young, educated, second-generation, uprooted Muslims, and it has taken a strongly supranational stance, proselytizing for the revival of the Caliphate (Khilafat). It is, nowadays, a mainly western party. It embraces the radical rhetoric of the revolutionary Islamist parties (the Hizb ut-Tahrir claims to be a political party and to promote Islamic "ideology"),[9] but contrary to the traditional Islamist parties, it does not enter the field of politics and promotes *dawa*, or preaching. Hizb ut-Tahrir members are organized in small circles (*da'ira*) of five to seven people, headed by a Mushrif. Each group member knows only the members of his or her circle and only the Mushrif knows the next-higher-ranking superior. It recruits in Uzbekistan, Tajikistan, and Kyrgyzstan, mainly among the dropouts of a failed educational system. It is typically a generational phenomenon that cuts across regional identities and even national lines (but with no impact in Turkmenistan and Kazakhstan). Although it does not promote armed struggle, its members are persecuted by the authorities. It had no contact with the Afghan Taliban and had no involvement in the Afghan campaign in fall 2001. It did, however, vigorously condemn the U.S. bombings in Afghanistan and supported the Taliban, though it did not endorse the 11 September terrorist attacks.[10]

In fact, Hizb ut-Tahrir, although advocating a "pacifist" approach, has many points in common with Al-Qaida's ideology, including an anti-Christian and anti-Semitic dimension, totally absent from the IRP's ideology. They are activists, have a narrow conception of what Islam is, consider people who do not follow them to be either bad Muslim or non-Muslims, and, more significantly, reject the idea of creating an Islamic state in any particular country. This last point is probably the most important difference between Hizb ut-Tahrir and the more the militant tradition of political Islam as practiced by the Muslim Brothers and IRP. Hizb ut-Tahrir, as well as Al-Qaida, are fighting for the immediate re-creation of the Muslim Ummah, by calling to all the Muslims in the world. Ummah and *shariat* are their common vocabulary, but Hizb ut-Tahrir is more cautious on *jihad*. By contrast, *jihad* was the main precept of Osama bin Laden.

The Islamic dimension of internecine struggles in Central Asia has undergone change. The IRP and IMU (whose main base of support was Ferghana) arose largely as expressions of disgruntled regional factions, where an old tradition of Muslim conservatism still predominated. One has been integrated into national politics, the other has chosen the "wrong" side in regional geopolitics. The time of armed Islamist guerrilla movements seems to have faded away, but a new form of radical Islamization is on the move and seems bound to be both more successful over the long term and more resistant to repression, because of its underground nature. It is urban, recruiting among educated youth, transcending traditional divisions, based on predication and propaganda, and working at the grassroots level of the society. The destruction of the armed Islamist organization by the military campaign in Afghanistan has coincided with and accelerated the changing patterns of Islamic militancy in Central Asia; it is now evolving from armed struggle to underground militant predication.

Olivier Roy is a researcher at the French Center for Scientific Research and the author of The New Central Asia, the Creation of Nations *(2000). He served as head of the OSCE mission to Tajikistan in 1993–1994.*

Notes

1. The declaration of *jihad* against the government of Uzbekistan was issued on 25 August 1999 by the *amir* of the Harakat-ul Islam (Islamic Movement), Tahir Faruq Yoldashev. The statement said that "the primary objective of this declaration of jihad is the establishment of an Islamic state with the application of the sharia" (web site of IMU).

2. The asymmetry of terms is a clear indication. One never pits "Christians" against "Muslims" in Central Asia, but "Muslims" versus "Russian-speakers," which include all "Europeans," including the Tatars, who, although nominally Muslims, are identified (and identify themselves) with Russians (they live in Russian neighborhoods). But this opposition knows some particularities: while "European" Jews (Ashkenaz), all Russian-speakers, are identified with Russians, local Jews (Bukharan

Jews), who speak Tajik and Uzbek, are seen as indigenous (*mahalli*); the same patterns of "nativization" may extend to Koreans, who, although exclusively Russian-speakers and never Muslims, are sometimes included in the indigenous population (as well as, strangely enough, some remaining Germans). The rationale for the two latter groups is that they are rural settlers, managing their own ethnic *kolkhozes*, and had never been part of the Russian local elites.

3. The official newspaper *Tâjikistân-i shuravi* (Soviet Tajikistan) condemned, in its headline, the announcement of the creation of the Tajik branch of IRP, under the title "A Provincial Clandestine Committee Under the Banner of Islam" (17 May 1991).

4. Ahmed Rashid, *Central Asia*. London: Zed Books, 1994, p. 122.

5. The party's program has been published in several languages. My source is the journal *Hedayat,* in Tajik, no. 1, June 1990 (no place of publication). All the following quotations are from this issue.

6. Olivier Roy, *The Failure of Political Islam.* Cambridge, MA: Harvard University Press, 1995.

7. Quadi Akbar Turajonzoda, "Religion: The Pillar of Society," in *Central Asia: Conflict Resolution and Change,* edited by Roald Sagdeev and Susan Eisenhower. Washington, DC: The Center for Political and Strategic Studies, 1995: www.cpss.org/cabook.htm.

8. Ibid.

9. On Hizb ut-Tahrir, see Suha Taji-Farouki, *A Fundamental Quest, Hizb al-Tahrir and the Search for the Islamic Caliphate,* London: Grey Seal, 1996. See also the web site www.khilafa.com.

10. See "The Campaign to Subvert Islam as an Ideology and a System," written by the members of Hizb ut-Tahrir, in the November issue of the *Khilafah Magazine* (London, 2001). See also: www.khilafah.com.

6.5

Afghanistan:
The Challenge of "Winning the Peace"[1]

Mohammed Haneef Atmar & Jonathan Goodhand

Before the events of 11 September 2001, Afghanistan was one of the world's "orphaned" conflicts in terms of the priorities of the international community. The overriding response since the end of the Cold War had been one of strategic withdrawal or containment. After more than twenty years of fighting, up to 1.5 million deaths, mass displacement, and the breakdown of the institutions of the state and civil society, Afghanistan appeared to be stuck in a no-exit cycle of chronic political instability. However the military and political landscape has changed dramatically following the U.S.-led military intervention and renewed diplomatic engagement. This has led to the fall of the Taliban, the signing of the "Provisional Arrangements" in Bonn, Germany, on 5 December 2001, and the promise of a major reconstruction package for Afghanistan. While some of the immediate objectives of the "war on terrorism" have been achieved, it is clear that the longer-term challenge yet to be addressed is "winning the peace." This can only be secured through robust and sustained international action at a regional level.

Present-day Afghanistan originated when the great powers drew its borders to create a buffer between the British and Russian empires. Its identity reflected the relations of force and strategic needs of the imperial powers rather than the political or social structures within its borders.[2] The weak centralized Afghan state that developed in the first half of the twentieth century was dependent on external resources. Its power was circumscribed by the traditionalist power structures in rural areas; indeed, conflict between rural and urban elites is a recurring feature of Afghan history. The contradictions inherent in the process of state formation produced a growing radicalism, which by the early 1970s had resulted in the emergence of the socialist and Islamist movements. These became the contending forces in the Afghan conflict.

Of the leftist groups emerging in the 1970s, the Soviet-supported People's Democratic Party of Afghanistan (PDPA) became preeminent. In April 1978

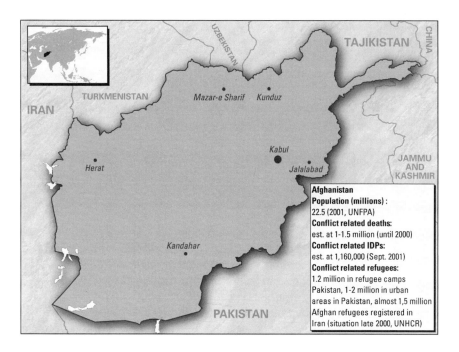

Afghanistan
Population (millions):
22.5 (2001, UNFPA)
Conflict related deaths:
est. at 1-1.5 million (until 2000)
Conflict related IDPs:
est. at 1,160,000 (Sept. 2001)
Conflict related refugees:
1.2 million in refugee camps
Pakistan, 1-2 million in urban
areas in Pakistan, almost 1,5 million
Afghan refugees registered in
Iran (situation late 2000, UNHCR)

the PDPA came to power through a coup (the Saur Revolution) and initiated a reform program. This drew violent resistance from the Islamists and the population of the countryside and *mujahedeen* groups set up training camps in Pakistan. In September 1979 a second coup took place as opposing groups within the PDPA (the Khalq and Parcham factions) fought for power. Growing revolt and increased instability led to the Soviet invasion in December 1979.

The Afghan war can be viewed as having five main periods since 1979.[3]

1. *1979–1988: Jihad in a Cold War context.* The Afghan rural resistance fights the Soviet-backed Kabul regime. The Sunni resistance parties receive military and financial support from Pakistan, the United States, and Saudi Arabia. More than 5 million Afghans become refugees in Iran and Pakistan. The Geneva agreements of 1988 pave the way for the Soviet withdrawal. An interim government, composed of the Sunni parties and excluding the Shia parties, is set up under the aegis of the United States, Pakistan, and Saudi Arabia.

2. *1989–1992: Jihad among Afghans.* After the Soviet withdrawal an internal war between the Soviet-supported government of President Najibullah and the various Afghan factions ensues with continued support from Russia and the United States. However, the collapse of the USSR and the ending of U.S. aid alters the balance of power. The Najibullah regime collapses when Dostam and his Uzbek militia switch allegiance from the Kabul regime to the *mujahedeen*, who enter the capital.

3. *1993–1996: Factional war among Afghans.* The *mujahedeen* government is fractured by internal power battles and shifting alliances among the

major party leaders. As superpower influence declines, regional power interests reassert themselves and the conflict assumes the characteristics of both a regional proxy war and a civil war. In late 1994 the Taliban emerge, with a stated objective of restoring stability. In September 1996 they take Kabul.

4. *1996–2001: Talibanization.* Fighting continues between the primarily Pashtun Taliban, backed by Pakistan, and the primarily non-Pashtun United Front[4] (UF), backed by Iran, Russia, Uzbekistan, Tajikistan, and India. The Taliban control roughly 90 percent of the territory, and the UF occupy the remaining pockets of land. Both sides have access to external aid and international markets, and continue to pursue their objectives through military means.

The presence of radical Islamic groups in Taliban-controlled territory (and in neighboring countries) including Osama bin Laden's Al-Qaida network and the Islamic Movement of Uzbekistan (IMU) adds an additional layer of complexity to international involvement in Afghanistan. Increased concern from both the United States and Russian about bin Laden's support for international terrorist activities contributes to the imposition in 1999 of international sanctions. More stringent sanctions are subsequently introduced in 2000.[5]

5. *2001–present: Post-Taliban?* On 9 September 2001, Ahmad Shah Massoud, a leading military commander of the UF is assassinated by suicide bombers in northeastern Afghanistan. Attacks two days later on the World Trade Center and Pentagon, allegedly by Al-Qaida, focus world attention on Afghanistan. A U.S.-led coalition simultaneously applies diplomatic pressure on Pakistan and the Taliban to hand over bin Laden, while preparing for military strikes. The Afghan-Pakistan border is closed and the coalition presses Pakistan to cut financial and military support for the Taliban. Military strikes begin on 7 October with the twin objectives of destroying Al-Qaida's networks and undermining the Taliban's military capability. Shortly afterwards, Pakistan's president Pervez Musharraf reshuffles his military command with the aim of marginalizing Islamist generals.[6]

On 9 November, Mazar-i-Sharrif falls to the United Front, quickly followed by Kabul, the capital, and the main provincial cities. The Taliban heartland of Kandahar falls in early December, marking the military and political defeat of the Taliban. The security situation, however, remains fluid and uncertain. At the time of this writing Osama bin Laden, many of his foreign fighters, and the Taliban leadership including the leader Mullah Omar have not been captured. Warlords from the pre-Taliban years have reemerged and established themselves as de facto power holders in many areas. Tensions between Pakistan and India have increased following an attack on the Indian parliament on 13 December by radical Islamic groups thought to have bases in Pakistan. Furthermore, there is uncertainty over whether the "war on terrorism" will be extended to other "rogue states" such as Iraq and Somalia. In addition to the security and political crisis there is a profound humanitarian crisis. The World Food Program has estimated that between 5 and 7 million people are in danger of starvation during the winter months of 2001–2002. This crisis is due to a combination of factors, including a three-year-old drought and internal displacement as a result of military activity, which has in turn prevented effective aid delivery.

On the positive side, following talks in Bonn, an Interim Authority, led by Hamed Karzai, has assumed power. This will be in place until mid-2002, when a *loya jirga* (grand council) will determine composition of a Transitional Authority, which will hold power until elections take place within two years. Discussions are also taking place, led by the United Nations Development Program (UNDP) and the World Bank, with the aim of developing a long-term reconstruction plan for Afghanistan.

Afghanistan is a largely mountainous country situated at the western edge of the Himalayan massif. There are six major ethnic groups: the Pashtun, Tajiks, Uzbeks, Turkmens, Hazaras, and Baluch. Although Islam has been a unifying factor, there are tensions, particularly between a Sunni Muslim majority and a Shia Muslim minority. Agriculture is the predominant activity and in 1978, the year before the Soviet invasion, an estimated 85 percent of the population lived in rural areas.[7] Deeply impoverished, Afghanistan ranks 170th out of 174 in the 1995 UNDP's Human Development Index. Subsistence takes place within an economy dominated by war and with a collapsed state unable to provide basic services for its population.

Conflict Dynamics

The Afghan conflict been constantly evolving over time. It is not currently clear whether this latest phase represents the beginning of a transition from war to peace or a return to the warlordism and chronic instability of the early 1990s. While there may be some room for cautious optimism, it is important to note that the Afghan war did not start with the Taliban, nor is it likely to finish simply by removing them. Stopping the fighting and securing a peace agreement are essential starting points, but peacebuilding must involve tackling the underlying causes and dynamics of the Afghan conflict. In the following section we examine conflict dynamics at the global/regional, national, and local levels.

The Global/Regional Level

Afghanistan is part of a multilayered and interdependent regional conflict system, characterized by great volatility and constantly shifting alliances that have a ripple effect on the whole system.[8] Conflicts and civil unrest in Kashmir, Pakistan, Tajikistan, and Uzbekistan are all, in various ways, part of this regional conflict formation.[9]

There are multiple state and nonstate interests in Afghanistan. In recent times the interests of the United States and Russia have converged around the issues of drugs, antiterrorism, and regional stability. Pakistan had provided support to the Taliban in the belief that a stable and pliant regime in Afghanistan would give Pakistan "strategic depth" in its confrontation with India over

Maria Söderberg/Panos

Afghan refugees, Malalai hospital in Quetta, Pakistan.

Kashmir,[10] and also facilitate the opening up of land routes (and potentially oil pipelines) to Central Asia. To counter the influence of Pakistan and the Taliban, a Russia-Iran-Uzbekistan-Tajikistan-India axis has developed, with Russia and Iran in particular providing significant military and financial support to the United Front.[11]

The states in the region compete with nonstate entities such as religious networks, long-distance trading leagues (contraband and otherwise), transborder diasporas or military groups, rogue agencies, and local solidarity networks of various types.[12] Afghanistan has become both a "safe haven" and a "training field" for Islamic groups connected to transnational networks. A "dynamic of *jihad*" drives a wider process of "Talibanization" within the region[13]— perhaps most dangerously in Pakistan where the government (in particular the military) have been tolerant of, if not actively supportive of, proto-Taliban forces.[14] This dynamic of *jihad* could well persist or even accelerate with the defeat of the Taliban.

This regional conflict system had proved relatively impervious to external attempts to bring peace. The international community has had only limited influence on the competing state and nonstate entities.[15] It has also been argued that the West lacked the necessary political resolve to address the underlying causes of the conflict. International policy from 1992 focused more on containment than resolution, and humanitarian aid became a substitute for state-led political action. There has clearly been a shift in recent months toward reengagement. However, the region-wide, interconnected security problems remain. The clear lesson for future intervention is that peacebuilding must take place within a regional framework and balance the competing interests of neighboring powers.

The National Level: The Afghan State and the War Economy
Most of the institutions of the nation-state have collapsed. This power vacuum has been filled by regionally based nonstate entities. With the decline of superpower patronage in the early 1990s, controls on nonstate entities have declined and such groups have increasingly had to generate their own resources to support their military activities and patronage networks. The war years have been characterized by a rapid monetization of the economy, and the conflict has created tremendous incentives to find cash-producing activities including opium production, money laundering, and transborder trade, particularly in drugs, smuggling, and in the case of the United Front, the gem trade.[16] In 1999 Afghanistan produced three times as much raw opium as all the rest of the world's production put together.[17] A ban on poppy cultivation decreed by Taliban leader Mullah Omar did have significant impact,[18] but with the fall of the Taliban, a significant increase in poppy production is forecast for 2002.[19]

According to a World Bank study,[20] in 1997 the transborder trade between Afghanistan and Pakistan generated around $2.5 billion per annum; however, by 2000 this had fallen to $930 million. The Taliban exacted a tax of about 6 percent on the opium and smuggling activities.[21]

As Rubin notes, the war is sustained by the availability of lootable or taxable resources and the low cost of recruiting fighters.[22] Peace would disrupt the systems of production and exchange that provide warlords and their followers with livelihoods. One could therefore argue that economic forces have become more central to the dynamic of the Afghan conflict since the early 1990s, but that doesn't mean that state power was altogether irrelevant. Evidently, international recognition was one of the few bargaining chips that the international community had in dealing with the Taliban. Internationally recognized sovereignty affords access to major external resources, such as financing for the Turkmenistan-Pakistan gas pipeline and the reconstruction aid.

A central challenge now is reconstituting the Afghan state—at the heart of the Afghan conflict is the crisis in the legitimacy and capacity of the state. This process must be informed by an examination of the incentives and disincentives for putting the state back together. The war economy has created strong incentives for misgovernment [23] and clearly the interests of those who profit from continued instability need to be addressed.

The Local Level: Afghan Society
An appreciation of the international and national dimensions of the Afghan conflict should be complemented by a "fine grained" analysis of Afghan society. This is frequently missing in analyses of the Afghan war; conflict is seen as exogenous to the society, causing breakdown and "social capital depletion." However, the relationship between conflict and society is more subtle and complex than the "breakdown" model suggests. There are important continuities with the past, while at the same time there have been profound social transformations that have fed back into the conflict.

For instance, Afghan social networks have been extremely resilient and adapted to the changing context. Historically, the state has both utilized, and been colonized by, such networks.[24] For example, Pakistan's Inter Services Intelligence Directorate (ISI) utilized such networks when channeling arms to the resistance and the *mujahedeen* drew upon such relationships to mobilize fighters; more recently, such networks and relationships have also been used for drug smuggling and other criminal activities.

On the other hand, conflict has been a force for social change. The war brought intense ideological struggles into the most remote valleys.[25] It precipitated a new leadership, the reworking of traditional patron-client relationships, and an adherence to larger-scale identities based on religion, ethnicity, and political grouping.[26] One can identify a number of fault lines and tensions within Afghan civil society, which feed into the wider dynamic of the war. These include tensions over resources, ethnicity, tribal affiliation, and religion. Conflict entrepreneurs and external powers have effectively used ethnic tools to mobilize groups and the war has led to a shift in the balance of power among the different ethnic groups.[27] Although ethnicity is not an underlying cause of the war, it has frequently been conducted along ethnic lines.[28] This has had a corrosive effect on Afghan society and impedes the search for a solution to the conflict.[29]

In many other respects the conflict has reworked social identities and challenged power hierarchies. The Taliban victory represented a "social revolution" in which the sons of poor tribes and clans were able to overthrow a tribal aristocracy.[30] In a dramatic reversal of previous patterns of change, it was the countryside who ruled the capital.[31] Violence was thus viewed as a means to restore status and power.[32]

Finally, the conflict has had a profound effect on gender roles and identities. The instrumentalization and politicization of Afghan women preceded the Taliban; although not as severely, the *mujahedeen* regime also restricted women's activities in the name of Islam.[33] Conflicting views on the role of women are symptomatic of ongoing tensions between tradition and modernity in Afghan society. In many respects the experience of exile has raised the expectations of women in terms of basic services such as education and health care and also their political role in the future. Peacebuilding strategies must provide women with the opportunity to play an active role in the public realm. The fact that places have been reserved for women in the Interim Administration is an encouraging start.

Therefore, a peace process that only involves the political elites is unlikely to bring long-term peace. A bottom-up approach to rebuilding civil society and "demilitarize the mind" is also necessary. This, however, must be based on an appreciation of the social transformations caused by the conflict; reconciliation and reconstruction are not about reverting to the status quo ante.

The Rise and Fall of the Taliban

"Taliban" is derived from the Arabic word *talib,* meaning "religious student." The Taliban's core leaders belong to a common political network, the Deobandi *madrassas* (religious seminaries for training of *ulama*) in the Pashtun tribal areas of Afghanistan and Pakistan. Since emerging as a military force in Kandahar in 1994, the Taliban, by 2001, controlled roughly 90 percent of Afghanistan (subsequently renamed the Islamic Emirate of Afghanistan in 1997). The government was only ever recognized by Pakistan, Saudi Arabia, and the United Arab Emirates. The Taliban's preeminence in Afghanistan consolidated a number of the regional and national trends described above. First, it confirmed the regional nature of the conflict, with neighboring countries increasingly intervening inside Afghanistan. Second, the security provided by the Taliban enabled the consolidation and enlargement of the war economy.

A complex mix of factors, both internal and external, traditional and modern, contributed to the rise of the Taliban. On the one hand, they drew support from a network of *madrassas*. During the twentieth century the *madrassas* had become marginalized by state modernization programs, but were reinvigorated and became autonomous as a result of exile in Pakistan and the experience of warlord-dominated Afghanistan.[34] On the other hand, the Taliban's military and political ascendancy was clearly facilitated by external actors, and especially official, quasi-official, and private groups in Pakistan.[35] The Taliban were supported militarily and politically first by the Bhutto and then the Sharif administrations as they were seen to represent a Pashtun front sympathetic to Pakistan's interests.[36] It is estimated that by 1999 up to 30 percent of the Taliban troops were Pakistani volunteers.[37] By 2001 there were thought to be between 8,000 and 15,000 non-Afghan Taliban fighters.[38]

The Taliban arose out of an extremely parochial and conservative milieu.[39] However, growing confrontation with the international community and ever-closer links with transnational Islamic groups pushed them toward a more radical agenda. Even before 11 September, experts were warning of the increased risk to regional stability as the pace of radicalization quickened.[40] The Taliban were a symptom of a deeper malaise—they represented a political response to an extreme situation.[41] Although the Taliban collapsed relatively quickly, the dynamic of Talibanization within the region is likely to outlive the Taliban regime itself.

Official Conflict Management

Attempts to resolve the Afghan crisis have been ongoing, involving various actors and strategies, and mediation efforts by state and nonstate actors at several levels. In the Cold War years, the diplomatic focus was on the United States and the Soviet Union, with support roles played by Pakistan and the Afghan regime. Later, it shifted to the neighboring regional powers. There have also been a number of civil-society and diaspora-led initiatives. However, the primary role has been assumed by the United Nations, operating in Afghanistan with little collaboration or competition from other intergovernmental organizations, which tend to be weak throughout Asia.[42]

It is important to note that there has never been one single UN body with a unified mandate and policy toward Afghanistan. In 2001 for instance, one could distinguish at least three distinct (and contradictory) policies toward the Afghan conflict. The UN Security Council (UNSC), spurred by the United

States and Russia, imposed one-sided sanctions against the Taliban, while the UN Special Mission for Afghanistan (UNSMA, established in 1993 as successor organization to the "Good Offices Mission" created in the late 1980s) attempted to mediate between the Taliban and UF. The sanctions, however, undermined the ability of UNSMA to act as a neutral and impartial mediator. Meanwhile, the UN Office for the Coordination of Humanitarian Affairs (UNOCHA) was charged with delivering humanitarian assistance to the Afghan population and, to achieve its goals, had been willing to engage the Taliban (and compromise principles according to its critics) to a greater extent than the other two UN bodies. In addition, the special rapporteur on Afghanistan reported on human-rights violations to the UN Human Rights Commission.[43]

Since the end of the Cold War, there has been a fundamental shift in the UN's efforts to resolve the Afghan conflict from bipolar approaches to multipolar approaches. After 1997 more attention was focused on the regional dimensions to the conflict with the initiation of the "six-plus-two talks" (the six neighboring powers, plus the United States and Russia).

The UN strategy aimed to (1) achieve a cessation of hostilities, (2) seek a regional political consensus in support of the peace process, and (3) seek direct negotiations between all parties on a political settlement.[44] In order to achieve these objectives, UNSMA pursued a three-track strategy for negotiation and mediation, i.e., the Central Track (dialogue between the main Afghan warring parties), Parallel Track (engagement with non-UN peacemaking initiatives), and the External Track (in the form of six-plus-two arrangement between the six Afghanistan neighbors and Russia and the United States).[45] Through regional consensus building and intra-Afghan dialogue, the UN aimed to:

- Establish a durable cease-fire
- Enforce a comprehensive arms and ammunition embargo
- Form a broad-based representative government
- Initiate reconstruction

In terms of achieving these policy objectives, the UN peace process has been a failure, and Afghanistan has proved to be a "graveyard for UN negotiation."[46]

William Maley identified three main reasons behind the failure of the UN mission:

1. *The inherent weakness of traditional peacemaking in contemporary wars.* Orthodox mediation is based on the premise of interstate relations and dialogue. Bilateral negotiations or talks within the six-plus-two framework, however, have a limited impact, because of the transnational and nonstate entities that are an integral part of the conflict. Such "non-state actors may deny the authority of the very framework of rules and norms within which conversations between states occur."[47]

2. *The history of UN involvement in mediation.* The UN has limited credibility with the different actors because of its previous failures, its limited

capacities (both in terms of individual performance and political muscle), and, on occasion, a perceived bias.

3. *The focus of UN mediation.* The UN has often failed to understand that the crisis in Afghanistan runs deeper than the mere composition of the government. As one NGO worker commented, UNSMA are "looking at any people who will sit round a table and talk to each other." It aims to call a cease-fire, form a broad-based government, hold elections, and move into reconstruction. How this peace package will address the interests of the nonstate entities is not clear, however, since they may have little interest or need of a unitary Afghan state.

In recent years, there have also been a number of non-UN peace initiatives by Afghans and third parties, including three parallel processes that were launched by Afghans, primarily from outside Afghanistan and with support from foreign governments and nonstate actors. These were the "Rome process," which focused around the former king Zahir Shah; the "Cypress process"; and the "Bonn process." Pakistan, Iran, the Organization of the Islamic Conference, and others have also been engaged in peacemaking efforts, but these initiatives have all have foundered, primarily because of the competing agendas of these "peacemakers" and the absence of a robust Track One process—due, in turn, to the insufficient support from UNSC members, notably the United States and Russia.

Although one can be critical of the UN role, without the political will of the international community, its impact was always going to be limited. As the UN Secretary-General commented in 1997, "It could be argued that . . . the role of the United Nations in Afghanistan is little more than that of an alibi to provide cover for the inaction—or worse—of the international community at large."[48]

The overriding policy response from the Western powers in the post–Cold War years was either one of strategic withdrawal and containment or an aggressive single-issue focus. While governments failed to address fundamental structural causes of the conflict, the interconnected security problems deepened. The stakes in the conflict system have grown year by year, as have the opportunity costs of not acting to resolve the problem. The Taliban, Osama bin Laden, and the U.S. bombing of 1998 did bring Afghanistan back "on the map," but the focus was still on containing the conflict rather than resolving it.

There were signs in the months before 11 September that donor governments were beginning to comprehend the need to provide tangible incentives for peace through a reconstruction package and the creation of institutions of governance necessary to transform the war economy into a peace economy.[49] The basic preconditions now appear to be in place for a peacebuilding strategy that has the potential to address the underlying structural dimensions of the regional conflict system. These include: the appointment of Lakdar Brahimi on 3 October 2001 as the overall coordinator of diplomatic and humanitarian efforts; the signing of the Bonn agreement and the investiture of the Interim

Authority in Kabul on 22 December; an agreement on the need for an international security force, part of which had arrived in Afghanistan by the end
of 2001; and the commitments by major donors to establish a reconstruction
trust fund.

All the main international and local players have aligned themselves behind the formation of a broad-based government and a "Marshall Plan" for
Afghanistan. The effectiveness of the UN in the peacebuilding process will depend partly on institutional capacity, but even more on political will. Maintaining and sustaining the political momentum that has been generated in recent months will be a critical challenge.

Multi-Track Diplomacy

Our analysis of the official conflict-management process points to the need for
a more inclusive multi-track approach that involves all levels of Afghan society. In theory, peace promotion should involve a number of parallel but coordinated tracks that involve a wide range of state and nonstate actors, but such
a multi-track has proved difficult in the Afghan context. It assumes common
interests on the part of intervening agencies, a shared understanding of peace
and a mechanism for coordinating tracks. In practice, international engagement
in Afghanistan has lacked consistency and coherence. Interests in the region
have fluctuated according to perceived strategic interests (from anticommunism,
to oil pipelines, to drugs, etc.); peace initiatives, often linked to other agendas,
have had limited credibility among Afghans; and coordination of multi-track approaches in a collapsed state context has proved extremely difficult.

The Role of Humanitarian Aid

In parallel to the diplomatic response to the Afghan war, there has been a
major humanitarian aid program, in response to massive humanitarian needs,
but also motivated by political agendas. In the 1980s, refugee and cross-border programs were seen by many as the nonlethal component of aid to the
Afghan resistance. By the early 1990s, as international interest in the Afghan
conflict waned, the peace process and humanitarian aid program were, to a
large extent, delinked, both politically and institutionally. By the mid-1990s,
international attention had been revived due a range of factors including the
Taliban, Osama Bin Laden, oil pipelines, human rights, and the growing drug
trade, accompanied by renewed interest in peacebuilding, multi-track diplomacy, and strengthening the link between aid and diplomacy.

With the Strategic Framework (SF) for Afghanistan, the international
community endeavored to more explicitly link diplomatic and aid programs.[50]
In 1998 a Strategic Framework document, produced after months of consultation among UN agencies, NGOs, and other actors, was endorsed by the Afghanistan Support Group (ASG)[51] in London. With an overarching goal of facilitating the transition from a state of internal conflict to a just and sustainable
peace, the SF brings together the three strategies (i.e., political, assistance, and

human rights) of the UN to address the crisis. The SF defines the principles, general policies, and institutional arrangements for a coherent and effective response.[52] Principled Common Programming (PCP), on the other hand, applies only to the assistance sphere and is a mechanism for establishing the assistance community's priorities, programs, and projects.

Together, SF and PCP represent in many respects an innovative response to the challenges of working in a chronically unstable environment, where the establishment of an institutional framework is needed to ensure coherence and complementarity of action. The lessons generated by this exercise have much wider relevance and should be studied carefully. While it is too early to come to definitive conclusions, the last three years have highlighted the practical problems of operationalizing such a framework.

There are, broadly, two sets of criticisms of the current process—those related to the macro issues of policy coherence and the politics of aid, and those related to organizational and bureaucratic constraints. First, the SF is based on the assumption that a robust and coherent political strategy will run in parallel with the assistance program; each in theory should exploit synergies with and support the other, but in practice the political process has faltered. In the absence of any real political process, attention has been focused largely on the assistance program. The result, critics say, has been a politicization of aid with humanitarianism being used as a substitute for robust political action. Strict conditionalities have been applied on aid to leverage political changes. It is argued that aid is being asked to do things that are beyond its remit and are normally left to diplomatic actors. Ethically, this is unsound since humanitarian principles are corrupted. Also, pragmatically, its effects are questionable; humanitarian assistance has limited leverage over the incentive systems of the warring groups, particularly if one juxtaposes the estimated $300 million per year in aid with the magnitude of resource flows generated by the war economy.[53]

A second set of criticisms relates to organizational constraints, notably the inability of the assistance community to coordinate effectively, perhaps due in part to interorganizational competition and an unwillingness to relinquish sovereignty. It may also be due to the perception, amongst NGOs that the process has been a very top-down one with limited input from the field. In the absence of a centralized, statelike entity, agencies had a great deal of autonomy, and few are now willing to take direction from a more central authority. While the PCP has made progress in terms of developing agreement on broad principles and frameworks, less has been achieved where the "hard interests" of agencies are at stake.

A 2001 evaluation of the Strategic Framework process pointed to continuing tensions between the diplomatic and aid communities.[54] The report argued that there was continued distrust and antagonism between the political and aid actors. Most important was their differing assessments of the context. While UNSMA viewed Afghanistan as a "rogue state," the aid community conceptualized it as a "failed state." Differing analyses led to differing prescriptions, with UNSMA promoting isolation of the Taliban and the aid community arguing for engagement.[55]

The Role of NGOs

For many years NGOs have been the mechanism of choice for donor governments unable or unwilling to engage directly with Afghan actors and institutions. Therefore, a multi-track approach to peacebuilding clearly depends to a great extent on the willingness and capacity of the NGO sector.

Currently, the NGO community can be divided into three broad categories: international, Afghani, and Islamic NGOs. Over 250 NGOs are members of one of six NGO Coordination Bodies.[56] Including nonmember NGOs, the number probably reaches 300. The ACBAR Directory of Humanitarian Agencies Working for Afghans 2000 covers 160 NGOs of all categories, from seventeen countries, with 23,413 staff members (22,377 Afghans, 705 Pakistanis, and 331 expatriates), and total expenditures between 1997 and 1999 of $376.4 million. NGOs' 1999 budget came from the UN (33 percent), the EU (20 percent), bilateral donors (20 percent), overseas international NGOs (20 percent), and others. In 1999, 91 percent of their budget was spent for Afghans inside Afghanistan and 9 percent for the refugee programs outside the country. In 1999, 45 key NGOs (14 Afghan, 4 Islamic, and 27 international Western) employed 73 percent of the total NGO staff and accounted for 75 percent of the total NGO budget.

The major areas of NGO work include health services, mine action, education, food security, (agriculture, irrigation, livestock, etc.) emergency response, rehabilitation, shelter, income generation, infrastructure, environment, community development work, and human rights. In addition to the six NGO coordination bodies in the country, British Agencies Afghanistan Group based in London provides information for the assistance community and engages with advocacy on behalf of the member NGOs.

Table 6.5.1 outlines a range of approaches adopted by NGOs and donor agencies to conflict management and peacebuilding in Afghanistan. We have divided the approaches into those that may have an indirect effect on peacebuilding processes and those that have an explicit and sole focus on peace.

Most NGOs are now more conflict-sensitive than they were in the 1980s and there has also been a trend toward longer-term developmental programming that aims to support local livelihoods and institutions. Such programs may aid recovery and reconstruction in the event of a peace process. However, programs with developmental and peacebuilding objectives represent a very small part of the overall aid portfolio; most funding goes to short-term humanitarian programs. The programs that do have peacebuilding objectives tend to be quite disparate and have only localized impacts.

Whether such micro projects can have a cumulative impact on conflict and peace dynamics is open to debate. The problem faced by both development and conflict-resolution NGOs is one of sustaining and scaling up impacts in a context of chronic instability. There are virtually no institutional stabilizing points at the level above the village for agencies to build upon. Therefore, peacebuilding and development projects often represent small-scale islands of success, dependent on ongoing funding and support from NGOs.

The evidence to date suggests that one should be realistic about the capacity of aid actors to influence incentive systems and institutions at the meso or

Table 6.5.1 Approaches to Conflict Management and Peacebuilding[57]

Type	Approach	Features/Organizations	Assumptions	Key Results	Constraints
INDIRECT APPROACHES	**Community development/ empowerment**	Aims at providing alternative livelihoods & social services, developing community organizations, strengthening social capital, and building good governance. Notable agencies are UNDP PEACE Initiative, UNHCS/Habitat, DACAAR, CARE, NCA, ADA, CoAR, NPO/RRAA	Community development will contribute to peacebuilding by creating sustainable livelihoods, decreasing competition over resources and developing alternative forms of leadership and governance.	Focusing on tens of rural and urban districts. Establishment and strengthening of community institutions. Generating rural and urban livelihood for tens of thousands. Reconstruction of key sectors of agriculture, irrigation, health, education, etc.	Community initiatives may not have cumulative effects and are likely to be destroyed by top-down violence. Suspicion of Afghan communities toward attempts at social engineering.
	Civil society strengthening	Capacity-building support for intermediary organizations such as Afghan NGOs, community Shuras or Forums. Notable agencies are NCA, Novib, CA/EO, UNDP	Supporting intermediary organizations will help mobilize countervailing voices in civil society and contribute to the development of social capital within Afghan society.	Organizational strengthening of around 30 Afghan national NGOs, creation and strengthening of hundreds of community-based organizations.	Perception of Afghan communities of NGOs. NGOs may be too transient and lack the analytical capacities to support social capital formation.
	Do no harm	Incorporating "do no harm" methodology into ongoing relief and development activities—but looking for peacebuilding opportunities as well as mitigating risks. Examples are NCA, UNDP, UNHCS, ADA, NPO/RRAA, CoAR	All societies have "connectors" and local capacities for peace. Aid agencies can support "pro peace" constituencies.	Training of tens of aid agencies on the "do no harm" methodology with a couple practicing it. A number of cases of aid agencies resolving local disputes/conflicts through aid programs.	The potential leverage and impact of aid may be overstated. Possible tension between the humanitarian imperative and peacebuilding objectives. While agencies may support the approach, many have not translated this into changed practice.

(continues)

Table 6.5.1 contd.

Type	Approach	Features/Organizations	Assumptions	Key Results	Constraints
INDIRECT APPROACHES	Protection/human rights	Incorporating rights-based approaches into ongoing relief and development programs. Notable are CARE, Save the Children (US) and SCF (UK).	Helping create an environment where basic rights are respected and promoted will in the long term help create sustainable peace.	Implementation of tens of rights-based programs enhancing and protecting the rights of selected vulnerable groups.	Aid has had a limited effect on behavioral change of the parties guilty of human-rights abuses. Because of security concerns aid agencies have had to evacuate when their watchdog role was most needed.
	Cooperation on IHL & public welfare	The warring parties have been brought to a negotiation table in Switzerland to discuss and agree on common concerns on humanitarian access and public welfare. Facilitating agency was SDC of Switzerland.	Cooperation between warring parties on humanitarian access and public welfare may lead to greater cooperation on political issues.	While a series of meetings have been held, there has not been any major agreement reached.	Political and military agendas of the parties take precedence over humanitarian concerns. Warring parties act with impunity and there are few if any mechanisms for unaccountability.
	Tranquility days for immunization	Calling for a temporary cease-fire between warring parties for humanitarian activities. Key actor is UNICEF with its national immunization campaigns.	Such events will not create peace per se but will create opportunities to broker cease-fires and establish a level of understanding and respect for IHL.	Tens of national immunization campaigns launched with most accompanied by a cease-fire.	Has little impact on the wider dynamics of the conflict. Cease-fires may provide warring groups with a strategic pause to regroup and launch new offensives.

(continues)

Table 6.5.1 contd.

Type	Approach	Features/Organizations	Assumptions	Key Results	Constraints
DIRECT APPROACHES	**Training on working with conflict**	Training for NGO workers and community members in conflict-resolution and mediation techniques. CPAU is one of the key training providers.	Conflict is the result of a breakdown of communication. Conflict-resolution skills will facilitate better communication.	Training of hundreds of aid workers, community leaders, and activists who play an active role in resolution of local disputes and conflicts.	Understates the political and economic factors driving conflict. Questions about the appropriateness of Western models. Problems related to mainstreaming—what happens after the training?
	Peace education	Peace education through schools, literature, and media. Key actors are BBC New Home–New Life, SIEAL, CPAU.	Given the prowar contents of education during the war years, peace education is needed to build future capital for peace.	While peace education through schools reaches tens of thousands, New Home–New Life is the most popular soap opera in the country.	By itself it cannot address the underlying political economy of the conflict and violence. Lack of follow-up or understanding of impact.
	Peace-conditional aid	As a carrot, offering large-scale reconstruction and development aid on the condition of a durable peace. Notable are the government of Japan and the EC.	Poverty and the lack of economic alternatives to warfare are driving the conflict. Reconstruction funding will provide an incentive to warlords to stop fighting.	No political agreement among the warring parties has been reached.	The package is not sufficient to wean warlords away from the war economy. The warring factions have limited interest in "putting the state back together."

macro levels. Multi-track approaches will achieve little if the central track is dormant or not functioning. Evidently there are things that aid agencies can do to improve the way they "do business," such as developing longer-term approaches, improving accountability, becoming more responsive to civil-society actors, and strengthening their advocacy strategies to influence the donor community and the international media. However, to an extent, the wider impact of their work depends on factors further up the economic and political chain. Unless political and economic incentives are changed through a combination of sticks and carrots by international and regional actors, aid represents at best a "holding operation"; it may play a role in supporting livelihoods and strengthening social capital, but it cannot be a leading edge in the peace process.

The Role of Civil Society

Over the last twenty years, peace negotiations have been conducted at the international and national level and Afghan civil society has had virtually no voice in the process. Whether a just peace can be arrived at as a result of negotiations between outsiders and warring parties with a record of human-rights violations is questionable. One of the aims of the Strategic Framework process was, by linking the political and assistance strategies, to stimulate involvement from a wider cross section of the Afghan population. In practice this has been difficult, partly because of the nature of the conflict and civil society in Afghanistan and partly because of deficiencies within the aid system.

First, in the second decade of the war economic agendas have become a central part of the conflict dynamic. A regional war economy has developed, along with a new leadership whose power is based upon establishing a monopoly of violence and controlling this economy. Leadership, therefore, is based on coercion rather than consent. Since civil society appears to have only a limited influence on the current dynamics of the conflict, it is difficult to see it becoming a leading edge in a peacebuilding process. The potential for exerting pressure "from below" to influence the incentive systems of leaders and promote humanitarian principles appears to be limited.

Second, Western notions of "civil society" do not transfer easily to the Afghan context. The idea of building a broad civil-society constituency for peace may only be possible in contexts where civil society is composed of vertically and horizontally integrated formal, rule-based organizations. Moreover, research from elsewhere suggests that where the state is weak and fractured, civil society will be similarly divided and lacking in voice; a strong healthy state is usually the precondition for a strong and healthy civil society. In Afghanistan, by contrast, the state has collapsed and civil society predominantly consists of a complex web of informal, norm-based networks based on blood, kinship, tribal, religious, cultural, and ethnic ties. Notable among these are the institutions of elders, Jirga (an assembly or council of Pasthun or Baluchi headmen and elders), Shura[58] (an Islamic consultative council), and religious networks. The interests and power base of such networks tend to be highly localized. To an extent, such institutions have enabled Afghan communities to construct a so-called mud curtain[59] to keep an interfering and often repressive state at bay. The fact that such institutions have survived over centuries and are remarkably resilient and adaptable is attributed to their stable legitimacy with Afghan communities in meeting essential societal needs, including local governance. This might be contrasted with modern civil formations, especially the political parties, which became increasingly irrelevant during the 1990s.

Historically based institutions such as the elders' Jirga play a role in local governance, conflict resolution, resource management, and management of state-society relationships in local spheres. Such institutions manage diverse local conflicts between individuals, families, and communities, and between communities and the state. Conflict resolution takes place through negotiation, arbitration, and adjudication by applying *sharia*,[60] local laws and norms. The state has historically respected the role of these institutions and this practice continued under the Taliban and United Front. In a number of instances, local institutions resisted externally imposed policies. In Khost, for instance, in 1998–1999, there was popular resistance to the Taliban-imposed local authorities. However, the capacity of such institutions to address conflict on a wider scale is limited.

Therefore, peacebuilding efforts need to be based upon a realistic assessment of the potential and limitations of civil society. Civil-society support programs in postconflict societies can run the risk of diverting funding and support away from the central task of state building. What is needed is a more strategic, sustained, and nuanced engagement with Afghan civil society than has occurred in the past. Particular attention should be focused on the peacemaking role of the Loya Jirga (Grand Assembly), and strengthening of the bottom-up peacebuilding impacts of civic groups.

The Loya Jirga[61] clearly has an important role to play in the eyes of most Afghans. Over the last three centuries, there have been sixteen Loya Jirgas (three in the eighteenth century, two in the nineteenth century, and eleven in the twentieth century, including two convened by the communist leaders). Issues addressed by these Loya Jirgas included appointing and legitimizing national leaders (e.g., kings and presidents), national strategies for liberation and defense against foreign aggression, national policies and governments, national constitutions, etc.

The Bonn agreement of 5 December 2001 reaffirms the role of the Loya Jirga. Two national meetings are to be held, one (an emergency Loya Jirga) to decide on the composition of a Transitional Authority for the next two years and a second (a constitutional Loya Jirga) to adopt a new constitution for the country.[62] The success of the emergency Loya Jirga in establishing the Transitional Authority will depend on (1) inclusive representation from all sections of the Afghan society, and (2) its ability to demand compliance and enforce implementation of its decisions. For the former, the legitimacy, integrity, and competence of the Special Independent Commission for the Convening of the Emergency Loya Jirga is critical. This is to be established during the Interim Administration. However, the latter will depend on first rebuilding the national state institutions, including national law enforcement institutions, and second, the commitment of the international community to support the implementation of the Bonn agreements. International engagement is particularly important during this initial period when there is an absence of national state institutions.

The second area of engagement with civil society is a bottom-up approach to peacebuilding with the aim of strengthening social capital and rebuilding the linkages between Afghan society and the state. In the past, aid agencies have looked to civil-society institutions as interlocutors for managing local welfare and recovery assistance programs. However, aid agencies were often too transient and had insufficient understanding of community-level dynamics to work with them. The result of such an approach was the disappearance of thousands of project-based and externally funded Shuras once the funding stopped. Moreover, uncritical support for "traditional" institutions has had un-intended impacts; for instance it has led to the exclusion of women or support for ethnically based groups, sometimes fueling tensions at the local level. A more sophisticated analysis is required, including, especially, nurturing women's organizations (with a real constituency in Afghan society) and other nonsectar-ian civic groups that have crosscutting ties. Donors will need to embrace a broad view of "civil society" and to develop mechanisms for engaging with less for-mal bodies in rural areas that may not mirror their ideal models of an NGO. However, the role of NGOs, particularly Afghan NGOs, is likely to be a critical component of the peacebuilding effort. To an extent, one of the primary sources of Afghan leadership has been held in "cold storage" during the war years, within the NGO sector. This leadership must be nurtured and encouraged to take on new roles, whether in the public, private, or civic sectors.

Prospects

The dynamics of the Afghan conflict have been transformed as a result of re-cent events. In the space of three months the negative military and political stalemate of the previous three years has been shifted. From being an "or-phaned" conflict, Afghanistan has become the focus of world attention. For the first time in the history of the war, there appears to be the collective will and the promise of sufficient resources to get to grips with the dynamics of the conflict.

While there is reason for cautious optimism in view of recent develop-ments, this optimism should be tempered by a realistic assessment of the task ahead. Our previous analysis highlighted the continuing existence of the fac-tors that caused and sustained the conflict. These include the competing agen-das of regional powers, the continuing Talibanization of Islamic groups in Central and Southern Asia (despite the demise of the Taliban), an expanding war economy, the crisis of states within the region, and deepening poverty. Unless these interlocking crises are addressed, violent conflicts will continue to be a feature of an extremely volatile regional conflict system.

Therefore, winning the peace depends on addressing root causes and en-tails a transition from peacemaking to peacebuilding. Peace processes elsewhere have often faltered when key actors failed to look beyond the peace settlement. Evidently, peace involves more than simply ending the fighting and peacebuilding must involve a discussion about what kind of peace should be built, how it will be defined, and who will be involved in the debate. Experience from elsewhere (and the lessons of past failures in Afghanistan) suggest that these debates should be as inclusive as possible—peace processes that marginalize groups in society are likely to generate grievances that lead to renewed conflict.

Given the deep-seated nature of the regional conflict system, there is unlikely to be a smooth transition from war to peace in Afghanistan. Chronic political instability for a number of years to come is quite likely. In many postconflict settings (South Africa, for example) there has been a shift from militarized violence to widespread social violence. The worst-case scenario (apart from a major armed confrontation between Pakistan and India) would be a return to the warlordism of the mid-1990s. There are indications that this is already occurring, with warlords establishing their power bases and reports of roadblocks, robberies, and the looting of aid in a number of areas.

Which scenario is acted out will depend to a great extent on whether international engagement is sustained and whether it is the right kind of engagement. In the past, international action has often been part of the problem rather than the solution. It has been halfhearted, uncoordinated, often one-sided, and has frequently created the wrong kinds of incentives. Of all the great powers, the United States has been the most inconsistent and inattentive in its policies toward the region.[63] Continued support by the United States for a UN-led peacebuilding process is essential. Without Western commitment and international attention, the competing interests of neighboring powers and the negative dynamic of the war economy will reassert themselves. The track record of the international community is poor in terms of the gap between the promise and the delivery of reconstruction packages.

Even if international attention is sustained, it must be the right kind of engagement. Politically driven aid helped create the tensions within Afghan society that led to the conflict in the first place and sustained it during the *jihad* years. There are dangers that a major injection of aid resources into a conflictual and resource-scarce environment will exacerbate tensions and renew the cycle of violence. Aid actors should avoid at all costs the mistake of recreating the Afghan rentier state, in which a small group of "shareholders" benefit from the peace dividend.

We have used the words "cautious optimism," but the greatest stress should perhaps be placed on the word "cautious." As research shows, societies that have a legacy of war are more likely to experience violent conflict in the future.[64] Afghanistan is a country that is geared up for war and a profound transformation is required for it to become a country that is "geared up" for peace.

Recommendations
In this final section we outline recommendations for how the international community can best support the transition from war to peace in Afghanistan.

The international community has limited understanding of why states collapse, and even less about how to put them back together again. Therefore the need for realism and humility should be emphasized—international action cannot engineer long-term peace, but the right kinds of intervention may increase the probabilities of this happening.

Although our focus has been primarily on the international community, we recognize that the key actors are the Afghans themselves. International support should be geared toward creating the preconditions that enable legitimate representatives of the Afghan people to make decisions about their future without external interference.[65]

Peacebuilding Principles
There are both short-term and long-term priorities. However, all forms of intervention—whether in the security, political, socioeconomic, or humanitarian spheres—need to apply the following peacebuilding principles.[66]

- *Provide sustained support.* The key question is, are the Western powers in this for the long haul? Can the diplomatic and political momentum be sustained? We are talking here about a decade or more of sustained and consistent support—politically and financially. The major powers must make concrete commitments of long-term support, to which they should be held accountable.
- *Tackle underlying causes.* While the war has changed over time, leading to new dynamics and incentive systems, the central task remains the reconstitution of a legitimate state with a monopoly of force—it was the crisis in the legitimacy and capacity of the state that led to the outbreak of war in the first place and if unaddressed is likely to contribute to renewed violence. Short-term priorities should not distract attention from the central task of rebuilding institutions (a political transition), transforming the war economy into a peace economy, and dealing with the legacy of violence (a socioeconomic transition).
- *Address the regional dynamics.* The Bonn agreements must be complemented by international agreements among the regional powers to ensure noninterference and the pursuit of legitimate interests in Afghanistan through peaceful means, which conform to international legal frameworks and respect the Afghan right of self-determination. Robust support for attempts to resolve neighboring conflicts (e.g., Kashmir) and to prevent renewed or emergent conflicts (e.g., Tajikistan, Ferghana Valley) should be provided and complemented by efforts to address the conditions that are leading to instability in the region, such as Talibanization, growing poverty, and state crises.
- *A comprehensive approach.* As outlined above, previous efforts at peacemaking and peacebuilding tended to undercut one another, creating the wrong types of incentives/disincentives. Efforts must be directed toward developing a common analysis, leading to a comprehensive and coherent peacebuilding framework. This does not mean repeating the mistakes of the Strategic Framework, which attempted to create a monolithic management framework. There does need to be room for separate, complementary approaches and initiatives,

but a patchwork of unrelated and uncoordinated interventions in the name of "independence" and "flexibility" is simply not good enough. The UN and NGOs must be prepared to sacrifice a level of sovereignty to ensure better co-ordination. There will be new actors entering the field (not least the Afghan state, but also new international donors), leading to overlapping coordination and accountability mechanisms. Strong UN leadership and particularly the role of Brahimi will be central, as will the development of a centralized funding mechanism, perhaps in the form of a Strategic Recovery facility.

• *Conflict sensitivity.* All forms of assistance should be designed and im-plemented so that they are sensitive to the dynamics of conflict and peace. Peacebuilding is not necessarily synonymous with development; the wrong kind of development may be conflict-producing. Conflict sensitivity is likely to mean a range of things and could include: developing the capacity to con-duct high-quality analysis; monitoring the distributional effects of aid (partic-ularly impacts on intergroup tensions); building in ownership and inclusive-ness to aid programs; developing "do no harm" and peace and conflict impact assessment (PCIA) tools; and disseminating information through the media about peacebuilding efforts.

• *Accountability, ownership, and learning.* In the rush to establish pro-grams and profile, there is a danger that agencies will repeat past errors and not place a sufficient premium on understanding the context or reflecting on lessons from the past. The Strategic Monitoring Unit (SMU) established in 2000 to improve learning and accountability should be a central player, but it is likely to be sidelined by new and better-resourced actors. We recommend that sufficient political and financial backing be provided to the SMU so that it has the profile and capacity to ensure that learning and accountability are built into the aid effort from the beginning. Second, we recommend the estab-lishment of a government body, a "National Reconstruction Auditor," within the Ministry of Reconstruction to ensure accountability in the planning and implementation of reconstruction. We have already pointed to the dangers of a small group of shareholders being the main beneficiaries of the potential peace dividend. Donors need to develop high standards of accountability and trans-parency for themselves. Similarly, they must set clear standards in terms of governance to ensure that the new Afghan state is accountable and responsive to its citizens.

Short-Term Challenges

A critical factor in war-to-peace transitions is the sequencing and mix of short-term and long-term activities. Quick and credible incentives for peace need to be created, while, simultaneously, longer-term structural issues are addressed. Getting the right balance is going to be difficult; while "buying out" the war-lords may be necessary in the short term, it is important not to lose sight of the need for justice and reconciliation. Some of the key short-term and long-term challenges ahead include:

• *Security.* Establishing a legitimate monopoly of force is the first priority. Security is the absolute precondition for a viable peacebuilding process. With the fall of the Taliban, old patterns of insecurity, lawlessness, criminality, and human-rights abuses have reemerged. An immediate and long-term priority will be the reestablishment of the state security institutions. The role of the International Security Assistance Force (ISAF) as a catalyst, supporter, and trainer will be critically important in the reestablishment of national law enforcement bodies. Rather than a classical demobilization strategy, in the long term a security-sector reform approach is necessary, linking security issues to a wider package of good governance measures.

• *Protection.* In many parts of the country there appears to be a growing protection vacuum as local warlords reassert their control and lawlessness and human-rights abuses increase. The international community must not turn a blind eye to this. There is an urgent need for human-rights monitoring and enforcement. The ISAF must be able to operate outside of Kabul to support Afghan security forces in keeping the peace and enabling human-rights groups and aid agencies to be operational throughout the country.

• *Humanitarian action.* The drought- and security-induced humanitarian crisis continues. Delivering massive quantities of humanitarian aid into Afghanistan is essential both in terms of saving lives and winning the peace. International actors must make this an absolute priority. Aid agencies should be provided with the resources and political space to deliver an effective aid program. This cannot happen while aid is seen as a strategic tool—part of the "war against terrorism." It must be separated out from the military and diplomatic action. Humanitarian actors should also ensure the efficacy of the humanitarian assistance program. Finally, emergency work should be designed so that it lays the groundwork for subsequent development activities. There will be a need to follow humanitarian assistance with quick-impact transitional activities that can support livelihoods and create alternatives to the war economy.

Long-Term Challenges

The key medium- to long-term challenge is to effect a transition toward national governance. Support for a broad-based coalition is essential. This has to be based upon a sophisticated understanding of the incentives and disincentives for peace (and an understanding of what kind of peace different external and internal actors wish to see established). This applies at all levels, from the Afghan farmer choosing whether to grow onions or poppies, to the warlord choosing whether to become part of the government or reestablish his fiefdom, to the regional power choosing whether to support the coalition as a whole or to promote certain elements within the coalition. While we have argued that the international community cannot engineer peace, it can help tip the balance in favor of collaboration by creating the right incentives—and enforcing penalties on the spoilers.

The record of the international community in terms of promoting good governance has been, at best, mixed, even in stable settings, because of a lack of local ownership, a formulaic approach, short time frames, and an inconsistent application of "bottom lines." Clearly, Afghan governance must be homegrown and not based on "off the shelf models" of Western liberal democracy. Some underlying principles can perhaps be taken as universal, including international norms on human rights, women's participation, and broad involvement of all sections of Afghan society. These ideals can be worked toward over time and achieved in different ways; however, an insistence on Western forms of governance may actually impede the establishment of more important underlying democratic "norms." Elections, for example, should not be viewed as the "be-all-and-end-all." In a number of postconflict settings, they have been destabilizing and counterproductive. Decentralized or federal systems may appear attractive to many Western analysts, but in the short to medium term, we feel the priority must be to build a strong central state with a legitimate monopoly of force. Support for a federal solution at this stage would cause massive tensions between the center and the regions. This is not an argument for a return to the centralized but weak state that led to the Afghan crisis. However, a strong center is a precondition for supporting and strengthening the state at the local level—in the same way that a vibrant civil society tends to mirror a strong and legitimate state.

Central to the task of establishing legitimacy will be the need to develop the capacity of the state to deliver services—this includes establishing a governance framework that would help transform the war economy into a peace economy and create opportunities for licit livelihoods. Support for the agricultural sector will be central to kick starting the Afghan economy. The state must also be supported in delivering education and health services to its population. Modern schooling, not just in Afghanistan but throughout the region, is a critical priority. The *madrassas* that fuel the dynamic of *jihad* have flourished because of the decay of the state school system. This is in no small part due to the policy prescriptions and market dogma of the international financial institutions. The multilaterals must learn from these failures—the standardized structural-adjustment package may be conflict-producing.

Finally, Afghanistan in the long run will not develop itself through aid funds. Development in the end will depend on the expansion of the private sector. Afghanistan's role as a bridge between Central and Southern Asia will need to be exploited, particularly in terms of trade and oil pipelines. Greater opportunities for regional cooperation may result, but they should be accompanied by measures such as oil trust funds to ensure that the profits are equitably distributed.

Resources

Newsletters and Periodicals
Afghanistan Consolidated Appeals, Office of the UN Coordinator for Afghanistan
Afghanistan Outlook, Office of the UN Coordinator for Afghanistan
ARIN, British Agencies Afghanistan Group, London

Reports
Carnegie Endowment for International Peace
"Preventing New Afghanistans: A Regional Strategy for Reconstruction," by Martha Brill Olcott, January 2002.
"Rebuilding Afghanistan: Fantasy versus Reality," by Marina Ottaway and Anatol Lieven, Janaury 2002.
Christian Michelse Institute, *Peace-Building Strategies for Afghanistan Part I: Lessons from Past Experiences in Afghanistan,* by Astri Suhrke, Arne Strand, and Kristian Berg Harpviken, January 2002.
Conflict Prevention Network, *Talibanization: Extremism and Regional Instability in South and Central Asia,* CPN In-Depth Study, September 2001.
Human Rights Watch
Afghanistan. Crisis of Impunity. The Role of Pakistan, Russia and Iran in Fueling the Civil War, July 2001.
Cluster Bombs in Afghanistan, October 2001.
Humanity Denied, Systematic Violations of Women's Rights in Afghanistan, October 2001.
Recommendations to the International Conference on Reconstruction Assistance to Afghanistan, Tokyo, 21–22 January 2002, 17 January 2002.
International Centre for Humanitarian Reporting, *Afghanistan, Essential Field Guides to Humanitarian and Conflict Zones,* edited by E. Girardet and J. Walter, Crosslines Global Report, Geneva/Dublin, 1998.
International Crisis Group, *Afghanistan and Central Asia: Priorities for Reconstruction and Development,* Osh/Brussels, 27 November 2001.
International Peace Academy, *Prospects for Peace in Afghanistan: The Role of Pakistan,* by A. Jan, 1999.
OECD, *The Limits and Scope for the Use of Development Assistance Incentives and Disincentives for Influencing Conflict Situations: Case Study: Afghanistan,* by K. Van Brabant and T. Killick, Paris, 1999.
Overseas Development Institute
Shifting Sands: The Search for "Coherence" Between Political and Humanitarian Responses to Complex Emergencies, by J. Macrae and N. Leader, HPG Report 8, London, 2000.
The Changing Role of NGOs in the Provision of Relief and Rehabilitation Assistance: *Case Study 1—Afghanistan/Pakistan,* by N. Nicholds Borton, UK, 1994.
"Security and Cash for Afghanistan Right Away," comment by William Shawcross, *The International Herald Tribune.* 31 January 2002.
Swedish Institute for Development Assistance, *Understanding the Economy of Afghanistan: An Exploratory Study,* by Ostrom, January 1997.
Swiss Peace Foundation, *Afghanistan: Reconstruction and Peacebuilding in a Regional Framework,* by Barnett Rubin, Ashraf Ghani, William Maley, Ahmed Rashid, and Olivier Roy, Koff Peacebuilding Reports, January 2001.
United Nations Department of Humanitarian Affairs, *Afghanistan, Coordination in a Fragmented State,* by A. Donini, E. Dudley, and R. Ockwell, A Lesson Learned Report, 1996.
UNDP/World Bank, "Study Report: Afghanistan's International Trade Relations with Neighboring Countries," *Afghanistan Watching Brief,* by M. Z. Khan, June 2001.
United States Institute for Peace, *Rebuilding Afghanistan—A Framework for Establishing Security and the Rule of Law,* 15 January 2002.
UNOCHA
Afghanistan—1998 Consolidated Appeal, 1998.
Afghanistan—1999 Appeal, 1998.

Afghanistan—2000 Appeal, 1999.
Initial Inter-Agency Humanitarian Emergency Assistance Plan for Afghans in Afghanistan and in Neighboring Countries, October 2001–March 2002.

Other Publications

Afghanistan, by L. Dupree. Princeton, NJ, Princetown University Press, 1980.
"Afghanistan Under the Taliban," by Barnett Rubin. *Current History* 98(625), 1999, pp. 79–91.
"Agreement on Provisional Arrangements in Afghanistan Pending the Re-establishment of Permanent Government Institutions," by Kofi Annan, *UN Secretary General Letter*, 5 December 2001 to the President of the Security General, 2001.
"Beyond the Taliban? The Afghan Conflict and United Nations Peacemaking," by M. Fielden and Jonathan Goodhand. *Conflict, Security, Development* 1(3), 2001.
"Coherence or Cooption? Politics, Aid and Peacebuilding in Afghanistan," by Haneef Atmar and Jonathan Goodhand. *The Journal of Humanitarian Assistance*, 2001, online: www.jha.ac/articles/a069.htm.
"Doing Well Out of War," by Paul Collier. In M. Berdal and Malone (eds.), *Greed and Grievance. Economic Agendas in Civil Wars*, Boulder, CO, Lynne Rienner Publishers, 2000.
"From Holy War to Opium War? A Case Study of the Opium Economy in North Eastern Afghanistan," by Jonathan Goodhand. *Central Asian Survey* 19(2), 2000, pp. 265–280.
From Rhetoric to Reality: The Role of Aid in Local Peacebuilding in Afghanistan, by Haneef Atmar, Sultan Barakat, and Arne Strand. York, UK, University of York, 1998.
Fundamentalism Reborn? Afghanistan and the Taliban, edited by William Maley. London, Hurst & Company, 1998.
Islam and Politics in Afghanistan, by A. Oleson. UK, Curzon Press, 1995.
NGOs and Peace Building in Afghanistan, by Sultan Barakat, Ehsan, and Arne Strand. Workshop report, The University of York, 1999.
NGOs and Peace Building in Complex Political Emergencies—Afghanistan Study, by Jonathan Goodhand. UK, University of Manchester/INTRAC, 2000, online: idpm. man.ac.uk/idpm/idpm-dp.htm.
Review of the Strategic Framework for Afghanistan, by M. Duffield, P. Grossman, and N. Leader, Commissioned by the Strategic Monitoring Unit, Afghanistan, 2001.
Taliban: Islam, Oil and the New Great Game in Central Asia, by Ahmed Rashid. London, I. B. Tauris, 2000.
The Chimera of Ethnicity in Afghanistan: Ethnic Affiliation No Basis for a New Regime, by C. Schetter, NZZ Online, 10 December 2001, www.nzz.ch/english.
The Emergence of Modern Afghanistan: Politics of Reform and Modernization, 1880–1946, by L. S. Vartan Gregorian, Stanford, Stanford University Press, 1967.
The Fragmentation of Afghanistan: State Formation and Collapse in the International System, by Barnett Rubin, Ashraf Ghani, William Maley, Ahmed Rashid, and Olivier Roy. New Haven/London, Yale University Press, 2001.
"The Political Economy of War and Peace in Afghanistan," by Barnett R. Rubin. *World Development* 28(10), 2000, pp. 1789–1803.
The Search for Peace in Afghanistan: From Buffer State to Failed State, by Barnett Rubin. New Haven/London, Yale University Press, 1995.
"The Taliban: Exporting Extremism," by Ahmed Rashid. *Current Affairs Digest*, book 66, February 2000.

Selected Internet Sites

www.afgha.com/ (Northern Alliance site)
www.afghanan.net/ (AfghanNet)

www.afghan-info.com/afghnews.htm (Afghanistan Information Center)
www.afghanistan.org/ (Afghanistan Peace Organization)
www.afghanradio.com/azadi.html (Azadi Afghan Radio)
www.afghan-web.com/aop/today.html (Afghanistan Online news)
www.afghan-web.com/politics/ (Afghan Politics)
www.crisisweb.org (International Crisis Group with reports on Central Asia online)
www.eurasianet.org/ (An Open Society Institute site that provides an independent
    source of news and analysis about Tajikistan)
www.fas.harvard.edu/~centasia (Perhaps the richest and most concentrated source of
    information on Central Asian studies worldwide)
www.incore.ulst.ac.uk/cds/countries/afghan.html (INCORE guide to Internet sources
    on conflict in Afghanistan)
www.institute-for-afghan-studies.org/ (Institute for Afghan Studies)
www.iwpr.net (Institute for War and Peace reporting)
www.loyajirga.com (Loya Jirga site)
www.omaid.com/ (Afghan newspaper with international distribution)
www.pcpafg.org (Office of the UN Co-ordinator for Afghanistan)
www.preventconflict.org/portal/centralasia/ (A conflict prevention initiative by Harvard
    scholars with detailed a detailed data base of summarized articles and links)
www.reliefweb.int (ReliefWeb Afghanistan)
www.usip.org/library/regions/afghan.html (Excellent overview of Taliban and Afghan-
    istan Web Links)

Resource Contacts

Rehman Baba, University Town, Peshawar, Pakistan
Nancy Dupree, e-mail: acbaar@radio.brain.net.pk
Simon Fisher, Responding to Conflict, e-mail: simon@respond.org
William Maley, School of Politics, University College, Australian Defense Force, e-mail:
    w-maley@adfa.edu.au
Peter Marsden, British Agencies Afghanistan Group, e-mail: peter.marsden@refugeecouncil.
    org.uk
Ahmed Rashid, e-mail: review@brain.net.pk
Olivier Roy, French Center for Scientific Research, e-mail: oroy@princeton.edu
Barnett R. Rubin, Center on International Cooperation, New York University, e-mail:
    Barnett.Rubin@nyu.edu
Susanne Schmeidl, Swiss Peace Foundation, e-mail: schmeidl@swisspeace.unibe.ch
Elizabeth Winter, British Agencies Afghanistan Group, e-mail: elizabeth.winter@www.
    baag.org.uk

Organizations

Office of the UN Co-ordinator for Afghanistan
H 292, St 55, Sector F-10/4
Islamabad, Pakistan
Tel +92-51-2211451
Web site: www.pcpafg.org

Data on the following organizations can be found in the Directory section

In Pakistan
    Afghan Development Association
    Afghan NGO's Coordination Bureau
    Agency Coordinating Body for Afghan Relief

Co-operation Center for Afghanistan
Co-operation for Peace and Unity
Islamic Coordination Council
Program on Peace Studies & Conflict Resolution
Research and Advisory Council of Afghanistan
Revolutionary Association of the Women of Afghanistan

In the United States
Afghanistan Foundation
Afghanistan Peace Association
Human Rights Watch
Institute for Multi-Track Diplomacy
Women's Alliance for Peace and Human Rights in Afghanistan
United States Institute of Peace

Others
British Agencies Afghanistan Group
Post-War Reconstruction and Development Unit
Swiss Peace Foundation

Jonathan Goodhand is currently a lecturer in the Department of Development Studies at the School of Oriental and African Studies, University of London. He previously conducted research with University of Manchester, INTRAC, and DFID on aid, conflict, and peacebuilding, and has managed NGO programs in South and Central Asia. Mohammed Haneef Atmar has an M.A. in Post-War Recovery Studies, University of York, United Kingdom. He is currently deputy country director of the International Rescue Committee (IRC) in Afghanistan. He has written extensively on aid policy and practice, aid policy and peacebuilding in Afghanistan, and institutional development of NGOs, among others.

Notes

1. This chapter builds upon research funded by the Department for International Development (UK) on NGOs and peacebuilding and subsequent research funded by International Alert on aid, conflict, and peacebuilding. The authors would also like to thank the following people who gave substantive comments on an earlier version of this paper: William Maley, Ahmed Rashid, Barnett Rubin, Elizabeth Winter, and Mohammed Ehsan Zia. They bear no responsibility for the views expressed herein, which are those of the authors alone.

2. Barnett R. Rubin, *The Search for Peace in Afghanistan: From Buffer State to Failed State*. New Haven and London: Yale University Press, 1995.

3. Adapted from Haneef Atmar, Sultan Barakat and Arne Strand, *From Rhetoric to Reality: The Role of Aid in Local Peacebuilding in Afghanistan*, York: University of York Press, 1998; and Koenraad Van Brabant and Tony Killick, *The Limits and Scope for the Use of Development Assistance Incentives and Disincentives for Influencing Conflict Situations: Case Study: Afghanistan*, Paris: OECD, 1999.

4. The United National Islamic Front for the Salvation of Afghanistan (Jabha-yi Muttahid-i Islami-yi Milli barayi Nijat-i Afghanistan). The UF was formed in 1996 as an alliance of the groups opposed to the Taliban. The president of the ousted government, Burhanuddin Rabbani, remained the president of Afghanistan and the titular head of the UF, although real power lay with Commander Ahmad Shah Massoud, the minister for defense (Human Rights Watch, 2001: 12).

5. The United Nations Security Council passed Resolutions 1267 on 15 October 1999 and 1333 on 19 December 2000. It has been argued that these were largely driven

by the United States and followed the August 1998 bombing of the U.S. embassies in Kenya and Tanzania, allegedly by bin Laden's Al-Qaida network. Resolution 1333 involved one-sided sanctions that aimed to disrupt the Taliban's capacity to conduct military operations (William Maley, "Talibanization and Pakistan," in *Talibanisation: Extremism and Regional Instability in South and Central Asia,* edited by Conflict Prevention Network, Berlin and Brussels: Conflict Prevention Network, 2001, p. 66).

6. Matthew Fielden and Jonathan Goodhand, *Peace Making in the New World Disorder: A Study of the Afghan Conflict and Attempts to Resolve It.* Manchester: Institute for Development Policy and Management, 2001, p. 11.

7. C. Johnson, *Afghanistan. A Land in Shadow.* Oxford: An Oxfam Country Profile, 1998.

8. Jonathan Goodhand, "From Holy War to Opium War? A Case Study of the Opium Economy in North Eastern Afghanistan," *Central Asian Survey* 19(2), 1999, p. 267.

9. Barnett R. Rubin, "Regional Instability in South and Central Asia," in *Talibanisation: Extremism and Regional Instability in South and Central Asia.* Berlin and Brussels: Conflict Prevention Network, 2001, pp. 13–32.

10. See Maley, "Talibanization and Pakistan," pp. 53–74; and Ameen Jan, *Prospects for Peace in Afghanistan: The Role of Pakistan,* New York: International Peace Academy, 1999.

11. Human Rights Watch, *Afghanistan: Crisis of Impunity, The Role of Pakistan, Russia and Iran in Fueling the Civil War* 13(3C), July 2001.

12. Rubin, "Regional Instability in South and Central Asia," p. 81.

13. Olivier Roy, "The Transnational Dimension of Radical Islamic Movements," in *Talibanization: Extremism and Regional Instability in South and Central Asia.* Berlin: Conflict Prevention Network, September, 2001, p. 81.

14. Maley, "Talibanization and Pakistan," p. 70. As Maley notes, such groups have been used by the Pakistani army, especially Inter Services Intelligence (ISI), as a tool of regional policy. For example, Harakat ul Mujahidin and Lashkar I Tayyeva became the main fighting units in Kashimr after 1995 with the full support of the Pakistani army, at the expense of the more nationalist Kashmiri groups (p. 83).

15. This has led some to argue that rather than attempting to engineer peace, external parties should give "war a chance" (Roy Licklider, "The Consequences of Negotiated Settlements in Civil Wars, 1945–1993," *American Political Science Review* 89[3], September 1995, pp. 681–690.)

16. Barnett R. Rubin, "The Political Economy of War and Peace in Afghanistan," *World Development* 28(10), 2000, p. 1797.

17. UNOCHA, *Afghanistan–2000 Appeal,* UNOCHA, 1999, p. 1.

18. Rubin, "Regional Instability," p. 14.

19. There are already reports of poppy planting in newly "liberated" areas. Given the level of poverty and the lack of alternative livelihoods this is hardly surprising. It was estimated that before the Taliban opium edict, between 3 and 4 million Afghans— or about 20% of the population—were dependent on poppy for their livelihoods.

20. A. F. Naqvi, *Afghanistan-Pakistan Trade Relations,* Islamabad: World Bank, 1999.

21. M. Z. Khan, "Study Report: Afghanistan's International Trade Relations with Neighboring Countries," *Afghanistan Watching Brief,* UNDP/World Bank, June, 2001.

22. Rubin, "Regional Instability," p. 17. It has been estimated that upwards of half a million people are directly dependent on war-related activities for their living (John H. Ostrom, *Understanding the Economy of Afghanistan: An Exploratory Study.* Stockhom: Swedish Institute for Development Assistance, 1997).

23. Rubin, "The Political Economy of War," p. 1799.

24. The dynastic patrimony of Amir Abdul Rahman (1880–1901) is a case in point. As Oleson argues, the "Iron Amir's" rule was characterized by an ongoing strug-

gle to establish a modern centralized state, independent of traditional Durrani tribal structures (the "tribal state') who had previously formed the military and political backbone of the Afghan state (Asta Oleson, *Islam and Politics in Afghanistan*. London: Curzon Press, 1995, p. 89.).

25. Kristian Harpviken, "War and Change in Afghanistan: Reflections on Research Priorities," in *Return to Silk Routes: Current Scandinavian Research on Central Asia*, edited by Mira Juntunen and Birgit Schlyter. London: Kegan Paul, 1999, p. 169.

26. Kristian Harpviken, "War and Change in Afghanistan: Reflections on Research Priorities," in *Return to Silk Routes: Current Scandinavian Research on Central Asia*, edited by Mira Juntunen and Birgit Schlyter. London: Kegan Paul, 1999, p. 170.

27. Before the war, the Pashtuns dominated the Afghan state. However, the conflict brought a new assertiveness from non-Pasthun minorities such as the Tajiks and Hazaras who mounted an effective resistance to the Soviet invasion. There has been a shift in the ethnic balance of power during the course of the war and the Interim Authority is strongly represented by non-Pasthun minorities from the UF. For the dangers of an essentialist notion of ethnicity, leading to a belief in ethnic quotas for governance, see Conrad Schetter, "The Chimera of Ethnicity in Afghanistan: Ethinic Affiliation no basis for a new Regime," NZZ Online, 2001: www.nzz.ch/english.

28. Human Rights Watch have documented numerous human rights abuses during the course of the war including Taliban discrimination against, and massacres of, Hazaras.

29. See Barnett R. Rubin, Ashraf Ghani, William Maley, Ahmed Rashid and Olivier Roy, *The Fragmentation of Afghanistan: State Formation and Collapse in the International System*. New Haven and London: Yale University Press, 2001, p. 6, and Fielden and Goodhand, *Peace Making in the New World Disorder*, p. 10.

30. Rubin et al., *The Fragmentation of Afghanistan*, p. 11; Fielden and Goodhand, *Peace Making in the New World Disorder*.

31. Barnett R. Rubin, "Afghanistan Under the Taliban" *Current History* 98(625), 1999, pp. 79–91.

32. Fielden and Goodhand, *Peace Making in the New World Disorder*, p. 15.

33. Nancy H. Dupree, "Afghan Women Under the Taliban," in *Fundamentalism Reborn? Afghanistan and the Taliban*, edited by William Maley, London: Hurst & Company, 1998; and Human Rights Watch, *Afghanistan: Crisis of Impunity, the Role of Pakistan, Russia and Iran in Fueling the Civil War* 13(3) July 2001.

34. Rubin, "Afghanistan Under the Taliban."

35. A. Davis, "How the Taliban Became a Military Force," in *Fundamentalism Reborn? Afghanistan and the Taliban*, edited by W. Maley, London: Hurst & Company, 1998; and Human Rights Watch, *Afghanistan: Crisis of Impunity, the Role of Pakistan, Russia and Iran in Fueling the Civil War*, vol. 13, no. 3(C), July 2001.

36. Jan, *Prospects for Peace in Afghanistan*.

37. Ahmed Rashid, *Taliban: Islam, Oil and the New Great Game in Central Asia*. London: I. B. Tauris, 2000, p. 100.

38. Human Rights Watch, *Afghanistan: Crisis of Impunity*, p. 11.

39. Rubin, "Regional Instabililty," p. 17.

40. Roy, "The Transnational Dimension of Radical Islamic Movements," p. 88.

41. See Ibid., and Rubin, "Regional Instability," p. 15.

42. Rubin, "Afghanistan Under the Taliban."

43. Rubin et al., *The Fragmentation of Afghanistan*, p. 25.

44. UNOCHA, *Afghanistan–1999 Appeal*, UNOCHA, 1998.

45. See Fielden and J. Goodhand, *Peace Making in the New World Disorder*, for a detailed discussion on this.

46. William Maley (ed.), *Fundamentalism Reborn? Afghanistan and the Taliban*. London: Hurst & Company, 1998, p. 183.

47. Ibid., p. 186.

48. Cited in Ibid., p. 198.

49. Rubin et al., *The Fragmentation of Afghanistan*.

50. Another impetus for change was the realization by the United Nations of the need for internal reform.

51. ASG (Afghanistan Support Group) is a donor states' forum with sixteen members established in 1997 that meets usually twice a year to discuss key issues concerning emerging humanitarian situations, donor policies, assistance provision, coordination, etc.

52. A. Donini, *The Strategic Framework for Afghanistan; A Preliminary Assessment,* unpublished paper, 2000.

53. On the other hand, one should not underplay the symbolic and practical importance of aid in Afghanistan. There is no longer a functioning state and all public welfare functions are being performed by aid agencies, with the UN becoming in effect a surrogate government. Humanitarian aid agencies have in fact been criticized for sustaining the conflict as they enable warring groups to free up resources that they would otherwise have to allocate for Afghan communities. Aid, after agriculture, is the second most important sector of the licit economy. Aid agencies employ around 22,000 Afghans and are one of the main providers of off-farm employment in Afghanistan. Furthermore, the entire national budget of the Taliban administration for public healthcare in 2001 was said to be around $1 million, a figure dwarfed by the annual expenditure of the aid community on healthcare, which was estimated to be $23.6 million in 1997, $20.2 million in 1998, $10.8 million in 1999 (Haneef Atmar and Jonathan Goodhand, "Coherence or Cooption? Politics, Aid and Peacebuilding in Afghanistan," *The Journal of Humanitarian Assistance,* 2001, online: www.jha.ac/articles/a069.htm.).

54. Mark Duffield, Patricia Grossman, and Nicholas Leader, *Review of the Strategic Framework for Afghanistan,* Commissioned by the Strategic Monitoring Unit, Afghanistan, September 2001.

55. Fielden and Goodhand, *Peace Making in the New World Disorder.*

56. ACBAR, ANCB, SWABAD, ICC, NCB (Herat), and NGO Forum Kabul.

57. Adapted from Atmar and Goodhand, "Coherence or Cooption? Politics, Aid and Peacebuilding in Afghanistan."

58. The debate on "traditional" Afghan institutions is a contested one. The authors have stressed that war and social change have profoundly reshaped Afghan institutions. However there are also important continuities with the past. The *shura* is a case in point, representing perhaps, the "reinvention of tradition" in the sense that contemporary actors have revitalized such institutions by drawing upon historical and religious traditions. Whether we view it as "new" or "traditional," the *shura* constitutes an important consultative and decisionmaking institution, albeit with variations in terms of local context.

59. L. Dupree, *Afghanistan*. Princeton, NJ: Princeton University Press, 1980.

60. The Islamic code of religious law, based on the teachings of the Koran and the traditional sayings of Muhammad.

61. During the last two decades, the Loya Jirga has been continually invoked as a mechanism for establishing a national consensus. However, without a strong central track process the Loya Jirga had limited leverage over the warring groups. It could perhaps play a role in legitimating a consensus but was unable to create one.

62. K. A. Annan, UN Secretary General Letter 5 December 2001 to the President of the Security General, re "Agreement on Provisional Arrangements in Afghanistan Pending the Re-establishment of Permanent Government Institutions," 2001.

63. G. Austen, "Great Power Geo-Strategic Roles in South and Central Asia," in *Talibanization: Extremism and Regional Instability in South and Central Asia,* CPN In-Depth Study, September 2001, p. 112.

64. Paul Collier, "Doing Well Out of War," in *Greed and Grievance. Economic*

Agendas in Civil Wars, edited by Mats Berdal and David Malone. Boulder, CO: Lynne Rienner Publishers, 2000.

65. Fielden and Goodhand, *Peace Making in the New World Disorder.*

66. Many principles could have been included in this section. We have picked out some of the essential ones.

6.6

The Ferghana Valley: In the Midst of a Host of Crises

Randa M. Slim

The borders of the three countries within the Ferghana Valley were artificially drawn between 1924 and 1936 by the Soviet authorities in Moscow, with Tajiks, Uzbeks, and Kyrgyz living on all sides. This is one of at least six major sources of present tension in the valley. Most international attention focuses on the threat of Islamic extremism. However, official attempts at conflict management through repressive measures and crackdowns against Islamic groups and civil society organizations are fueling rather than dampening people's anger and frustration. Effective conflict prevention might still push the Ferghana Valley away from the precipice to which it is now heading.

Throughout Central Asia's history, the Ferghana Valley provided an important center for merchants trading with China and the Mediterranean. A branch of the Great Silk Road linking China to the Middle East, the Mediterranean, and Europe passed through the Ferghana Valley. Initially part of the Timurid empire, after Timur's death the Ferghana Valley became a single political unit under the Kokand Khanate from the late sixteenth to the midnineteenth century. Tsarist Russia's advance into Central Asia by the midnineteenth century was fueled by "expansionist imperial policy, ambition to rule the entire continent east of Moscow, and unrelenting economic pressure from merchants, bankers, and industrialists."[1] Russian merchants were interested that Moscow secured supplies of Central Asian cotton. With the Bolshevik revolution and the introduction of Soviet rule into Central Asia, the social and political relations in the region were fundamentally altered. Prior to their assuming control of the region, people in Central Asia identified themselves in terms of their region and locale, religious practices, and family or clan. The Soviet policies in the region "precipitated nationalities from a range of less codified identities that had existed before, giving them their own distinct literary languages written in variants of the Cyrillic alphabet."[2] Borders were artificially drawn in such a way that Tajiks, Uzbeks, and Kyrgyz were found on all sides. This

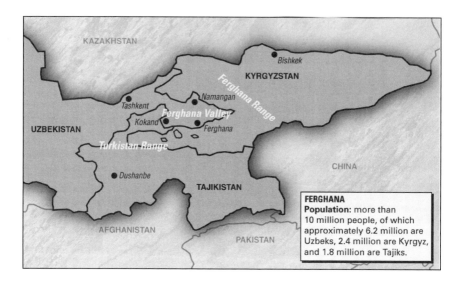

FERGHANA
Population: more than
10 million people, of which
approximately 6.2 million are
Uzbeks, 2.4 million are Kyrgyz,
and 1.8 million are Tajiks.

enabled the Soviet authorities to continuously be called upon by the people in the region to help them manage conflicts that were bound to emerge as a result of these artificial divisions.

Home to more than 10 million people, the Ferghana Valley is divided among three Central Asian republics: Uzbekistan, Tajikistan, and Kyrgyzstan. About 60 percent of the valley's territory lies in Uzbekistan (4.3 percent of Uzbek territory), 25 percent in Tajikistan (18.2 percent of state territory), and the remaining 15 percent in Kyrgyzstan (42.2 percent of state territory). The Ferghana Valley lies in the heart of the Tien-Shan range with the Syr-Darya River flowing through it. It is 350 kilometers long and 100 kilometers wide. There are seven administrative provinces in the valley—three are Uzbek (Andijan, Ferghana, and Namangan), three Kyrgyz (Batken, Osh, and Jalal Abad), and one Tajik (Sughd, formerly Leninabad). Complicating the boundary issue in the valley is the presence of seven small enclaves.

From the beginning, the Muslim people of Central Asia deeply mistrusted the Soviet ideology. Islam arrived in Central Asia in the eighth century and has since then played an important role in the cultural, social, and political development of the Ferghana Valley. In February 1918, the Basmachi Muslim rebel movement was created in the aftermath of an aggression by Soviet troops against the population of Kokand. The Basmachis were local military groups also led by *mullahs* who tried to overthrow Soviet rule and the old regional political elites in the name of an Islamic Turkistan. The Basmachi rebellion lasted until 1924 in most of Central Asia and was sustained in many parts of the Ferghana Valley until 1928. In 1991, following the collapse of the Soviet Union, the different states of Central Asia declared their independence and later introduced their national currencies.

Today, the Ferghana Valley remains the part of Central Asia with the highest level of Muslim observance. Although the level of knowledge of Islamic theology and *shari'a* is quite limited among the general population, this has been increasing in the last several years. Seventy-five years of Soviet rule and constant attempts at suppressing Islam have in a small way paid off. What now remains strong in the valley is a ritualistic form of Islam. The Ferghana Valley is also the region in Central Asia that suffered most from independence, due to the imposition of territorial borders in an area that was economically interwoven during the Soviet times. As noted by an International Crisis Group report, "What were once internal administrative borders, across which flowed lively social and economic exchange and across which individual collective farms or villages had expanded, became new national borders."[3]Acute conflicts over water and land resources, old ethnic rivalries, and steep decline in people's living standards make this region most prone to violence.

This is a quick review of some of the conflicts that have occurred in the past thirteen years, 1989–2001.

1989

Ethnic clashes occurred in the Uzbekistan part of the valley between ethnic Uzbeks and Meskhetian Turks. Meskhetian Turks belong to a small ethnic group deported from the Caucasus to Uzbekistan by Stalin. One hundred and three people died and over a thousand were reported wounded. The pretext for the fighting was a quarrel in the local market in the Kuvasay bazaar in the Ferghana district over the price of strawberries. Most of the Meskhetian residents had to flee the valley back to Russia and other Central Asian countries.

Ethnic clashes also occurred in Samarkandek (on the Kyrgyzstan part of the valley) between Tajiks and Kyrgyz over land distribution and water allocation. Several people were killed and injured. Violent tensions have also occurred between Tajik refugees and local Kyrgyz residents in the Batken province. Tensions erupted over water allocation.

1990

Riots occurred between Kyrgyz and Uzbeks in Osh and Uzgen, Kyrgyzstan. Hundreds were killed. The causes of this conflict involved control over land and housing, the underrepresentation of ethnic Uzbeks in local and regional authority structures (while Uzbeks at the time made up 29 percent of the region's population), and demands for greater Uzbek autonomy as it relates to preservation of Uzbek culture and language.

1991–1992

The conflict involved a takeover of the Namangan regional administration by an unofficial militant organization called Adolat. The takeover was a protest by the local devout Muslim group against the official clergy's decision to endorse Islam Karimov's presidential candidacy. A wave of arrests followed the takeover and most of Adolat's supporters fled to Tajikistan, Afghanistan, and Iran.

1996–1998

A series of riots, protests, and eventually a military coup attempt occurred in Leninabad (recently renamed Soghd), Tajikistan. In May 1996, violent demonstrations were held in Khujand and (Öra-Teppa demanding the removal of unpopular local officials. In April 1997, prison riots occurred in Khujand prison that led the deaths of a large number of prisoners. On 30 April 1997, Tajik president Imomali Rakhmanov was injured along with seventy others in an assassination attempt in Khujand. In November 1998, rebels led by ethnic Uzbek leader Mahmud Khudoiberdiev crossed into Leninabad from Uzbekistan, seized control of the security installations in Khujand, and occupied a regional airport in Chkalovsk. The main reason behind these events was the growing dissatisfaction by the Khujandis over the Kölabi-run government's attempts to undermine the northern region's traditional role in Tajikistan's political life. The Tajik government accused Uzbek president Islam Karimov of supporting the rebels.

A series of assassinations of police and local officials in Namangan, in the Uzbekistan sector of the valley, led to a massive crackdown in Namangan and Andijan including hundreds of arrests of suspected Islamic terrorists. The Uzbek government charged "foreign-trained Wahhabis" with responsibility for the assassinations.

1999

In August 1999, rebels crossed from Tajikistan into the Batken district in Kyrgyzstan, kidnapped foreign nationals, and engaged in clashes with the Kyrgyz and Uzbek troops. It is now believed that the rebel group included members of the Islamic Movement of Uzbekistan (IMU), an Uzbek opposition Islamic group and former Tajik opposition fighters. They demanded a free corridor through the territory of Kyrgyzstan to Uzbekistan. The rebels eventually released the hostages after obtaining a ransom.

On 16 February 1999, six car bombs targeting Uzbekistani government facilities exploded in different parts of Tashkent, Uzbekistan's capital, killing sixteen persons and wounding more than a hundred others. Uzbek official circles blamed the attacks on the IMU. The government used these bombing incidents as an excuse to launch a crackdown on the militants in the Ferghana Valley. Eleven people were sentenced to death and more than 120 others received long prison sentences. Despite the official version for these incidents, it is now strongly believed these bombings were part of an internal power struggle in Uzbekistan, and were aimed at shoring up the influence of one clique in the ruling elite.

In November 1999, clashes occurred in Yangiabad, in the Uzbekistan part of the Ferghana Valley. A group of fifteen to twenty gunmen also believed to be members of the IMU killed six people in clashes with the Uzbek security and Interior Ministry troops in the mountainous areas around Angren. The gunmen were killed. Violence erupted over water allocation between Tajik refugees and local Kyrgyz residents in the villages of Chet-Kyzil and Bai-Karabak in the Batken province.

2000

Violent tensions occurred in Samarkandek, Kyrgyzstan, over housing and land allocation pitting Kyrgyz against Tajik villagers.

In August 2000 small units of IMU rebels raided small villages over a wide area along the Uzbek, Kyrgyz, and Tajik borders. The rebels are now believed to be stationed in parts of Tajikistan and the highlands of southern Kyrgyzstan.

2001

Under pressure from the international community, Tajikistan expelled the IMU militants from Tavildara in the Karategin Valley where the group had reportedly been based for several years. The militants along with their leaders were escorted to Afghanistan.[4]

Skirmishes have occurred in July between Kyrgyz government forces and IMU militants. That summer's raids were occurring nearer to Kyrgyz-Uzbek border regions, and indicate a shift in IMU tactics.[5] IMU members seem now to have settled among the local population in these border areas inside Kyrgyzstan.

Conflict Dynamics

The three countries sharing the Ferghana Valley are in the midst of a host of crises. A legitimacy crisis undermines the people's confidence in their leaders' ability to represent their interests in a fair and inclusive manner. An economic crisis worsens that prevents these countries' leadership from meeting the basic needs of their population, thus giving way to the rise and eventual dominance of an informal or shadow economy. A security crisis, which causes these governments to divert scarce resources away from the development field and toward the military sector, still plagues the area's government. And finally, a mounting crisis of traditional values that have always governed these societies and by which traditional methods of decisionmaking in communities such as the council of elders have worked is of growing concern. These crises present the background against which we must view and analyze past and potential future conflicts in the Ferghana Valley. As Lubin and Rubin note, conflicts in the Ferghana Valley were "caused less by ethnic animosities than by a mix of elements—economic, social, political—embedded in a complex political and ethnic strata that formed the fault lines along which these conflicts eventually exploded."[6] Most analysts focus on seven sources of tension in the valley: borders, overpopulation and "creeping migration," water, unemployment, Islamic militant groups, ethnicity, and a criminal cluster including drug trafficking, corruption, and organized crime.

Borders

Stalin drew the borders in the region in the 1920s, based on political and economic considerations and without respect for ethnic balance (many different groups were deported by Stalin, which complicated the border issues). These lines had little practical impact for most of the valley's residents when they were all part of the Soviet Union. Overnight with independence, these lines became the international borders of three sovereign countries, thus disrupting the ordinary flow of people, goods, and trade in the Ferghana Valley. Numerous border posts have been established between the different parts of the valley. As the United Nations Development Program/International Labor Organization social-policy review paper (1995–1996) noted, "The borders, being artificial, created ethnic groups and nationalities, not the other way around, and these divisions were perpetuated when the five Central Asian republics became independent. Where once there was unity, today there is national division and rivalry, at least potentially."

In response to growing IMU activity, Uzbekistan has imposed a visa regime and moreover mined its borders. Kyrgyzstan has also mined its borders with Tajikistan and blown up mountain passes in order to make them impenetrable by IMU militants. These actions make people's daily lives extremely difficult. They disrupt trade routes and hamper cross-border economic activities. By February 2001, it was reported that border mines had killed thirty civilians along the Tajik-Uzbek border. Border guards' abusive behavior and corruption indirectly foment interethnic tensions as blame for their behavior is displaced on neighboring villages of similar ethnic backgrounds. Local leadership in the valley is pushing their respective national government to take tough stands on the border issues and is applying increasing pressure on them to solve this problem.

There are also currently a number of border disputes among the three countries sharing the different parts of the valley that need to be addressed within some forms of multilateral or bilateral official mechanisms. There are close to 140 unresolved border disputes between Uzbekistan and Kyrgyzstan. In April 2001, reports of a land swap between the two countries, enabling Uzbekistan to establish a land corridor to its Sokh enclave located in Kyrgyzstan's Batken district, drew ire from the local population and antagonized the Kyrgyz parliament.[7]

Overpopulation and "Creeping Migration"

With a young and rapidly growing population in a small region with limited arable land, the Ferghana Valley faces tremendous demographic pressures. The highest population density in Central Asia is now found in the valley—up to 250 inhabitants per square kilometer compared with the average of 14 inhabitants per square kilometer in Central Asia. Observers are witnessing a rural exodus to Osh in Kyrgyzstan, especially from the Batken province and among ethnic Kyrgyz who reside in Tajikistan, to Khujand in Tajikistan from the Jirgatal and Murghab regions, and to Andijan, Ferghana, and Namangan provinces in Uzbekistan. There is also a brain drain in the valley as Russians and Russian-speaking residents are emigrating to Russia and other Commonwealth of Independent States countries due to unemployment and deteriorating living conditions in the valley.

Competition for land is also rising as a result of demographic pressures. This problem is most acute in the case of Kyrgyzstan. This competition is taking on an ethnic dimension. There is a "creeping migration" phenomenon as Tajik citizens cross borders and try to purchase land and build houses on Kyrgyz farmland. They usually buy the land from Kyrgyz farmers only to discover later that the sale was illegal. This has lately caused a number of small-scale violent clashes in southern Kyrgyzstan among Kyrgyz and ethnic Tajiks who live in these border communities. Similar problems are arising among ethnic Uzbeks and Kyrgyz in the Osh region. In the Uzbekistan part of the valley, it is being claimed that land is being reallocated to Uzbeks to the disadvantage of ethnic Kyrgyz and Tajiks who live in the area.

Water

Water is a cause of many of the small-scale conflicts that are currently unfolding in the valley, especially between northern Tajikistan and southern Kyrgyzstan. During Soviet times, the different parts of the valley were made interdependent through a infrastructural network of water, energy, and transportation lines. The three countries "often have contrary needs for scarce water supplies: Kyrgyzstan uses one of the main rivers, the Syr-Darya, for energy production, but Kazakhstan and Uzbekistan need the water for irrigation of their large cotton and fruit crops."[8] In 2000, agricultural production fell by 30 percent due mainly to limited water resources. Though water allocation is discussed each year in bilateral summits and agreements, the latter are often violated. Most water reservoirs are season-regulated and 90 percent of their water is for irrigation. Both Tajikistan and Kyrgyzstan, while water-rich, are dependent on imported electricity from Uzbekistan and Turkmenistan. This dependence has created many tensions among the three countries. On 23 July 2001, President Akayev of Kyrgyzstan signed a new law, "On the Interstate Use of Water Installations, Water Resources and Hydro Facilities in the Kyrgyz Republic," seeking to impose charges on countries such as Uzbekistan for Kyrgyz water usage. This new law will further weaken the already frail relationship between Kyrgyzstan and Uzbekistan.

Water scarcity is further exacerbated by the inefficient use of water in farming in the valley—the malfunctioning and in some cases totally destroyed drainage system and irrigation channels built by the Soviet Union. This has led to periodic flooding, rising water tables, and increased soil salinity, thus directly contributing to increased ethnic tensions among border communities.

Unemployment

Unemployment is high in the Ferghana Valley, particularly among youth. The collapse of the Soviet Union had a major impact on the economies of Central Asia, mainly in depriving the region of its network of suppliers and distributors and markets that used to be scattered throughout the former Soviet Union. Many industries in the valley are now idle. According to unofficial reports, the unemployment rate in the Batken province in the Kyrgyz part of the valley runs from 50 to 80 percent. It is estimated that 35 percent of the work force in the Uzbekistan part of the valley is unemployed, including the majority of those under the age of twenty-five. An unemployed and hungry youth is readily attracted to popular movements and ready to engage in criminal and violent activities. It has been reported that the unemployment problem has taken on an ethnic character. For example, in the Kyrgyzstan part of the valley, it has been observed that the rate of unemployment is higher among ethnic Uzbeks than Kyrgyz residents.[9]

Islamic Militant Groups

Islam has always been an inalienable part of the Central Asian culture, and more so in the Ferghana Valley. Although the Soviet Union tried over seventy-five years of its rule to co-opt local clergy and control them, underground Islamic networks that survived the Soviet times have now come to the surface and are playing a major role in the growth of militant Islamic groups in the valley. The two largest underground opposition Islamic movements known to be currently operating in the valley are the Islamic Movement of Uzbekistan (IMU) and the Hizb ut-Tahrir (Islamic Liberation Party). They both appear to be pan-Islamists with a vision for creating an Islamic caliphate in the historical region of Turkestan based on *shari'a* law. They are ideologically influenced by the Wahhabi Islamic tradition of Saudi Arabia, though a leader of Hizb ut-Tahrir has recently claimed that though they agree on the goals, they differ with the Wahhabi movement over the means to achieve their goals. The latter believe in a guerrilla war and the creation of an Islamic army to do that while the former espouses a peaceful, long-term strategy of ideological work at the community level.

Hizb ut-Tahrir was founded in Palestine in the 1950s and remained underground during the Soviet times.[10] It operates in small five-man cells, is highly secretive, and believes in peaceful political change through a mass revolt against the Central Asian regimes, while not excluding the possibility of using violent means if repression continues. The party has growing support in Tajikistan, Uzbekistan, and Kyrgyzstan. Recently, more than twenty followers were sentenced to different prison terms in Khujand, Tajikistan. The IMU core leadership consists of former members of banned Islamic parties in Uzbekistan who had to flee the Ferghana Valley to Tajikistan, Afghanistan, and Iran in 1992 during the harsh crackdown on the opposition by Uzbekistan's government. IMU members fought with the United Tajik opposition during Tajikistan's civil war (1992–1997). When the Tajik civil war ended in 1997, the Uzbek fighters refused to lay down their arms, claiming that their goal now is to engage in an armed struggle to topple the Uzbek government and establish an Islamic state in Uzbekistan.

Until recently, it was believed that IMU members maintained their bases in eastern Tajikistan, from where it is convenient to pass into Kyrgyzstan and Uzbekistan. Following their incursions into the Batken region in Kyrgyzstan in 2000 and 2001, and under strong pressure from neighboring Central Asian states, the government of Tajikistan is reported to have expelled the IMU's leader and some of his followers, who were flown aboard Russian helicopters to Afghanistan. It is now clear that the IMU did receive some support from the Taliban in Afghanistan and it is reported that other funders included Osama bin Laden and private Islamic groups in Pakistan and Saudi Arabia.[11] As pointed out earlier, skirmishes in July 2001 between IMU and the Kyrgyz government forces point out that militants are now operating inside Kyrgyzstan. Strategically, this tactical shift indicates that the IMU leadership now regards Kyrgyzstan as a military objective in its own right, aiming to embroil it in a wider regional conflict. Many analysts tend to argue that Islamic militancy now represents the most serious threat to stability in the region. Others feel, however, that it is the harsh repressive regimes of Central Asia and the economic crisis in the region rather than Islamic militancy that are the real cause of instability in the region. Furthermore, an International Crisis Group report correctly argues that "the [Islamic] insurgency is a reflection of the economic hardships and discontent affecting a part of the population and a reaction to the severe crackdown on Islamic activities which has pitted observant but otherwise moderate Muslims against their state."[12]

Ethnicity

A gap exists between the ethnic divisions and the political boundaries in the Ferghana Valley. For example, 700,000 ethnic Uzbeks live today in southern Kyrgyzstan, 300,000 ethnic Kyrgyz reside in Uzbekistan, and more than 1.4 million ethnic Uzbeks live in Tajikistan. The threat of interethnic tensions is more likely in southern Kyrgyzstan. Osh residents still remember the 1990 clashes between ethnic Uzbeks and Kyrgyz. Close to 30 percent of Kyrgyzstan's southern provinces are non-Kyrgyz. The largest minority group consists of Uzbeks (close to 15 percent), while Russians and Tajiks make up about 2–3 percent each. Despite Kyrgyzstan's publicly touted efforts toward diminishing the importance of ethnicity, ethnic Uzbeks in their part of the valley believe they have been increasingly discriminated against in allocation of official position, access to redistributed land, and access to other employment opportunities in the private sector such as the bazaar. It is also an alarming trend that many of the resource-based conflicts in the valley, and in particular in the Kyrgyz-Tajik border communities, are being expressed along ethnic lines. It has been noted that there is "sufficient tension based on discrimination, differential access to resources and the memory of past conflict to make the reoccurrence of such clashes a distinct possibility."[13]

Criminal Cluster: Drug Trafficking, Corruption, and Organized Crime

Drug trafficking and criminal activities are some of the main factors contributing to present and future instability in the Ferghana Valley. Drug trafficking has grown as a business as the economy in the region has declined. Drought, the wars in Afghanistan and Tajikistan, and the absence of economic and social reforms have plunged the region into poverty. This phenomenon is aided by the informal economy known as the "shadow economy" that has developed over decades in the former Soviet sphere including Central Asia.

The national governments in Kyrgyzstan and Uzbekistan claim that the drug trade is also funding the radical Islamic movements operating in the valley, including the IMU. There is as yet no firm evidence to support this claim.

Drug cultivation, production, and transportation have started to create a culture of consumption in the valley, especially among the unemployed youth. Today's typical drug addict in the valley is aged between thirteen and twenty-two and is unemployed. More women are becoming drug addicts as they are being used as couriers. The fear is that the increasing drug business will in the future contribute to further corruption of the power and security structures in this region. On 2 March 2001, a former Tajik embassy official was convicted of carrying 68 kilograms of heroin.

There is an ongoing intense competition among various criminal groups for control of the best trafficking routes. According to Agence France-Presse, over a hundred new organized criminal drug-smuggling groups have sprung up in Tajikistan alone. One explanation for the murder of Tajikistan deputy interior minister Habib Sanginov on 11 April 2001 relates to intensifying competition among Tajikistan's drug lords. According to analysts, the greatest struggle now centers on the road running northeast from Tajikistan's capital, Dushanbe, connecting the Garm region with southern Kyrgyzstan.[14] At present, large numbers of people are involved in these activities and the local state structures throughout the valley seem helpless at this point in containing this trade. Though one analyst points out that the drug trade in the Ferghana Valley presents one of the few examples of "coordinated interethnic cooperation," one might speculate whether in the future competing drug gangs will engage in turf wars that might take on an interethnic character.[15]

Official Conflict Management

National governments sharing the Ferghana Valley have in the past used and are now using different strategies and tactics for tackling sources of tension in the valley. This section will focus on the official attempts to deal with three major sources of tension: the economy (including land and unemployment), water, and Islamic militancy.

On the economic front, all three states have officially embraced economic reform policies. However, the implementation of such policies has varied in practice from one country to another, and within each country from one region to another. As far as the Ferghana Valley is concerned, these economic reforms have had a negative impact. As noted by Lubin and Rubin, "Customs controls, the establishment of separate currencies, and differences in rates and means of economic liberalization are all policy decisions that tear at the fabric that has woven the valley together over the course of centuries."[16] The imposition of customs controls, especially by Uzbekistan, has impeded cross-border regional trade and exacerbated corruption and given border guards free reign to make people's lives very difficult.

Land privatization has proceeded slowly in both the Uzbek and Kyrgyz parts of the valley. In the Uzbek part of the valley, "privatized" collective farms are still required to produce cotton and wheat for sale exclusively to the state at well below market prices. In southern Kyrgyzstan, privatization has proceeded slowly given the history of the 1990 ethnic rioting in Osh over land allocation policies. There is a fear among Kyrgyz that ethnic Uzbeks will use their economic advantage to buy more Kyrgyz land, while Uzbeks fear that local officials in the valley will use the privatization process as a pretext to chase them out of prime agricultural land. The industrial sector is not faring better in the Ferghana Valley. Similar to the rest of Central Asia, industries (both primary and secondary) need to be overhauled and restructured. Local firms lack investment funds and an efficient infrastructure. Potential large-scale foreign investment is being withheld, especially in the Uzbek part of the valley, due to that country's restrictive economic policies. These economic woes are further compounded by the lack of good transportation links between the different regions in the valley and their respective national centers. It is fair to say that the valley's main economic activities remain centered on agriculture, and the sector is in bad need of reform.

As far as water reform is concerned, the major obstacles to effective management lie mainly in the lack of political will to tackle such a complex issue. This holds especially on the part of the regional and local authorities that derive much of their power from their control over water allocation in their respective localities. In addition, any successful attempts at dealing with water-based conflict will require an input of funds and expertise that are currently lacking in the region. These are necessary to overhaul a water supply system that is in sore need of restructuring and in some cases total rebuilding.

Conflicts over water resources manifest themselves in the valley at both the national and the regional/local levels. Some of the resource-based conflicts at the local level are in some cases amenable to a localized, affordable solution that need not involve the national authorities. Many of these conflicts over water have taken on an ethnic character at the local level. In southern Kyrgyzstan, many of the local conflicts over water pit Kyrgyz villagers against ethnic Tajiks or Tajik refugees living in Kyrgyzstan. They also involve border communities in southern Kyrgyzstan and northern Tajikistan. The potential of these local conflicts to escalate into widespread ethnic rioting in these parts of the valley is high, but are easily preventable with a site-specific, intercommunal, low-cost intervention. One of the few success stories in the Ferghana Valley has been a project funded by the Swiss Development Agency that focuses on local resource-based conflicts. This project will be presented in detail in the following section on multi-track diplomacy.

At the national level, water reform must be addressed within the framework of a multi-issue, multiparty negotiation process linking border, water, and energy issues. A multiparty process is essential due to the fact that the Amu Darya and Syr Darya basins go through all six countries in the region—Afghanistan, Kazakhstan, Kyrgyzstan, Tajikistan, Turkmenistan, and Uzbekistan. Due to the crisscrossed infrastructure links set up by the Russian Federation among its former republics in Central Asia, countries in the Ferghana

Valley are interdependent in the supply of resources such as water and gas. Uzbekistan is totally dependent on Kyrgyzstan and Tajikistan for irrigation water, while the latter depend on their gas supplies from the former. Economic relations among the three countries have been lately the subject of tit-for-tat games over these resources. While bilateral swap agreements on water resources and energy (e.g., the agreement between Kyrgyzstan and Uzbekistan signed in December 2000) have averted major crises in the short term, they have proven to be dysfunctional in the long term due to complex political and economic problems between the upstream and downstream countries. Uzbekistan has imposed a gas embargo on Kyrgyzstan in winter 2000–2001 in order to coerce the latter into settling a territorial dispute over the Sokh enclave. To compensate for gas shortages, Kyrgyzstan diverted water resources into hydroelectric power generation, resulting in decreasing water supplies to Uzbek farms across the border.

A regional, integrative approach to dealing with resource-based conflicts has so far been rejected by Uzbekistan. The latter has also rejected international assistance in helping the countries reach consensus on a regionwide water management system. It fears that outside intervention will increase the bargaining power of the two weaker parties in this relationship, i.e., Kyrgyzstan and Tajikistan. Water is the one resource that gives Kyrgyzstan, and to some extent Tajikistan, leverage over its powerful neighbor. Uzbekistan's position has been that all Central Asia's water resources are "common wealth" that must be provided by the upstream countries, Kyrgyzstan and Tajikistan, at no cost. Kyrgyzstan has proceeded to defend its water resources. In March 2001, Kyrgyzstan declared that it was ready to provide 750 million cubic meters of water instead of the previously agreed-upon 2.3 billion cubic meters. Combined with the drought that has plagued the region for the last two years, this is having a devastating impact on Uzbekistan's cotton harvest. As stated earlier, President Akaev has signed on 23 July 2001 a law that seeks to impose charges for water usage in line with world prices. Both Tajikistan and Kyrgyzstan have proceeded to decrease their dependence on Uzbekistan for their energy supplies. The Kyrgyz government hopes to invest in the building of new hydropower stations over the next four years. The hope is that by 2005, Kyrgyzstan will produce enough electricity to meet its domestic needs. Tajikistan is making strong efforts to attract foreign investment in the hydropower sector. With its rich hydropower resources (presumed to have the eighth-highest concentration of such resources in the world), Tajikistan still relies on neighboring countries such as Uzbekistan to meet 20 percent of its energy needs. In order to attract investment into prospective hydropower projects, Tajikistan is considering a variety of options from joint ventures to direct investment. It has already transformed twenty-four power stations into joint stock companies, with the government holding all the initial shares. It has recently turned over the management of these shares to the Ministry of Power Engineering.[17] Enacting a new water management regime will be directly linked to the land privatization efforts. Unless farmers in the valley start using water more efficiently, any water management system will fail. Creating such incentives among the valley's farmers is tightly linked to a "real" land privatization effort by the government. So far, governments have seemed content to continue subsidizing the agricultural sector rather than privatize the land.

In dealing with the Islamic insurgency, the three countries sharing the Ferghana Valley differed in their assessment of the threat and consequently in their response to it. After fostering an Islamic revival in the 1990s following the Soviet collapse, Uzbekistan has recently come to perceive Islamic militancy as the most serious threat to its national security. Its official strategy for dealing with this threat has so far centered on repressive military measures. It has recently closed down more than nine hundred mosques in the Ferghana Valley region. Regional authorities regularly conduct house-to-house raids and mass arrests of groups of men who assemble in public. Government agents monitor mosques, even "official" ones, and men shave their beards for fear they will be labeled Islamic radicals. In Namangan, nearly everyone has a family member or friend who has been arrested. Recently, the Uzbek government has admitted that detention camps exist, though it is impossible to determine the exact number of detainees, believed to be in the thousands.[18] Recently, in Andijan more than three hundred people demonstrated in front of municipal administrations demanding that their relatives be released from jail.[19] In order to stem the cross-border IMU incursions, the Uzbek government has mined its borders with both Kyrgyzstan and Tajikistan, causing many civilian deaths. It has also imposed a strict visa regime that hampers cross-border trade in the valley. In March 2001, fifty ethnic Uzbeks holding Tajik citizenship and living in Uzbekistan were deported to the Tajik border on suspicion that they are IMU collaborators. In response to the August 1999 IMU incursion, Uzbekistan bombed territory in Tajikistan thought to be occupied by IMU followers, thus increasing the tensions that already existed between the two countries. Uzbekistan is still pursuing its policy of mining mountainous areas along the borders with Kyrgyzstan and Tajikistan, further indicating its intent to deal unilaterally with the IMU threat. Many observers believe that the increasing popularity of the militant groups in the valley, particularly of the IMU and Hizb ut-Tahrir, is as much a result of the government's repressive tactics and people's discontent with the region's economic decline.

Recent reports indicate that the IMU has changed its professed view of Kyrgyz territory as purely a corridor into Uzbekistan, and is now seeking to embroil Kyrgyzstan in a wider regional conflict. Kyrgyzstan's government has so far adopted a two-pronged approach to its interactions with the IMU: On the one hand, it has been building up its defense capabilities, while on the other, they made overtures to the IMU about negotiating a nonviolence pact.[20] However, negotiation overtures came to a halt after a Kyrgyz military court sentenced two IMU fighters to death for their participation in the August 2000 raids. The IMU had warned of retaliation if the death sentences are carried out. Kyrgyzstan' policy toward Islamic activists has recently become more restrictive. Distinctions are being made between "official" Islam and the independent

Muslim clergy. The latter are being closely monitored, especially in southern Kyrgyzstan. Following the 1999 incursions, a closer collaboration was established between the Kyrgyz Ministry for National Security and the Uzbek National Security Service. With the recent IMU incursions showing that the IMU is now operating inside the Kyrgyz territory, the Kyrgyz government is bound to increase its repressive tactics in southern Kyrgyzstan.

Tajikistan is the only country in Central Asia that has involved Islamists in its governing coalition. The 1997 peace accord between the government and the United Tajik opposition stipulated that 30 percent of the official posts be allocated to members of the opposition, which consisted mostly of Islamic Revival Party members. The current minister of emergencies, Mirza Ziyayev, is reputed to have fought alongside IMU leader Joma Namangani during the 1992–1997 Tajik civil war. There is now ample evidence that former United Tajik opposition militants have been involved with the IMU in the actual fighting in Kyrgyzstan and Uzbekistan. In May 2000, under pressure from its neighbors, Tajikistan expelled IMU fighters from its territories where they have been based for years. However, there are some in the Uzbek and Kyrgyz military who still believe that the IMU is utilizing bases in Tajikistan. Tajikistan's government is more threatened by Uzbekistan's policies than by the IMU. Uzbek raids inside Tajikistan in 1999 against IMU bases there killed civilians and damaged homes. Its strict visa regime has restricted Tajik citizens' travel throughout the region, given the fact that Tajikistan is almost exclusively dependent on Uzbekistan for transportation links to the outside world. Its mining of the borders has caused close to thirty civilian deaths in Tajikistan to date. Continuous accusations by the Uzbek president that Tajikistan is supporting the IMU is further exacerbating tensions between the two governments. Recently, he demanded that the Tajik government relieve its minister of emergency situations from his post on the grounds that he is a close ally of IMU leader Juma Namangani.[21] Tajikistan's government views the IMU's presence in Tajikistan as providing it with some leverage vis-à-vis the Uzbek government, which still harbors a dissident army officer, Mahmud Khudaiberdiyev, who attempted a coup in 1998 against the ruling elite. Both the Tajikistani government and the leadership of the Islamic Revival Party are now more worried about the activities of the Hizb ut-Tahrir in northern Tajikistan. A number of Hizb ut-Tahrir followers were captured in November 2000 and sentenced to terms in prison. Other followers of Hizb ut-Tahrir were recently captured in Dushanbe.

Due to different assessments in the three countries of the seriousness of the Islamic threat vis-à-vis their respective national security, multilateral regional attempts to counter this threat are likely to be limited. In June 2001, at a summit of the Shanghai Five, Uzbekistan joined the newly created Shanghai Cooperation Organization (SCO). In addition to Uzbekistan, SCO's members include China, Kazakhstan, Kyrgyzstan, Russia, and Tajikistan. One of the major aims of the SCO is to improve the regional response to radical Islam in Central Asia, including the creation of a regional antiterrorist center in Bishkek. However, recent statements by Uzbek president Karimov and Russian officials already attest to the difficulties facing the newly created organization.[22] The Uzbek president has expressed concern that the SCO should not become a Russian instrument to mount anti-U.S. initiatives in the region. Previous border demarcation agreements between China on the one hand and Kyrgyzstan and Tajikistan on the other are being reexamined, creating tensions among the three governments. Russia is becoming more concerned with Beijing's growing influence in the region and is concerned that the SCO might become a venue for China to pursue its ambitions in Central Asia. Furthermore, financial resources needed for the implementation of regional agreements such as the regional antiterrorist center have yet to materialize. A far more serious implication of the Islamic threat to the valley lies in the fact that it has provided the governments in the region the opportunity for diverting scarce governmental resources away from the developmental field and toward the security and military sectors.

Multi-Track Diplomacy

This section will focus on the efforts being undertaken by international governmental and nongovernmental organizations to manage some of the sources of tension in the Ferghana Valley. Few of these projects have involved cross-border partnerships, mostly due to Uzbekistan's resistance. Due to their mandate, some donor agencies, such as USAID, work mostly bilaterally with partners in the other states. Hence, they will find it hard to fund a regional project. Regional projects have so far been limited to two parts of the valley: southern Kyrgyzstan and northern Tajikistan. One or two projects are truly regional in their action plan and implementation policies in that they involve joint Kyrgyz-Tajik analytical and implementation teams. Southern Kyrgyzstan has benefited from much international aid and development assistance due to the fact that the Islamic insurgencies have hit it most in the past two years. Though many donor agencies now profess funding conflict-prevention projects, few are committed to the long-term agenda of a conflict-prevention program. To succeed, a conflict-prevention program cannot be subordinated to the three-to-five-year funding cycle of most development agencies. As correctly noted by Barnett Rubin, "The evolution of perceptions of Central Asia illustrates . . . a tendency to overemphasize operational prevention—intervention to halt escalation of violence—and under-emphasize structural prevention—establishing programs to strengthen fundamental factors that prevent conflict, such as governance and equitable development."[23] This section will discuss in brief the two projects that first brought the ideas of structural conflict prevention in the Ferghana Valley to the attention of Western policymakers, and then present four projects that promise much hope for long-term conflict prevention in the valley.

The United Nations—Ferghana Valley Development Program

This is the first international project to call for a comprehensive conflict-prevention approach in the Ferghana Valley. The project discusses three major challenges facing the Ferghana Valley: maintaining the interethnic peace and good community relations; promoting regional dialogue and cooperation on issues such as Islamic militancy and drug trafficking; and building regional institutions covering both the official and the civil-society sectors. The program called for a regional, trilateral program focusing on issues dealing with growth and sustainable development. The programmatic areas advocated by the program were five: (1) job creation and income generation; (2) establishing joint interethnic confidence-building measures; (3) regulation of cross-border trade and a related dialogue on the maintenance of transparent boundaries; (4) regional cooperation in the fields of language and education; and (5) revival of a common cultural heritage in the region. The program further advocated cross-border partnerships in the valley among NGOs and other civil-society organizations working in the region. The project officially began in August 1998, established its headquarters in Osh (Kyrgyzstan), and set up a bilingual website at <www.ferghana.elcat.kg>. Tajikistan and Kyrgyzstan participated in the program. The United Nations Development Program was the lead agency and funder in the countries where the program operated. Uzbekistan refused to participate in the program, and couched its refusal in terms of opposition to external conflict prevention in the valley. In reality, analysts now note that Uzbekistan's rejection of the program was due to its perception that this effort was a Kyrgyz attempt to intervene in Uzbekistan's affairs through international agencies.[24]

Center for Preventive Action (CPA) Project on the Ferghana Valley

The purpose of this project was to assess the potential for conflict in Central Asia by studying one of its most volatile areas and provide recommendations for policymakers on conflict prevention in the region. In addition to the interethnic schisms, this project's key premise focuses on "a range of economic, political, social, organized crime, environmental, security, and other factors that have long proved incendiary in this part of the world."[25] A project working group was assembled, chaired by former U.S. senator Sam Nunn, a very influential and widely respected policymaker, that included policy experts, business executives, journalists, national security experts, and members of the nongovernmental sector. A delegation of the working group traveled to the region in March 1997, visiting the Uzbek and Kyrgyz parts of the valley. Other members of the working group visited northern Tajikistan in May 1998. The working group report was issued in the form of a 1999 book titled *Calming the Ferghana Valley—Development and Dialogue in the Heart of Central Asia*. It recommended the following conflict-preventive measures in the valley: (1) creation of an information clearinghouse on the Ferghana Valley to assist both investment and foreign assistance; (2) promotion of cross-border civil-society initiatives in the fields of governance and human rights; (3) supporting efforts at regional intercultural dialogues; (4) focusing foreign development assistance on cross-border regional projects while maintaining bilateral aid; and (5) promoting foreign direct investment in the valley by pressing Uzbekistan to relax its currency and border restrictions.

The UNDP and the CPA projects were critical in putting the Ferghana Valley on policymakers' agendas, especially in the West, and in promoting an active interest and eventually engagement by the donor community in the valley.

Many of the ongoing development projects in the valley have adopted the principles and recommendations advocated by these first two initiatives. Following is a short description of four other projects that have much potential for regional conflict prevention in the Ferghana Valley.

Peace Promotion Program for Bordering Regions

This is one of the most ambitious, ongoing peace promotion programs, funded by the Swiss Agency for Development and Cooperation. It is a regional program involving a number of local NGOs in all three countries. It adopts a multifold strategy targeting the grass roots, and middle-level leadership in the region. This program includes a number of civil-society initiatives.

Cross-Border Conflict Prevention Project at the Community Level

Initiated in June 1999 and implemented by the Kyrgyz NGO Foundation for Tolerance International and Tajik NGO Ittifok, this program has offices in Batken and Leilek (southern Kyrgyzstan) and Isfara and Khujand (northern Tajikistan). It targets border communities that have manifested a potential for interethnic violence, and it promotes the prevention of such conflicts through:

- Application of consensus-building processes and the cultivation of the tradition of good neighborhood and mutual trust in managing emerging disputes
- Organization of joint educational, cultural, and social programs among neighboring communities
- Establishment and institutionalization of a regional network of community mediators who can help de-escalate local disputes
- Attracting public attention in the border communities to nonviolent methods of conflict resolution.

Goodwill Ambassadors Networks Project

This initiative's aim is to set up three national networks of unofficial diplomats in Uzbekistan, Tajikistan, and Kyrgyzstan. These unofficial networks promote conflict prevention through:

- Field visits to the Ferghana Valley, on the basis of which they can provide their former colleagues in the official sector with a more accurate analysis of the causes of conflict and sources of tension
- Sharing their experience with conflict management with the local leadership in the different communities, in the hope that this might help reduce the tensions
- Lobbying state authorities about the persistent problems
- Disseminating new ideas and approaches for conflict prevention and management in the decisionmaking bodies of the three countries

This project was initiated in June 2000 and has now established the three national networks. The networks have offices in Bishkek, Dushanbe, and Tashkent.

The project is being funded in collaboration with the Peace-Building Section of the Swiss Ministry of Foreign Affairs.

Rehabilitation of Physical Infrastructure Project
This initiative is being implemented by UNDP in Tajikistan and Kyrgyzstan through the United Nations Office for Project Services (UNOPS) and focuses on cross-border social infrastructure rehabilitation, mainly drinking water and irrigation.

Central Asia Media Support Project
This initiative promotes a regional dialogue among journalists, holds training seminars for journalists from all three countries on producing balanced and accurate news on regional issues, and produces bulletins on subregional media issues. It is a joint collaboration between the Geneva-based CIMERA Network and the Osh Media Resource Center.

Preventive Development in the South of Kyrgyzstan Program
The overall objectives of this program are to support the government of Kyrgyzstan and local communities in the south, to identify the root causes of conflict, and take the necessary measures for conflict prevention. It was established by the UNDP and the government of Kyrgyzstan. Though only focusing on four municipalities in the Batken province in south Kyrgyzstan, it is hoped that in the future this program will extend to other areas in the south of the country as well as to Tajikistan. It involves a three-pronged approach:

1. Establish a preventive development center to be equipped with an early warning system.
2. Support community-based organizations in carrying out community-wide projects through microcredit programs. Community members will receive training in the creation and management of small business enterprises.
3 Strengthen the law-enforcing capacities of the Batken provincial police department through provision of equipment, training, and vehicles.

The International Crisis Group Central Asia Project
The International Crisis Group (ICG) is a private multinational organization committed to strengthening the capacity of the international community to understand and act to prevent conflicts. The ICG project contributes to crisis prevention in the Ferghana Valley through:

- Research and analysis on political and socioeconomic trends in the valley and in the region in general. It opened an office in Osh in October 2000 where its staff conducts field research involving a wide range of sources.
- Publications in the forms of regular briefings and analytical reports including practical recommendations for international decisionmakers. It has so far published five reports on Central Asia and one briefing.

- Lobbying decisionmakers and the international media to keep the former informed about events as they unfold in the region and to build momentum for international action to avert a surge of violence regionwide.

Organization for Security and Cooperation in Europe (OSCE)
The OSCE has held a number of training workshops for the purpose of disseminating information about conflict analysis and prevention. Such seminars include a human-rights training program for Kyrgyz border guards, and training in the field of interethnic relations targeting officials in provincial and local administrations in south Kyrgyzstan as well as major ethnic communities. Monthly early warning reports by local monitors trained and employed by the OSCE are sent to the OSCE Commissioner on National Minorities.

Prospects
When covering the Ferghana Valley, the Western media has placed much emphasis on the Islamic threat in Central Asia, which diverted attention away from the root causes of conflict in that region. The root causes lie in poverty, repressive measures being undertaken against opposition and civil-society groups, corruption in the official sector creating a total disconnection between the governors and the governed, and poorly maintained and badly built infrastructure networks in the region. Official policies that focus solely on the Islamic threat and neglecting the root causes previously mentioned further exacerbate tensions and will, if sustained in the long term, lead to conflict escalation.

Official attempts at conflict management through repressive measures and crackdowns against Islamic groups and civil-society organizations are fueling rather than dampening people's anger and frustration. Visa regimes and mining of borders are further exacerbating simmering social and political frustrations and daily increasing the risks of local outbreaks of violence. Following 11 September 2001, repressive measures against Islamic groups have been on the rise, especially in Uzbekistan. There are valid concerns among the human-rights community that increased cooperation between the United States and Uzbekistan would result in less U.S. scrutiny of Uzbekistan's human-rights record. In the past, the United States has been one of Uzbekistan's strongest critics on human-rights violations. In February 2001, the U.S. State Department reported that the Uzbek government's poor human-rights record worsened, primarily due to the iron-fisted assault on independent political and religious expression. But as cooperation between the two countries increased following the launching of the U.S.-led antiterrorism war, official disapproval in Washington over Uzbek human-rights violations has turned silent. In October 2001, the U.S. State Department chose not to designate Uzbekistan as one of the countries of particular concern. An intensification of the government crackdown on all forms of religious expression might lead to increased popular support for militant movements such as the Islamic Movement of Uzbekistan and the Hizb ut-Tahrir. It might also lead to consolidation of efforts among the two movements and further radicalization of those such as Hizb ut-Tahrir, who have until now espoused nonviolent forms of opposition to the Uzbek government.

Following the U.S.-led antiterrorism campaign, countries in the region, including the three sharing the Ferghana Valley, have imposed additional restrictions on population movements across borders and a crackdown on illegal migration. These new security measures mean more hardship for residents of the Ferghana Valley, impeding cross-border trade and visits. Farmers who have previously depended on cross-border trade are now trying to find new sources of income. People find it very hard to visit relatives in neighboring countries. Border soldiers are trying to supplement their meager salaries with bribes imposed on those who want to cross to neighboring villages. A black-market economy is flourishing, especially in border communities, as small-scale entrepreneurs try to resell scarce goods purchased at a lower price across the border. Local economies in the valley are suffering due to decreased cross-border trade. There is a fear in the valley that poor economic conditions, especially in places such as Osh in Kyrgyzstan, might foster renewed interethnic tensions between Kyrgyz and Uzbeks similar to the ones that occurred in 1990.

Governments in the region have also stepped up their crackdown on illegal migrants as of late September 2001. Kyrgyzstan, for example, deported three hundred undocumented foreigners, mostly Tajiks and Afghans. This behavior has increased interstate friction in the region. Until recently, the drug trade has provided some funding to the militant groups. It has also contributed to the increase in criminal behavior, especially among the youth. Drug addiction is also on the increase, further weakening the region's economy due to the diversion of human and financial resources away from more productive sectors such as agriculture and industry. It is hoped that one of the positive outcomes of the U.S.-led antiterrorism campaign is a termination of Afghanistan's drugs industry. If that were to happen, there would be an urgent need to inject funds into the valley to provide alternative jobs for youth who used to be engaged in drug trafficking and to provide drug rehabilitation and treatment for drug addicts. Otherwise these unemployed youth will become eager recruits to Islamic militant movements. The real threats in the Ferghana Valley remain rooted in internal factors, mainly economic deprivation, lack of employment opportunities, total distrust in their government's ability and/or willingness to improve their living conditions, and anger at their government's repressive measures. One of the few valid generalizations in the literature on social protests and collective mobilizations is that social, violent mobilization of groups occurs when aggrieved groups cannot work through established channels, such as political parties or civil-society groups, to communicate new claims into the political process of authoritative decisionmaking.[26] Other factors that contribute to success of violent mobilization efforts include the intensity of deprivation, the resources of the mobilizing actors, the militants' strategic skills, and the counterstrategies of the opponents, i.e., governments. All these factors apply to today's situation in the Ferghana Valley. These factors are further exacerbated by a feeling of hopelessness that is quickly spreading among the population. People do not believe anymore that their respective governments are fair, willing to be inclusive, able to relate to their people, and/or willing to reform themselves to become less corrupt and more accountable. History has shown us that when people feel they are pushed against the wall and they have nothing to lose, they usually resort to drastic and violent measures.

The Ferghana Valley is now at a critical juncture where effective conflict-prevention efforts might push it away from the precipice to which it is now heading. An effective conflict-prevention intervention must be multisector and multilevel, and focus on structural rehabilitation, institutional reform, and attitudinal and behavioral change. A multilevel approach will involve simultaneously the national governments, the regional/local leaderships, and the civil-society organizations. A multisector intervention will focus on making information more accessible, promoting participation in decisionmaking processes, reforming education, restructuring national and local economies, and promoting governance and decentralization of the decisionmaking process. Structural rehabilitation will involve overhauling and in some cases rebuilding the infrastructure networks that are currently at the root of many of the local ethnic tensions in the valley. Institutional reform aims at eliminating the corruption that is rampant in official circles at the national, regional, and local levels. Corruption has eroded people's trust in their government and contributed to the feelings of injustice that fuel people's support for the Islamic militant groups.

Attitudinal and behavioral change is often bypassed or paid lip service in institutional efforts at conflict prevention. However, sustainability of conflict-prevention efforts rests on the success of programs that aim at changing people's attitudes about others and the conflict in general. Specifically, this implies creating mechanisms for nonviolent adjudication of conflict at the community level, introducing different habits for dealing with conflict, changing people's attitudes toward the enemy however the latter is defined, and strengthening people's collaborative problem-solving capacities and skills.

Recommendations

An effective conflict-prevention strategy should focus on the following tasks:

• Governments and donor agencies working in the region must reinvigorate economic reforms, target immediate humanitarian support to those sectors of the population living in extreme poverty, and create jobs through the promotion of better investment environments. While continuing to push for reforms at the macro level, donor agencies must focus at the micro level on promoting and strengthening the capacities and resources of existing community-based organizations to become the engines of economic growth in their communities.

• Establish a joint expert committee from Tajikistan, Uzbekistan, and Kyrgyzstan to assess the impact of the travel restrictions and border controls recently established in the valley. This committee should be funded by the international community and provided with outside expertise and training. While these controls should continue in the short-term to be part of the security measures to counter terrorist and drug-trafficking activities, in the long term they might prove to be counterproductive if they continue to limit cross-border trade and fuel people's anger and frustrations due to the humiliations inflicted on them by the border guards.

• Judicial systems in each of the three countries are in need of serious reform. The judicial systems must be allowed to be truly independent from the executive structures; judges must be better trained and paid, and subject to stiff sanctions if they were to accept bribes. In the Ferghana Valley, people view the judicial system as corrupt, inefficient, and incapable of providing an impartial venue for channeling their grievances. In such a context, it is no wonder that people resort to violence.

• Efforts at reducing corruption in the administrative and security state structures must be strengthened. Such efforts could take the form of strict legal sanctions for those officials who accept bribes, electing rather than appointing local officials, new standards of personnel management to ensure an educated work force, transparent hiring practices to ensure that ethnic minorities are not discriminated against, and better pay for personnel to help them meet their family basic needs. In the Ferghana Valley, border and customs officers are most notable for their corrupt and humiliating practices.

• Establish a multi-issue, multiparty negotiation process to simultaneously address border, water, and energy issues in the valley. This process should be held under the aegis of a respected, impartial third party. In July 2001, a regional effort at dealing with energy issues paid off when representatives from the five Central Asian energy ministries signed a treaty in Bishkek forming a regional energy grid. This grid should foster efficient trading of power resources among the five Central Asian states and is likely to be of benefit to the Ferghana Valley energy problems. This approach should also allow more efficient production and distribution of power throughout the region and facilitate quick decisions about when and where to send surplus power.[27] However this regional treaty does not deal with the water issues in the region. Unlike energy, some governments in the region are neither ready nor willing to pay for water. In particular, Kazakhstan and Uzbekistan announced that they find the idea of paying for water to be "unacceptable" and a violation of international norms. The United States Agency for International Development has been pushing for a solution linking water and energy, which Uzbekistan has so far found unacceptable. An unofficial process involving trusted experts from the three countries, and moderated by international experts in these issues, could be promoted and funded by the international community.

• Governments in the region should abandon the repressive measures against their clergy, the political opposition, and members of the civil society. They need take a look at the modern history of neighboring Iran and conclude that such measures did not help the shah in preventing the Islamic opposition from assuming power. There is a fear that U.S.-led efforts to counter terrorism in Afghanistan have led regimes in Central Asia to believe that all forms of oppression against their opposition, as long as the latter are labeled Islamist, would be accepted by the international community. The international community must send a strong message that such behavior is unacceptable. Islam is an integral part of Central Asian societies, and won't go away. Seventy years of communism failed to achieve that and any efforts by these three governments to suppress it will likely fail and eventually backfire on them. The donor community must push for a dialogue in each of these countries involving the government, the Islamic clergy, and the civil-society structures. However, it is extremely important that this dialogue not involve outside voices or "experts." Unless it is locally owned, initiated, and facilitated, such a dialogue will be labeled as a Western attempt at containing the Islamic revival movement in Central Asia.

• In addressing the structural causes of conflicts in the region, especially water-based disputes, donors must adopt a twofold strategy. In the long term, the Soviet-built irrigation and water supply networks must be totally overhauled. In the short term, they must focus on the localities where water-based conflicts have taken on an ethnic character and which, if not addressed, might provide the spark for regionwide interethnic violence. Needs-assessment teams including engineers and conflict-management specialists must work together in identifying those communities in the valley most at risk for this type of conflict. The Swiss Development Corporation has been most successful in following this strategy in its "peace promotion for bordering regions" project.

• Training in conflict-management techniques must be organized at all levels in the valley, involving the regional and local official leaders, community leaders, and civil-society organizations. These training workshops must focus on fostering in the participants skills of conflict analysis and collaborative problem-solving behavior. Conflict prevention is most successful if done quickly and locally. This requires certain skills and abilities: skills in conflict monitoring, conflict analysis, dispute system design, consensus building, negotiation and mediation, and strategic planning. Civil-society organizations and local experts in "conflictology" lack minimal expertise in this field. It is important that such training programs be designed for regional and local officials, members of traditional institutions such as the council of elders, local staff of nongovernmental organizations, teachers, and high school and university students. These local stakeholders can then provide a local cadre working to promote different attitudes about the "enemy" and new habits of collaborative problem-solving behavior.

• Free information flow is essential for equal opportunity, consensus building, and keeping the state structures accountable. Governments in the region must be pushed to honor the freedom of the press and combat the harassment of journalists.

• Drug addiction and consequently AIDS are on the increase in the different regions of the valley. Regional antidrug educational programs must target the at-risk communities, mostly involving unemployed youth. Young men and women get drafted into the business due to lack of other employment opportunities and the good pay. It is hoped that with increased attention focused on the region, more aid will flow into drug prevention programs and projects to create alternative sources of employment for the Ferghana Valley's unemployed youth.

Resources

Newsletters and Periodicals

Central Asia and the Caucasus–Journal of Social and Political Studies, Central Asia and the Caucasus Information and Analytical Center, Sweden

Central Asia–Caucasus Analyst, the Central Asia–Caucasus Institute of the Johns Hopkins University, the Nitze School of Advanced International Studies

Central Asia Monitor

Information Analytical Bulletin, International Centre Interbilim, Bishkek

Reporting Central Asia, Institute for War and Peace Reporting, London

The Central Eurasian Studies Review, the Central Eurasian Studies Society

Turkistan Newsletter, Research Center for Turkistan, Azerbaijan, Crimea, Caucasus and Siberia in the Netherlands

Reports

International Crisis Group's Central Asia Project

"Afghanistan and Central Asia: Priorities for Reconstruction and Development." *Asia Report* No. 26, 27 November 2001.

"Central Asian Perspectives on 11 September and the Afghan Crisis," briefing, 28 September 2001.

"Central Asia: Crisis Conditions in Three States," *Asia Report* No. 7, 7 August 2000.

"Central Asia: Drugs and Conflict." *Asia Report* No. 25, 26 November 2001.

"Central Asia: Fault Lines in the New Security Map," *Asia Report* No. 20, 4 July 2001.

"Incubators of Conflict: Central Asia's Localized Poverty and Social Unrest," *Asia Report* No. 16, 8 June 2001.

"Islamist Mobilisation and Regional Security," *Asia Report* No. 14, 1 March 2001.

"Kyrgyzstan at Ten—Trouble in the 'Island of Democracy,'" *Asia Report* No. 22, 28 August 2001.

"Recent Violence in Central Asia: Causes and Consequences," *Central Asia Briefing,* 18 October 2000.

"Uzbekistan at Ten—Repression and Instability," *Asia Report* No. 21, 21 August 2001.

Royal Institute for International Affairs, *Western Engagement in the Caucasus and Central Asia,* by Neil MacFarlane, 1999.

United Nations Development Program

Kyrgyzstan Human Development Report, 1998, 1999, and 2000.

Tajikistan Human Development Report, 1998, 1999, and 2000.

Uzbekistan Human Development Report, 1998, 1999, and 2000.

United States Institute of Peace, *The Challenges of Regional Cooperation in Central Asia: Preventing Ethnic Conflict in the Ferghana Valley,* by Anara Tabyshalieva, June 1999.

Other Publications

Calming the Ferghana Valley: Development and Dialogue in the Heart of Central Asia, by Sam Nunn, Nancy Lubin, and Barnett Rubin. New York, The Century Foundation Press, 1999.

Central Asia: Conflict, Resolution, and Change, edited by Roald Sagdeev and Susan Eisenhower. Chevy Chase, MD, Center for Post-Soviet Studies, January 1995.

Central Asia's New States: Independence, Foreign Policy, and Regional Security, by Martha Brill Olcott. Washington, DC, United States Institute of Peace, October 1997.

Civil Society in Central Asia, edited by M. Holt Ruffin and Daniel Waugh. Seattle, University of Washington Press, 1999.

Conflict, Cleavage and Change in Central Asia and the Caucasus, edited by Karen Dawisha and Bruce Parrott. Cambridge, Cambridge University Press, 1997.

Islam and Central Asia: An Enduring Legacy or an Evolving Threat? edited by Susan Eisenhower and Roald Sagdeev. Washington, DC, The Center for Political and Strategic Studies, June 2000.

Political Islam and Conflicts in Russia and Central Asia, by Lena Johnson and Murad Esenov. Stockholm, The Swedish Institute of International Affairs, 1999.

The New Central Asia: The Creation of Nations, by Olivier Roy. New York, New York University Press, 1999.

The Resurgence of Central Asia: Islam or Nationalism? by Ahmad Rashid. Karachi, Oxford University Press, May 1999.

Selected Internet Sites

www.camsp.osh.kg/ (Central Asia Media Support Project)

www.crisisweb.org/ (ICG's Asia reports are available at this site)

www.eurasianet.org/ (An Open Society Institute site that provides an independent source of news and analysis about Central Asia and the Caucasus)

www.fas.harvard.edu/~casww/ICG-CAP.html (The International Crisis Group's Central Asia Project website)

www.fas.harvard.edu/~cess/ (The website of the Central Eurasian Studies Society)

www.ferghana.elcat.kg/ (Ferghana Valley Development Programme)

www.fti.kyrnet.kg/ (The Foundation of Tolerance International, Ferghana Valley List-server Archive, by date)

www.icarp.org (Interactive Central Asia Research Project)

www.internews.ru/ (An independent news service that covers events in Central Asia)

www.iwpr.net/index.pl?centasia_index.html (Institute for War and Peace Reporting, Central Eurasia Resource Pages)

www.times.kg (Online version of the weekly English language newspaper *The Times of Central Asia*)

Resource Contacts

Vicken Cheterian, CIMERA, e-mail: vicken.cheterian@cimera.org

John Gely, Swiss Agency for Development and Cooperation, Tashkent, e-mail: johan.gely@tas.rep.admin.ch

Jonathan Goodhand, INTRAC, e-mail: intrac@gn.apc.org

Altaaf Hasham, Agha Khan Foundation, e-mail: akfgarm@atge.automail.com

Raya Kadyrova, Foundation Tolerance International, e-mail: fti@infotel.kg

Kamol Kamilov, Center of Youth Initiatives, e-mail: davron@cyi.khj.tajik.net

Irene Leibundgut, Swiss Coordination Office, e-mail: irene@swisscoop.kg

Rasoul Rakhimov, United Nations Office for Drug Control and Crime Prevention, e-mail: rakhimov@odccp.tojikiston.com

Elena Sadovkaya, Center for Conflict Management, e-mail: ccm@online.ru

John Schoeberlein, Forum for Central Asian Studies, Harvard University, e-mail: schoeber@fas.harvard.edu

Anara Tabyshalieva, Institute for Regional Studies, e-mail: ifrs@elcat.kg

Data on the following organizations can be found in the Directory section:

In Kyrgyzstan
Foundation for Tolerance International
Institute for Regional Studies
Osh Media Resource Center

In Tajikistan
Center for Youth Initiatives, Ittifok

International
CIMERA
International Crisis Group
Office of the OSCE High Commissioner on National Minorities

Randa Slim (Dayton, Ohio, USA) focuses on consulting and training in the fields of conflict management and public participation. Since 1993, Slim has been a member of the Inter-Tajik Dialogue, an unofficial dialogue focusing on the conflict in Tajikistan. She is currently the principal consultant for the Inter-Tajik Dialogue civic initiative, a three-year project funded by a consortium of U.S. foundations. She is also a consultant for the Peace Promotion Project in the Ferghana Valley funded by the Swiss Agency for Development and Cooperation. Randa Slim can be reached at <randaslim@aol.com>

Notes

1. Ahmed Rashid, *The Resurgence of Central Asia—Islam or Nationalism?* Cambridge, Oxford University Press, 1994, p. 17.

2. Nancy Lubin and Barnett Rubin, *Calming the Ferghana Valley: Development and Dialogue in the Heart of Central Asia*, New York, The Council on Foreign Relations, 1999, p. 41.

3. ICG, "Central Asia: Crisis Conditions in Three States," *Asia Report* No 7, August 2000, p. 2.

4. Asad Sadulloyev, "SOS: Jaga Is Going Out," *Central Asian News* from Ferghana, 2 February 2001.

5. Arslan Koichiev, "Skirmishes Suggest IMU Is Changing Tactics," *Eurasia Insight,* 6 August 2001.

6. Lubin and Rubin, *Calming the Ferghana Valley*, p. 59.

7. Arslan Koichiev, "Batken Residents Furious over Secret Kyrgyz-Uzbek Deal," *Eurasia Insight,* 25 April 2001.

8. Anara Tabyshalieva, *The Challenges of Regional Cooperation in Central Asia—Preventing Ethnic Conflict in the Ferghana Valley,* Washington, DC, United States Institute of Peace, 1999, p. 26.

9. Lubin and Rubin, *Calming the Ferghana Valley,* p. 66; "Incubators of Conflict: Central Asia's Localised Poverty and Social Unrest," *International Crisis Group Report,* no. 16, 8 June 2001, p. 8.

10. Ahmed Rashid, "Confrontation Brews Among Islamic Militants in Central Asia," *Turkistan Newsletter,* 22 November 2000.

11. ICG, *Asia Report* No 14, p. 11; Rashid, "Confrontation Brews."

12. ICG, *Asia Report* No 14, p. 11.

13. ICG, "Central Asia: Fault Lines in the New Security Map," *Asia Report* No. 20, 4 July 2001, p. 6.

14. Gregory Gleason, "Tajikistan Minister's Murder Points to Drug-Route Conflict," *Eurasia Insight,* 16 April 2001.

15. Tabyshalieva, *The Challenges of Regional Cooperation,* p. 27.

16. Lubin and Rubin, *Calming the Ferghana Valley,* p. 79.

17. Daler Nurkhanov, "Tajikistan, Kyrgyzstan Seek to Bolster Power Generating Capacity, Break Energy Dependence," *Eurasia Insight,* 2 August 2001.

18. ICG, *Asia Report* No. 14, p. 7.

19. Musaev Bakhodir, "Uzbeks Losing Patience: Uzbeks Take to the Streets to Air Anti-Government Grievances," *Reporting Central Asia,* no. 47, 10 April 2001.

20. Arslan Koichiev, "Kyrgyz Soldiers Reportedly Clash with IMU Fighters," *Eurasia Insight,* 26 July 2001.

21. "Uzbek President Urges Tajik Authorities to Sack Opposition Minister," Voice of the Islamic Republic of Iran, via BBC Worldwide Monitoring, 12 August 2001.

22. "Russia Has Misgivings About Shanghai Cooperation Organization," *Eurasia Insight,* 20 June 2001.

23. Barnett Rubin, unpublished document, 2001, p. 36.

24. Ibid., p. 27.

25. Lubin and Rubin, *Calming the Ferghana Valley,* p. xii.

26. Herbert Kitschelt, "Social Movements, Political Parties, and Democratic Theory," *Annals of the American Academy of Political and Social Science,* no. 528, July 1993.

27. Gregory Gleason, "Mixing Oil and Water: Central Asia's Emerging Energy Market," *Eurasia Insight,* 27 August 2001.

6.7

Tajikistan: From Civil War to Peacebuilding

Randa M. Slim & Faredun Hodizoda

Tajikistan, along with other former Soviet republics, declared its independence in September 1991. With a weak state structure, independence engendered a struggle for power and national identity resulting in civil war and the installation of an authoritarian regime run by former members of the Communist Party of Tajikistan. This war has resulted in thousands of deaths and thousands of refugees who have fled their country to neighboring Afghanistan, Pakistan, and Russia. In the conflict, the government and its allies were confronted by a loosely united Tajik opposition including Islamists, democrats, and nationalists. In April 1994, a United Nations mediation effort was launched for the purpose of bringing a lasting peaceful settlement to the conflict. This mediation effort lasted three years and ended on 27 June 1997 with the signing in Moscow of the General Agreement on the Establishment of Peace and National Accord in Tajikistan. Tajikistan is now in the midst of a postconflict peacebuilding phase that will determine the future sustainability of the 1997 general agreement.

The causes of the Tajik civil war are many. Some are rooted in the history of Tajikistan, some in the breakdown of the Soviet Union, some in regional politics, and some in the historical events that led to the establishment of today's Tajikistan. As Olivier Roy puts it, "Most of the difficulties of present-day Tajikistan are linked to the very definitions of what is Tajikistan and what is a Tajik."[1] Tajikistan appeared on the map in the mid-1920s, along with the other countries of Central Asia, when the Soviets territorially divided Turkestan, which they inherited from the tsars and the Emirates of Bukhara and Kokand. The present Tajik republic was first divided between the Soviet Republic of Turkestan (created in 1918) and the People's Republic of Bukhara (1920). Later, it became an autonomous region of the new Republic of Uzbekistan, then an autonomous republic in Uzbekistan (1925), and in 1929, a full Soviet Socialist Republic.

TAJIKISTAN
Population (millions): 6.1 (2001, UNFPA)
Conflict related deaths: 157,000 (2000)
Conflict related IDPs: 600,000
Repatriated refugees by 1999: 50,000

The 1920s division was not fair to Tajikistan. Only a small portion of the total Tajik population lived in the newly established state, and the Tajik's two most important intellectual and cultural centers, Bukhara and Samarkand, were placed within the borders of Uzbekistan. Instead, the small city of Dushanbe became the capital of the new republic. Stripping Tajikistan of its cultural centers undermined the formation of a Tajik intelligentsia and deprived Tajikistan of critical human resources for state building. It also hindered the development of a strong ethnic Tajik identity and strengthened the influence of local and regional affiliations on political loyalties, a phenomenon referred to by the Tajiks as *mahalgerai* ("localism"). Furthermore, a poorly developed transportation infrastructure reinforced the isolation of the different Tajik regions, impeding the establishment of relations among them.

Tajikistan was the center of the Basmachi resistance movement against the Bolsheviks and Soviet control of Central Asia in 1918–1928. A period of repression and collectivization followed that led to the depopulation and forced resettlement of certain groups in the republic. Stalin further insisted on staffing the Communist Party and the state apparatus with ethnic Tajiks. Thousands of Tajiks with limited Marxist education were enlisted in the party apparatus. The traditional regional networks of authority, power, and benefits soon infiltrated the Soviet power machinery in Tajikistan. The primary base of power for the new regime in the 1940s became the district of Khujand, renamed Leninabad. Though part of Tajikistan, the region had always been more closely linked by geography and trade to Uzbekistan than to the rest of Tajikistan. Throughout Soviet rule, the north was the economic powerhouse of Tajikistan, and the home of all republican Communist Party first secretaries from 1943 until independence in 1991. The Khujandis endorsed localism as the basis of their policy in Tajikistan and channeled the majority of their allocations from the central budget to industrial development in their province. During Soviet rule, northern Tajikistan prospered in comparison to the south, a tendency reinforced by a large-scale Soviet resettlement policy imposed to meet labor needs. Following World War II, many people from the Karategin Valley and Gorno-Badakhshan were moved into the southwestern province of Qurghan-Teppa, leading to tension and resentment on the part of the locals, mainly Kölabis, toward the newly settled groups. In the 1970s, the Communist Party leaders sought to broaden their political base and started involving people from the southern conservative district of Kölab, motivated, quite probably, by a desire to broaden their political base and forge an alliance with the south. Following the invasion of Afghanistan, elites from Gorno-Badakhshan were promoted by the Russian KGB in the ranks of the local KGB. Few political elites were recruited from other regions of Tajikistan.

The monopoly on political power exercised by the Khujand-Kölab alliance created much resentment among the intelligentsia of the other regions and led, with the advent of *perestroika*, to the formation of opposition movements. In 1991, these opposition forces included the Islamic Renaissance Party, the Democratic Party of Tajikistan, the La'li Badakhshon and Nosiri Khusraw societies, as well as forces loyal to the republic's official Islamic clergy. In 1991, they formed an opposition coalition with the aim of rooting out localism, uniting the nation, and building an independent democratic nation. With the exception of La'li Badakhshon and Nosiri Khusraw, which were regionally based nonpolitical associations, all other opposition forces operated as national parties.

Officially registered in December 1991, the Islamic Renaissance Party (IRP) called for the revival of the role of Islam in both political and everyday life. It declared Islam the guiding principle of the party while its immediate tasks involved establishing a legal and democratic state. Two other opposition parties were the nationalist Rastokhez Popular Movement and the Democratic Party of Tajikistan, an anti-Marxist reformist party calling for an end to totalitarianism and localism, and supporting democracy, a market economy, and a more equitable distribution of power.

In addition to these local actors, Russia and Uzbekistan played crucial roles in the developing conflict by taking sides with the governing coalition against the opposition. As Sergei Gretsky puts it, "It was outside interference that turned civic strife in Tajikistan into civil war." Russia's "Near Abroad Policy" aimed to (1) protect the interests of Russians living in those areas, (2) stop migration to Russia from those areas, and (3) maintain stability in neighboring regions, especially on Russia's southern borders. A variety of Russian interest groups, including officers in the Russian 201st Motorized Rifle Division based in Tajikistan, were able to make the argument inside the Kremlin that Russia must support the government coalition to prevent the spread of Islamic fundamentalism in Central Asia and an exodus of Russians from Tajikistan.

Two factors prompted Uzbekistan's leader, Islam Karimov, to back the Tajik government. *Perestroika* brought a revival of age-old rivalries between the Tajiks and Uzbeks, and with *glasnost* came demands in Tajikistan, Bukhara, and Samarkand for the return of these two intellectual and cultural centers to Tajikistan and for the protection of the rights of the Tajik population living in Uzbekistan. At the same time, Karimov faced domestic opposition and feared that any opposition success in Tajikistan might send the wrong message to the Uzbek opposition.

Conflict Dynamics

In February 1990, two weeks prior to Tajikistan's first parliamentary elections, violent riots erupted in Dushanbe, sparked by public anger in response to rumors that large numbers of refugees from the Armenian earthquake were to be rehoused in the capital. Blaming the Rastokhez Popular Movement for instigating the riots, the government banned opposition parties from the upcoming elections. In March 1990, those elections produced a Communist Party–dominated parliament. In December 1990, a multiparty system was adopted, and new political parties and movements were subsequently established, including the Democratic Party of Tajikistan and the IRP. In August 1991, after president Quahhar Mahkamov backed the coup attempt in Moscow, angry protesters in Dushanbe demanded his resignation. On 9 September 1991, the Tajik Supreme Soviet declared Tajikistan's independence and Mahkamov immediately resigned. He was replaced by Kadreddin Aslonov, who suspended Communist Party activities and froze its assets, but Aslonov was then ousted by parliament and replaced by former party first secretary Rahmon Nabiev.

However, after fourteen days of street protests, Nabiev stepped down and called for presidential elections. During the November 1991 elections, opposition parties including the Democratic Party and IRP, and the Rastokhez Popular Movement united and presented an opposition candidate, Davlat Khudonazarov,

Stephen Dupont/Panos Pictures

Tajik refugees in North Afghanistan

who was defeated in what most observers considered to be seriously flawed elections. Former communists from the Khujand and Kölab regions were over-represented in the new regime under the leadership of Nabiev. Soon after, a series of repressive measures was implemented preventing opposition forces from assuming any role in the governing structure. In March 1992, opposition followers began a fifty-two-day rally in Shahidon Square. Pro-government forces responded with their own demonstrations and in May 1992, opposition and pro-government forces clashed violently, with the Russian military, still present in the country, supplying arms to the government. In an attempt to prevent further escalation of the conflict, President Nabiev put together a coalition government, the Government of National Reconciliation (GNR), with a third of the ministerial posts allocated to the opposition. But hard-line elements, primarily from Kölab and Khujand, opposed the move and declared the new government to be invalid because it had not been approved by parliament. In mid-May 1992, the armed conflict shifted to the south, and by June fierce fighting had broken out across the country between the supporters of the coalition government and forces loyal to the old Soviet order. In September 1992, Popular Front militiamen broke through the blockade of Kölab and killed a large number of opposition supporters in the Qurghan-Teppa region, causing hundreds of thousands to flee to neighboring countries.

There followed a period of instability, during which President Nabiev was forced to resign. A government of "national reconciliation" was formed under parliament chairman Akbarsho Iskandarov, and the government survived a coup attempt. A the end of 1992, Iskandarov resigned and a new government was formed, headed by the chairman of the parliament, the Kölabi Imomali Rahmonov. With no representation from the opposition, this government was comprised almost exclusively of Kölabis and Leninabadi Communist Party members. It soon repealed all previous GNR legislation, banned opposition parties and newspapers, and merged Qurghan-Teppa and Kölab into the newly created Khatlon Province.

The Uzbek and Russian governments decided that their national interests were being jeopardized by the chaotic situation in Tajikistan, and agreed, along with the governments of Kazakhstan and Kyrgyzstan, to intervene with peacekeeping forces from the Commonwealth of Independent States (CIS). These forces included troops from the Russian 201st Motorized Rifle Division and additional troops from Uzbekistan, Kyrgyzstan, and Kazakhstan. In early December 1992, after days of brutal fighting, the Kölabi Popular Front troops, supported by Russian and Uzbek troops, entered Dushanbe. When Rahmonov was named head of state, a Kölabi headed Tajikistan for the first time in modern history. Kölabi troops conducted a campaign of murder and terror against the pro-opposition Pamiris and Karateginis. This resulted in mass displacement of refugees into Afghanistan. Arrest warrants and death sentences were issued for the opposition leaders, who were blamed for the war. The opposition leadership fled to Moscow, Iran, and Afghanistan. During the period of March through August 1993, the government consolidated its power throughout the country. Opposition groups, now stationed in Afghanistan, launched an offensive across the Panj River from Afghanistan into southern Tajikistan, targeting both Russian and pro-government forces.

Between 1993 and the signing of the peace accords in June 1997, the opposition forces constantly skirmished with Russian border guards and pro-government forces. A number of cease-fire agreements were signed following the launch of UN-mediated negotiations in April 1994. During this period, the pro-government bloc was wracked by dissension, with a split between the Kölabi governing leadership and what came to be called the new or third force, the Khujandis, and a further split within the Kölabi camp itself. Although the Democratic Party of Tajikistan also splintered and differences emerged between the political and military wings of the opposition, overall relations within the opposition forces remained cooperative and civil.

The governing coalition was first forged in 1992 when the Khujandis, seeking military support, invited economic leaders and crime bosses from Kölab to join a coalition against the Islamic-democratic opposition. The Kölabis were rewarded when Rahmonov was named head of state in December 1992 and in the new government, the Kölabis were a majority. The Khujandis, who still maintained control over the important economic and security posts, assumed that once the opposition was taken care of, they could reinstate a Khujandi as head of state. But regional factors including a shift in Russia's policy toward Uzbekistan and its allies in the region disrupted their political calculations. Russia threw its support to Rahmonov and in 1993 Abdulmajid Dostiev, Rahmonov's first deputy, formed a pro-Kölab People's Party of Tajikistan. Rahmonov eventually forced the dismissal of his prime minister, Abdumalik Abdullajanov, a powerful Khujandi political leader. Most political and security officials in the province of Leninabad were sacked and replaced by Kölabis.

In November 1994, Rahmonov defeated his opponent, Abdumalik Abdullajanov, in a presidential election, and in February 1995 his supporters won an overwhelming victory in parliamentary elections. But because of both fraud and legislative restrictions, these elections were widely condemned by outside observers.

In May 1996, in the first significant sign of northern concern about the Kölabi-dominated government, there was serious unrest, including riots, in Khujand and Öra-Teppe, followed by the arrest and imprisonment without trial of hundreds of demonstrators. The riots were sparked by the murder of a prominent Leninabadi businessman, but soon developed into political protests over the disproportionate influence of Kölabis in Leninabad. In July 1996, Abdumalik Abdullojanov and two other prime ministers from northern Tajikistan, Abdujalil Samadov and Jamshed Karimov, formed the National Revival Movement, which constituted a "third force" in Tajik politics. In mid-April 1997, a protest in the Khujand prison involving the jailed leaders of the May 1996 riots was violently suppressed and it is estimated that more than 150 inmates died. These events culminated on 30 April 1997 in an assassination attempt on Rahmonov. Two people died in a grenade attack and seventy-three were injured, including the president. Using the attack as an excuse, the Tajik government immediately initiated a widespread crackdown on the "new" opposition in the Leninabad region, including arrests, beatings, and disappearances.

A similar split occurred within the Kölabi camp. The Kölabi militia, the Popular Front of Tajikistan, consisted of two major factions: Kölabi and Hisari. The Hisari group included units from districts with a substantial ethnic Uzbek population, where the communists had always enjoyed support. In 1993, the relations between the two factions turned sour when the government of Tajikistan declared its intention to form the armed forces of Tajikistan out of Kölabi units only. In May 1994, Kölabis and Hisaris battled each other just outside Dushanbe—an indication that localism prevailed not only at the regional level, but had also permeated the lower administrative echelons of the society to the district level.

The exiled opposition forces concentrated themselves in Afghanistan, Moscow, and Gorno-Badakhshan, with some troops operating in the Karategin Valley. The Islamic military forces, headed by Said Abdullah Nurwere, were located in Afghanistan, and consisted of forces loyal to the Muslim cleric Qazi Kalan A. Turajonzoda and IRP supporters. The political/secular opposition was based in Moscow. Now called the Coordinating Center of Tajik Democratic forces in the CIS, it united members of the Democratic Party, Rastokhez, different Pamiri groups, and other activists and intellectuals. Otakhon Latifi, former deputy prime minister of Tajikistan, headed the center. In July 1995, the various groups forming the opposition created the United Tajik Opposition, headed by Said Abdullah Nuri. The United Tajik Opposition (UTO) then became the main interlocutor for the opposition during negotiations.

Official Conflict Management

UN involvement in the Tajikistan war was initiated in September 1992 by the address of Uzbek president Islam Karimov to the UN Secretary-General, supported by Finnish president Mauno Koivisto. A mission visited Tajikistan in October, and then in January 1993 a small United Nations unit of political, military, and humanitarian officers was dispatched to monitor the situation on the ground. Ismat Kittani was appointed special envoy to Tajikistan in April 1993, followed in January 1994 by Ramiro Pirez-Ballon. Their efforts at promoting peacemaking bore fruit when both sides to the conflict agreed to come to negotiations in Moscow in April 1994. The special envoy chaired three rounds of talks, leading to a temporary cease-fire and the establishment of a joint commission to oversee its implementation. In December, the Security Council established the United Nations Mission of Observers to Tajikistan to monitor the implementation of cease-fire, maintain contact with the conflicting parties, and support the efforts of the UN Secretary-General's special envoy.

In February 1994, the Organization for Security and Cooperation in Europe also opened a permanent office in Tajikistan with a mandate to promote institution building, assist in establishing a constitution, organize democratic elections, and survey human-rights conditions. The mission was given the status of observer at ongoing UN-mediated talks.

The Inter-Tajik Dialogue on national reconciliation lasted until June 1997. From the beginning, they were held under the auspices of the United Nations. Representatives of Russia, Uzbekistan, Iran, Pakistan, Kazakhstan, Kyrgyzstan, Afghanistan, and Turkmenistan, with the OSCE and the Organization of Islamic Conference (OIC) participating as observers. The venue of the talks shifted among the capitals of the observer countries. Having these countries as observers helped mitigate the potential negative influence of some of the neighboring countries' policies on the domestic actors. Both Russia and Iran played important roles at critical junctures by persuading their allies to make necessary compromises.

The General Agreement on the Establishment of Peace and National Accord in Tajikistan (hereafter, General Agreement) is the name given to a package of nine documents that were signed in the course of eight rounds of negotiations between the delegations of the government of Tajikistan and the UTO, and numerous other meetings. The General Agreement stipulated a transition period of twelve to eighteen months during which all the protocols of the agreement were to be implemented. During the transitional period, the following provisions would be implemented:

- 30 percent UTO representation in government executive structures
- Voluntary and safe return of all refugees and internally displaced people
- Disbanding, disarmament, and reintegration of opposition forces into government power structures
- Reform of government structures
- Constitutional amendments
- Amendments to the law on elections, the law on political parties legalizing banned opposition and other political parties and movements, and the law on mass media allowing the functioning of free and objective mass media
- Full exchange of prisoners of war and other forcibly detained people
- Adoption of an Amnesty Law and an Act on Mutual Forgiveness
- Establishment of a Central Electoral Commission for conducting elections and referenda, with 25 percent UTO representation in its composition
- Setting the date for new parliamentary elections

The principal mechanism for the implementation of the General Agreement was the Commission on National Reconciliation (CNR). The CNR was established with equal representation from both sides (thirteen members each). The CNR chairman was the UTO leader, Said Abdullah Nuri, with the first deputy speaker of parliament, Abdulmajid Dostiev, as deputy chairman. Following the first plenary meeting in Moscow in July 1997, the CNR's mandate went into full effect on 15 September 1997, with a working plan prepared by its four subcommissions to complete the schedule of implementation within twelve to eighteen months. The four subcommissions respectively dealt with the protocols concerning political, legal, military, and refugee issues. Two subcommissions were headed by government representatives and two by UTO representatives. An expert group was also established in September 1997 to administer the Amnesty Law. Each subcommission and the expert group consisted of six members, based on equal representation of the government and UTO.

The main monitoring entity of the implementation of the General Agreement was the Contact Group (CG), consisting of eight states (Afghanistan, Iran, Kazakhstan, Kyrgyzstan, Pakistan, Russia, Turkmenistan, and Uzbekistan) and three international organizations (OIC, OSCE, and the UN) with the special representative of the UN Secretary-General serving as coordinator. In addition to its monitoring functions, CG provided expertise, advice, good offices, and recommendations on ways to ensure the parties' compliance with the General Agreement.

Multi-Track Diplomacy

The Inter-Tajik Dialogue

The Inter-Tajik Dialogue, which first met in Moscow in March 1993, was established to provide a forum for pro-government and pro-opposition Tajikistani citizens to come together and discuss the root causes of the Tajik conflict. The objective then was to see whether a group could be formed from within the civil conflict to design a peace process for their own country. The dialogue was conducted under the auspices of the Dartmouth Conference Regional Conflicts Task Force[2] by a subgroup organized by the U.S.-based Kettering Foundation and the Russian Center for Strategic Research and International Studies of the Institute of Oriental Studies in Moscow. A third-party team that included three Americans and three Russians facilitated the Inter-Tajik Dialogue. The meetings were alternately chaired by the Russian and American cochairs. The dialogue involved a core of eight to ten citizens of Tajikistan divided between the pro-government and pro-opposition camps. When the dialogue began, the majority of the pro-opposition members were in exile in Moscow. Two members of the dialogue group eventually became formal delegates to the UN-mediated negotiations.

The cochairs and the rest of the team members facilitated the discussions by setting the agenda at the beginning of every meeting, raising questions at critical times during the discussions, asking for clarifications about certain ideas and proposals when needed, helping to put down on paper the ideas articulated during the meeting, and (when emotions flared up) trying to help the participants deal constructively with their anger. At the end of every meeting, the U.S. team drafted a report and shared it with UN agencies and other interested official bodies in the United States and Russia.

During meetings between March and August 1993, participants discussed the origins and conduct of the civil war. They concluded in August 1993 by agreeing on the need to start a negotiation between the government and the opposition about creating conditions for the safe return of refugees. In January 1994, opposition participants came to the dialogue with the new platform for a United Tajik Opposition. Pro-government participants grilled them for over two days. The pro-government participants left the meeting feeling that the basis for negotiations now existed and promised to report the meeting discussions to the government. One month later, the government of Tajikistan accepted the special envoy's invitation to join UN-mediated peace talks. A high-level Tajikistani official later said, "After six meetings of the Dialogue, it was no longer possible to argue credibly that negotiations between the government and the opposition were impossible."

During meetings in March 1994, the dialogue participants produced their first joint memorandum, which recommended the creation of four working groups to focus on refugee, political, military, and economic issues—an idea that became part of the General Agreement. When official negotiations started in April 1994, the dialogue redefined its objectives as "designing a political process of national reconciliation for the country." They also addressed issues that caused stalemate in the official negotiations. In March 1995, the dialogue began using the idea of "a transitional period." The General Agreement adopted that concept to describe the twelve-to-eighteen-month post-accord phase during which the CNR would try to implement the provisions of the General Agreement. In May 1996, the Inter-Tajik Dialogue stated in a joint memorandum: "Participants believe that the primary obstacle to peace in Tajikistan is the absence of an adequate understanding on sharing power among the regions, political parties and movements, and nationalities in Tajikistan." Beginning in the summer of 1995, the dialogue repeatedly recommended the creation of a Consultative Forum for the Peoples of Tajikistan as a mechanism for bringing together different regions and political forces for deliberations on the kind of country they envisioned. Although the forum has never come into being, it was agreed in 1996 in a memorandum signed by President Rahmonov and UTO leader Nuri that such a forum should be created.

When the CNR was formed, four participants in the dialogue were members. In March 1993, the dialogue provided the only channel of communication across factional lines and relations were acrimonious. At the end of 2000, after twenty-nine meetings, the Inter-Tajik Dialogue was still meeting and had become what we call "a mind at work in the midst of a country making itself." Through these eight years, dialogue participants have played significant roles at all levels in a multilevel peace process that includes government negotiators, highly informed citizens outside government, and grassroots organizations.

There can be no doubt that the Inter-Tajik Dialogue played a role in the peace process in Tajikistan, but determining exactly what that role was illustrates one of the continuing problems in assessing the impact of unofficial dialogues. One of the lessons learned from the Tajikistan peace process, observes Gerd Merrem, former special envoy to Tajikistan and the official mediator at the UN-mediated Inter-Tajik Dialogue, is that "in a two-track approach, an NGO-facilitated dialogue between Tajiks on existing political and socio-economic antagonisms enabled these personalities within the polarized conflict to look beyond what separates them. This exercise, facilitated by a former U.S. official with skill and perseverance, has clearly facilitated compromise at the negotiation table."[3]

International Nongovernmental Organizations

International nongovernmental organizations (INGOs) played an important role in the promotion and then implementation of the peace agreement. The main ones are as follows.

The Aga Khan Foundation. The Aga Khan Foundation has focused its efforts in the early stages of the war on providing humanitarian assistance to the Ismaili population in the Gorno-Badakhshan province. Throughout the official negotiations, UN special envoys consulted frequently with His Highness Prince Karim Aga Khan on issues related to the peace process. The prince's visits to Tajikistan (in particular in May 1995) had a moderating influence on some of the negotiating parties. Since the signing of the peace accords, the foundation has launched an impressive array of long-term programs focusing on community-based economic development, a new humanities curriculum at Tajikistani universities, and support for civil society. They are also launching a Western-style Central Asian university with a main campus in Kharugh (Tajikistan) and satellite campuses in Kyrgyzstan and Kazakhstan.

United States Institute of Peace. The United States Institute of Peace organized a number of forums and study groups on the prospects for negotiations to end the Tajikistan conflict. It also published a report on the prospects for conflict and opportunities for peacemaking in the southern tier of former Soviet republics. In June 1995 it organized a forum on the conflict with U.S. ambassador to Tajikistan Stanley T. Escudero and former OSCE head of mission in Tajikistan Olivier Roy, later publishing its findings, and in June 1996, it hosted a discussion involving the Inter-Tajik Dialogue participants. Its contribution to the peace process has been in providing analysis and a forum for ideas.

International Committee of the Red Cross. The International Committee of the Red Cross (ICRC) played a significant role in implementing the agreement on prisoner exchange, which served an important confidence-building function. These agreements were reached during the third and fourth rounds of the official negotiations in late 1994 and 1995. The ICRC could assume this task because of its vast experience with such exchanges, and the respect it enjoyed among all parties to the negotiations. Beyond this role, it was also involved informally throughout the negotiation process in discussions on humanitarian issues.

Local Nongovernmental Organizations

NGOs are a relatively new phenomenon in Tajikistan. Since 1994, there has been a rapid increase in their activity and 415 NGOs representing a wide variety of interests (e.g., youth, civil society, education, women, health, social protection and poverty elimination, environment, culture, business training, mass media, science) have been established in the past five years.

Historically, civil society in Tajikistan is rooted in local institutions. Each Tajik rural community or village has a council called *mahalla* council where all local problems were discussed and wherever possible, solved by the people themselves.[4] The *mahalla* council is supplemented by informal meetings, forums, and small group conversations around common dinners held in a mosque where adult males gather, each bringing food.

Though useful in providing venues for people to get together and solve local problems, the *mahallas* could do little to bind the different regions of Tajikistan together. This local civic infrastructure reinforces the problem of localism by failing to provide sufficient incentives for common national or interregional collaboration and by shaping the average Tajikistani citizen's mind-set where the terms of reference are a narrow circle of relatives, neighbors and community members.

Many of Tajikistan's NGOs were established in 1997 following the signing of the General Agreement. Some of them, like the Oli Somon Cultural and Intellectual Foundation, were established during the war, but their effect on the course of events during the civil war was, in our opinion, minimal. They were hampered by fear of retaliation from the militia structures, lack of human and financial resources, lack of professional knowledge about the third sector and its role in a democratic society, and a weak legal framework to protect the integrity of their activities.

During the transition period (June 1997–February 2000), the local NGOs played a major role in the preelection process. In collaboration with the OSCE mission in Dushanbe, local NGOs trained by OSCE experts and staff organized hundreds of training seminars focusing on civic, gender, and human-rights topics. A network of thirteen local NGOs trained in the field of conflict resolution was organized by Counterpart Consortium, with financial assistance from the U.S. Agency for International Development. In our opinion, these two programs, targeting the entire country and focused on promoting skills and knowledge critical to the establishment of a nonviolent civic culture, have played a supporting role in the grassroots consolidation of the official agreements.

But Tajikistan's NGOs still suffer from a number of weaknesses:

1. The majority of NGOs (at least the more professional ones) are still concentrated in the two largest cities in the country, Dushanbe and Khujand. Few are established in small towns and in rural areas. The weak transportation and communication infrastructure as well as lack of local funding sources present the major obstacles to the emergence and sustainability of NGOs in rural areas.

2. All local NGOs in Tajikistan are far from being self-sustaining. They are still dependent on outside funding and the funders' priority areas mostly

drive their programs. As funders change their funding priorities (from gender issues, to drug prevention, to HIV/AIDS prevention), local NGOs follow suit. How to achieve local NGOs' long-term sustainability is one of the most challenging issues facing the donor community today.

3. Members of the intellectual and academic intelligentsia founded many of these organizations. The majority of their leaders are Russian-educated and lack real connections to the local strata of the society, especially to people living in rural areas. They have no close or ongoing relationship with the traditional civic networks and local *mahalla* councils. It is our opinion that the basis of civil society in Tajikistan are these *mahalla* councils, and unless NGOs shift their area of operation to these local units, their efforts at strengthening and building civil society will not be sustainable.

Prospects

The main task facing Tajikistan today is that of building a democratic civil society. The obstacles to this task lie in an unaccountable and centralized governing structure, unemployed ex-combatants, and the illegal drug trade.

According to the government of Tajikistan, the stipulations of the General Agreement have been implemented. In August 1999, the UTO announced that no further opposition military units existed—all had been disarmed and integrated into existing government units. That announcement led the government to lift the ban on opposition parties. On 26 September 1999, a referendum was held on constitutional amendments with about 73 percent supporting the proposed amendments. The constitutional amendments created a new two-chamber parliament where the parliamentarians would be no match for the executive branch since the presidential appointees in the upper chamber (eight members) and the members of the president's party in the lower chamber could effectively uphold any veto.

The presidential election was held on 6 November 1999. Though there was one other candidate on the ballot, President Rahmonov ran, in effect, unopposed, receiving close to 97 percent of the vote. Parliamentary elections followed in February 2000. Of the sixty-three seats in the lower chamber, the pro-presidential People's Democratic Party garnered thirty seats, the Communist Party thirteen, the Islamic Renaissance Party two, and a group of nonpartisan candidates believed to be pro-presidential garnered fifteen seats. Although the election process was not considered fair, it was the first multiparty election ever held in Tajikistan, with the Islamic Renaissance Party participating for the first time in the post-Soviet era. More importantly, the new parliament now includes some experts with strong intellectual and experiential credentials.

The CNR ended its work when the new parliament took office. However, international observers in Tajikistan judge that implementation of the General Agreement of 1997 has not really been completed despite a proclamation by the government to that effect. Most political observers do consider that the protocol on refugee issues has been successfully implemented. Both government and the UTO shared an interest, though for different reasons, in having the refugees return home.

Implementation of the military and political protocols has been less successful. The military protocol aimed both to integrate Tajikistan's many armed forces into a unified military and to promote decommissioning and demobilization. One could argue that the defeat of a November 1998 uprising in the Leninabad region was a test for the newly integrated armed forces. Nonetheless, former UTO commanders, though supportive of the peace process, are not satisfied with the current situation. Many of the integrated UTO units are poorly housed, clothed, and fed. An esprit de corps has failed to develop among the armed forces. Rank and file are still loyal to their former military commanders and many rank and file in the Tajik army did not even know the names of their formal commanding officers. A hostage-taking incident in June 2001, engineered by former Tajik opposition fighters, provides further support to this argument. Despite the progress made by the United Nations Mission of Observers to Tajikistan and United Nations Organization for Project Services in reintegrating ex-combatants, the government is now challenged to find salaried jobs for all ex-combatants.

The main task now facing Tajikistan is to build a democratic civil society. It must begin by building democratic institutions and democratizing the structures of power. Tajik political institutions are now more centralized than they were before. The president and his administration control the decisionmaking process with minimal influence from the legislative and judicial bodies. The decisionmaking process is far from transparent and is perceived to be corrupt. The president's party, People's Democratic Party (PDP), enjoys privileged access to government resources. In three recent by-elections, only PDP candidates were allowed to run, with opposition candidates barred on technicalities. The IRP is now suffering from a lack of resources. As one IRP senior official stated privately, "It is easier to fund the *kalashnikov* than to support political and social platforms." There is an ongoing internal debate between the hawks, who are still motivated by the *jihad* mentality, and the young Turks, who are calling for professionalization of IRP political activities. Today, three political parties dominate Tajikistan's political scene, though they do not enjoy equal stature and access to resources. The most prominent is the PDP. The two other parties with some support base are the Communist Party and the IRP. The Democratic Party is split into many factions, and many of its leading figures are now in government.

According to official statistics, the economy is on the road to recovery. According to the United Nations Development Program *2000 Human Development Report,* "Since 1997, the government has managed to achieve positive economic growth and an improvement in the well-being of the population." Yet Tajikistan still remains the poorest country in the CIS, with the lowest income per capita and more than 80 percent of the population living in poverty.

The illegal drug trade is undermining Tajikistan's moral fabric, pushing its youth into criminal activities, and infiltrating its governing and judicial bodies. Tajikistan is a major conduit for narcotics produced in Afghanistan. According to UN estimates, Afghanistan's poppy harvest in 2000 was about 3,000 metric tons, making the country the largest producer of heroin in the world. Despite official efforts to stop the flow of narcotics into Tajikistan, drug trafficking has been increasing, and Russian Federal Border Service guards patrolling part of the Tajik-Afghan border confiscated more than 1,300 kilograms of drugs, including 970 kilograms of heroin, in the first half of 2001. This amount exceeds the amount seized during all of 2000. A similar trend is seen in drug-related criminal activities, with major increases in the cultivation, use, and sale of narcotics. According to official statistics, 135,000 people are estimated to be drug addicts, representing about 2.3 percent of Tajikistan's population.

The process of nation building is just now beginning again after an abortive start in the nineteenth century. This process will be affected by regional events including military and political developments in Afghanistan and the ongoing power struggle in Uzbekistan. Following the 11 September 2001 events, and with the launching of the antiterrorism war in Afghanistan, the future of Tajikistan is likely to be affected by the new realities in the region. Following the assassination of the Northern Alliance's commander Ahmad Shah Masoud and the launching of the U.S.-led antiterrorism war, there were widespread fears in Tajikistan of a potential massive influx of refugees into the country. Such fears have so far proven to be unfounded. However, such fears are not completely eliminated. If, in the future, UN efforts to promote a multiethnic governing process in Afghanistan fail and the country once again plunges into interethnic and interfactional fighting, Afghan refugees might again head toward the Afghan-Tajik border. Any influx of refugees in Tajikistan in the short- to long-term future will threaten the fragile economic and political infrastructure of the country.

In October 2001, during a visit to the region by U.S. Secretary of Defense Donald Rumsfeld, Tajikistan agreed to grant basing rights to the U.S. military and to provide assistance to the U.S.-led coalition in intelligence gathering and various types of military-to-military cooperation. In return, Tajikistan's leadership was promised increased U.S. economic assistance, and now expects Washington's help in using its influence to help them to gain access to development aid offered by international financial institutions. However, unless the United States and other donor agencies tie future economic assistance to improved social and economic conditions, additional development funds might instead end up exacerbating popular frustrations. On the security front, destruction of the Al-Qaida network by the U.S.-led coalition eliminated a major source of logistic and economic assistance for Central Asia's Islamic militants, including the Islamic Movement of Uzbekistan and Hizb ut-Tahrir; both movements have been active in Tajikistan. Without such support, it is still too early to say how these movements will react in the long term. In the short term, it is fair to say that they will cease their military and recruiting activities and wait to see how these events in Afghanistan shape up.

It is certain that the United States will expect from any future Afghan government, in exchange for its military support, an elimination of Afghanistan's drug industry. Ending Afghanistan's drug industry will have a dual impact on

Tajikistan. On the one hand, Tajikistani youths who have in the past engaged in drug trafficking will now find themselves unemployed. Many of these young people are also drug addicts. Unless these young people are provided jobs and drug rehabilitation facilities, they can be a source of major trouble, including being recruits for Islamic militant groups in the future. On the other hand, this will assist ongoing efforts to put an end to the corruption and criminal activities that have infiltrated Tajikistan's society and leadership structures as a result of drug money. Well before 11 September, Russia has been reasserting its power in Central Asia. A Russian threat assessment in 1999 identified Central Asia as of vital importance for its security and economic well-being, and it is now seizing the initiative. Most importantly, until recently Moscow has seen the region as a bulwark against radical Islamic movements emanating from Afghanistan and Pakistan, and is, therefore, willing to commit considerable resources to securing the southern border. The Central Asian leaders agree with Russian president Putin on the need to stop the rise of militant Islam in the region. At a meeting of the Shanghai Five (Russia, China, Kyrgyzstan, Kazakhstan, and Tajikistan) in June 2001, all leaders, plus the Uzbek president, adopted a framework for cooperation in battling Islamic insurgency. The organization was then transformed into the Shanghai Cooperation Organization (SCO) with the addition of Uzbekistan. One of the major aims of the SCO is to improve the regional response to different problems connected with radical Islam. Such concerns have been heightened in the wake of 11 September. However, anti-insurgency efforts in the region have so far been hampered by a lack of coordination among the countries' security forces and by disputes among the members over borders and resources. It is safe to say that the course of future events in Tajikistan will be significantly influenced by the actions of these regional players. It is hoped that with increased attention focused on the region, more aid will flow into drug prevention programs and projects to create alternative sources of employment for the Ferghana Valley's unemployed youth.

Recommendations

The period between now and the next round of elections in 2004–2005 can be viewed as a new transition period for Tajikistan. As Tajikistan moves into this new transition phase, the following are priority tasks.

• Strengthening the continuing peace process and the public involvement in it. In particular, attention must now be paid to broaden the political base of the government both in terms of regional representation and opposition forces. The recent forays made by Hizb ut-Tahrir in Khujand attest to the feelings of marginalization that this region still feels. The regime has strengthened its position in the north and the secession scenario is less applicable today than it was in 1997. Any negative developments in north Tajikistan will in the future have an immediate and severe impact on border countries. The international community must convince the Tajik government, through the use of carrots and sticks, to truly implement a policy of inclusion embracing all political forces and movements in the decisionmaking processes. Laws on elections and political parties must be revised in order to enable wider participation.

• Strengthening the capacities of the parliament to perform its legislative duties well by establishing a training academy for the parliamentarians and their staff.

• Widening and deepening the process of democratization in the society by promoting democratic self-governing institutions via legislation to protect the role and function of entities such as *mahallas.*

• Facilitating development of a free and independent press by continuing to expand access to alternative sources of information through the granting of licenses for private radio and TV broadcasting stations.

• Encouraging professionalization of political parties. Parties also need to extend their reach beyond Dushanbe. Only the People's Democratic Party and the Islamic Renaissance Party have branches outside Dushanbe. Other parties must be encouraged to do so through adequate training and availability of resources, both of which could be provided by the international community.

• Advancing economic reform by broadening involvement of citizens in the economic life of the country.

• Military reform and preservation of the security of citizens with particular attention to integrating former soldiers into the economy. Close to 1,500 former UTO armed fighters are still in the Karategin Valley, unemployed and marginalized.

• Professionalization, with encouragement of the donor community, of the NGO sector. We estimate that less than 10 percent of the NGOs currently registered in Tajikistan have the necessary skills to engage in strategic planning and project design, and few of them are sustainable financially in the long term. It is time for the donors to recognize that quality and not quantity should be the rule of thumb in the development of a healthy civil-society sector. NGOs are not necessarily the best elements of a strong civil society. Community-based organizations, especially the ones developed and promoted by local *mahallas,* might be a more sustainable element in Tajikistan's civil society.

• The establishment of closer connections between citizens and government, that is, the building of "some sort of bridge" that government must not fear as a rival. Both government and NGOs must be involved in the building of a new national identity. Localism and regionalism are still prevalent in Tajikistani political life. Now might be the time to reintroduce the idea of a Consultative Forum of the Peoples of Tajikistan as a parallel power structure to involve representatives from all regions of Tajikistan, all ethnic groups, and representatives of civil society and of government.

• A whole array of activities must be promoted to deal with the growing drug problem and HIV/AIDS crisis.

• Lastly, the international community must send a strong message about its low tolerance for the criminalization of Tajikistani society through drug money. Different layers of Tajikistan's political, security, and economic structures are now involved in the narco-trafficking business. The international community could link future loans and economic assistance to the willingness of the government to rid its structures of elements that are known to be involved in the drug business.

Resources

Newsletters and Periodicals

Central Asia and the Caucasus, Journal of Social and Political Studies, Information and Analytical Center, Sweden

Central Asia–Caucasus Analyst, the Central Asia–Caucasus Institute of the Johns Hopkins University, the Nitze School of Advanced International Studies

Central Asia Monitor

Current History, some of its issues focused on Central Asia

Turkistan Newsletter, Research Center for Turkistan, Azerbaijan, Crimea, Caucasus and Siberia, the Netherlands

Reports

Conciliation Resources, *The Tajikistan Peace Process, Accord,* issue 10, 2001.

Human Rights Watch, *Conflict in the Soviet Union: Tadzhikistan,* July 1991.

International Crisis Group
"Incubators of Conflict: Central Asia's Localised Poverty and Social Unrest," in *Central Asia: Fault Lines in the New Security Map,* July 2001.
"Tajikistan: An Uncertain Peace." *Asia Report* no. 30, 24 December 2001.

The Civil War in Tajikistan: Causes and Implications, by Olivier Roy, December 1993.

The War in Tajikistan Three Years On, Special Report, November 1995.

United Nations Development Program, *Tajikistan Human Development Reports,* 1998, 1999, 2000.

United Nations Mission of Observers in Tajikistan, *General Agreement on the Establishment of Peace and National Accord in Tajikistan—What Does It Say?* September 1997.

Other Publications

A Public Peace Process, by Harold H. Saunders. New York, St. Martin's Press, 1999.

Central Asia and the Transcaucasia: Ethnicity and Conflict, edited by Vitaly V. Naumkin. Westport, CT, Greenwood Press, May 1994.

Central Asia: Conflict, Resolution, and Change, edited by Roald Sagdeev and Susan Eisenhower. Chevy Chase, MD, Center for Post-Soviet Studies, January 1995.

Central Asia's New States: Independence, Foreign Policy, and Regional Security, by Martha Brill Olcott. Washington, DC, United States Institute for Peace, October 1997.

Civil Society in Central Asia, edited by M. Holt Ruffin and Daniel Waugh. Seattle, University of Washington Press, 1999.

Islam and Central Asia, edited by Susan Eisenhower and Roald Sagdeev. Washington, DC, Center for Political and Strategic Studies, June 2000.

"Managing Conflict in Divided Societies: Lessons from Tajikistan," by Randa M. Slim and Harold H. Saunders. *Negotiation Journal* 12, no. 1, January 1996.

Tajikistan: Disintegration or Reconciliation? by Shirin Akiner, London: The Royal Institute of International Affairs, 2001.

The New Central Asia: The Creation of Nations, by Olivier Roy. New York: New York University Press, May 2000.

The Resurgence of Central Asia: Islam or Nationalism? by Ahmad Rashid. Karachi, Oxford University Press, May 1999.

The Subtlest Battle: Islam in Soviet Tajikistan, by Muriel Atkin. Philadelphia, Foreign Policy Research Institute, 1989.

The Tajik War: A Challenge to Russian Policy, by Lena Jonson. London, Royal Institute of International Affairs, 1998.

Selected Internet Sites

www.angelfire.com/sd/tajikistanupdate (The Tajikistan update includes sections on news, culture, discussion, analytical articles, and a message board)

www.crisisweb.org (International Crisis Group with reports on Central Asia online)

www.eurasianet.org/ (An Open Society Institute site that provides an independent source of news and analysis about Tajikistan)

www.fas.harvard.edu/~centasia (Perhaps the richest and most concentrated source of information on Central Asian studies worldwide)

www.friends-partners.org/~ccsi/nisorgs/tajik/taj (List of organizations in Tajikistan)

www.icarp.com/tajik.html/ (An online resource for original reference and curricular materials, analytical materials, and annotated links to Tajikistan and Central Asia)

www.incore.ulst.ac.uk/cds/countries/tajik.html (INCORE guide to internet sources on conflict and ethnicity in Tajikistan)

www.internews.ru/ASIA-PLUS (An independent news service in Tajikistan)

www.iwpr.net (Institute for War and Peace Reporting)

www.reliefweb.int/ (Reports from WHO, OCHA, IFRC, and other agencies on humanitarian disasters in Tajikistan from 1997 to the present)

www.rferl.org/bd/ta/index.html (Daily news, analysis and real audio broadcasts covering the developments in Tajikistan)

www.times.kg (Online version of the weekly English-language newspaper covering Central Asia)

www.un.org/dept/dpko/missions/unmot.html (Information on the United Mission of Observers in Tajikistan)

Resource Contacts

Abdelaziz Abdelaziz, Organization for Security and Cooperation in Europe, Dusti field office, e-mail: azizaziz@mail.com

Zuhra Halimova, Tajik Branch of Open Society Institute Assistance Foundation, e-mail: zhalimov@osi.tajik.net

Mirza Jahani, Agha Khan Foundation, e-mail: mirzajahani@atge.automail.com

Ibodullo Kalonov, Khujand Madreseh, tel: 3422 65236, 3422 64457

Shamsiddin Karimov, Global Training for Development Project, e-mail: shams@tajnet.com

Christine Kiernan, Internews, e-mail: kiernan@internews.ru

Abdugani Mamadazimov, National Association of Political Scientists of Tajikistan, e-mail: abdu@napst.td.silk.org

Parviz Mullajanov, Public Committee for the Promotion of Democratic Processes, e-mail: okpdv@tajik.net

Stephane Nicolas, ACTED, e-mail: stephane.nicolas@acted.org

Muzaffar Olimov, Sharq Center, e-mail: olimov@tajik.net

Randall Olson, Counterpart Consortium, e-mail: rolson@counterpart-tj.org

John Schoeberlein, Forum for Central Asian Studies, Harvard University, e-mail: schoeber@fas.harvard.edu

Akbar Usmani, United Nations Development Program, e-mail: akbar.usmani@undp.org

Daniel Zust, Swiss Coordination Office, Dushanbe, e-mail: zud@sdc.tojikiston.com

Data on the following organizations can be found in the Directory section:

Asia Plus

Centre for Conflict Studies and Regional Research

Centre for Social Technologies

Fidokor
Foundation to Support Civil Initiatives
Manizha Information and Education Centre
National Association of Political Scientists of Tajikistan
Public Committee for the Promotion of Democratic Processes
Sharq Reserach and Analysis Center
Silk Road—Road of Consolidation
Sudmand
Tajikistan Center for Citizenship Education
Traditions and Modernity

Randa M. Slim (of Dayton, Ohio, USA) focuses on consulting and training in the fields of conflict management and public participation. Since 1993, Slim has been a member of the Inter-Tajik Dialogue, an unofficial dialogue focusing on the conflict in Tajikistan. She is currently the principal consultant for the Inter-Tajik Dialogue civic initiative, a three-year project funded by a consortium of U.S. foundations. She is also a consultant for the Peace Promotion Project in the Ferghana Valley, funded by the Swiss Agency for Development and Cooperation. Faredun Hodizoda is currently the national coordinator of the Goodwill Ambassadors project, funded by the Swiss Agency for Development and Cooperation. He holds a doctorate from the Rudaki Institute of Language and Literature of the Tajikistan Academy of Sciences. Randa Slim can be reached at <randaslim@aol.com>

Notes

1. Olivier Roy, *The Civil War in Tajikistan: Causes and Implications.* Washington, DC: United States Institute of Peace, 1993, p. 13.

2. The Dartmouth Conference, which began in 1960, is the longest continuous bilateral dialogue between Soviet (now Russian) and U.S. citizens. The regional conflicts task force was formed in 1981 to probe the dynamics of Soviet-U.S. interactions in such regional conflicts as those in southern Africa, the Middle East, and Afghanistan. It was cochaired until 1988 by Yevgeny Primakov and Harold Saunders. Gennady Chufrin succeeded Primakov in 1989. The task force has met every six months since August 1982. In 1992, the task force decided to conceptualize the process of dialogue that it learned through more than twenty meetings and to apply that process to one of the conflicts that had broken out on the territory of the former Soviet Union.

3. Gerd Merrem, "The Tajikistan Peace Process: UN Achievements to Date and Challenges Ahead," unpublished document, March 1999, p. 14.

4. Parviz Mullojanov, "Civil Society and Peacebuilding," in *Conciliation Resources: The Tajikistan Peace Process, Accord,* issue 10, 2001, pp. 60–63.

6.8

Uzbekistan: Authoritarianism and Conflict

David Lewis

Uzbekistan's regime has promoted political stability above political or economic reform. Paradoxically, its repressive policies and its failing economy have produced a situation in which internal conflict is now a serious threat. The official policy of a strong political center and gradual economic reform has stagnated into a repressive regime in which security forces play a powerful role and the economy is governed by a small corrupt clique of vested interests. Its pivotal role in the region, as the major military power in Central Asia, ensures that its policies have a major impact on its neighbors. External military and financial support by the international community is only likely to increase tensions, as the government uses security issues to avoid vital economic and political liberalization.

The present Uzbek state is a largely artificial creation, containing large numbers of ethnic minorities, and with ill-defined borders in many regions. Prior to the Soviet period there was no unified Uzbek state, and throughout its history regional loyalties have been more important than national identities.

The heart of the territory of present-day Uzbekistan is formed by the region between the two great rivers of the Central Asian region: the Amu-Darya and the Syr-Darya. This area, known to ancient historians as Transoxiana, has been inhabited for thousands of years. Islam came to the region in the seventh century, and over the next four hundred years a high level of scholarship and learning developed, particularly in cities such as Bukhara and Khorezm.

Much of this civilization—including elaborate irrigation systems and great oasis cities—was destroyed by the invasions of Genghis Khan in the thirteenth century. One of Genghis Khan's descendents, Timur the Lame (Timurelane), united much of central Asia from his base in Samarkand. Following his rule, however, his empire gradually declined into more or less independent principalities and city-states. By the early sixteenth century, Uzbek tribes from the north took control of many of these autonomous kingdoms.

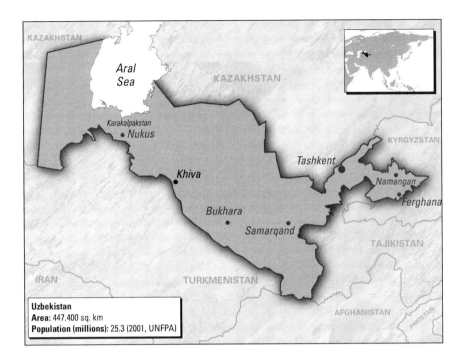

Uzbekistan
Area: 447.400 sq. km
Population (millions): 25.3 (2001, UNFPA)

The Uzbek kingdom also fragmented and by the eighteenth century, a number of powerful principalities or *khanates* had emerged on its territory. Foremost among them were the khanates of Bukhara, in the Zeravshan Valley, Khiva in the northwest, and Kokand in the Ferghana Valley

There were early failed attempts by the Russians to expand into the region in the eighteenth century, but Russian imperialism gained a firm hold in Turkestan in the midnineteenth century. In 1865 Russian troops seized Tashkent, and by 1876 Russia had turned Khiva and Bukhara into protectorates, and absorbed Kokand into the empire. Many of the significant socioeconomic features of the present began under Russian colonial rule. Foremost among them was the establishment of widespread cotton production, based on the rehabilitation of irrigation systems. Railways were built from the Russian heartland to Tashkent, to allow for cotton exports. Tashkent became the center of Russian power in the region, and an increasing number of Slavs emigrated to the city.

With the Bolshevik Revolution in 1917, a Tashkent Soviet formally seized power and suppressed nascent nationalist movements based in Kokand and elsewhere. A guerrilla war ensued between so-called basmachi rebels and Soviet forces, but by late 1919 the Soviets controlled most of what is now Uzbekistan. In 1924 an Uzbek Soviet Socialist Republic was formed, consisting largely of the territories of the three former khanates of Bukhara, Khiva, and Kokand, but also including the territory of present-day Tajikistan as an autonomous republic. In 1929 Tajikistan was given the status of a full union republic, and in 1936 the present-day boundaries of Uzbekistan were established, when Karakalpakstan was incorporated as an autonomous republic.

Soviet colonial policy imitated prerevolutionary rule in many ways, expanding cotton production and importing greater numbers of Slavs to run new industry and to control parts of the political and security apparatus. However, the Soviet regime also strongly promoted ethnic Uzbeks into the elite. In the 1930s, many of this new leadership were executed or imprisoned in the Stalinist purges, labeled as nationalists. Moscow never entirely rooted out nationalist elites from Uzbekistan, and in the 1970s the Uzbek leadership had considerable autonomy in its rule. Under Sharif Rashadov, leader of the Uzbek Communist Party from 1954 to 1983, the elite gained considerable control over local policy and over the local economy. This permitted the growth of huge levels of corruption, notably in the cotton sector. High levels of falsification led to a major anticorruption drive in the 1980s, in which many senior officials were dismissed.

By the late 1980s social discontent was making itself felt through increasing interethnic tension. In June 1989 Meskhetian Turks were the targets of riots in the Ferghana Valley and elsewhere, and there were further outbreaks of disorder in the Tashkent region in March 1990. In 1989 Islam Karimov was appointed first secretary of the Communist Party, and given a mandate to restore order in the republic. In March 1990 Karimov was elected to the position of executive president of the republic by the Supreme Soviet (legislature). On 31 August 1991 the Supreme Soviet voted to declare Uzbekistan an independent state.

In the first decade of independence, Karimov intensified his control over all aspects of political life. On the surface, the political situation has been largely stable, and the government has sought strong relations with the West and foreign investment. However, a combination of inept economic policy, social problems, and political repression has provoked radical opposition to the regime, undermined international relations, and made any succession to Karimov fraught with danger.

In particular, the state initiated serious repression of Muslim believers, particularly after a series of violent incidents linked to the armed militant group, the Islamic Movement of Uzbekistan (IMU) in 1998–1999. Uzbekistan has claimed that actions against the IMU have been part of a legitimate antiterrorism policy, but many innocent believers have been caught up in government

---

Uzbekistan is divided into twelve *viloyats* (provinces), and the autonomous province of Karakalpakstan. Local governors (*hakims*), who are appointed directly by the president, rule the regions. Roughly a quarter of the population lives in the densely populated Ferghana Valley. Some 2.5 million live in the capital Tashkent. Thirty-six percent of the population is under the age of fourteen. Much of the rest of the country is desert, interspersed by oasis cities, such as Samarkand and Bukhara, the historic and cultural centers of the country.

repressions, and the hard-line policy has only engendered more support for the radical opposition.

Conflict Dynamics

That the conflict in Uzbekistan poses a threat is largely a result of government policies that have led to a combination of authoritarian rule, economic decline, social discontent, and a polarized political arena in which radical Islamist groups have begun to occupy an important underground role. These domestic pressures are played against a backdrop of poor relations with neighboring states, and in a region characterized by instability.

Authoritarian Rule

The government is highly centralized and personalized around President Karimov. Policies are developed largely in an informal circle of close allies of the president, rather than through the formal government and parliamentary structures. The regime is extremely authoritarian and suppresses all forms of dissent and opposition. There is widespread evidence of human-rights abuses by the security forces against political opponents of the regime.

Under this system, there is very little opportunity for dissent to be voiced. The media is strictly controlled by prepublication censorship, and by arrests and harassment of independent journalists. The press is no more open than it was under Soviet rule. Formal political mechanisms, such as elections, have little impact on the actual policymaking process. Most political disputes are conducted away from the public eye, in behind-the-scenes informal environments.

Elections have been held both to the presidency and to parliament, but none have met international standards of free and fair elections. The first elections, held in December 1991, were relatively open, with a contest between Karimov and Erk Party leader Mohammed Salih. In March 1995 Karimov cancelled the presidential elections due in 1996, and instead called a referendum to extend his term in office until 2000. In January 2000 Karimov won presidential elections with 92 percent of the vote. Even his sole opponent admitted that he had voted for Karimov. In January 2002 Karimov extended his term in office from 2005 to 2007 through a referendum.

There are virtually no legal channels for any protest against the government. The two main opposition parties that were formed in the early 1990s, Erk and Birlik, are banned, and their leaders remain in exile. There are a few Birlik members still active, and they are mainly engaged in collecting information regarding human-rights abuses. They are often members of the Human Rights Society of Uzbekistan, which maintains a rivalry with the International Human Rights Society of Uzbekistan, which is affiliated with Erk. Tense relations between the two main opposition groupings have merely facilitated the regime's control over political life.

Parliament is little more than a rubber stamp on the activities of the executive, and a bicameral legislature planned for 2002 is not expected to pose any more opposition to the regime than its predecessor. Most parliamentary deputies are elected indirectly or from party lists. The ruling People's Democratic Party of Uzbekistan (PDPU) and a number of affiliated "official" parties dominate parliament, but the parties have little or no role in political life.

In this environment there is an obvious danger of festering discontent being channeled into illegal and violent political activity. There is no scope for public involvement in political decisionmaking through formal, constitutional means. Even traditional community leaderships, such as the mahalla (community) chairmen, have been increasingly taken under the control of the state, and appointed rather than elected by local people. This all-embracing authoritarianism has provoked the growing memberships of groups such as Hizb ut-Tahrir, as one of the few channels for the expression of dissatisfaction with the regime. The lack of openness has also badly affected the efficiency of governance. With no opposition or critical media, there is little incentive for officials to do much except use their positions for self-advancement and self-enrichment.

Radical Islam

Since the suppression of virtually all secular political opposition, radical Islam has become the only nationwide grassroots opposition movement. According to official figures, 88 percent of the population is Muslim, and Islam in Uzbekistan has revived significantly since independence in 1991. In the late 1980s and early 1990s in particular, foreign Islamic groups funded the rebuilding of mosques, provided Islamic education, and funded education for young people in Islamic schools abroad. Radical Islamic ideas gained some following, particularly among young people, and particularly in areas such as the eastern Ferghana Valley, which has always been a center of Islamic piety in the region, and rural parts of southern Uzbekistan, such as the Surkhan-Darya region.

Since 1992 the government has led a campaign against independent Islamic and Islamist groups, while providing support for loyal Islamic structures. The government strictly controls the Muslim Board, which represents the official Muslim hierarchy, and has disbanded all other Islamic groups. A number of independent Islamist movements emerged in 1990–1991, advocating the introduction of an Islamic state including the imposition of *sharia* law. The groups were crushed by a campaign against independent Islamic groups, particularly those with political aims, in 1992. Many members of such groups fled the country, and formed the basis for radical groupings in exile such as the IMU.

It is difficult to ascertain the real level of support for radical Islamist groups. The government has been active in pursuing alleged Islamic radicals, but according to human-rights groups, many of those implicated by the security forces have been largely innocent of any attachment to radical groups, further increasing dissatisfaction with the government. There is evidence of minority support for more radical Islamist ideas, particularly in areas of the Ferghana Valley. In the present political context, there is no outlet for these ideas, but there is the potential for rapid emergence of new radical groups in the case of conflict, or indeed of liberalization of the political environment.

Two major groups opposed to the regime have been active since 1997–1998. These are the IMU and Hizb ut-Tahrir.

Islamic Movement of Uzbekistan (IMU)

The origins of the IMU lie in the Ferghana Valley, in particularly the Namangan region. In the late 1980s, probably with the support of foreign religious emissaries from Saudi Arabia and elsewhere, small groups were established espousing radical Islamist ideas. Groups such as Tovba (Repentance), Adolat (Justice), and Islam Lashkalari (Warriors of Islam) had similar ideas of introducing radical Islamist principles as the basis of the state. Leaders of such groups who escaped imprisonment in the government crackdown in 1992 moved into exile, often to Tajikistan, where many fought in the civil war on the side of the United Tajik Opposition.

In 1997 some members of these groups coalesced into the IMU led by Juma Namangani and Tohir Yuldash. They were mainly based in Tajikistan and Afghanistan, and became heavily involved in criminal activities, in particular narcotics smuggling. Their stated aim was overthrow of the Karimov regime and the establishment of an Islamic state in the whole Ferghana Valley region. The IMU was allegedly involved in several military actions against the regime, although the extent of its activities and its capabilities were always in doubt.

The first proof of real terrorist capabilities, allegedly carried out by the IMU, came on 16 February 1999, when seven bomb explosions were reported in Tashkent. At least 16 people were killed in the explosions, and about 150 people were injured. Fifty administrative and residential buildings were damaged, some severely. Those killed and injured in the bombings were mainly bystanders. The two initial car bombs may have been part of an attempt to assassinate Karimov. Whether the attacks were the work of the IMU remains unproven: the ease of access apparently enjoyed by the attackers to highly secure environments suggested at least a degree of involvement by elements in official structures.

In August 1999 a group of several hundred gunmen from the IMU crossed the border from Tajikistan into Kyrgyzstan and occupied several villages and mountain valleys in the southern Batken district of the Osh region. It was widely believed that the gunmen were attempting to open a corridor through to Uzbekistan, with the intention of provoking an uprising or staging a terrorist attack and cross-border incursions. During the attack the rebels kidnapped several local soldiers and officials, and four Japanese geologists. In October the rebels retreated back across the border into Tajikistan, and the Japanese nationals were released, apparently after a large ransom was paid.

A group of gunmen, claimed by the government to be linked to the IMU, attacked a police post in Yangiyabad, about 80 kilometers east of Tashkent, near the border with Tajikistan, on 15 November 1999, killing four policemen and three civilians. The attack may have been related to the Islamic militants' involvement in the drug trade. Some 1,500 troops were involved in tracking down the gunmen.

In 2000 there were incursions by small groups of IMU fighters into Uzbekistan. Fighting was reported in the hills close to Tashkent, and on a pass on the road to Ferghana. There was also fighting in the Surkhan-Darya region of southern Uzbekistan, apparently between Uzbek military forces and IMU units from Tajikistan. Uzbekistan responded by laying mines on much of its border with Kyrgyzstan and Tajikistan, which have led to the deaths of scores of local people.

In 2001 there was little sign of IMU activity in Central Asia, and they seem to have become closely involved in the Taliban campaign against the Northern Alliance inside Afghanistan. Many members of the IMU are believed to have been killed in military action in Afghanistan, and their leader, Namangani, was reportedly killed during fighting in Kunduz. This does not necessarily mean that Uzbekistan has rid itself of the IMU. Remnants will no doubt return to Central Asia. More importantly, the preconditions that gave rise to the IMU—socioeconomic decline, government repression, and a search for identity—remain in place.

Hizb ut-Tahrir

One of the fastest-growing political groups in Uzbekistan is Hizb ut-Tahrir, a clandestine organization founded in the Middle East in the early 1960s. It aims to establish a borderless Islamic caliphate in the region. The group is banned in many Middle Eastern countries, but has a considerable following throughout the Muslim world, including in Western countries.

Hizb ut-Tahrir has a very different ideology from that of the IMU. It is based on a particular interpretation of Islamic history that is opposed in principle to the division of Islamic peoples into nation-states. Instead it advocates the re-creation of the Islamic caliphate throughout the region. Hizb ut-Tahrir would be largely a fringe party in any normally functioning democracy, but in repressive states they have gained influence through their underground cell structure and their strong campaigns against corruption and injustice.

The extent of support for the movement is unknown, though some sources have suggested that membership in the region may have reached 12,000–15,000. Its own leaders have alleged that it has up to 80,000 supporters, including senior officials. Most of its work takes place in secret, but it has staged occasional demonstrations. In July 2001 several hundred activists were arrested after staging demonstrations in Tashkent against the arrests of Hizb ut-Tahrir members.

Hizb ut-Tahrir concentrates on propaganda activities, as opposed to the overt armed struggle conducted by the IMU. Its aversion to violence is both ideological and tactical—it has observed the lack of success enjoyed by the IMU against the regime through armed struggle. Its opposition to violence is not absolute—its members are free to take part in *jihad* against anti-Islamic aggressors, for example. But it seems unlikely that it will resort to terrorist activity against the Uzbek regime in the short term. It probably has more to gain by building up a wide support base and attempting to infiltrate the regime from within.

Whatever regime is in power in Uzbekistan, radical Islamist ideas will be part of the political spectrum. However, in a pluralistic society, they are unlikely to gain the support of more than a small minority of the population. High levels of government repression, socioeconomic decline, and the lack of freedom provided to authoritative Islamic teachers and scholars have all contributed to the growth of radical Islamism. The lack of viable alternative political opposition groups has also contributed to rapid growth, and Islamist groups will now be a major player in any potential conflict scenario.

Regional Divisions

Clan networks and regional groupings play an important role in Uzbek politics, although the exact nature of these networks is much disputed by scholars. In the most simplistic form, there are four important clans, based on particular regions. These are the Samarkand-Bukhara clan, the Tashkent clan, the Ferghana clan, and the Kashkadar clan. These clans continued to exert influence throughout the Soviet period, and particularly in the 1960s and 1970s when ethnic Uzbeks gained more influence in the political elite.

Karimov came to power in 1989 as a result of a compromise among different clan leaders. However, his roots are in Samarkand, and his rise to power owed much to a leader of the Samarkand clan, I. Jurabekov. Since 1992, when the leader of the Tashkent clan, Shukrullo Mirsaidov, attempted to oust Karimov, rival clans have not dared to challenge the supremacy of the Samarkand clan in politics.

Karimov has attempted to achieve a certain balance among the rival groupings, while ensuring the preeminence of the Samarkand grouping. Prime Minister Utkur Sultanov is a representative of the Tashkent clan, though he does not wield significant authority in the government. Minister of Foreign Affairs Abdulaziz Komolov is also from the Tashkent clan, and is believed to be a close ally of Karimov and to wield considerable influence in the inner circles of power. The Ferghana and Kashkadar clans wield largely regional authority. Clan representatives excluded from political power have achieved influence in business and economics, which has somewhat lessened tension in the political sphere.

In the long term, Karimov seems intent on reducing the influence of clans in politics. He rotates personnel with considerable frequency, both in the central government and in the regions, aiming to avoid any regional leaders building up their own power bases and networks that could challenge his central authority. However, clan allegiances and loyalties are firmly rooted, and there is a danger that clans who feel excluded from political and economic power will attempt to regain political influence by other means. Such a scenario would be particularly pertinent in any succession struggle.

The most dangerous scenario is an unholy alliance of excluded regional leaders and radical forces outside the state, including Islamic radical forces. There is some suspicion that just such an alliance was behind the Tashkent bombings in 1999. Whether true or not, there is clearly the scope for a very complex alliance of opposition to the present regime that would include disaffected regions.

Human-Rights Abuses

There is considerable evidence of widespread abuses of human rights by the security forces. According to information collected by local and international human-rights groups, there are about seven thousand possible political prisoners in Uzbekistan. Not only are many of those arrested and sentenced innocent of involvement in violent activity against the state, but many of those arrested are beaten or otherwise abused while in police custody. Mass arrests of men believed to be part of independent Islamic movements peaked in 1998, and again in 1999 after the Tashkent bombings. There is no sign that government repression has lessened following the September 2001 terrorist attacks in the United States: if anything the government seems to be even less concerned by criticism by the international community.

Human-rights abuses not only undermine the legitimacy of the government; in Uzbekistan, they are also direct contributors to instability. Many members of the IMU and Hizb ut-Tahrir have been radicalized by the actions of the government against friends and relatives. Severe government repression has been one of the key elements of conflict promotion. The sentences given to prisoners accused of acting against the regime tend to be long and arduous. Several prison camps are believed to exist in which political prisoners are kept. Amnesty International has confirmed the existence of one of these prison camps—Yaslik—located in a former Soviet army barracks in the Karakalpakstan Autonomous Republic. Conditions are said to be cruel, inhuman, and degrading. The treatment of prisoners in such conditions inevitably produces further radicalization and anger. Whatever their views when sentenced, prisoners released after spending time in an Uzbek prison are unlikely to take up moderate political positions.

Socioeconomic Decline

Most opposition to the regime in the early 1990s came from intellectuals in Tashkent or from young people drawn to Islamist ideas in the cities of the Ferghana Valley. As the economic situation has declined, there is evidence of growing dissatisfaction among other social groups, notably agricultural workers and the rural poor, who are suffering disproportionately from the state's failure to improve living standards for the mass of the population.

Uzbekistan has failed to develop a serious reform program to achieve the transition from a centrally planned economy to a market economy. Uzbekistan has significant precious-metal resources, including gold and platinum. Its substantial gas and oil reserves—it is the tenth-largest gas exporter in the world—have prompted the government to make self-sufficiency in energy a strategic priority. These resources, and comparative agricultural wealth, did much to ensure that the economy did not contract as much as the other postindependence former Soviet economies. In some ways this lessened the initial shock of economic transition, but ten years later it is clear that this economic policy is no longer sustainable, and is contributing directly to instability.

The growth of corruption at all levels of the government and ill-advised, grandiose construction projects in the capital have prevented a fair distribution of what wealth is being generated. Recent plans to diversify agriculture with a view to increasing self-sufficiency in staple products such as grain have suffered from poor weather conditions and inadequately maintained irrigation and distribution networks. Surveys aimed at identifying further reserves of gold and other minerals have met with discouraging results. Meanwhile, the narcotics trade has grown enormously, with production increasing massively in Tajikistan, and gradually increasing in Uzbekistan.

Government policy has aimed at ensuring political stability by avoiding "shock therapy." This has preserved a role for domestic producers and avoided too cataclysmic a fall in people's incomes. However, this policy is not compatible with long-term aims of developing the economy. Many domestic producers are unviable in the long term, and structural readjustment will be necessary. Little real economic reform has been carried out, and there is little encouragement for private enterprise or individual initiative. The bureaucracy is overstaffed, and many officials retain a Soviet-era approach to economic problems. High levels of regulation, lack of legislative reform, and widespread corruption have limited the development of an open economy, while government policy has not yet achieved significant liberalization of exchange controls or other elements of state intervention. The lack of convertibility of the currency has discouraged significant foreign investment and made regional economic cooperation even more difficult.

Jeremy Hartley/Panos

Young women fetch water from a
dilapidated standpipe in Korasub Hospital's courtyard.

Without new government policies on the economy, there will be no reversal in the present decline in living standards, particularly in rural areas. Conditions in many regions of the country are now worse than in neighboring states, despite Uzbekistan's significant advantages in industrial development and in resources. Karakalpakstan and Khorezm have undergone one of the worst droughts in recent memory. In 2001 there were substantial crop losses, and a severe impact on animal husbandry. In both these regions, economic problems have been accompanied by serious problems in environmental matters and in health. Other areas, notably in southern Uzbekistan, are also facing serious economic difficulty that is leading to social discontent.

Even if the government discovers the political will to implement the changes urged by international financial institutions, it will face serious obstacles. Implementing currency convertibility would inevitably lead to a sharp fall in the value of the *som,* a rise in prices on many basic goods, and a lowering of living standards for much of the population. The government is understandably concerned that this will increase social discontent and political opposition. Yet doing nothing is equally dangerous. An almost unprecedented protest organized by farmers in Jizzakh province in July 2001 could be the precursor of future unrest unless major changes in policy are made.

Interstate Relations

Many of the problems faced by Uzbekistan are difficult to resolve on a national basis. Economic, security, environmental issues, and disputes over water and energy supplies, all have a regional dimension. However, Uzbekistan has tended to shun regional organizations, and attempted to achieve results in interstate relations largely on a bilateral basis.

Following the bombings in February 1999, Uzbekistan took on an even more isolationist line. When IMU militants invaded southern Kyrgyzstan in August 1999, the Uzbek air force bombed a village in Kyrgyzstan, and mounted several raids into Tajikistan. It has also mined much of its borders with Kyrgyzstan and Tajikistan, and sharply increased border security, badly damaging regional trade. Such actions have severely limited regional cooperation, and hamper any regional efforts at overcoming conflict pressures.

Other regional issues also leave cause for concern. Disputes over natural-resource allocation, notably water, pose a major threat for the future. While Kyrgyzstan produces much of the water used in Uzbekistan's irrigation systems, it receives no compensation for the reservoir network that it maintains. Kyrgyzstan has attempted to increase the amount of water it can use under old Soviet allocation allowances, both for hydroelectric power and for irrigation. But increased use in upstream countries badly affects the amounts available for irrigation downstream, particularly for the vital cotton harvest. As a result, there have been frequent tensions between the two countries. A barter agreement is supposed to provide Kyrgyzstan with gas, to limit its need to generate electricity, while Uzbekistan receives adequate water. In practice, neither side has adequately fulfilled the agreement. The issue is unlikely to lead to interstate conflict, but it creates local tensions and worsens relations between the two countries. Similar problems are evident between Uzbekistan and Turkmenistan over water sharing and borders.

The increasing support for Uzbekistan by the international community may make international cooperation even more difficult. Its Central Asian neighbors are concerned that increased financial and military support for Uzbekistan will provoke a more aggressive policy in the region, and lessen its need for regional cooperation. The international community needs to emphasize the dangers of unilateral policymaking in conflict areas, while remaining realistic about the potential for successful regional conflict-prevention programs.

Official Conflict Management

The nature of potential conflict in Uzbekistan makes official conflict management policies particularly difficult. The government remains convinced that its official policy of strong security measures and tight government control over society is the most effective means for preventing conflict. It seeks assistance on a bilateral basis, largely in the field of security cooperation, where its main partners have been the United States, Israel, and Turkey.

Regional efforts at conflict management have revolved almost exclusively around security developments. Uzbekistan has been wary of any organizations that seem to act as channels for Russian influence in the region, notably the Russian Commonwealth of Independent States Security Pact (which it left in 1999) and the Shanghai Cooperation Organization (SCO), which unites the central Asian states (except Turkmenistan), Russia, and China. The SCO is based almost exclusively on security cooperation, with the political philosophies of Russian and China being most prevalent. A joint peacekeeping force formed by Uzbekistan, Kyrgyzstan, and Kazakhstan has hardly been functional.

Russian involvement in Uzbekistan's policymaking has sharply declined, and relations between the two countries are often difficult. Russia shares Uzbekistan's fear of Islamist extremist groups undermining stability in the region, but differing geostrategic positions have limited their cooperation. Uzbekistan has largely sought Western assistance in its security policies, but until September 2001, this assistance has been limited to occasional aid and some political support. Relations with China are good, based largely on similar attitudes to what both states view as a security threat from Islamist groups. This confluence of views on the "Islamist threat" has only increased since 11 September, with Uzbekistan enjoying greater international support, including from Western countries.

U.S. policies on human rights and broader approaches to security have often been viewed by local leaders as mere rhetoric since there has been little linkage between U.S. economic and military assistance and human rights or democratic progress. During an official visit in 2000, then Secretary of State Madeleine Albright was extremely critical of the government's record on human rights, and stressed the need for a distinction between Islamic extremists and innocent believers. Since 11 September, there has been a downplaying of U.S. concern over human rights, although the U.S. embassy in Tashkent has been attempting to keep the issue on the agenda. Secretary of State Colin Powell visited in December 2001, but in the context of the international campaign against terrorism, the U.S. agenda seemed to be set by Department of Defense representatives emphasizing military and security cooperation. Other international governments have also been largely silent about the failings of Uzbekistan's policy toward its religious and political opposition.

Neither the UN nor the Organization for Security and Cooperation in Europe (OSCE) has been able to engage Uzbekistan successfully with regard to conflict management programs. UN agencies have been criticized for their failure to stress democratization and rule of law as critical to development and security. The United Nations Development Program (UNDP) has been particularly weak in this regard. Its main emphasis, understandably, has been on socioeconomic development, but it has been criticized in the past for lacking any overall political view, and for becoming too closely entwined with the authorities. In 2000 the UNDP was strongly criticized in a report by independent consultants, who objected to its exclusion of independent human-rights groups from projects, and its contributions of some $2 million to official human-rights bodies. These attempts to bolster its position vis-à-vis the authorities have not given it any useful leverage. In 1998 the UNDP attempted to develop a program in the Ferghana Valley, involving Uzbekistan, Kyrgyzstan, and Tajikistan, but it was largely blocked by the Uzbek authorities, which feared that it impinged on their sovereignty. The program has a strong conflict-prevention element, and would have offered some real cross-border projects in the area for the first time. This was only the most obvious example of the reluctance of Uzbekistan to become involved in regional programs, and its failure has marred further development of cross-border contacts.

The OSCE's work on human rights and democratic development is viewed with suspicion by the Uzbek government, and it has faced considerable difficulties in expanding its work. In contrast to the UNDP, it is respected by local human-rights organizations, and is the one international organization that has consistently supported independent groups. Its initial work stressed its Human Dimension priorities—human rights and democratization—but since the late 1990s it has attempted to expand other areas of its mandate, including security issues and environmental and economic aspects of security. Its attempts to become involved in regional mediation, in water for example, have largely failed, and it has not been involved in any of the interstate disputes in the region over borders or other issues.

The European Union (EU) has played a fairly weak role in Uzbekistan, limiting itself to a small Technical Assistance for the Commonwealth of Independent States program. It did attempt to begin a wider political dialogue with Uzbekistan under negotiations for a Partnership and Cooperation Agreement (PCA), signed in 1999. But the EU's attempt to link the PCA to improvements in human rights and political and economic reform have failed.

The PCA has been only implemented formally, with some discussions on trade and finance, but has had no discernible impact upon government policy in the area of human rights. The Cooperation Council of the PCA was suspended in 2000, but was revived in January 2002, with the EU promising to raise issues of human rights and democracy, alongside security concerns.

NATO's Partnership for Peace program includes elements of preventive diplomacy and confidence building, but most of its work is focused on formal exchanges and education. In the absence of any understanding from the authorities of the dangers of such policies, the international community needs to act in ways that bolster stability largely independent of government policy.

Multi-Track Diplomacy

NGOs have faced considerable problems in establishing any level of conflict-prevention capability. The lack of government recognition of the problem, and a latent suspicion toward nonofficial actors, have combined to limit NGOs largely to the sphere of social and economic development. Even in these fields, it has sometimes been difficult for NGOs to obtain legal registration, although attitudes in government structures are changing, and NGOs are becoming more sophisticated, with training from organizations such as Counterpart Consortium. In many areas, the government has become more willing to contemplate cooperation, and some local governments have become active in attracting NGO involvement.

Nevertheless, in such an environment, it seems unlikely that a successful multi-track diplomacy approach could work. The best hope is that a range of projects aimed at social activism, civil-society building, economic development, education, and information provision will be able to strengthen society to ensure that future stresses and potential conflicts are resolved peacefully. The Soros Foundation runs a number of projects of this nature, ranging from education and academic exchanges, to economic development programs. One of the most promising Soros programs is an Internet access project that will develop wider and better access to the Web outside the capital. This program is also supported by UNDP and NATO, which is offering satellite and communications assistance. The Internet is becoming one of the key tools in countering government censorship, and many Uzbek sites are emerging. The government still blocks opposition sites, where it is able, but it is also supportive of wider expansion of the Internet for educational purposes. It has yet to resolve these two contradictory impulses, and there may be further clampdowns on Internet provision in the future.

Despite such programs, Internet access will remain unavailable to much of the population, and there is still a need for much more open media, in print, radio, and television. One of the few successful NGOs working in this area is Internews, which runs training for journalists and also has a team producing weekly programs for independent television stations. This is a useful combination since much training for journalists does not give them an outlet for their skills. Internews gives them an opportunity to produce their own programs, but there is no similar program for radio or print. CIMERA runs training programs for print journalists, but faces the problem of limited outlets for their work.

Social activism is now a core aim of UNDP programs, and this area offers some hope for the development of grassroots decisionmaking. The aim is to include local communities in the decisionmaking process. In many ways this involves working through the *mahalla* institution. The *mahalla* is a traditional form of local government in which all the local population have some say. In practice, the *mahalla* has often been taken over by the state and democracy is limited, but it still provides a potentially useful forum for grassroots activism. Counterpart Consortium is also active in developing grassroots participation. Its *mahalla* development program provides grants to local communities of up to $5,000. The grants are awarded on the basis of local collective decisionmaking on priorities for a local community. As a sideline, Counterpart also supports local NGOs in advocacy programs, providing them with skills in lobbying local government for local needs. This kind of program is a useful form of proto-politics from below, with local communities hopefully becoming more aware and protective of their rights.

Nevertheless, where NGOs have attempted to become involved in political activity, they have inevitably faced strong opposition from the state. In monitoring human-rights violations, the most active groups are the Independent Human Rights Organization of Uzbekistan (IHROU) and the Human Rights Society of Uzbekistan (HRSU). Neither is officially registered, and their members often face harassment, detention, or other forms of police persecution. Their main activity is producing accounts of police ill-treatment, unlawful arrest, assistance to families of prisoners, and advice on legal rights. Some other legal-advice centers are beginning, and the American Bar Association has had some projects in this field. Human Rights Watch (HRW) and Amnesty International are both active in monitoring human rights, and also in advocacy toward Western governments on their policies toward Uzbekistan. HRW, in particular, has been consistently pressing the U.S. government to attach more conditionality and consistency to its relationships with the government.

In a separate category, the International Crisis Group (ICG) produces regular reports on the political and socioeconomic situation in Uzbekistan from the point of view of conflict prevention. A considerable part of the work of ICG is spent in advocacy in Europe, Japan, and North America, with a focus on UN, OSCE, and other international institutions, as well as major governments. ICG produces some of the few in-depth reports on the region that address issues from the policymakers' perspective, and they are also active in advocacy within the region.

There is little NGO activity on issues of economic reform, but considerable interest in business development and poverty-alleviation programs. The local Association of Businesswomen has advice and consultancy services for women in business, while Counterpart also supports NGOs active in these fields. Among the most promising poverty-alleviation programs are microcredit schemes, such as those run by the UNDP in Karakalpakistan or Mercy Corps in Namangan. These provide ways for the poor to achieve income generation without resorting to predatory banks or high interest rates from unofficial moneylenders. In most cases, these offer small loans of $50–$150 to women, with groups of women banding together to guarantee each others' loans. Most of these are small-scale pilot schemes, and there is huge room for expansion. Mercy Corps is already expanding its existing scheme to four new offices, and considering similar projects in the vulnerable southern region of Surkhan Darya.

In regions such as Karakalpakistan, environmental and health problems are major promoters of emigration and social degradation. Médecins Sans Frontières (MSF) and others have significant projects here, but many projects associated with the Aral Sea have been failures, owing to lack of coordination between agencies and a failure to involve local people.

Following the failure of the UNDP program in the Ferghana Valley, few NGOs have been able to build up regional linkages. However, the United States Agency for Intenational Development (USAID) has funded a major Ferghana Valley program based in Andijan, the Peaceful Communities Initiative, which is run by Mercy Corps. It will attempt to establish cross-border cooperation in neutral areas, such as sports; includes similar local community initiatives to those promoted by Counterpart, including small grants for projects implementing solutions to basic problems of access to water, food security, sanitation, and hygiene; and address other problems identified by the communities themselves. This type of creative program offers a real chance for intercommunity relations to develop, initially at a low level, and provides financial incentives for interethnic cooperation.

Most NGOs have noticed an improvement in the environment in the past two to three years, as local governments come to understand the advantages that their programs can offer. Yet there is a long way to go. Government bureaucracy, corruption, and state interference pose major challenges. Local NGOs are still relatively weak, compared with neighboring Kyrgyzstan, and require further training and support. Competition between them for grants can give rise to an unhealthy rivalry, and there is sometimes a lack of coordination between international NGOs. Yet the sector is growing, and it is no longer true to say that there is no capacity for further international assistance. The main problem is that without major policy change, the NGO sector can still only have a very limited impact on democratization and economic prospects.

Prospects

Scenarios for potential conflict are largely on two levels. At the highest political level, the most likely sources of conflict will be concerned with future succession to President Karimov, and the role of regional groupings that have been largely excluded from power. The latter aspect may be manageable if the economy is sufficiently successful to provide all regional leaders with some rewards from economic activity. If the economic situation worsens, tensions between rival regional groupings over limited resources will grow and could lead to high-level political conflict.

At the lower level, the greatest danger is of social and civil unrest, prompted by economic decline. Such protests have been occurring very sporadically and at a very limited level. Without political leadership, civil unrest is unlikely to challenge the state, but it could be used by dissatisfied elites to their own advantage. The state is clearly willing to contemplate repressive measures where necessary, but it is unlikely to be successful in the long term if serious unrest develops.

Between these two extremes, there is a continuing danger of terrorist groups developing on the basis of Islamist radicalism and finding support from the socially excluded and economically deprived. Hizb ut-Tahrir does not pose a threat of violence at present, but some of its members may potentially turn to arms if repression continues. The destruction of many of the IMU in Afghanistan does not mean the end of that organization, and it may return in a more dangerous mode, using small cells and classic terrorist techniques.

On the level of civil society, the challenge will be to challenge mentalities and develop grassroots activism. Some developments in this field are evident, with community involvement in micro projects, but much more is possible. Despite the difficulties that NGOs find in working in Uzbekistan, experience demonstrates that progress can be made, particularly in developing social activism at a grassroots level.

Recommendations

The main issues facing the international community are centered around how to conduct conflict-prevention programs in their widest understanding under a government that refuses to recognize the concept. The problems facing Western relations with Uzbekistan have become yet more difficult following U.S.-led intervention in Afghanistan. The United States and other states have offered financial support in exchange for Uzbekistan's cooperation in providing air bases and support for the military campaign in Afghanistan. This support has few conditions attached, and may provide the government with yet another breathing space that will allow it to avoid making difficult decisions regarding economic reform or political liberalization.

It is vital that the international community does not provide funds and support that would enable the government merely to prolong its present policies. There is a danger that announcements in December 2001 of increased bilateral support by the United States will merely cushion the government temporarily from the consequences of its ill-advised economic policies. This may provide some respite in the short term, but the longer reform is delayed, the worse the accompanying difficulties in terms of social unrest or political upheaval are likely to be. All aid to Uzbekistan should be provided with conditions attached. Otherwise, it will merely heighten the risk of future social upheaval and civil unrest.

The challenge for the international community should focus on three areas:

1. *Economic development and poverty alleviation.* In this sphere, much depends on government policy, although there are some areas where the international community can do more without government assistance. At the top of the agenda will be the attempts by Western governments and the international financial institutions (IFIs) to encourage structural reform. Although there have been serious problems with the IFIs' reform plans for many post-Soviet states, in general their ideas for Uzbekistan are realistic and necessary. Primarily, this involves the increasing liberalization of the economy from state control. One of the first policies that will be advocated will be the move toward a liberalization of exchange controls, which are blocking inward investment and making it difficult for Uzbekistan to maintain constructive economic relations with its neighbors. The main players in this program will be the IMF and the World Bank. A proposed IMF reform program could attract the support of the World Bank and other IFIs to support moves toward currency convertibility and structural reform. This needs to be pushed politically by the United States and other parties, while offering financial support to counteract negative consequences. Without significant support, any moves toward major reforms are likely to spark social unrest.

2. *Social infrastructure development, including health and education.* Although not normally a priority in conflict-prevention programs, in Uzbekistan it is partly the decline in social infrastructure that is producing a new generation, disillusioned, ill-educated, and lacking in employment skills. It is this generation that poses the greatest danger of involvement in criminal activities, including drug trafficking, and radical political and religious groups. These areas are easier for the international community to operate in: about half of USAID's budget goes to health programs, and there are successful projects being implemented by MSF and others. Poverty, lack of government attention, and a stress on ideological training are all taking their toll on the effectiveness of national education. In many areas of development work, the local community organizations—*mahallas*—have been used as channels by international organizations. As the basic building block of society and the political system, this approach makes sense. But in many cases, *mahallas* have become extensions of government control over society, and are often used by the security forces to maintain surveillance and limit the activities of political opponents. When aid focuses on *mahallas,* it is important that it be channeled in ways that supports the *mahalla* as a potential component in civil society rather than as an instrument of the state or the security forces.

3. *Political pluralism and human-rights activity, including support for independent media.* This is a much more difficult area in which to work, but it is vital for future conflict prevention. Without increased information about the world, some groups in the population are vulnerable to manipulation by extremist forces. The United States and other governments provide some support

in this area, but U.S. funding for democracy programs has been cut in recent years. The OSCE's program is relatively small, and other agencies, such as the UNDP, have very little impact with their good governance and similar programs. NGOs such as Internews provide a vital service in supporting semi-independent media, and should be strongly supported. Human-rights groups are also worthy of support, despite their internal differences. Above all, the international community needs to remind the Uzbek government constantly that its present policies are not producing long-term political stability and are unacceptable to other states with interests in the region. It may seem to be politically expedient to downplay differences over political pluralism and rule of law for short-term gains in the campaign in Afghanistan, but in the long term international indifference to the internal situation in Uzbekistan will come back to haunt Western policymakers in the future.

Resources

Newsletters and Periodicals
Central Asia and the Caucasus, Journal of Social and Political Studies. Information and Analytical Center, Sweden
Central Asia–Caucasus Analyst, Central Asia–Caucasus Institute of the Johns Hopkins University, Nitze School of Advanced International Studies
Central Asia Monitor

Reports
International Crisis Group
    Uzbekistan at Ten—Repression and Instability, Brussels/Osh, 21 August 2001.
    The IMU and the Hizb-ut-Tahrir: Implications of the Afghanistan Campaign, Brussels/Osh, 30 January 2002.
U.S. Department of State, *Uzbekistan Country Report on Human Rights Practices* (2000).
See also reports on Uzbekistan by Human Rights Watch (www.hrw.org)

Other Publications
Central Asia: Conflict, Resolution, and Change, edited by Roald Sagdeev and Susan Eisenhower. Washington, DC: The Center for Political and Strategic Studies, January 1995: www.cpss.org/cabook.htm.
Central Asian Security: The New International Context, edited by Roy Allison and Lena Jonson. London, RIIA, 2001.
Central Asia's New States: Independence, Foreign Policy, and Regional Security, by Martha Brill Olcott. Washington, DC: United States Institute of Peace, 1997.
Civil Society in Central Asia, edited by M. Holt Ruffin and Daniel Waugh. Seattle, Center for Civil Society International, 1999.
Islam and Central Asia, edited by Susan Eisenhower and Roald Sagdeev. Washington, DC, The Eisenhower Institute, 2000.
"Political Development in Uzbekistan: Democratization?" by William Fierman. In Karen Dawisha and Bruce Parrot (eds.), *Conflict, Cleavage and Change in Central Asia and the Caucasus,* Cambridge, Cambridge University Press, 1997.
Security Dilemmas in Russia and Eurasia, edited by Roy Allison and Christoph Bluth. London, RIIA, 2001.
The Modern Uzbeks: From the Fourteenth Century to the Present: A Cultural History, by Edward Allworth. Stanford, CA, Hoover Press Publications, 1990.

The New Central Asia: The Creation of Nations, by Olivier Roy. London, I. B. Tauris, 2000.
The Resurgence of Central Asia: Islam or Nationalism? by Ahmad Rashid. London, Zed Books, 1999.
Uzbekistan: Politics and Foreign Policy, by Annette Bohr. London, Royal Institute of International Affairs, 1998.
Uzbekistan: Transition to Authoritarianism on the Silk Road, by Neil J. Melvin. Amsterdam, Harwood, 2000.

Selected Internet Sites
www.birlik.net (Opposition party web site)
www.cango.net.uz (Counterpart Consortium web site of Uzbekistan's NGOs)
www.crisisweb.org (Contains International Crisis Group reports on Central Asia)
www.eurasianet.org (Analytical coverage of Uzbekistan)
www.fewer.org (Reports on conflict prevention in Central Asia)
www.hizb-ut-tahrir.org (Official web site of the transnational Islamist group)
www.internews.uz (Internews programs and information on electronic media)
www.mercycorps.org (Wide range of programs in Uzbekistan, including conflict prevention)
www.msf.org/aralsea (Information on Médecins Sans Frontières programs and state of Aral Sea)
www.osce.org (OCSE Centre in Tashkent)
www.preventconflict.org/portal/centralasia/ (A conflict-prevention initiative by Harvard scholars with a detailed data base of summarized articles and links)
www.rferl.org (Daily news and analysis)
www.soros.org/osi.html (Open Society Institute programs in Uzbekistan)
www.undp.uz (Information on UNDP programs in Uzbekistan)
www.usaid.gov/country/ee/uz/ (USAID's program in Uzbekistan)
www.uzbekistanerk.org (Opposition party web site)
www.uznews.com (Official government site)
www.worldbank.org (Information on programs, economic situation)

Resource Contacts
Mikhail Ardzinov, Independent Human Rights Society of Uzbekistan, e-mail: iron@mik.silk.org
Richard Conroy, Country Representative UNDP, e-mail: Richard.Conroy@undp.org
Alisher Ilkhanov, Open Society Institute, e-mail: osi@osi.uz
Soroush Javadi, Counterpart Consortium, e-mail: soroush@cpart.uz
Annette Legutke, OSCE Centre in Tashkent, e-mail: alegutke@osce.sand.uz
David Lewis, International Crisis Group, Central Asia Project, e-mail: icgosh@crisisweb.org
Joshua Machleder, Country Representative Internews, e-mail: Josh@internews.uz
Roy Male, Médecins Sans Frontières, e-mail: cm@msfh-tashkent.uz
Murat Mirzaev, Swiss Cooperation Office, e-mail: Murat.Mirzaev@tas.rep.admin.ch
Susan Savage, Mercy Corps International, e-mail: savage@naytov.com
Jon Thiele, Eurasia Foundation Tashkent Regional Office, e-mail: jont@ef.freenet.uz
Tolib Yakubov, Human Rights Society of Uzbekistan, e-mail support@hrsu.uz

Data on the following organizations can be found in the Directory section:

In Uzbekistan
  Association of Uzbekistan for Sustainable Water Resources Development
  Union for Defence of the Aral Sea and the Amudarya

Outside Uzbekistan
  Central Asia and the Caucasus Information and Analytical Center
  Center for Conflict Management

EastWest Institute
Human Rights Watch
Institute for Multi-Track Diplomacy
International Crisis Group
Office of the OSCE High Commissioner on National Minorities
Open Society Institute
OSCE
United States Institute of Peace

David Lewis is director of the International Crisis Group's Central Asia Project, based in Osh, Kyrgyzstan. The project produces analytical reports on the political and socioeconomic situation in the region, and conducts advocacy programs among policymakers from its offices in Brussels, New York, and Washington, DC.

7

SOUTH ASIA

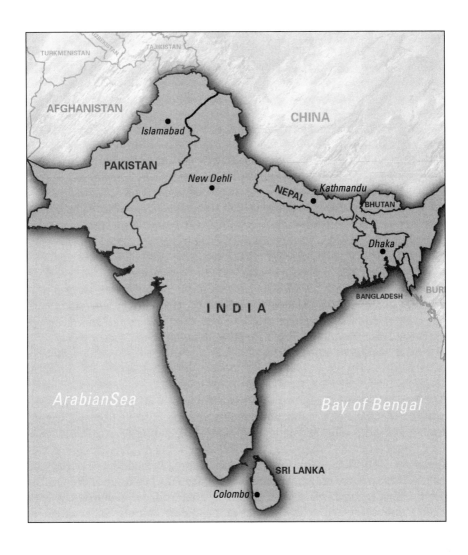

7.1

Forging New Solidarities:
Nonofficial Dialogues

Navnita Chadha Behera

South Asia is at the crossroads today. While the concept of regional integration through the South Asian Association for Regional Cooperation has been deadlocked since 1999, the idea of South Asia and a South Asian consciousness is beginning to take root among the attentive public and politically conscious segments of the civil society in the region. The inability of the governments, and their lack of flexibility to find viable solutions to several key issues, has led to nonofficial initiatives by South Asians. Civil society is convinced of the inevitability, benefits, and imperative of peace and cooperation. It is also eager and prepared to play a constructive role in creating an opinion and acting as an advocacy group in the interest of the peoples in the region. This chapter seeks to understand and analyze the evolution of the nonofficial dialogue processes in terms of how these have come about. What are its important features, its changing character, and future prospects?

The basic theoretical argument is that regionalism in South Asia, pursued within a functionalist paradigm and mainly through official channels, remains hostage to protecting the "national identity," defending the "national interests," preserving the sanctity of "national borders," and safeguarding the "national security." The nationalist discourse accords precedence to nation and nationalism over the region. Without the philosophical ethos underpinning the South Asian regionalism, the political leadership of these countries has been unable to imagine and evolve a mind-set that could be truly characterized as "South Asian." That is why the task of creating a South Asian mind and the necessary political and social milieu to forge a South Asian regional consciousness and develop a South Asian community must be rooted in the domain of civil society. Unfettered by the nation-state ideology, the players in the civil society are better placed to conceive, shape, and nurture the idea of "South Asia."

South Asia is a well-defined geographical region with a shared social, cultural, and civilizational past, but its postcolonial history, mired in interstate conflicts, has deeply divided the region. The entire nation-building project sundered the integrated social, economic, political, and foreign-policy system of the Indian subcontinent, making South Asia a unique region that "entered the 20th century as a community and leaves this century as seven nation-states divided by their historical inheritance."[1] It was only in the 1980s when changing power equations, global realities, and growing voices of civil society at home brought back the agenda of re-creating a South Asian community. The end of the Cold War and a bipolar global divide gave way to a multipolar world, characterized by the increasing power and influence of regional groupings such as the North American Free Trade Agreement (NAFTA), European Union, and Asia-Pacific Economic Commission (APEC) rather than nation-states. South Asia Association for Regional Cooperation (SAARC) was born in 1986 but has not been a pacesetter in changing the political or social dynamics of intraregional relations. As the political leadership failed to meet the challenge, the civil-society actors are taking initiative in forging links and communication channels at the people-to-people level. Several developments within the region and its nation-states have facilitated this task.

Supportive Mechanisms and Processes

First and foremost, the growing autonomy of the civil society is evident from the ascendance of market forces that are "overtaking the state as an arbiter of intra–South Asian economic relations."[2] For instance, while Pakistan continues to regulate its bilateral trade with India through denial of the Most Favored Nation status, their informal trade far exceeds the formal trade routed through third countries such as Dubai and Singapore. Similarly, informal trade between India and Bangladesh nearly equals the official trade statistics. The story of Indo-Nepal trade is no different. The informal trade is serviced by an increasingly efficient informal capital market, operating outside the purview of the monetary authorities, which finances $2–3 billion worth of intraregional transactions in goods and services. Along with this, the large-scale movements of people across borders in search of better livelihood and the resultant integration of the labor markets of South Asia have undercut the barriers of national boundaries. The private sector is another catalyst for change. Conscious of the enormous potential of intraregional trade and increasing importance of regional economic blocs in global trading, private enterprise and business associations are setting the pace in transforming regional relationships and establishing the institutional framework for regional cooperation and networks.

The communications revolution in satellite technology has challenged the notion of state sovereignty, including the power to control radio waves and television signals within a nation's borders, and drastically undercut the governments' monopoly over controlling the flow of information. The satellite medium is playing a critical role in exposing people to diverse viewpoints and breaking down several myths about the "enemy country."

The phenomenal growth of NGOs across the South Asian region has opened a multitude of communication channels, at the grassroots level, on a broad spectrum of issues ranging from gender issues and human-rights violations to ecology. They play an active role in civic mobilization and public advocacy and in organizing activities across national boundaries in these areas.

Cross-border trafficking in women and children, smuggling of arms and drugs, and most important, spillover of ethnic conflicts causing huge outflows of refugees, such as Tamils from Sri Lanka into India, Bhutanese refugees into Nepal, and so on, have exposed the flaws of carving state boundaries, cutting across communities, tribes, and ethnic groups. Likewise, the three major river systems—the Indus, Ganges, and the Brahmaputra—divided between India, Pakistan, Nepal, and Bangladesh have resulted in disputes over water sharing. Such transnational problems defy national solutions, forcing state governments to develop regional strategies of management.

The Changing Character of the Dialogue Process

Civil-society voices are acquiring a new dynamism in the region. There has been a phenomenal growth in popular interactions among various segments of South Asian society. The most remarkable feature of this dialogue process pertains to their broad range and diversity in terms of objectives, strategies, outreach, institutional bases, and networks. Before undertaking a multifaceted classification of these dialogues, let us first map out certain definitional parameters.

Definitional Parameters

In the "Track One–Track Two" paradigm of peacemaking activities, Track One pertains to diplomatic efforts to resolve conflicts through official channels of government. Track Two pertains to policy-related discussions that are nongovernmental, informal, and unofficial in nature, but which are close to governmental agendas and often involve the participation of government officials in their private capacities, with the explicit intention of influencing or informing public policy. As a form of "shadow diplomacy," they seek to provide a second line of communication between conflicting states and seek to bridge the gap between official government positions by serving as "testing grounds" for new policy initiatives. The term "Track Two," however, does not adequately represent the complexity and varied range of unofficial interactions among citizens. For example, in South Asia, people-to-people dialogues characterized as "Track Three" activities involve groups that explicitly function apart from or beyond governments, aiming to build new constituencies for peace to reorder national security priorities. These rarely have direct access to the relevant foreign offices, but instead aim to change public attitudes and mobilize public pressure on their respective governments to resolve differences and disputes.

In this overview, the broader category of nonofficial dialogues is used as a generic term that includes both Track Two and Track Three efforts, along with a host of other activities such as various kinds of meetings, exchanges, and training programs that have been conducted on both a bilateral and multi-lateral basis. The criterion is not the kind of setting but the *intention to converse on sensitive issues across the borders* with a shared belief of improving the relations between the countries. A second criterion is that only those dialogues that are *continuing on a sustained basis* have been included. Finally, the review has taken into account only those dialogues that have *originated within South Asia*, on a bilateral or a multilateral basis. It does not include the dialogues that involved South Asians or the foreign experts on South Asia, but were born outside the region.

Objectives and Strategies
The institutions and players involved in nonofficial dialogues have pursued two sets of objectives and employed two broad, albeit not mutually exclusive, strategies. The first school of thought stresses the "policy impact" of the dialogues. There are, however, no institutional forums where the Track Two professionals formally report or brief government officials or policymakers, along the lines, for example, of the Track Two processes connected with the Association of South East Asian Nations Regional Forum or the Council for Security Cooperation in Asia Pacific. Nor do government officials participate in such meetings in their personal and private capacities.

Most of such professionals, including retired bureaucrats or army officers, have informal contacts with the policymakers through personal connections. The most widely known examples are that of the Neemrana dialogue between India and Pakistan and the Coalition for Action on South Asian Cooperation (CASAC)—a regional initiative. A more recent example is that of the nuclear-risk reduction talks led by the Delhi Policy Group on the Indian side, that seeks to develop "a shared and agreed lexicon" on nuclear concepts such as "minimum nuclear deterrence" and prepare the ground for bilateral negotiations between the two governments. The foreign offices on both sides were regularly briefed. Another example is that of the Indian chapter of the India-Pakistan Soldiers Peace Initiative who, following a visit to Pakistan in early 2001, met Prime Minister Atal Behari Vajpayee, as well as External Affairs Minister Jaswant Singh, national security advisor and principal secretary to the prime minister, Brajesh Mishra, chief of the army staff, General Padmanabhan, and the chief of the naval staff, Admiral Sushil Kumar. The delegation also met a cross-section of political leaders from the government and opposition political parties.

In the highly polarized political realities of South Asia, generating bipartisan support could prove to be a critical factor for ensuring success. The India-Bangladesh Dialogues—the single most important success story of Track Two dialogues—that facilitated the resolution of the Farakka Barrage dispute between India and Bangladesh was a case in point. For example, the dialogue participants such as A. Moyeen Khan, who was the state minister for planning, M. Rahman, who was the finance minister, and M. Morshed Khan, who was the special envoy to the prime minister, later became front-bench members of the opposition party in Bangladesh's national parliament, the Jatyo Sangshad.

More significantly, there was an unusual and unprecedented movement of the Track Two participants to the first track of the official dialogues. For instance, from the Indian side, I. K. Gujral, who participated in the dialogue series, subsequently became foreign minister and then the prime minister of India. S.A.M.S. Kibria from Bangladesh was part of the Dhaka delegation to the first two rounds of the dialogue in Delhi and Dhaka on economic relations, and then became the finance minister of Bangladesh. This, as we will discuss later, is a rare phenomenon in the South Asian context. It was, according to Gujral, very helpful in the top political leadership to "acquire a first-hand understanding of the conflict as well as alternative policy options for resolving the same," which proved to be a critical factor in the subsequent signing of the Ganges Water Treaty.[3] It is important, however, to also take note of a totally different picture presented by another set of policymakers, the bureaucrats especially from the South Bloc. While acknowledging the important role played by "good friends like Ramaswamy Iyer," Salman Haider, the then foreign secretary of India, who negotiated the treaty, gives credit to the Center for Policy Research (CPR) "to get the thinking going on the subject," and conveying a "clear sense that the problem was soluble," but no further. Once the negotiations got under way, he insisted, "the specific solutions suggested by the CPR and others did not apply."[4]

Haider and others also pointed to a fortuitous constellation of several political developments that helped create a conducive political environment for resolving the dispute. The Sheikh Hasina–led Awami League had, after a twenty-year gap, come to power in Bangladesh, and the Indian government was keen to strengthen her position. Resolving the long-standing Farakka dispute would, no doubt, go a long way in achieving that objective. Another critical variable was that the Indian prime minister Gujral was able to garner the support of the West Bengal government led by Jyoti Basu, whose finance minister played a critical role in outlining the parameters of a "politically saleable" solution to their own constituency. It was, then, a combination of several factors at the political, governmental, and nongovernmental levels that led to the ultimate breakthrough, and perhaps that is why the success story of Track Two India-Bangladesh Dialogues has not been replicated elsewhere in South Asia.

The second school of thought underlines the importance of "knowledge creation" as part of the process and product of nonofficial dialogues. This is based on three varying sets of premises. The first believes that the real challenge lies in forging a South Asian consciousness. To this stream belongs the idea of creating a South Asian university, with issue-oriented faculties such as water management, peace research, human rights and duties, gender politics, communications, and others, spread throughout the region.[5]

Students and researchers will be "people of South Asia first and last," and would look into the issues from a "South Asian perspective, indeed, over and beyond the modern state to which they all belong." The idea is to "create a South Asian mind" that would look into the business of organizing cooperation in diverse fields within South Asia, not from the standpoint of nations and states but from the standpoint of people.[6]

Fellowships in South Asian Alternatives, a project being implemented through a networking of nongovernmental institutions such as the Center for Alternatives, Dhaka; Center for Study of Developing Societies, New Delhi; Nepal Water Conservation Foundation, Kathmandu; Regional Center for Strategic Studies, Colombo; and Sustainable Development Policy Institute, Islamabad, is a step in this direction.

The second viewpoint is that there is a need to mobilize the rich intellectual resources of the region to develop a shared capacity to service the process of developing a South Asian community. The task, accordingly, is to create a body of knowledge regarding the cost-benefit analysis of bilateral and regional cooperation in order to help policymakers make better-informed decisions. To this genre belong the South Asian research institutes and networks such as the Regional Center for Strategic Studies (RCSS), South Asia Center for Policy Studies (SACEPS), and South Asia Network of Economic Institutes (SANEI), which seek to facilitate interstate cooperation in South Asia through policy research, structured dialogue, and interaction. The driving force behind SACEPS, for example, was to institutionalize a South Asia think tank, since the experiences of the 1980s and 1990s had shown that most initiatives such as the Committee on Studies for Cooperation and Development (CSCD), the South Asian Dialogue, Independent Group for South Asian Cooperation (IGSAC), and others were short-lived functional regional entities with a sectoral focus. While they helped to build a community of South Asian professionals and generated a body of useful ideas, many withered away once the funding dried up, thus leaving behind no institutional memory. The idea was, therefore, to design institutional arrangements for reaccumulating South Asia's human resources within the region and also mobilize well-established national institutions to build a shared capacity to service the process of South Asian cooperation.

Third, it is argued that since partition in 1947, an entire generation of Indians and Pakistanis has grown up with virtually no direct knowledge or experience of each other's society. Hence the importance of exchanges between schoolchildren and youth. The Network of South Asian Writers was born out of such concerns that people in the region knew less about the literatures of neighboring countries than about those in West. Using language as a primary vehicle of creativity, which can bond beyond political boundaries and engender better understanding among people, the underlying philosophy of these initiatives is that there can be no better force than writers and intellectuals of the region to work toward achieving a culture of peace in South Asia. An annual conference of SAARC writers now provides an institutional forum to bring about greater awareness among writers, poets, and scholars about their role in creating regional identities and enhancing regional cooperation.

Levels of the Dialogue Process
This discussion includes both bilateral and multilateral dialogues originating within the South Asian region. A large share of bilateral dialogues continue to be held between India and Pakistan, such as the Neemrana Dialogue, the India-Pakistan Peoples Forum for Peace and Democracy, and others, as outlined in the following sections. However, the practice of dialogues among significant segments of civil society level is by no means restricted to the Indo-Pak equation. For example, there was the Patna Initiative and the India-Bangladesh Dialogue series. Clearly, though, there is a need for more such dialogues among the smaller neighbors. India's large size and presence looms large in such dialogue processes.

Track-Two Dialogues at the Bilateral Level

India-Pakistan Soldiers Initiative for Peace
Formed by the Pakistan Peace Coalition at Karachi in 1999, the retired armed forces personnel from India and Pakistan who are its founders hope to function as "soldiers of peace." A group of retired Pakistani officers visited Kolkatta and New Delhi in January 2000. In a reciprocal visit, a group of twenty-one Indian officers visited Lahore, Rawalpindi, Islamabad, and Abbottabad in February–March 2001. On their return to India, the delegation members met a cross section of political leaders from the government and the opposition political parties.

RIMCO Old Boys' Network
This association of the Royal Military College (RIMCO), Dehradun, exchanged visits in April 1996 and 1997. The association uses its members' connections as a forum to discuss effective means of improving bilateral cooperation. The network has not brought out any publications.

India–Sri Lanka Joint Business Council
Created by the Federation of Indian Chambers of Commerce and Industry (FICCI), and its counterpart in Sri Lanka in 1980, the Joint Business Council (JBC) works toward better economic cooperation between India and Sri Lanka. The sixth meeting of the JBC was held in November 1999 at Bangalore. The apex federations have received suggestions from the JBC for joint ventures and increased commodity trade and more frequent trade fairs and exhibitions. It also investigates practical difficulties for businesspersons such as visa, travel restrictions, and poor communication links. The recommendations of the JBC remain largely confidential.

PHD Chambers of Commerce and Industry India-Pakistan Desk
Set up in 1982, the Desk plays an active role in promoting bilateral trade and maintains close contacts with the trade ministries and the high commissions in New Delhi and Islamabad, respectively. It organizes exchanges with various

chambers of commerce in Pakistan; advises the India-Pakistan Joint Commission on trade; and arranges seminars and discussions on trade between the two countries. The Desk recently hosted a visit to India by the Peshawar Women's delegation of entrepreneurs in April 2001. PHD has set up an Indo-Pakistan business committee to oversee the Desk. Vineet Vermani is the current chairperson of the committee and Shabnam Pareek is secretary to this committee.

Jang Initiatives
Jang, the Pakistani Urdu newspaper, has organized two large-scale exchanges of parliamentarians and journalists, in February and July 2000 respectively.

India-Pakistan Friendship Society
Founded in 1987 and chaired by I. K. Gujral, the society seeks to create a peoples-level forum for political-cultural interaction between the two countries. It has facilitated visits by Pakistani cultural groups to India, organized discussions with each other's high commissioners, and held annual lectures in memory of its founder, Kewal Singh. The society has met its modest costs with donations from private business groups supplemented by the society members' personal funds.

India-Pakistan Neemrana Initiative
Launched in 1991, the initiative serves as a forum in which former diplomats, military personnel, and academics from both countries regularly meet, twice a year, to discuss contentious issues. Each round has discussed a broad thematic area of bilateral relations including national polity, economy and society, press and cultural issues, women's status, industrial cooperation and trade, visa and communication difficulties, and science and technology. A joint policy paper outlining options for Kashmir was presented to the governments of India and Pakistan. Other papers have been written on trade and media issues. The Neemrana dialogues are co-chaired by A. M. Khusro, a former member of the Indian Planning Commission, and Niaz Naik, a former Pakistani foreign secretary. The Neemrana Initiative has been funded by the United States Information Services (USIS), the Ford Foundation, and German foundations at different stages.

India-Bangladesh Joint Chambers of Commerce and Industry
This was upgraded from a Joint Business Council in 1999. Its first meeting took place in Calcutta in December 1999. Four meetings have been held so far, the most recent one was also organized in Calcutta in December 2000.

Indo-Bangladesh Dialogues
Initiated in 1994–1995, it has enabled politicians, diplomats, academics, and media personnel from both countries to meet in a time-bound framework to explore ways to improve bilateral relations in four areas—economic relations, water resources and river-water sharing, political and security relations, and

demographic and migration-related issues. Six rounds of dialogues have been held so far. The dialogue facilitated the resolution of the long-standing Farakka Barrage dispute between India and Bangladesh. Its recommendations on trade and economic issues were presented to the Parliament Committee on Foreign Affairs in the Indian Lok Sabha, by I. K. Gujral. The Indian co-chair is B. G. Verghese and the Bangladeshi co-chair is Rehman Sobhan of the Center for Policy Dialogue. The Ford Foundation has supported these dialogues.

Peoples of Asia Forum
This forum brings together eleven Indians and eleven Pakistanis in a face-to-face discussion to explore various issues including the idea of a Union of South Asia. The first session of the forum was held in 1996. The forum plans to conduct more focused studies of bilateral relations in a workshop environment and hold fewer press conferences and public meetings. Its recommendations are intended to be placed before the governments of India and Pakistan, with whom several of the participants have close connections. The principal Indian organizers of the forum are Balraj Puri and Nirmala Deshpande.

India-Pakistan Joint Chambers of Commerce and Industry
Upgraded from a joint business council in 1999, this association works to improve bilateral economic relations. It comprises representatives of the federations and is specifically intended to promote bilateral trade and investment. A Pakistani delegation visited India and the first meeting was held at FICCI, New Delhi, in April 1999. A return visit by FICCI to Islamabad took place in May 2001.

Multilateral Dialogues
The multilateral dialogues are usually designed to suggest directions and policy options for the SAARC process. There is an implicit assumption that the government channels of the SAARC process have often failed to deliver and it needs "outside" or supplementary support in terms of ideas, processes, and mechanisms from the nonofficial players. SAARC has, for example, discussed and accepted the Independent Group for South Asian Cooperation's policy recommendations for establishment of a Poverty Alleviation Fund, a Regional Fund, a Regional Free Trade Zone–SAPTA, and Regional Food Security. More such examples are outlined below.

South Asia Network of Economic Research Institutes (SANEI)
This is a regional initiative to foster networking among economic institutions in the South Asia region that was initiated with assistance from the World Bank in June 1998. It seeks to establish strong research interlinkages among its forty-member-strong diverse economic research institutes in the region. Indian Council for Research on International Economic Relations (ICRIER) plays a nodal role in administering the network. SANEI acts as a nodal agency for dissemination of information on economic issues in the South Asia region and plans to organize summer school and training workshops.

South Asia Regional Initiative/Energy

This $50 million USAID-designed initiative works to encourage regional co-operation in South Asia in energy development and promoting trade in energy resources with partner countries including Bangladesh, India, and Nepal. The program's first phase that began in 2000 seeks to improve the institutional capacity to make decisions in sustainable-energy development; promote private-sector participation in, and civil society support for, energy development; and create as well as strengthen regional forums, networks, and associations for cooperation and advocacy on energy development.

South Asia Labour Forum (SALF)

Formed by the labor organizations in May 1996 to forge better economic co-operation in the South Asian region and toward building a South Asian Regional economic bloc, it has taken up issues of globalization, international trade, and labor laws. The formation of SALF was preceded by separate national consultations. In India, two consultations in March and October 1995 were held in which more than hundred participants from all major trade unions and social movements participated and three working groups on labor standards, environmental standards, and human rights were constituted. The Sri Lankan and Pakistani national consultations were held in May 1996. SALF seeks to form a South Asian labor rights charter and its members are drawn from various trade unions in India, Nepal, Pakistan, and Sri Lanka. The forum may seek the status of a SAARC Regional Apex Body of long-term regional cooperation with the SAARC Secretariat.

SAARC Chambers of Commerce and Industry

Established in 1989 by common agreement of the seven SAARC nations and their apex business federations, this association seeks to bring about greater economic cooperation in South Asia. It is recognized as the apex body of all the national federations of Chambers of Commerce and Industry by the SAARC secretariat. It has organized seminars, commissioned research studies on trade and investment issues, and provided inputs to South Asian commerce ministries. The chamber brings out a handbook of business and commercial information on each South Asian country. Executive committee meetings take place three times a year and are paid for by the federations themselves. The most recent meeting took place in Kathmandu in February 2001. Friedrich Naumann Stiftung had provided core support to the organization, which now generates its own funds. Its current president is Qasim Ibrahim from Maldives. It has a permanent secretariat in Islamabad.

South Asia Human-Rights Documentation Center

Set up in 1989–1990 to investigate and research human rights issues, this organization maintains an informal network of individuals and partner human rights organizations in other South Asian countries with which it attempts to develop common approaches to human rights issues. Consultations between the center and the partner organizations take place every two years. The center produces a number of publications. Its funds come principally from fees that it charges for its research and investigative work and by mobilizing small donations.

Regional Center for Strategic Studies Initiatives (RCSS)

Set up in 1992 to serve as a networking and research institute for strategic and security issues in South Asia, the center aims to build linkages between South Asian and other scholars and institutions. Its summer school workshop on Defence, Technology, and Cooperative Security in South Asia, and its winter workshop on Nonmilitary Sources of Conflict in South Asia are annually held events, targeting the young professionals in the field. RCSS also organizes conferences and workshops and has published several monographs and books. It also brings out a newsletter and has an interactive web site.

Coalition for Action on South Asian Cooperation (CASAC)

Founded in December 1994, CASAC is an independent, nonprofit, public-policy network of South Asian opinion- and policymakers committed to the promotion of regional cooperation in South Asia. It seeks to contribute to the mobilization of political will for furthering regional cooperation with the help of civil society, media, parliamentarians, and political institutions; strengthening of people-level contacts; and enhancement of the role of the private sector in fostering trade and economic cooperation. Its activities are carried out in a decentralized manner through its national chapters, while overall coordination is done by an executive committee at the regional level.

Network of South Asian Writers

The Academy of Fine Arts and Literature organized the first SAARC Writers Conference in New Delhi in April 2000 to explore the possibilities of creating effective machinery to facilitate the institutionalization of such scholarly exchanges among South Asian writers. The second SAARC Writers Conference was held in Kathmandu in November 2000, followed by the third meeting held at Dhaka in March 2001. The last meeting was held at Colombo in June 2001. It envisions an exchange program involving visits of prominent writers among the South Asian countries to engage in formal lectures to students and scholars, and to participate in creative writing and translations workshops and cultural evenings of music and poetry recitals at selected universities.

HIMAL

HIMAL is a South Asian review magazine that began publication in 1987. From its base in Kathmandu, Nepal, *HIMAL* provides a platform for information and debate on pressing issues and significant trends in the South Asian region from a nonnationalistic perspective that covers regional issues not covered extensively by the mainstream media in the region. *HIMAL* has also been a catalyst for other media-related initiatives such as the promotion of documentary films, public radio, and journalism training.

SAARC Association of Speakers and Parliamentarians
Formed in 1992, this association holds an annual conference for speakers and elected representatives that provide opportunities for political leaders to interact informally. They are funded by the SAARC governments.

South Asian Media Association (SAMA)
Established in December 1991 by a group of prominent editors, journalists, scholars, and filmmakers, media activists, and artists, this association aims at addressing ways in which the media can help resolve conflicts within the nation-states of South Asia. SAMA projects include seminars, workshops, study tours, and research activities.

Climate Asia Network South Asia
This network was established by the Bangladesh Center for Advanced Studies (BCAS), for training groups in South and Southeast Asia on greenhouse inventories. BCAS is the regional center for CAN-SA and produces a quarterly newsletter (Clime Asia) that is distributed throughout the subcontinent. BCAS collaborates with institutions such as the Rajiv Gandhi Foundation, Tata Energy Research Institute at New Delhi, Sustainable Development Policy Institute in Pakistan, and Royal Nepalese Academy of Science and Technology in Nepal.

Center for Science and Environment (CSE):
Bilateral and South Asian Initiatives
CSE is an Indian environmental research and activist organization. Since 1989, it has organized periodic interactions with NGOs in other South Asian countries to discuss common environmental problems. CSE organized a meeting of South Asian NGOs before the Earth Summit in 1992 to develop a common regional position on environmental issues, as well as a follow-up conference in 1993 to discuss emerging patterns of global environmental governance. In 1995, CSE facilitated South Asia–wide meetings in Nepal, with International Union for the Conservation of Nature–Nepal, and in India on behalf of the International NGO Forum. Further meetings are to be held in Sri Lanka. The 1995 meetings resulted in decisions by South Asian environmental NGOs to develop common agendas and action programs to identify further areas of regional cooperation, launch a newsletter, and improve communication and networking among South Asian NGOs. The funding for South Asia initiatives comes from a variety of sources including CSE itself, IUCN, and participating NGOs.

SAARC LAW
Formed in 1991 and recognized by the SAARC in 1994, SAARC LAW is comprised of legal luminaries and scholars from the various South Asian nations and works to spread knowledge about different South Asian legal systems among the legal communities in these countries. It has affiliated country

chapters in Bangladesh, India, Nepal, Pakistan, and Sri Lanka. SAARC LAW chapters have been formed. It has five hundred individual members. The 8th SAARC LAW conference was held in Kathmandu in September 2000.

South Asia Center for Policy Studies (SACEPS)

Formed at the initiative of a group of eminent persons in the region in 1999, SACEPS is a network of regional organizations including the Center for Policy Research, New Delhi; Institute of Integrated Development Studies (IIDS), Kathmandu; Lahore University of Management Sciences (LUMS), Lahore; Institute for Policy Studies and Marga Institute in Colombo; and Center of Policy Dialogue, Dhaka, that is working as its secretariat. SACEPS aims to promote regional cooperation in the field of development-policy research, policy studies, and policy advocacy by building business and professional networks with some of the well-established national institutions in the region. It was formally launched in Dhaka in January 2001. A seven-member executive committee oversees its activities. Six task forces have been formed to conduct studies on issues such as South Asia free trade costs and benefits, common investment strategy for South Asia, South Asia's strategy for WTO negotiations, and energy cooperation in South Asia.

South Asia Forum for Human Rights

The South Asia Forum for Human Rights was set up in 1992 to promote international standards of human rights and monitor their enforcement. It serves as a lobbying and monitoring organization network, looking into the problems of refugees and statelessness in South Asia, ways to train human-rights activists, and greater transparency and participation within SAARC. The forum has published pamphlets and bulletins on its work and plans to build up a regular dossier on regional human rights. The forum is advised by a governing board of two members each from India, Pakistan, Bangladesh, Nepal, and Sri Lanka. It works through a network of forty partner civil-society organizations and its programs are structured around regional dialogues, research and training workshops, publications, and advocacy campaigns. Funding for the forum comes principally from Dutch and German donor organizations.

Duryog Nivaran

Duryog Nivaran is a South Asian initiative on disaster management set up in 1994. Its network members include Intermediate Technology (ITDG) Nepal, ITDG Bangladesh, ITDG Sri Lanka, and Disaster Mitigation Institute and Center for Science and Environment in India. Duryog Nivaran aims to reduce the vulnerability of communities to disasters and conflicts by integrating alternative perspectives at the conceptual, policy, and implementation levels of disaster mitigation and development programs in the region. The network has organized regular seminars in all member countries, with the first one taking place in Kathmandu in 1994. Each session has focused on a broad area of disaster management and research has been carried out in the area of floods, road traffic, gender vulnerability, induced and natural risk, and effectiveness of relief mechanisms.

Fellowship in South Asian Alternatives

The fellowship is a collaborative effort among a number of South Asian policy institutes, including the Center for Alternatives, Dhaka; Regional Center for Strategic Studies, Colombo; Center for the Study of Developing Societies, New Delhi; Sustainable Development Policy Institute, Islamabad; and the Nepal Water Conservation Foundation in Kathmandu. The fellowships are intended to promote research by younger scholars on common themes of South Asian concern. Apart from practical work of dialogue, interaction, information, and advocacy at the field level, fellows from more than one country are jointly working on three main issues: water, power, and people; life and death in nuclear space; and ethnicity.

Citizens' Commission for South Asia

Set up by CASAC with eminent personalities of the region, the commission held its first meeting in December 2000 and aims at intensified South Asian regional cooperation through increased public awareness and civil-society participation. The next meeting is planned for 2001 when its members propose to take up several studies on issues such as globalization and its impact on South Asia; democracy and good governance including effective measures to tackle poverty; potential of biotechnology; and regional cooperation in energy.

Outreach

In terms of the outreach, the dialogues could be analyzed from a functional perspective or the nature and kind of participants involved in them. From a functional viewpoint, the dialogues range from the cultural arena such as Network of South Asian Writers and the Sanskriti Pratishthan that aim to use their pen or art to lobby for peace. At the other end of the spectrum, there are attempts, for example, by the Delhi Policy Group to engage the Pakistanis in nuclear-risk-reduction talks. Another important set of initiatives are those that seek to strengthen business links. These efforts in network building are usually cooperative ventures involving well-established business fora such as the Confederation of Indian Industries (CII), the Lahore Chamber of Commerce, or regional ones including the SAARC Chambers of Commerce and Industry. Yet another set of dialogues focuses on sharing of natural resources and environment-related issues. These include Duryog Nivaran, Eastern Himalayan Rivers Study, and the like.

There is also an elite vis-à-vis grassroots argument. As pointed out earlier, typically the Track Two dialogues seek to target the intelligentsia and reach out to those who have access to the policymakers or the corridors of power in general. To that extent, their outreach may be limited to certain segments of elites, but perhaps that is why, it is argued, they are more effective in terms of influencing the decisionmaking processes. On the other hand, the Pakistan-India

Peoples Forum for Peace and Democracy (PIPFD) believes in spreading the dialogue process horizontally to various segments of the society at the grassroots level. They therefore try to involve people from all walks of life—journalists, artists, lawyers, writers, activists, political leaders, trade unionists, and army officers. The sheer territorial spread of the PIPFD in terms of its local chapters in different parts of the two countries remains to be matched by any other dialogue.

Track-Three Dialogues

Pakistan-India People's Forum for Peace and Democracy (PIPFD)
Created in 1994–1995 to act as a mass-based pressure group, PIPFD has since held five conventions involving hundreds of delegates from both sides. The next meeting is planned to be held in Pakistan. The forum has debated issues such as confrontation in Kashmir, demilitarization and peace, and intolerance and governance. The PIPFD publishes pamphlets and books, campaigns for the exchange of artists and activists, and engages in publicity and network campaigns to broaden public awareness of its aims. It has regional chapters in Jaipur, Varanasi, Hyderabad, Mumbai, Kolkata, Patna, Madras, New Delhi, and Jammu in India; and Karachi, Lahore, Quetta, Peshawar, Islamabad, and Hyderabad in Pakistan.

Women's Initiative for Peace in South Asia (WIPSA)
Led by Ms. Nirmala Deshpande and Ms. Asma Jehangir in India and Pakistan respectively, groups of the Women's Initiative have exchanged delegations. An Indian delegation of twenty-four women had visited Pakistan in March 2000, and a return visit of Pakistani women's delegation came to India in May 2000. Both visits attracted wide media coverage. WIPSA has published two reports on these visits and another on "Kashmir: The Journey in Quest for Peace."

Doon School Old Boys' Society
This network emerged in 1985, at the time of the school's golden jubilee, and delegations of Indian and Pakistani former schoolmates have since visited each other's countries at regular intervals. The group has refrained from discussing bilateral relations at their meetings, placing a higher value on their personal relationships, and maintain a newsletter of personal information. While delegation members pay for their own travel, hospitality in the host country is provided privately. The network was initiated by Gulab Ramchandani, a former Doon School headmaster.

Action Committee Against Arms Race (ACAAR)
ACAAR was formed in 1998 in Islamabad to chalk out a program to mobilize public opinion against the nuclearization of the subcontinent and the conventional arms race. At its general body meeting on 22 May 1999, it denounced the government for celebrating the Chagai nuclear tests and 6 and 9 August

2000; it organized public meetings to observe the Hiroshima and Nagasaki days respectively.

The Pakistan-India People's Solidarity Conference

This conference focuses on the nuclear issues, democracy, and the Kashmir issue between India and Pakistan, and works toward promoting greater people-to-people contacts. Its joint declaration on peace was endorsed by more than two hundred organizations in South Asia in July 2001. The main organizers included Movement in India for Nuclear Disarmament (MIND), the Coalition for Nuclear Disarmament and Peace (CNDP), Women's Initiative for Peace in South Asia (WIPSA), Center for Dialogue and Reconciliation, and the Pakistan-India People's Forum for Peace and Democracy.

Last but not least, some initiatives have, over the years, found an institutional home, while others continue to be primarily networking groups. Institutions such as RCSS and SACEPS have a regional character and outlook. These institutions seek to mobilize professional resources and national institutions within the region to generate the critical mass needed to build South Asian institutions which could serve as the common centers of learning and research. This is important from the point of view of capacity building, especially in smaller countries. More such institutions are required in South Asia that have the analytic capacity and independence to initiate policy-related research and collaborative projects with the government. At the same time, initiatives such as CASAC and PIPFD have their local chapters in respective member countries but continue to work as "networks."

Funding the Dialogues

Much of the funding of nonofficial dialogues continues to originate outside the region from donors such as the Ford Foundation, Friedrich Ebert Stiftung (FES), Friedrich Normann Stiftung (FNS), Japan Foundation, W. Alton Jones Foundation, Rockefeller Foundation, and aid agencies such as the Canadian International Development Agency and USAID. There are sensitivities within the region about the funding issue and perceptions of external interference. "These were most commonly raised about U.S. funding, and, to a much lesser extent, European, Japanese and Canadian."[7] This is important because some dialogues have simply died after the foreign funding ceased. South Asia Dialogues is a case in point. A counterexample is that of the Neemrana Dialogue, which managed to sustain the process after the USIS and the Ford Foundation funding had dried up, by diversifying its sources of funding. Yet another important dialogue—India-Bangladesh Dialogues—stands at a critical juncture today. They have completed six rounds of discussion funded by the Ford Foundation, and as of now their future is uncertain. Some initiatives have, however, become self-financed while others rely on indigenous sources such as local philanthropy and industry. PIPFD members, for instance, finance their own travel while the hosts, with locally raised funds, provide the hospitality.

Critical Evaluation

The widely varying form, substance, and objectives of South Asian dialogues make it difficult to come to any simple assessment of their overall value. An earlier review[8] enlisted their achievements to include:

- Exploring alternatives for conflict management at a nongovernmental level
- Acting as informal channels for exploring policy options without committing the government
- Influencing public discussion on regional issues
- Prompting government action by calling public attention to escalating problems
- Lowering barriers between officials and citizens, especially on economic issues
- Creating new connections among research institutes and among NGOs in the region, and
- Serving as a formative influence ground for those individuals who would later play leading national roles

At a more tangible level, the idea of nonofficial dialogues had taken off and grown exponentially among the elite segments of the civil society in South Asia. An earlier review had noted forty dialogues that were under way in 1996. In 2001, the numbers have increased both at the bilateral and regional level.

Critics, however, point that the nonofficial dialogues have not produced any dramatic breakthroughs on contentious regional issues nor brought any qualitative transformation in the calculus of bilateral and regional cooperation. They have not had any kind of cumulative effect or achieved a systematic influence on governmental thinking and interactions. The channels of communication between Track One and Track Two continue to be informal, ad hoc, and of a personalized nature. An interesting recent trend in Track Two diplomacy has been that of individual initiatives, the most prominent example being that of Mr. R. K. Mishra, chairman of the Observer group of newspapers, apparently with the blessings of the Indian prime minister's office. In 1999, for example, Mishra was involved in exploring a possible solution to the Kashmir and Kargil conflicts with Niaz Naik, who was reportedly functioning with the blessings of Pakistan prime minister's office.

With the exception of Bangladesh, perhaps, bureaucracies have not been pressured from above or below into accepting Track Two or other dialogue processes as a routine part of business, and tend to see few advantages in doing so. "They are rarely the governmental instrument of choice or a major part of the diplomacy of the region. Track Two processes have almost never served as fora surrogate or proxy negotiations occurring in concert with formal governmental negotiations, as they have, for example, in the Middle East peace process. Nor have they often been used, as in the Asia-Pacific, as a forum for discussing threat perceptions as part of a process of confidence building and mutual reassurance."9

Why have these dialogues not succeeded in realizing their larger goal of creating a broad-based peace constituency in the region? At a fundamental level, one may argue that there are two critical flaws in conceptualizing the strategy and outreach, or perhaps the vision of such dialogues' processes. The first relates to certain erroneous assumptions about the players, sites, and dynamics of policymaking in the South Asian context. To begin with, it is important to understand its qualitatively different character from, say, that of the United States and Asia-Pacific, where the idea of Track Two diplomacy first originated and has proven to be a successful venture. In the United States, there is a very large and influential policymaking community outside the State Department that includes the Council on Foreign Relations, the Rand Corporation, the Brookings Institution, and a vast network of think tanks. This, along with its well-established practices of frequent and lateral traffic between academia and the government, has, over the years, put in place the necessary infrastructure and mechanisms that could be used for influencing the policymaking processes. In Asia-Pacific, the government officials participate in such Track Two processes in their private capacities. South Asia has none of these features.

Hence it is important to understand the power structure, the players within the establishment, and its equations with those "outside"—media, academia, think tanks, and the small but prominent community of ex-bureaucrats and ex-military officials—in the specific South Asian context. In India, the foreign-policy bureaucracy, since the Nehru days, has traditionally been the only institution groomed in the task of foreign policymaking. This along with the institutional hurdle of the absence of lateral entry into key bureaucratic positions has resulted in often thick and impermeable barriers between officials and public—an "iron curtain" dividing those "inside" the establishment and those "outside," that is, the civil society. This is true for every country in South Asia including Pakistan, Sri Lanka, Bangladesh, Nepal, Bhutan, and Maldives.

The two live in separate, almost self-contained worlds that operate from fundamentally different information bases. There is no sharing of memory, no reliance on institutional memory, and no light thrown on the decisionmaking processes. No government in South Asia respects a freedom of information act; classified documents are *never* made public. The author's interaction with serving or retired government officials pointed to the structural problems inherent in this situation: the government information base remains too narrow; and that of the nongovernment sources is wide but not well-informed. As a result, there is considerable mutual suspicion rather than mutual interaction. Many believe that the government uses people to hear what it wants to hear and those challenging the government positions are quickly and effectively sidelined and marginalized. Clearly, it is not a healthy relationship.

In our interactions with the policymakers for an earlier review of the nonofficial dialogues, many had expressed a disinterest bordering on contempt for involvement of outsiders described in one discussion as "naïve meddlers and amateurs" lacking the skills and information to manage sensitive issues. Another official spoke of "well-intentioned people wasting their time and ours." Their views were not universal but they were a recurrent refrain.[10] Little has changed after five more years of Track Two dialogues.

A long-lasting and perhaps more effective way out might, therefore, be to first create and institutionalize new mechanisms for interactions between the government and civil society within each country. It is important, however, to use a much more inclusive conception of civil society than is currently understood in popular parlance. It must, as a leading intellectual lamented, "explore the world outside the Saturday Club of the India International Center." This has been the second critical lacuna of the Track Two diplomacy, that is, it failed to make any connections with the enormous potential of a vast network of social movements at the grassroots level. The tragedy of the Track Two initiatives has been that by involving people too close to the establishment, by debating issues close to the governmental agendas and perspectives, and trying to help the government through backdoor channels, they too started reflecting the status quo governmental thinking.

Cold-shouldered by the establishment, the Track Two professionals were also divorced from the social realities on the ground. It became essentially a "managerial approach," not a radical one that questions the governmental assumption and seeks to provide any meaningful alternative to the governments. "The bureaucrats have played the game for so long that despite the RRS (Retired Radical Syndrome) factor, it was pointed out, they could only tell you how to play the game but would never question the rules of the game."[11] The mantle of this responsibility has been borne by the social movements since the early 1980s. But then the amorphous entity of "people" hardly has anything to do with the domain of international politics, especially foreign policymaking. The counterargument runs like this: the critical inputs for a new understanding of security are indeed emerging from critical social movements, which are often focused on local issues but sensitive to the wider picture. They also raise fundamentally important issues concerning the possibilities of imagining political community and forging new solidarities, which act in ways that transcend the boundaries of blocs and states working to promote international collaboration irrespective of state policies.

A large population of such social activists, highly educated and skilled, drawn from across the social spectrum and from across regional, linguistic, cultural, and even national boundaries, have been active in peace and antinuclear armaments, the environmental movement, the women's movements, or the movements for autonomy and self-determination of cultural groups, minorities, and tribes. Writing in the early 1980s, D. L. Sheth described them as "blazing a new trail, illuminating a new terrain of policies and evolving a new mode of politics, bypassing legal and territorial definitions and bringing new constituencies into the political arena, around new definitions of the issues and context of policies."

What is different in the twenty-first century—the era of globalization—is a growing awareness among these intellectuals and activists about the vertical linkages between their life situations and global economic power structures and the country's elites. They realize that the local power structures, which they are fighting in their respective areas, derive their power vertically from the macro structures of the prevalent national and international order. Such problems as the threat of nuclear warfare and ecological destruction, which still appeared to many at the national level (scientists, politicians, journalists) as remote concerns, are fast becoming a part of their political consciousness. This is indeed the constituency that the Track Three, or as a scholar put it, "professionals trying to move from Track V to Track X, rather than Track II to Track I," have sought to mobilize. While a beginning has been made, there is a long way to go.

At the same time, one must recognize that the nonofficial dialogues per se are still at a comparatively nascent stage and it is premature to expect quick results, especially when formal diplomatic efforts are, for the last five decades, still grappling with the same issues. The dialogue process has also not become resilient enough to withstand the unpredictable changes in political environment in the region. The Kargil crisis in 1999 delivered a serious blow to not only official but also nonofficial interactions. For example, while members of the RIMC Old Boys' Network have kept in touch on an individual and personal basis, they could not sustain organized and group-level interactions with their Pakistani counterparts. The Peoples Forum for Peace and Democracy also did not hold an annual convention in 1999. Some participants of the Neemrana Dialogue felt that gains painstainkingly made over years of close interactions were negated rather quickly as some of their members started resorting to "nationalistic" positions in the dialogue process.

There is, however, another side of this picture. In the aftermath of nuclear tests in India, PIPFD and others organized protest marches. An Action Committee Against Arms Race (ACAAR) was formed to chalk out a program to mobilize public opinion against the nuclearization of the subcontinent. MIND was born in India. The South Asian Against Nukes web site was set up to bring together information resources for peace and antinuclear activists from all over South Asia. On the eve of the Agra summit between Pakistan's president general Pervez Musharraf and Indian prime minister Atal Bihari Vajpayee, citizens of the two countries organized an India-Pakistan People's Solidarity Conference. Its joint declaration was endorsed by 147 Indian organizations, 46 Pakistani organizations, and 8 South Asian and Pak-India groups based abroad.

Governmental resistance to nonofficial dialogues on policy-sensitive matters, as argued earlier, remains a major obstacle. Some even debunk them as harmful to the "national interests." The Pakistan-India Forum's convention at New Delhi was criticized by Pakistan's Foreign Office, Ministry of Information, and members of the Kashmir Committee as "inappropriate and questionable [in its] timing, tenor and size."[12]

On a positive note, the dialogue process has, over the years, broadened its base in terms of participation. Some of the lacuna identified earlier, pertaining to the underrepresentation of some groups including "women, the generation under forty, those who live outside the national capitals, and those who do not speak in English," has been addressed to some extent.[13] The constituency of women have been mobilized by groups such as WIPSA and initiatives such as WISCOMP (Women in Security, Conflict and Peace Management) in India and FOWSIA (Forum on Women in Security and International Affairs) in Bangladesh. Similar initiatives are planned for countries such as Sri Lanka and Pakistan.

Dialogues such as the summer workshop on Science, Technology, and Arms Control and the winter school on Non-Military Sources of Conflict in South Asia are especially for younger South Asians. The emergence of a new generation of Indians and Pakistanis—"the Midnight's Grandchildren"—is of special significance. They do not carry the psychological baggage of the partition trauma. The third generation has been exposed to a wide variety of international influences through films, music, travel, and more recently, satellite television. There is a growing trend of an expatriate generation of students, returning home with stronger commitment to South Asian connections and possibilities. The third generation does not, of course, constitute a monolithic social group. Widespread differences in upbringing, education, social mobility, and regional and ethnic preferences separate them to a great degree from peers in their own countries. However, the post-1971 generation of educated urban middle class is more cosmopolitan and liberal in outlook. They neither perceive the "other side" as "the root of all evil" nor, are they prepared to "sacrifice the future to get even."[14] Contact is also being established between the fourth generation of Indians and Pakistanis. The schoolchildren of Karachi and Bombay interact through a letter exchange program called "Peace Pals."

Yet another set of dialogues have sought to involve the parliamentarians. In 1992, the speakers of the parliaments of South Asian countries met in Sri Lanka and Nepal to form the Association of SAARC Speakers and Parliamentarians. In 1994, the International Center for Peace Initiatives collaborated with Parliamentarians for Global Action and the International Peace Academy for their program of workshops in peacemaking and preventive diplomacy for parliamentarians in South Asia. The first workshop was held in Kathmandu in May 1994 and the second in the Maldives in May 1995. In November 1996, CASAC held a workshop for parliamentarians on appropriate measures for conflict resolution and confidence building in South Asia. In February 1999, the Jang group of newspapers organized a meeting of parliamentarians from India and Pakistan. One of the proposals that have been discussed over the years is a nonlegislative parliament for South Asia.

Last but not least, an attempt to reach out to the erstwhile neglected constituency of indigenous and regional language media of India, Pakistan, and Sri Lanka together, was made through a unique gathering of the editors of newspapers from the Sinhalese, Tamil, Hindi, Marathi, Malayalam, Punjabi, Sindhi, Urdu, and Baluchi press of the three countries. This was organized by the North-South Security program of King's College, London, and the South Asian Media Association (SAMA) of Colombo, Sri Lanka, in cooperation with International Center for Peace Initiatives, Mumbai and Citizens Media Commission,

Karachi, in June 1999. A number of concrete initiatives were agreed upon, including the setting up of a South Asian Editor's Forum that would develop the guidelines to develop a South Asian ethos in the press. In 1999, the Sanskriti Pratishthan in New Delhi launched a residency program for scholars, writers, and artists from South Asia.

The Internet has provided a new and active platform for networking among South Asians. Despite its inherent limitations of being accessible to only those who can afford it, it is beginning to play an important role in providing a common forum for exchanging views and building bridges among the people of the region. South Asia Citizens' Web is an independent space on the Net to promote dialogue and information exchange between and about South Asian citizens under the main rubrics of civil society, peace, democracy, secularism, social movements, the women's movement, environmental campaigns, labor movement activism, human-rights groups and campaigns, citizens action against communalism and religious fundamentalism, news, films, and research projects. SAWNET is another such example.

Overall, the process of developing a critical mass of people who believe in the idea of South Asia is well under way. The road map to the future remains difficult, but with people thinking ahead of the governments, the future prospects of nonofficial dialogues in the region are bright.

Resources

Other Publications

Beyond Boundaries: A Report on the State of Non-Official Dialogues on Peace, Security and Cooperation in South Asia, by Navnita Chadha Behera, Paul M. Evans and Gowher Rizvi. Ontario, University of Toronto/York University, Joint Center for Asia-Pacific Studies, 1997.

Crisis Prevention, Confidence Building and Reconciliation in South Asia, edited by Michael Krepon and Amit Sevak. Washington, DC, Henry L. Stimson Center, 1996.

"Non-Official Dialogues Between India and Pakistan: Prospects and Problems," *ACDIS Occasional Paper,* August 1997.

"People's Initiative: An Idea Whose Time Has Come," by Gautam Navlakha. *Economic and Political Weekly,* 11 March 1995, pp. 484–485.

People-to-People Contacts in South Asia, by Navnita Chadha Behera et al. New Delhi, Monohar, 2000.

Perspectives on South Asia, by Navnita Chadha Behera and V. A. Pai Panandikar (eds.). New Delhi, Konark, 2000.

Political Leaders and Track Two Diplomacy in South Asia. New Delhi, International Center for Peace Initiatives, December 1995.

Rediscovering a South Asian Community: Civil Society in Search of Its Future, by Rehman Sobhan. Colombo, International Center of Ethnic Studies, 1998.

SAARC: Beyond State-Centric Cooperation, edited by Imtiaz Ahmed and Meghna Guhathakurta. Dhaka, Center for Social Studies, 1992.

Studying Asia Pacific Security: The Future of Research, Training and Dialogue Activities, edited by Paul M. Evans. Ontario, University of Toronto/York University, 1994.

Track Two Diplomacy in South Asia, by Sundeep Waslekar. 2d ed. Urbana, IL, ACDIS Occasional Paper, Program in Arms Control, Disarmament and International Security, University of Illinois and Urbana-Champaign, October 1995.

Organizations

Action Committee Against Arms Race
Yusuf Mustikhan, Convener (ACAAR)
43/3-C, Shah Abdul Latif Road, Block-6, PECHS
Karachi, Pakistan
E-mail: B. M. Kutty (Secretary) at b.m.kutty@cyber.net.pk
Web site: www.mnet.fr/aiindex/acaar.html

Center for Science and Environment
Sunita Narain
41 Tughlaqabad Institutional Area
New Delhi–110062, India
Tel: +91-11-6981110
Fax: +91-11-6985879
E-mail: cse@sdalt.ernet.in
Web site: www.cseindia.org

Citizens' Commission for South Asia
Sridhar Khatri
P.O. Box 10619, Sanogauchar Gyaneshwar
Kathmandu, Nepal
Tel/Fax: 977-1-412477
E-mail: sridhar@ccsl.com.np
Web site: www.fesindia.org/casacmain1.htm

Climate Asia Network South Asia
Atiq Rahman, CAN-SA
H.No. 23, Road 10A, Dhanmondi R/A
Dhaka-1209, Bangladesh
Tel: +880-2-8115829
Fax: +880-2-8111344
E-mail: atiq.r@bdcom.com
Web site: www.climatenetwork.org/CANSA/CANSouthAsia.html

Coalition for Action on South Asian Cooperation
Sridhar Khatri
P.O. Box 10619, Sanogauchar Gyancshwar
Kathmandu, Nepal
Tel/Fax: +977-1-412477
E-mail: sridhar@ccsl.com.np

Doon School Old Boys' Society
Gulab Ramchandani
UdayanVillage & P.O. Jhajra
Dehra Dun, U.P. 248007, India
Tel: Dehra Dun-683267
Fax: 683309

Duryog Nivaran
Madhavi Ariyabandu, Duryog Nivaran Secretariat
5 Lionel Edirisinghe Mawatha Kirulapone
Colombo-5, Sri Lanka
Tel: +94-1-852149
Fax: +94-1-856188
E-mail: madhavi@itdg.lanka.net

Fellowship in South Asian Alternatives
Prof. Imtiaz Ahmed
E-mail: imtiaz@bangla.net

HIMAL
Kanak Dixit, Himal Media Pvt. Ltd
GPO Box 7251
Kathmandu, Nepal
Tel: +977-1-543333
Fax: +977-1-52101
Web site: www.himalmag.com

Indo-Bangladesh Dialogues
B. G.Verghese, Center for Policy Research
Dharma Marg, Chanakyapuri
New Delhi-110021, India
Tel: +91-11-3015276
Web site: www.cpd-bangladesh.org

India-Bangladesh Joint Chambers of Commerce and Industry
Amita Sarkar, FICCI, SAARC Cell
Federation House, Tansen Marg
Ncw Delhi-110001, India
Tel: +91-11-3738760/70

India-Pakistan Joint Chambers of Commerce and Industry
Amita Sarkar, FICCI, SAARC Cell
Federation House, Tansen Marg
New Delhi-110001, India
Tel: +91-11-3738760/70

India-Pakistan Neemrana Initiative
A. M. Khusro, The Aga Khan Foundation
Sarojini House, Bhagwan Das Road
New Delhi-110001, India
Tel: +91-11-3782173
Fax: +91-11-3782174

India-Pakistan Soldiers Initiative for Peace
Ms Nirmala Despande, South Asia Gandhi Ashram
Kingsway Camp
New Delhi–110009, India
Tel: +91-11-7434514
E-mail: nirmala@sansad.nic.in

India–Sri Lanka Joint Business Council
Amita Sarkar, FICCI, SAARC Cell
Federation House
Tansen Marg, New Delhi-110001, India
Tel: +91-11-3738760/70

Network of South Asian Writers
Ajeet Cour, Academy of Fine Arts and Literature
4/6 Siri Fort Institutional Area
New Delhi, India
Tel: +91-11-6498070
Fax: +91-11-6496542

Pakistan-India People's Forum for Peace and Democracy
Tapan Bose, Pakistan-India People's Forum
K-14 Green Park Extension
New Delhi–110016, India
Tel: +91-11-6863830
or I. A. Rehman, Co-Chairperson, PIPFPD
11-Temple Road
Lahore, Pakistan
Tel: +92-42-735-7926
Fax: +92-42-722-3455
E-mail: pakindo@brain.net.pk
Web site: www.brain.net.pk/~pakindo/

Pakistan-India People's Solidarity Conference
Sonia Jabbar
D-41 Jungpura Extn
New Delhi–110014, India
Tel: +91-11-4310511
Fax: +91-11-4626699
E-mail: info@pakindpeace.org
Web site: www.pakindpeace.org

Peoples of Asia Forum
Balraj Puri
(Tel: Jammu-542687)
and Nirmala Deshpande, South Asia Gandhi Ashram
Kingsway Camp
New Delhi–110009, India
Tel: +91-11-7434514
E-mail: nirmala@sansad.nic.in

PHD Chambers of Commerce and Industry India-Pakistan Desk
PHD House
4/2 Opposite Asian Games Village
New Delhi-110016 India
Tel: +91-11-6863801/3802
Fax: +91-11-6863135

Regional Center for Strategic Studies Initiatives
Gen. Dipanker Banerjee, Executive Director
Regional Center for Strategic Studies, 2, Elibank Road
Colombo 5, Sri Lanka
Tel: +94-1-599734/5
Fax: +94-1-599993
E-mail: rcss@sri.lanka.net
Web site: www.rcss.org

RIMCO Old Boys' Network
General Ashok Mehta
Tel: +91-11-4456122/23

SAARC Chambers of Commerce and Industry
H.No 5, Street No. 59, F-8/4
Islamabad, Pakistan
Tel: +92-51-2281395/6
Fax: +92-51-2281390

E-mail: saarcnet@ficci.com
Web site: www.saarcnet.org

SAARC LAW
Bharat Raj Upreti
SAARC LAW Secretariat, GPO Box 6561
Kathmandu, Nepal
Tel: +977-1-433411
Fax: +977-1-436328
E-mail: saarclaw@ntc.net.np
Web site: www.saarclaw.org

South Asia Center for Policy Studies
Prof. Rehman Sobhan, Executive Director, SACEPS
H.No 40-C, Road No. 1, Dhanmondi R/A
Dhaka 1205, Bangladesh
Tel: +880-2-8124770
Web site: www.cpd-bangladesh.org/saceps

South Asia Forum for Human Rights
Tapan Bose
GPO Box 12855
Kathmandu, Nepal
Tel: +977-1-541026
Fax: +977-1-527852
E-mail: tapan@safhr.org
Web site: www.safhr.org

South Asia Human-Rights Documentation Center
Ravi Nair
B-6/6, Safdarjang Enclave Extension
New Delhi–110029, India
Tel: +91-11-6191120/2717
Fax: +91-11-6191120
E-mail: hrdc_online@hotmail.com
Web site: www.hri.ca/partners/sahrdc

South Asia Network of Economic Research Institutes
Dr. Isher Judge Ahluwalia, Director and Chief Executive
ICRIER, Core 6 A, Fourth Floor
India Habitat Center, Lodhi Road
New Delhi–110003, India
Tel: +91-11-4645218/20
Fax: +91-11- 4620180
Web site: www.saneinetwork.org

South Asian Media Association
PO Box 1263
No. 16, Barnes Place
Colombo-7, Sri Lanka
Tel: +94-1-699166/7
Fax: +94-1-686315

South Asia Regional Initiative/Energy
Robert W. Beckman, Regional Coordinator and Program Manager, USAID
American Embassy, Shantipath, Chankyapuri

New Delhi–110021, India
Tel: +91-11-4198469
Fax: +91-11-4198545
E-mail: rbeckman@usaid.gov
Web site: www.sari-energy.org

Women's Initiative for Peace in South Asia
Nirmala Despande, South Asia Gandhi Ashram
Kingsway Camp
New Delhi–110009, India
Tel: +91-11-7434514
E-mail: nirmala@sansad.nic.in

Navnita Chadha Behera is a visiting fellow at the Brookings Institution. She has been an assistant research professor at the Centre for Policy Research, and assistant director, Women in Security, Conflict Management and Peace (WISCOMP), New Delhi. Dr. Chadha has also served as a consultant to the Ford Foundation at the New Delhi office. She has published widely in India and abroad. She is the author of State, Identity and Violence: Jammu, Kashmir and Ladakh *(2000),* State, People and Security: The South Asian Context *(editor, 2001),* Perspectives on South Asia *(coeditor, 2000),* People-to-People Dialogues in South Asia *(coauthor, 2000) and,* Beyond Boundaries: A Report on the State of Non-Official Dialogues on Peace, Security and Co-operation in South Asia *(coauthor, 1997).*

Notes

1. Rehman Sobhan, *Rediscovering a South Asian Community: Civil Society in Search of Its Future.* Colombo: International Center of Ethnic Studies, 1998.

2. Ibid.

3. Interview with author.

4. Based on confidential interviews with government officials.

5. Imtiaz Ahmed and Meghna Guhathakurta (eds.), *SAARC: Beyond State-Centric Cooperation.* Dhaka: Center for Social Studies, 1992.

6. Based on personal conversations with Imtiaz Ahmed.

7. Navnita Chadha Behera, Paul M. Evans, and Gowher Rizvi, *Beyond Boundaries: A Report on the State of Non-Official Dialogues on Peace, Security and Cooperation in South Asia.* Ontario: University of Toronto/York University, Joint Center for Asia-Pacific Studies, 1997.

8. Ibid.

9. Ibid.

10. Ibid.

11. Based on confidential interviews with senior scholars.

12. Ibid.

13. Behera, Evans, and Rizvi, *Beyond Boundaries.*

14. Sundeep Waslekar, *Track Two Diplomacy in South Asia.* Urbana, IL: ACDIS Occasional Paper, Program in Arms Control, Disarmament and International Security, University of Illinois and Urbana-Champaign, October 1995.

7.2

The Need for Confidence-Building Measures

P. R. Chari

Mistrust between India and Pakistan aggravates what is, in any case, an extremely dangerous security situation in South Asia. Confidence-building measures (CBMs) offer one strategy for building trust and creating an atmosphere more conducive to the peaceful resolution of conflicts, or at the very least, the reduction of tensions in the region. There are, nonetheless, a number of problems inherent in the CBM modality that must be considered. In particular, of course, CBMs will not have an appreciable effect if the two sides are not, for political reasons, committed to resolving their differences and ending the "culture of adversarial politics." But other objections, as well as a number of paradoxes related to the CBM approach, also need to be considered. For instance, "trust" is a prerequisite for reaching agreement on confidence-building measures, whose purpose is to increase trust, and the very CBMs put in place to prevent tensions from boiling over (a hotline, for example) may be ignored or neglected during the crisis. Nonetheless, with so much at stake in South Asia, the CBM approach should not be ignored.

Confidence-building measures are recognized to be "arrangements designed to enhance assurance of mind and belief in the trust-worthiness of states . . . confidence is the product of much broader patterns of relations than those which relate to military strategy. In fact the latter have to be woven into a complex texture of economic, cultural, technical and social relationships."[1] Nations in asymmetric situations, therefore, can enhance mutual trust and reduce tensions between themselves by negotiating military, including nuclear, and nonmilitary CBMs. They are classifiable into those that increase communications, transparency, and border security, or involve notifications, consultations, and declarations to promote mutual faith.[2] A counsel of perfection would advise their pursuit in all these directions. However, wisdom also lies in appreciating that

Confidence-building Measures are pragmatic steps toward ideal objectives. Those steps will necessarily be small at the outset if serious grievances must be bridged. A broad CBM negotiating framework that facilitates linkages and trade-offs is advisable, but when central security concerns are at issue, and when states have powerful military establishments, military-related steps tend to dominate at the outset. Ultimately, however, success in negotiating CBMs in the military sphere will depend on multiple initiatives.[3]

CBMs have gained universal acceptance, and commend themselves for achieving national and regional security—at relatively low cost. It might be supposed that national leaders will strive to minimize expenditures for maintaining security. But the reality is very different. Powerful domestic constituencies erode their political will to either reduce military expenditures or pursue the CBM route to establishing peace and stability. In India, for instance, these constituencies are recognized to constitute a "strategic enclave,"[4] a situation common, with local variations, in other South Asian countries. Their strength in the national polity is apparent, and is responsible for the limited progress made by the CBM process in the region. The intrinsic nature of the regional security problem underlines the difficulty in forging a "security consensus" in South Asia, and extending the CBM modality to establish confidence between its adversarial nations.

The Security Situation in South Asia

Four features distinguish the South Asian security situation. First are the serious tensions and instabilities characterizing Indo-Pakistani (Indo-Pak) relations since their birth. This occasioned armed conflicts in 1947–1948, 1965 (twice), 1971, and 1999, apart from recurring armed clashes along the line of control in Kashmir. Since 1989 a proxy war has been waged by Pakistan in Kashmir, and earlier in Punjab. This has completely skewed the foreign policies of India and Pakistan, with both perceiving each other as the major national security threat, and spending inordinately on defense budget, to the detriment of social and economic development. Both countries occupy the lower ends of the Human Development Index, while the South Asian region is only better than sub-Saharan Africa in this regard.

Second, Indo-Pak tensions and instabilities have acquired a nuclear edge since May 1998, when both countries exploded nuclear devices. A possible nuclear arms race between India and Pakistan was adjudged as "the most probable prospect for future use of weapons of mass destruction, including nuclear weapons . . . A nuclear exchange on the subcontinent would be devastating . . . particularly as each side strives to develop missiles with which to reach deeper into the other's territory."[5] It was also believed that an open-ended nuclear arms race could ensue "unless Indo-Pakistani relations improve and the threats posed by their respective nuclear programs are reduced through the adoption of mutual confidence-building measures or related strategies."[6] These predictions came true in 1999; India's discovery of Pakistani intrusions into the Kargil sector of Kashmir led to a two-month conflict between the two countries during which nuclear threats were held out[7] and escalatory actions taken[8]; they could easily have triggered a larger conflagration. For these reasons South Asia is rightly designated as the most dangerous, conflict-prone region in the world.

Third, the geostrategic reality obtains that India dominates the region in terms of size, population, natural resources, gross domestic product, and other attributes of national power. Additionally, by a quirk of geography, no two of its neighbors have common borders with each other, but India has land or maritime boundaries with all of them. This has led to an ingrained insecurity complex in India's neighbors regarding its "hegemonic" desire to impose a version of the Monroe Doctrine on the region. A strategic writer has commented that "India's regional strategy suggests two core perceptions: India will not allow a neighboring state to undertake any action in foreign affairs or defense policy that India deems potentially inimical to Indian security. India will not permit foreign governments to establish a presence or influence in a neighboring state that India views as unfriendly."[9]

This is a maximalist opinion; but such perceptions do inform the ruling elites in India's neighboring countries. Hence, CBMs should be initiated between India and neighbors Nepal, Bangladesh, and Sri Lanka.

The Case for and Against CBMs in South Asia

The experience of other regions is relevant for South Asia. For instance, the Helsinki Final Act (1975) envisaged inviting observers to NATO–Warsaw Pact military exercises. The Stockholm Accord (1986) mandated such invitations and required that an annual calendar of military exercises be provided in advance. The Vienna Agreements (1990 and 1992) enlarged their transparency by calling for information on force deployments, major weapons programs, and military budgets, and requiring demonstrations of new types of military equipment.[10] Inadvertently, no doubt, a variant of these agreements occurs in the "Agreement on Advance Notice of Military Exercises, Manoeuvres and Troop Movements" reached between India and Pakistan in April 1991.[11] Further, the two countries decided in their Lahore Declaration (February 1999) "to notify each other immediately in the event of any accidental, unauthorized or unexplained incident that could create the risk of . . . an outbreak of a nuclear war between the two countries."[12] This formulation replicates the language in Article 2 of the "Agreement on Measures to Reduce the Risk of Outbreak of Nuclear War" reached by the United States and the erstwhile Soviet Union in September 1971.[13] The difficulties often expressed in transposing CBMs from other regions into South Asia, therefore, is highly exaggerated; wisdom suggests that whatever is relevant to the region can and should be accepted.

Arguments for pursuing the CBM modality in South Asia include the need to address crushing levels of poverty; risk of nuclear annihilation; an environment where confrontational attitudes contribute to to religious extremism, ethnic conflict, and Marxist violence; and the need to inspire confidence in external powers to invest in the region. Significantly, the emergence of a nuclearized subcontinent places a premium on nuclear deterrence, which "rests on a combination of accommodation and reassurance, not on nuclear threats alone . . . Reassurance and accommodation will involve diplomatic steps that heretofore might have been unnecessary . . . In this environment, New Delhi and Islamabad will need to find ways to convince each other that each is secure, not that each is threatened; the relationship must be one of coordination and mutual dependence, not just conflict."[14] All these requirements provide a context for negotiating CBMs to mitigate the mistrust and suspicions that cause tensions and instabilities in South Asia.

Questions regarding the CBM modality should not be ignored. Obviously CBMs in the Indo-Pak context cannot mitigate tensions or conflict if both nations are determined to pursue them for internal political or systemic reasons. Besides, the existing CBMs between India and Pakistan have often been breached in letter and in spirit. In fact, "demanding proper implementing of CBMs between India and Pakistan is viewed by many military officials as a belittling and fruitless exercise. Unless there is a greater sense of ownership of CBMs and some relief from the culture of adversarial politics, South Asia will continue to lag well behind other regions that have normalized long-adversarial relations."[15] Skepticism regarding the CBM modality is, more significantly, also due to exaggerated claims about their efficacy in containing the East-West rivalry; their being recognized only after the Cold War ended, and their "harmlessness," which makes it easy to paint them in positive colors. More significantly, CBMs have been "so loosely defined that they go far beyond confidence building to encompass virtually everything from war prevention to peace building. Almost every declaration, agreement or measure between rival states is being portrayed as a CBM."[16] There are further reasons for the resistance to the CBM process in South Asia; they comprise a zero-sum perspective in Indo-Pak relations, suggesting that "any step that benefits an adversary must necessarily be bad for the home side."[17] Hence "conflict-avoidance measures appear to have been accepted not so much for their intrinsic merit, but because they would do little harm while satisfying well-meaning outsiders and aid donors."[18] Further, CBMs could "freeze rather than unfreeze a quarrel"; are "perceived as a sign of weakness by one's enemies"; they "risk giving too much away"; they could be used as "a form for strategic deception rather than reassurance"; they are superfluous in times of peace and redundant in times of war; and, "they actually curtail the diplomatic and military room for maneuver."[19]

However, with the fragile security situation in South Asia, any measures that may reduce the present danger merit consideration, including CBMs. The incentive for states to do so exists under the following six conditions:

- When they are involved in an enduring dispute in which the stakes are high
- When there is a substantial probability or expectation that the dispute will lead to hostilities
- When military technologies and strategies favor the offense over the defense, i.e., when there are incentives to strike first

- When conventional and nuclear weaponry, which may be used offensively or defensively, make the costs of war disproportionate to any reasonable goals in the dispute
- When there is the fear that misperceptions—arising from various technical problems or cognitive failures—could lead to inadvertent war
- When neither outright war nor a comprehensive peace seems plausible.[20]

Clearly, these preconditions apply fully to the nuclear standoff between India and Pakistan.

Nature and Paradoxes of the CBM Modality in South Asia[21]

Several paradoxes obtain in pursuing the CBM route to peace and stability in South Asia. Before discussing them, three broad but unique features of the CBMs already established in the region might be noticed.

1. Their almost exclusive pursuit in the bilateral Indo-Pak context, resulting in a heavy emphasis on military CBMs. The empirical evidence reveals that their negotiation and emplacement has generally followed serious military crises, e.g., after the Brasstacks Exercise (1987),[22] and the Kashmir-related Spring crisis (1990).[23] These CBMs include the agreement not to attack each other's designated nuclear facilities and installations (1988); advance notification of military exercises, maneuvers, and movements (1991); prevention of airspace violations and permitting overflights/landings by military aircraft (1991); upgrading hotline communications between the directors-general of military operations (1991); and joint declaration not to use, produce, or stock chemical weapons, or transfer the related technology to others (1992).[24] Besides, important nonmilitary CBMs have been negotiated, postcrises, between India and Pakistan; they include the Indus Waters Treaty (1960),[25] and the Tashkent (1966) and Simla (1972) agreements.[26] Significant agreements were also reached by them immediately after the trauma of their partition, such as the 14 December 1948 Accord relating to the protection of life and property of minority communities, boundary disputes, evacuee property, insurance policies, museums, and stores; and the Liaquat-Nehru Agreement (8 April 1950) to ensure the rights of minorities to personal security and equal opportunities in the two countries.[27] These were landmark understandings reached in an environment shrouded by hatred and communal violence.

2. Inadequate appreciation accrues about the several momentous nonmilitary CBMs reached between India and its other neighbors. They include the Indo-Bangladesh Agreement (1997) to share the Ganges waters; the Indo-Bhutanese Agreement (1974) to construct the Chukha hydroelectric project and establish a power-sharing arrangement; the Indo-Nepal Agreement (1996) to undertake the integrated development of the Mahakali River; and the Indo–Sri Lanka Agreement (1998) envisaging a free-trade zone. A decision to effect the sale of surplus power by Pakistan to India (1998) is under negotiation.

3. A pernicious belief holds that contentious issues must first be resolved before the CBM process addresses other issues in dispute. The Farakka dispute,

for instance, remained in contention for over two decades before its resolution by the Indo-Bangladesh Accord in 1997. The Kashmir issue has impeded the normalization of Indo-Pak relations since their birth. Pakistan identifies Kashmir as the "core" issue that must first be settled before the bilateral CBM process can evolve. India, for its part, favors a multipronged approach in which the Kashmir issue finds inclusion within a broad agenda pertaining to other bilateral contentions. Besides, Pakistan would like external mediation to resolve the Kashmir dispute, while India wishes to proceed on the basis of strict bilateralism. Conversion of the line of control into an international border, effecting, thereby a geopolitical partition of Kashmir, could be a *via media* solution to resolve the impasse, but this is not unacceptable to either country at present. Wisdom requires pursuit of an incremental step-by-step approach to promote the CBM process, rather than binding it to the prior resolution of a single issue.

Four unresolved paradoxes of the CBM modality can now be identified in South Asia, that are also relevant in other conflict-ridden regions.

1. CBMs admittedly "provide the atmospherics for improving inter-State relations, and providing the instrumentality to proceed further with an arms control and disarmament process."[28] They can also establish trust between adversarial nations; but paradoxically, trust is necessary before a CBM process can even be initiated. The logic then becomes circular as to which comes first, which militates against the CBM modality succeeding between states in an asymmetric situation with each other.

2. CBMs established under duress or without conviction are easy to disrupt. The empirical evidence reveals that the hotline established between the directors-general of military operation became nonfunctional during the Indo-Pak war of 1971, with telephones either being left unattended or manned by junior officers with no authority to make decisions. During the Brasstacks crisis (1987), "information shared through the hotline was deemed unreliable because of mutual suspicions; hence, information supplied on Pakistani request was only minimally complied with."[29] So it is that CBMs work satisfactorily in times of peace, but fail in their objectives in times of emergency and conflict.

3. Public declarations are obviously useful mechanisms to reduce tensions and enhance trust; they "can take the form of joint summit statements, negotiated agreements of a declaratory nature—such as non-attack pledges—and/or unilateral statements."[30] But the historical record shows that the leaders in India, Pakistan, and other South Asian countries as well routinely make inflammatory statements to garner domestic support in the context of electoral politics. Conciliatory statements, on the other hand, are often designed to impress the international community, or lower the adversary's guard. In this bitter terrain the paradox emerges: "rather than promote security and confidence building, such declarations have often exacerbated existing regional tensions."[31]

4. The empirical evidence also reveals the ease with which India and Pakistan adopt each other's negotiating positions, suggesting that they are primarily guided by tactical considerations of immediate gains and losses and not by any calculations of long-term policy. Two examples are cited here. First, India has traditionally insisted on the principle of bilateralism during Indo-Pak negotiations, whereas Pakistan has always sought the intervention of outside powers. However, India did accept mediation by the World Bank in the case of the Indus Waters Treaty[32] and the Soviet Union in negotiating the Tashkent Agreement (1966). For its part, Pakistan has always insisted that the "core" issue of Kashmir must be resolved first, before other Indo-Pakistani disputes are discussed; India has insisted on addressing Kashmir along with other issues. During the Simla Agreement negotiations, however, these positions were reversed. Pakistan called for a step-by-step discussion, and India rescinded its claims to the whole of Kashmir by accepting the conversion of the line of control into an international border.[33]

Lessons and Recommendations

What then can be learned from the CBM process in South Asia that could further this process in the region, and be applied, *mutatis mutandis,* to other conflict-prone regions in the world?

First, contestants must be assured that instituting CBMs constitutes a win-win situation. For instance, the promise of massive economic aid to India from the World Bank and a consortium of developed countries to implement its Second Five Year Plan greatly facilitated India's acceptance of the division of the Indus River Basin; this permitted the finalization of the Indus Waters Treaty. Pakistan, as the lower riparian state, could not risk a breakdown in the negotiations, lest it cause an interruption in water flows. Consequently, the World Bank "was able to make both India and Pakistan winners in the Indus Waters settlement, since each country received more irrigation water as a result of the agreement."[34] Despite the state of tensions and instabilities marking their relationship over the years, the Indus Waters Treaty has been faithfully implemented. Similarly, the Agreement on the Prohibition of Attack Against Nuclear Facilities (1988) has been scrupulously observed. The reason is obvious—neither country wishes its nuclear establishments to be targeted, since the radioactivity released would be catastrophic for their populations.

Second, for the CBM process, both secret diplomacy and open diplomacy are accompanied by particular risks. With respect to India and Pakistan, secret diplomacy is very difficult to carry out; in the charged atmosphere, such activities rarely remain confidential, and their discovery can worsen the political situation. Frequently then, open diplomacy becomes public diplomacy, inflaming emotional issues such as Kashmir. Leaders are also tempted to make harsh, uncompromising statements to please a skeptical population, leaving little room for retreat when negotiations commence. Similar difficulties arise from blanket declarations, plainly designed for cosmetic purposes, about a willingness to negotiate at "any level, at any time and in any place."[35] What can still be done in this unpropitious milieu to promote negotiations and the CBM process? The modality of emissary-level talks before substantive meetings are held is a useful middle way between secret and open diplomacy; this was effectively utilized in 1972 when accredited representatives of India and Pakistan met earlier in Murree (near Islamabad) to thrash out the agenda and negotiating positions of the two sides before the Simla Summit took place.[36]

Third, the thesis can be advanced, based on the empirical evidence, that the resolution of continuing Indo-Pakistani disputes is more likely to be reached after new governments assume power in either or both countries. Z. A. Bhutto, for instance, negotiated the Simla Agreement less than seven months after assuming power. Similarly, a compromise on the Salal project, which is an offshoot of the Indus Waters Treaty, was reached in 1977 by the Janata government, which had just come to power in India. The salubrious agreement on sharing Ganges waters, resulting in a resolution of the long-enduring Farraka dispute, was reached in 1996 by the Deve Gowda government in India and the Sheikh Hasina government in Bangladesh; both had just assumed power. The reason for this phenomenon is obvious. New governments can adopt innovative approaches to resolving old disputes before getting enmeshed in divisive internal politics and the intrigues of vested interests with a stake in continuing adversarial relations. New governments could therefore consider making early affirmations of their commitment to improving bilateral relations with their neighbors.[37]

Fourth, past experience in implementing CBMs shows that "an evolutionary step-by-step approach seems to work best, at least until core security issues must be tackled."[38] A building-block approach could be useful to build upon military CBMs already established between India and Pakistan. For instance:

- The agreement not to attack each other's nuclear facilities and installations could be extended to identified population and economic targets
- The agreement on providing advance notice of military exercises could be extended to associating military observers with these exercises, providing an annual timetable in advance, and establishing crisis management centers
- The agreement on preventing airspace violations could be enlarged into an "open skies" arrangement to allow joint aerial surveillance of the line of control

Fifth, a greater emphasis seems necessary on nonmilitary CBMs. Clearly, military CBMs cannot be neglected, but, nonmilitary CBMs can reduce suspicion and generate an atmosphere conducive to peace and stability. The newer sources of insecurity such as migration, arms and drugs smuggling, money laundering, transnational crime, and environmental degradation, moreover, require the accent to be placed on the negotiation of nonmilitary CBMs.

Sixth, taking unilateral conciliatory steps might be politically unfeasible when mistrust and suspicion prevails. An alternative, however, would be to pursue a "Graduated Reduction in Tensions" strategy (GRIT) that would "encompass initiating a positive action in order to elicit an appropriate reciprocation move from the adversary."[39] Should this positive action not be reciprocated, it would be withdrawn at the end of a specified time. Examples would be the reduction of troops in a designated border zone on the premise that the adversary would do the same within a defined period, or lowering tariffs on certain goods in the expectation that the neighboring country would reciprocate within a specified period, a modality that would encourage more engagement among the South Asian countries through commerce and joint development projects, and greater regional and subregional cooperation.

Seventh, the establishment of nuclear weapons–related CBMs by India and Pakistan are essential for the security of the region. This is because "nuclear equations are most unsettled and tension-producing at the outset of any such pairing,"[40] as the early nuclear history of the United States and the Soviet Union informs us. The Memorandum of Understanding accompanying the Lahore Declaration envisaged India and Pakistan providing each other "advance notification in respect of ballistic missile flight tests"; notifying any "accidental, unauthorized or unexplained incident"; maintaining a "unilateral moratorium on conducting further nuclear test explosions"; concluding "an agreement on prevention of incidents at sea"; reviewing "the implementation of existing Confidence Building Measures"; reviewing "existing communications links . . . with a view to upgrading and improving these links"; and, most significantly, engaging "in bilateral consultations on security, disarmament and non-proliferation issues."[41] These technical and complex issues need urgent attention to establish nuclear restraint and a nuclear risk reduction regime in South Asia.

Conclusions

That mistrust and suspicion are the bane of South Asia and the chief reason for the CBM process achieving very modest success is an obvious platitude. This also becomes apparent from their failure to implement existing CBMs, such as not altering the Line of Control unilaterally, "irrespective of mutual differences and legal interpretations," as inscribed in the Simla Agreement. This provision has routinely been violated; indeed, Pakistani intrusions across the Line of Control were the prescient cause for the Kargil conflict. Neither have the two countries sought to "prevent hostile propaganda directed against each other," as they pledged in the 14 December 1948 Accord, the Tashkent Declaration, and the Simla Agreement.

Still, a joint statement in a future SAARC summit that all the South Asian states "shall prevent the organization, assistance or encouragement of any acts detrimental to the maintenance of peace and harmonious relations" would go far toward creating favorable conditions for settling differences and invigorating a CBM process. Similarly, innovative measures such as establishing emissary-level talks, affirming their commitment to improving bilateral relations, building upon existing CBMs, or undertaking the GRIT modality can easily be pursued by these countries. All that is lacking is political will. Increasingly, governments in South Asia are coalition governments; they feel too weak to launch bold initiatives in the domestic or external sphere. Further, the bane of plebiscitory politics afflicts the region; opposition parties oppose everything the party in power supports. It can only be hoped that, eventually, wisdom will prevail and political parties will reach a consensus to pursue national goals such as peace and stability by invigorating the CBM process.

In the current dark atmosphere, there are a few rays of hope: the growing desire of the people for a better quality of life; the growing recognition that a purely military approach to transnational threats to security is inadequate; the establishment of trade, cultural, and professional ties across national borders; and so on. A new generation is assuming positions of power and influence in the region; this generation would, hopefully, pursue socioeconomic progress as a priority, rather than dwell on the hate and bitter memories of the past.

P. R. Chari is a former member of the Indian Administrative Service and served in several senior positions at the central and state level. He was director of the Institute for Defence Studies and Analyses, New Delhi (1975–1980); international fellow, Centre for International Affairs, Harvard University (1983–1984); and research professor, Centre for Policy Research (1992–1996). Currently he is firector of the Institute of Peace and Conflict Studies. He has worked extensively on nuclear disarmament, nonproliferation, and Indian defense issues. He has published extensively in newspapers, web sites, and written over a hundred monographs and major papers in learned journals/chapters in books in India and abroad. Examples of his work include: coauthor and coeditor, Nuclear Non-Proliferation in India and Pakistan: South Asian Perspectives (1996); *editor,* Perspectives on National Security in South Asia: In Search of a New Paradigm *(1999); and editor,* Security and Governance in South Asia *(2001). He is currently working on a coauthored book,* Human Security in South Asia.

Notes

1. Johan Jorgen Holst, "Confidence Building Measures: A Conceptual Framework," *Survival* 25(1), January–February 1983, pp. 2, 4.

2. A list of confidence-building measures established between India and Pakistan is available in Michael Krepon, Dominique M. McCoy, Matthew C. J. Rudolph (eds.), *A Handbook of Confidence-Building Measures for Regional Security,* Handbook No. 1. Washington, DC: The Henry L. Stimson Center, September 1993, pp. 46–48. [Hereafter *Handbook, 1993*]

3. Michael Krepon, "The Decade for Confidence-Building Measures," in *Handbook, 1993,* p. 9.

4. This expression has been defined as "a subset of the Indian military-security complex—specifically, the set of research establishments and production facilities that are responsible for the development of these new [military R&D] programs" in Itty Abraham, "India's 'Strategic Enclave': Civilian Scientists and Military Technologies," *Armed Forces and Society* 18(2), winter 1992, p. 233. More broadly, the "strategic enclave" comprises a loose collection of retired civil and military officials, defense correspondents, right-wing politicians, and scientists in the defense and nuclear establishments. They are bound together by a common faith in the pursuit of a militaristic approach to national security, a "realist foreign" policy, and the value of nuclear weapons.

5. *Hearing of the [U.S.] Senate Government Affairs Committee.* Witness: James Woolsey, Director, Central Intelligence Agency: February 24, 1993, p. 2.

6. Leonard S. Spector, *The Undeclared Bomb*. Cambridge, MA, Ballinger Publishing Company, 1988, p. 70.

7. Apropos, Pakistan's foreign secretary had warned during the course of this conflict that "any weapon" in its arsenal could be used to defend the country's territorial integrity. *The Hindu*, 1 June 1999.

8. Apparently, "India then [during the Kargil conflict] activated all its three types of nuclear delivery vehicles and kept them at what is known as readiness State 3—meaning some nuclear bombs would be ready to be mated with the delivery vehicle at short notice." Cf. Raj Chengappa, *Weapons of Peace: The Secret Story of India's Quest to be a Nuclear Power*. New Delhi: HarperCollins Publishers India, 2000, p. 437.

9. George K. Tanham, *Indian Strategic Thought: An Interpretive Essay*. Santa Monica, CA: Rand, 1992, p. 29.

10. Michael Krepon, "Conflict Avoidance, Confidence-Building, and Peacemaking," in *A Handbook of Confidence-Building Measures for Regional Security*, 3d ed., edited by Michael Krepon, Khurshid Khoja, Michael Newbill, and Jenny S. Drezin, Handbook No. 1. Washington, DC: The Henry L. Stimson Center, March 1998, p. 2. [Hereafter *Handbook, 1998*]

11. Text of Agreement may be seen in Michael Krepon and Amit Sevak, *Crisis Prevention, Confidence Building and Reconciliation in South Asia*, New Delhi: Manohar, 1996, pp. 255–257.

12. This was expressed in the Memorandum of Understanding accompanying the Lahore Declaration. Text may be seen in *The Hindu*, 22 February 1999.

13. Text of Agreement available in *Arms Control and Disarmament Agreements: Texts and History of Negotiations*, Washington, DC: U.S. Arms Control and Disarmament Agency, 1996 edition, pp. 88–89.

14. Neil Joeck, "Nuclear Relations in South Asia," in *Repairing the Regime: Preventing the Spread of Weapons of Mass Destruction*, edited by Joseph Cirincione. Washington, DC: Carnegie Endowment for International Peace, 2000, pp. 1–2.

15. Michael Krepon, "South Asia: A Time of Trouble, A Time of Need," in *Regional Confidence Building in 1995: South Asia, the Middle East, and Latin America*, edited by Jill R. Junnola and Michael Krepon, Report No. 20. Washington, DC: The Henry L. Stimson Center, December 1995, pp. 7–8. [Hereafter, *Report, 1995*]

16. Brahma Chellaney, "CBMs—A Critical Appraisal," in *Confidence Building Measures in South Asia*, edited by Dipankar Banerjee. Colombo: Regional Centre for Strategic Studies, 1999, p. 25.

17. Michael Krepon, "South Asia: A Time of Trouble, A Time of Need," *Report, 1995*, p. 7.

18. Ibid.

19. These grounds for apprehension about CBMs are noted in Kanti Bajpai, "CBMs: Contexts, Achievements, Functions," in *Confidence Building Measures in South Asia*, edited by Dipankar Banerjeepp. Colombo: Regional Centre for Strategic Studies, 1999, pp. 16–17.

20. Kanti P. Bajpai, "Conflict, Cooperation, and CSBMs with Pakistan and China: A View from New Delhi," in *Mending Fences: Confidence- and Security-Building Measures in South Asia*, edited by Sumit Ganguly and Ted Greenwood. Delhi: Oxford University Press, 1997, p. 31.

21. This section draws heavily upon my earlier essay entitled "CBMs in Post Cold War South Asia," in *Confidence Building Measures in South Asia*, edited by Dipankar Banerjee. Colombo: Regional Centre for Strategic Studies, 1999, pp. 44–64.

22. See Kanti P. Bajpai, P. R.Chari, Pervaiz Iqbal Cheema, Stephen P. Cohen, Sumit Ganguly, *Brasstacks and Beyond: Perception and Management of Crisis in South Asia*. New Delhi: Manohar, 1996.

23. See Devin T. Hagerty, "Nuclear Deterrence in South Asia: The 1990 Indo-Pakistani Crisis," *International Security* 20(3), winter 1995–1996. This crisis is the

subject of a forthcoming study by P. R. Chari, Pervaiz Iqbal Cheema, and Stephen P. Cohen.

24. Text of all these agreements may be seen in Michael Krepon and Amit Sevak (eds.), *Crisis Prevention, Confidence Building, and Reconciliation in South Asia,* New Delhi: Manohar, 1996, pp. 254–261.

25. See Michael Krepon and Amit Sevak (eds.), *Crisis Prevention, Confidence Building, and Reconciliation in South Asia.* New Delhi: Manohar, 1996, pp. 245–250.

26. Ibid., pp. 250–253.

27. A brief description of these agreements may be seen in P. R. Chari, "Declaratory Statements and Confidence Building in South Asia" in *Declaratory Diplomacy: Rhetorical Initiatives and Confidence Building,* edited by Michael Krepon, Jenny S. Drezin, and Michael Newbill, Report No. 27. Washington, DC: The Henry L. Stimson Center, April 1999, pp. 94–96.

28. P. R.Chari, Navnita Chadha, Maroof Raza, *Confidence-Building Measures in South Asia.* New Delhi: Centre for Policy Research, January 1995, p. 10.

29. Kanti P. Bajpai, et al., *Brasstacks and Beyond,* p. 41.

30. Michael Krepon and Jenny S. Drezin, "Introduction," in *Declaratory Diplomacy: Rhetorical Initiatives and Confidence Building,* edited by Michael Krepon, Jenny S. Drezin, and Michael Newbill, Report No. 27. Washington, DC: The Henry L. Stimson Center, April 1999, p. xi.

31. Chari, "Declaratory Statements and Confidence Building in South Asia," p. 130.

32. Dennis Kux, *Estranged Democracies: India and the United States, 1941–1991.* New Delhi: Sage Publications, 1993, pp. 150–152; Jagat S. Mehta, "The Indus Waters Treaty: A Case Study in the Resolution of an International River Basin Conflict," *Natural Resources Forum* 12(1), February 1988, p. 70.

33. This episode, admittedly controversial, is described in P. R. Chari and Pervaiz Iqbal Cheema, *The Simla Agreement 1972: Its Wasted Promise,* New Delhi: Manohar, 2001, esp. pp. 56–60.

34. Kux, *Estranged Democracies,* p. 152.

35. This offer has repeatedly been made in recent months by General Pervez Musharraf seeking a dialogue with India, without specifying either an agenda or any compromise on the outstanding issues in contention. In the absence of prior consultations, their rejection by India was almost axiomatic, which has then been used by Pakistan for propaganda purposes.

36. Chari and Cheema, *The Simla Agreement 1972,* pp. 30–34.

37. Chari, "Declaratory Statements and Confidence Building in South Asia," p. 133.

38. Krepon et al., *Handbook 1993,* p. 10.

39. Arun P. Elhance and Moonis Ahmar, "Nonmilitary CBMs," in *Crisis Prevention, Confidence Building, and Reconciliation in South Asia,* by Michael Krepon an Amit Sevak, New Delhi: Manohar, 1996, p. 147, citing Alexander L. George, *Bridging the Gap: Theory and Practice in Foreign Policy,* Washington, DC: United States Institute of Peace Press, 1993, p. 52.

40. Krepon, "South Asia: A Time of Trouble," p. 6.

41. Text may be seen in *The Hindu,* 22 February 1999.

7.3

Border Conflicts and Regional Disputes

Sushil K. Pillai

In South Asia, border conflicts[1] flare up for a variety of reasons: (1) pre- and postcolonial border alignments, the legacies of which are fiercely defended by their inheritors; (2) ethnic and religious conflicts and the employment of terrorism and fundamentalism (which ignore boundaries) as a means to resolve them; (3) large-scale migrations of populations and refugees across boundaries that are difficult to guard because of rugged or open terrain; and (4) competing claims on land and maritime territories that are rich in natural resources or have po-litical or sociocultural importance. Factors such as organized crime, the drug trade, political instability, and interference by other nations tend to exacerbate such conflicts.

Significantly, in South Asia, ethnic nationalism and resulting conflicts to re-define boundaries have arisen out of collective fears of ethnic groups that their freedom to control their resources and way of life will be taken away by the dominant majority of their country.[2] Often, bilateral border conflicts in South Asian countries are supported covertly or overtly by other countries acting in their "national interests." When sanctuaries are provided in contiguous coun-tries, conflicts get prolonged. A marked feature of the contemporary strategic environment has been the resolution of border conflicts through international pressure.

Border conflicts are linked to poor governance, but international and do-mestic efforts to resolve border conflicts focus more on political, economic, and military factors than governance issues.

The serious problem of refugees in South Asia has not yet been tackled ef-fectively by the countries concerned. Host countries have in some cases armed some refugees and pushed them back to fight insurgent movements. The human dimension of the refugee problem is of a grave nature.

An Overview

Afghanistan

Afghanistan, which shares borders with Iran (936 kilometers), Turkmenistan (744 kilometers), Uzbekistan (137 kilometers), Tajikistan (1,206 kilometers), China (76 kilometers), and Pakistan (2,430 kilometers) has unresolved border disputes with Pakistan and Iran. Its rugged and mountainous frontiers significantly affect border conflicts. There are no major conflicts along Afghanistan's northern boundaries with the Central Asian states, or with China. In 1946, the mid-channel of the Amu Darya River was fixed as the boundary between the former USSR and Afghanistan. That agreement remains in effect with the successor states.

The sociopolitical situation in Afghanistan is quite complex, characterized by various loyalties within tribes. The five main Afghan demographic groups are not monolithic.[3] The Pashtuns, for example, are a group of two confederations of tribes in addition to five affiliated tribes. The overlap of ethnicities with all its neighboring countries, the divide between Shia and Sunni Muslims, its location astride strategic overland Central Asian trade routes, and its natural resources are among the causes of border conflicts. In addition, of course, Afghanistan has endured years of internal conflict, exacerbated by numerous foreign interventions, the rise and fall of the fundamentalist Taliban regime between 1994 and 2001, and the use of Afghanistan as a staging area for terrorism by Osama bin Laden and the Al-Qaida organization.

The collapse of the institutions of governance and the abject poverty of the people of Afghanistan are in themselves sources of conflict. Since October 2001, a coalition of European nations and the United Nations are playing a significant role in conflict resolution through a battery of political, economic, mititary, and humanitarian measures. But uncoordinated international efforts to bring peace and a disunited, unstable post-Taliban government may not be sufficient to prevent the contagion of instability spreading from Afghanistan to its neighbors. Unless a minimum peace plan is forged that is acceptable to most parties to the conflict, the situation in Afghanistan will remain critical.

Pakistan

Pakistan shares borders with four countries: Iran (909 kilometers), Afghanistan (2,430 kilometers), China (523 kilometers), and India (3,147 kilometers). Pakistan's major boundary conflicts concern Afghanistan and India. Previously, Pakistan also had disputes with Iran and China. Iran had claimed some areas in Baluchistan, but this dispute was resolved by a Frontier Agreement in 1957. In 1963, in drawing the boundary with China, Pakistan ceded 5,180 square kilometers of territory (claimed, in fact, by India) to China. China accepted this with a proviso that it would be renegotiated once the Kashmir conflict with India was resolved.

The conflicts with India concern Jammu and Kashmir and the Sir Creek in the northwestern Indian state of Gujarat. These issues have been discussed in six rounds of negotiations[4] between the two countries. Maritime boundary disputes with India have also occurred; the two nations have waged war four times (1947, 1965, 1971, 1999) and have been engaged in continuous low-intensity conflict in Jammu and Kashmir since 1947. India and Pakistan both conducted nuclear tests in 1998, changing the global strategic environment.

India
With the exception of Afghanistan, India shares boundaries with all the countries of South Asia, including land boundaries with Pakistan (3,147 kilometers), Nepal (1,751 kilometers), Bhutan (699 kilometers), and Bangladesh (4,351 kilometers), and maritime boundaries with the Maldives and Sri Lanka. It also borders on Myanmar (1,643 kilometers) and China (4,056 kilometers). India's inherited colonial legacy has left some sectors of its boundaries unresolved with all countries except the Maldives, but only its disputes with Pakistan and China are serious.

Nepal
The kingdom of Nepal shares borders with India (1,690 kilometers) and China (1,236 kilometers). It has minor boundary disputes with India. Its borders with China were defined by the Nepal-China Border Agreement of 1961 and the Sino-Nepal Border Protocols of 1963 and 1979. The large-scale migrations of Nepalese across the India-Nepal border into Bhutan poses a problem to both countries.

Apart from its boundary disputes with India, there are a variety of other bilateral disputes, but Nepal enjoys generally good relations with India. Movement of trade across its borders is of importance to landlocked Nepal, and talks with India to reach agreement on a new trade treaty are under way. At issue, in particular, are Indian concerns about duty-free Nepali products flooding the Indian market.

Nepal's relationships with China are stable, though China does complain that Nepal takes inadequate action against activists of the Free Tibet Movement who use Nepal as a route to and from Tibet.

Internally, the growth of a strong Maoist insurgency since 1996, allegedly with assistance from North Korea and Peru's Shining Path, poses a grave threat to Nepal's constitutional monarchy. If the security situation were to badly deteriorate, there might be a risk of intervention from China or India.

Bhutan
Bhutan has a 470-kilometer boundary with China, parts of which are in dispute. It also shares a 699-kilometer border with India. There is no boundary conflict with India, and an Indo-Bhutan Treaty of Friendship is in effect. Internally, Bhutan's security problems are related to internal ethnic conflicts and dealing with insurgent groups[5] from India who have established sanctuaries in the forests of Bhutan.

Bhutan has a population of 1.9 million divided into three main ethnic groups: the Ngalongs (17 percent) in western Bhutan, who form the country's elite including the monarchy; the Sharchops (30 percent) in eastern Bhutan, who claim to be the original inhabitants; and the Lotshampas (28 percent) of southern Bhutan, who are of Nepali origin and demand greater representation in politics. A 1985 Citizenship Act mandates the wearing of Bhutanese national dress at public places and at state occasions, and fluency in Dzonkha, the national language, for all Bhutanese, irrespective of their origin, while banishing the Nepali language from the school curriculum. After a census in 1988, some 96,500 noncitizens (mostly of Nepali origin) were expelled and now live in refugee camps in eastern Nepal. Despite ten rounds of Bhutan-Nepal talks, the fate of the Nepali migrants has not been resolved beyond an attempt at classifying the types of refugees.

Security is also threatened by the presence in Bhutan of about one thousand armed Nepali youth who have taken to violence, and Northeastern Indian insurgent groups. Though Bhutan has assured India that these groups will be evicted, they continue to use the forests of Bhutan as sanctuaries. Bhutan's long-term security depends on its ability to resolve its internal ethnic conflicts, and to cope with transborder insurgent groups seeking sanctuary on its territory, as well as discovering ways to find a balance between maintaining traditions and managing economic and social development.

Bangladesh

Bangladesh, which seceded from Pakistan in 1971, shares boundaries with India (4,053 kilometers) and Myanmar (193 kilometers). High population density (1,956 persons per square kilometer) and severe poverty are important factors in issues related to land claims, sharing of natural resources, and large-scale migration to other countries. These are central to the four categories of boundary conflict between Bangladesh and India: (1) nonratification of the 1974 Indo-Bangladesh Land Boundary Agreement; (2) nondelineation of maritime boundaries in the Bay of Bengal; (3) ownership of Talpatty Island (referred to as New Moore Island by India); and (4) sharing of river waters that flow from India to Bangladesh. Its conflict with Myanmar is related to mass migrations of Muslims from Myanmar to Bangladesh.

Sri Lanka

The island nation of Sri Lanka, off the southeastern coast of India, has no land and maritime boundary conflicts with its larger neighbor. Internally, the nation has endured a long conflict between the Sri Lankan Tamils (3.2 million) and the Liberation Tigers of Tamil Eelam (LTTE) with the Sinhalese (14 million).[6] India has been involved because of ethnic links with the nearby Indian state of Tamil Nadu. This highlights an aspect of conflict dynamics that even when there is no boundary conflict, a country can get drawn into conflict involving an internal problem of a neighboring state. An Indian peacekeeping force operated in Sri Lanka from July 1987 to 1989 and was able to ensure local elections in the Tamil area. This was a temporary reprieve. Since then the LTTE has virtually neutralized all other Tamil groups. Norway (which hosts about ten thousand Sri Lankan refugees) is mediating as a third party to help resolve the conflict. A cease-fire was declared between the government of Sri Lanka and the LTTE on 23 February 2002. The cease-fire is being monitored by a sixteen-member team from Scandinavian countries. Peace negotiations brokered by Norway are scheduled to commence in May 2002.

The Maldives

The Indian Ocean nation of the Maldives consists of 1,200 small coral islands grouped in nineteen atolls. It lies 675 kilometers southwest of Sri Lanka. Due to its strategic location, the United Kingdom, France, and the United States have an interest in the islands. Other littoral countries such as India, Pakistan, and Sri Lanka have also recognized its strategic importance in the control of shipping lanes in the Indian Ocean and in providing bases for any action in South Asia. Britain established an air base at Gan in the southern Addu atoll during World War II, but gave it up in 1976 due to budgetary pressures. The Maldives gained its independence in July 1965 and became a republic in November 1968. Conscious of its strategic importance, the country strives to keep out of any alliance and refused permission to provide an air base to the USSR at Gan in 1997. There are no boundary conflicts between the Republic of Maldives and other littoral countries.

Security threats to the Maldives are internal. There were two attempted coups in 1980 and 1983. In November 1988, a Maldavian businessman led a seaborne mercenary force of Sri Lankan Tamils to capture the capital, Male. Indian intervention was requested and provided promptly. The coup was put down and the troops returned to India.

Given the importance of its fishing industry, it was necessary for the Maldives to establish clear maritime boundaries. These were arranged among Maldives, India, and Sri Lanka by the maritime treaties of 22 November 1976 and 28 December 1976. The existence of an international framework of boundaries combined with the Maldives' strict policy of neutrality has kept the islands free of conflicts. However, the danger that isolated islands could be used as staging points for arms or drug running does exist. If this threat can be managed, and barring individual or small-scale power struggles, the Maldives are likely to remain islands of peace.

Border Conflicts in Detail

Afghanistan-Iran

The major border conflict between Afghanistan and Iran concerns the sharing of river waters of the Helmand River in the area of the Hamun lakes with the upstream riparian Afghan area. An agreement to resolve the long-standing dispute over the distribution of these waters was reached in the Treaty of 13 March 1973, but wasn't implemented as it was followed by a coup in July 1973. This treaty could thus form the basis for a future settlement. In September 1998, following the killing of Iranians by the Taliban during their capture of Mazar-e Sharif, 70,000 Iranian troops were deployed on the border, ostensibly for an exercise. However, no fighting took place. Iran's interest in the Helmand province and Herat continues in post-Taliban Afghanistan for economic and religious reasons. This region remains a potential source of conflict.

Afghanistan-Pakistan

The British delineated the Durand Line as Afghanistan's southern boundary between India (now Pakistan) and Afghanistan in 1893. This divided the Pashtuns or Pushto-speaking people who live in that area and created dissatisfaction. On independence, Pakistan inherited this border problem and rejected the demand for an independent Pashtunistan. In 1947, Afghanistan voted against inclusion of Pakistan in the UN because of the border dispute. Afghanistan's prime minister, Mohammed Daoud Khan, supported secessionist movements in Pakistan's NorthWest Frontier Province until 1975, when then-president Daoud and Pakistan's prime minister, Zulfikar Ali Bhutto, reached an "accommodation." After the Soviets invaded Afghanistan, Pakistan became a frontline state and U.S. surrogate for anti-Soviet aid to noncommunist groups in Afghanistan.

The Durand Line is by no means uniformly well defined on the ground. Some portions of the line were demarcated during the period 1894–1895 but other areas still have not been demarcated because of local tribal resistance. In July 1949, a Loya Jirga (Council of Tribes) repudiated all treaties with the British, including the Durand Line. Pakistan objected and broke off trade and transit ties with Afghanistan in 1950. Tensions on the border increased. In 1963, Iran mediated the restoration of cordial relations between the two countries.

During the years of conflict beginning with the Soviet invasion in 1979 and continuing, for the most part, up to the present, the Durand Line has ceased to exist in any real sense on account of the massive flow of refugees and *mujahedeen* across it. Indeed, in 1994, a century after it had been established, the Durand Line became defunct coinciding with the ascendancy of the Taliban. While in power, the Taliban tried to renegotiate a new boundary, but Pakistan continued to support maintenance of the status quo, and in April 2000 Pakistan reestablished the Durand Line as a de facto boundary with the formality of entry points, passports, and visas.

The reestablishment of the Durand Line has significance not only for relations between Afghanistan and Pakistan, but also for the complex conflict dynamics of the region, which revolve around religious factionalism, ethnic differences, and a fierce tradition of independent tribal identities situated in an area of considerable geostrategic importance. An undefined boundary with Pakistan with a possibility of a renewed movement for an independent Pashtunistan or a resurgent Taliban could plunge the region into conflict. This, combined with the possibility of the spread of fundamentalism beyond the Islamic crescent into India and Southeast Asia, together with continued violence against the United States and its allies, could plunge the region in further turmoil.

Pakistan-India

Resolved conflicts between India and Pakistan include:

1. Sharing of waters, Indus Water Treaty 1960[7]
2. Tashkent Accord, 3 January 1966
3. Rann of Kutch boundary dispute resolved by a three-member commission in Geneva, 1968
4. Simla Agreement, 2 July 1972
5. Salal Dam Agreement, 1978
6. Agreement on "no attack on mutual nuclear installations," 31 December 1988

Many others, however, remain unresolved.

Pakistan-India: Jammu and Kashmir[8]

The ongoing conflict in Jammu and Kashmir over the unresolved status of the region has resulted in frequent fighting along the Line of Control (LOC), which both parties accepted in the 1972 Simla Agreement following the 1971 war. (The LOC replaced a Cease Fire Line mutually agreed upon in 1949.) Both nations have maintained troops along the line. Consequent to the occupation of the Siachen area (the Saltoro Range with heights ranging from 18,000 to 22,000 feet) by Indian and Pakistani troops in April 1984, this portion was termed as the Actual Ground Position Line (AGPL). The eastern boundary of Pakistan is thus a line composed of the International Boundary,

Kashmir separatists praying.

the LOC, and the AGPL. Despite six rounds of bilateral negotiations, no solution has been found nor is one likely to be found unless the two countries moderate their present positions.

Pakistan-India: Siachen

The Shimla Agreement defined a fresh Line of Control. The LOC agreed upon in 1972 was not clearly defined in the Saltoro Range overlooking the Siachen Glacier. Both countries claimed the region and sent troops to assert their claims. In November 1992 they nearly reached agreement on the first phase of a resolution that envisaged (1) pulling back troops from the Saltoro Range, (2) avoidance of force, and (3) determination of future positions on the ground to conform to the Shimla Agreement. Unexpectedly the agreement did not take place, with both sides blaming the other for stalling the agreement. The dispute remains unresolved.

Pakistan-India: Wular Barrage/Tulbul Navigation Project

The Wular Barrage (referred to by India as the Tulbul Navigation Project) is a project started by India in 1984 at the mouth of the Wular Lake downstream from the Jhelum River. It consists of a dam with a navigation lock to permit navigation during the lean winter months. Work was stopped in 1987 following a protest by Pakistan that this was a violation of the Indus Water Treaty of 1960, in that it was meant for water storage. India's stand is that the construction is meant to enhance navigation, which is permissible under the treaty.

Eight rounds of talks have been held so far but an agreement has remained elusive. An agreement was almost reached in 1991 but before it could be ratified Pakistan added a provision unacceptable to India. As with the Siachen issue, the failure to conclude an agreement is indicative of lack of political will and refusal to accommodate the other's needs.

Pakistan-India: Sir Creek

The 60-kilometer-long Sir Creek lies on the boundary between Pakistan and India in the marshes of the Rann of Kutch and flows into the Arabian Sea. It was not included in the 1968 Tribunal Award on the Indo-Pakistan Western Boundary because both sides had agreed to exclude the area from the deliberations of the tribunal.

The area adjoining the creeks is rich in fish, is a breeding ground for prawns, and may also be rich in hydrocarbon deposits. Any change in the land boundary will greatly affect the Extended Economic Zone (EEZ) of either country. Though Sir Creek involves a disputed area of only about 4–5 kilometers of marshy swamp, resulting changes with respect to the ocean and ocean bed could be significant.

The dispute is over the interpretation of the boundary line dividing the creek. The Pakistani view is that a mid-channel boundary (Thalweg Doctrine) is not applicable as the creek is not navigable. Therefore the boundary should run along the eastern bank of the creek, giving it full possession of the creek.

The Indian view is that the creek is navigable at high tide and is in fact being used by fishing boats. Therefore the mid-channel principle should apply. The two countries' proposals for resolution are not mutually acceptable. As per the UN Convention on the Law of the Seas, India and Pakistan must demarcate the Continental Shelf by 2004 or they will be subject to third-party arbitration. In the meantime, fishermen of both counties are being regularly apprehended and jailed by both sides in the creek area, leaving their families without breadwinners.

Pakistan-India: Factors for Consideration

In the conflict between India and Pakistan along their common border, five factors are of particular importance:

1. The international boundaries separating India from Pakistan were determined primarily on the basis of theocratic (rather than geographic) considerations. One result is that Pakistan lacks strategic depth to its vulnerable northern and eastern borders. As a number of authors have pointed out, Kashmir thus assumes particular geostrategic importance for Pakistan.[9]

2. In a dispute between a theocratic state and a secular one, it is particularly difficult to find common ground.

3. The danger of a nuclear exchange is omnipresent. The possession of nuclear weapons has quite possibly reduced the risk of conventional war, but possession of nuclear weapons does not stop low-intensity wars and terrorism.

4. Based on captured militants and documents, India alleges that Pakistan is actively supporting the various militant foreign and indigenous groups engaged in cross-border terrorist activities in Kashmir. Pakistan denies this and maintains that the allegations presented are unproved and that the Kashmir movement is an indigenous fight for freedom.

5. Despite earlier bilateral peace talks between the governments and efforts by NGOs, the stands taken by both sides have not appreciably changed. A terrorist raid on the Indian Parliament building on 13 December 2001 has led to a full-scale deployment of the two armies on their respective sides of the border. Pakistan has offered to hold talks with India primarily on the core issue of Kashmir. This has been rejected by an Indian precondition that state-sponsored cross-border terrorism should cease before a meaningful dialogue could take place. As the impasse continues, tensions between the two countries remains dangerously high.

India-China

Following the 1962 war between India and China over the delineation of their common 4,056-kilometer border, China assumed control of large chunks of disputed territory. The boundary as it stands today is known as the Line of Actual Control (LAC) and is subdivided into three sectors—the 2,176-kilometer western (Ladakh/Aksai-chin), 554-kilometer central (Uttar and Himachal Pradesh), and the 1,326-kilometer eastern (Sikkim and Arunachal Pradesh) sectors. In addition, territory claimed by India in the Karakoram area has been ceded by Pakistan to China. China recognizes neither the Indian state of Arunachal Pradesh (as it claims all the area north of the Brahmaputra River) nor the merger of the Kingdom of Sikkim with India. Thus the boundary disputes with nuclear China are on a far larger scale than the Kashmir conflict, but since 1962, the two countries have eschewed violence and opted for restraint in addressing the disputes.

Following the communist victory in 1949, China pushed for renegotiation of boundaries drawn by the British, while India accepted the traditional boundaries on the watershed principle and the 1914 MacMohan Line in the east. In 1951, China constructed the strategic Aksai-chin–Xinjiang Highway[10] through an area claimed by India. China's claim to this area was announced in 1954 and followed its claims for Ladakh and Arunachal Pradesh in early 1959. These claims resulted in a month-long war with China (October-November 1962) ending in a military defeat for India. A unilateral cease-fire was declared by China on 21 November 1962.

Since 1962, the situation has been stable along what is known as the LAC, and the sides have engaged in bilateral negotiations to resolve the conflict. In November 1988 a Joint Working Group (JWG) was set up to resolve the border dispute, and to date twelve meetings have taken place.[11] The two sides have rejected the use of force to solve the dispute in agreements in 1993 and 1996. A number of confidence-building measures have been put into place. India advocates a sectoral approach to the dispute while China has preferred to address the dispute as a "package." Since 1985, however, it has largely accepted India's sectoral approach (while stressing the need for a holistic approach), accepting the MacMohan Line as a basis for discussion in the eastern sector and the 1899 Macartney-MacDonald Line (which roughly conforms to China's former claim line) for Ladakh.

In September 1993 a high-level Sino-Indian Expert Group was set up to assist the JWG. Following India's nuclear tests on 11 and 13 May 1998, Sino-Indian relations deteriorated but have since improved. In November 2000, for the first time, maps were exchanged showing each side's perception of the border, and in January 2001 it was agreed that the process of border delineation would be hastened. High-level visits from both sides during 2001 and 2002 have appreciably created an environment suitable for a peaceful resolution of conflicts. Unlike the Indo-Pakistan dispute, a certain amount of flexibility, reciprocity, and restraint have marked the efforts for conflict resolution.

India-Myanmar

A similar approach marks the resolution of border conflicts with Myanmar. India and Myanmar amicably renegotiated their colonial boundaries in 1967. A 128-kilometer Indo-Myanmar stretch from India's tri-junction with Myanmar and China is unresolved as it is linked to the Indo-China boundary dispute. Free movement of the border population 20 kilometers on either side of the Indo-Myanmar boundary is permitted. In 2001 two roads from India to

Myanmar were constructed, linking their respective road networks in order to facilitate trade and closer relationships.

Nepal-India

The India-Nepal border is an open one, testimony to traditionally friendly Indo-Nepal relations. However, the open border results in illegal settlers, drug running, arms and explosives smuggling, and recently a change in the demographic pattern in the southern Indo-Nepal border region with about 34,000 people of Indian origin staying illegally in the Terai region. These include Muslim settlers from India and Bangladesh crossing into Nepal. Islamic religious schools (*madrassas*) have been opened in the Terai and are allegedly being used for anti-Indian activity with Pakistan's assistance.

Indo-Nepal border disputes are related primarily to water-sharing issues, treaties governing trade, and other relationships, and the problems caused by an open border.

Kalapani Border Area

The 35-kilometer-long boundary in the Kalapani area near the western trijunction of India, Nepal, and China is the main Indo-Nepal boundary dispute. It gained importance after the 1962 Indo-China war. A traditional route from India to Tibet runs through the Kalapani area via the all-weather strategic Lipu Lekh Pass, which provides a military entry point.

The Indian stand, based on an 1816 treaty, is that Kalapani is Indian territory, but Nepal points to maps that show the area in Nepal, and claims the boundary runs 5.5 kilometers west of Kalapani toward the Lipu Lekh Pass. It advocates a trilateral agreement with China to resolve the dispute. The Indian stand is that it is a bilateral issue.

To resolve the dispute, a JWG and a Joint Technical Boundary Committee were set up in 1982 and meet twice a year. A time-bound schedule was drawn up in August 2000. It was agreed that fieldwork for the delineation of the boundary would be completed by 2002, and final strip maps will be prepared by 2003.

Bhutan-China

Boundary disputes between Bhutan and China exist mainly over grazing areas for yaks. Twelve rounds of bilateral talks since 1984 have reduced the disputed areas from 1,128 square kilometers to 269 square kilometers in three areas in northwest Bhutan. At the end of the twelfth round of border talks, Bhutan and China signed an Agreement of Friendship.

India-Bangladesh

In 1947 the Radcliffe Award delineated the boundaries between India and East Pakistan. In 1974, following independence, a comprehensive new boundary agreement, the Indo-Bangladesh Land Boundary Agreement, was signed by the prime ministers of Bangladesh and India, but it has yet to be ratified. To date there is no maritime boundary agreement between the two countries.

The 1974 Indo-Bangladesh Agreement. The 4,351-kilometer boundary between India and Bangladesh, of which 180 kilometers runs along river lines, has yet to be fully delineated. A dispute over a 6.5-kilometer stretch of floodplain shared with the Indian state of Tripura has yet to be resolved. Ratification of the boundary agreement has been delayed due to the existence of 111 Indian enclaves in Bangladesh and 51 Bangladesh enclaves in India, complicating the process of delineating the boundary line. These enclaves, which were not taken into account by the Radcliffe Award, came into being when the previous rulers of the princely states of Cooch Behar (which merged with India) and Rongpur (which merged with East Pakistan) gambled away portions of their lands to each other. The problem is further complicated by shifting river courses. The locals mistakenly think that the boundary runs in the mid-channel of a river irrespective of subsequent changes in the river course. As a result, border people of either side take possession of land that has fallen on their side as a result of a change in the river course. Heated disputes and exchanges of fire from the border outposts have occurred. A recent conflict between border forces in April 2001 at Pyridwah and Boraibari raised tensions but was handled with restraint by both governments.

Maritime boundaries and Talpatty (New Moore) Island. Maritime boundary negotiations commenced in 1974 but have stalled because of differing perceptions on the applicability of the principles of international law in delimiting the maritime boundary. According to international practice, territorial waters extend 12 nautical miles into sea. Thereafter, water areas with a depth of 70 fathoms are considered as the continental shelf, after which an EEZ of 200 nautical miles is measured. Nations therefore pay particular attention to the drawing up of a baseline for finalizing maritime boundaries, as it has important effect on the total area of the EEZ.

The continental shelf of Bangladesh is enlarging because of an annual deposit of around 2.2 billion tons of sediment deposited into the sea by its river systems. This not only gives hope for land reclamation but also for exploiting seabed resources of hydrocarbon and mineral deposits.

Talpatty/New Moore Island is 2 square kilometers of uninhabited offshore island at the mouth of a river flowing between an Indian and a Bangladesh district,[12] which is visible only during low water. It emerged in 1970 as a result of a tectonic upheaval of the seabed. There is considerable fishing activity in the area. The island assumes significance because possession of the island provides the potential for offshore exploration of oil. Bangladesh belatedly laid claim to it in 1979. In 1981, a tense situation was calmed through diplomacy and by vacating the island, but resolution of the dispute and delineation of the maritime boundaries are priorities.

Sharing of river waters.[13] The waters of fifty-six rivers from the Ganges and the Brahmaputra river systems flow from India to Bangladesh. Water from the Ganges plays a vital role in both countries and has been a source of conflict particularly when the flow of water is low during summer. A long-standing dispute over the waters was resolved by the Ganges Water Sharing Treaty of 12 December 1996, nineteen years after the dispute had arisen. The treaty has validity for thirty years with periodic five-year reviews, and incorporates fail-safe mechanisms that oblige India to release water amounting to no less than 90 percent of Bangladesh's share. The treaty has been hailed as an example of conflict resolution, though it is not without its critics. A more comprehensive and equitable water-sharing agreement encompassing the two main river systems and their tributaries still must be worked out.

Migrants to India. Though not related to a boundary problem, the influx of migrants and Chakma (Buddhist) refugees from Bangladesh into India is causing serious demographic changes in India's northeastern border states. Following an accord between the Chakmas and the government of Bangladesh in December 1997, many Chakma refugees returned to Bangladesh, but a large number still remain in India.

Positive developments. Since 1996, a number of positive developments in Indo-Bangladeshi relations have taken place, including:

1. The Indo-Bangladesh Water Sharing Treaty, 1996
2. India lifts nontariff barriers, 9 December 1998
3. Road and rail links between India and Bangladesh have been established, effective from June and December 1999 respectively
4. A Joint Indo-Bangladesh Chamber of Commerce has been established. India has provided a 20 million rupee credit line for three years in June 1999.
5. Transshipment rights through Bangladesh for goods to northeast India have been allowed since July 1999

Bangladesh-Myanmar

From 1991 onwards about 400,000 ethnic Rohingya Muslim refugees have fled from religious persecution in Myanmar and streamed into Bangladesh. Population tensions in Bangladesh have led to clashes between them and the local population. Between mid-1992 and 1997, 230,000 Rohingyas were repatriated back. There is also the problem of 300,000 Bihari Muslims who are living in abject poverty who are stranded in Bangladesh because they are not accepted in Pakistan.

Sri Lanka–India

The narrow Palk Straits separating India and Sri Lanka have served as traditional fishing grounds for both countries. A long-standing dispute over the ownership of a 3.75-square-kilometer island, Kacchativu, 12 nautical miles off the Indian coast and 10.5 nautical miles off the Sri Lankan coast, was resolved in 1976 by a bilateral agreement awarding the island to Sri Lanka. Two maritime agreements of 1974 and 1976 define the maritime boundaries between the two countries.

Prospects

Afghanistan, Pakistan, and India will remain the major flashpoints in South Asia, followed by the civil war in Sri Lanka.

The boundary conflict between India and China, which covers an area far larger than that of Afghanistan and Pakistan put together, does not fall into this pattern because of the post-1962 restraint generally shown by both sides. Also it is largely a bilateral, secular, political issue unsullied by terrorism. There is not much space for other countries to become players in the issue. Any strategic conflict of interests between the two countries will likely be played out elsewhere.

The boundary conflicts between India and Pakistan are unlikely to be resolved in the near future because of different perceptions on the approach to resolve the conflicts—e.g.,"holistic" versus tackling "core" issues. The dispute has become ossified by hardened attitudes and lack of fresh initiatives. Conflict resolution helped by a third-party initiative is unlikely.

By far the most serious threat arising out of a border conflict in South Asia is that of a nuclear exchange between Pakistan and India. The whole escalation process, starting from a localized border incident to a limited conventional war based on brinkmanship, and an assessment of the other side's nuclear threshold, is fraught with danger. Compounded by the short flight time of missiles, the scenario is grim.

India, as one of the key players in South Asia, has had to deal with a wide range of border conflicts and has approached each situation differently. Some lessons learned in the process have a larger applicability.

Having "open borders," though attractive theoretically, has its dangers in the South Asian context. Open borders with friendly Nepal have created serious problems. On the other hand, the limited free border zone between Mizoram, Nagaland, in India and Myanmar is workable even if the same approach won't work on the Indo-Bangladesh border. Opening up and enlarging border trade does not automatically improve a security situation unless its area-specific effects are correctly assessed.

India has managed its maritime boundary issues satisfactorily. Since independence it has fixed its maritime boundaries with Thailand, Indonesia, Myanmar, Sri Lanka, and the Maldives. Bangladesh and Pakistan are the only two countries with which it has maritime boundary disputes. India has generally chosen bilateral agreements as a means to solving border disputes. However, when disputes are prolonged, arbitration is advisable, as was done in the case of a portion of the Rann of Kutch. The future increase in trade and shipping in the Indian Ocean for the littoral South Asian countries makes it an economic imperative to stabilize maritime boundaries as soon as possible. The option of joint ventures with neighboring countries in exploiting ocean bed resources is better than fighting for the same resources.

With globalization, international pressures on resolving bilateral border conflicts will increase.

Recommendations

Conflict resolution activities undertaken by governments follow time-honored techniques. Politicians and bureaucrats trapped in their own logic bubbles gather relevant facts and also prepare logical refutations of the other side's arguments. A holistic view is rarely taken, therefore eliminating the possibilities of joint management or sharing. Thus when controlling migration flows are being considered, it is easier to arrive at short-term solutions such as border fencing rather than the establishment of joint ventures, development aid, and other measures to improve the economy of the region. A similar holistic view has to be taken to help resolve the problems of ethnic groups straddling the boundary, without compromising the political boundary itself.

Information flows and mass awareness programs have yet to mature in South Asia. Similarly, region- and area-specific organizations for training in conflict management, development of negotiation and interpersonal skills, and availability of objective data bases for the purpose are yet to be widely used in governance. The growth of independent think tanks in the region is an encouraging sign.

Concept reviews by each country on their specific conflict areas need to be done, especially in the case of long-standing disputes, since the working concepts themselves may be impeding conflict resolution. Detailed case studies of long-standing conflicts need to be prepared and studied to identify "breakthrough" factors that led to conflict resolution and to understand how and why these factors became effective. The Ganges Water Sharing Treaty between India and Bangladesh, which took nineteen years to finalize, and the 1957 Pakistan-Iran Frontier Agreement on the Baluchistan area might be useful case studies.

Most South Asian countries have until now resolved their conflicts bilaterally. Globalization, developments in information technology, the worldwide connections of terrorists, "freedom fighters," and the underground drug and arms economy are factors that make bilateralism an option instead of a negotiating principle. The implications of this require greater attention from governments and various official and nonofficial organizations.

Lieutenant General (Retired) Sushil K. Pillai was a former deputy chief of army staff and director general of infantry in the Indian Army. After retirement in 1991, he has written extensively on counterinsurgencies in India's Northeastern region. He is consulting editor of Faultlines, *a journal on conflict management of the Institute for Conflict Management, New Delhi, India.*

Resources

Other Publications
Boundary Conflicts and Preventative Diplomacy, by Kjell-Ake Nordquist. Washington, DC, Carnegie Commission on Preventing Deadly Conflict, n.d.
Conflicts: A Better Way to Resolve Them, by Edward De Bono. London, Harrap, 1985.
"Containing Fear. The Origins and Management of Ethnic Conflict," by David A. Lake and Donald Rothchild, *International Security* 21(2), fall 1996.
Dirty Wars, by Leroy Thompson. London, BCA, 1991.
L'eau Source de Conflits en Asie du Sud 1947–1999, Defense Nationale monographs (in French) on South Asian countries by Comite d'etudes de Defense Nationale, Paris, Fax +33-1-44423189, E-mail: cednrevu@worldnet.fr.
The Cost of Conflicts, edited by Michael Cranna. London, Earthscan, 1994.
The Fearful State: Power, People and Internal War in South Asia, by S. Mahmud Ali. London, Zed Press, 1993.

Afghanistan
Afghanistan, by Louis Dupree. Princeton, NJ, Princeton University Press, 1980.
Afghanistan, by Sharifah Enayat Ali and Sharifah B. Ali. Tarrytown, NY, Benchmark Books, September 1995.
Afghanistan: Mullah, Marx & Mujahids, by Ralph Magnus and Eden Naby. Boulder, CO, Westview, 1998.
The Fragmentation of Afghanistan, by Barnett R. Rubin. New Haven, Yale University Press, 1995.
The Pathans 500 BC–AD 1957, by Sir Olaf Caroe. Cambridge, Oxford University Press, July 1984.
Taliban: The Story of the Afghan Warlords, by Ahmad Rashid. London, Pan Books, 2001.

Bangladesh
Harnessing Eastern Himalayan Rivers: Regional Co-operation in South Asia, by B. G. Verghese and R Iyer. Delhi, Konark, 1993.
The Betrayal of East Pakistan, by Lt. Gen. A. A. K. Niazi. New Delhi, Manohar, 1998.
The Sacred and the Secular, by T. M Mursdid. Cambridge, Oxford University Press, 1995.
Waters of Hope, by B. G. Verghese. Delhi, Konark, 1990.
Women and Islam in Bangladesh, by Taj Hashmi. Basingstoke, Hampshire, Macmillan, 2000.

Bhutan
Bhutan: Society and Polity, by Ramakant and Misra. New Delhi, Indus, 1996.
Ethnic Conflict in Bhutan, by Mathew Joseph C. New Delhi, Nirala's Publication, 1998.

India
India's China War, by Neville Maxwell. Bombay, Jaico, 1970.
Kashmir: The Troubled Frontiers, by Maj. Gen. Afsir Karim, AVSM. New Delhi, Lancer, 1994.
Kashmir 1947, by P. S. Jha. Delhi, Oxford University Press, 1998.
Ministry of Defence, "The Official History of Operations in J&K 1947–48," Controller Publications, 1987.
Rites of Passage: Border Crossings, Imagined Homelands: India's East and Bangladesh, by Sanjoy Hazarika. New Delhi, Penguin Books India, 2000.
India's North East Resurgent, by B. G. Verghese. Delhi, Konark, 1996.

Maldives
Les Maldives: Un archipel en plein developpement, by Alain Lamballe. Defense Nationale, a monograph, December 1997.

Nepal
Faces of Nepal, by Salter and Gurung. Lalitpur, Himal Books, 1996.
Nationalism & Ethnicity in a Hindu Kingdom, by David Gellner. Amsterdam, Harwood 1997.
Society and State Building in Nepal, by R. S. Chauhan. New Delhi, Sterling Publications, 1989.
The Political Development in Nepal, 1950–70: Conflict Between Tradition and Modernity, by R. S. Chauhan. New Delhi, Associated Publication House, 1971.

Pakistan
Contemporary Problems of Pakistan, edited by J. Henry Korson. Boulder, CO, Westview, 1993.
Historical Dictionary of Pakistan, by Shahid Javed Burki. Metuchen, NJ, Methuen Scarecrow, 1991.
Pakistan, by David Taylor. Oxford, Clio Press, 1990.
Pakistan: A Country Study, by Ed RF Nyrop. Washington, DC, American University, 1984.
Quest for Identity, by Muhammed Sher Ali Khan Pataudi. Lahore, Al–Kitab Press, 1984.

Sri Lanka
Assignment Colombo, by J. N. Dixit. Delhi, Konark, 1997.
India, Sri Lanka and the Tamil Crisis 1976–1994, by Alan Bullion. London, Pinter, 1995.
Reaping the Whirlwind, by K. M. De Silva. New Delhi, Penguin India, 1998.

Selected Internet Sites
www.idsa-india.org (Institute of Defence and Strategic Analysis)
www.ipcs.org (Institute of Peace and Conflict Studies)
www.satp.org (South Asia Terrorism Portal)

Notes
1. For the sake of clarity, in this chapter the author accepts the definitions of boundaries and borders as spelled out by Kjell-Ake Nordquist in *Boundary Conflicts and Preventative Diplomacy,* Washington, DC: Carnegie Commission on Preventing Deadly Conflict, n.d. (Chapter 2). *Boundary* refers to the line separating two states, irrespective of its degree of implementation (delineation or definition on paper and demarcation or marking on the ground). *Border* refers to an area surrounding a boundary and *frontier* is the area where two states meet in interests and penetration, while not necessarily with an agreed territorial limit for their aspirations. Where boundaries are not defined, some sort of line is tacitly accepted by both parties and called by another name, e.g., Line of Control or Actual Ground Position Line, or even as a "working boundary." Boundaries are based on internal and international legislation. A boundary agreement is an international legal document even if its making and ratification is exclusively an internal political process.
2. See David Lake and Donald Rothchild "Containing Fear," *International Security* 21(2), fall 1996.
3. Louis Dupree mentions twenty-one Afghan ethnic groups in his book *Afghanistan,* Princeton, NJ, Princeton University Press, 1980.
4. 3 January 1966; 2 July 1972; January 1994; 28 March 1997; 18 October 1998; and 16 July 2001.
5. United Liberation Front of Assam (ULFA) and the United Democratic Front of Bodoland (NDFB).
6. See Nick Lewer and Joe Williams, "Sri Lanka," in this volume for a more detailed discussion of this conflict.
7. See Ramaswamy R. Iyer, "Water-Related Conflicts," in this volume.

8. See Kristoffel Lieten, "Jammu and Kashmir," in this volume for an in-depth analysis of the conflict.

9. For example, Maj. Gen. Akbar Khan *Raiders in Kashmir,* Karachi: DSO Pak Publishers, 1970, and archival papers of Lt. Gen. Arthur Smith Chief of General Staff, British Army in India (quoted in Lt. Gen. S. L. Menezes, *Honour & Fidelity*, Oxford: Oxford University Press, 1999).

10. The road provides the main logistics link to the four Chinese armies in Tibet and links to Lop Nor, the Chinese nuclear and missile testing site, and facilitates trade along an old silk route.

11. The last meeting was held on 8 February 2001.

12. The Hariabhanga River that separates two districts—the 24-Parganas (in the Indian state of West Bengal) and Khulna (in Bangladesh).

13. See Ramaswamy R. Iyer, "Water-Related Conflicts," Chapter 7.5 of this volume.

7.4

Protecting the Victims of Forced Migration: Mixed Flows and Massive Flows

Ranabir Samadar

The phenomenon of mixed flows of forced migration in South Asia raises significant issues for "humanitarian politics"—a name under which the international work on protection and care of the victims of violence, discrimination, environmental degradation, disaster, famine, and economic deprivation goes. There is a new mix of forced and unwanted population flows and this new phenomenon is not adequately appreciated in refugee protection policies, particularly in a region such as South Asia.[1]

The forced migration situation in South Asia raises the problem of method from several angles. It is important to note the following in this context:

1. Studies of forced population movements, particularly in South Asia, have been hitherto pursued from economic and demographic angles. The link between state politics and population flows cannot be seen through rose-tinted glasses.

2. The notion of force is so narrowly defined that the structural violence permeating these societies escapes our attention, though violence and coercion are considered as benchmarks in the determination of refugees' status.

3. Only the present of any conflict envelops our minds, and the history of the enmeshing of peoples recedes into some hoary past in which contemporary scholars engaged in fixing problems and finding solutions have little interest.

4. The politics of a humanitarian regime do not allow expansion of the institutional framework to ensure full justification of the notion of humanitarianism. There is now a great urgency to address these questions in the context of our region, and take general note of the inadequacy of the frameworks, practices, and received notions.

Protection policies in this region have to take into account the imperatives of peace and reconciliation—imperatives that supposedly were not concerns of a protection regime. We must remember that the present system grew in the wake of the Cold War and possesses no capacity to respond to the imperatives of justice and reconciliation.

We also have to take note of the non-gender-specific nature of humanitarian practices and law. Nowhere it is more apparent, as several reports on refugee care and the care of the internally displaced people in South Asia bear out, than in the way women feature as refugee subjects in refugee management. The non-gender-specific nature of fear, persecution, and threat as outlined in *The UNHCR Handbook on Procedures and Criteria on Determining Refugee Status* does not think deeply on the fears of violence, of state, of law, of assault, nor of the breakdown of security and lifeways faced by more than half of the refugees on earth.

The Non-Entrée Regime in South Asia

The massive refugee flow, forced repatriation, decline of liberal asylum practices, and the creation of a virtual non-entrée regime in this region, following European examples, indicates that the "fortress Europe" mentality is engulfing the region. The Convention Relating to the Status of Refugees of 1951 was intended for Europe, and did not consider the millions fleeing homes in the wake of decolonization, partition, and the emergence of new states in South Asia. No United Nations High Commission on Refugees (UNHCR) was there to take care of the refugees as this region was being decolonized. A report in the *Human Rights Tribune* describes in detail the charade of the Dublin Convention, the Amsterdam Treaty, and the new Charter of the Fundamental Rights of the European Union that do not take into account the rights of non-European citizens. Likewise, in South Asia, each state is free to devise guidelines for the conduct of its security forces. The country-specific protection regimes in South Asia, as elsewhere, are unable to administer quick and proper care of the thousands fleeing from violence, terror, environmental devastation, and other insecurities. The situation is aggravated because states sometimes administer care to a victim group quickly while ignoring the same group at other times, in tune with diplomatic and security considerations. In the face of the structural adjustment policies that produce what scholars have termed "new slavery," and with the entire subcontinent being populated today by aliens leading a submerged existence—whom, following Eric Wolf, we may call "people without history"[2]—it is meaningless to stick to current citizenship policies. The current controversy over citizenship in Nepal, India (particularly the Northeast), Pakistan, and Sri Lanka—in each of these cases, vast numbers of people remain disenfranchised—reinforces the need to study the mixed phenomenon of forced migrants, unwanted migrants, and migrants of the submerged world within the country and across the country. Given the situation in the subregion, the relevance of the current state of institutionalized care and protection is suspect.

As Judge Geoffrey Care of the International Association of Refugee Law Judges has demonstrated, the peculiar nature of the Convention of 1951 leaves a tremendous burden on jurisprudence and enormous freedom to the state. He

Howard Davies/Panos

Bhutanese refugee in Beldangi Refugee Camp, Nepal. Holding her ID card, this woman is confirming her Bhutanese citizenship. In the early 1990s, Bhutan dispossessed and expelled one-sixth of its population, over 100,000 ethnic Nepali, who had lived in Bhutan for several generations. The majority now live in refugee camps in southeast Nepal.

has commented that the courts and tribunals have increasingly given interpretations of the states' obligations under the convention that are not always in conformity with the views of the executive sector of those states. The convention is applied with the reality for the individual himself or herself in mind. Today, refugee determination procedures on an individual basis and the resulting unequal burden sharing have produced confused, traumatized, and nervous shelter seekers who rarely travel with supportive documents and land in alien systems that are in, Judge Care's words, "frequently hostile or incredulous" hosts.[3] The more fundamental question is to what extent decisions of determination of refugee status on an individual basis contribute to setting up an international ethic and framework of care, hospitality, and kindness, taking on broad collective political, economic, and cultural considerations. How would law in such cases settle on proof? The method of evaluation is not one of hard facts. It requires knowledge not only of the asylum applicant's own tale, and what is accepted of it, but a whole range of other factual matters. A more fundamental structural issue is at stake here. Refugees flee in fear from the induced violence of the state, private armies, systemic discriminatory institutions, environmental disasters, and developmental catastrophes. They flee from a state where they are citizens and land in another state where there is a system that tries to frame the rules of the game. How can an ethic of care and kindness and a framework of responsibility grow from that? If it can at all, it will develop very incrementally.

People displaced by agencies or other people are, prima facie, wronged. How shall we judge the moral obligation of others, in this case other states, toward the wronged, the actual and potential victims? We have here not only the relevance of the ethic of care, kindness, and hospitality, but an added ethic, that of responsibility. This responsibility has two implications—responsibility of the state and of the international community. The word, *responsibility,* carries two senses—responsibility of the host and that of the expelling state, or the state that allows the "nice exit." Ethically, the issues they must confront are concerned with what is morally owed to the victims of displacement. How do we place and apportion responsibility for man-made disasters, a dam, a highway, a famine, or a flood? What are the politics of reparation in these cases? And what will be the norm of responsibility in the more complex cases of indirect displacement and repeated displacements? What will be the method? How shall we settle for what is known as minimal justice? These are questions of ethics standing before those who have held that issues of care, kindness, and hospitality are matters of a systematic and humanitarian doctrine. While there may be substantial agreement about preferred values, there is a clear lack of agreement over strategies to meet the emerging situation, marked by the following three conditions.

1. Refugees are today a phenomenon of mass flight, mass movement, and massive displacement, but individual determination of the status of the shelter seeker that comes as a shadow of the principle of "no forcible return" overwhelms the principle of care of the victims of forced migration.
2. The movement of the displaced is so mixed that, while states today no longer claim an absolute right to return the displaced to persecution and peril, there is a greater freedom of action made available to states because the terminology of refugee protection has been rendered obsolete with the rise of new words such as "displaced persons," "illegal immigrants," "economic migrants," "safe third country," "visa requirements," "carrier sanctions," and finally the "internally guaranteed security zones."
3. Hospitality is now subject to rules, procedures, laws, and practices that must be thought anew in terms of the imperatives of the ethic of hospitality.

Raising these questions means taking into account emerging policies and perspectives relating to conflicts, collective actions, and human-rights perspectives. We must interrogate the way in which states in South Asia respond to inflows of refugees and other kinds of forced migrants. There is, admittedly, a difference between a "Northern approach" and a "Southern approach." By Northern approach we imply individual determination, emphasis on law and procedure, a host of administrative and quasi-judicial mechanisms, and attempts to adhere to the 1951 Convention and the 1967 Protocol. By Southern approach we indicate the prevalence of heavy reliance on bilateral methods to resolve refugee crises (the India–Sri Lanka Accord being one such example), group determination, community care and protection, and an almost deliberate reluctance to legally stabilize a related situation. While acknowledging the truth of the difference in the two sets of practices, a human-rights perspective would demand that the emerging reality of mixed flows of forced migration, the increasing reluctance of states to offer shelter to the victims, and the woefully inadequate institutionalization of practices of care and protection be recognized. Steps should be suggested for a broader and coordinated approach. Such a perspective would encourage new insights, involving these questions: Who are they—refugees, asylum seekers, economic migrants, students, or nomads? Should they be classified in this way or should all the reasons that have driven them to leave their countries of origin be taken into account? And would not a humanitarian policy of the state demand that attention also be paid to economic, demographic, social, and health issues? Further, it would encourage the policy planners to face the reality that a refugee cannot be defined by a single event that has supposedly produced the shelter-seeker. The partition of 1947 has produced refugees long after the states had thought that the event was dead in terms of producing refugees. Yet research, including mine, on the linkages between various phases of forced migration in the subcontinent show how long after the states stopped concerning themselves with that bygone event, it continued to produce escapees prompted by fear and insecurity. This realization should have political and legal implications.[4]

A South Asian Forced-Migration Observatory

All these examples show that there is, in the first place, the need to take account of the various streams of forced migration, their dimensions, and their mixed nature in order to grasp the complexity of the challenges to humanitarian tasks. One way of gaining such an account may be to set up a South Asian migration observatory and to conduct a feasibility study for such an observatory for Europe. A feasibility study will establish and connect various research institutions and organizations active in the field of forced migration, thus producing a wealth of information on migration within the region and outside. It will also facilitate the analysis of the information systems used by policymakers and others, and identify the relative importance of specific information sources and networks. It will show that, for policymakers, the main problems are inherent in the sheer volume and diversity of information on migration. Sources of information are frequently unknown or inaccessible to them, or there is a lack of resources to digest and evaluate what is available.

There may be several gaps in the information on forced migration, or in the information available to users. The first may be related to access to and coordination of existing information. The second may be the lack of a comprehensive and up-to-date sources on national policy, legislation, case laws, and administrative and quasi-judicial orders relating to forced migration. A South Asian forced-migration observatory can easily fill these gaps. A third gap relates to the need, especially of policymakers, for more timely, reliable, and harmonized statistics. A migration observatory would be unlikely to produce many more up-to-date statistics, but it could enable other improvements, notably by serving as a catalyst for data harmonization. A fourth gap may be in the provision of analyses of trends and patterns of migration. An observatory would be able to perform a series of analytical roles and develop ways of enhancing statistical data bases that would improve the depth and quality of its analyses. The shortage and inadequacy of country reports, which can support the development of an early warning system, constitutes a fifth gap. The proposed observatory would ameliorate this problem by compiling its own reports, by signposting existing country-based information, and by synthesizing reports already in existence. A sixth gap can be the lack of a comprehensive source of information on what research is currently being done or planned, and the identification of gaps in the current research effort that may necessitate reorientation of funding.

The mandate for such an observatory should be to make the information that already exists more accessible. It should primarily serve the needs of policymakers, analysts, human-rights groups, and multilateral humanitarian agencies for information on all aspects of forced migration in the region. To be able to do this, it has to be an open institution, based on up-to-date information technology, network-based, with a clearly defined set of analytical tasks. A forced-migration observatory with such a mandate will go a long way in facilitating not only information needs for humanitarian tasks, but also help in indicating the trend of current legislation, court pronouncements, and administrative practices, and the trend of proper direction of all these. An annotated directory of services and persons involved can be the first step toward such an observatory.

Innovative and Democratic
Border Management by Easing Labor Inflow

The second suggestion offered in this chapter relates to democratic border management effected by easing labor inflow between countries, primarily of working populations driven by insecurities of various kinds. As an example, we can refer to the situation obtaining between India and Bangladesh. Both India and Bangladesh have proved woefully inadequate in dealing with the reality of the border between the two countries. The border, with its long history of movements between people, cultures, beliefs, ideas, and customs, was completely unreal from the beginning. There were farms within 40 yards on either side. There are fifty-three rivers in the region that make the functionality of the border more complicated. Almost all of India's disputes with East Pakistan are related to this border. Each country had its enclaves within the boundary of the other, meaning that the border was rife with potential problems. After the liberation of Bangladesh, it was hoped that the border would lose much of its potential for creating disputes. Sadly, even more than twenty-five years after the birth of Bangladesh, almost all the outstanding issues between India and Bangladesh continue to be related to their common border. These include sharing of water resources of common rivers, the demarcation of maritime boundaries, illegal cross-border activities, illegal migration, and the granting of entry/exit facilities. Convictions about the sanctity of the border are weaker in this region than elsewhere in India. Out of despair and under political pressure, the government of India has built barbed-wire fencing on parts of both Assam and the West Bengal sides of the border, well over 500 kilometers in all. Other measures such as regular patrolling and checkpoints continue. But these have not stemmed the flow of people or goods; indeed, it is no secret that border guards on either side accept and demand bribes from those seeking to cross illegally. As a result of the influx, the size of which is difficult to estimate, a constant state of tension exists in the Northeast between migrants, perceived migrants, and the host communities. If one is to accept that migration is a natural human phenomenon that occurs in varying degrees worldwide, one must also accept the fact that few countries in the world have successfully contained it, be it a superpower such as the United States or a medium power such as Germany. One must actually go a step further and say that it can only be contained or regulated. Or rather, it can be negotiated through a process of meaningful economic activities, exchanges, regulatory mechanisms, and above all through dialogue.

One can think of certain policy suggestions. First, a system of identity cards acceptable to the local population, particularly those living on the border in the eastern and the northeastern regions, has to be ensured. Second, while the system of visas for nationals of either country will continue, for those who cannot or do not want to use the visa system, a specific, time-bound legal system sanctioning their presence in the host area has to be devised. We can take the specific case of the Indian border districts that share rivers or land with Bangladesh, where the process of acquiring a passport and a visa are both cumbersome and time-consuming, as an example. Third, the development of a scheme to allow migrants to come legally into the region on the basis of work permits issued by a central work-permit authority. This can be done with the backing of the relevant state and set up by an act of parliament, with specific clauses involving the officials of the local state and village-level administrators. This could be worked out in association with the Home Ministry as well as the Ministry for Law and Company Affairs. A retired supreme court/high court judge may head such a panel and a member of the National Human Rights Commission may be associated with it.

Since the permits are intended to discourage illegal migration and promote healthy economic cooperation at subregional and local levels on both sides, the preliminary step may be that the permits be issued to groups (of say twenty or so) rather than to individuals. This practice should be allowed in the following fields: agricultural operations at harvest time, construction, boat-building, and fishing and allied activities. Work permits could be issued at border posts set up for this purpose by cells that would include a representative of the district magistrate, with members gleaned from the following sources: one senior member of the local *panchayat* (village council system), a police officer, a member of an NGO or some other public organization, a representative of the labor board, and a person representing labor organizations—with at least two of these five being women. Since the border is long, a system of such posts needs to be worked out, situating them either at existing checkpoints or beside them.

The permits would be issued on the spot after verification of the following documents: (1) the identity of the applicant(s) as proof of nationality/residency; (2) a clear statement on the place they will be residing for the next year (work permits would be given for a maximum of one year to begin with) and the name of the employer, who must be present (in person or by a representative) for the issue of the permit with supporting documents from his or her side; and (3) a document stating the employer's responsibility for the immigrant(s). If the permit is to be extended, it can be done by the district commission or the labor commissioner of the relevant district, for a period not beyond another two years. Permit holders would have no voting or political rights, but would have access to the courts of the host country if their civil rights are injured in any way, and would be permitted to receive payment for services at the same level as local workers and repatriate their savings to their home country.

For the Indo-Bangladesh border, an autonomous binational commission could be formed to act as a flexible instrument for formulating strategies of cooperation. Such a commission would form temporary working groups of local parallels as existing between West Bengal/Assam/Meghalaya/India and Bangladesh on matters of landholdings, employment, and social and economic resources, and formulate policies based on commonalities and the market. The ultimate goal would be to hand over local administration to largely decentralized administrative units that can work with greater competence and stability in comparison to the vested-interest groups, and consequently the promotion of an atmosphere of greater understanding between two countries and also throughout the subregion.

In brief, the example of such a proposal, worked out in detail by four researchers in *Economic and Political Weekly,* 4 September 1999, shows that care and protection policy for victims of forced migration can be innovatively widened if the attending factors, such as labor market linkages, work permits, local cooperation, and decentralization of border management and control, are considered, and national and military security is not held up as the cornerstone of state policy toward illegal immigrants who are mostly deprived of livelihood and remain victims of insecurities of all kinds.

A Mixed Situation Needs
Mixed Response and Mixed Policies

The above analysis and examples of innovative measures suggest that the mixed situation in forced migration calls for a new outlook on the overall protection framework in the region. This region grapples with a whole raft of issues: mass influx, prima facie determination on group basis, temporary protection, the need for combining the rules of protection with the need for reconciliation, operational measures to enhance security of the victims of forced migration, sharing of responsibility, and planning for durable solutions based on gender equity. A human rights–based approach calls for deep reflection on all these issues. Clearly South Asia has to seek its own model while learning from these examples in terms of coping with mass displacement and influx. The civilian character of protection will be enhanced when the human rights–based approach is given priority; justice to the victims will become the prime value, and roles and responsibilities will be democratized. The refugee will not be an object of protective administration only, but the subject of a humanitarian framework.

Mass influx in South Asia will continue to affect not only host states, but also the entire regional community. Besides adopting international tools, there is therefore a current need to further develop them. This is particularly necessary in order to cope with the task of determining the prima facie status for groups of victims of forced migration. They will have to be provided with temporary protection through better harmonization of approaches, with acceptable standards and a degree of flexibility in protection-based response to mass influx in the region. This will require that both national mechanisms and regional cooperation be in tune with international standards for sharing responsibilities and burdens in mass influx situations. Policies will have to be framed for democratizing citizenship issues, resettlement of the victims, humanitarian transfers, and other appropriate procedural mechanisms. It is important in all these cases that we proceed from local best practices and local experiences and burdens. Only then will we be able to proceed toward sharing responsibilities more equitably and coordinating refugee-protection mechanisms with other protection policies such as the UN International Convention on the Protection of the Rights of all Migrant Workers and Members of Their Families. This is where an immigration policy based on human rights must begin. From a simple protection framework for refugees who are mostly determined individually and sometimes collectively, it becomes a framework against racism, oppression of migrants, trafficking of women and children, and other various discriminations—a framework for tolerance and greater enjoyment of economic, social, and cultural rights.

In dealing with mixed and massive flows of forced migrants based on a fundamental concern for the victims, the choice is between a human-rights and care-oriented approach and a state security–oriented approach. A fundamentally state security–oriented approach will not be able to contain, mitigate, and tackle conflicts on a cooperative basis. Since responsibility sharing and care, protection, hospitality, settlement, resettlement, and perhaps voluntary return are the only appropriate ways to protect the victims of forced migration, a justice and human rights–based approach is the only option. It will not only help humanitarians to cope with the paradoxes of humanitarian politics, but will also help the political societies of the region to realize that conflicts occur not due to demography or population flow, but because of a nation-state security-centric attitude that forecloses all possibilities of cooperation, coexistence, and the envisioning of new avenues of accommodation.

Ranabir Samadar is the director of the Peace Studies Program at the South Asia Forum for Human Rights, Kathmandu. He has worked extensively on conflicts in South Asia. His particular research has been on migration and refugee studies, the theory and practices of dialogue, nationalism and postcolonial statehood in South Asia, and technological restructuring and global labor flows. He serves on the editorial board of several journals and is the founding editor of Refugee Watch. *Examples of his publications are* Marginal Nation: Trans-border Migration from Bangladesh to India *(1999) and* Whose Asia Is It Anyway? Region and the Nation in South Asia *(1996).*

Notes

1. I am indebted to Paula Banerjee, Sanjoy Hazarika, and Monirul Hussain, with whom I had earlier worked on democratic management of borders in South Asia, for some of the ideas presented here. Similarly, I remain indebted to Augustine Mahiga and Wei Ming Lim-Kaaba, the chief and deputy chief of mission of the UNHCR in New Delhi, for inviting me to the Eminent Persons Group meeting at Colombo, 2001, that gave me the opportunity to first frame my ideas in the present form.

2. Eric Wolf, *Europe and the People Without History.* Berkeley, CA: University of California Press, 1982.

3. Geoffrey Care, "Transnational Refugee Recognitions—A Judicial Perspective," unpublished paper, presented at the International Conference on Forced Migration, Displacement and Conflict Resolution, Calcutta, University of Jadavpur, 20–22 April 2000.

4. See in this context the Report of the Asia-Pacific Seminar of Experts on Migrants and Trafficking in Persons, with Particular Reference to Women and Children, 5–7 September 2000, Bangkok, which in Paragraph 1 of its conclusions admitted that "migration concerned the movement of people within *and* across national borders and that people migrated inter alia because of poverty, perceived deprivation, racial discrimination, internal conflicts, lack of opportunity, discrimination against women, and to reunite separated families." The same report also spoke of legislative and other institutional inadequacies in protecting migrants and victims of trafficking in persons.

7.5

Water-Related Conflicts: Factors, Aspects, Issues

Ramaswamy R. Iyer

This chapter examines, in broad and general terms, various water-related conflicts in the South Asian context. It begins with a discussion of riparian conflicts—essentially disputes over the rights to the waters of a flowing river claimed by different users located alongside or in the vicinity of that river. This issue can arise at the level of households, farms, communities, villages, or towns, but has most serious implications at the level of political or administrative units within a country, or between "coriparian" countries.[1]

The Cauvery Dispute

The Cauvery Dispute, an interstate conflict within the quasi-federal structure of India, is a typical case in point for discussing intrastate water-related conflicts. The Cauvery is an important river system in the southern India. The essence of the dispute, which dates back to the nineteenth century, is a conflict of interests between the downstream state of Tamil Nadu, which has long been using the Cauvery waters for irrigated agriculture, and the upstream state of Karnataka, which started later with irrigated agriculture but has been making rapid progress. Kerala, an upstream state with a relatively modest demand for Cauvery water, and Pondicherry, furthest downstream and with a very small demand, have also become parties. Any fair sharing would have to provide for the legitimate interests of all four parties. Unfortunately, the governments of the principal contending states have exploited the issue for political purposes, which has impeded negotiating freedom and flexibility on both sides. In both states, all political parties tend to take a strong stand on this issue, making it risky for any party in power to show weakness. This makes the dispute an intractable one. It has been under adjudication by a tribunal set up by the government of India. In 1991, an interim order passed by the tribunal generated a secondary dispute that led to some violence. That secondary dispute has partially settled and adjudication on the main water-sharing issue has been proceeding, but it is uncertain if a final decision will be accepted, or lead to further conflict. It is difficult to say whether good sense will prevail, or pressure from an ill-informed public and the shortsighted calculations by politicians will preclude rationality.

The Indus Treaty of 1960

The India-Pakistan dispute over the waters of the Indus, resolved through a treaty in 1960, is representative of a water dispute at the international level. The 1947 Line of Partition cut across the Indus River system, necessitating an understanding between the two new countries on the sharing of the waters and steps to be taken in response to the disruption of well-established irrigation systems. Prolonged talks between the two governments, assisted by the good offices of the World Bank, led to the signing of the Indus Treaty in 1960. Water sharing under the treaty was quite simple: the three western rivers (the Jhelum, the Chenab, and the Indus itself) were allocated to Pakistan, and the three eastern rivers (the Ravi, the Beas, and the Sutlej) were allocated to India. As the headwaters of all the rivers lay in India (the upper riparian), it was necessary to allay the apprehensions of Pakistan (the lower riparian). Accordingly, India was not allowed to build storage reservoirs on the rivers allocated to Pakistan, except to a very limited extent. Restrictions were also imposed on the extension of irrigation development in India. Relatively fewer significant restrictions were imposed on Pakistan. There were also provisions regarding the exchange of data on project operation, extent of irrigated agriculture, and institutional arrangements. A permanent Indus Commission was established, consisting of a commissioner each for India and for Pakistan. The treaty also provided for periodic meetings and exchanges of visits. Provisions were included for conflict resolution: differences, if any arose, were to be resolved within the commission; if agreement could not be reached at the commission level, the dispute was to be referred to the two governments; if they too failed to reach agreement, the treaty provided an arbitration mechanism. The settlement also included the provision of international financial assistance to Pakistan for the development of irrigation works for utilizing the waters allocated to it, and India too paid a fairly large sum.

The treaty has been working reasonably well despite the difficult political relationship between the two countries, and has not been abrogated even during periods of war. Differences do arise from time to time, but these usually get resolved within the framework of the treaty. There has been no recourse to the arbitration provisions so far. At present, there is an unresolved dispute regarding what is known as the Tulbul Navigation Project (or the Wular Barrage Project). The intergovernmental talks on the subject have not so far been successful, but doubtless this dispute too, like the earlier one relating to the Salal Project, will eventually be resolved.

It could be argued that the division of the river system into two segments, one for Pakistan and one for India, was not the best solution, and that there should have been a sharing on all the rivers, or a joint integrated planning and management of the totality of the system by the two countries. However, such possibilities were probably ruled out by the state of relations between the two countries, and the treaty doubtless represents the best arrangement that was negotiable.

The Ganges Water-Sharing Treaty, 1996

In the relationship between India and Bangladesh, the dispute over the waters of the Ganges River was for two decades an important—perhaps the most important—component. Though it now stands resolved by the Treaty on the Sharing of the Waters of the Ganges of December 1996, it would be a mistake to regard it as having wholly disappeared.

Bangladesh accused India of exploiting its size and power to carry out a "unilateral diversion" of the waters of the Ganges at Farakka Barrage, with severe adverse effects on Bangladesh, its smaller and weaker neighbor. A national sense of grievance cutting across all kinds of divisions within Bangladesh grew and became a significant factor in electoral politics. In its most extreme expression, India was demonized and Farakka blamed for such afflictions as drought and flooding. On the Indian side, the government felt that Bangladesh was rigid and unreasonable on this issue; that it was claiming a disproportionate share of the waters; that it tended to exaggerate the adverse effects of reduced flows; and that by turning the dispute into a domestic political issue, it had made intergovernmental negotiations difficult. Furthermore, state governments felt that the central government had failed to pay adequate heed to their interests and had been too generous to Bangladesh at their expense. To a lesser degree than in Bangladesh, then, the conflict became an issue in state politics.

The deteriorating political relationship between the two countries rendered this problem a very difficult one, and in turn the water dispute contributed to the further deterioration of the relationship. In the late 1980s and early 1990s the problem seemed almost insoluble. With changes in the governments of both countries, circumstances in mid-1996 appeared favorable for reaching an agreement. Despite some difficulties, the Treaty on the Sharing of the Waters of the Ganges, agreed to by India and Bangladesh on 12 December 1996, was a more significant document than most people had considered possible. Behind that success lay several factors: the friendly relations between the two new governments; their desire to find a solution to this vexing problem; the wisdom and courage of the Bangladeshi prime minister Sheikh Hasina in tackling an issue fraught with considerable political risk; the high priority that the new Indian foreign minister attached to this matter; the constructive and sagacious role played by the chief minister of West Bengal; and last but not least, facilitation extended at nonofficial levels by certain institutions in the two countries. The treaty had a shaky start in the lean season of 1997 because of very low flows in the river, but the flows ranged from "good" to "very good" in the ensuing three lean seasons (1998, 1999, 2000), and the two governments have expressed satisfaction with the working of the treaty.

Currently, flows appear to be stable, and the sharing formula should be generally easy to operate. Even if a low-flow situation (as in 1997) were to occur again, as it might once in every four years or so, all that is needed is an understanding between the two governments on how to share those flows, which should be achievable, assuming that goodwill and good sense continue to prevail. However, if political relations between the two countries were to worsen for any reason, the operation of the treaty would also come under a strain. In other words, it is politics and not water that will determine the future of the treaty.

India-Nepal

Though water sharing has never been a source of serious conflict in the relations between India and Nepal, efforts to cooperate in deriving benefits from the water resources by way of hydropower, irrigation, flood management, and navigation have led to conflict. Two early projects (on the Kosi and Gandak rivers), far from promoting good relations between the two countries, caused serious strains in that relationship. The Kosi/Gandak agreements, initially signed in 1954/1959, were amended in 1966/1964 to take care of Nepalese concerns, but the sense of grievance was not wholly removed. The bitterness generated by these experiences colored all subsequent dealings between India and Nepal. That mistrust and suspicion led to the inclusion of a provision in Nepal's constitution requiring parliamentary ratification by a two-thirds majority for any treaty or agreement relating to natural resources that was likely to "affect the country in a pervasively grave manner or on a long-term basis," as opposed to a simple majority for treaties of "an ordinary nature."

The Tanakpur episode represents another example of misunderstanding. In this case, India failed to inform Nepal that it was making use of a very small piece of Nepalese territory—just 2.9 hectares—for the construction of an embankment whose purpose was to protect Nepalese territory from possible backwater effects from the Tanakpur Barrage (which itself was wholly in Indian territory and did not involve the consumptive use of water). India attempted to remedy its oversight by reaffirming Nepalese sovereignty over the territory, and agreeing to provide some free electricity and water to Nepal, but Tanakpur nonetheless came to loom large in the Nepalese consciousness, and the issue contributed to the fall of the government. Indeed, it was more a matter of domestic politics than an Indo-Nepal controversy, but it still had the potential to sour Indo-Nepal relations. The supreme court of Nepal, in response to a petition, ruled that the Memorandum of Understanding between the two prime ministers on Tanakpur was indeed in the nature of a treaty or agreement, but left it to the executive government and parliament to decide whether ratification by a simple or two-thirds majority was needed. Quite wisely, this was not put to the test; instead the Tanakpur controversy was subsumed in a larger negotiation regarding the Mahakali River.

A new chapter in Indo-Nepal relations appeared to open with the Mahakali Treaty of February 1996. The signing of the treaty was preceded not merely by negotiations between the two governments but also by extensive informal consultations covering all parties in Nepal so as to facilitate the process of parliamentary ratification. Ratification by a two-thirds majority was achieved, but additional parliamentary resolutions weakened that ratification. Though the treaty is said to be in force and implementation proceeding, in fact implementation has been stalled because of differences between the parties, there seem to be no signs of concerted efforts to sort out those differences, and matters remain unsettled. Furthermore, despite the parliamentary "ratification," it seems that the validity of the treaty is not universally accepted in Nepal. As a result, a very confused situation prevails, with a potential for reintroducing severe strains in the relationship between the two countries.

Some Observations

From these examples, it is clear that different approaches to disputes over water rights are possible. For instance, in the Indus case, there was a simple onetime bifurcation of the river system; in the India-Bangladesh case concerning the Ganges, there was an allocation of the waters of a single river, implying a continuous process of sharing (under joint monitoring); in the Cauvery case, if the final order of the tribunal is ultimately accepted, resolution will entail a similar allocation of flows; and in the India-Nepal case, there was a project-centered agreement for utilization of the Mahakali River.

There were also differences in the approaches to conflict resolution. Mediation by the World Bank played an important part in the Indus case. Facilitation by respected, nonofficial research institutions was important in the processes leading to agreement on the Ganges Treaty between India and Bangladesh. The Mahakali Treaty between India and Nepal was entirely the result of bilateral intergovernmental negotiations, though nonofficial "Track Two" efforts have since been important in the processes of resolving certain post-treaty differences. In the Cauvery case, adjudication by a constitutionally mandated mechanism is in progress.

Despite these differences, some general reflections suggest themselves. With the riparian perspective, a limitation is that it seems generally to lead to an allocation of waters among the different parties, rather than to a joint, cooperative, integrated planning and management of the river as a system. However, agreement or even adjudication is better than dispute and discord, and if the ideal is not feasible, then the second-best solution should be welcome.

Another limitation of the riparian perspective is that it tends to focus exclusively on the river and ignores everything else: groundwater aquifers, land, and the ecological system of which the river is a part. The riparian perspective cannot be dismissed as irrelevant or unimportant, but its limitations should be kept in mind.

Evolution of Water Conflicts

It is instructive to consider how conflicts in relation to water or over water-resource development projects arise, whether between countries or between constituent units within a country (assuming that there is no deliberate intention on the part of any party to cause harm to others). One or more of the following causes may be of import:

- Wrong principles (assertion in an absolute manner of the Harmon Doctrine of territorial sovereignty, prior appropriation, prescriptive rights, etc.)
- Limited vision (myopic nationalism, blind assertion of local perceptions)
- Lack of sensitivity on the part of the stronger party, excessive touchiness on the part of the weaker
- Inadequate understanding of implications and consequences; failure to study these fully
- Ignorance; lack of data/information
- Unwillingness to share information; failure to consult all concerned; failure of imagination about others' needs, rights, or concerns, and
- Politicization, i.e., the tendency for differences over water or environmental concerns to become elements in domestic electoral politics (and of political issues or frictions to impact on water issues)

How can such conflicts be avoided or minimized? From a hydrological perspective, it is best to ignore national or political boundaries; a hydrological unit such as a basin or sub-basin should be taken as a whole, and there should be integrated water-resource planning for such a unit. From a political/economic perspective, regional planning is viewed as superior to national planning. Though there is much to be said for these principles, there are also some difficulties that must considered.

The advocacy of regionalism tends to become doctrinaire. Some problems and issues are best dealt with on a national or local basis; some call for cooperation between two countries or units; and others demand a regional approach. The circumstances vary from case to case, and in each case the most appropriate route needs to be followed. Rigid bilateralism such as that adopted by the government of India may be unwise and unduly self-limiting, but a dogmatic advocacy of regionalism can unnecessarily complicate simple issues and render resolution more difficult. What is called for is pragmatism rather than doctrine.

The "basin" approach is theoretically sound, but some basins are too large and have to be broken down into sub-basins. Besides, "basin planning" and the talk of "integration" carry with them an implicit bias toward gigantism and technology-driven approaches. We need to be conscious of this danger. Further, a hydrological approach that ignores political boundaries may sound right in theory but may be impractical. An element of realism may need to be injected into a theoretically correct approach. The best need not be the enemy of the good. Integration may be ideal, but it may sometimes be necessary to settle for the second-best option of "coordination." Similarly, enlightened nationalism or bilateralism may be the first step toward eventual regionalism.

With regard to principles, neither the Harmon Doctrine (that of territorial sovereignty) nor that of prescriptive rights or prior appropriation has found general approval. What commands a fair degree of international acceptance is the language of the old Helsinki Rules on equitable apportionment for beneficial uses. The UN Convention on the Non-Navigational Uses of International Water Courses, passed by the General Assembly in 1997, but still awaiting ratification, requires the watercourse states to "utilize an international watercourse in an equitable and reasonable manner" (the idea of "apportionment" has disappeared) and to "participate in the use, development and protection of an international watercourse in an equitable and reasonable manner" (where the word *protection* suggests "sustainable development"). There is, of course, enormous scope for differences in interpretation of "equitable," but there is some merit in a general subscription to the principles of equity and reasonableness. Similarly, a general admonition to the upper riparian on the question of causing harm to the lower riparian is unexceptionable.

The point here is that if countries or other administrative units wish to avoid conflict while planning a project affecting a river basin or sub-basin, there are enough principles and guidelines to go by. Briefly stated, the upper riparian, in exercising its powers of control over waters, cannot ignore the *rights* of the lower riparian; and the lower riparian, in asserting its rights over the waters, cannot ignore the *needs* of the upper riparian. Given that kind of understanding, conflicts will either not arise at all or can be resolved without much difficulty when they do.

As regards institutional mechanisms, there are many models to choose from: bilateral or multilateral commissions; purely governmental bodies or bodies with a large nonofficial component; advisory or empowered bodies; private-sector projects; and so on. The feasible solution will reflect and serve the felt needs and the facts of geography on the one hand, as well as the state of political relations between the countries concerned. It is important that institutional mechanisms appropriate to a given case should be established very early, before differences of perception grow sharp and attitudes harden.

Regarded simply as disputes relating to water sharing, it is clear that they are not particularly difficult to resolve: a reasonable agreement can always be reached. But often, reasonable agreements are impeded by political exigencies.

A currently fashionable thesis postulates that conflicts over scarce resources, particularly water, can lead to severe political problems, and even wars. These commonly held views concerning water wars may be debatable, but there is little doubt that a complex interaction between water issues and political relations exists. It is not always a case of conflicts over water resources leading to a worsening of political relations, though that may happen on occasion; it is more often a case of a difficult political relationship rendering the water issue more intractable. This is particularly so when other issues become prominent from time to time: for instance, Nepal's grievances as a landlocked country and its concerns over trade and transit issues; or India's security concerns and its apprehensions about Nepal's relations with China; or in the Indo-Bangladesh context, the question of illegal immigrants, Chakma refugees, insurgency operations, border demarcation issues, trade balance, etc. Water issues in turn can become the most dominant factor at certain times, and can have an impact on the general political relationship.

More than anything else, one factor tends to influence Indo-Nepal and Indo-Bangladesh relations, namely, India's size. India's relations with its smaller neighbors have doubtless improved significantly in recent years, but in Nepal or in Bangladesh the old distrust of the "Big Brother" has not wholly disappeared. The twin dangers of big-country insensitivity or arrogance and small-country touchiness, diffidence, and suspicion are the Scylla and Charybdis that can wreck even a good relationship.

Narmada (Sardar Sarovar) Project

An Indian project that has caused considerable conflict and become an international cause célèbre is the Narmada (Sardar Sarovar) project in the state of Gujarat. The project had its origins in a riparian conflict but its subsequent history includes conflicts of other kinds.

The Narmada River is an "inter-state river" in terms of Indian law: Madhya Pradesh, Maharashtra, and Gujarat are the riparian states. Each state wished to make use of the river for planned projects. After prolonged interstate negotiations, reports by expert committees, and unsuccessful efforts at conflict resolution by the central government, a tribunal was established in 1969 to adjudicate the dispute. It took until 1979 for the tribunal to issue a final decision, which accepted and incorporated the determination of the available flows in the river as agreed upon by the three riparian state governments, and allocated those flows among them, with a small allocation to the nonriparian state of Rajasthan. The features and dimensions of two projects (Sardar Sarovar in Gujarat and Narmada Sagar in Madhya Pradesh) were fixed in the decision, and therefore became "mandated." The tribunal also broke new ground by making detailed recommendations on the subject of the displacement of people by the projects and their resettlement and rehabilitation. Project planning began, a World Bank loan was negotiated, and work on the ground began in the 1980s; but then the project became subject to new requirements associated with environmental concerns, leading eventually to the issue of what came to be known as "conditional clearances" for the project in 1987.

Meanwhile, in the late 1980s, the project became the target of criticism related to the displacement and resettlement of people, as well as some environmental concerns. This criticism soon burgeoned into a big movement against the project. The organization spearheading it, the Narmada Bachao Andolan (NBA) ("Save the Narmada Movement"), became internationally known, and the case came to symbolize the more generalized controversy surrounding big dams, their environmental impacts and human-rights implications, and the kind of developmental philosophy and relationship to nature that they represent.

The impasse on the project led to the establishment of an independent review (the Morse Commission) by the World Bank, and the commission's report (1992) was severely critical of the project. The government of India rejected the report and decided not to draw further funds from the World Bank loan, and the World Bank too decided to withdraw from the project. Both the implementation of the project and the movement against it continued. A Five Member Group (FMG) set up by the government of India submitted a report in

April 1994. Meanwhile, the NBA had filed a writ petition before the supreme court of India, charging the project authorities and governments with many lapses and failures and called for a comprehensive review of what in its view was a badly flawed project. At the request of the supreme court, the FMG (with one member excusing himself) submitted a further report in April 1995. During the course of the case, the MP government proposed a reduction of the height of the dam with a view to reducing the magnitude of the displacement/rehabilitation problem, but the Gujarat government opposed this.

Ultimately, in October 2000, the supreme court issued a decision, accompanied by a minority opinion written by one of the three judges. The minority opinion held that the processes of examination and approval of the project in 1987 were deficient, and called for a fresh examination and clearance. However the prevailing majority judgment was essentially a rejection of the NBA's writ petition and a direction that the project should proceed further as mandated by the tribunal (with some provisions for looking after environmental and displacement/rehabilitation aspects).

It can be said that the interstate riparian dispute has been resolved with the tribunal's award, although the government of MP could still press its demand for a new tribunal. However, in all such large dam projects, there are always a number of potential and real sources of conflict:

1. Conflict between development resulting from the project and nature (forests, flora and fauna, aquatic life, the microclimate, the quality and morphology of water, the downstream river regime, estuarine ecology, and so on) that accordingly implies an inherent conflict between present and future generations
2. Conflicting interests of the beneficiaries of the project and those adversely affected by it in one way or another
3. Conflicting interests of those who are being resettled and the host communities in the resettlement area
4. Conflicts arising from objections of the inhabitants of the areas where environmental remedial measures (catchment area treatment, compensatory afforestation, alternative habitats or sanctuaries for wildlife, etc.) will occur
5. Conflicting interest of different beneficiary groups within the command area of the project
6. Competing claims on the water (for instance, more villages and townships are to receive drinking water, necessitating adjustments in the allocation for irrigation); and finally
7. Conflicts between the people and the state, particularly in the context of the human rights of the projected affected people, particularly those of the poor, the disadvantaged, and tribal communities.

Many of these issues figured in the submissions are made before the court, but the judgment can be viewed as rejecting the petitioner's claims. The judgment has been criticized by many (including this writer) for failing to do justice to the issues brought before the court, but the judgment of the highest court remains the law of the land. From a strictly legal point of view, it can therefore be plausibly argued that with the riparian conflicts resolved by the tribunal, the other kinds of conflicts referred to above have been "resolved" as well. However, these conflicts do not disappear magically. The hardships experienced by people, and their sense of suffering and injustice, do not vanish because a judgment has been pronounced; they continue to cause pain and indignation. Popular discontent in the Narmada Valley continues to simmer. It is difficult to say what the future holds, and it is difficult to say what the right course of action would be for NBA.

Project-Affected People

Beyond the specifics of the Narmada case, a few general observations may not be out of place. There are two kinds of theoretical responses to the hardships inflicted by such projects on the affected people, who are often poor, backward, and disadvantaged, and in many cases belong to tribal communities. One response is to say that while everything must be done to mitigate their hardship, development does involve difficult choices, and that some groups may have to accept a measure of hardship ("sacrifice") for the greater interests of the nation. However, "sacrifice" seems the wrong word to use for an involuntary displacement from land and homestead, and the *imposition* of such a "sacrifice" seems morally indefensible. Equity surely demands that project-affected persons (PAPs) must have the first claim on benefits arising from the project.

This leads to the second possible response, providing for "stakeholder consultation/participation." This approach, endorsed in the Dublin/Rio principles, has gained much currency in recent years. Most policy documents and guidelines would now include this as a matter of course and it has become fashionable to refer to PAPs as "partners in development." Unfortunately, these sanctimonious formulations bear little resemblance to reality. Efforts to involve PAPs in decisionmaking and to give them their rightful share of the benefits of the projects that impose hardships on them have either been unsuccessful or have not been seriously pursued.

It should also be noted that the very concept of "stakeholder" is flawed, with great potential for misuse. First, as an analogy drawn from prospecting for oil or minerals, it carries a connotation of an individualistic claim that may, implicitly, be contested. Second, it is an ethically neutral concept that lumps together every person or party having any kind of connection or concern with a project. The term encompasses not only those likely to suffer adversely of benefit from a project, but a wide range of others, such as politicians, bureaucrats, engineers, consultants, and contractors, who are in some way involved. The interests and concerns of these diverse categories may not in all cases be benign and legitimate, and some may have a more vital "stake" than others, but the term "stakeholder" makes no distinctions: it legitimizes and levels all kinds of "stakeholding" so that primacy is not granted to those whose lands and habitats are taken away and who suffer a traumatic uprooting.

Thus, the vital distinction between project-affected people and prospective beneficiaries tends to get blurred when the bland assimilating term "stakeholders" is employed. There is a cruel irony in describing the involuntary and helpless victims of a project as "stakeholders," and this is compounded when they are put on the same footing as the potential beneficiaries of the project. In the case of the former, *existing* rights—natural and often centuries-old rights of access and livelihood—are taken away, whereas in the case of the latter, the project confers *new* rights not earlier enjoyed. The former are thus "stakelosers," whereas the latter are "stake-gainers."

Potential for resolution may depend on a truly "participatory," consultative, people-centered, holistic approach to project planning. The principle of "informed prior consent" and the "rights and risks" approach recommended by the World Commission on Dams (WCD) in its report *Dams and Development* seems the right course to follow. However, the government of India and many other governments in the developing world consider the guidelines recommended by WCD unworkable. One must hope, following further debate, consensus on the future course of action will be reached.

Reviving Old Traditions

There are also possibilities of conflict between the state and civil-society institutions and initiatives. India has historically had a wide range of community-managed systems and practices of local water conservation and management. However, first the colonial rulers and later the successor state assumed control over natural resources, and their management passed into the hands of government officials and engineers. The modern state began to build big, technology driven, centralized projects, and concomitantly the traditional, community-managed systems and practices went into decline. Now there is a move to revive some of those traditions, and to promote new community initiatives in local water harvesting and management. These efforts are often hampered by the unhelpful and sometimes hostile attitude of governments toward such initiatives and toward the NGOs inspiring or supporting them. NGOs in turn sometimes adopt confrontational attitudes.

Where river waters are concerned, the irrigation acts of the various Indian states vest ultimate control over the uses of these waters in the state governments. This "eminent domain" makes community initiatives problematic. In the state of Rajasthan, when community initiatives resulted in water reappearing in rivers and streams that had been dry for years, the state claimed the right of control over those waters. In one instance, the people making use of the waters of the Arvari (a small river in Rajasthan) have established the "Arvari Parliament" as a decisionmaking and conflict-resolution body. This "parliament" is purely an informal body without statutory backing, and any authority it has acquired by common consent in civil society can be negated if the state so desires. Still, the Arvari Parliament exemplifies a useful and innovative development that might well be replicated in other places.

It must be recognized that the present legal framework in India is indifferent if not hostile to such community initiatives. For one thing, administrative divisions do not always coincide with hydrological units or sociocultural groupings. Also, apart from the formal laws of the state there are also informal traditions, conventions, customs, practices, institutions, and so on, and locally, some of these have the virtual force of law. Bureaucracies and technocracies are not always aware of or sympathetic to these customs, traditions, and practices; and formal and informal laws are not always congruent—what is known as legal pluralism is not always accepted.

Development Versus Sustainability

Conflicts relating to water can also arise in other contexts and at other levels: between uses or between areas (e.g., agriculture and industry; irrigation/power generation and flood moderation; diversion for irrigation and maintenance of downstream flows for various purposes; rural versus urban needs; and so on). There are also conflicts in the context of access to groundwater and its exploitation, use, and marketing; and flood-control initiatives. The pollution and contamination of water sources and supplies can also be a source of serious conflict.

Above all, conflict can and does arise between "development," including (perhaps especially) water-resources development, and "sustainability," meaning, ultimately, the long-term health and survival of earth and its inhabitants. That is a topic far too large for further discussion here, but it merits this brief mention.

In this context, it may be instructive to consider an epigrammatic remark of Mahatma Gandhi: "The world has enough for everyone's need but not enough for anyone's greed." By "greed" he meant the desire for higher levels of consumption than needed, his definition of "need" being quite austere. In reply to a speculative question of what would happen if India were to attain the standards of consumption reached in the West, he is said to have remarked: "My God! We shall soon strip the earth bare, like locusts." Those were prescient words and early intimations of the environmental movement that was to emerge much later. Conflicts, the theme of this chapter, often arise from the "greed" (in Gandhi's sense) that underlies the prevailing notions of "development" and makes unsustainable demands on nature. We cannot learn to live in harmony with our neighbors until we have learned to live in harmony with nature.

Resources

Newsletters and Periodicals

"A Judgment of Grave Import," by Ramaswamy R. Iyer. Commentary on the supreme court's judgment on the Narmada (Sardar Sarovar) case, *Economic and Political Weekly,* Bombay, 4 November 2000.

"An Important Collection of Papers," by Ramaswamy R. Iyer. Review of "Common Management and Sharing of Resources," *South Asia Forum for Human Rights* in collaboration with Nepal Water Conservation Foundation, Kathmandu, *The Book Review,* New Delhi, October 2000.

"Bridge over Troubled Waters? Conflict and Cooperation over the Waters of South Asia," by Ben Crow. *Regional Cooperation in South Asia: Prospects and Problems,* edited by Sony Devabhaktuni, *Occasional Paper No. 32,* Washington, DC, The Henry L. Stimson Center, February 1997.

"Conflict Resolution: Three River Treaties," by Ramaswamy R. Iyer. *Economic and Political Weekly,* Bombay, 12 June 1999.

"Delay and Drift on the Mahakali," Ramaswamy R. Iyer, *HIMAL,* Kathmandu, June 2001.

"Fight for the Last Drop: Inter-State River Disputes in India," by Ashok Swain. *Contemporary South Asia* 7(2), July 1998, pp. 67–180.

"How Not to Do a South Asian Treaty," by Dipak Gyawali and Ajaya Dixit. *HIMAL* 14(4), Kathmandu, April 2001.

"Hydro-Politics in South Asia: A Comparative Analysis of the Mahakali and the Ganges Treaties," by Salman M. A. Salman and Kishor Uprety. *Natural Resources Journal* 39(2), spring 1999, pp. 295–343.

"Indian Federalism and Water Resources," by Ramaswamy R. Iyer. *International Journal of Water Resources Development* 10(2), Oxford, 1994.

"Inter State River Water Disputes: Some Suggestions," by Ramaswamy R. Iyer. *Mainstream,* New Delhi, 5 June 1999.

"Perspectives of the Indus Waters Treaty," by K. Warikoo. In *Peace as Process,* edited by Ranabir Samaddar and Helmut Reifield, Delhi, Manohar, 2001.

"Pluralist Politics Under Monistic Designs—Water Accords in South Asia," by D. Gyawali. In *Peace as Process,* edited by Ranabir Samaddar and Helmut Reifield, Delhi, Manohar, 2001.

"Water Conflicts in the Middle East and South Asia," by Miriam R. Lowi. In *Environment and Security: Discourses and Practices,* edited by M. Lowi and B. Shaw, London, Macmillan, 2000.

"Water: Conflicts and Accommodation," by Ramaswamy R. Iyer. Review of *Negotiating Water Rights,* edited by Bryan Randolph Bruns and Ruth S. Meinzen Dick, *Economic and Political Weekly,* 28 October 2000.

"Watersheds, State and Society," by Ramaswamy R. Iyer. Review of *Participatory Watershed Development: Challenges for the Twenty-First Century,* edited by John Farrington, Cathryn Turton, and A. J. James (Oxford University Press, New Delhi, 1999), *The Book Review* XXV(3), New Delhi, March 2001.

Reports

Department of Peace and Conflict Research. *The Environmental Trap: The Ganges River Diversion, Bangladeshi Migration and Conflicts in India,* by Ashok Swain. Uppsala, Report No. 41, 1996.

Government of India (unpublished, submitted to the Supreme Court of India). *Further Report of the FMG on Certain Issues Relating to the Sardar Sarovar Project,* 1995.

International Conference on Water and Environment. *Dublin Statement,* Dublin, 1992.

Ministry of Power, Government of India. *Report of the Expert Committee on the Environmental and Rehabilitation Aspects of the Tehri Hydro-Electric Project,* New Delhi, 1997 (unpublished).

Ministry of Water Resources, Government of India. *Report of the Five Member Group on Various Issues Relating to the Sardar Sarovar Project,* 1994.

United Nations. *UN Convention on the Non-Navigational Uses of International Water Courses,* 1997.

World Commission on Dams. *Dams and Development,* London, Earthscan Publications, November 2000.

Other Publications

Converting Water into Wealth, edited by B. G. Verghese, Ramaswamy R Iyer, Q. K Ahmad, S. K. Malla, and B. B. Pradhan. New Delhi (also published simultaneously at Dhaka and Kathmandu), Konark, 1994.

Cooperation on the Eastern Himalayan Rivers: Opportunities and Challenges, edited by K. B. Adhikary, Q. K. Ahmad, S. K. Malla, B. B. Pradhan, Rahman Khalilur, R. Rangachari, K. B. Sajjadur Rasheed, and B. G. Verghese. New Delhi, Konark Publishers, Dhaka, under the auspices of Bangladesh Unnayan Parishad, New Delhi, Centre for Policy Research, and Kathmandu, Institute for Integrated Development Studies, 2000.

Harnessing the Eastern Himalayan Rivers: Regional Cooperation in South Asia, by B. G. Verghese and Ramaswamy R. Iyer. New Delhi, Konark Publishers Pvt. Ltd., Centre for Policy Research, 1993.

Indus Waters Treaty, by N. D. Gulhati. New Delhi, Allied Publishers Private Ltd., 1973.

Politics of Himalayan River Waters: An Analysis of the River Water Issues of Nepal, India and Bangladesh, by B. C. Upreti. Jaipur, Nirala, 1993.

Sardar Sarovar: The Report of the Independent Review, by Bradford Morse and Thomas Berger. Canada, Resource Futures International, 1992.

Sharing the Ganges: The Politics and Technology of River Development, by Ben Crow with Alan Lindquist and David Wilson. New Delhi, Sage Publications, 1995.

Singh Shekhar: Large Dams: India's Experience, A Report to the World Commission on Dams, by R. Rangachari, Nirmal Sengupta, Ramaswamy R. Iyer, and Pranab Banerji, June 2000.

The Cauvery Dispute, by Ramaswamy R. Iyer, a monograph brought out by the Centre for Policy Research, New Delhi, May 1996.

The Cauvery River Dispute—Towards Conciliation, by S. Guhan. Madras, Frontline Publications, 1993.

The Dam and the Nation: Displacement and Resettlement in the Narmada Valley, edited by J. Dreze, Meera Samson, and Satyajit Singh. Delhi, Oxford University Press, 1997.

Selected Internet Sites

www.fao.org/landandwater/swlwpnr/y_sa/sa.htm (FAO South Asia link)

www.irn.org (International River Network)

Ramaswamy R. Iyer is the former secretary of water resources in the government of India. Until recently he was research professor (now honorary research professor) at the Centre for Policy Research, New Delhi. He was also a consultant for the World Bank in a review of water-sector strategy, a consultant to the World Commission on Dams for a study of India's experience with large dams, a member of India's National Commission on Integrated Water Resource Planning, and a member of the "Vision 2020 Committee" of India's Planning Commission.

Note

1. Comments by R. Rangachari and Himanshu Thakkar on the first draft of this paper are gratefully acknowledged; they bear no responsibility for the views expressed or any errors that may remain.

7.6

Understanding Religious Conflicts

Rajmohan Gandhi

Conflicts pitting people of different religions against one another have caused untold pain and bloodshed in South Asia. Western readers may view such conflicts primarily as "religious" conflicts, but such categorizations oversimplify the reality. The Hindu-Muslim conflict in India, the various sectarian conflicts in Pakistan, the ongoing conflict between India and Pakistan over the Kashmir region, various other sectarian conflicts in India (Sikh-Hindu, and especially in the Northeast, Hindu-Christian or Muslim-Christian), conflict between Muslims and Hindus in Bangladesh, and the devastating war between Hindu Tamils and Buddhist Sinhalese in Sri Lanka are religious conflicts in the sense that the opposing sides are adherents of differing religious beliefs, but they can only be fully understood when the ethnic, national, social, and political dimensions are taken into consideration.

Conflicts bearing religious labels have long been common in South Asia, a region where society is deeply religious. Given these two realities, some Western scholars have drawn the conclusion that a natural connection exists between religion and South Asian violence.

It is a link that some Indians too have stressed, including the well-known author and sometime activist Arundhati Roy. After India conducted a series of nuclear tests in 1998, Roy linked India's atomic bomb, and the violence generally witnessed in postindependence India, to the mixing of religion with India's recent politics, and also to the role that religion played in India's freedom movement. "Ram and Rahim," Roy wrote, using Hindu and Muslim names for God, were invited to take part in "human politics and India's war of independence against the British," and the result was "freedom, the carnage of Partition and the Hindu nuclear bomb."[1]

However, most South Asians, Indians included, are unwilling to conclude that religion has caused the conflicts taking place around them. Convinced of the benign character of their religious beliefs, South Asians are generally inclined to

Tibetan refugees demonstrating against
Chinese occupation of Tibet, Dharamsala, India

blame politicians or poverty for the conflicts. Sometimes an external source, a near or distant neighbor, is held responsible. This chapter examines the character of some of the prominent South Asian conflicts.

The barest of descriptions is enough to convey South Asia's religious, ethnic, and constitutional variety. Accounting for over 77 percent of South Asia's population, India has adhered for more than fifty years to a secular constitution that promises democracy, federalism, and equality. In theory at any rate, and at times in practice, a woman, an atheist, a Muslim, a Christian, a Sikh, or an untouchable can rise to a high state office in India. So of course can one of India's Hindus, who constitute about 83 percent of the population of more than 1 billion. The remainder includes Muslims, at around 12 percent, and Christians and Sikhs, between 2 and 3 percent each. The former untouchables are about 15 percent. Most of these are counted as Hindus, but sections have embraced Buddhism or Christianity. India's "tribal" or "indigenous" groups, scattered across the land and amounting to about 7 percent of the total, are also generally seen as Hindus, while some of them, especially in the Northeast of India, are Christians.

Nepal, with a population of roughly 24 million, is the world's sole Hindu kingdom. Buddhists form a significant minority in this Himalayan land where an elected parliament has shared power with the monarchy.

Pakistan, with a population of around 138 million, 97 percent of whom are Muslim, has oscillated between democratic and military rule since its creation in 1947. It is an Islamic state where, however, the judiciary, the print media, women's groups, and other civil-society organizations have remained active.

While reserving a special place in its constitution for Islam, Bangladesh accords equal rights to the country's Muslim and non-Muslim citizens. It has a population of 130 million, of whom about 12 percent are Hindu, and a much smaller percentage Buddhist or Christian.

In the island nation of Sri Lanka, with a population of about 19 million, a large majority belong to the Buddhist faith and speak the Sinhalese language, though there are also many Sinhalese-speaking Christians. Sri Lanka's Tamil speakers, who are mostly Hindus but include some Muslims or Christians, probably comprise about 20 percent of the population. Buddhism receives specific mention in the Sri Lankan constitution.

Two small countries, the mountain kingdom of Bhutan (a Buddhist land) and the ocean republic of the Maldive Islands (whose inhabitants are predominantly Muslim), make up the rest of South Asia.

This attempt at an overview of the region's conflicts is not, of course, comprehensive. It does not endeavor to examine religious conflict in Nepal, Bhutan, or the Maldives, nor does it address two other vital issues, caste and gender. It may, nonetheless, help the reader to better understand the relationship between religion and conflict in South Asia.

India's Hindu-Muslim Conflict

The 1947 partition and independence of the Indian subcontinent, which had been ruled by the British from the 1760s, took place in a context of Hindu-Muslim mistrust. Living all across the Indian subcontinent but forming a majority only in its northwestern and eastern portions, Muslims were receptive to the argument that their future would be insecure in a free India ruled by its Hindu majority. The Muslim League, a political party then representing the bulk of the subcontinent's Muslims, successfully campaigned for an independent Muslim homeland, Pakistan, comprising the (separated) Muslim-majority areas. Around half a million people were killed in riots that accompanied the 1947 Partition, most of them in the northern Punjab province that was divided into its Pakistani and Indian halves. Muslims and non-Muslims (Sikhs and Hindus) were killed in equal numbers. In addition, between August and December 1947, about 5 million Hindus and Sikhs left Pakistan for India, and around 6 million Muslims migrated to Pakistan from Hindu-majority areas.

The trauma of the 1947 massacres and migrations, often recalled in films, fiction, and political discourse, continues to affect today's South Asia. The recollection is usually selective, with "the other" held more responsible. Frequently, the stories of 1947 are placed in a long "historical" context, starting from the eighth century, of Hindu-Muslim discord, of desecration of Hindu temples by invading or ruling Muslims, or of Hindu notions that Muslims were unclean and untouchable.

The Muslim League's call for partition, first articulated in March 1940 and pursued with tenacity by its president, Muhammad Ali Jinnah, was opposed by some Muslims, by most Hindus and Sikhs, and especially by Mohandas Karamchand Gandhi (1869–1948) and the organization nurtured by

Gandhi, the Indian National Congress. However, the league's view that the subcontinent's Muslims were "a separate nation" was shared by some Hindu leaders, including Lala Lajpat Rai of the Punjab and Vinayak Damodar Savarkar of Maharashtra. Three years before the league's call for India's division, Savarkar, president of the Hindu Mahasabha ("Great Assembly"), had declared that Hindus and Muslims were two nations.

An influential ideologue of Hindu nationalism, Savarkar defined a good Indian as one who saw India as both his homeland and his holy land. This emotional definition joined religion to nationalism and made Hinduism synonymous with India. Also, it placed Buddhists, Sikhs, and Jains, along with Hindus, in the category of faithful Indians, for their religions had been founded in India, while casting doubt on the loyalty of Muslims and Christians, whose holy sites were located outside India's geographical boundaries.

The Muslim League, the Hindu Mahasabha, and the para-political Hindu organization founded in 1925, the Rashtriya Swayamsevak Sangh ("National Volunteer Association" or the RSS), succeeded, between them, in polarizing India around rival notions of Muslim and Hindu nationalism and in frustrating Gandhi's bid for independence for a united Hindu-Muslim India. Five months after India's independence and partition, Gandhi was assassinated by Hindus loyal to Savarkar, who had links to the RSS and thought that Gandhi was too friendly to Muslims.

The assassination discredited Hindu nationalism. For fifty years after independence, India was ruled by individuals and parties subscribing to the vision of a pluralist and secular India bequeathed by Gandhi and by his political heir, Jawaharlal Nehru, India's prime minister from 1947 to 1964. But since the late 1990s, India has been governed by a coalition headed by the Bharatiya Janata Party ("Indian People's Party" or BJP), many of whose leaders were members of the RSS. Though it swears by the secular Indian constitution, the BJP is sympathetic to Hindu nationalism and to the notion that while Hindus are ipso facto loyal to their country, India's Muslims and Christians have to prove their patriotism.

It was a nationwide campaign focusing on a sixteenth-century mosque allegedly built on a sacred Hindu site in Ayodhya in the state of Uttar Pradesh (UP) that brought the BJP to power. The campaign, mounted in the 1980s and early 1990s, revived Hindu memories of ancient Muslim wrongs. It was asserted that Hindu and Indian honor required substituting a Hindu temple for the mosque in Ayodhya, and the BJP for the Congress Party in New Delhi.

In December 1991 a frenzied Hindu mob razed the Ayodhya mosque to the ground even as the BJP's national and Uttar Pradesh leadership watched the exercise from ringside seats, and police units of the BJP-run UP government looked away. Though warned in advance of what was afoot, and empowered to dismiss the state government or send its own forces to Ayodhya, the congress-controlled federal government chose not to intervene in the crisis. It did not want to risk losing the Hindu vote.

Riots in the wake of the demolition took more than a thousand lives in different parts of India. Most victims were Muslims angrily protesting the demolition, but a series of revenge bombings in Mumbai in March 1992 claimed over two hundred lives, mostly Hindu.

Unwilling to acknowledge what was happening, the federal government tried at first to dismiss the Mumbai blasts as an *economic* challenge to the liberalization that the government had just launched, but no one was deceived. Polarization between the Hindu and Muslim communities was occurring, accompanied by an increase in violence and the radicalization of Muslim and Hindu youth. All these developments seemed to benefit the BJP. Gaining steadily in polls, the party secured national power in 1998, and again in fresh elections called in 1999, but then only at the head of a coalition with a number of small or regional parties, not all of whom were enthusiastic about Hindu nationalism.

The result is a more moderate program that omits earlier references to mosques built on sites sacred to Hindus and other items that might make Muslims insecure. On occasion the BJP's leaders have offered apologies for the demolition, but the proximity of elections, whether provincial or national, frequently entices some in the party to revive the temple-in-place-of-the-mosque campaign.

And while Prime Minister Atal Behari Vajpayee and the BJP's spokespersons maintain that building a temple on the flattened site of the Ayodhya mosque is not on the party's agenda, its "nonpolitical" allies such as the Vishwa Hindu Parishad ("World Hindu Council") periodically announce progress in readying stones and carvings for the proposed grand temple. Each announcement of this kind is capable of sparking off a disturbance somewhere in India, for in most parts of the country, Hindus and Muslims live in close proximity to one another, with the resiliency of the peace between communities varying considerably from place to place.

Why Hindu-Muslim riots and other violent incidents occur in some places and not elsewhere has been examined by several observers. Studies confirm that an alert police, and neighborhood Hindu-Muslim and citizen-police committees can prevent or reduce conflict, while violence is exacerbated by unemployment, scarcity of space, a biased or apathetic police, and collapsing municipal services, e.g., the absence of public toilets.

Many of India's Hindus entertain an image of Hinduism as a peace-fostering religion and of Hindus as a people abhorring violence, and an opposite image of Islam and of Muslims. Though also a key Buddhist and Jain expression, *ahimsa* (noninjury or nonviolence) is undoubtedly given a high place in Hindu texts. But Hindu epics, accounts of past Hindu dynasties, and studies of modern Hindu societies reveal a good deal of violence and oppression as well. The killings in the summer of 2001 of members of Nepal's royal family, a fair proportion of the grim killings that continue in Sri Lanka, some of the killings in India's northeast, and resistance to the demand for equal rights by India's untouchables, constitute examples of Hindu violence.

Pakistan's Regional and Sectarian Conflicts

A Pakistan ("Land of the Pure") where the British no longer ruled, Hindus no longer dominated, and good Muslims were to manage a mostly Muslim nation has not turned out to be conflict-free. The notion that a common religion would ensure mutual accommodation in Pakistan received a rude jolt soon after the new nation was born. East Pakistan, containing a majority of the country's population, was alienated from the west when a demand for equal status for its language, Bengali, with Pakistan's official language, Urdu, was rejected. The agitation that followed, the repression with which the agitation was countered, and the liberation struggle triggered by the repression led finally, in 1971–1972, to the emergence of Bangladesh as an independent nation.

But Pakistan seemed reluctant to draw any lessons from the separation of Bangladesh, and its history books tended to dismiss the event as the work of Indian agents and the Indian military. A recent Pakistani study notes that: "As an independent nation, Pakistan largely ignored the social diversity of its people and the economic disparities of its regions. It constructed a 'national ideology' based on a mechanical notion of unity and simplistic ideas of cultural homogeneity. This neglect of social diversity and disregard of ethnic and regional interests has exacted a heavy cost from Pakistan."[2]

Pakistanis are distributed by language or ethnicity into Punjabis, Seraikis, Sindhis, Pathans, Baluchis, and Urdu-speaking Mohajirs (migrants from India), to mention only some principal categories; by class into landowners, peasants, entrepreneurs, artisans, workers, government employees, officers, and soldiers; and by sect into Sunni Muslims of diverse kinds and Shia Muslims, also of different subsects. Conflicts occur from time to time across these ethnic, class, and sectarian lines.

The army has fought Sindhis aggrieved by grants of land to Punjabi farmers in Sindh province and by Mohajir dominance in the cities of their province. Armed Mohajirs have clashed in cities such as Karachi and Hyderabad with soldiers trying to curb them, or with Sindhis resentful of the Mohajir presence, or with Pathans or Punjabis competing with Mohajirs for influence in Karachi. Baluchi tribesmen have exchanged fire with army units.

Sectarian conflict has matched ethnic ones. Clashes between Shias and Sunnis and between Sunni groups have occurred in different parts of the Punjab and in Karachi, resulting in loss of life. Neighbors have rarely been involved, however, and many of the killings have been caused by drive-by shooting or shelling. Studies suggest that bazaar merchants finance the violent activity, which is conducted by *madrassa* (religious school) students or unemployed youth, but involvement by elements outside Pakistan is also alleged. Noteworthy, too, are instances of discrimination against Pakistan's Hindus, a small minority living mostly in Sindh, and of attacks on the country's Christians, most of whom are poor.

It is not easy to assess the influence of the radical fundamentalism in Pakistan of neighboring Afghanistan's deposed Taliban leadership. *Madrassas* functioning across Pakistan are said to have spread the Taliban's ideas, which are also believed to have found a hearing in sections of a hitherto professional and modern army. However, sizeable segments in Pakistan prize personal freedom and opportunities.

Kashmir and the India-Pakistan Wars

India and Pakistan have engaged in four wars, in 1947–1948, 1965, 1971, and 1999. Except for the 1971 war, all were fought over Kashmir, the large, beautiful, and mountainous "head" of the subcontinent. Kashmir, or the state of Jammu and Kashmir, to give the full name, was a theater for the 1971 war too, which was linked to the demand for a separate Bangladesh. In May 1998, concern was expressed worldwide when nuclear tests were successfully conducted by India and a few days later by Pakistan.

Both India and Pakistan had violated some of their principles when, in 1947–1948, the subcontinent's princes and maharajas, ruling more than five hundred principalities, faced the choice of joining India or Pakistan or attempting independence. Though asking for a Pakistan comprising Muslim-majority areas, Jinnah and the Muslim League were willing to take in Hindu rulers such as Maharaja Hari Singh, who ruled over Muslim-majority Jammu and Kashmir, as well as Hindu-majority principalities ruled by Muslims, such as Hyderabad in southern India and Junagadh in western India.

Holding that a principality's people, whether Hindus or Muslims, were the final arbiters, India declared that a ruler's decision could be challenged. On this basis, India supported popular movements for joining India in Junagadh, whose ruler had acceded to Pakistan, and in Hyderabad, where the ruler desired independence. Following Indian intervention, Junagadh and Hyderabad became parts of India.

Hari Singh too had hoped for independence for Kashmir but he acceded to India after Pakistan-aided tribal fighters invaded his land in October 1947. Calling the accession provisional, the Indian government said that eventually the people of Jammu and Kashmir would have the opportunity to express their own wishes. Meanwhile India and Pakistan were at war on Kashmir's soil. At the end of 1948, when a UN-backed cease-fire halted the war, India was in possession of slightly less than two-thirds of the territory of Jammu and Kashmir, and Pakistan held the remaining portion. Apart from small alterations effected by subsequent wars, this division, demarcated by a Line of Control (LOC), has survived to the present day.

Many in Jammu and Kashmir, and in Pakistan, have challenged Kashmir's accession to India and criticized India for not allowing the territory's people to decide their fate. Poor governance and rigged elections have contributed over the years to the anti-Indian sentiment in Kashmir. Pakistan provides moral, political, diplomatic, and, according to India, military support to insurgent groups in Kashmir battling against the Indian state. India charges that among the insurgents are non-Kashmiris including *mujahedeen* from Afghanistan, Sudan, and the Middle East.

India devotes large resources and security forces to maintaining its position in Jammu and Kashmir, but ceding parts of Kashmir is not an option that the Indian parliament and public are likely to accept. Moreover, such a choice could trigger separatism elsewhere in India and also invite reprisals directed at vulnerable Muslims across India. Concluding that agreement on altering borders is not likely at this stage, although some have proposed greater autonomy for both parts of Jammu and Kashmir, and a softening of the LOC between the two.

Jammu and Kashmir is a heterogeneous land with diverse languages and ethnicities. The portion that Pakistan administers is of at least three distinct types, inhabited by Sunni and Shia Muslims speaking three or four languages. Likewise, Indian-administered Kashmir has at least three distinct regions, Jammu (where 60 percent are Hindus), Ladakh (a large tract with Buddhist and Shia Muslim halves), and the Vale of Kashmir (overwhelmingly Sunni Muslim), which is small, bewitching, and densely populated. The migration from the Vale of Kashmir of most members of a Hindu minority with ancient links to the land, the Pandits, has tended to harden Indian attitudes. No solution can work that ignores such diversity and facts.

Indians counter the Pakistani argument that as a Muslim-majority area Kashmir is entitled to leave India by stressing the secular character of the Indian nation and the presence in India of as many Muslims as Pakistan contains. If the cause is greater autonomy or self-determination for the Kashmiri people, a political argument is more likely to advance it than a religious one.

Disappointment was caused by the failure to move toward a resolution of the Kashmir question at the Indo-Pak summit held in July 2001 in the shade of the Taj Mahal in Agra. It had been thought that as a member of the BJP, Prime Minister Vajpayee might have been in a position to offer concessions that previous prime ministers could not risk, and similarly that as a military chief President Pervez Musharraf might be capable of taking bold steps.

Such hopes for action from the summit's star characters were not realized. The leaders could not free themselves wholly from their political and bureaucratic establishments, or from the perceived pulls of their domestic constituencies. The India-Pakistan relationship is characterized by wounds that require healing, and images that call for rectification, even if it also encompasses cultural ties, an immense trade potential, and the imperative of avoiding a nuclear clash.

Sikh Militancy in the Punjab and Elsewhere

Concentrated in India's Punjab state but also living elsewhere in India, and in significant numbers in North America and the UK, the Sikhs, who follow the Sikh religion (founded in the fifteenth century by Guru Nanak) and speak the Punjabi language, retain memories of the first four decades of the nineteenth century when they ruled much of northwestern India from Lahore, now one of Pakistan's premier cities. The British subdued this fighting community in the 1840s but only after two tough wars.

The 1947 Partition brought almost all the Sikhs of Pakistan's West Punjab into India's East Punjab, which was the Sikh base, yet Hindus were more numerous in East Punjab until 1966, when a smaller Punjabi-speaking state with a Sikh majority was formed. However, Sikh restiveness continued, partly because the leading Sikh party, the Akali Dal, which saw religion and politics as interconnected, failed to win political power. Enlisting most Hindus, who constituted more than 40 percent of the state's population, and some Sikhs, the Congress Party retained power in a series of elections.

A declining share in the Indian army and fears that the Punjab's waters would be diverted to other states added to the restiveness, but it was the rise of a charismatic young leader, Jarnail Singh Bhindranwale, that made Sikh militancy a force to reckon with from the late 1970s to the middle of the 1990s. Ironically, Bhindranwale's emergence was to begin with the work of congress, which wanted to counter the Akalis with a Sikh leader possessing religious appeal. Playing on fears that Sikhs would lose their identity in a modernizing India—that young Sikh men would forsake Sikh tradition and start cutting their hair—Bhindranwale recruited numerous activists from the ranks of devout Sikhs and the unemployed.

In the end he and his followers could only be defeated by an assault by the Indian army on Sikhism's holiest shrine, the Golden Temple of Amritsar, where Bhindranwale and thousands of his supporters had taken sanctuary and stored arms, and from where assassinations in different parts of Punjab were said to be directed. Several hundred militants including Bhindranwale, and about a hundred Indian soldiers, were killed in the action, which took place in June 1984. In some parts of the country, Sikh soldiers of the Indian army reacted to the attack on the shrine by deserting their regiments, and in a later reaction in October 1984, Indira Gandhi, the prime minister who had sanctioned the Golden Temple operation, was killed by Sikh members of her bodyguard.

The prime minister's assassination was followed by three days of arson, looting, and murder in New Delhi, where up to three thousand Sikhs were killed. In one form or another, insurgency in Punjab continued for some years, but Punjab's Sikh peasants seemed to turn against the militants by the early 1990s. In elections held in 1997, the Akalis won comfortably and their leader, Parkash Singh Badal, became chief minister; but while the state has remained largely free of violence, any assumption that Sikh resentment has disappeared forever must be regarded as premature.

The Northeast

The hills and jungles where India and Bangladesh approach China and Burma also comprise the terrain where a large number of ethnicities meet—not necessarily peacefully. The region's conflicts can be linked to enmities handed down from the past; to clashes over land; to migration across tribal or national borders; to a conviction of separateness and of independent histories; to distance from, ignorance in, and neglect by New Delhi; and to corruption in the local governments of Arunachal Pradesh, Assam, Manipur, Meghalaya, Mizoram, Nagaland, and Tripura, the so-called seven sisters of the Northeast.

Some conflicts in the Northeast have grown into insurgencies and independence movements, to which Indian security forces have reacted. Some insurgencies have lasted for decades while others have given a place to power sharing. Parties to a conflict in the Northeast may subscribe to Hindu, Christian, Muslim, or local traditional beliefs, but religion as such is not necessarily a crucial factor in the Northeast, though it is used now and again to arouse emotions. Elsewhere in India, the Northeast's clashes are at times presented in Hindu-Muslim, Hindu-Christian, or Muslim-Christian terms, and sometimes it is charged that Western missionaries fuel separatism in the Northeast (although, in fact, hardly any Western missionaries are left in the region).

Some idea of the Northeast's complexity may be obtained from the course of the protracted peace talks between New Delhi and the Naga Socialist Council of Nagaland (NSCN). When it was announced in the summer of 2001 that a cease-fire observed for about two years by Indian and NSCN forces in the state of Nagaland would be extended to Naga-inhabited areas in neighboring states including Manipur and Assam, life in Manipur (and in parts of Assam) was totally disrupted by opponents of the decision. Manipur's Meitei majority felt that the cease-fire's extension would give legitimacy to Naga claims to the hilly region of Manipur state. Yielding to the sharp protests, the government of India withdrew the extension.

Like the Nagas, the Meiteis are a Mongol group. Unlike the Nagas, many of whom became Christian in the last hundred years or so, the Meiteis have been Hindus from the nineteenth century; and while the Nagas tend to live in the hills, including in the hilly parts of Manipur state, the Meiteis inhabit the Manipur Valley. Some Indians outside the Northeast not only saw this latest manifestation of the Northeast's tribulations in Hindu-Christian terms, but, assuming that "Hindu" was synonymous with loyal and "Christian" with suspect, they also wondered why a BJP government had seemed ready to prefer Christians to Hindus.

What they failed to consider was the fact that the "Hindu" Meiteis, like the "Christian" Nagas, also had their armed pro-independence outfits, or that "Christian" Kukis were fighting "Christian" Nagas in the Manipur hills, or that the Northeast's challenge was primarily one of accommodation among a whole variety of ethnic, aggrieved, and rebellious "others," any two of whom were capable of fighting each other. And they overlooked the fact that the United Liberation Front of Assam (ULFA), involved for well over a decade in a separatist insurgency in the largest of the Northeast's "seven sisters," Assam, is comprised primarily of Hindus.

Bangladesh

Bangladeshis migrating into India's West Bengal state and into the Indian Northeast are a factor in India's political controversies, but Bangladesh, home to cyclones, floods, and a flourishing NGO movement, also has its own internal conflicts. Religion is involved in some of these. The country's Hindu percentage has been slowly declining. While Muslims too have moved from Bangladesh into India, the proportion of Hindus doing so has been higher. The rhetoric of Islamization frightens Bangladeshi Hindus, even when it emanates only from nongovernmental quarters.

In the hill tracts of eastern Bangladesh, the Buddhism of many of the tribal groups, whose relationship with the government of Bangladesh is uneasy and at times hostile, gives the tribal unrest a religious color. Some alienated tribal groups have moved to camps in India's Northeast. As in these areas of India, questions of control over land and political accommodation between Bangladesh's tribal entities and its nontribal entities are probably more significant than religion.

More central in Bangladesh, and more bitter, is the conflict between rival mainstream claimants to national power. Unresolved suspicions about involvement in past tragedies seem to fuel the bitterness. Standing on one side is the Awami League led by Sheikh Hasina Wajed, prime minister from 1996 to 2001 and daughter of the man seen as the nation's founder and principal liberator, Sheikh Mujib. The other side features the Bangladesh National Party (BNP) led by Begum Khaleda Zia, prime minister from 1991 to 1996 and widow of general Zia-ur-Rahman, who ruled Bangladesh from 1975 to 1981. Both Mujib and Zia were assassinated.

Not confined to the two political parties and their respective allies, Bangladesh's internal rivalry—or enmity, to use a more accurate word—seems to be reflected in civil society as well—in the bureaucracy, in the professions, and in the media. Religion is perhaps an element in the division. While the BNP also counts Hindus among its supporters, the Awami League is generally seen as being more willing than the BNP to acknowledge the country's religious pluralism and to accord the Hindus, 12 percent or so of the population, some social and political space. Yet the need for an enemy appears to be the basic drive, and the chief political opponent fits the bill.

Sri Lanka

Considering the scale, duration, and global awareness of the tragic Sri Lankan conflict between the forces of the government and the Liberation Tigers of Tamil Eelam (LTTE), which is also portrayed as a clash between the island's Sinhalese-speaking majority and the minority who speak Tamil, some might think that the conflict is merely the extension of an ancient story. However, scholars stress the relatively modern character of the Sinhala-Tamil divide and suggest that the picture of Sri Lanka as a Buddhist nation of Sinhalese-speaking ethnic Aryans containing a minority of Tamil-speaking Dravidians is a misleading one.

Whatever the differences in language, racially the island is not so divided. Common blood probably flows in the veins of Sinhalese- and Tamil-speakers. Vijaya, the supposed father of the Sinhalese/Aryan race, may indeed have migrated from northern or eastern India, but the island of Sri Lanka was mostly peopled by migrants from southern India, many of whom became Buddhist and started speaking Sinhalese. As for the religious divide, Sri Lanka's Buddhists continue to propitiate several Hindu gods, though seeing them as subservient to the Buddha, while Hindus accept the Buddha as an incarnation of one of their chief Gods, Vishnu.

During the colonial period, when the Portuguese, the Dutch, and the British controlled Sri Lanka, the "other" for most Sri Lankans was the white outsider.

In fact it has been claimed that "throughout the colonial period, there was no (internal) ethnic conflict, with the sole exception of the 1915 Sinhalese-Muslim clashes, in which, strange as it may seem today, the Tamil leadership took the side of the Sinhalese."[3]

But we know that Tamils and Sinhalese have been portrayed for about fifty years as the ethnic "other" of each, and the portrayal has been accompanied by much bloodshed. Yet surprise assaults and suicide attacks have been punctuated by talks for a peace settlement, with facilitation on occasion by representatives of other lands.

We know too that a watershed moment was the "Sinhala only" language policy championed in the mid-1950s, which engendered insecurity in Tamils. The notion of a Sinhalese-speaking "nation" was countered by a struggle on behalf of a Tamil "nation." Most Sinhalese are Buddhists, and most Tamils are Hindus, but "a religious conflict" is an unconvincing description of what is occurring in Sri Lanka. At bottom the struggle is for power sharing, with, of course, linguistic, ethnic, and religious overtones.

The Sri Lankan struggle shows that "nationalism" inflames animosities existing across the religious or linguistic divide. It raises crucial questions, for one side, of the folly of refusing to recognize a competing nationalism and of delaying a compromise with it; while for the other side, it raises equally crucial questions of the means of struggle, of the use of fear and terror, of the freedom granted to or withheld from participants in the struggle. Meanwhile Tamils and Sinhalese alike remain locked in a painful and risky conflict.

Conclusion

From the foregoing overview, a number of conclusions can be drawn. For one thing, the conflicts of South Asia are struggles among the region's diverse groups for a share of power, and are linked to the success or failure of efforts at dialogue and mutual accommodation. Second, the differences are of linguistic, religious, ethnic, and national character, and conflicts seem possible across any one of these divides. Third, when nationalism is introduced into the equation, the result can be an intensification of what is fundamentally a linguistic, ethnic, or religious dispute. Therefore, Muslim nationalism, Hindu nationalism, Bangladeshi nationalism, Kashmiri nationalism, Sikh nationalism, Naga nationalism, Sinhala nationalism, and Tamil nationalism (the list is not exhaustive) are, or can be, powerful and at times explosive impulses. Fourth, on its own religion is not necessarily a cause for conflict. And finally, if they remain unhealed, the wounds of history can exacerbate current conflicts, especially when history is manipulated by politicians seeking power for themselves.

Though this chapter has focused on conflicts and not on possible solutions, some ideas for resolving these conflicts suggest themselves. Generous offers may be effective if made in time. Acting on their own, statesmen or stateswomen seem to have limited scope for resolving a conflict. They need support from national establishments, the media, and citizens. For healing wounds and correcting stereotypes of the "other," political leaders may require the support of the creative thinker, doer, or artist—someone who can offer a gesture or make a proposal that penetrates deeper than mere words, something that may move the "other" by its unexpectedness or genuineness.

Rajmohan Gandhi is a writer, a former member of the Indian Parliament, an occasional visiting professor, and an activist for human rights and conflict resolution. He is also the co-chair of the Centre for Dialogue and Reconciliation in India, and a member of the international council of Initiatives of Change (formerly, Moral Re-Armament). His last book, published in 1999, was Revenge and Reconciliation: Understanding South Asian History.

Notes

1. *Frontline,* Chennai, 14 August 1998.

2. From the foreword by Mohammed Qadeer in *Ethnicity and Politics in Pakistan,* by Feroz Ahmed, Oxford: Karachi, 1998.

3. V. Suryanarayan, in *Religion, Politics and Society in South and Southeast Asia,* edited by N. N. Vohra and J. N. Dixit. New Delhi: Shipra Publications, 1999.

7.7

Bangladesh: Indigenous Struggle in the Chittagong Hill Tracts

Jenneke Arens and Kirti Nishan Chakma[1]

The Chittagong Hill Tracts (CHT) in the southeast differs from the rest of Bangladesh, both in physical characteristics and population. The twelve ethnic groups that originally comprised 98 percent of the population in the hills each have their own distinct culture, religion, and language. The British, who annexed the area in 1860, gave the area a special status, acknowledging the distinct identity of the indigenous population. After independence from British rule in 1947, the successive governments of East Pakistan and later Bangladesh failed to acknowledge the deteriorating situation and the legitimate demands of the indigenous peoples for recognition of their separate identity. Instead, during Pakistani rule the Kaptai Dam was constructed, displacing one-fifth of the indigenous population, and the special status of the area was abolished. After the independence of Bangladesh in 1971, the indigenous peoples in the CHT were refused constitutional recognition of their separate identity and from 1976 onward the Bangladesh government's reaction was militarization and flooding the area with landless Bengalis from the plains. These policies resulted in an escalation of the conflict and a further alienation between the Bengali majority in the plains and the indigenous people who took up arms in defense. Negotiations between indigenous leaders and successive governments of Bangladesh repeatedly failed, but on 2 December 1997 a peace accord was signed. Slow implementation and nonacceptance of the accord by a section of the indigenous population, however, remain factors of instability in the area. Moreover, the Bangladesh Nationalist Party (BNP), which has headed the government since October 2001, has earlier agitated strongly against the peace accord, and since the present government came to power it has already taken several measures in violation of the accord.

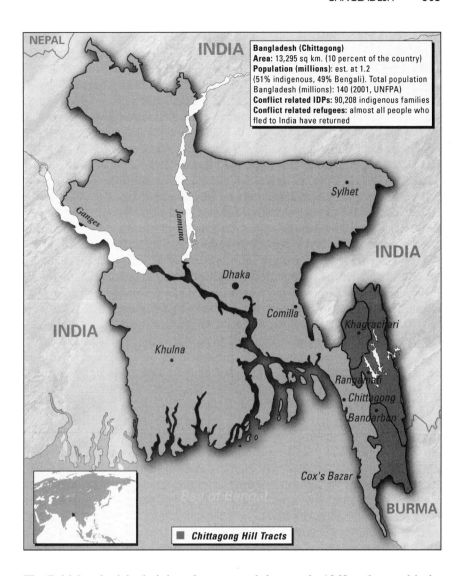

Bangladesh (Chittagong)
Area: 13,295 sq km. (10 percent of the country)
Population (millions): est. at 1.2
(51% indigenous, 49% Bengali). Total population
Bangladesh (millions): 140 (2001, UNFPA)
Conflict related IDPs: 90,208 indigenous families
Conflict related refugees: almost all people who
fled to India have returned

■ *Chittagong Hill Tracts*

The British colonial administration annexed the area in 1860 and named it the
Chittagong Hill Tracts. In 1900 the British passed the so-called 1900 Regulation,
which gave the area special status, restricting settlement of non-"tribals" in the
hills and separating the administration. Although the British had their own interests in mind, the indigenous people still regard this 1900 Regulation as a
recognition and protection of their land rights, separate identity, and culture.

When British India gained independence in 1947, the country was split
between Hindu-dominated India and Muslim-dominated Pakistan. The hill
people hoisted the Indian flag in the CHT on 15 August, as they had been assured repeatedly that the CHT, with a 93 percent non-Muslim population,
would be included in India. Only on 17 August, two days after independence,

was it announced that the Chittagong Hill Tracts had been included in East Pakistan, together with East Bengal. The Pakistani government amended the 1900 Regulation several times, slowly eroding the special status of the CHT. In 1960 the construction of a hydroelectric dam at Kaptai was completed, flooding 40 percent of the land available for plough cultivation in the CHT and displacing some hundred thousand people. In 1964 the special status of the CHT was completely abolished, although some special treatment still continued.

In the early 1950s the Pakistani government, seated in West Pakistan, declared Urdu the national language, ignoring the Bengali-speaking majority population in East Pakistan. Moreover, although most of the foreign exchange was earned in East Pakistan, this part remained largely deprived of economic development. The growing dissatisfaction of the Bengali population that was being denied its own identity, culture, and development finally culminated in a bloody war of liberation, in which some 3 million Bengalis were killed. Bangladesh won independence from Pakistan in 1971 with the help of the Indian army. Indigenous people in the CHT had joined the liberation forces and played an active role in the liberation of Bangladesh. However, Chakma Raja (King) Tridiv Roy—a member of the national parliament—had sided with Pakistan, as he thought that this would better serve his people's interests. This led to a general suspicion of Bengalis toward the indigenous people in the CHT who were, unjustly, regarded as traitors. Both the flag-hoisting incident in 1947 and the collaboration of the Chakma Raja with Pakistan are still sensitive issues and taken by Bengalis as an indication of disloyalty of the indigenous hill peoples to the Bangladesh state.

In 1972 a delegation of the indigenous people, led by the late Chakma MP Manobendra Narayan Larma, requested autonomy for the CHT, retention of the 1900 Regulation, and a ban on the influx of Bengalis. However, Prime Minister Sheikh Mujibur Rahman, who himself had led the Bengali people in the struggle for their own Bengali identity and culture, now failed to recognize the legitimacy of a similar demand from the indigenous peoples. He told them to forget their ethnic identities and to be "Bengalis." He also threatened to flood

---

The Chittagong Hill Tracts (CHT) is very different from the fertile alluvial plains of Bangladesh, both in physical characteristics and its population. The hilly area is rich in forest and mineral resources, such as oil, gas, copper, and uranium. Until the mid-1970s the CHT was mainly inhabited by twelve ethnic groups, numbering about 600,000 people, each with its own distinct culture, religion, and language. The Chakma, by far the largest group, Marma, and Taunchengya are Buddhist; the Tripura and Riang/Brong are Hindu; the Bawm, Pankhua, and Lushai are Christian; and the Chak, Mru, Khumi, and Khyang mostly practice their own traditional religions. They all practice mixed farming of plough cultivation in the fertile valleys and swidden agriculture on the hill slopes, known as *jhum* cultivation.

the area with Bengalis and military troops if the hill people insisted on sticking to their demands. Following Mujib's denial, the indigenous people formed the Parbatya Chottogram Jana Samhati Samiti (PCJSS, or the Chittagong Hill Tracts People's United Party) in 1972, and a year later its armed wing, the Shanti Bahini (Peace Brigade). The PCJSS introduced the term "Jumma" as a collective name for the twelve different ethnic groups—referring to the traditional *jhum* ("swidden") cultivation practiced in the hills. Misinterpreting the legitimate demands of the PCJSS for recognition of their identity and protection of their rights, the Bangladesh government accused the PCJSS of being secessionist. The militarization of the CHT and large-scale settlement of Bengalis that Mujib had threatened, however, did not take place until after Mujib and most of his family had been killed in a coup d'etat in 1975.

Conflict Dynamics
After General Ziaur Rahman ("Zia") came to power through a military coup in 1975, the conflict between the indigenous people and the Bengali government turned from a democratic struggle into a low-intensity armed conflict. Zia ordered full militarization of the CHT and simultaneously development of the "backward tribal" area. Next to road construction and telecommunication, settlement programs of the indigenous population in model villages (similar to the "strategic hamlets" erected during the war in Vietnam) were carried out. The fact that the CHT Development Board, set up by Zia, was headed by the military commander in charge of the CHT illustrates that these development programs were an instrument of counterinsurgency. From 1976 the CHT became an area under military occupation and a training ground for counterinsurgency. Many army officers received training in the United States and the United Kingdom. The security forces controlled the administration, as well as all development programs.

The Indian government, worried about the military takeover in Bangladesh in 1975 (having lost its earlier influence over the Bangladesh government and fearing that the CHT might again become a hideout for insurgents from Northeast India), provided the PCJSS training and safe havens in the neighboring northeastern Indian state of Tripura. In late 1976, the Shanti Bahini carried out its first armed attack on a military outpost in the CHT.

In the name of counterinsurgency against the Shanti Bahini, the Bangladesh security forces perpetrated massive human-rights violations—massacres, killings, torture, rape, arson, forced relocation, forced marriages to Bengalis, and cultural and religious oppression of the indigenous people. In April 1979 the first of a series of massacres took place in Kanungopara, where reportedly 25 indigenous people were killed by the army and eighty houses were burnt down. In a second massacre on 25 March 1980, indigenous people in Kalampati/Kaukhali were forced to line up and then the army opened fire. Reports about the number of indigenous people killed in Kaukhali vary between 50 and 300. Young women were held by the army for days and raped. In the 1980s, 10 percent of the indigenous population fled to neighboring India, and others fled to isolated jungle areas. More than ten major massacres have taken place between 1979 and 1993 in which an estimated 1,200 to 2,000 indigenous people have been killed. These and subsequent massacres formed part of the counterinsurgency strategy to drive out the indigenous population and settle Bengalis on their land. One of the army generals reportedly said in 1977: "We want the land, not the people."

Another main element in the counterinsurgency strategy was the settlement of some 400,000 landless Bengalis from the plains in the CHT between 1979 and 1985 under a secret government transmigration program. This dramatically changed the composition of the population: the percentage of Bengalis in the CHT rose from 26 percent in 1974 to 41 percent in 1981. Moreover, Bengalis illegally occupied indigenous people's land on a large scale. This further escalated the conflict. Land became one of the main sources of conflict between the indigenous people and Bengali settlers and the army. The PCJSS reacted to the militarization and Bengalization of the CHT by stepping up its armed actions.

General Ershad who had come to power in yet another military coup in 1982, declared a general amnesty and a special five-year plan for the CHT after a split had occurred within the PCJSS in 1983 and Manobendra Larma, leader of the PCJSS, had been killed by the dissident faction. Manobendra's brother Jyotirindra Bodhipriya (Santu) Larma took over the leadership of the PCJSS. A large number of dissidents surrendered between 1983 and 1985. Repression and human-rights violations by the security forces in the CHT, however, continued as before. Some of the worst massacres took place in 1984 and 1986. Repressive measures restricted, for example, the freedom of movement and the selling and buying of essentials to prevent the delivery of supplies to the Shanti Bahini. The indigenous population was forcefully relocated in "model villages" (as a so-called rehabilitation measure to stop environmentally damaging *jhum* cultivation, but in fact to be better able to control them). Bengalis who could not be accommodated on the land that the fleeing and relocated indigenous people had left behind were settled in "cluster villages," usually next to a military camp where they served as a protective shield for the military. In defense of their rights and their land, the Shanti Bahini started carrying out attacks on Bengali settlers, trying to drive them out and prevent more settlers from coming to the CHT.

These rehabilitation schemes, as well as road construction and afforestation programs, were largely funded by the Asian Development Bank. A few other donors, such as UNICEF and UNDP, also funded "development" programs in the CHT. The Swedish and Australian governments pulled out of road construction and afforestation programs in the CHT in the early 1980s after the repressive government policies seeped to the outside world and it became clear that these programs were not at all in the interest of the indigenous peoples.

Partly due to international pressure, negotiations between the respective governments and the PCJSS have taken place since 1985 without, however, coming to any agreement. The main demands of the PCJSS were regional autonomy and constitutional recognition of the Jumma identity; withdrawal of the army from the CHT; and removal of the Bengali settlers from the CHT.

Jenneke Arens

Repatriated refugees whose land has not yet been returned.
They still live in a transit camp under very poor conditions.

Only in 1997 was a peace accord signed between the PCJSS and Sheikh
Hasina's Awami League government that had won the national elections in
1996. The opposition parties led by the BNP and Bengali settlers opposed the
accord as a sellout and campaigned fiercely against it.

On totally different grounds, a section of the indigenous people who had
earlier supported the PCJSS rejected the accord on the grounds that the main
demands of the Jumma peoples had not been fulfilled and declared their intention to continue the struggle for autonomy by democratic means. They
formed the United Peoples Democratic Front (UPDF) in December 1998.

The major part of the peace accord has yet to be implemented and so far
the government elected in October 2001 has taken several measures that are in
violation of the accord. For instance, Prime Minister Khaleda Zia has appointed
herself as minister for CHT affairs and a Jumma representative only as deputy
minister. The peace accord stipulates that the minister's post should be given
to an indigenous representative from the CHT. Similarly, the government unilaterally appointed one of the CHT MPs, a Bengali settler and BNP member,
as chairman of the CHT Development Board, bypassing the indigenous MP
who should have been given preference as specified in the accord. BNP members have also been appointed unilaterally as chairmen of the three Hill District Councils and still no provisions have been made for elections of these
district councils.

Official Conflict Management
From 1983 the International Labour Organization (ILO) criticized the Bangladesh government annually for inadequate reporting with regard to ILO Con-

vention 107 on Indigenous and Tribal Populations to which Bangladesh is a signatory. The CHT issue was also raised annually in the UN Working Group on Indigenous Populations, and the Bangladesh government was questioned in the UN Human Rights Commission and the UN Sub-Commission on Prevention of Discrimination and Protection of Minorities. In 1987, the PCJSS demanded the deployment of a UN Peace-Keeping Force and implementation of its demands for withdrawal of the security forces and the Bengali settlers under the auspices of the UN. The successive governments, however, ignored this demand. No foreigners were allowed in the CHT and news coming out of the CHT was heavily censored.

Dialogues between the PCJSS and the respective Bangladesh governments have taken place since 1985. After six dialogues between the PCJSS and the Ershad government in which the government remained inflexible to the demands of the indigenous people, the government coerced other indigenous leaders in 1989 into consent with the enactment of the three Hill District Councils, one for each of the three Hill Districts into which the CHT had been split up by then. In contrast to the rest of the country, the Hill District Councils were to be elected and the majority of the seats were designated for indigenous ("tribal") people. The government claimed to have thus given autonomy to the CHT. The PCJSS rejected the Hill District Councils outright. Their main arguments were that the councils had no constitutional basis and therefore could be repealed anytime; that they formalized and legitimized the illegal settlement of 400,000 Bengalis in the hills; and that only minor powers were given to the councils and the land rights of the indigenous people were not safeguarded. The Hill District Council elections in 1989 and its outcome were fully controlled by the Bangladesh army, refuting all claims of having given autonomy.

In December 1990, Ershad was ousted by a mass movement that ended almost fifteen years of military rule in Bangladesh. In August 1992 the PCJSS unilaterally declared a cease-fire and from November 1992 several rounds of negotiations with the elected BNP government headed by Khaleda Zia were held, without any concrete results.

Finally, in December 1997, negotiations with the Awami League government of Sheikh Hasina (daughter of the murdered Sheikh Mujibur Rahman), elected in 1996, culminated in the signing of a peace accord. Changes in the government in India were a factor in this as well. There were a few high-level meetings between the governments of Bangladesh and India, and India put pressure on the PCJSS to come to an agreement.

The main points of the peace accord are:

- Modification of the three Hill District Council Acts of 1989 and an indirectly elected Regional Council with a two-thirds majority of indigenous members to coordinate and supervise the District Councils
- Withdrawal of all security-force personnel to the six permanent cantonments in the CHT

- Land to be placed under the jurisdiction of the Hill District Councils, and installation of a Land Commission to resolve all land disputes
- Rehabilitation of surrendered PCJSS and Shanti Bahini members
- Repatriation and rehabilitation of refugees from India and internally displaced persons

The main weaknesses of the accord are:

- No constitutional provision for the ethnic identity, nor for the councils, so these can be repealed any time
- No deadline for the withdrawal of the security forces and no provisions for proper investigation of past and future human-rights violations
- No timetable for implementation of the accord and no provision for independent monitoring of the peace process
- The Land Commission has the near-impossible task of resolving the massive land disputes
- The crucial issue of the Bengali settlers remains largely unresolved

The PCJSS claims that during the negotiations a verbal agreement was made with the government to resettle the Bengali settlers outside the CHT. However, the government denies having made such an agreement.

In 1996, the European Parliament had adopted an amendment to earmark part of the aid to Bangladesh "for the repatriation of Bengali settlers in the CHT back to the plains." Although the Bangladesh government had expressed its willingness to repatriate the Bengali settlers if funds were provided, according to the European Parliament, the government has so far failed to table any such proposal.

The European Union and several other donor governments have made implementation of the peace accord conditional on funding development programs in the CHT.

Four years after the signing of the accord, many of its provisions have yet to be implemented and there is disagreement between the government and the PCJSS on several points.

The slow implementation of the peace accord as well as the violent conflict between the PCJSS and the UPDF add to the continuing instability in the area.

Multi-Track Diplomacy

A combination of historical factors, successive government policies—both colonial and postcolonial administrations—and the particular development of "Bengali" nationalism[2] that has finally led to the emergence of the eastern part of Pakistan as independent Bangladesh, have contributed to the development of the political and social collective identity of indigenous peoples in isolation from the mainstream Bengali society.[3] This is not to say that both societies did not interact. But these interactions have been at best superficial; overwhelming portions of both societies remained unconcerned with each other's plight and existence.

Because of the particular background to the situation of the indigenous peoples in the CHT, instances of multi-track diplomacy were few and far between during the pre-accord period. Nor was the tight, often heavy-handed, control of the government's administrative machinery over the region helpful in developing a congenial environment in this regard. But in order to put the role of the civil society in perspective, an outline of the role of civil society in the context of the CHT is in order.

Civil Society

Civil society in Bangladesh has a long and distinguished heritage. Communities and associations have continued to play a significant part in the sociopolitical life of the territory from the distant past. Even during the British colonial time these entities articulated the feelings and demands of the society at large and made significant direct and indirect contributions to shaping official policy. Civil society continued to play a strong role during the period when Bangladesh was part of Pakistan and made important contributions to the flowering of the movement for autonomy and eventually independence of the territory.

However, at this stage all the efforts of the civil society were concentrated on the autonomy movement of the "Bengali" people and civilization—a logical consequence to distinguishing it from the West Pakistani–dominated venture of building Pakistan on an Islamic religious model. But this ethnocentric effort of the predominant Bengali civil society hardly left any room for accommodating the aspirations of their ethnic minority brethren. It is, then, not surprising to find, immediately after the independence of Bangladesh, the failure of the newborn nation to take account of the demands of the CHT MP, Manabendra Narayan Larma, for a separate autonomous status for his region by providing constitutional safeguards for ensuring distinct identities of its indigenous ethnic minority inhabitants. One cannot overlook the irony in the fact that the same people who gained independence in the name of cultural self-determination failed to respond to the aspirations of people in a similar situation in its own territory.

Although the events of 1975 and the subsequent intrusion of the military into the politics of postliberation Bangladesh seriously disrupted the process of growth and development of civil society, it continued to maintain a steady existence. Despite obstacles, sociocultural, human-rights, civic, and community organizations participated consistently in the struggle for restoration and strengthening of democracy in the country during the mid-1980s and mid-1990s. However, this important component of the Bangladeshi society remained mostly silent or ignored the events of militarization and military atrocities in the Chittagong Hill Tracts. A possible explanation might be its ethnocentric origins (these civil-society organizations are mostly composed of and led by Bengalis and have little or no participation from their indigenous counterparts) and also its preoccupation with the struggle for restoring democracy in the country following the tragic events of 1975, which was considered more important.[4]

The tight military control and brutal repression did not allow either the intervention of outside organizations—national or international—in the conflicts of the Chittagong Hill Tracts or to the growth of any such indigenous organizations. The few organizations of the latter category were built up either by the military or with direct support from them, as a result of which none of these organizations could claim any legitimacy in the eyes of the indigenous inhabitants of the region.

Another reason for the silence of civil-society organizations on the CHT conflict may have been the paucity of factual information because of the situations of armed conflict and violence.

There were, however, a few notable examples where civil society played a bold and courageous role. One such example is the series of events immediately following the Kalampati massacre in 1980. The subsequent inquiry by a commission, comprised of the then member of parliament from the CHT along with other prominent representatives of civil society, disclosed to the outside world the gruesome, cold-blooded killing of innocent indigenous civilians, perpetrated jointly by the Bangladesh army and the local Bengali settlers.

From the late 1980s and during the 1990s, civil-rights organizations and activists started to become more and more vocal and raised their concerns on the prevailing situation in the Chittagong Hill Tracts and the violation of human rights of its indigenous inhabitants. Besides, the individual activists who worked to strengthen this trend included prominent personalities such as poet Shamsur Rahman and political personality Rashed Khan Menon of the left-wing party alliance. From the mid-1990s onward, the involvement of the civil society became even stronger, and with the signing of the peace accord in 1997 this momentum could only grow as the NGO sector continues to play a proactive role. In particular, the National Committee for the Protection of Fundamental Rights in the CHT has, since the early 1990s, supported the Jumma peoples' rights and demands and continues to do so. Since the return to parliamentary democracy in 1991, more information about the past and present situation in the CHT has become available, although the issue of indigenous peoples' rights, in particular in the CHT, remains sensitive.

From 1989, Jumma people organized themselves in three organizations: first, the Hill Students' Council, and a few years later the Hill People's Council and Hill Women's Federation. They campaigned for the PCJSS demands and the Jumma people's rights from a democratic platform, withstanding severe repression. They formed alliances with progressive Bengali forces. The Hill Women's Federation addressed in particular the oppression—rape, sexual violence, forced marriages, etc.—of their women in the armed conflict, as well as the issue of equality and respect for women within their own societies.

In the year following the peace accord, the Hill Students' Council, Hill People's Council, and Hill Women's Federation split into two factions, one supporting the accord and one rejecting it. The latter formed their own political party in December 1998, the United Peoples Democratic Front (UPDF). The UPDF has met with severe repression and there is continuing rivalry between the PCJSS and the UPDF, regularly culminating in violent confrontations. Mediation attempts by Jumma elders between the two groups have so far failed to stop the attacks, let alone bring about an agreement.

From the early 1980s onward, several international NGOs, such as the Anti-Slavery Society, Survival International, the International Work Group for Indigenous Affairs, the Minority Rights Group, and Amnesty International, have brought out reports on the human-rights violations in the CHT. In 1990 the international Chittagong Hill Tracts Commission carried out an independent investigation in the refugee camps in Tripura and also managed to get into the CHT. The commission reported extensively on the background and development of the conflict and the massive human-rights violations. International aid agencies and donor governments, alarmed by the reports, started questioning the Bangladesh government and gradually international pressure was put on Bangladesh to come to a political solution of the conflict.

Because of the ongoing conflicts very few development organizations were working in the CHT area before the accord of 1997. However, in the postaccord era many big national NGOs[5] have expanded their activities and services in the region. Further, a number of locally inspired NGOs have come into being—founded mostly by the local indigenous inhabitants. At the moment, there are fifty-two registered NGOs at work in the CHT. If nonregistered NGOs are considered, the number may be as high as three hundred, as estimated by the Asian Development Bank (ADB).

The bulk of these NGOs focus on health, education, water, and sanitation, with microcredit activities mostly done by the big national NGOs with little or no participation by the local indigenous NGOs. Apart from this, NGOs are intervening in diverse areas such as agriculture, horticulture, afforestation, fisheries, poultry farms, microcredit, education, women in development, income generation, the environment, and training and development in general.

Reflection on NGO Initiatives

Unlike all other regions of Bangladesh, the armed conflicts of the past decades have severely restricted the activities of NGOs in the CHT. As a result, while there are a good number of NGOs with divergent interests working in the region, most of them are just evolving and gaining experience. This is particularly true of the local indigenous NGOs who have been able to start their activities only during the last couple of years. This fact is all the more important given the need for gigantic reconstruction and other developmental work in the region. The involvement of the NGOs—particularly the local indigenous NGOs—will be crucial if development projects are to meaningfully address the frustrations and aspirations of the indigenous peoples. Moreover, many of the indigenous peoples feel that their frustrations, problems, and aspirations cannot be truly addressed by organizations from the outside because of the particularity of the problems—ethnic, social, cultural, geographic, religious, etc. Such worries have already been raised on several occasions.[6] It has also been indicated that the bureaucratic and administrative rigidity of the large national NGOs[7] may not be appropriate to the particularity of the CHT peoples. So, unless the genuine participation of the indigenous peoples and their representative organizations can be ensured in any development process, their aspirations are likely to remain unfulfilled. The local indigenous NGOs are thought to be representative—specifically for the developmental activities.

However, such a view of the local indigenous NGOs also puts them in a difficult position with respect to the government, as has been witnessed in the accusations and counteraccusations in March–April 2001 between the government and indigenous NGO leaders in the national media. The government accused some local indigenous NGOs[8] of working against the stipulations of the peace accord and involvement in activities subversive to the state of Bangladesh. The NGOs concerned vehemently denied these accusations and protested against government measures to have them supervised by the security agencies. They described these measures as denying the right to development and universally recognized fundamental human rights of the indigenous peoples.

But despite this tussle between the government and indigenous NGOs, the government seems to have accepted the principle of "particularity" regarding the activities of NGOs in the CHT region. As per the stipulation of the peace accord, the former Special Affairs Division has been converted to a new, full-fledged ministry with the name of the Chittagong Hill Tracts Affairs Ministry, to be headed by an indigenous representatives of the CHT. This ministry is vested with power to look after the activities of the NGOs in the region.

In the long run, much will depend on how much the local indigenous NGOs can grow. Despite their recent existence and small size, it is rightly argued that they represent many of the genuine concerns, voice, and aspirations of the indigenous peoples of the CHT—especially in matters related to development activities. Another point to be observed is whether the development of the local indigenous NGOs in the CHT could follow the path of their predecessors at the national level and, starting with small-scale relief and rehabilitation operations, grow into larger service delivery and/or social-mobilization organizations, fully integrating themselves with the civil society of the country—in fact, even becoming one of the dominant voices of the civil society. In a country such as Bangladesh, ridden with political schisms and intolerance, a robust and burgeoning civil society may be one of the best guarantees for ensuring its often-threatened democracy and the civil and political rights of its peoples. Similarly, in a region that has been bogged down in a bloody civil war for the last two decades, a robust and vibrant NGO sector capable of bridging between the civil society of the country and the concerns and aspirations of the peoples of the region is highly desirable.

In a country that often becomes diametrically divided along lines of political affiliation, voices of moderation are one of the most precious things to be nurtured. And most would agree that it is the failure to listen to the voice of moderation of Manabendra Larma—recognition of the specific rights of the indigenous peoples of the CHT within the constitutional framework of the country—that led to the bloodshed of the past decades. Now, in the aftermath of the peace accord, it seems vital to support the indigenous NGOs of the CHT to follow this line of moderation, to continue in representing certain concerns and aspirations of the people of the region within the larger fabric of the nation.

Prospects

With the signing of the accord in 1997, two strategic developments for the better—the surrender of arms and the return of refugees and their rehabilitation—have taken place. Although it should be noted that many refugees are still not properly rehabilitated, many have not yet had their land returned and some are still living in transit camps. When the accord was signed, it was widely hoped that it would usher in a new age for the people of the region with a greater pace of socioeconomic development. The accord, by and large, has been accepted by the peoples of the region and by the donor community as well—though one section of the indigenous people has explicitly rejected the accord and has formed the United Peoples' Democratic Front, which continues the demand for autonomy (within the state of Bangladesh). Accordingly, a good number of representatives from donor country/agencies and multilateral development agencies have visited the region, and some of these agencies have started to disburse funds for different development projects. Alongside these initiatives, a number of NGOs—both local and national—are also undertaking development programs. Prospects for peace in the CHT have at least become brighter.

However, it should be noted that the government and the PCJSS has already fallen apart politically. The PCJSS claims that most of the provisions of the accord (to the extent of 98 percent) remain unimplemented. The government, in turn, counters that a similar portion of the accord has already been implemented. The PCJSS further claims that in addition to the stipulations agreed upon in the peace accord, there has been an unwritten agreement between the government and PCJSS on several other matters, most notably on relocation of the settlers. The PCJSS is also extremely critical of the government's failure to withdraw as many as five hundred temporary army camps and of the continuation of the de facto army rule in the CHT. While the accord requires that any settlement or acquisition of land should be done with the consent of the District Council, the PCJSS complains that the government has acquired huge tracts of land for setting up a new army training ground and an air force base in Bandarban district, violating the existing laws and most importantly, the spirit of the peace accord. The government has also expanded the Reserve Forest and is planning to declare more land as Reserve Forest.

But the main point of disagreement between the two parties is on the relocation of the Bengali settlers and subsequently the preparation of a voters' list for the region, based on the stipulation agreed in the peace accord. The alleged noncooperation by the government on the latter issue has even led the PCJSS to boycott the last national parliamentary elections.

As part of the stipulation of the peace accord, the government has formed a Task Force on Rehabilitation of Returnee Refugees and Internally Displaced Persons, chaired by the MP for Rangamati in 1998. But almost immediately after the formation of this task force, its interventions led to controversy and disagreement because it also wanted to declare a large number of Bengali settlers as internally displaced persons and provide for their rehabilitation. As a result, the PCJSS, one of its key members, has boycotted the meetings of the task force since its last session eighteen months ago. Similarly, a land commission is supposed to start to work on settling land disputes in the region. But although it has been formally declared, nearly four years after the signing of the peace accord it has yet to begin work. With the change of power in the government following the last parliamentary elections in October 2001, the initiatives of the new government of the BNP for tackling these impending issues should be noted.

As per the provisions of the peace accord, a ministry of CHT affairs and a regional council have been constituted. While the former is coordinating and supervising the overall development and administrative activities of the region, the latter has been marginalized, allegedly due to the unwillingness of the government, although according to the peace accord the regional council is supposed to play a crucial role in the development and administrative activities of the region.

Another worrying point for the people of the region in the post-accord period is the general deterioration in law and order, aggravated by the division among the indigenous people—the rivalry between the PCJSS and the UPDF. The power vacuum created by the surrender of arms by the PCJSS and consequently their return to normal life has not been filled either by the law-and-order enforcement agencies or by any local representative bodies, such as the regional council or the local district councils. As a result, extortion and rent-seeking activities have multiplied. Many of these problems owe their origins to the slow implementation of the provisions of the accord.

In light of this situation, it might be asked, what possibility is there that the situation will relapse into conflict? The accord certainly envisages a political process that has been, by and large, accepted by the public. Second, it will be difficult for the PCJSS and Shanti Bahini leaderships simply to go back to the jungle and resume insurgency. So instead, one should ask how the situation in the CHT might evolve in the near future.

If a power vacuum is not properly filled, the risk of anarchy always remains potent, and that is exactly what is happening at present in the CHT. The present law-and-order situation and the activities of the UPDF[9] may be seen as symptoms of a "residual insurgency" from which the region is suffering at present. If the root causes of the conflict are not properly addressed, any fault-line conflicts always have the potential to rekindle at any moment. Furthermore, one should keep in mind that, geopolitically, the CHT straddles an active cross-border insurgency area. Hence, continuing frustration may provide incentives for regrouping and the resumption of violence, perhaps not necessarily with insurgency but with other equally disruptive forms for the society as a whole.

Recommendations

From the point of view of conflict prevention, the key concern is to undertake measures so that conflict is not resumed. Now that the Peace Accord of 1997 is an established fact, the key recommendation will be to continue implementation of the accord without setbacks. Key issues creating the major stumbling block between the government and the PCJSS are settlement of land disputes, rehabilitation of the remaining refugees, and the voter list. The government must show deep commitment and take bold steps in resolving these problems. One recommendation is for the government to show political commitment to the implementation process. For this, the National Implementation Committee should meet and there should not be any lack of visible interest on the part of the government to implement the accord. Further, the government must initiate the appropriate relocation of the Bengali settlers who had been rehabilitated there by the government as counterinsurgency measures in the late 1970s and 1980s. Unless, the issue of the settlers can be definitively settled, the seeds for further discontent, and thus violence, will always remain potent among the indigenous people of the region. The reported news of assurance from several donor agencies for funding initiatives for relocation of Bengali settlers elsewhere should be seen as a great facilitating process.

Over the past two years, the PCJSS leadership seems to have become disillusioned with the government and it seems that national electoral politics are the main reason. The government's political priorities seem to get preference over its commitment to the accord, leading to alienation and lack of confidence. The PCJSS, with which the government signed the accord, has become the ruling party's opponent in the context of national politics. The victory of the BNP-led coalition in the last election and the subsequent formation of a new government by this coalition, may lead to the revision of government policy on the CHT, as it declared in its electoral manifesto. Such revision of policies must not abrogate the provisions and hamper the spirit of the peace accord. Add to this the lack of progress on two other vital issues—the land commission, and army camps and virtual army rule—and the situation in the CHT has the potential to degenerate further.

One of the most pertinent answers to redress the above discontent would be to institute the local democratic process through elections to the district councils and the regional council. The democratic process will mitigate a lot of these grievances. Concomitant to the elections in the district and regional councils, the government must initiate a rapid handing over of powers to these institutions, as stipulated in the provisions of the peace accord. The existence of a crippled regional council and district councils might provoke more violence in the long run than no such councils at all. The provisions of the accord with regard to withdrawal of army camps should also be implemented. The visibility of the army should be reduced.

The land commission should be set in operation. Settling the land disputes is going to be a very complicated and lengthy process. But initiation of the land commission will go a long way in neutralizing some of the opposition to the accord. Wherever any injustice has taken place, it should be mitigated with boldness.

There should also be a policy of encouraging the activities of the local indigenous NGOs in the area, as long as their areas of intervention remain within the purview of the provisions of the peace accord. While this may outrage the hawks concerned with the security and sovereignty of the nation, in the long run such an approach might prove far more effective in circumscribing and venting the anger and frustrations of the indigenous peoples in a more constructive and productive manner. Such a policy must also target regular meetings and exchanges with their peers at the national level and the civil society at large.

The accord signified an important and bold step toward conflict resolution through negotiation and peaceful means. It also demonstrated that the political process should be allowed to function in the CHT. Such a process will ultimately also be beneficial in cultivating mutual tolerance and respect between the different factions among the indigenous people. Finally, the sooner the elected district councils and the regional council start functioning and the provisions of the peace accord are fully implemented, the quicker will be the mitigation of many of the existing problems and the elimination of the causes of potential conflict.

We would also recommend that the indigenous people stop the infighting between the PCJSS and UPDF, which has already led to some forty deaths and several kidnappings on both sides after the accord.

Resources

Newsletters and Periodicals
Kheyang, Tribal Cultural Institute, Rangamati, Bangladesh

Reports
Anti-Slavery Society, *The Chittagong Hill Tracts: Militarization, Oppression and the Tribes,* Series 2, London, Indigenous Peoples and Development, 1984.
Asian Development Bank
    Chittagong Hill Tracts Region Development Plan, Interim Main Report (ADB TA#3328–BAN), Rangamati, November, 2000.
    Chittagong Hill Tracts Rural Development Project, Vols. 1–3, Dhaka, 2000.
AusAid, *AusAid Capacity Building Project, Feasibility Study Report,* Dhaka, Australian High Commission, 2000.
Bangladesh Centre for Development Journalism and Communication, *Life in the Chittagong Hill Tracts,* Dhaka, 1994.
Centre for Development Research, Bangladesh (CDRB), *The Chittagong Hill Tracts of Bangladesh: The Untold Stories,* by Mizanur Rahman Shelley, 1992.
DANIDA, *Report of the Interim Planning Mission on Watershed Development in the CHTs,* Dhaka, Royal Danish Embassy, 2000.
Defence Services Command and Staff College, *Counter Insurgency Operations,* Restricted papers and proceedings of Annual Seminar of the Staff College, in Dhaka on 5–6 December 1994.
Government of Bangladesh, *Government Response to the Demands of the PCJSS,* Dhaka, 1993.
Government of Bangladesh—Ministry of CHT Affairs
    A Report on the Problems of Chittagong Hill Tracts and Bangladesh Responses for Their Resolution, Dhaka, 1993.
    Situation in the Chittagong Hill Tracts, Dhaka, October, 2000.
Green Hill, *Need Assessment Survey Report on Hygiene Education, Sustainable Safe Water and Sanitary Status of the Hill People of Rangamati Hill District,* Rangamati, 1999.

Institute of Bangladesh Studies, *Tribal Cultures in Bangladesh,* edited by Mahmud Shah Qureshi, Rajshahi, Rajshahi University, 1984.

International Working Group on Indigenous Affairs, *Land Rights of the Indigenous Peoples of the Chittagong Hill Tracts, Bangladesh,* by Rajkumari Chandra Roy, Document No. 99, Copenhagen, Denmark, 2000.

Parbattya Chattagram Janasanghati Samity (PCJSS)
*Dabeenama (*Charter of Demands to the Government), Rangamati, 1993.
*Dabeenama (*Charter of Demands to the Government), Rangamati, 1996.
Situation in the Chittagong Hill Tracts, Khagrachhari, Information and Publicity Department, 2000.

Society for Environment and Human Development
Bangladesh: Land, Forest and Forest People, edited by Philip Gain, Dhaka, 1995.
The Chittagong Hill Tracts: Life and Nature at Risk, by Raja Devasish Roy, Meghna Guhathakurta, Amena Mohsin, Prashanta Tripura, and Philip Gain, Dhaka, 2001.

South Asia Forum for Human Rights, *Living On The Edge: Essays on the Chittagong Hill Tracts,* by Subhir Bhaumik, Meghna Guhathakurta, Sabyasachi Basu, and Ray Chaudhury, Kathmandu, 1997.

Tebtebba Foundation, *The CHT: Road to Lasting Peace,* Baguio City (Phillipines), 2000.

The CHT Commission, *Life Is Not Ours: Land and Human Rights in the Chittagong Hill Tracts, Bangladesh,* 1991. Updates in 1992, 1994, 1997, and 2000. Distributed by the International Working Group on Indigenous Affairs, Denmark, and the Organising Committee Chittagong Hill Tracts Campaign, Netherlands.

Other Publications

"Bangladesh's Chittagong Hill Tracts Peace Accord: Institutional Features and Strategic Concerns," by M. Rashiduzaman. *Asian Survey* XXXVIII, no. 7, July 1998, pp. 653–670.

Counting the Hills: Assessing Development in Chittagong Hill Tracts, edited by Mohammad Rafi and A. Mustaque R. Chowdhury. Dhaka, University Press Ltd., 2001.

Ethnic Insurgency and National Integration: A Study of Selected Ethnic Problems in South Asia, by Mahfuzul Huque. Dhaka, University Press Ltd., 1998.

"Insurgency and Counterinsurgency: Bangladesh Experience in Regional Perspective—The CHT," by Syed Muhammad Ibrahim. *Military Papers,* Issue No. 4, Dhaka, AHQ MT Directorate, 1991.

Insurgency in Chittagong Hill Tracts: Modalities for a Solution, by Abdul Muyeed Chowdhury. Paper presented at the Seminar on Counter-Insurgency Operations organized by Defence Services Command and Staff College, Dhaka, 5–6 December 1994.

"Land Rights of the Indigenous Peoples of the Chittagong Hill Tracts," by Raja Devasish Roy. *Land* 1(1) (quarterly journal of the Association of Land Reforms and Development, Dhaka), 1994.

"Modernity, Alienation and the Environment: The Experiences of the Hill People," by Amena Mohsin and Imtiaz Ahmed. *Journal of the Asiatic Society of Bangladesh,* December 1996.

"Problems of National Integration in Bangladesh," by S. A. Ahsan and Bhumitra Chakma. *Asian Survey* XXIX, no. 10, October 1989.

"Resource Development and Ethnic Conflict in Bangladesh: The Case of Chakmas in the Chittagong Hill Tracts," by Peter J. Bertocci. In Dhirendra Vajpeyi and Yogendra K. Malik (eds.), *Religious and Ethnic Minority Politics in South Asia,* New Delhi, 1989, pp. 160–161.

"Sustainable Land Management with Rubber-Based Agro-Forestry: A Bangladeshi Example of Uplands Community Development," by N. A. Khan and S. K. Khisa, *Sustainable Development* 8(1), 2000.

The Chittagong Hill Tracts: Living in a Borderland, by Willem Van Schendel, Wolfgang Mey, and Aditya Kumar Dewan. Dhaka, University Press Ltd., 2001.

"The Invention of the 'Jummas': State Formation and Ethnicity in South Eastern Bang-ladesh," by Willem Van Schendel. In *Indigenous Peoples of Asia*, edited by R. H. Barnes, Andrew Gray, and Benedict Kingsbury, Ann Arbor, Michigan, Association of Asian Studies Inc., University of Michigan, 1995.

The Politics of Nationalism: The Case of the Chittagong Hill Tracts, Bangladesh, by Amena Mohsin. Dhaka, University Press Ltd., 1997.

"The Problems of Tribal Separatism and Constitutional Reform in Bangladesh," by Mohammad Humayun Kabir. In Iftekharuzzaman (ed.), *Ethnicity and Constitutional Reform in South Asia*, New Delhi, Manohar, 1998.

"Tribal/Non-Tribal Discourses on Ethnicity in Bangladesh," by Prasanta Tripura and Ishrat Jahan. *Asian Studies*, June 1992.

Resource Contacts

Shapan Adnan, National University of Singapore, e-mail: sadnan@nus.edu.sg, or saras@bttb.net.bd

Imtiaz Ahmed, Centre for Alternatives, e-mail: calter@bangla.net

Bhumitra Chakma, Department of International Relationship, e-mail: pratmuna@yahoo. com

Pradanendu Bikash Chakma, Department of Management, Dhaka University, e-mail: pradanik@bdonline.com

Philip Gain, Society for Environment and Human Development, e-mail: sehd@citecho. net

Sadeka Halim, Department of Sociology, Dhaka University, e-mail: sadeka@bangla.net

Amena Mohsin, Centre for Alternatives, e-mail: calter@bangla.net

Yoshihiko Murata, Japan Committee for CHT, e-mail: jcchti@alles.or.jp

Raja Devasish Roy, Taungya, e-mail: devasish@citecho.net

Willem van Schendel, Department of Asia Studies, Amsterdam University, e-mail: vanschen@pscw.uva.nl

Prashanta Tripura, Department of Anthropology, Jahangirnagar University, e-mail: ptripura@juniv.edu

Organizations

Bangladesh Adivashi Forum
Contact: Mr. Sanjib Drong, General Secretary
e-mail: sdrong@bangla.net

CARITAS, Dhaka
Contact: Father Timm
e-mail: hlbtimm@citecho.net

Center for Indigenous Peoples Development (CIPD), Rangamati
Contact: Rupayan Dewan
e-mail: cipd@aitbd.net

Committee for the Protection of Forest and Land Rights (CPFLR)
Contact: Mr. Gautam Dewan, Former Chairman of Rangamati District Council

Green Hill, Rangamati
Contact: Mr. Moung Thowi Ching, Coordinator
e-mail: greenhil@citechco.net

Organising Committee CHT Campaign
P. O. Box 11699
1001 G Amsterdam, Netherlands
Fax +31-20-664 5584
e-mail: occhtc@xs4all.nl

Research and Development Collective (devotes itself actively at the field level on land-related issues)
Contact: Dr. Mesbah Kamal, Department of History, University of Dhaka
e-mail: rdcsc@bol-online.com

Taungya, Rangamati
Contact: Raja Devasish Roy
e-mail: devasish@citecho.net

Tribal Cultural Institute, Rangamati (a government organization set up for promoting tribal culture in the CHT). The institute, among others, publishes a quarterly journal, Kheyang.

Trinamul
Contact: Mangol Kumar Chakma, Executive Director
e-mail: mktripura@hotmail.com

Selected Internet Sites

www.bangladeshgov.org/mochta/ (Official site of Ministry of Chittagong Hill Tracks Affairs)
www.banglarights.net/ (Bangladesh Human Rights Network)
www.hrdc.net/ (South Asia Human Rights Documentation Center [SAHRDC])
www.iwgia.org (International Workgroup for Indigenous Affairs)
www.meghbarta.net (Online Forum for Activism)
www.satp.org (Site of Institute for Conflict Management)
www.unpo.org/member/chitta/chitta.html (Info on CHT from UNPO)

Data on the following organizations can be found in the Directory section:

In Bangladesh
  Bangladesh Institute of International and Strategic Studies
  Bangladesh Inter-Religious Council for Peace and Justice
  Centre for Alternatives
  Center for Development Research
  Centre for Policy Dialogue
  Centre for the Study of Peace
  Coordinating Council for Human Rights in Bangladesh
  Peace for All
  Society for Environment and Human Development
  South Asia Partnership
  Technical Assistance for Rural Development

Outside Bangladesh
  International Center for Ethnic Studies
  International Work Group for Indigenous Affairs
  South Asia Forum for Human Rights

Jenneke Arens has been involved with the Netherlands-based Organising Committee CHT Campaign since it was formed in 1985. She is also a resource person of the CHT Commission and participated in its investigation into the refugee camps in India and all three districts of the CHT in November–December 1990. She has published several articles on the CHT. Kirti Nishan Chakma belongs to one of the indigenous groups of Chittagong Hill Tracts. He is an NGO and development activist for the indigenous inhabitants of the region. He is currently serving with Save the Children–UK in Bangladesh as Research and Advocacy Manager.

Notes

1. The writing in this chapter is supported by earlier drafts supplied by Mizanur Rahman Shelley, Centre for Development Research, Bangladesh, and Abdur Rob Khan and Mohammad Humayun Kabir of the Bangladesh Institute for International and Strategic Studies.

2. A detailed and interesting discussion on this topic can be found in "The Politics of Nationalism: The Case of Chittagong Hill Tracts, Bangladesh" by Amena Mohsin, Dhaka: University Press Ltd., 1997.

3. See "The Invention of the 'Jummas': State Formation and Ethnicity in Southeastern Bangladesh," by Willem Van Schendel, in *Indigenous Peoples of Asia,* edited by R. H. Barnes, Andrew Gray, and Benedict Kingsbury, Ann Arbor, MI: Association for Asian Studies Inc., Monograph 48, 1995.

4. This last point has been repeatedly raised to the author as a principal argument in many formal and informal meetings/discussions with several prominent representatives of the civil society in the country. This argument seems quite plausible given the fact that it is usually the liberal section of the society that tends to remain the most vocal on the rights if the indigenous peoples, the kind of people who are generally associated with Awami League or leftist politics. Following the events of 1975, this section of the society has been continually sidelined and/or repressed by the following successive regimes.

5. Most prominent are Bangladesh Rural Advancement Committee (BRAC), PROSHIKA, Integrated Development Fund (IDF), CARITAS, World Vision, Community Health Care Project (CHCP), etc.

6. One such comment seems particularly poignant and pertinent. It was made in a conference in Rangamati in 1998 by an indigenous elder: "We have remained 25 years in Bangladesh without any development. If necessary, we can wait 20 more years (for development). But any development for us must be meaningful to us and have to be in conformity with our aspirations and demands."

7. The years of 1998–1999 witnessed reports in the media of sporadic cases of attack by the indigenous villagers on workers of BRAC and other national NGOs against certain of their administrative practices that, reportedly, go against the cultural habits of the indigenous peoples.

8. These are Taungya, Indigenous Multi-Purpose Development Organisation (IMDO), Jabarang, Centre for Indigenous Peoples Development (CIPD), Trinamul, and Hill Tracts NGO Forum (HTNF).

9. The factions of PCJSS opposing the peace accord have regrouped themselves under this newly formed organization.

7.8

India

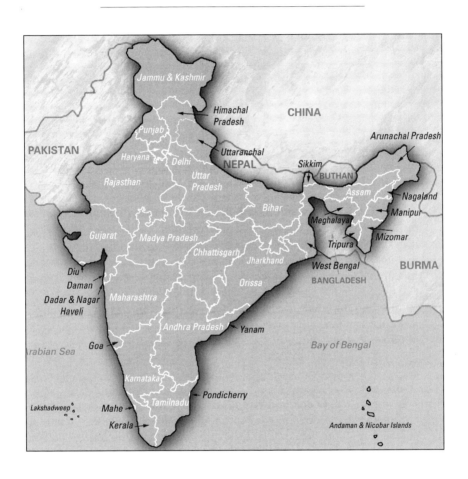

7.8.1

Multiculturalism in India: Diverse Dots in a Multiple Mosaic

N. Manoharan

It is an empirical reality that the majority of countries are multi-cultural in character. Only 10 to 15 percent of all countries can be reasonably classified as ethnically homogenous. It is also true that, even as the notion of a "global society" becomes more and more a reality, ethnocentrism and identity assertion are also on the ascendancy. In the modern world, negotiation with diverse groups within the confines of state boundaries is unavoidable. In this regard, new concepts such as "multiculturalism" (in Europe generally referred to as "interculturalism") have evolved, been discussed, and officially sanctioned by developed societies to tackle the problems of diversity. Canada became the first Western country to adopt multiculturalism as an official state policy in 1971, and Australia followed in 1977. But what about developing multiethnic societies such as India? How is India managing its diversities?

The Concept

To begin with, a discussion of the concept of "multiculturalism" may be useful. Multiculturalism refers to the doctrine that "cultural diversity should be recognized as a permanent and valuable part of political societies," and endorses the idea of difference and heterogeneity that is embodied in "diversity." Though it distinguishes between the majority and minority communities, it argues for the granting of equality to all within the boundaries of both the public and political arenas. In other words, "equality" and "nondiscrimination" are the watchwords of multiculturalism. The concept centers around three basic ideas:

1. Human beings live and organize their lives within a culturally structured world and their worldview will fall within that culture.
2. Since every culture presents only a limited range of worldviews, the assistance of other cultures is required not only to understand the world better,

but also to enrich its own culture and expand the horizon of general understanding. The world demands "cultural interdependence" rather than "cultural autarchy."

3. No culture is wholly worthless; each carries some value for its members. This, in turn, also means that no culture is perfect enough to justify imposing its values on others.

Multiculturalism assumes that society is composed not only of individuals but also of groups, each with a particular culture. Paradoxically, one group manages to establish its cultural norms (which is termed "universalization" or "hegemony") over the others and thus tries to impose its supremacy. The role of multiculturalism here is to erode the dominance of one group and empower or give voice to the other groups that are oppressed. "It is," as Nathan Glazer puts it, "a position that rejects assimilation and the 'melting pot' image as an imposition of the dominant culture, and instead prefers such metaphors as the 'salad bowl' or the 'glorious mosaic,' in which each ethnic and racial element in the population maintains its distinctiveness."[1]

Thus, a multicultural society is

> one of mutual and multiple recognitions where individuals are neither subjected to the tyrannies of compulsive cultural traditions nor [are] cultural groups subjected to the oppression of either the state or a dominant group within it. It is a decent society where there is a continued effort to eliminate humiliation and institute rights and dignity in the lives of individuals and groups. It is a society, which is respectful both of its internal as well as its external "other," one which is animated by reaching out to the "other" with grace, love and participation.[2]

In other words, it constitutes an extensive effort to cope with diversity democratically.

The efforts also engenders stiff resistance to the homogenizing moves either by the state or the dominant community. Forceful assimilation, it is held, is the antithesis of willing loyalty on the part of minorities toward the state, and leads to secession. Thus, the sense of "belonging" and loyalty toward a country can only be achieved through genuine recognition—public and institutional—of the many cultural groups and their rights, rather than mere acknowledgement of their existence. In other words, providing equal space and opportunity for different cultures to sustain themselves through institutional and legal support is as important as respect for diversity. The multiculturalists argue that if every cultural group is given its rightful access to resources, opportunities to retain, express, and develop their own culture, and institutional protection, it is possible to avoid divisive frictions and ensuing conflicts.

The Context
India is a culturally diverse country. This diversity manifests itself in every respect—religion, language, caste, region, and other social particularities. The

Bonded laborers' liberation dance, Tamil Nadu, India.

situation in India is not the same as that in developed and official multicultural societies such as Australia or Canada. Indian society incorporates a bewildering number of minorities, whose boundaries have always been fluid and overlapping. So diverse is the society that it might be more difficult to characterize the majority than the minorities. And compared to Western societies, there is not the same degree of consensus regarding a national political culture and identity. Hence, at independence many prophesized that due to innumerable ethnic, religious, linguistic, regional, tribal, and caste differences India would soon break apart, or that disunity could only be prevented by military or authoritarian rule, and certainly not in a democracy.

Yet, to the surprise of all, India has defied the prognostications that it was an "historic impossibility." How has it managed to maintain what Weiner terms a "baffling democratic exceptionalism"?[3] What factors have been responsible for this multicultural coexistence of diverse ethnicities within one political unit?

Above all, it is because of the foresight of the founding fathers of the republic that India has been able to maintain its multicultural character. While some developed Western countries pride themselves on their multicultural policies, India recognized the importance of multiculturalism as early as in 1928 when the All-Parties Conference finalized a scheme for the Indian constitution in the form of the Nehru Report. It recommended inter alia equal rights for women, freedom to form unions, and dissociation of the state from religion in any form. The character of multiculturalism was evident in the set of nineteen rights recommended by the report. Not surprisingly, ten of those nineteen rights were later included in the constitution. Thus, early on, the national leadership showed a strong desire for a postindependence polity to be based on "unity in diversity."

In the formative years, the national leadership also displayed tremendous capacity for accommodating the interests of diverse communities without any prejudice or self-interest. Decisions were arrived at by consensus on all major issues. This tact in fact was inherited during the course of the struggle for national independence. For instance, Jawaharlal Nehru, Sardar Vallabhai Patel, Rajendra Prasad, Vinoba Bhave, Radhakrishnan, Rajagopalachari, Jayaprakash Narayan, B. R. Ambedkar, Shyama Prasad Mookerjee, Narendra Dev, P. C. Joshi, and many other leaders of great caliber, though belonging to different parties, ideologies, and opinions, were interested in and worked for the higher goals of unity, national integration, democracy, and development. In addition, they enjoyed tremendous support and popularity from every sector of the society.

Unconsciously, the national legacy acted as a strong force for "multiculturalism." (India's first prime minister, Jawaharlal Nehru, for instance, pronounced that "the glory of India has been the way in which it manages to keep two things going at the same time: 'infinite variety' and 'unity in that variety.'"[4]) While nation building was to be based on a common struggle against colonialism and the existing challenges confronting the nation, the country's rich cultural, linguistic, religious, ethnic, and regional diversity was acknowledged and appreciated. While the other newly independent states at that period were influenced by the "dominant model" of nineteenth-century France, Italy, and Germany in the name of building a strong nation, the Indian leadership considered "diversity" and "multiple identities" as positive features and a source of strength for Indian culture, civilization, and the emerging Indian nationhood.

The Indian National Congress, which spearheaded the Indian freedom movement, articulated a secular and inclusive nationalism in which there would be "equal respect, equal opportunities and equal liberty for all, regardless of their religious affiliations or social location."[5] It was argued that its inclusive and syncretic character was evident in the principles of Indian civilization. In this regard, a leading congress nationalist and the first vice-president of India, S. Radhakrishnan, noted, "No religion should be given preferential status of unique distinction. No person should suffer any form of disability or discrimination because of his religion but all alike should be free to share to the fullest degree in the common life. Secularism as here defined is in accordance with the ancient religious tradition of India."[6] It was an unstated policy that "no state is civilized except a secular state." The talk of "Hindu Raj" or a state based on one culture was considered "mad."

At the organizational level, the structure and strength of the Indian National Congress Party also provided a strong base that discouraged mobilization on multiple lines, at least in the formative years. In other words, its amorphous structure enabled it to accommodate various groups and subgroups reflecting India's diversity. Its social base extended to all religions, castes, and regions. Its all-India appeal was deeply rooted and so it wasn't difficult for the party to sustain the policy of multiculturalism during its nearly four decades in power following independence. The party allowed dissent and encouraged different views and opinions, and free discussion.

The national leadership's commitment to transforming an India that was "multicultural by accident" into an India that was "multicultural by design" was evident in the constitutional debates and the subsequent passage of a "multicultural constitution" guaranteeing to all cultural groups both "equality of treatment" as a general rule and "differential treatment" in special circumstances. For instance, constitutional recognition and protection was offered to religious, cultural, and linguistic minorities. Equal respect, fairness, and nondiscrimination were to be the guiding principles of state policies toward minorities. Article 29 of the constitution protected the right of any group "having a distinct language, script or culture . . . to conserve the same." Article 30 enshrined the right of "minorities, whether based on religion or language . . . to establish and administer educational institutions of their choice," and extended statutory recognition to the religious and linguistic minorities.

But it is interesting to note here that differences based on caste and class were not recognized. In fact, in this regard the constitution embraced a policy of assimilation and affirmative action. The constitution prohibited the practice of untouchability in any form (Article 17), further empowering the state to make any law "providing for social welfare and reform or the throwing open of Hindu religious institutions of a public character to all classes and sections of Hindus" (Article 25.2b). At the same time, special privileges were provided to the "Scheduled Castes" and "Scheduled Tribes," including the reservation of seats in the parliament and the legislative assemblies (such reservations, which were initially stipulated for only ten years, were later extended to further periods of ten years as a formality) and in jobs, promotions, and educational institutions. These privileges were extended on the grounds of the backwardness of the beneficiaries. Thus, the constitution was, significantly, committing the state to ensure the protection and welfare of the weaker and more vulnerable sectors of the society.

Interestingly, language assertion, which was one of the important mobilization factors in postindependence India, posing a threat to national integrity, subsequently turned out to be a source of stability. In the postindependence polity, there were two camps vis-à-vis the linguistic reorganization of states and the establishment of a single national language. Supporters of a single language and script argued, "For thousands of years one and the same culture has all along been obtaining here. . . . It is in order to maintain this tradition that we want one language and one script for the whole country."[7] It was felt that any attempt toward linguistic reorganization might threaten national integrity and might also be administratively inconvenient, and two high-level committees recommended against linguistic reorganization.

However, the support for local languages was stronger, especially in the south, as language was closely related to culture, and therefore to the customs of the people. And so recognition was extended to regional languages. Later it was even stated that "a linguistic mosaic might well provide a firm base for national unity." A single language was also not imposed. India adopted a three-language formula—Hindi was to be the national language and English, the link language, alongside the respective languages of the states (where "state" means the federal units within the Indian Union, e.g., Andhra Pradesh, Jammu and Kashmir, Manipur, Bihar, etc.).

But there was a problem of the status of linguistic minorities (those who speak a language other than the official language of the state) in each state. To avoid any integrationist or discriminatory practices by the states, certain fundamental rights were provided in the constitution itself. Article 30 provides that "all minorities, whether based on religion or language, shall have the right to establish and administer educational institutions of their choice . . . The state shall not, in granting aid to educational institutions, discriminate against any educational institution on the ground that it is under the management of a minority, whether based on religion or language."

The contribution of a highly professional, but apolitical, civil and military bureaucracy, an effective parliament, an independent judiciary, and a free press also contributed significantly to the maintenance of diversity in Indian society.

Though the bureaucracy confronted congress time and again prior to independence, in the postindependence polity congress gained the upper hand. And if the bureaucracy was by nature inflexible and conservative, it showed no favoritism toward any communal or ethnic groups in the formative years.

In parliament, though congress was dominant, the opposition parties' views were heard and even respected. The debates in the House were conducted at a high level and policies were formulated only after intensive debate and discussion. Such consensual opinions on contentious issues indirectly prevented factional infighting among the competing political groups.

As far as the judiciary was concerned, except for a brief period of time during Indira Gandhi's regime, it always served to protect the vulnerable and weak. Time and again, the apex court asserted its duty to safeguard the "basic features" of the constitution. Judicial rulings, in fact, have extended the rights of minorities. For instance, in *Commissioner, Hindu Religious Endowments v. Lakshmindra case* (1954) it was held by the supreme court that what was guaranteed by Articles 25 and 26 was not only the right of the individual to practice and propagate matters of faith or belief, but also all those rituals and observances that adherents regard as integral parts of a religion. At the same time, in a different case (*Stanislaus vs Madhya Pradesh,* 1977) it was held that right of propagation was not the right to proselytize, as that would be a violation of others' rights to freedom of religion. Thus the judiciary was responsible for maintaining a balance between freedom of faith and the right to propagate. The provision of autonomous bodies such as the National Commission for Minorities, the National Commission for Scheduled Castes and Scheduled Tribes, and the National Human Rights Commission has reinforced multiculturalism in the sense that these commissions act as vigilantes of pluralism.

As for the media, it has generally functioned without restriction and advanced informed criticism and debate on vital issues in society. In the absence of a vigilant press, it would have become difficult to gauge if multiculturalism and other policies really worked. Through the efforts of the "Fourth Estate," various attacks on the minorities in the name of "Hindutva" have been brought to light and opposed.

Despite these successes in maintaining and managing diversity, why have a "million mutinies" multiplied? Why is there an impression, of late, that the intolerance of multiplicity has arisen in India? Again, this is due to the erosion of the foundations upon which the multicultural society was based.

Multiculturalism in Contemporary India

For one thing, the dominant legacy of the national movement has come to be challenged. In recent years the political discourse in India has been colored by the intense struggle for power between competing political groups. Various strategies are being pursued—the most common being "Minority Appeasement." The Hindutva forces question the Nehruvian model of secularism and multiculturalism which, they allege, posed a threat to the well-being of the nation. They stir suspicions that Indian Muslims are more attached to Pakistan than their motherland or, alternatively, they argue for "unity" rather than "diversity." In fact, they insist on Hinduism being the national character of "Hindustan" rather than *videshi* (foreign) cultures.

Today there is a reverse movement and the process of "othering" at work, where even those who are within the space of the nation-state-society are being excluded one by one. A "thick" notion of ethnic nationalism has gained currency. According to this perception, minorities would have to accept a formulation of "national culture" in which their contribution is not recognized, and is either assimilated or accorded very limited rights of self-determination. Equal citizenship is not extended to all (although elimination of minorities need not be envisaged). Religious majoritarianism in this context, then, should be seen as a political project for state power rather than a fundamentalist one with religious aims. Though these ethnic or cultural conflicts are very deep-rooted, they still require intensive analysis. In India it is politics that influences and fine-tunes identity. Ethnic conflicts are nothing but power conflicts. In other words, they are only a subset of larger political conflicts.

Second, a fair amount of deinstitutionalization occurred in the 1970s and the 1980s at all levels. The Indian National Congress, as a party carrying forward the traditions of the national movement, faced splits with the demise of Jawaharlal Nehru, which resulted, from 1969, in the emergence of numerous splinter groups. Thus was born the strategy of electoral appeal on the basis of identity. Later, in the 1980s, the growing weakness of the Congress Party and its exclusive appeal to Muslim electorates strengthened the parties that sought support exclusively on a Hindu plank. Various identities found expression in numerous parties, and consequently competitive politics. As the Bharatiya Janata Party ("Indian People's Party," BJP) settled for Hindu votes, the Congress, the Janata Dal, and its splinter groups sought votes among the religious minorities and the backward and lower-caste groups and divided the Hindu constituency. To strengthen their base and to fill the political vacuum left by the Congress Party, while the BJP took up the cause of Ram and Ayodhya, the Janata Dal implemented the Madal Commission Report in 1990. This further encouraged the political parties to appeal to various manufactured identities. Thus a vicious cycle of political parties and various groups based on special identities proliferated.

Third, the quality of leadership also deteriorated gradually. After Nehru and his contemporaries, many of the second-generation leadership lacked national appeal or a larger vision of the interests of the country as a whole. Instead, the new leadership appealed to the primordial emotions of the masses so as to achieve shot-term gains. Thus, for instance, Laloo Prasad Yadav is associated with the Yadava community of Bihar, Mayawati with the Dalits of northern India, Ramdoss with the Vaniyars of Tamil Nadu, and so on. With very few exceptions, the present leadership has lacked nationwide appeal and reach. Obviously, this has hindered the efforts to assert moral authority against majoritarianism.

Fourth, though the Indian constitution has stood the test of time, it did not anticipate that one day the majority community, by virtue of its numerical superiority, might monopolize state power by collective assertion. The constitution assumed that the state would remain "neutral" and "impartial" forever. While the constitution granted wide-ranging powers to the state in reforming Hindu social practices, it included no provisions empowering such intervention in Muslim or Christian society. For instance, under Article 25.2b the state was empowered to make any law "providing for social welfare and reform or the throwing open of Hindu religious institutions of a public character to all classes and sections of Hindus." This does not apply to other religious minorities, though Sikhs, Jains, and Buddhists were included under "Hindus."

Thus the state was placed in a unique position. Some of the objectives of the constitution are being questioned today. The present BJP-led government has even appointed a commission to review some provisions of the constitution, who submitted its report to the government in March 2002. The constitution provides no guidance for the resolution of problems such as the Uniform Civil Code, cow slaughter, national language, recognition of the identity of certain minorities like Sikhs, and religious conversions. (A proposal to include a ban on conversions was omitted from the constitution, while "the right freely to profess, practice and propagate religion" was included. One majoritarian congressman, Lokanath Misra, denounced the provision as "a charter for Hindu enslavement.") Efforts to bring some clarity to the issue via the judiciary were stymied because, without legislative endorsement, there was not the sort of mandate required in a multicultural society.

And the parliament, which is considered the watchdog of government policies, has now become a mere talking shop where effective action is impossible. Thus the government pushes its agenda at any cost, the opposition tries to disrupt them, and policies to advance the common good fall by the wayside.

Deinstitutionalization has also affected the autonomy of the judiciary, which has been sensitive to social issues and social justice. In the 1970s and 1980s, previous governments pushing populist policies ignored the law of the land. When the judiciary tried to defend the fundamental rights of the people, its independence was encroached upon by the executive. However, in recent years the judiciary has had more success maintaining its independence.

The process of politicization has permeated the bureaucracy, with efforts to convert it from a "neutral" player into a "committed" body. Apart from politicization, bureaucracy has been "casteized," communalized, and regionalized. Once a highly professional force, these processes have had an increasingly divisive effect on the bureaucracy. Of late, communalism has also penetrated the ranks of the police. During communal disturbances, they either stand by as mere spectators or act against the minorities. The Krishna Commission Report, to cite one example, found that the police played a role in the communal riots in Mumbai (formerly Bombay) in the wake of the Babri Masjid demolition in December 1992. This has been the case of many such riots in the country, in Gurajat, to cite a recent example.

Concluding Remarks

To summarize, India offers the model of a multicultural developing democracy. The character of multiculturalism is derived from its legal-institutional and national legacy. It was due to this policy that the country could survive as one entity for so long, contrary to predictions that it would disintegrate. But of late, multiculturalism has been under threat, especially with the increase in political competition, and the exploitation of ethnic issues by rightist forces. The ethnic conflicts are basically power conflicts and are a subset of larger political conflicts.

To regain and retain its multicultural character, India should not abandon its historical commitments. To assure the protection of India's minorities, commitment to equal rights and social justice, and the embrace and implementation of nondiscriminatory policies, may be as important as the recognition of differences. The rise of religious majoritarian forces agitating against minorities and attributing mythical threats to them makes principled adherence to the multicultural tradition a moral imperative.

Still, some shifts in approach to Indian multiculturalism are necessary. Focusing on cultural differences without exploring the possible linkages between cultural deprivation and other forms of deprivations leads to a somewhat "culturalist" and limited approach to the problem of increasing social antagonism in Indian society. Granting recognition to minority groups without addressing the other social and political causes of hostility in society, and without emphasizing the need for democratization, could increase, rather than reduce, hostility and fragmentation in society. We need to correct this anomaly immediately, given the fact that increasing conflict in society is frequently attributable to poor access to resources. In this regard, the Indian state should be prepared to devolve more power to the village communities to enable the multicultural policy to develop from below.

The building of a multicultural society calls for continued democratic struggle and spiritual strivings. Along with listening, it calls for the ability to identify with the suffering of each other and, through this, to understand each other more fully and graciously, and to contribute to the building of a common future. Identification with suffering demands much more than does the glorification of identity politics and a triumphalist approach.

At the theoretical level, if multiculturalism is to become a true conflict-prevention and management activity, then the existing political and social theories, concepts, and vocabularies are not enough. The immediate task is to find a way to forge political unity without disturbing cultural differences. While no simple formula exists, states such as India probably need to simultaneously pursue a range of objectives including freedom and equality, as well as respect for the contributions of minorities to a shared national culture.

Feminists argue that Indian society is not purely multicultural, as women continue to be discriminated against. They point out that multiculturalism is silent on the issue of implicit bias against women in society. Hence, it is also important to take into consideration, in any multicultural policy, the removal of intracultural discrimination. Provisions to reserve seats in legislative bodies for women should be passed. Such affirmative action might initially benefit upper-class women, but judging from the success of affirmative action for women in Panchayat bodies, this situation would only prevail for a short time.

Multicultural education in the curriculum needs to be strengthened. Of late there has been an attempt to change the character of secular education in the name of "standardization." But such an act of manufacturing "cohesion and consent" is a way to silence dissident voices and discourage diversity and tolerance. The aim of education is not just to impart information and to equip students for their careers, but also to help make the world a better place in which to live, and to impart a sense of responsibility toward one's fellow human beings. Most importantly, studies and research on multiculturalism should be encouraged so as to facilitate the development and dissemination of more information in the field.

N. Manoharan is research officer at the Institute of Peace and Conflict Studies, New Delhi, India. His areas of interest and expertise are multiculturalism, minorities, ethnicity, human rights, and Sri Lanka. He has written extensively on Indian and international affairs in general and on Sri Lankan issues in particular.

Notes

1. Nathan Glazer, *We Are All Multiculturalists Now.* Cambridge, MA: Harvard University Press, 1997, p. 10.

2. Ananta Kumar Giri, "Promoting Multiculturalism," *The Hindu,* New Delhi, 3 February 2001.

3. Myron Weiner, *The Indian Paradox: Essays in Indian Politics.* London: Sage Publications, 1989, p. 30.

4. See *Constituent Assembly Debates,* Constituent Assembly of India, New Delhi, vol. VII, p. 323.

5. Sarah Joseph, "Of Minorities and Majorities," *Seminar,* New Delhi, no. 484, 1999, p. 33.

6. S. Radhakrishnan, *Religion and Society.* London: George Allen and Unwin Ltd., 1947, pp. 52–55.

7. Speech by Seth Govind Das, the strong proponent of Hindi as a national language, in *Constituent Assembly Debates,* Constituent Assembly of India, New Delhi, vol. IX, p. 1328.

7.8.2

Religious Conflict:
A Brief Survey of the Hindu-Muslim Problem

Asghar Ali Engineer

The Hindu-Muslim conflict is the product of colonial India, although it is presented as a centuries-old struggle by the communal forces. The Hindu communalists believe that the conflict between Hindus and Muslims started with the invasion of the Arab general Muhammad bin Qasim in the seventh century A.D. They believe that the Muslims invaded and plundered the motherland of the Hindus, and that they violated its sanctity and demolished their temples. According to this communalist view, there has subsequently been no respite in the ensuing bloody religious conflict. These forces even depict liberal rulers such as Akbar as tyrants who persecuted Hindus and forcibly married their daughters. They particularly revile rulers such as Babar and Aurangzeb who demolished their temples and humiliated them. The manifestations of this communalist view of history and the present are the subject of this chapter.

"Communalism" and "secularism" in an Indian context have different connotations than in Europe. In a European context communalism is a positive word, meaning to be associated with one's own community or to work for the good of one's own community. However, in the Indian context it is used negatively. To be communal is not only to be a partisan of one's own community, but also to be hostile to the other community. Second, it is political rather than religious in nature, though it pertains to the principal religious communities of India—Hindus and Muslims. Communalism relates to a political struggle for power between the elites of the two communities. Thus we can define communalism as the use or misuse of religion for secular ends, i.e., for grabbing political or economic power.

"Secularism," on the other hand, is a positive term in an Indian context. In the Indian context, secularism indicates the state's and the political parties' neutrality toward religion and religious beliefs. A citizen, whatever his/her religion, will have equal rights. The state favors no religion, according to the Indian constitution. This is the essence of Indian secularism.

336

Thus communalism and secularism are antithetical in the Indian context. A secularist, while respecting religious beliefs, would not politicize them or use or misuse them for political ends. The political parties are supposed to stay neutral toward religion. Any party using religious propaganda would be construed a "communal party." The country's past should also be understood in terms of historical, social, and political dynamics rather than religious dynamics. The communal parties and scholars, social scientists, or historians associated with communal parties or communal ideologies, on the other hand, glorify or condemn the country's past in terms of religious dynamics. Thus the present religiopolitical conflicts are projected into the past by the communal parties. History is communalized and interpreted as such.

Secular scholars reject this communal interpretation of history, arguing that such an interpretation is not only simplistic but is also prejudicial. It takes no account of complex social forces or the motives of the rulers. It assumes that the religious beliefs of the rulers were a main motivating factor. These secular scholars believe that the communal narrative is the product of colonial history writing with its own agenda. It was the British rulers with their divide-and-rule policy who encouraged through their own officers and historians the communal narrative of history so as to create conflicts between Hindus and Muslims. History has been one of the most powerful tools for promoting communal cleavage between the two principal communities of India. During the 1880s this communal historical narrative was used by the communal forces to polarize Hindus and Muslims and to cause a great deal of bloodshed along communal lines.

The cleavage created between Hindus and Muslims was so deep that it ultimately resulted in the partition of India along communal lines in 1947. This partition has left bitter memories and it rankles in the minds of the members of the majority community. Memories of partition are invoked repeatedly to embitter relations between the two communities.

Internal Cleavages

Secular scholars believe that it is wrong to homogenize a community on the basis of religion. In other words, it is patently wrong to believe that all Muslims are united on the one hand, and all Hindus, on the other. No religious community can be homogenous without internal cleavages and conflicts. The Hindus are divided among themselves along caste, regional, and linguistic lines. The same can be said of the Muslims. While caste cleavages are very pronounced among Hindus, sectarian strife is common among Muslims.

Political divisions are also quite pronounced among Hindus and Muslims, particularly among the Hindus. Not all Hindus support one party, much less the Bhartiya Janata Party (BJP), which provides the political leadership of what is today known as the Sangh Parivar, or the Saffron family. This consists of a number of religious, cultural, and political groups including the Vishwa Hindu Parishad (VHP), Bajrang Dal, Rashtriya Sevak Sangh (RSS), and the BJP. While the BJP is political leader of the family, the RSS provides its ideological leadership and nothing can be done against the wishes of the RSS or the ideology laid down by it.

The RSS believes in the Hindu view of India and totally rejects the secular viewpoint. For the RSS, secularism is an alien ideology imported from the West by some Westernized leaders of the Congress Party. It believes in the establishment of a Hindu Rashtra, or Hindu nation, based on the laws laid down for Hindu society by the sage Manu. Those upholding the RSS view are also referred to as Manuwaids, especially by the Dalit leaders who denounce the RSS ideology as an essentially upper caste–oriented ideology. There is sharp cleavage between the Dalits and upper-caste Hindus, particularly of the RSS variety.

The RSS viewpoint was at one time considered a fringe viewpoint. Of late it has moved to center stage, and while it is still not dominant, it has certainly acquired far greater credibility than previously. Though it is essentially an upper-caste point of view, the RSS is also trying hard to sell it to the lower-caste Hindus in order to widen its political base. The RSS is aware that it cannot acquire political hegemony with a narrow base among the upper castes. The percentage of upper-caste Hindus is no more than 18 percent of all the Hindu population. Yet this upper-caste stratum is culturally, educationally, and economically advanced compared to the lower-caste Hindus. It is for this reason that the upper-caste Hindus hold sway over Indian politics and the RSS represents their point of view. The lower-caste Hindus, on the other hand, are mostly poor, illiterate, and economically backward. Though they are far more numerous, they are highly stratified along various subcastes and hence disunited. Among them, too, there are sharp contradictions.

The Muslims in India are also divided along caste and sectarian lines, although caste divisions are less sharp than with the Hindus. The caste divisions among them have become somewhat blurred, especially after partition, although after the implementation of what is known as the *Mandal Commission Report* (reserving official positions for the other lower castes), some sense of caste identities has emerged among Muslims as well. Minority consciousness among Muslims overrides their caste consciousness. In communal riots the purveyors of violence make no distinction between lower- and upper-caste Muslims. Fear of communal forces compels them to close their ranks.

Just as the RSS believes all Hindus are one, it believes all Muslims too are united and homogenous. It hardly recognizes any caste or sectarian cleavages among the Muslims. All Muslims, either poor and backward or those belonging to more influential sections from wealthier social strata, are treated as one. RSS, the ideological leader of the Hindutva forces, believes that all Muslims cling to their religion fanatically and do not treat India as their *pitra* and *pavitra bhoomi* (i.e., fatherland and sacred land). The RSS ideologues believe that only Hindus view India in this light. And since Muslims do not treat India as their sacred land, they cannot be true patriots. The RSS not only suspect their loyalty but also feel they are pro-Pakistan and basically their loyalty is toward their Islamic neighbor. Hence they often talk of Indianizing Muslims. They demand from Muslims that they respect the Hindu "mainstream culture" and consider the Hindu gods such as Rama and Krishna as their own heroes. They even demand that the Indian Muslims describe themselves as "Mohammedan Hindus," thereby asserting their Hindu identity and their Hindu cultural heritage.

It is, to reiterate, wrong to think that Indian Muslims are culturally homogenous. There is a sharp dividing line, between Muslims from the north of India and from the south. In south India too, Kerala Muslims and Tamil Muslims have very different identities. Also, there are cultural differences between urban and rural Muslims. Rural Muslims are far more rooted in the indigenous culture. There are some cultural differences between Hindus and Muslims in urban areas, but hardly any in rural areas. Also, in urban areas there is more Hindu and Muslim consciousness among the elite than among the urban poor. The urban poor are closer to each other, compared to the Hindu and Muslim elites.

Partition

The partition project was mainly a political rather than a religious project. It is important to note that the Partition of 1947 was the result of the failure of power-sharing arrangements between the Hindu and Muslim elites of northern urban India. It was *not,* basically, a religious divide. No prominent Muslim theologian supported the partition movement. It was the Muslim power elite around Jinnah and his colleagues who were in the forefront of the partition movement. Neither the Muslim masses nor the religious elite showed interest in Jinnah's "Two-Nation" theory. The Islamic organization Jamiat-ul-'Ulama-i-Hind (i.e., the organization of the Muslim theologians of India) remained an ally of the Indian National Congress and its leaders, all prominent Muslim theologians of the subcontinent, vigorously opposed the creation of Pakistan.

However, Hindu communal forces refuse to understand the real causes of the partition of India and treat it as a religious and not a political phenomenon. They think that Muslims are fundamentally separatists and are always intent on creating a separate country and an Islamic state. They think that Pakistan is an Islamic Rashtra (nation) and hence the Hindus have every right to create a Hindu Rashtra. So the RSS leaders are vigorously engaged in creating the India of their dreams, i.e., the Hindu India.

India has been a strongly multireligious, multicultural, and multilingual country for centuries. It was administratively united by the Mughals and, even more so, by the British. India was not a nation in the classical sense of the word. It was a multinational entity. As a nation state today, its multireligious, multicultural character can be protected, promoted, and consolidated only as a secular state and hence the founding fathers of the Indian constitution rightly made it a secular state. The model of Indian secularism has been generally referred to as a Nehruvian model. Jawahrlal Nehru, the first prime minister of India, was a passionate champion of secularism. He even earned the wrath of the Hindu fundamentalists, but remained firm in his secular commitment. He pushed through modern reforms in Hindu society. He was the real architect of modern India. He was convinced that to build a really modern India one had to strengthen the secular state structure. Nehru also believed that promoting modern scientific education would promote secularism and secular values.

However, this turned out to be a rather simplistic assumption on the part of Nehru. There has been no direct, one-to-one relationship between modern education and a modern secular attitude. The educated middle class is in fact more communal than the illiterate masses. Communalism is a modern phenomenon rather than a religious one, and it is mainly promoted by the educated middle classes to promote their own interests. Religion plays only an instrumental role.

The upper-caste Hindu middle class is using the Hindu religion as a cover to create a Hindu Rashtra, to promote its own interests. Secularism did not come under serious challenge until the early 1980s, when the Hindu middle class expanded numerically and also the minorities and lower castes became more conscious of their rights. They began to demand their share in power and economic development, thereby challenging the unquestioned monopoly of power of the upper-caste Hindus.

Communal Violence
The Muslims in India remained relatively subdued after partition. There was a great deal of communal violence during the partition riots and Muslims felt quite insecure. Thus they kept a very low profile throughout the 1950s. However, after a decade of independence they felt more confident and began to assert themselves. This assertion through democratic institutions aroused Hindu communalism. In a democracy, political competition between two religious communities often results in communal strife. Communalism is thus basically a political phenomenon. Hindu communal forces became more aggressive from the early 1960s, which resulted in communal riots in several cities in India. The first major communal riot in independent India took place in 1962 in Jabalpur in central India.

The Jabalpur riot was quite ferocious and shook even Jawahrlal Nehru, who thought communal violence would not occur in modern secular India. The Jabalpur riot was followed by a series of riots in several places during the 1960s. Communal feelings were further aggravated by the war with Pakistan in 1965. The ideologues of Hindu communalism always suspected the loyalty of Muslims toward India. Any conflict with Pakistan would create tension between Hindus and Muslims, often resulting in outbursts of communal violence.

Hindu communalism became even more aggressive in the late 1960s when Indira Gandhi took over as prime minister and split the Congress Party to reinforce her authority. She appealed to all secular forces to support her and all minorities rallied round her. Thus Indira Gandhi was seen by insecure minorities as the champion of secularism, like her father Nehru. The more she asserted her secularism, the more the communal forces showed their aggression against minorities. As if to throw a challenge to her secular leadership and to weaken her political authority, a communal riot of major proportion was engineered in Ahmedabad in Gujarat in 1969. In this riot more than 1,100 people were killed, mostly Muslims. This riot was followed by another cataclysmic outburst of communal violence in Bhivandi, 40 kilometers from Bombay. In this riot, a prominent role was played by a newly formed political outfit called Shiv Sena, a communal and regional chauvinistic party formed with the backing of some congressmen opposed to Nehruvian progressive secular policies.

Shiv Sena's storm troopers not only broke strikes, but also preached hatred against minorities and those who came to work in Bombay from the south of India. Thus it promoted both regional and communal chauvinism. Bal Thackaray, the Sena chief, was a cartoonist in an English daily from Bombay and was financed to form Shiv Sena by a top Congress Party leader from Bombay and a non-Maharashtrian industrialist. The aim of forming this party was twofold: to break the stranglehold of Nehruvian ideology on one hand, and to break the left-controlled trade unions, on the other.

The Bhivandi-Jalgaon riots once again shook the nation. It was through these riots that this political outfit acquired political moorings in Maharashtra. A strong communal climate was created, particularly in the state of Maharashtra, by Shiv Sena. It used abusive language particularly against Muslims. The communal massacres in Bhivandi and Jalgaon made Muslims terribly insecure. The Shiv Sainiks were dreaded most by them.

In comparison, the period between 1970 and 1976 saw less communal violence. There were very few riots for various reasons. In 1970 the Bangladesh war of liberation began, with much Indian involvement. In 1971, Pakistan was defeated and Bangladesh came into existence. Indira Gandhi emerged as a leader of great prestige. Even the Jan Sangh (as the BJP was then called) had to admire her for breaking Pakistan into two. But this lasted for less than a year and a mass movement was started against her by Jay Prakash Narayan, a socialist leader.

When her position was threatened by this mass movement and a court judgment unseated her from parliament, she proclaimed a state of emergency in 1975, which lasted for two-and-a-half years, during which the democracy was throttled. During this emergency, she arrested all important opposition leaders including those of Jan Sangh and Jamat-e-Islami, leaving no one to provoke further violence. Thus the emergency period saw no communal violence whatsoever.

However, when elections were held in 1977 Indira Gandhi lost heavily and the Janata Party took over. The Janata Party was formed by merging various opposition parties, including the Jan Sangh, which took an oath on Mahatma Gandhi's Samadhi that it would renounce its communal politics and would accept secularism and Gandhian socialism. But this experiment was also short-lived. The Janata Party government was voted out on the question of the Jan Sangh members maintaining their RSS membership. Thus the oath taken on the Samadhi of Mahatma Gandhi was broken and the Jan Sangh members had not really renounced their communal ideology. During the Janata Party rule, four major communal riots took place from 1977 to 1979, in which several hundred Muslims were killed.

Democracy Deepened

After breaking away from the Janata Party, the Jan Sangh leaders launched a new political party in 1980 called the Bhartiya Janata Party and again swore to be secular. But it is a strange irony that the more the BJP pretended to be secular, the more it became aggressively communal. In fact, the 1980s saw the most aggressive face of BJP communalism. There were number of reasons for this.

First, Indira Gandhi, for fear of losing the Muslim vote, began to woo Hindu voters, particularly those who had traditionally voted for the Jan Sangh (now the BJP) and newly emerging lower-caste Hindus. Even the RSS, which is the most militant Hindu organization, began to favor Indira Gandhi as a savior of Hindus. This frightened the BJP leaders and forced them to take more militant communal postures to compete with Gandhi and to convince the RSS ideologues that they had not weakened their Hindu moorings by adopting "secular politics."

Second, in the early 1980s another factor emerged to alter the political scene. Indian democracy had by now deepened and established firm roots, bringing greater awareness of rights and bargaining powers to the weaker sections of society and minorities. This in turn led upper-caste Hindus to fear that they would have to share a greater degree of power with these sections of society. These sections saw the BJP as the savior of their interests and a section of the upper-caste Hindus that had traditionally voted for Congress switched their support to the BJP.

The Sikh militants in Punjab demanding Khalistan, the student movement in Assam, and the militant Muslim agitation against the Shah Bano judgment of the supreme court, which ultimately forced the Rajiv Gandhi government to reverse the judgment by enacting a new law, frightened upper-caste Hindus. It pushed them further into the fold of the BJP, the so-called champion of the "Hindu cause." This was the third important factor strengthening Hindu communalism and sharpening the religious conflict in India.

The fourth and most important factor was the implementation of the *Mandal Commission Report* in 1990, which ensured reserved official positions for the other lower-class Hindus. The upper-caste Hindus thought their share of government jobs had been further reduced and more of them switched their loyalty to the BJP. Its implementation also worried the BJP, as it thought it would lose these lower-caste votes to the Janata Dal.

The BJP, which was merely an upper-caste urban party, had realized that it would need to extend its political base if it was to take power. It thus decided to widen its political base among lower-caste and rural voters. The best way to do this was to use the Ramjanambhoomi issue (related to the disputed Ram temple in Ayodhya), as Ram is universally respected, particularly in the north of India. Thus it intensified the Ramjanambhoomi movement in the late 1980s to overcome caste fragmentation and create an illusion of "Hindu unity." For the time being, it was tremendously successful.

All this sharpened the communal divide during the 1980s in India and resulted in large-scale communal violence. The 1980s was the most dangerous decade, seeing communal rioting with a frequency and scale never previously witnessed in the postindependence period. During this decade hardly any year passed without a major communal riot. As a result of violent agitation for the construction of the Ramjanambhoomi temple led by the Sangh family, Babri Masjid was demolished on 6 December 1992. This demolition shocked the entire nation, particularly Muslims, and Bombay witnessed horrible riots in which more than a thousand persons perished. Again it was the Shiv Sena that was mainly responsible for the Bombay riots. Communal violence in Bombay surpassed all riots before and put the entire nation to shame. Bal Thackaray openly incited violence against Muslims.

The Bombay riots terrified the Indian Muslims and made them increasingly insecure. It was as a result of such sectarian and communal movements that ultimately the BJP-led government was established. In the post–Babri demolition period there have been no major communal riots, but the arrival of the BJP-led National Democratic Alliance government in power at the center and BJP governments in states such as Gujarat has worsened the communal situation. Greatly emboldened, the Sangh Parivar have appointed their personnel to key positions, especially in the highly sensitive educational and research institutions and police and armed forces. The RSS has also spread its tentacles throughout India, even reaching into those states where it had previously been unable to find a grip. More and more young people are being recruited by the RSS. The Vishwa Hindu Parishad has become highly aggressive and is again frustrating the Ramjanambhoomi temple construction, thereby intensifying communal tension. The communal situation is a cause for concern, even grave anxiety.

A New Front Against the Christian Minority

The Sangh Parivar has now opened a new front with fierce attacks on the Christian minority. It has accused Christian missionaries of converting Hindus to Christianity. An Australian Christian priest, Graham Staines, was burned alive along with two of his young sons in January 2000 by a local VHP leader in a small tribal village in Orrisa. Graham was falsely accused of converting the tribal people. In fact, he was working among the lepers in the village. In many such incidents, Christian priests have been targeted and some of them killed. A number of nuns have also been raped, including those in the Jhabua district of Madha Pradesh.

Because the BJP has a simple majority in Gujarat and can rule by itself without a coalition partner, the Sangh Parivar has become very aggressive in that area. The first attacks on Christians took place in the Dang district in Gujarat. Some Christian churches were demolished on Christmas Eve in 1999. In several other Gujarati towns, Christian priests, nuns, and churches were also attacked and these attacks are continuing. Various Christian groups and secular organizations have documented these attacks, which generally take place in remote village areas. The police, especially in Gujarat, are quite partisan. Either they remain spectators when Christian priests or institutions are attacked or they may even side with the attackers. The Christian community in India is very small—less than three percent—compared to the Muslims who are about 15 percent. And it is not possible to organize communal riots against them as in the case of Muslims. But the Sangh Parivar has generated a debate on conversions throughout India. As the Ram temple has become an issue, conversion too has become a political issue. The Ram temple conversion issue is also being blown out of all proportions. Conversions do take place, but they are few and far between. In fact the census data show that the Christian population has decreased. The anti-Christian tirade is mainly aimed at keeping the hard-core Hindu flock together, as the anti-Muslim tirade has lost its appeal to some extent.

Meeting the Challenge

The communal mobilization is mainly intended to capture power at the center and in various other states and to fulfill the dream of one day establishing a Hindu Rashtra. The Hindu middle class supports the Sangh Parivar as it opens the door of political and economic opportunities for them. The Muslim middle class supported the Muslim League for the same reasons in 1947. It is necessary to understand this play of forces to successfully fight communal forces in India. This conflict is not religious or theological in nature. As noted before, it is a misuse of religion for the purpose of grabbing political power and economic resources. In many cases, it is a feigned fanaticism.

Some NGOs are fighting against the menace of communalism, but their number is extremely limited. Very few NGOs, such as the Centre for Study of Society and Secularism[1] and Communalism Combat[2] from Bombay, devote themselves exclusively to this purpose. Most other NGOs join forces only in the event of a major communal riot. There are no concerted efforts to wage a single-minded battle against the communalist forces. The RSS carries on its communal campaign with missionary zeal. It has vast resources at its disposal, including human power. The NGOs can never match these resources. But they need to coordinate and network with each other. Only then will they be able to meet this challenge.

Asghar Ali Engineer is a civil engineer by profession, but gave up this career to be involved full time in academic work, and in activism for interreligious harmony. He is the chair of the Centre for Study of Society and Secularism, Bombay, and also director of the Institute of Islamic Studies. His research covers the communal problem in South Asia and Islamic issues, both theological and social. Asghar Ali Engineer has written and edited about forty-five books on these issues.

Notes

1. This organization regularly publishes *Secular Perspectives,* writings on communalism and secularism. See the Directory section in this volume for more information on this organization.
2. See: http://sabrang.com/cc/.

7.8.3

Demands for Autonomy: Internal Weaknesses of a Multiethnic, Multicultural, and Multinational State

Ashok Behuria

The greatest strength of Indian polity is its gravest weakness. India is hailed by many as a shining example of a multicultural, multiethnic, and multinational democratic state, which has successfully weathered many internal threats of disintegration. But still, the assertive face of multiple ethnocultural identities has worried many observers. Analysts have hinted at the Indian state's[1] diminishing capacity to address the developmental aspirations of the multiple ethnonational groups, who have begun to assert their right to autonomous self-administration within the broader framework of the Indian state. The unfolding internal divisions, characterized by lack of trust (if not distrust) among diverse ethnocultural groups, have threatened to wreck the Indian state from within. The assertive diversity of Indian society is thus perceived to be weakening the unitarian fabric of the Indian state.

In addition to internal demands that seek to redraw the internal borders, there have been demands for secession from the Indian state, which seek to redraw the external frontiers. The state, in spite of its nuclear strength, is thus confronted with problems that threaten to redefine its territorial configuration.

In this chapter an attempt is made to present the cases of demands for autonomy and analyze them critically. The demands for secession will be dealt with separately and comparison between the two will be made toward the end of the discussion.

Autonomy in the Indian Context

The issue of autonomy changes its connotation in the context of Indian polity and in this sociopolitical milieu has to be studied in a federal context. Autonomy in the classical sense would mean a community's legitimate, sovereign right to self-determination or self-legislation, unimpeded by any external

345

intervention. However, any attempt to study "autonomy" in the classical sense in the Indian case is bound to lead to conceptual delusions and contradictory conclusions. Autonomy in the Indian case has been primarily used to denote the demands of plural regional-ethno-national identities for a greater degree of self-administration within the larger federal framework of the Indian constitution. The other form of autonomy, which seeks to promote the idea of self-determination outside the purview of the Indian federation, is usually termed secessionist, antistatist, and antinational. For a clearer understanding, one could term the former an "integrationist model of autonomy" and the later a "disintegrationist model of autonomy."

Integrationist autonomy within the Indian union, without altering the central preponderance in the federal domain—which means dependence on (and not autonomous independence from) the central administration—has been accommodated, even after initial hesitation. In many cases, after the initial sanctioning of autonomous councils, the Indian state has granted statehood (status of a full-fledged federating unit with representative governance within the Indian union) to such autonomous units. Demands for "autonomy" within the Indian union but which seek to redefine the center-state (federation-unit) relations in favor of the states (units), have been viewed with suspicion and as a prelude to secession, which could lead to the breakup of the Indian state in the long term. This has often provoked the coercive might of the Indian state. In cases of demands for secession, the secessionist forces have often agreed to demands of greater autonomy, which would mean redefining the center-state relations. But the Indian state has not yet grown out of the postcolonial inertia of unitarian federalism to the degree that it can accommodate such demands. The obsession with a unitarian federal system has paralyzed the state's capacity to tackle such problems without violence. It is helpful to have a brief historical overview to elucidate these points.

Background

The Indian state was confronted with demands for the reorganization of the states (provinces or federating units) immediately after independence. Upon the recommendation of the States Reorganisation Committee (SRC) of 1953, headed by Fazal Ali, the provinces were reorganized on the basis of language. By the 1960s, the provinces seemed to have settled down within the redrawn boundaries. The larger province of Bombay was divided into Marathi-speaking Maharastra and Gujrati-speaking Gujrat. Punjab was trifurcated into a Punjabi-speaking Punjab, Hindi-speaking Haryana, and Pahari-speaking Himachal Pradesh. The Kannada-speaking areas of Bombay were transferred to the state of Mysore/Karnataka, and similarly, Telugu-speaking areas of the Madras province were transferred to Andhra Pradesh. The linguistic reorganization looked complete and the first phase of reorganization of the states within the Indian union was over.

Then came the demands for autonomy in the northeastern region. The aspirations of the tribal groups were soon recognized by the Indian state. The states of Manipur, Tripura, and Meghalay were formed in the late 1970s. The North Eastern Frontier Agency (NEFA) was granted statehood under the name of Arunachal Pradesh in 1987. The restive Nagas and the Mizos, however, were granted statehood only after violent encounters with the Indian state. The Naga insurgency continues until the present day, even after the formation of the state of Nagaland in 1956. The Mizo insurgency subsided after the 1973 agreement, which declared the Mizo district of Assam as a Union Territory. Mizoram was later granted full state status after the 1986 agreement with the rebel leader Laldenga.

However, this did not completely exhaust the aspirations for autonomous administration or statehood by many groups. The cultural differences within the overarching linguistic unity, in many cases, led to demands for statehood within the primarily language-based federating units of the Indian union.

The Telengana movement raged on until the 1980s in the less developed Telugu-speaking region in western Andhra Pradesh, which was under the rule of the Nizam of Hyderabad and was later merged with the more economically developed, Telugu-speaking, coastal Andhra Pradesh. The less assertive Kosala movement in western Orissa still continues. Similarly, the movements for Chhatisgarh in Madhya Pradesh, the Jharkhand movement in Bihar, Orissa, and Madhya Pradesh, and the movement for Uttaranchal/Uttarakhand in Uttar Pradesh, have been active since the 1950s until they were granted statehood in 2001. This has led to an intensification of demands for autonomy from other ethnocultural groupings within Indian society. Recent forceful demands for statehood for Vindhyanchal, Vidarbha, Haritdesh, Coorg, Kamtapur, Gorkhaland, Madhyadesh, Bundelkhand, and Purvanchal have demonstrated the rising aspirations of subcultural groupings to have their own autonomous administrative units.

In the 1950s and 1960s, in the wake of the movement for constitutional recognition of Hindi as the national language, there was a lurking suspicion in the minds of the political elite in the southern states of India that the elite of the northern region—perceived to be mainly of Aryan racial stock—were intent on subjugating the predominantly Dravidian south through their language policy. The anti-Hindi movement in the south had assumed violent proportions and there were demands for the secession of southern states and establishment of Drvidastan. The Indian state demonstrated remarkable wisdom in accommodating the demands of the southerners and recognized English as an official language along with Hindi.

However, this spirit of accommodation gradually gave way to a statist-integrationist zeal and all demands for autonomy were treated with force, leading to complications further down the line. The unwillingness of the state to share its authority with the constituent units was the primary reason for this "siege" attitude. During the 1980s, an increasingly closed and paranoid Indian state adopted a siege mentality when confronted by demands for autonomy, which bordered on secession. The demands for autonomous statehood within the Indian union were also unfavorably received by the central administration.

The 1980s saw the rise of secessionist movements in Punjab, Kashmir, and some of the northeastern states (Nagaland, Manipur, and Tripura). The movements for autonomy in several regions—Jharkhand, Chhatisgarh, Uttaranchal, and Gorkhaland—also gathered momentum and made their presence felt on the political horizon. The response of the ruling Congress Party under Rajiv Gandhi was to negotiate with the leaders of the more assertive movements. There were a series of accords with the Akali Dal leadership in Punjab, with the All Assam Students' Union (which later became Assam Gana Parishad), and with Gorkha leader Subhas Ghising in 1985. In all these cases, the central government led by the Congress Party seemed accommodating and granted some amount of autonomy to the assertive units. In the case of Jharkhand, the Congress tried to absorb the assertive leadership and thus defuse the movement.

However, during the 1990s when the movements for Uttaranchal, Jharkhand, and Chhatisgarh came to the fore, Congress was rather undecided about the question of granting autonomy to these regions. But the Bharatiya Janata Party (BJP)—the party currently leading the coalition in power in India—during the days of its ascendancy in the 1990s, exhibited a spirit of accommodation and openly supported the idea of statehood for aspiring groups. This also helped it gain political footholds in areas such as Jharkhand, western Orissa, and Uttaranchal. The reservations of the Congress leadership in December 1998 led the BJP to withdraw the Vananchal/Jharkhand Bill. However, the grant of statehood to Jharkhand, Uttaranchal, and Chhatisgarh in the year 2000 has conveyed an attitude of sympathy toward such assertions from the opposition as well as the parties in power at the center.

Three New States Within India

Jharkhand

The movement for the recognition of Jharkhand or Vananchal, as it was later called, had been supported for over fifty years by the Adivasi people of the Chhotanagpur Plateau–Santhal Parganas belt, which included eighteen districts from Bihar, four from Madhya Pradesh, three from West Bengal, and two from Orissa. This larger concept of Jharkhand was later dismissed in 1998 by the BJP's principal spokesperson for the cause, Babulal Marandi, the then union minister of state for environment and forests, as "politically unfeasible." In December the BJP had brought in a states reorganization bill to accord statehood on Jharkhand, but under stiff resistance from Rashtriya Janata Dal (RJD) and noncooperation from Congress, the bill fell through. In August 2000, Congress support was unanimous and with its pressure on RJD the bill was safely carried through both the houses of the Indian parliament. In November 2000, the state of Jharkhand came into being. Ironically, Babulal Marandi was one of the principal bidders for the chief minister's post in the new state. However, the present state of Jharkhand was carved out of the state of Bihar and did not comprise the districts from Orissa, West Bengal, and Madhya Pradesh.

Chhattisgarh

The Chhattisgarh (literally meaning "thirty-six forts") was formerly known as Dandakaranya, Gondvana, Dakshin Kaushal. Since Madhya Pradesh was constituted in 1956, at different times, various movements have agitated for the creation of Chhattisgarh state under the leadership of several leaders. Finally, the Madhya Pradesh state assembly, dominated by the Congress Party, passed a unanimous resolution to this effect on 18 March 1994. Subsequently, the BJP also took up the issue and reaped their political reward in the 1997 elections. In August 2000, the region was granted statehood by the Indian parliament.

Uttaranchal

The movement for Uttarakhand/Uttaranchal began in the early 1950s and came up for discussion in the States Reorganisation Committee in its deliberations between 1953 and 1955. It picked up recently after the reservation policy of the Mayawati government in Uttar Pradesh to reserve a quota of 27 percent for "other backward castes" in the Uttar Pradesh (UP) government services. Uttaranchal has a majority of higher-caste population (nearly 85 percent) and they objected to this policy for they feared marginalization of their share in governmental services. The local BJP unit promptly advocated the cause of a separate state of Uttarakhand and surprisingly the lower-caste parties such as the Bahujan Samaj Party of Mayawati and Samajwadi Janata Party of Mulayam Singh Yadav also supported the idea. This state also came into being in the year 2000.

The Apprehension

The openness of the political leadership to the idea of the formation of smaller states for electoral gains has led many analysts to conclude that such steps will open up a Pandora's box and demands for autonomous units will proliferate. This could well lead to a "remapping" of the Indian federation. In fact, the assertions by people of Kamtapur in West Bengal and the renewed demands of Gorkhas for a separate state have strengthened such suspicions. There have also been demands for statehood from other regions (Vidarbha, Harit Desh, Coorg, Vindhyanchal, Purvanchal). Many others are in the offing: Malwa, Kutch, Saurastra, Mithilanchal, Kosala (Western Orissa), etc. It may be useful to outline some of these upcoming demands for autonomy/statehood.

Vidarbha

Situated in northeast Maharastra, Vidarbha is an economically backward region but rich in mineral and forest resources. The economic viability of the Vidarbha region as a separate province was recognized by the State Reorganisation Committee in 1953–1955. However, the demand for a separate state/province for Vidarbha (which predates the Chhatisgarh and Uttaranchal movements) was subsumed in the Samyukta Maharastra movement (a movement for unification of all Marathi-speaking areas) in the 1960s and it was absorbed in the state of Maharastra. However, the demand for a Vidarbha state continued to be raised intermittently.

The Vidarbha Rajya Sangharsha Samiti ("Struggle for the Separate State of Vidarbha") and Maha-Vidarbha Sangharsha Samity ("Association for the Struggle for Greater Vidarbha"), the organizations that led this movement, gathered speed in the 1990s when BJP supported the idea of a separate Vidarbha state. A statutory development board for the region came into existence in 1994 in recognition of the need for developmental initiatives in the region. The BJP's advocacy had a political motive—it wanted to penetrate into the Vidarbha region, traditionally regarded as a bastion of the Congress Party. The BJP advocacy was, however, contested by its ally Shiv Sena in Maharastra, which is still wedded to the idea of preserving and nurturing "the emotional and linguistic unity of all Maharashtrians." In fact, in 1996, when the Vidarbha demand was raised, Shiv Sena supremo Bal Thackeray had vowed to lead the movement for statehood himself if the region's developmental backlog was not cleared within two years. Since the creation of three new states in August 2000, the demand for the Vidarbha state has gathered further momentum. The decision of the Congress Party apart from other parties on the issue will determine the course of the movement in the near future.

Vindhya Pradesh

Since the creation of Chhattisgarh state, a demand for "Vindhya Pradesh" has been raised by the politicians from the region headed by the speaker of the Madhya Pradesh legislative assembly, Srinivas Tiwari. Tiwari reportedly called twenty-five MLAs (members of the legislative assembly) to his residence in March 2000 to discuss the issue of a separate state of Vindhya Pradesh. This would comprise six districts of the Vindhya region: Datia, Tikamgarh, Rewa, Seedhi, Shehdol, and Satna. After the independence of India from the colonial rule, Vindhya Pradesh came into existence in 1948 and a government was installed in the state after the 1952 elections. However, it was merged with Madhya Pradesh in 1956. Thousands of people had protested the move and were jailed. On 10 March 2000, the state assembly unanimously adopted the nongovernment resolution to carve out a Vindhya state. The resolution had been forwarded to the central government in New Delhi and the center has yet to make a decision on this.

Coorg

The Kodagu Rajya Mukti Morcha (KRMM), which roughly translated means the Movement for the Liberation of the State of Kodagu, is an organization led by N. U. Nachappa that has campaigned for a separate state of Coorg to be carved out of the present state of Karnataka. The declaration by Deve Gowda, the then prime minister of India, in 1996 that Uttarakhand would soon be granted statehood, gave a further boost to this movement. The Kodagu or Coorg district is the smallest district in the southwest of the Karnataka state. Until its amalgamation into the Kannada state of Mysore (now Karnataka) on linguistic grounds following the recommendation of the States Reorganization Commission, the Coorg functioned as a Part "C" state from January 1952 to

1 November 1956—slightly less than five years. The KRMM sponsored the "Madikeri Declaration" of 22 November 1996, projected as the Cauveryland charter of rights, followed soon after the "Gowda Declaration," which formed the framework and the inspiration for the KRMM to lead Coorg to the "liberation of Kodagu and its creation as a separate Ethnic State." The KRMM was later known as the Coorg National Council (CNC) with Nachappa as its secretary-general. The CNC also has a web site to promote its cause.

Purvanchal

Purvanchal Mukti Morcha—roughly translated as Liberation Front for Purvanchal—headed by Raj Kumar Singh, first demanded a separate state of Purvanchal comprising twenty districts of eastern UP in 1996. This is a relatively backward area, and the "green revolution" that brought agricultural prosperity to the western districts of the state could not touch this area. The people in this area speak a local dialect, "Bhojpuri." The leaders of this area have often held the discriminatory policy of the Uttar Pradesh government responsible for the backwardness of the area. This has led them to demand a separate state. The Pragatisheel Bhojpur Samaj ("Progressive Bhojpuri Society") has made frequent demands for an even larger Bhojpur, comprising twenty-five districts of eastern UP and neighboring Bihar, with Varanasi as its capital, and inclusion of the Bhojpuri language in the Eighth Schedule of the Indian constitution.

Harit Desh

The SRC of 1953 debated the possibility of creating a separate state of Western Uttar Pradesh (Paschim Pradesh) and 97 out of the 100 MLAs from this region then submitted a memorandum to the SRC demanding the separation of the western districts. But it was discouraged by the Congress leadership of the time on the excuse that there was no public support behind the issue. This region has benefited most during the green revolution and the planned economy of the Nehru era and is a prosperous area. Recently, Ajit Singh, son of former prime minister Charan Singh and leader of the farmers, has called this region Harit Desh (the "Green Country") and convened a meeting of western UP leaders on 19 August 2000 to forcefully put his demand for a Harit Pradesh. Recently the BJP leadership expressed its willingness to support the demand purely for electoral advantage. The issue of Harit Desh is being debated now in India with great enthusiasm. The future of this movement will depend on the political mobilization of the people in the region and the interests the leaders of the movement take in the issue.

Bundelkhand

The Bundelkhand region of central India encompasses twelve districts of northern Madhya Pradesh (MP) and five districts of southern Uttar Pradesh. The area once known in history as Bundelkhand is identified with the districts of Jhansi, Lalitpur, Jalaun, Hamirpur, Banda, and Mahoba in Uttar Pradesh, Sagar, Chattarpur, Tikamgarh, Panna, and Damoh in Madhya Pradesh and parts of Gwalior, Datia, Shivpuri, and Chanderi. It is located in the central Hindi belt, south of the Yamuna River, between the fertile Gangetic plain stretching across northern UP and the highlands of central MP. This region has recently witnessed a movement for the recognition of the separate state of Bundelkhand led by Raja Bundela, a film actor.

Kamtapur

The movement for creating a separate state of Kamtapur from the state of West Bengal is being spearheaded by the Koch-Rajbangshis, who mainly inhabit areas in north Bengal and parts of Assam. Besides statehood, they are also demanding the inclusion of the Kamtapuri language in the Eighth Schedule and the propagation of the Kamtapuri language and culture through state-controlled radio and television. The two organizations taking the lead in this field are the Kamtapur Peoples' Party (KPP) and the Kamtapur Liberation Organisation (KLO). The former is more moderate; yet its leader, Atul Roy, reportedly said recently: "We will not abandon our demand for statehood, and if Rajbongshi mothers have to lose their sons for achieving the goal of statehood, so be it."[2]

The KLO is allegedly coordinating its militant activities with the United Liberation Front of Assam (ULFA), which is demanding formation of an independent Assam. The fledgling KLO militants are reportedly being groomed by seasoned militants from the ULFA in the Dooars region (known for its teas), the Buxa reserve forests, Cooch Behar and North Bengal's bordering areas with Assam, and Bangladesh. Recently, KLO activists have launched a number of attacks on Communist Party workers. The situation became so critical that police teams from Assam and West Bengal launched a joint operation code-named "Operation Shadow" in mid-November 2000 to arrest the activists. On 6 November 2000, Kamtapur activists descended in the thousands on the Nilmoni Airport in Cooch Behar town in support of the demand for a separate state of Kamtapur, and held a hugely successful mass rally. The movement for a Kamtapur state is progressing quickly at present. The Kamtapuris have also resorted to violence to uphold their cause.

Gorkhaland

Gorkhaland was granted autonomous council status in August 1985. However, in the wake of the recent formation of three new states, the Gorkhas have renewed demands for a separate state for the Gorkha people, comprising parts of the hill subdivisions of Darjeeling, Kurseong, and Kalimpong. The Gorkha National Liberation Front and the Gorkhaland United Front have recently marked the renewal of their agitation for Gorkhaland with a series of strikes.

Bodoland

Several Bodo insurgent groups have been working since the 1960s for goals that range from the establishment of a Bodo autonomous council, to a separate Bodo state within India, to total independence from India. The Bodos were granted an autonomous council in February 1993, but were unsatisfied with the amount of autonomy in this arrangement and demanded a separate state, which soon led to demands for "a sovereign Bodoland." The Bodos have taken to violence to drive their points home. Their violent expulsion of non-Bodos from the region has resulted in the displacement of more than 87,000 ethnic Santhals, and a smaller number of Bengalis and Nepalis have been displaced by the violent conflict between Bodo insurgents and non-Bodos in western Assam. Ethnic tension is rife in Assam, which is home to many ethnic groups. Some groups, such as the Assamese and Bodos, have lived in the region for many centuries. Others, including Bengalis, Santhals, and ethnic Nepalese, migrated there during the 1800s.

The campaign for Bodoland and its attendant violence continues unabated. However, the government's initiative to bring the Bodos to the discussion table is showing some promise. The recent meeting of some of the Bodo leaders with the Indian home affairs minister showed that the center is powerless as the Assam legislature would not approve a separate state of Bodoland at present. However, it may not be long before a separate state of Bodoland is carved out of Assam within the purview of the Indian constitution. On 18 January 2001, Mainao Daimary, publicity secretary of the Bodo Liberation Tigers, expressed satisfaction at the progress of peace talks between the outfit and the Indian government.

Disintegrationist Autonomy

The unity and integrity of the Indian state, mostly understood in the territorial sense, has clouded the central government's approach toward demands for confederal autonomy. In some cases, the movements for maximum autonomy have confronted the coercive might of the state and have become violent in nature. In such cases, the fear of disintegration has often led the state to react to such demands with a reflexive statist attitude—with sweeping, indiscriminate military aggression. In the case of Jammu and Kashmir and some of the northeastern states (such as Nagaland, Manipur, Assam, and Tripura) external support for autonomist-turned-secessionist demands has further complicated matters, compelling the defense mechanism of the Indian state to resort to intense counterinsurgency operations.

But research shows that in many cases, apart from external intervention, unimaginative handling of demands for "autonomy" within the Indian union has itself led to violence. Often it is this descent into violence that has invited external forces to fish in troubled waters. The unending cycle of violence has assumed an "autonomy" of its own and refuses to subside. The example of Kashmir and many instances from the northeast corroborate such a point of view. The autonomy provision for the state of Jammu and Kashmir that is written into the Indian constitution via Article 370 and the articles that seek to determine the relative autonomy of the northeastern states have time and again emerged as irritants for the central administration.

Threats of Secessionism and the State's Response

Threats of secession from certain sections of the population in Jammu and Kashmir, Punjab, and Nagaland in the Northeast played a great role in legitimizing the centralization of power throughout the 1980s and even in the 1990s. The influence of external forces in all these cases and the tendency of such subversion to spread into other autonomist movements in neighboring areas (Manipur, Tripura, Assam) has further strengthened the arguments favoring a strong center in India in recent years. This has pushed other evolving paradigms of federalism onto the back burner.

On the other hand, the prejudiced response of the Indian state has aggravated many autonomist movements. Any assertion on religious or ethnic grounds has been regarded as inimical to the central principle of unity and integrity of the state and treated with disdain and force. This has worsened matters in Punjab, the Northeast, and even in Jammu and Kashmir. Examination of the initial demands of the autonomists (the Sikhs in the Anandpursahib resolution, the Kashmir resolution for autonomy, or even the demands of the ULFA and Bodos) shows that "threats of secessionism" were mostly made as a bargaining chip. The reactive policies of the state then prepared the grounds for external intervention. The hostile militarism of the state has either induced militancy in some cases or sustained preexisting militancy in some other cases. It is important to note here that in some cases, such as Punjab, the central government has unwittingly nurtured future militants. Congress Party patronage to Jarnail Singh Bhindranwale is a case in point.

The Case of Kashmir

Any demand for autonomy from the people of Kashmir—the state that began as a special federating unit in the Indian union—has been treated as an act of disloyalty toward the union. Ironically, such autonomy was granted to the Kashmiris in Article 370 of the Indian constitution and reinforced by the Jawaharlal Nehru–Sheikh Abdullah accord in 1952 and the Mirza Afzal Beg–G. Parthasarathy talks of 1977. The summary rejection of an autonomy bill, passed in the Jammu and Kashmir assembly by the central BJP dispensation in 2000, suggests the strength of the fundamental suspicion with which the Kashmiri people are regarded.

However, the notion of confederal autonomy initially granted by Article 370 has kept the Kashmiri passion for autonomy alive to the present day. In fact, "autonomy" has cropped up as a safety valve on many occasions. Seeking to absorb Kashmiri disenchantment with the Indian union on the one hand, and ignite the flames of secession or independence on the other, the call for autonomy has proved a halfway house between irrevocable union with the Indian state and complete *azadi* (independence). The recent espousal of the autonomy cause by Farooq Abdullah, the chief minister of Kashmir, and the rise of popular support for autonomy in the Gallup polls, prove this contention.

The saddest aspect of the whole Kashmir-centric discourse on autonomy has been the overwhelming resistance it has evoked from various quarters to the idea of such a confederal proposition, advocating a rather loose union with the central administration. Any idea of refederalizing the Indian polity with the grant of a greater share of residuary powers has been rejected as an almost blasphemous suggestion. In the face of shrinking economic power with the onset of globalization, perhaps the Indian state has been reluctant to shed its political power lest that would in the long term crystallize disruptive forces at the peripheries and weaken its bases of unity and integrity.

Analysis

It is useful to analyze the causes of rising ethnocultural assertions in the Indian case. The preceding discussion covers some empirical cases and each case is unique and deserves separate analytical study. However, for the benefit of understanding such autonomist and/or secessionist movements, it is immensely helpful to draw upon the analyses of various scholars and look for the common strands of explanation. Various studies on the movements covered here reveal that the demands for autonomy arise out of the following causes:

• Decline of the capacity of the state to cater to the rising aspirations of ethnocultural groups and an attendant temptation to legitimize violence/force as a means of resolving crises arising out of demands placed on the state.

• The spread of political awareness naturally leads people to make demands for their rights. And such claims of rights have been viewed with suspicion by the ruling elite in many occasions, compelling the claimants to adopt violent postures leading to subversion and insurgencies.

• Growing political awareness has also made people aware of their socioeconomic conditions and the causes of their disadvantages or advantages. In many cases, in the existing states there is a system of what Marxist scholars of development would call "internal colonization" in both economic and cultural senses. Awareness of real or perceived discrimination tends to ignite aspirations for self-legislation and autonomy among a marginalized population.

• Rising economic insecurities that have visited many developing and underdeveloped states in the wake of globalization have created the bases for popular disaffection and expanded the bases of political mobilization on grounds of primordial loyalties.

• Globalization has also weakened the capacity of the sate to manage such socioeconomic crises with competence.

• The system of democracy that is practiced in many of the developing and underdeveloped societies in the Third World puts more emphasis on the mechanism of democratic governance than on values of democracy and liberalism. The consequent calculus of electoral politics has led to the growth of an immensely stratified entrepreneurial elite, especially in multicultural/pluralist societies like India, who have sought to build their constituencies on ever-proliferating ethnocultural identities. This has fractured the existing civil society and ruptured the uniting links and necessitated the introduction of fresh and refined bonds of unity. The state with its inertial status-quo-ism has failed to take the lead by redefining its relations of power with the constituent units. This has led to systemic violence.

• The Indian federation has temperamentally behaved as a "union" and not a "federation." However, the leadership in the country has to take care to adopt federal principles to judge such cases of autonomy and gradually devolve powers (especially financial powers) to the units if it is to contain such ethno-cultural assertions.

Among all these explanations there is a common thread of argument that says that the shrinking capacity of the state, underdevelopment, and the politicization of plural peripheral identities, together with the search for power by neo-elites at the margins, have snapped the interethnic and intercultural bonds that have so far drawn them together. This has created new identities and led to an overwhelming craze for autonomy or self-legislation. It is interesting to note that the concessions of statehood in the recent cases were conditioned by sheer electoral calculations and not by considerations of economic viability. And these concessions in no way altered the basic constitutionally guaranteed relationship between the federation and the units, which is lopsided in favor of the federation. Creation of "dependent" states will in no way improve the conditions, and the passion for a greater degree of autonomy will haunt the Indian states until a genuinely devolved refederalized system of governance grows out of the present system of unitarian federal democracy in India.

Ashok K. Behuria is assistant director, International Centre for Peace Studies, New Delhi. He has a Ph.D. in international relations from Jawaharlal Nehru University, New Delhi, and has written extensively on India-Pakistan relations, the autonomy issue in Kashmir, refugees and human rights, and interstate relations in South Asia.

Notes

1. Unless categorically mentioned as the Indian state, "state" will mean federating units in the discussion.

2. See Atol Roy, quoted online in *India Abroad,* 8 August 2000: http://www.indiaabroad.com.

7.8.4

The Background to the
Violent Conflicts in India

Kristoffel Lieten

Attention has regularly been drawn to armed conflicts in India. In addition to the recurrent border conflict with Pakistan, there have been communal clashes (involving Hindus and Muslims), ethnic conflicts (particularly in Northeast India between various tribal groupings and immigrant populations), homeland movements (Bodo in Assam and Bru in Mizoram), independence movements (as in Kashmir and Nagaland), and agrarian class conflicts (Senas in Bihar and Naxalites) in some other states as well.

It is a multifaceted field of conflict and the various conflicts have intricate causes. They are related to the enormity of the subcontinent, the multiethnicity of its population, and the political and economic feeding grounds of discontent. Political expedience and the profusion of examples for imitation have added a dynamism of their own.

The government of India has been dealing with such conflicts since independence in 1947. It may be argued that, in view of the various challenges mentioned above, it has not done too badly. Some of the conflicts in the past have been solved and other conflicts have been contained within reasonable limits. Conflicts could have escalated and could have triggered further conflicts, but, by and large, this has not happened. Most areas in the country are peaceful and subject to law and order.

If one attempts to explain the relative absence of conflicts—we shall see shortly that there are nevertheless intractable and dramatic conflicts—one could suggest the following elements. The New Delhi government's state machinery is reasonably functional, and its decentralized governance means that a number of responsibilities have been delegated to the state governments. It had also ensured, at least until the 1990s when neoliberal policies were introduced, that regional disparities were kept in check and that class and caste polarization did not escalate. This was done by reallocating resources, by positive discrimination, by state intervention in the agrarian system, and by directing (private and government) investment to backward areas.

Underlying the relative stability was also a sense of unity that most Indians, despite regional subnationalisms, had about their Indianness. This perception of a common Indian nation was forged in the course of the long struggle for independence. An important element in this respect was the growth of a civil society long before the concept entered Western development theory. Students, peasants, workers, women, youth, artists, and other sections of society had their own organizations, usually front organizations for political parties. They mobilized the people below and put pressure on the government institutions above. By the late 1980s, externally financed NGOs began to play an important role and took up various human-rights and advocacy causes.

However, there are also a number of factors that have helped to stimulate conflicts and violence. The insurgency in some parts of the country, where civil society organizations could have contributed immensely to a de-escalation of the conflict, has seriously damaged the impartiality of the NGOs and the local front organizations. Their impartiality in the conflicts has frequently turned out to be suspect. Civil-society organizations were often caught up in the sectarian agenda of the insurgents' groups. Human-rights activists and oppositional voices within the insurgent communities not infrequently have been the first victims of violent attacks; many persons and institutions that were seeking to build moderate, democratic, and secular structures have been silenced.

In the very same regions, unfortunately, the state structures and the political parties also have been affected by the terrorist organizations and insurgent groups. Many of the movements are linked to overground organizations, contractors, political parties, and even the lower and higher echelons in the state bureaucracy, who in exchange for protection and indirect or direct support are willing to cooperate with gangs and even actively stimulate them.

This cooperation causes destruction and bloodshed, but the human suffering usually occurs at the fringes, rather than around the corridors of power: in the remote countryside and in the far-flung provinces. Deaths in foreign incidents and disasters sometimes receive wider press coverage than the killings in Bihar or Tripura. These conflicts may be regarded merely as distant thunder, and the resolution of such conflicts may then require less urgency.

Political conflicts in India have always involved political parties and hence political parties will have to be part of the solution of any conflict. Herein lies an opportunity but also a basic weakness in conflict resolution. Political parties indeed often have a hand in manipulating conflicts.

It is not uncommon for the government of India to refer to the "foreign hand." In the distant past, the U.S. CIA was often quoted as the instigator behind the various conflicts in Kashmir and in Northeast India. China has also been accused of involvement in the latter conflict and in the Naxalite Maoist rebellion. And the ISI (Pakistani secret service) has, of course, been accused of supporting terrorist incidents in Kashmir, Punjab, and the Northeast.

Some evidence has been provided for foreign interference. External scapegoating, however, has also served political purposes. The external hand more often than not has been an internal hand, namely the ruling party at the center (the union government in New Delhi). In its ambition to remain in power, and weaken opposition forces, the Indian National Congress (INC), when it was still dominant in Indian politics, repeatedly worked with reactionary, sectarian, and violent organizations in order to steal the thunder of the opposition parties.

For example, the alliance of the INC with the National Alliance, the ruling party in Kashmir, has invoked all kinds of undemocratic means in order to prevent political alternatives from emerging. Indira Gandhi was particularly deft at these political games. It was she who released Sheikh Abdullah, the Kashmir leader, from jail after having signed a deal with him that tied his hands. It was she who groomed Bhindrawale, who was responsible for the orgy of violence that disrupted Punjab in the 1980s. She increasingly sought to make deals with ethnic groupings in order to get them on her side politically. Her son, Rajiv Gandhi, continued this policy. The so-called communalization of politics (the reliance on religious communities) took place during his period of governance.

The government led by the Bharatiya Janata Party BJP from 1998 onwards has behaved no differently. While the ethnic violence escalated in Tripura and the state government, which was then led by the Communist Party, requested the army and the Central Reserve Police Force (CRFP) to intervene, particularly during local elections in May 2000, the central government refused to do so. It allowed the election rigging, the killings, and the kidnappings to continue. While massacres took place in the "killing fields" of Bihar (in confrontations between the Naxalites and the Ranvir Sena), deployment of the CRFP to the

Islamabad, Pakistan: Poster opposing the Indian "occupation" of Kashmir

center-left government in the state was also withheld. The BJP has repeatedly been accused of having a political understanding with the Ranvir Sena, Bodo tribal movement, and the Naga insurgents, among others.

Particularly at the periphery, India's centralized federalism has been most seriously tested and the machinations of Congress and BJP politicians have worked to damage the integrity of India. Rather than working with the moderate elements in the states, political expediency has too often eliminated these moderate elements and has preferred some kind of settlement with the extremist movement.

In the regional conflicts, there thus appears to have been an internal hand. However there has also been a form of foreign involvement that can be termed long-distance nationalism. Expatriate Indians in foreign lands often tend to cultivate their roots, and in the process become more ethnically conscious than they would have been in India. In other words, while abroad, rather than emphasizing their shared national identity, they fall back on their regional roots, especially when their emigration was politically motivated. The long-distance nationalism of Kashmiri and Naga émigrés, for example, operates on the basis of an international network that helps feed the nationalists at home and that tends to be more uncompromising and more fixed on cultural symbols than the people back home.

Leaders of the movements based in India itself usually belong to the middle classes—student organizations are prominently in the forefront—who wish to set themselves apart from others by focusing on the unique ethnic identities that are said to be threatened by the nationalist state, the other ethnic people, and the inchoate cultural "mainstream." They claim to lead a "freedom struggle" against a homogenizing state. The underlying motives and ideologies are often more correctly interpreted in terms of conflicting competition over limited resources, especially land and (government) employment. Various questions of cultural identity, political autonomy, and economic exploitation combine as an explanation for the conflicts. It is common for the middle class leadership to accentuate the culture of differences rather than the common economic interests that unite most of the poor people in the area concerned.

A disturbing trend, moreover, is the widening network of extortion, criminal and quasi-legal operations that the leadership of these organizations now commands. These activities not only fuel and finance militancy, but, more significantly, have had an extremely corrosive and corrupting impact on democratic institutions and structures in the state. There has also been a continuous process of "lumpenization" as growing numbers of common criminals join in the activities of the organization. This has been the case not only with right-wing organizations, including most "insurgents" in Northeast India, but also with left-wing organizations such as the Naxalites.

Many of the conflicts remain intractable. The various cases *discussed* in this volume (Kashmir, Naxalites, Ranvir Sena, and the multiple insurgencies in Northeast India) illustrate how, so far, conflict dynamics have outstripped conflict solution.

Kristoffel Lieten (Belgium, 1946) is an associate professor at the Amsterdam School of Social Sciences of the University of Amsterdam (lieten@pscw.uva.nl). Since his studies at the Jawaharlal Nehru University in New Delhi in the early 1970s, he has done extensive research on political and social developments in South Asia. He has worked as the South Asia correspondent of the Dutch and Belgian Radio and has become a regular media commentator. He has cofounded the Dutch National India Committee and has written several books on various aspects of politics, history, and rural development in India.

7.8.5

Jammu and Kashmir:
Half a Century of Conflict

Kristoffel Lieten[1]

For more than half a century the territory of Kashmir has been contested by India and Pakistan. In 1947 it was split between two countries that have been at loggerheads ever since. Since the late 1980s, the emergence of a violent militant movement has intensified internal strife, resulting in at least 30,000 deaths at the hands of the Indian army and the various terrorist organizations. The decision by India and Pakistan in 1999 to restart their bilateral dialogue has created the preconditions for a movement toward a political settlement, and developments within Pakistan under President Musharraf appeared to have reduced the support for a Muslim jihad in Kashmir. Over the last three years, periods of cease-fire declared by the insurgents or by the Indian government have alternated with an escalation in violence. The war against Afghanistan may once again have changed the equations in Jammu and Kashmir. In January 2002 Musharraf banned five extremist organizations that have been responsible for much of the violence in Kashmir and that brought the two countries to the brink of a new war after a terrorist attack on the Indian parliament in December 2001.

The modern history of Kashmir can be traced to the Treaty of Amritsar, signed between the British government and Maharaja Gulab Singh in 1846. According to Article 1 of the treaty, the British government transferred to the maharaja the mountainous country with its dependencies situated eastward of the River Indus and westward of the River Ravi. The descendants of the maharaja continued as sovereign princes until British colonial power left the Indian subcontinent in August 1947. The subcontinent was partitioned between India and Pakistan, and the more than 550 princely states, which had not been incorporated in British India and some of which were on the borderline between India and Pakistan, had to decide on their future allegiance.

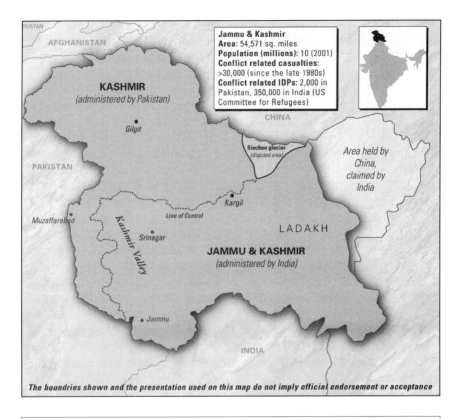

Jammu & Kashmir
Area: 54,571 sq. miles
Population (millions): 10 (2001)
Conflict related casualties:
>30,000 (since the late 1980s)
Conflict related IDPs: 2,000 in
Pakistan, 350,000 in India (US
Committee for Refugees)

KASHMIR
(administered by Pakistan)

Gilgit

CHINA

Siachen glacier
(disputed area)

Area held by
China,
claimed by
India

PAKISTAN

Kargil

Line of Control

LADAKH

Muzaffarabad

Srinagar

Kashmir Valley

JAMMU & KASHMIR
(administered by India)

Jammu

INDIA

The boundries shown and the presentation used on this map do not imply official endorsement or acceptance

Jammu and Kashmir, on the Indian side of the line of demarcation (or LOC: line of control) between Indian and Pakistan, comprise three distinct regions: Jammu, the Kashmir Valley, and Ladakh. Indian nationalists prefer to add three more regions outside the Indian borders: Azad Kashmir, the Northern Areas (Gilgit and Baltistan), and Aksai Chin (China). The Sunni Muslims constitute the majority in the valley and in Azad Kashmir; the Kashmiri Brahmins, Dogras, and Sikhs are the most significant groups in the Jammu region. In addition, there are Buddhists, living mainly in the Ladakh region; Shia Muslims, settled around Kargil; and Sunni and Ismaili in the Northern Areas.

Some of the districts that fall within India are heavily populated; other districts such as Kargil (eight people per square mile) are sparsely populated. Around 65 percent of the population are Muslims, most of whom live in the Kashmir Valley. Hindus (33 percent of the population) are more populous in the Jammu region, but a number of districts in that region also have a Muslim majority. Population growth per decade is quite high: around 30 percent. The literacy rate in 2001 of 66 percent for males and 54 percent for females was the second lowest of all Indian states. Politics in Jammu and Kashmir has been dominated by the family of Sheikh Abdullah, the founder of the National Conference (NC), and his son Farooq Abdullah. The absence of democracy within the party and the weakness of the parliamentary opposition have kept political allies of New Dehli, like the Abdullah family, in power and have allowed high levels of corruption and nepotism to continue.

The Hindu ruler Maharaja Hari Singh then held dominion over Jammu and Kashmir. Four actors staked their claim to political dominance over the princely state. The government of India wanted to include the Muslim-dominated territory as proof of the multireligious, secular character of India. It was supported by Sheikh Abdullah, who in 1932 had founded the All Jammu and Kashmir Muslim Conference, and later, significantly had changed the name to All Jammu and Kashmir National Conference (NC). The NC was fighting for a representative government within independent India and was supported by the Indian National Congress led by Jawaharlal Nehru. The third actor, Pakistan, claimed to provide a nation-state to Muslims and thus to Kashmiri Muslims as well. The fourth actor was the autocratic ruler Maharaja Gulab Singh, who initially preferred to continue the autonomy of his princely state.

While the maharaja was deliberating on which option to take, Pushto (Pathan) tribesmen and other Pakistani armed intruders sought to capture Kashmir by force. They occupied Muzafarabad on 22 October 1947, and then headed for Srinagar. The maharaja appealed to India for help. The authorities in New Delhi decided that Indian troops could be sent only after Kashmir acceded to India. Around 26 October 1947, Maharaja Hari Singh signed the Instrument of Accession. With the political support of the undisputed popular leader of Kashmir, Sheikh Abdullah, the Indian army pushed the intruders back. India accused Pakistan of aiding the intruders and entered Pakistani territory in pursuit of the invaders. Full-scale fighting between the armies of both countries continued until December 1947, with one-third of the bigger Kashmir territory remaining under the control of Pakistan. The old princedom had been effectively bifurcated.

The Indian government decided to refer the case to the UN Security Council and lodged a complaint on 1 January 1948. The UN Commission for India and Pakistan (UNCIP) was established to investigate and mediate the dispute. A benchmark UNCIP decision on 13 August 1948 called for an immediate cease-fire and asked for the withdrawal of Pakistani troops from the disputed area. The withdrawal of troops was to take place in two stages. Only after the vacation of the Pakistani side was complete would India withdraw its own troops from the occupied territory, except for a minimum force needed to maintain law and order within the lines existing at the moment of cease-fire. A third part of the resolution stated that the future of Kashmir would be decided "in accordance with the will of the people." Pakistan objected to withdrawing its forces ahead of an Indian pullout.

Except for the first phase envisaged by the resolution (the withdrawal of Pakistani forces), there has been no progress regarding the other two provisions of the 13 August resolution. The cease-fire was able to preserve the peace until 1965. Following the two Indo-Pakistani wars of 1965 and 1971, India and Pakistan reached two major agreements regarding Kashmir. The 1965 war resulted in an agreement in Tashkent in January 1966 reaffirming the commitment of both the countries to settle their disputes through peaceful means, and to respect the cease-fire lines. The 1972 Simla Declaration, which followed the 1971 war, was more specific. Both India and Pakistan agreed on the exact location of the Line of Control (LOC).

During the 1970s and the 1980s, the two countries refrained from open confrontation. As allies of the two antagonistic power blocs in the Cold War, India and Pakistan strengthened their armies and positioned their army divisions along the LOC. Occasional skirmishes and artillery exchanges have occurred, but usually of little significance. In the 1990s, conflicts tended to multiply, and in May 1999, the Indian army began a military offensive that came quite close to a new war. The offensive was said to be a reaction to what India called the incursion by "Pakistani irregulars and troops" in the high mountain ranges around Kargil, overlooking the Leh-Srinagar highway. Fighting, involving combat aircraft, continued for three months and ended with the withdrawal of the irregulars. Again, in October 2001, while the U.S. secretary of state was visiting both countries to shore up support for the "war on terrorism," Indian artillery pounded Pakistani positions along the LOC, and a serious exchange of fire followed. Both sides seemed intent on drawing the United States onto their side in tacit exchange for support, but by and large the LOC remains respected by both sides.

After the accession of the princely state to India, Sheikh Abdullah, often called the Sher-I-Kashmir (the "Lion of Kashmir"), and Jawaharlal Nehru negotiated the 1953 Delhi Agreement between the state and the Indian union. The government of India accorded Kashmir a special status, unlike the other Indian states, with the power to enact legislation on a residuary list of subjects, to elect its own governor, to have its own flag, to be outside the jurisdiction of the supreme court of India, and to have its own constitution. The union government in New Delhi soon thereafter, however, started retracting on its commitment and many of the special constitutional arrangements were suspended. For two long periods, Sheikh Abdullah was put in jail and when he was released from jail in 1975, he joined forces with Prime Minister Indira Gandhi, accepting the constitutional changes.

Politically, Jammu and Kashmir thereafter appeared to have joined the mainstream of Indian politics. The National Conference struck opportunistic alliances with whatever political grouping currently formed the union government in New Delhi and appeared to have electoral and popular support in the valley. Elections, however, except possibly for the 1977 elections, were rigged and faith in the democratic process receded. Discontent with faltering development, lack of democracy, and widespread corruption from around 1990 onward formed a breeding ground for pro-Pakistani and anti-Indian forces and terrorist organizations. Because of this danger, sensing a pro-Pakistani pull among the Kashmiri electorate, the government of India has never really allowed genuine democracy to take root.

Conflict Dynamics

The UNCIP was initially more sympathetic to the position of India. It did not ask for a simultaneous withdrawal, but instructed Pakistan to withdraw its troops prior to the Indian withdrawal. At that time India was closer to the United States than Pakistan was: whereas Nehru in 1949 was invited to visit the United States by President Harry Truman, his Pakistani counterpart, Liaquat Ali Khan, accepted an offer to visit Moscow. However, the equations soon started changing: India moved closer to the Soviet Union and became an important leader of the Movement of Non-Aligned Countries; Pakistan joined U.S.-led military organizations. This polarization, which followed in the wake of the intensification of the Cold War, was probably the reason behind the arrest of Sheikh Abdullah, the popular prime minister of Kashmir, who took a stronger position on independence than many of his cabinet colleagues. In 1953, after the visit of Adlai Stevenson, Sheikh Abdullah was arrested for his "subversive speeches."

Initially, in the early 1950s, India made a number of decisions that responded to the urge for autonomy in Kashmir. Kashmir was accorded an exceptional position, limiting the extent the union government could interfere with state legislation. Soon, however, the Indian government, when a section of the Kashmiri leadership called for further devolution of power, started victimizing the local leadership. Sher-I-Kashmir Sheikh Abdullah in August 1953 was put behind bars for his alleged conspiracy with the United States. When he was released in 1975 after three long terms of imprisonment, he agreed to officially sign an agreement in which a number of the exceptional regulations for Jammu and Kashmir were scrapped.

For thirty years after the mid-1950s, when gradually the exceptional status that Kashmir had been accorded was dissipated, the conflict had been lingering when toward the late 1980s, the first violent skirmishes, involving the Jammu and Kashmir Liberation Front (JKLF), took place. In late 1988 the JKLF started a campaign for independence that brought about a sudden and rapid escalation of violence, especially in the Kashmir Valley. Agitated mobs, carrying pictures of Zia-ul-Haq, the Pakistani military dictator, clashed with the police in Srinagar in February and March 1989. Strikes brought many cities to a standstill and in April of that year bands of militants for the first time confronted the police with AK-47 automatic weapons. The paradise on earth, as Kashmir was once called, was fast turning into a hell with bomb blasts, shoot-outs, and violent clashes involving angry mobs and the police. The situation dramatically returned to the conditions experienced in the period after Sheikh Abdullah was arrested in 1953 and when people took to the street in a similar wave of protest.

Two developments that led to the dramatic eruption of popular protest were internal to local politics and two were associated with national politics.

The absolute lack of democratic expression in Kashmir came into the open during the 1987 state assembly elections. Not only were the elections manipulated by the Abdullah family and the NC, this time in alliance with the Indian Congress Party, ruling at New Delhi, but in the aftermath of the elections, many leaders and activists of the opposition alliance were arrested on charges of antinational activities. The expression of anger against unemployment and corruption by decades of autocratic "family rule" was not allowed through the ballot box. The widespread alienation, especially among the unemployed youth, soon found expression in a more militant form. Abdul Ghani

Lone, the charismatic leader of the People's Conference, was quoted as saying: "If people are not allowed to cast their votes where will their venom go
except into expression of anti-national feelings?" The second development of
an internal nature was the numerous human-rights violations by the administration and especially by the police and the Border Security Force (BSF). Various reports by Amnesty International and Human Rights Watch have been
discarded by the government as foreign-instigated propaganda. Indian media,
however, have also reported numerous cases of discrediting behavior by the
administration and by the BSF. When, for example, Jagmohan, a governor
renowned for his toughness, was sent by New Delhi to Jammu and Kashmir
for a second term in 1990, *India Today* reported (February 1990):

> With Kashmir on fire, the new government has once again turned to Jagmo-
> han. In Jammu, people danced on the streets to celebrate his appointment. But
> the euphoria was short-lived. Even before Jagmohan could reach Srinagar,
> hundreds of police and paramilitary forces fanned out into downtown ghet-
> tos and conducted brutal house-to-house searches, smashing electronic items,
> insulting women and children by parading them in the cold.

Even more serious human-rights violations by the Indian army created a fertile soil for opposition forces, even for organizations with a more fundamentalist Muslim character.

The mobilization of secessionist sentiment took place in the context of
two external developments. A violent campaign, including gruesome terrorist
attacks, had been going on in the neighboring state of Punjab where radical
Sikhs claimed independence from India, and which led ultimately to the murder of Indira Gandhi. The other development was the *jihad* that was under way
in Afghanistan against the communist infidels of the Soviet-backed regime.
Fighters for Islamic purity, who had been trained in Pakistan for deployment
in Afghanistan from 1992 onwards, when the *mujahedeen* were victorious in
Kabul, were redirected toward Kashmir. The *jihadi* groups had little support on
the ground, but could thrive in conditions where the state and central governments had failed to arrest institutional decay and improve socioeconomic conditions. In the years that followed, the anti-India militancy had access to sophisticated weapons and was maintained by a unending stream of suicide squads. It
is difficult to judge how successful they were in enlisting the support of the people in the valley. They are possibly in the same position as the Indian security
forces who are also blamed for excesses, custodial deaths, and extortion.

The eruption of violence is clearly illustrated by the enclosed graph (Figure 7.8.5.1), which is based on official figures and may understate the number of victims. Some accounts put the number of people killed during the
1990s at 60,000, around double the official figures. Whatever the magnitude,
it is clear that before 1990 the Kashmir Valley was relatively free of violence.
What is also clear is that many of the people killed were innocent Hindu and
Muslim citizens. They were killed either as unlucky victims in encounters between armed forces or as targets of terrorist attacks. Moderate Muslims, Sikhs,
and Hindu Brahmins have been targeted intentionally. Among the latter group,

Figure 7.8.5.1   Insurgency-Related Casualties in Kashmir, 1988–2000

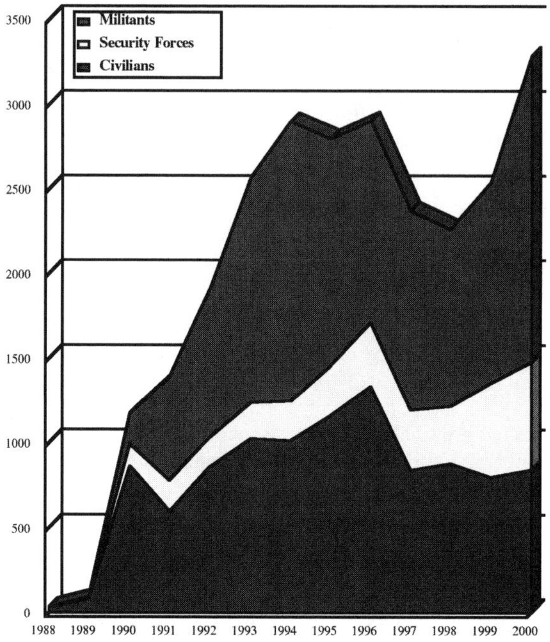

Source: http://www.satporg/india/J&K/Table.html, based on Government of India sources

the so-called *pundits,* many families starting leaving their ancestral living places and migrated to the Jammu region and to other places, including New Delhi. Poor Kashmiri Muslims had nowhere to go and remained caught up in unsettled conditions.

By the end of 1998 it was clear to most analysts that the political and security situation inside Jammu and Kashmir had changed. Despite occasional violent events, life in Kashmir seemed to be returning to "normal" (see also the dip in the accompanying graph). Elections were conducted in 1996, the NC of Farooq Abdullah tied up with the National Democratic Alliance led by the Hindu nationalist Bharatya Jana Party (BJP). An economic and political package to strengthen the economy and security of the region was implemented. The indications were that the administration of civil supplies has somewhat improved and that security forces maintained a lower profile, improving living conditions in the state. Much of the opportunity, however, was lost with the eruption of the Kargil war in May 1999.

After the Kargil war, after the failure of the Vajpayee/Musharraf summit in Agra, and particularly after the allied offensive against Afghanistan, violent attacks appear to have escalated. Particularly, the attack on Afghanistan helped to inflame sentiments in Kashmir and some terrorist organizations went on a spree of violence. A bomb set off in October 2001 in front of the legislative assembly killed thirty-eight people in one of the most gruesome scenes that the state has ever witnessed. An even more significant attack was the assault by five armed men on the Indian parliament in New Delhi on 13 December 2001. The government of India was quick to point out that the terrorists were members of the Pakistani organizations and started preparing for military retaliation on Pakistani territory. The government of Pakistan, unlike the government in New Delhi, wanted to solve the conflict through the intervention of the UN, but in its efforts was repeatedly rebuffed by a belligerent attitude on the Indian side. The danger of a new war lasted for one month, until President Musharraf announced his decision to ban five extremist organizations.

The nature of militancy in Kashmir had greatly changed. It was calculated that in 1998–1999, the majority of militants came from outside the region rather than from inside. In the early 1990s, the JKLF, a Kashmiri youth force, dominated militancy. In the mid-1990s, the Hizbul *mujahedeen,* which included also many elements from Azad Kashmir and some Pakistani elements from elsewhere, was the dominant force. Since 1996, coinciding with the Taliban takeover in Kabul, the Lashkar and other militant Islamic groups from Pakistan and Afghanistan have taken over. The Kashmir youths have joined these terrorist organizations as subsidiary forces. The implication is also that political control has become more and more external to Kashmiri society, and that negotiations have become even more difficult. The militant groups operating inside Kashmir on the Indian side of the LOC are not necessarily pro-Pakistan, but because of the military and logistic support received from within Pakistan during the 1990s, pro-Pakistani groups such as the Lashkar-e-Toiba, Hizbul *mujahedeen,* and Jaish-e-Mohammad have become more powerful. Lashkar e Toiba is the militant wing of a religious organization (Markaz), founded in 1987 by Arabs and Pakistanis. The Lashkar has resources including iron and garment factories to generate its own income, and is fairly independent of the Pakistani secret service (ISI) and the Pakistani government. The Harkat-ul-Mujahedeen was earlier known as the Harkat-ul-Ansar, but changed its name after the United States declared it a terrorist group in 1997, following the kidnapping of five Western tourists in Kashmir in 1995. The Harkat belongs to the Deobandi-Wahabi faith and has close links with the Taliban. Its members are mostly Afghans and have been trained in weapons operation, including Stinger missiles, by the ISI and the CIA to fight the Soviets in Afghanistan. When the Najibullah government was overrun by the *mujahedeen,* they were sent to other parts of the world, from Albania and Bosnia to Kashmir. Jaish-e-Mohammad was formed by Maulana Masood Azhar after he was released by India after negotiations following the hijacking of an Indian Airlines aircraft in December 1999. Maulana Masood Azar, a former member of the Harkat, has the support of a large number of Deobandi *madrassas* of Pakistan, and, like the Harkat, has close links with the Taliban. Finally, the Hizbul *mujahedeen,* founded in 1989, has strong links with the Jamiaat-i-Islami of Pakistan and Jammu and Kashmir. Though the Hizbul claims that its members are from Kashmir, there are a sizeable number of Afghans and Pakistanis in the outfit.

In a major address to the nation on 12 January 2002, President Musharraf made it clear that Pakistan would henceforth disassociate itself from terrorism and from the *jihad* culture. Five organizations (including the Lashkar and the Jaish) were banned and 2,000 known terrorists were arrested. After the crackdown by Pakistan, the Indian government has failed to reciprocate. It actually has intensified its repressive regime after the enactment of the Prevention of Terrorist Organizations (POTO) legislation in March 2002. The first "terrorist" to be arrested under POTO was the JKLF leader Yasin Malik, one of the more moderate leaders within the Kashmiri movement. At the time of his arrest, serious discussions were taking place on the issue of participating in the state assembly elections later in the year. Malik has a good public image and could give the National Conference a run for its money if he decided to take the plunge and contest elections. Many Kashmiri have regarded his arrest as a sign that the normal democratic process in the state remains to be scuttled.

Official Conflict Management
The Kashmir question was taken to the UN when India lodged a complaint in the Security Council on 1 January 1948. The Security Council, after having called on India and Pakistan to return to normalcy, appointed the UNCIP to investigate the facts and to bring about a cessation of hostilities. On 13 August 1948, the UNCIP passed an important resolution, comprising three parts. Part 1 dealt with the establishment of a cease-fire; Part 2 with the truce agreement; and Part 3 with the determination of the future status of Jammu and Kashmir in accordance with the will of the people. The acceptance of this resolution of August 1948 by India and Pakistan resulted in a cease-fire agreement coming into force on 1 January 1949. An agreement was also reached between the two countries on the demarcation of the cease-fire line on 27 July 1949.

Thereafter, the United Nations Military Observers Group in India and Pakistan has continued to patrol the cease-fire line, but as a mediator, the role of the UN was progressively minimized after the 1950s. In the war that intervened (in 1965), the Security Council, however, brokered the cease-fire on 22 September 1965, and Soviet premier Kosygin thereafter persuaded both parties to send representatives to Tashkent. Outside mediation resulted in an agreement between India and Pakistan. This was one of the instances in which outside mediation was accepted by India and Pakistan in order to ameliorate their seemingly intransigent positions regarding conflict and confrontation. Thereafter, India has consistently refused to have a third party involved in its dealings with Pakistan. The offer by the UN to send international observers to Kashmir at the time of the Kargil war was summarily rejected by Indian prime minister Vajpayee. The offer by Pakistan to refer the terrorist attack on the Indian parliament in December 2001 to the UN was equally dismissed by the government of India.

The Pakistani government fiercely disputes the legitimacy of the act of accession and officially focuses on the plebiscite mandated by the UNCIP Resolution of 1948, omitting the fact that it has to withdraw all forces as the precondition for the plebiscite. Pakistan until recently has insisted on third-party mediation. Pakistan has repeatedly tried to raise the issue of Kashmir in various international organizations, but has been largely unsuccessful, with the exception of such organizations as the Islamic Conference Organization, which has consistently endorsed the Pakistani position. The Indian insistence on the bilateral mode has reduced the possible role not only of the UN, but also of the Non-Aligned Movement and of the South-Asian Association of Regional Co-operation (SAARC). The SAARC, which otherwise could have become a fruitful forum for economic cooperation, partly because of the conflict overhang, has remained an ineffective organization.

The bilateral talks between the two countries have only succeeded in issuing joint statements and expressing their commitments to resolve the issue through dialogue. But outside the conference rooms, the stances of both sides have hardened. Particularly, the government of India has reacted in an unresponsive way to a number of offers made by the president of Pakistan in recent years. The stalemate between both countries has prevented the stimulation of processes that could have built a higher level of mutual confidence and a healthier interaction between the populations of both countries and between the population of Kashmir and the rest of the population within both countries.

In July 1989, the two youthful leaders, Rajiv Gandhi and Benazir Bhutto, met amidst high expectations. It was the first summit between the leaders of Pakistan and India since the Simla Agreement. In a joint communiqué both the leaders expressed their desire to work toward a comprehensive settlement to reduce the chances of conflict and the use of force, but no tangible solutions were proposed. The next meeting, between newly elected prime ministers Chandrashekar and Nawaz Sharif, on 21–23 November 1990, did not come much further than establishing a hot line between the two leaders, and resuming the foreign secretary–level talks on issues of bilateral importance between the two countries. Meetings were also held at various international meetings where leaders from both countries happened to be present, but, as a consequence of the increase in militant activities, the opposition of the two countries grew even more entrenched. The promise of a breakthrough came when the Indian left-of-center prime minister Gujral met his Pakistani counterpart Nawaz Sharif during the SAARC meeting in Male in May 1997. They decided to reactivate the hot line, and to constitute working groups on various issues as part of an "integrated approach," instead of focusing merely on Kashmir. Joint working groups were to discuss issues such as Kashmir, peace and security, the Sir Creek contested territory near the coastal area, terrorism and drug trafficking, economic cooperation, and the promotion of friendly exchanges.

The installation of the new government led by Atal Behari Vajpayee of the Hindu chauvinist party BJP in 1998 initially led to a dramatic deterioration in the relationship. After India had exploded nuclear devices, Pakistan did the same. Less than one year later, in February 1999, Vajpayee met Nawaz Sharif in Lahore, the Pakistani city just across the border. In the Lahore Declaration, both sides agreed to "intensify their efforts to resolve all issues, including the issue of Jammu and Kashmir." Both governments agreed to refrain from intervention and interference in each other's internal affairs and condemned terrorism "in all its forms and manifestations." They also agreed to work on confidence-building measures. The follow-up, however, was disappointing. Later in the year, the so-called Kargil war erupted. In late May, for the first time in twenty-seven years, the Indian army started to use air power across the high mountain ranges around Kargil in Kashmir, and in some other areas along the international border. On the Indian side, it was suggested that the Pakistani military was dissatisfied with the Lahore agreement, and that it therefore had provoked the Kargil war by pushing troops into Indian territory. The magnitude of the "infiltration," however, has never been made transparent in official documents and neither has the Indian government informed the UN or contacted the government of Pakistan before launching the strikes. The fact, however, is that when the military took over from the civil government in October 1999, the military leader General Pervez Musharraf appeared to make a number of conciliatory measures and proposed bilateral talks to solve all the issues. He, however, made it also clear that the unresolved Jammu and Kashmir dispute should form the central point of the discussions. The government of India thereupon invited the Pakistani leader for a peace summit, but the Vajpayee-Musharraf summit at Agra (14–16 July 2001) again failed in its objectives, because the Indian government continues to insist that Jammu and Kashmir is not a bilateral problem, and that the joint attack on terrorism should be the major point on the agenda.

Official conflict management in Jammu and Kashmir itself is also in a stalemate. The government of India continues to hold that Jammu and Kashmir is an integral part of India and that Pakistan should vacate the territory it has illegally occupied in "Azad Kashmir" and the Northern Areas. Any discussion on Kashmir with Pakistan will only be held strictly within the Shimla Agreement, which envisages a bilateral negotiating framework. In the meantime, the government of India hopes to bring back "normalcy" in Jammu and Kashmir and to slice off moderate elements for a separate deal with New Delhi. At the political level, presidential rule over the state was revoked in October 1996 and elections were conducted to the state assembly, which resulted in the National Conference of Farooq Abdullah coming to power.

The state government run by the NC favors continued association with India, albeit with more autonomy. After it won a two-third majority in the 1996 assembly elections, the government of Farooq Abdullah appointed two committees to make recommendations on the issues of state autonomy and regional autonomy. The "State Autonomy Report" was tabled in the state legislative assembly and was approved in June 2000. It stated that after 1953, forty-two constitutional amendments have undermined the powers of the state and have seriously affected the special status that Jammu and Kashmir once had. It is a very significant document, with a detailed list of complaints and remedies, but it has been rejected summarily in government circles in New Delhi. Only the left-wing parties showed some appreciation for the report.

They have argued that the overcentralization and increasing authoritarianism in India is a dangerous development that weakens the unity of the country, and regard greater autonomy for Jammu and Kashmir as an example of a more federal and decentralized Indian state. Government parties and the Congress opposition have condemned the "State Autonomy Report" outright as bordering on secession, and as setting a bad example that could encourage other movements in India to likewise seek autonomy. The report recommends a return to the constitutional relationship of the early 1950s, based on Article 370, which effectively means that, apart from defense, external affairs, and communications, other subjects could be negotiated between the state and the Indian union. The strong terms with which the union government has reacted to the report of the state assembly does not augur well for the demand of more autonomy within a strict parliamentarian approach.

Multi-Track Diplomacy

The government of India has always insisted on bilateral discussions with the government of Pakistan. As mentioned earlier, these contacts have not been fruitful. The most palpable breakthrough thus far has been the Tashkent Declaration, brokered by a third party (the president of the Soviet Union), when an agreement was reached on the LOC. Within India, negotiations involve many organizations, mainly political parties and militant groups. There are no other civil-society institutions that could provide a movement for an alternative solution. There is even a conspicuous absence of a peace movement. Some NGOs are active in rehabilitation work, but even their resources are limited

Martin Adler/Panos

Kashmir: Women protesting Indian "occupation"

and a number of them have given way to organizations that, if not directly militant, function as front organizations of a polarized political field.

The National Conference has played a major role in de-escalating the conflict and in defending the political and economic rights of the people of the Kashmir Valley, but on too many occasions the party has proved to be corrupt and vindictive and to observe an opportunistic relationship with New Delhi. Also internally, the absence of democratic procedures prevents a committed and independent leadership from standing up against the entrenched interests of the Abdullah family. Two other political parties are in a position to draw substantial support away from secessionist politics. They are the left-of-center People's Democratic Party (PDP) led by former home office minister of the union government, Mufti Mohammad Sayeed, and the Communist Party of India (Marxist) led by its state secretary, Tarigami. Both parties have been trying to mobilize secular and democratic forces in civil society. Together with Saifuddin Soz, the influential member of the Rajya Sabha (the upper house in New Delhi), they are forming an anti-NC coalition. Tarigami reaffirms the party's stand that there can be no military solution to the problem and that only the process of dialogue can bring about a peaceful resolution. The summary rejection by the government of India of the unanimous resolution of the Jammu and Kashmir state assembly on state autonomy is an indication that such dialogue remains a distant prospect.

Much depends on whether politicians from the secessionist platform of the All Party Hurriyat Conference (APHC) are willing to join forces with the secular parties. The APHC is a fractious coalition of various political, religious, and secessionist groups that are both overground and underground. Professor Abdul Ghani Bhat of the Muslim Conference acts as the chairman. The People's Conference, the Jamaat-e-Islami, the Ittihad-ul-Muslimeen, the Awami Action Committee, the Jammu and Kashmir Liberation Front, and the People's League are among its members. Most of them are pro-Pakistani. Formed in 1993, the APHC wants to resolve the problem in Kashmir through a dialogue involving the parties to the dispute—India, Pakistan, and the "genuine representatives" of the people of Jammu and Kashmir. It calls for the immediate and complete cessation of (Indian) military action and the reintroduction of the rule of law, inclusive of an end to custodial torture and killings. The alliance largely functions as a cooperative body with an executive council comprising seven members drawn from the main constituent outfits. The alliance claims to be the sole representative of the Kashmiri people. This claim has predictably been challenged by the NC and by established parliamentary parties such as the Communist Party of India–Marxist (CPI–M), and the PDP. It has also come under challenge from Pakistan-based militant outfits, which after the APHC's and Hizbul's positive response to the prime minister's cease-fire offer have questioned the Hurriyat's credentials. The terrorist activities of organizations such as Jaish-I-Mohammadi, Harkat-ul-Mujahedeen, and Lashkar-e-Toiba have intensified in the second half of 2001. The attack on the state assembly building in October 2001, the threat to attack women who do not wear veils, and the strike in support of the Taliban enforced on 21 September were all instances of terrorist activities that did not have mass support and actually were in defiance of the APHC.

The JKLF, although divided in at least two major factions (headed by Amanullah Khan and Yasin Malik respectively) was the most indigenous secessionist organization in Kashmir during 1989–1995. Both factions regard Kashmir as a question of national independence for around 15 million people in India and Pakistan, and not as a territorial dispute between India and Pakistan. Jammu-Kashmir (including all areas that were part of the territory just before independence in August 1947) is regarded as an indivisible political entity. Only the Kashmiri people, or their representatives duly elected for this purpose, have the right to decide about the future constitutional, political, social, and economic systems for the country and its relationship with foreign countries. Amanullah Khan, chairman of the JKLF based in Pakistan, firmly believes that the "third option," involving an independent and unified Kashmir, should be given serious thought by India and Pakistan. Also, former Jammu and Kashmir chief minister and leader of the Awami National Council, Ghulam Mohammad Shah, tends to support this position.

The main political tendency among non-Muslim political organizations in Jammu (such as the Gujjars United Front, the Dogra Sadar Sabha, and the Panthers Party) is for the separate statehood of the Jammu region within the Indian union. The Panun Kashmir is an organization of the Kashmiri Brahmins. Its objectives include the establishment of a "homeland" for Kashmiri Hindus in the Kashmir Valley. This homeland, to be placed under the central administration with a union territory status, is to comprise the southern region of the state to the north and east of the Jhelum River.

As mentioned earlier, civil society in Jammu and Kashmir is weakly developed. Among the more active organizations are involved with rehabilitation, relief, and social welfare. The more important ones are:

Society for Human Welfare and Education. This society was set up in 1941, and is one of the oldest social-welfare organizations in Kashmir. Its primary objective is providing education to children from poorer families.

Jammu and Kashmir Hussaini Relief Committee. This committee was established in 1972, and has a long record of serving the needy irrespective of caste and creed. It has some eight hundred volunteers in different parts of Kashmir, through whom it implements its relief programs. It regularly organizes blood-donation camps throughout Kashmir, the blood being provided to victims of violence and the injured.

Association of the Parents of Disappeared Persons. Established in 1994 by human-rights activist Pervez Imroze, the APDP investigates cases of people who have gone "missing" (generally supposed to have been killed) in the current turmoil in Kashmir. It also investigates human-rights abuses.

Kashmir Foundation for Peace and Development Studies (KFPDS). Established in 1999, this organization aims at restoring peace in Kashmir, investigating human-rights abuses, arranging for relief to victims of violence, strengthening democratic institutions in the state, and bringing people from the three regions of Jammu and Kashmir, representing various different ideologies, into dialogue with each other.

Prospects

After half a century of conflict and stalemate, the two countries that hold the key to the solution in Kashmir have not budged an inch from the positions they first assumed around 1950. The government of India, moreover, has not indicated that it is willing to reconsider the special status within the Indian union that Kashmir had in the early 1950s, and which gradually has been amended. Unless in both respects some reconsideration of the old positions takes place, the prospect for a solution of the problem remains bleak. On the other hand, terrorism may be reduced. The end of the Taliban regime in Afghanistan has been followed by a curb of the more fundamentalist Islamic groups operating in Kashmir from Pakistani territory. In April 2002, President Musharraf has been confirmed for a five-year term on the platform of economic and political reforms, which included the elimination religious intolerance and terrorism. The scale of violence witnessed in Kashmir during the 1990s is likely to drop to normal levels, but Pakistan will not possibly renounce its claims on the autonomy of the people in Kashmir. Concessions from the Indian side will increase the maneuverability on the Pakistani side. Such concessions will also help to assuage the feelings of alienation and mistreatment within the Indian union, which affect many Kashmiri. Unless the government of India enters into a dialogue with the leaders who have organized the resistance from Kashmiri soil, not much headway can be expected. The militant groups continue to call for the independence of Kashmir, and in the absence of any movement on the political front negotiations may prove elusive.

Recommendations

The role of the United Nations has been progressively minimized since the 1950s. After the first cease-fire in 1948, both India and Pakistan have not budged from their position. While the entire world has been in the process of rapid change, both countries still adhere to their maximalist positions.

1. The first step toward a solution is that the bifurcation, which exists now at all levels and in all spheres, be breached by minimal measures. Such measures could include:

> • Facilitation of contacts between families divided by the LOC: Kashmir is possibly the last region in the world where even kith and kin remain separated by a border conflict.
> • The borders of Kashmir with India and Pakistan should gradually be opened for the transit of people, goods, and services after working out the formalities.

• While the present Line of Control would remain in place until such time as both India and Pakistan decide to alter it in their mutual interest, both the countries should demilitarize the area included in the Kashmir entity; such a measure could be arranged on a bilateral basis or with regional (SAARC) or international (UN) supervision.

2. A political solution within the state of Jammu and Kashmir will require bold initiatives by the governments of both India and of Pakistan. The third option that has been proposed by certain groups in Kashmir, particularly by the JKLF, may not be a realistic option: one cannot expect both governments to sign away part of their territory. The plebiscite giving Kashmiri on both sides of the LOC a choice among accession to India, accession to Pakistan, or full sovereignty, is a long-term option only. It may by then have lost its urgency if the presently sealed borders between both areas of Kashmir have been opened so that Kashmiri have access to each other, even if living in two countries.

3. The demand of Kashmiris for greater autonomy has always been understood by the government of India as subversive. The accession of Kashmir to India has been on the basis of a separate constitutional agreement. It seems to be the overwhelming desire of the people of Kashmir to recapture some of the autonomy that has been usurped by the government. The absolute unwillingness of the Indian government, as again expressed in its reaction to the 2000 state assembly report, only helps to convince more and more Kashmiri people that normal parliamentary means do not work. The government should be prepared to sit down with the political and civil-society representatives of Kashmir and discuss what the special status of Kashmir within India could mean. This would go a long way in emotionally reintegrating the people in Kashmir with the Indian union.

4. The effective monitoring of human-rights violations and redress of the grievances of the people of Jammu and Kashmir should be put high on the agenda. The end of the Cold War may make the Indian government less jittery when it is confronted by (foreign) reports on human-rights abuse. It would be advisable to opt for a transparent policy and make it possible for all human-rights abuses, both by government organizations and by Kashmiri militants, to be investigated. This will be the surest way of convincing the people in Kashmir that the rule of law is paramount, also for them.

5. Other measures, such as stimulating economic development in the region, will be helpful. This, however, may not be the best policy to start with. As long as corruption is rampant in the state, it will rather lead to further polarization between the haves and the have-nots, and thus to more pent-up feelings of frustration.

6. Given the fact that neither country operating on its own has been able to inch closer to a solution for more than half a century, the governments of India and Pakistan could well benefit from a third party that facilitates the discussions and the agreements on confidence-building measures as a first step toward a more general solution.

Resources

Newsletters and Periodicals
Faultlines, Institute for Conflict Management
Informative Missive, Public Commission on Human Rights
Kashmir Quarterly, Kashmiri-Canadian Council
Kashmir Trends, Centre for Peace Studies
Peace Initiatives, International Centre for Peace Inititiaves

Reports
Amnesty International
   "India: Call for Restraint in Kashmir," London, 3 October 2001.
   "India: Civilian Deaths in Kashmir Are Unacceptable," London, 11 December 2001.
   "India: Use of the Public Security Act in Jammu and Kashmir," London, 18 June 2001.
   "India: Welcome Steps to End Impunity in Jammu and Kashmir," London, 2 November 2000.
   "Indo-Pakistan Summit: Plea to Put Human Rights in Jammu and Kashmir Firmly on the Agenda," London, 12 July 2001.
Centre for Policy Research, *Kashmir Question Revisited,* by A. G. Noorani, New Delhi, 1991.
Delhi Policy Group, *Jammu and Kashmir: An Agenda for the Future,* by Kanti Bajpai et al., New Delhi, mimeo, 1999.
Gandhi Peace Foundation, *Jammu and Kashmir: The Way Out,* New Delhi, 1996.
Human Rights Watch
   "Behind the Kashmir Conflict: Abuses by Indian Security Forces and Militant Groups Continue," 1 July 1999.
   "Cycle of Killings in Kashmir Fuels Conflict," New York, 1 July 1999.
   "India/Pakistan Summit: Call to Address Human Rights in Kashmir," New York, 14 July 2001.
   "Kashmir: Wave of Attacks on Civilians Condemned, All Parties Must Respect Civilians' Rights," New York, 21 August 2000.
   "Rights Abuses Behind Kashmir Fighting: India, Pakistan Both Guilty," New York, 16 July 1999.
Institute of Policy Studies, *Kashmir Problem: Challenge and Response,* by Tarik Jan and Ghulam Sarwar, 1990.
International Center for Peace Initiatives, *Next Steps in Kashmir: Give Peace a Chance,* Peace Initiatives, vol. 6, nos. 4–5, 2000.
Joan B. Kroc Institute for International Peace Studies, University of Notre Dame, *Kashmir and "The War on Terrorism,"* by Cynthia Mahmood, 2001, online: www. nd.edu/~krocinst/polbriefs/pbrief8.html.
Kashmir Study Group
"1947–1997, The Kashmir Dispute at Fifty: Charting Paths to Peace: Report on the Visit of an Independent Study Team to India and Pakistan," New York, 1997.
"Kashmir: A Way Forward," New York, 2000.
Pakistan-India People's Forum for Peace and Democracy, *Proceedings, Recommendations and Declaration of the Third Joint Convention,* Calcutta, 28–31 December 1996.
Program in Arms Control, Disarmament, and International Security, University of Illinois, *The Road to Peace in South Asia: Lessons for India and Pakistan from the Arab-Israeli Peace Process,* by Moonis Ahmar, ACDIS Occasional Papers, online: www.acdis.uiuc.edu/homepage_docs/pubs_doc/PDF_Files/Ahmar.pdf
South Asia Forum for Human Rights, *Ten Week War in Kargil: From the News Files,* by Sabyasachi Basu Chaudhury, and Shahids Fiaz, SAFHR paper series No. 7, 1999.

University of Azad Jammu and Kashmir, Muzzafarabad, *Fifty Years of the Kashmir Dispute,* edited by Suroosh Irfani (based on the proceedings of the International Seminar held at Muzaffarabad, Azad Jammu and Kashmir, 24–25 August 1997), 1997.

Other Publications

Breaking the Silence: Women and Kashmir, by Sumona DasGupta. New Delhi, Foundation for Universal Responsibility, 2000.

The Challenge in Kashmir: Democracy, Self-Determination and a Just Peace, by Sumantra Bose. New Delhi/London, Sage Publications, 1997.

Constitutional Autonomy. A Case of J&K, by K. K. Wadhawa. New Delhi, Bhawana Books, 2001.

India, Pakistan, and the Kashmir Dispute, by Robert G. Wirsing. New York, St. Martin's, 1998.

Jammu and Kashmir: The Way Out, edited by Gandhi Peace Foundation. New Delhi, Gandhi Peace Foundation, 1996.

Kargil: The Tables Turned, edited by Maj. Gen. Ashok Krishna and P. R. Chari. New Delhi, Manohar Publishers, 2001.

Kashmir and Indo-Pakistan Relations, by Ravi Nanda. New Delhi, Lancer Books, 2001.

Kashmir: A Disputed Legacy 1846–1990, by Alistair Lamb. Herfordshire, Roxford Books, 1991.

Kashmir: Behind the Veil, by M. J. Akbar. New Delhi, Penguin Books, 1991.

Kashmir in Conflict: India, Pakistan and the Unfinished War, by Victoria Schofield. London/New York, I. B. Tauris, 2000.

Kashmir in the Crossfire, by Victoria Schofield. London/New York, I. B. Tauris, 1996.

Political Development in Jammu, Kashmir and Ladakh, by Usha Sharma. New Delhi, Radha Publications, 2001.

Reclaiming the Past: The Search for Political and Cultural Unity in Contemporary Kashmir, by Vernon Marston Hewitt. London, Portland Books, 1995.

State, Identity and Violence: Jammu, Kashmir and Ladakh, by Navitna Chadha Behera. New Delhi, Manohar Publishers, 2000.

The Crisis in Kashmir: Portents of War, Hopes of Peace, by Sumit Ganguly. Cambridge, Cambridge University Press, 1977.

War and Diplomacy in Kashmir, 1947–8, by C. Dasgupta. New Delhi, Sage, 2002.

War at the Top of the World : The Struggle for Afghanistan, Kashmir and Tibet, by Eric S. Margolis. New York, Routledge, 2001.

Selected Internet Sites

jammukashmir.nic.in/ (Official web site of the Jammu and Kashmir government, India)

users.online.be/basjak/ (Belgian Association for Solidarity with Jammu and Kashmir)

www.imtd.org/initiatives-kashmir.htm (Kashmir initiatives of the IMTD)

www.ipcs.org (Web site of the Institute of Peace and Conflict Studies, on various countries)

www.jammukashmir.net/ (Independent web-based project providing research papers and documents)

www.jammukashmir.nic.in (The official web site of the state of Jammu and Kashmir)

www.kashmiri.com/ (Kashmir-American Council)

www.kic.org.pk/ (Kashmir Information Center)

www.krrc.org (Kashmir Record and Research Council, a network of research scholars basically supportive of the liberation of Kashmir)

www.mha.nic.in (The official web site of the Ministry of Home Affairs, India)

www.pak.gov.pk/public/kashmir/ (An excellent window on the official Pakistani position on Kashmir, with news from the non-Indian perspective)

www.pakistannews.org/ (A daily source of Pakistani newspaper articles)

www.satp.org (South Asia Terrorism Portal, a rich source of information on all ethnically based conflicts in South Asia) www.un.org/Depts/DPKO/Missions/unmogip.htm (United Nations Military Observer Group in India and Pakistan)

Resource Contacts

Naeem Ahmed, Department of International Relations, Karachi University, e-mail: naeemifti@hotmail.com

Paul Beersmans, Belgian Association for Solidarity with Jammu and Kashmir, basjak@glo.be

Nayana Bose, e-mail: nayanabose@hotmail.com

Alexander Evans, Centre for Defense Studies, e-mail: aevans@jammukashmir.net

Amitabh Mattoo, Jawaharlal Nehru University, e-mail: mattoo@jnuiv.ernet.in

John McDonald, Institue for Multi-Track Diplomacy, e-mail: imtd@imtd.org

K. N. Pandita, Friends of Kashmir International, e-mail: knpandita@hotmail.com

M. A. Raina, Jammu Kashmir National Awareness Campaign, e-mail: srinagar2000@yahoo.com

Karan Sawhny, International Center for Peace Initiatives, e-mail: karansawhny@bol.net.in

Farhan H. Siddiqi, Department of International Relations, Karachi University, e-mail: Farhan_74@hotmail.com

Organizations

Association of the Parents of Disappeared Persons
C/o Advocate Pervez Imroze, Lal Chowk
Srinagar, Kashmir

Jammu and Kashmir Hussaini Relief Committee
Alamgiri Bazaar
Srinagar 190001, Kashmir

Public Commission on Human Rights
The Bund, Amira Kadal
Srinagar, Kashmir
Tel/Fax +91-194-456381
E-mail: p_imroz@usa.net

Society for Human Welfare and Education
Silk Factory Road, Solina
Srinagar, Kashmir-190009

Data on the following organizations can be found in the Directory section:

In India:
   Centre for Dialogue and Reconciliation
   Centre for Policy Research
   Centre for Study of Society and Secularism
   Coordination Committee on Kashmir
   Delhi Policy Group
   Gandhi Peace Foundation
   Indian Institute for Peace, Disarmament & Environmental Protection
   Institute for Conflict Management
   Institute of Peace and Conflict Studies
   International Centre for Peace Initiatives
   International Centre for Peace Studies
   Kashmir Foundation for Peace and Development Studies
   Pakistan-India People Forum for Peace and Democracy

Women in Security, Conflict Management and Peace
Women's Initiative for Peace in South Asia

In Pakistan:
Human Rights Commission of Pakistan
Pakistan-India People Forum for Peace and Democracy—Pakistan chapter
Program on Peace Studies & Conflict Resolution

Outside India/Pakistan:
Institute for Multi-Track Diplomacy
Kashmiri-Canadian Council
Kashmir Council for Human Rights/Organisation for South Asian Peace

---

Kristoffel Lieten (Belgium, 1946) is an associate professor at the Amsterdam School of Social Sciences of the University of Amsterdam (lieten@pscw.uva.nl). Since his studies at the Jawaharlal Nehru University in New Delhi in the early 1970s, he has done extensive research on political and social developments in South Asia. He has worked as the South Asia correspondent of the Dutch and Belgian Radio and has become a regular media commentator. He has cofounded the Dutch National India Committee and has written several books on various aspects of politics, history, and rural development in India.

Note

1. The writing of this chapter was supported by reports supplied by Karan R. Sawhny, Suba Chandran, and Nidhi Narain of the International Centre for Peace Initiatives, New Delhi.

7.8.6

The Naxalite Movement

Suba Chandran & Mallika Joseph

In India, the term "Naxalite" refers to a variety of revolutionary rural struggles. The Naxalite movement shuns participation in electoral politics and attacks the landed classes directly in a bid to liberate entire territories from feudal and capitalist exploitation. Although it has an ideological following all over the country, it is mainly restricted to three states: Andhra Pradesh, Jharkhand, and Bihar. The Naxalite movement, which started in the late 1960s, has undergone numerous splits due to ideological and personal reasons. The efforts taken by the various state governments have contained the movement but "liberated zones" continue to exist. The Naxalites operate in areas that on one hand have very low levels of income and very low human development indicators, and on the other hand suffer from extreme forms of economic and social polarization. The state governments, rather than addressing the security needs of the landless laborers most affected by the violence or providing protection to villagers at risk, have approached it as a law-and-order problem. Civil-society sympathy for the Naxalites' cause and concern about the repression by police and the private armies of landlords (the so-called senas) is mixed, with misgivings about the more extremist tendencies within the Naxalite movement.

India has a long history of peasant uprisings. From the 1930s onwards, communist-inspired organizations and movements have been in the forefront of the struggle for land and tenancy reform. The agitation was especially powerful during the last years of colonial rule and during the first years of independence when the government of India dragged its feet on land reform and compromised with the feudal landlords. In 1946, Bengal witnessed a large-scale *tebhaga* ("three shares") movement among sharecroppers, which demanded the reduction of the landlords' share in the crop from a half to one-third. Landlords had been using force to take at least half the harvest. The peasants,

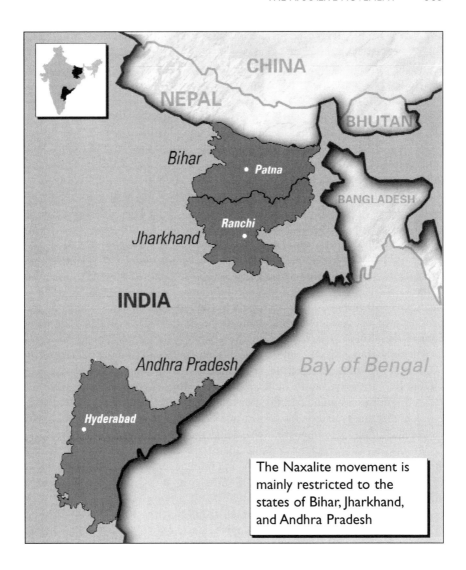

The Naxalite movement is mainly restricted to the states of Bihar, Jharkhand, and Andhra Pradesh

guided by the *kisan sabhas* (peasant unions), forcibly seized two-thirds of the harvest, leading to violent clashes. The landlords fled and the *kisan sabhas* temporarily established control in many rural areas.

In subsequent decades, the popularity of the communist peasant leaders declined in some areas, such as Punjab and Andhra Pradesh, but the movement has endured in Tripura, Kerala, and West Bengal, three states where communist parties have repeatedly headed popularly elected governments. When this happened for the first time in 1967 in West Bengal, a populous state plagued by feudal forms of exploitation and suppression in agriculture, a section of the leftist communist party, the Communist Party of India–Marxist (CPI–M), broke ranks and opted for a radical alternative. They rejected participation in multiparty governments, and electoral politics in general, and opted for a non-conciliatory attack on the landed classes.

While a left-dominated front was forming the government in Calcutta (in 1967), three sharecroppers with the help of 150 members of the breakaway wing of the CPI–M, armed with sticks, bows, and arrows, removed the entire stock of grain from a landlord's granary. This happened in the village of Naxalbari in the narrow corridor between Nepal and what is now Bangladesh that connects mainland India with the northeastern states. Peasants and tribals have continued to be oppressed by unscrupulous landlords and moneylenders, and the local leaders in Naxalbari considered government intervention too slow, too legalistic, and too moderate. Their revolt signaled the birth of a new armed struggle.

The struggle, inspired by the Chinese Communist Party, was initially led by the Communist Party of India–Marxist-Leninist (CPI–ML) under the chairmanship of Charu Mazumdar. Very soon, dissent erupted and gradually the party disintegrated into numerous breakaway factions, all claiming to be less revisionist in ideology and more revolutionary in practice than the others. Since then, all forms of armed struggle by such groups that have taken up the cause of socioeconomic development of the downtrodden rural masses have come to be termed "Naxalite."

In West Bengal itself, where the government has been quite successful in implementing land reforms, the movement did not endure beyond the late 1970s. In many other areas in eastern India, semifeudal conditions have remained. The semifeudal conditions have been exacerbated by the failing government machinery and by the formation of *senas* (armed squads) by the upper castes and classes to safeguard their socioeconomic and political interests.

Today, a dozen Naxalite groups operate primarily in the states of Bihar, Jharkhand, and Andhra Pradesh (AP), and in pockets in the neighboring states of Madhya Pradesh, Uttar Pradesh, Chattisgarh, and Orissa, although other states may also be incidentally affected. Most groups are disorganized, lack popular support, and continuously face splits, but the People's War Group (PWG) in AP and the Maoist Communist Centre (MCC) in Bihar and Jharkhand are the two best-organized, and most ruthless, Naxalite groups in India.

Conflict Dynamics

In Andhra Pradesh, the revolutionary peasant movement was of great significance at the time of independence. An armed struggle emerged as early as 1946 in the princely state of Hyderabad. The movement, first against the Nizam and then against the government of India, is known as the Telengana Armed Struggle. It started as a revolt against the continuation of feudal land ownership and the oppression of the poor peasantry and tribals by landlords. The communist-led movement "liberated" more than three thousand villages, but, ultimately, after more than four thousand revolutionaries lost their lives, was suppressed by the Indian army. Again in 1961, a violent movement under the banner of Srikakulam Armed Struggle sought to liberate the deprived hill people from the clutches of the plainsmen who had alienated them from their land and oppressed them economically. Coordinated police action resulted in the collapse of this movement.

Extremist activities in AP began once again with the formation of the People's War Group in 1980. Presently, fifteen of the twenty-three districts in AP are affected. The two parties to the conflict are the government, represented by the police, and approximately nineteen Naxalite groups. The PWG is predominant among them in terms of party organization, network, manpower, and striking capabilities: it has about one thousand full-time underground cadres, three thousand overground militants who are organized into four military platoons and further into *dalams* (forest squads).

In the last couple of years, activities have intensified after a decline in the mid-1990s. In October 2001, the Coca-Cola plant was attacked. The attack, in response to the U.S. bombing of Afghanistan, caused substantial damage without affecting the production process. One month earlier, in a single action, the PWG killed nine policemen in Guntur district.

The aim of the PWG is to capture power through the strategy of protracted armed struggle and an areawide seizure of power by initially building bases in rural and remote areas. These bases would eventually be transformed into guerrilla zones and later into liberated areas that would ultimately encircle the urban centers of power.

The security forces as well as police and government offices have been the main targets of the PWG, but most victims have been civilians. Of the nearly three thousand casualties since extremism started, less than five hundred are policemen, the rest being civilians. Analysis of the casualty list shows that only a quarter of the civil victims belonged to the high castes. The others belonged to the lower classes, "scheduled castes," and "scheduled tribes," the very sections whose cause the Naxalites are supposedly championing. Naxalite activities thus also appear to be associated with the struggle to eliminate the political influence of other organizations such as the parliamentary communist parties, among others.

In Bihar, similar conditions exist as in the most backward areas of AP. The feudal nexus of big landowner, rack-renting, and market control has left millions of poor peasants, sharecroppers, and agricultural laborers in abject poverty and oppression. Communist parties had been reasonably strong in some pockets of the state and mass movements were active, but revolutionary violence erupted only after the developments in Naxalbari. From West Bengal, revolutionaries went over into Bihar and assisted locally in the organization of revolutionary cells. The CPI–ML was formed at Musahari in 1967 under the leadership of S. N. Singh. After Singh left the organization in 1971, as in the neighboring West Bengal, the movement very soon underwent various splits. In the early 1980s there were at least three major Naxalite parties: the CPI–ML (Liberation), MCC, and CPI–ML (Party Unity).

CPI–ML (Liberation) is said to be active in thirty-six districts and to have five thousand full-timers and a membership of more than two hundred thousand.

It runs five organizations: the All-India Students Association, Bihar Pradesh Kisan Sabha, All-India Coordination Committee of Trade Unions, All-India Progressive Women's Association, and Jan Sanskriti Manch. Dipankar Bhattacharya is the Liberation's national general secretary. In 1977, the organization, then under the leadership of the influential Vinod Mishra, decided on a "rectification" program.

This program resulted in the creation of the Indian People's Front (IPF) and the decision to participate in elections. The first initiative (the IPF, meant to unite all anti-feudal and anti-imperialist forces) failed to attract other groups and the IPF was discontinued in 1994. The second initiative was reasonably successful. Particularly in Bihar, some of its candidates were elected to parliament. The other two major segments of the Naxalite movement (Party Unity and the MCC) have not "rectified" their political line and have continued to operate as underground movements.

The rectification by CPI–ML Liberation resulted in the MCC emerging as the most radical and militant of the Naxalite groups in Bihar. The Maoist Coordination Committee was originally established as the Bengal–Bihar Special Area Committee in the early 1970s, but was renamed the MCC in 1975. It became very powerful during the second half of the 1980s. The first major massacre in which the MCC was involved took place in 1987 when it brutally killed forty-two persons belonging to upper-caste Rajput families in the Aurangabad district of Bihar. The MCC has been fighting the upper-caste/class landlords in Bihar and their private armies (*senas*) ever since. It is said to be active in thirty districts, and to have three hundred professional revolutionaries, sixty armed squads, and thirty thousand members. Like the CPI–ML Liberation, it has various front organizations such as the Krantikari Chhatra League (students), Communist Yuva League (youth), Naari Mukti Sangh (women), and Mazdoor Mukti Sangh (workers). The organization has been banned since 1987.

The CPI–ML Party Unity was formed in 1978; after the mid-1980s it went through a number of splits and in 1999, it merged with the People's War Group. It is active in twenty-five districts, and has various front organizations including the Majdoor Kisan Sangrami Parishad (agricultural labor), Shramik Sangharsh Manch (workers), and Bharat Naujawan Sabha (youth).

The most gruesome killings in Bihar have been related to the ongoing caste-war, in which the *sena* (see Chapter 7.8.7 survey on this conflict) is one of its opponents. In March 1999, thirty-five upper-caste villagers were killed in Jehanabad in retaliation for thirty-three lower-caste killings by the *sena* earlier in the year. Other attacks, such as the attack by the MCC in Jharkand in September 2001, killing thirteen policemen, were aimed at the security forces.

It should be emphasized that the differences between these Naxalite groups that continue along the nonparliamentarian path have to do more with personal clashes among the leadership and less with their ideology. Invariably, all the Naxalite groups work toward the same objectives, and use the same methods.

The Naxalite groups have enough weapons to operate at the local level, but they do not pose a threat at the supralocal level. Some groups in Bihar, Jharkhand, and AP are equipped with sophisticated arms including AK-56s. These weapons, however, are few: according to a news report, the MCC possesses one thousand weapons, including more than a dozen AK-47s and AK-56s. Most of the weapons have been looted from licensed holders or snatched from the police during raids on police convoys. Interestingly, there may also be a nexus between established political parties and some Naxalite groups.

It is generally known that there is a nexus between leaders of several political parties and the rebel outfits, both in Bihar and AP. In return for votes or support in general, some leaders of the Bharatya Janata Party (BJP), the main party in the government coalition in New Delhi, may have gifted AK-47 rifles and money to Naxalite outfits. On the other hand, they are also supporting the private armies of the landlords, the so-called *senas*. Reports from other areas in the country also suggest that this may be the case. A report tabled in the Maharashtra assembly in December 2000 established that in the Naxal-affected districts (Gondia, Chandrapur, and Gadchiroli), forest contractors and local businessmen are being forced to fund Naxalites in their area. The report also suggested that most of the businessmen actually exploit tribals and consider funding the Naxalite groups operating in the region a good investment.

The Naxalite groups exploit the vacuum in the administrative machinery to attract the masses by their campaign against various social evils such as the dowry system, exploitation of lower castes by the upper castes, theft, rape, and prostitution. The failure of the government administration and the armed power of Naxalite groups such as the MCC and the CPI–ML "People's War" in a number of areas (for example in Palamu and Daltonganj in Bihar, and in Warangal, Adilabad, and Karimnagar in AP) has created a different type of law and order.

According to Arjun Prasad Singh, joint-secretary of the All-India People's Resistance Forum, law and order in the Naxalite-infested areas is far better than in other areas. Even some landlords have started supporting the Naxalites. According to a report in *The Week* (20 April 2000), out of the 3,207 villages in Palamu district, Naxalites operate in 1,700. There are only three big landlords left in the district, which once had nine kings, 2,100 zamindars, and six thousand landlords. Bonded labor has been abolished and no employer dares pay less than the wages fixed by the state government. The exploitation of tribal women and collection of tolls by local goons have also stopped. But it is a fact, the local reporter adds, that the ultra outfits collect money from forest contractors, traders, and landlords in exchange for peace. The contractors are only too happy to contribute to the Naxalite coffers. A contractor was quoted as staying: "Before the Naxalites came I had to grease the palms of policemen, forest officers and local criminals. Today I have to go to only one place." Top Naxalite leaders defended this by saying they have not used the money for committing crimes but for people-oriented schemes.

The MCC and Party Unity hold *jan adalats* (people's courts). *Jan adalats* are usually held at night after a notice is issued to the villagers. These "courts" are gaining in popularity since the settlement of cases in government courts is costly and time-consuming. Moreover, the Naxalites are able to deliver on their verdicts, which the government courts often fail to do. Similarly, in the field of education, Naxalite groups in a number of areas have taken over the educational system and have made sure that it works. They are often the people's only insurance against demanding policemen, criminals, and landlords, and against upper-caste teachers who had been drawing salaries without doing any teaching.

Conflict Management

In general, government intervention has concentrated on military efforts to eliminate the "Naxal problem" rather than focus on the demands that the revolutionary groups have raised. Extrajudicial executions by security and police forces have been documented by international human-rights organizations and Indian civil-liberties groups. The police routinely claim that the killings occur in so-called encounters. Moreover, the Naxalite threat has been used to justify state violence against all forms of peasant resistance and against other critics of state policy. A Human Rights Watch report has stated:

> Police have also repeatedly engaged in excessive use of force when dealing with Naxalites. Under the pretext of seeking out Naxalite militants police have conducted raids on Dalit villages and falsely arrested those accused of harboring Naxalites. In some cases, federal paramilitary forces have been deployed. Like the private militias, police have sexually assaulted women and attacked children who remained behind after the men fled the villages.[1]

The official response to the Naxalite problem takes place at three levels, first at the state level in which the individual states deal with the problem; second at the union level, in which the union government provide funds and security forces to tackle the Naxalite groups; and third at the intrastate level, where the states cooperate with each other to deal with the situation.

The government of the state of Bihar has banned all Naxalite organizations, except for CPI–ML Liberation, and has provided financial assistance to the families of the victims. The state government launched a number of centrally assisted schemes aimed at providing better infrastructure and communication facilities, and at providing employment, but ineffective administration, corruption, and class interests made them unproductive. In December 2000, the governments of Bihar and Jharkhand mounted a coordinated offensive against the Naxalites; Bihar also put together a special task force with 150 commandos for anti-Naxalite operations and deployed them in hypersensitive areas. Additional policemen are undergoing specialized commando training. They appear, thus, to be addressing the situation more as a security problem than as a socioeconomic problem.

The government of Andhra Pradesh has adopted a multipronged approach to the Naxalite problem. Since the issue has its origins in socioeconomic underdevelopment, attempts have been made to address this by special programs for youth, the formation of cooperative societies of tribals, the improvement of primary health centers, village water-tank repairs, the provision of drinking water, roads, schools, youth clubs, etc.

The police have formed a special anti-Naxal force (the Greyhounds), which is specially trained in guerrilla warfare and equipped with sophisticated weaponry. A coordinated and consistent police action has resulted in the elimination of most of the top leadership of the movement and the year 2000 saw extremist-related killings decrease by around 20 percent. The enforcement agencies are positive that the two-decade-old problem will soon be solved.

The AP government has also tried to win back the peasantry by redistributing some of the land in the north Telengana region and has initiated programs to lure the Naxalites into surrendering by helping them to reintegrate into the mainstream society. Since 1993, when the program started, nearly four thousand Naxalites have surrendered and more than one thousand have been rehabilitated. During the last couple of years, the government has approached the left-wing extremist problem less as a police (law-and-order) problem and more as a socioeconomic issue. Those who surrender are rehabilitated. The rewards include the distribution of Jeeps, tractors, and auto rickshaws along with financial assistance to start shops. For this purpose, rehabilitation *mela* (fairs) are organized, attended by politicians and officials.

The Naxalites are opposed to any form of representative government under the present constitution and have issued poll boycotts. In the last ten years nearly 250 political leaders belonging to various political parties have been killed. Since other leftist parties, particularly the parliamentary parties, are catering to the same classes, it is not uncommon for leaders of these parties to be targeted.

Still, some understanding exists between the Naxalites and some political parties: it is not uncommon for right-of-center parties to seek the help of the Naxalites for getting elected in Naxal-dominated areas in return for the release of Naxalites or their sympathizers from prison and stopping police action against them. In Bihar and Jharkhand, leaders of almost every political party, including some leaders of the BJP and of the Samata Party, have been making efforts to keep the Naxalite leaders on their side. The parties do not openly condemn the Naxalites at public meetings and refer to them as misguided brethren.

The extent of support accorded to the Naxalites by the main political parties in AP remains unclear as the policy keeps fluctuating. The Congress government banned the PWG in 1992. Four years later, all curbs were lifted and the PWG was permitted to operate freely and hold meetings without any restriction, before it was banned again. N. T. Rama Rao, founder of the Telegu Desam Party, which then came to power, offered the Naxalites a "red salute" and called them "true patriots, who have been misunderstood by [the] ruling classes." The current TDP chief minister Chandrababu Naidu has expressed his willingness to hold talks with the outlawed PWG or any other Naxalite group and help them to reintegrate in society. The underground leadership of the PWG had recently said that it was ready for talks with the government. However, the PWG had laid several preconditions for the talks, including the withdrawal of the ban on the group and action against police officials involved in "fake encounters."

The role of regional and international organizations in this issue is minimal. The regional organization—South Asian Association of Regional Cooperation (SAARC)—has no mandate to deal with these issues. India traditionally has been against any external involvement in its domestic issues. Besides, none of the other countries in the region or elsewhere has anything at stake in this ongoing conflict.

Multi-Track Diplomacy

Whenever a massacre is perpetrated by the Naxalites, there is widespread condemnation of both the Naxalites and the governments for their inability to come to a negotiated solution, but on the ground improvements over the last quarter century seem to have been minimal. The media do play an important role in reporting whatever gruesome murders have taken place, but otherwise by and large are silent on the various social and economic issues underlying the conflict.

The state governments' response has varied according to the policies of political parties in power and the scale of the problem. While AP has banned the PWG, formed an exclusive counter-Naxal police force, and made it a punishable offense to provide food or shelter to the Naxalites, Madhya Pradesh is keen to negotiate with the Naxalites in order to solve the problem. A result of these disparate responses is that Naxalites committing crimes in one place flee to another where government policy is favorable to them. Following the killing of a high-profile minister from AP in March 2000, the union home affairs ministry has set up a coordination committee of the seven states most affected by leftist extremism. Their police chiefs have been meeting regularly. The central government has already granted several proposals submitted by the states for developmental activities that would help tackle Naxalism at the social and economic levels.

In some areas, the Naxalites have been able to muster public support among the downtrodden people. The polarization between the have-nots and the landed elite is sharp in areas in Bihar and Jharkhand where the Naxalites operate. The upper section of civil society, the upper classes and castes, finds the Naxalites hostile to its social and economic interests, and it has organized private militia called *senas,* particularly the Ranvir Sena, to safeguard their interests. As defenders of the interests of the poor villagers, Naxalites can count on a more sympathetic response from the villagers themselves. They give them shelter against the forces of law and order. NGOs such as the People's Union for Democratic Rights (PUDR) have taken sides in this caste and class conflict. In one of its reports, the PUDR considers the birth of Marxist-Leninist organizations and their growing support among the peasantry a direct outcome of the social order and the failure of the state to implement its own laws. A similar position is being taken by the People's Revolutionary Front. This ideological alignment with the Naxalite movement has somewhat diminished the neutral status of the PUDR, but it remains one of the foremost human-rights organizations in the country.

In AP, the Committee of Concerned Citizens (CCC), People's Union for Civil Liberties (PUCL), Association for the Protection of Democratic Rights, AP Civil Liberties Committee (APCLC), and United Struggle Committee Against Fake Encounters are some of the organizations that have also raised their voices against police/government action against the Naxalites. They have frequently voiced their concern about the number of Naxalites who are killed in "encounters," labeling them "false encounters." In the wake of an "encounter" that left three central-committee members of the PWG dead in December 1999, civil-liberty activists were able to mobilize as many as forty-six different organizations and coordinate rallies protesting the police action.

The CCC and PUCL for years have been trying—unsuccessfully—to negotiate a settlement between the government and the Naxalites. However, as in Bihar, their position as a mediator is impaired by their focus on misbehavior by government staff and institutions, passing over terrorist acts by Naxalites. They have also tended to remain oblivious to the hardships caused to the people and damage to property by the Naxalites. The government therefore sees them as front organizations of the Naxalites. Consequently, their decade-long talks with the government have yielded little result. However, the reports they bring out and the press campaigns they organize are invaluable as sources that document the human-rights violations involved.

At the international level, Human Rights Watch (HRW) has been monitoring the problem for a long time and has made recommendations to the state and central governments. It has carried out a number of studies and investigations, and has approached the state government directly with a list of suggestions. These include the prosecution of senior officials found to be complicit in the attacks, the provision of full security to villagers, placing police pickets away from upper-caste areas, and creating independent commissions of investigation.

Prospects

The extremist communist movement is often analyzed as a highly fragmented and splintered movement without a proper road map, intent only on violence and destruction. Yet, in a number of districts, it has survived for many decades. The reasons for its endurance are related to a number of factors. First, land reforms have not been properly carried out and landlords have been left in effective control of land, credit, and labor markets. The major Naxalite outfits thrive on the issue of land redistribution and proper wages and labor treatment. Second, the governments, which are often controlled by the urban upper-class elites and the rural landlord class, have not extended infrastructural facilities to the remote and backward areas. Many villages in Jharkhand and Bihar are without even basic necessities such as schools, health centers, roads, electricity, and water. The government's failure has resulted in the growth of the Naxalite movement with its parallel governments there. In North

Telengana, conditions are somewhat better, and the issue is more a law-and-order than a socioeconomic problem. The extremist groups operating there have become more interested in extortion than in the socioeconomic improvement of poor tribals and peasants. Finally, the collusion between vested political interests and extremist politics may be an added reason.

Some progress has been made. In West Bengal, the cradle of the Naxalite movement, extremist tendencies have been brought under control through an effective socioeconomic program, including land reforms, and an effective (police) administration. The success achieved by counter-Naxalite operations in AP registering an 18 percent decline in the year 2000 is a pointer to the general optimism that the movement can be brought under control.

Leftist extremism in the 1960s could be tackled more effectively due to a strong centralized authority and because basically the same party (the Congress Party) was in power at the center and in the states. With political fragmentation and with decentralization, law and order being a state subject, the effective response to the problem has been lacking. The states with a Naxalite problem have woken up to the need for concerted action and have had a series of interstate meetings beginning in December 1999. With the states' responses getting more organized than in the past two decades, the extremist movement will face greater challenges.

Recommendations

An effective response to Naxalism would have to include strategies at three levels. The Naxalite movement can thrive in an environment where economic development is lagging, where the old exploitative classes (feudal lords, contractors, and traders) have not been dislodged by modernization and development, and where the government machinery has not been made transparent by the pressure of a functioning democracy.

At the first level, the lack of socioeconomic development provides a breeding ground for discontent and extremist solutions. The implementation of tenancy reforms, protecting the rights of sharecroppers, and the payment of minimum wages require urgent attention. In some of the areas, land redistribution should help to create sustenance for landless labor families and curtail the power of landlords. Governments must ensure that existing facilities are properly utilized: schools, primary health centers, and government extension facilities should be run in such a way that the most downtrodden people have unhindered access. A basic-needs strategy, including a network of roads that makes the areas more accessible, will help to open the remote and backward areas to the outside world. If these conditions are fulfilled, the breeding ground for violent resistance will be reduced.

Second, law and order being a state responsibility, efforts at countering the Naxalite problem have until recently been undertaken only at the state level. There is a need for coordinated and uniform policies and for coordinated police action, including resource and intelligence sharing across the states, to tackle the problem from a law-and-order angle. There is also a need for evenhandedness by the police and administration, who tend to come down heavily on Naxalites yet remain inactive when private armies of landlords (*senas*) resort to violence.

A case could be made for the modernization of the police force in order to increase their effectiveness and morale. The problem, however, is to distinguish between terrorist activities and poor-people's movements, and it is imperative for the police to be evenhanded. All too often repressive behavior by the elite has not been curtailed or punished, and this permissiveness had been a breeding ground for terrorist reactions. Citizens' vigilance committees should be given an official status so that they can help in separating legitimate action against terrorist and criminal outfits and human-rights abuse in actions against rightful political activities.

The often repressive onslaught, of which genuine Naxalite organizations have been the target, often in fake encounters, should be considered as a human-rights abuse, and should be allowed to be investigated as such. On the other hand, the various Naxalite outfits should also allow civil-society organizations, other than the human-rights groups associated with them, to investigate cases of manslaughter and large-scale killings. Their extremist political stand continues to prevent a united front of all organizations and political parties fighting for the poor and thus in fact sustains the very power of exploitative classes and castes.

Social and economic rehabilitation programs to bring the discontented Naxalites into the mainstream would be helpful. Currently, only AP has a comprehensive package for rehabilitating surrendered Naxalites. The problem with such programs is that it may reward those who have held villages at ransom, and who continue to do so in alignment with mainstream political leaders. The programs have also been utilized by mainstream politicians in a secret understanding with Naxalite leaders. Development finances meant for the general good of the poor people in the affected areas should not take second position to the individual buying out of Naxalites willing to surrender.

Resources

Reports
Human Rights Watch, *Broken People: Caste Violence Against India's Untouchables,* 1999: http://www.hrw.org/reports/1999/india/.

Other Publications
Imperialism and Revolution in South Asia, edited by Kathleen Gough and Hari P. Sharma. New York/London, Monthly Review Press, 1973.
India's Freedom Struggle Betrayed, by Suniti Kumar Ghosh. Calcutta, Rupe, 1998.
Inside India Today, by Dilip Hiro. London, Routledge, 1976.
"Love for the Outlaws," by Kanhaiah Bhelari. *The Week,* 30 April 2000: www.the-week.com/20apr30/events6.htm.
Maoism in India, by Mohan Ram. Delhi, Vikas Publications, 1971.
The Naxalites and Their Ideology, by Rabindra Ray. Delhi, Oxford University Press, 1988.
The Naxalite Movement, by Biplab Dasgupta. Bombay, Allied Publishers, 1974.
"30 Years of Naxalbari: An Epic of Heroic Struggle and Sacrifice": www.maoism.org/misc/india/cpiml/cpiml-pw/30years/30_Years.htm.

Selected Internet Sites

www.aiprf.purespace.de/ (Web site of the All-India People's Resistance Forum, claiming to provide research documents, mainly on the People's War)

www.cpim.org/ (The largest communist party, not involved in, but often victim of, Naxalite activities; good web site with linkages and regular updates)

www.cpiml.org/ (A good source of CPI–ML documents, including *Liberation*, the monthly magazine of the organization)

www.fas.org/irp/world/india/threat/naxalite.htm (Federation of American Scientists, Intelligence Resource Program; also info on MCC and PWG)

www.ipcs.org/nmt/nax-index.html (An excellent source providing comprehensive coverage of newspaper reports on Naxalites)

www.maoism.org/misc/india/india.htm (A couple of documents, mostly dated, of the CPI–ML People's War)

Resource Contacts

K. K. Mitra, IPS (Retd), tel: +91-11- 5616714

Ambrose Pinto, Indian Social Institute, e-mail: ambrose@unv.ernet.in

Ashwini K. Ray, School of Social Sciences, Jawaharlal Nehru University, New Delhi 110067, India

Shankar Sen, IPS (Retd), Institute of Social Sciences, e-mail: sankar@ndf.vsnl.net.in

Yogendra Singh, School of Social Sciences, Jawaharlal Nehru University, New Delhi 110067, India

Organization

Center for the Study of Developing Societies
29, Rajpur Road
Delhi, India 110054
Tel: +91-11-3951190
Fax: +91-11-2943450
E-mail: csds@del2.vsnl.net.in

Data on the following organizations can be found in the Directory section:

Center for Policy Research
Institute for Conflict Management
Institute of Peace and Conflict Studies
People's Union for Civil Liberties

Suba Chandran is a research officer at the Institute of Peace and Conflict Studies, New Delhi. His areas of expertise include Afghanistan, Pakistan, Kashmir, religious fundamentalism, and terrorism. He has contributed to publications on these issues and to the Landmine Monitor *2000 and 2001. Mallika Joseph is a research officer at the Institute of Peace and Conflict Studies, New Delhi. She has worked extensively on the issues of landmines and improvised explosive devices, particularly their use by nonstate actors including Naxalites. She has contributed to several publications and to the* Landmine Monitor *1999, 2000, and 2001 as the researcher for South Asia.*

Note

1. Human Rights Watch report: http://www.hrw.org/reports/1999/india/India994-06.htm.

7.8.7

Caste Violence and Class in Bihar: The Ranvir Sena

Suba Chandran & Alok Kumar Gupta

Sena *literally means "army." In the context of Bihar—one of the most underdeveloped states of India—it refers to the private militias of the upper caste. Bihar has seen conflict between the upper castes (the landowning feudal classes and business contractors) and the lower castes (usually powerless sharecroppers and agricultural laborers) ever since independence. The gradual empowerment of these lower classes has provoked a bloody reaction from the gangs* (sena) *surrounding upper-caste criminals. The ever-present repression and retaliation escalated in the second half of the 1990s, when the entire populations of a number of hamlets were massacred in outbursts of Naxalite and* sena *violence.*

Lack of effective state intervention and the political patronage of the upper-caste militias have worsened the situation described above. Patronage along caste lines by various political parties and organizations has exacerbated the problem of suppression and violence. In Bihar, civil society is organized along caste lines to a far greater degree than in other Indian states. This caste orientation reinforces the strong nexus between the landlords, contractors, criminals, politicians, and administrators.

Bihar, apart from being one of the biggest states (with 83 million inhabitants in 2001, after Jharkhand had been split off to form a separate state), is also the poorest state in terms of both per capita income and human-development indicators. Whereas India as a whole, and the surrounding states with a similar feudal past (Uttar Pradesh and West Bengal), have considerably reduced the percentage of people below the poverty line, Bihar has not. Male and female literacy in 2001 were as low as 60 percent and 34 percent respectively, which is far below the average of 76 percent and 54 percent of India as a whole.

This continuing poverty is due partly to the feudal rigidity in the agrarian structure of Bihar. The hold of the landlords has distorted the modernization of social and political structures. In addition to the Brahmins, the Bhumihar and

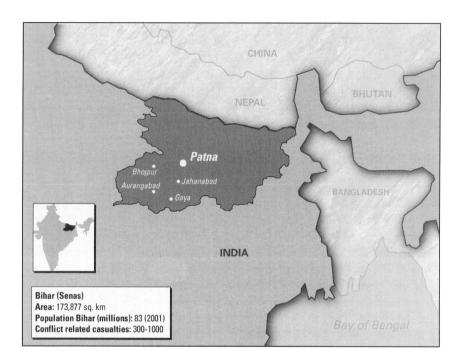

Bihar (Senas)
Area: 173,877 sq. km
Population Bihar (millions): 83 (2001)
Conflict related casualties: 300-1000

the Rajput are the dominant landed elite. For a long period in the history of the state, these zamindars (landlords) have dominated politics and have exploited their sharecroppers and agricultural laborers.

Popular resistance was formerly organized by the communist parties, which had a strong presence in many areas. From the late 1960s onwards, their role has been taken over partially by the Naxalites and partially by assertive low-caste politicians. Particularly, the emergence of the movement led by Jayaprakash Narayan in the 1970s and the promotion of low-caste politicians in the 1980s and 1990s to prime ministership (Laloo Prasad Yadav and his wife Rabri Devi of the Rashtriya Janata Dal [RJD]) has changed the political landscape in the state. The RJD (National People's Party) has risen to political prominence by championing the interests of traditionally repressed lower castes, but has remained largely inactive on the issue of land reforms and the implementation of minimum wages.

The emergence of the low caste as a political force has provoked a reaction among the landlords. Ever since the Rajputs in Bhojpur district formed the Kuer Sena in 1979, all upper castes and even some middle-caste groups have formed their own *sena*, mainly in order to suppress the lower castes and classes. In the 1990s their role was extended to defending the political interests of the caste, namely the defeat of the RJD. As such, the *senas* continue a long feudal tradition. Earlier, the zamindars had men called *lathaiths* (those armed with sticks) whose main job was to execute the orders of the landlords, keep the peasantry and sharecroppers under control, ensure that "taxes" and other payments were paid regularly, and enforce the settlement of local disputes. Bihar has regularly experienced gruesome murders of entire hamlets when impoverished laborers dared to stand up for their rights. In May 1977, for example, eleven people in Belchi village in the Patna district were stabbed to death. Today's *senas* however, are more powerful because of their structure and political patronage.

Three reasons could be cited for the emergence of *senas* in Bihar. First, the negative fallout of the "green revolution," which in the 1970s and 1980s resulted in greater agricultural productivity. It also resulted in increasing basic inequalities that existed between landlords and the landless. The poor and landless, mainly belonging to the lower classes, increased their demands for fair distribution of land and its produce, which led to the formation of *senas* by landlords to suppress them.

Second, the growth of the Naxalite movement in Bihar resulted in the lower caste and class openly challenging the age-old domination of the upper castes and classes. With the Naxalite groups openly advocating and indulging in armed activities, the landlords began cultivating *senas* to counter the opposition from both the Naxalites and the landless.

The third reason was the politicization of caste, especially through the "reservation policy" for the lower castes, which was introduced in 1990. While education and employment have not reached the entire lower-caste population, a small segment of the lowest castes (the ex-untouchables, nowadays renamed Dalit by the more radical sections) and of the backward castes has benefited, however. This lower-class elite has begun mobilizing the lower castes for their own political ends, sometimes with the help of the Naxalites. The powerful upper caste landlords could not tolerate this defiance by the low-caste elite and formed various *senas* to resist the gradual emergence of the lower castes in politics.

Conflict Dynamics

Besides Ranvir Sena, which is basically the private army of the landlords, there are a number of other armed gangs who represent the interests of the other castes. The Sunlight Sena is controlled by the Muslim Pathan landlords of Garwah, Palamau, and Gaya in alliance with the Rajput landlords of Palamau. The Bhoomi Sena was initially formed as the Kisan Suraksha Samiti in early 1980. Rich Kurmi landlords (a middle caste of the region), corrupt gentry, and professional criminals accumulated a huge quantity of arms, recruited some Kurmi youths, and launched a professional armed gang. The Bhoomi Sena is still powerful in some blocks in Patna district, but in other districts it has been eliminated by the armed squads of Maoist organizations. The Lorik Sena, of the backward-caste Yadavs, was formed in 1983 in Nalanda district but soon extended its activities and it is still powerful in Gaya and Dhanarua block in Patna. It appears to have degenerated into a gang that thrives on extortion from Yadav peasants.

Ranvir Sena, the most dreaded of all *senas*, is an organization of the upper-caste landlords. It came into existence in August 1994 in Belaur, a village with a population of twelve hundred in the central Bihar district of Bhojpur. The leader of the organization is Bharmeshwar Singh, who is also a Bharatiya Janata Party (BJP) activist, having previously been with the Congress Party during its period of national and regional government.

Estimates of the strength of the Ranvir Sena range from a few hundred to tens of thousands. The gangs are armed with knives, sickles, and home-produced guns and revolvers. Landlords finance it through "generous" contributions and subscriptions and members of the squads are reported to be drawing a monthly salary. The Ranvir Sena has also opted for the legal path by creating the Rashtravadi Kisan Mahasabha (RKMS), a peasant union that fields candidates for the elections, in alliance with the BJP and the Samata Party, both ruling parties in New Delhi.

The main objective of the Ranvir Sena and the RKMS is to intimidate the Dalits (the lower castes) and wipe out Naxalism. Ranvir Sena represents the Bhumihar and the Rajput, two major upper castes who have, in the past, been at loggerheads. The name Ranvir is actually associated with a nineteenth-century Bhumihar folk hero who fought against the Rajput landlords in Bhojpur. The common objective of oppressing the Dalits and the Naxalites and protecting their class interests has led them to heal their differences.

Since its formation in 1994, the Ranvir Sena has been involved in more than twenty-five massacres, in which, according to different reports, between

A Dalit woman manual laborer carrying stones, a job often done by untouchables

three hundred and one thousand persons have been killed. The raping of women is a common tactic employed by members of the Ranvir Sena and other caste militias to spread terror in lower-caste communities. In 1992, more than one hundred Dalit women in the Gaya district of Bihar were reportedly raped by the Savarna Liberation Front. Pregnant women and children have also been killed.

Some of the more gruesome murders in the years thereafter are the following:

• Within weeks after its formation, the Ranvir Sena was involved in clashes in the Bhojpur district. The first major incident occurred in Bathani Tola (Sahar block) on 11 July 1996, when nineteen CPI–ML supporters were killed by around sixty Sena activists armed with homemade firearms and cutting weapons. In previous months, numerous exchanges of fire took place leaving both sides with casualties. Two months earlier, nine Sena supporters were killed in a village in the same area.

• In late March and early April 1997, the Ranvir Sena killed ten Muslims in one village and eight Dalits in another village. On 20 April, two hundred armed persons belonging to the CPI–ML Party Unity attacked the village of a BJP member of the legislative assembly, allegedly responsible for the earlier attack, blew up his house, and killed six hard-core supporters of the *sena*.

• On 1 December 1997, sixty-three Dalits, including sixteen children, were killed in Laxmanpur Bathe village in Jehanabad; five teenage girls were raped before being shot in the chest. The village was raided in an overnight attack by two hundred and fifty Ranvir Sena members. The victims were sympathizers of the CPI–ML Liberation; in the area there had been an argument about the capture of government land by Bhumihars.

• In January 1999, twenty-two lower-caste men, women, and children were killed in Shankarbigha (Jehanabad district) when a Ranvir Sena gang entered their eight thatched huts and shot the inhabitants at point-blank range. The village is only 10 kilometers away from Laxmanpur Bathe.

• In April 1999, two groups of fifty men, each carrying sophisticated arms, attacked two hamlets in Sandani in Gaya district, killing twelve Yadavs, including a ten-year-old child; the killings were possibly a retaliation for the Bhumihars killed in Senari village one month earlier. Squads of the Maoist Communist Centre (MCC) then slit the throats of thirty-four Bhumihars in retaliation for two massacres carried out in MCC strongholds earlier in the year, claiming a further thirty-four lives.

• In June 2000, thirty-five Yadav men, women, and children were killed in Miapur, Aurangabad district, by a gang of two hundred Bhumihars. One week earlier, thirteen Bhumihars had been killed in Newada district, at a distance of 200 kilometers, in retaliation for the killing of three Kurmis.

The above list of massacres perpetrated by the Ranvir Sena reveals two trends. First, the scale of the killings has increased. There have been instances, in which the entire Dalit or Muslim population, including women and children, of one hamlet was slaughtered. Second, the geographical reach of the *sena*'s activities has been extended. Whereas initially, they focused on the Bhojpur district of Bihar, their operations are now spread over many other districts of Bihar and Jharkhand, especially Jehanabad, Patna, Gaya, and Aurangabad.

The political support of the upper castes to the Ranvir Sena and the RKMS has unfortunately also increased. The Ranvir Sena, as alleged by the Dalits, has the support of the major political parties in the state—the BJP, Congress, and even some sections in the ruling RJD. These allegations were raised in the press and by human-rights organizations. In October 2001, the Justice Amir Das Commission, constituted by the government three years earlier to investigate the nexus between political parties and the Ranvir Sena, confirmed the allegations. Notices have been issued to two federal ministers—including the powerful BJP minister Murli Manohar Joshi—and to twenty-two other politicians, of whom only two belong to the RJD.

The continuation of the conflict is also due to the involvement of local police officers, most of whom belong to the upper castes. The police are often on the scene of incidents but remain inactive. In his report on the 1996 attack in the Sahar block, the then home office minister Indrajit Gupta (a communist) remarked during the debates in the Lok Sabha (national parliament), on 19 July 1996 that "the failure of the district machinery was the immediate reason for the tragedy. In fact, it has been admitted by the state administration that despite the availability of intelligence about the impending tragedy and even the positioning of forces in the area, the massacre could not be averted due to connivance or lack of courage on the part of the law enforcing agencies."[1]

Official Conflict Management

Ministerial responsibilities in the Indian constitution have been divided between the union government and the state governments. Law and order is a function of the state, and as such, it is primarily the responsibility of the Bihar government to deal with the issue. Unfortunately, Bihar is one of the few states in India with a defective system of governance.

Bihar banned all caste-based private militias as long ago as 1986, resulting in the disappearance of a number of such groups in the first half of the 1990s. However, the government is finding it difficult to tackle the Ranvir Sena for various political and social reasons. In 1996, the state government, then headed by Laloo Prasad Yadav, banned the Ranvir Sena after the latter's involvement in the killing of six Dalits in Sarthna village in Bhojpur. But the government has not been able to control it.

The state government's response over the last six years has been reactive and short-term. After every major massacre, it has announced financial compensation to the families of the deceased, and the concerned officials have been either suspended or transferred. Occasionally, a new post was also created in the police to deal exclusively with this issue. After the Laxmanpur Bathe massacre (in which sixty-three people were killed in December 1997), the state government transferred the home secretary, suspended the superintendent of police in the district, and created a new post of additional director general of police to focus on the law-and-order problems. Similarly, the state government directed the administration to take up the construction of roads on a war footing. The absence of roads keeps the poor people in the remote areas in a precarious position and hinders the swift deployment of police forces.

At the judicial level, the state has appointed special courts for speedy trials. After the Sankarbigha massacre in January 1999, Chief Minister Rabri Devi announced the creation of a special court. A major problem is that many of the arrested *sena* members are known to be quickly released on bail and to have many sympathizers within the police and justice departments.

Committees have been formed at state and district levels, and they have come forward with various ideas, particularly stressing the need for the restoration of local self-government, the implementation of land reforms, and a meaningful development of the affected areas.

At the police level, the handling of the situation has been dismal. It is alleged that in several cases the police were unconcerned in dealing with the situation. For example, three police pickets were present during the attack in Bhatanitola in 1996, but they appeared to ignore the shots being fired. After an attack in Narayanpur where twelve Dalits were murdered by the Ranvir Sena in February 1999, it took the police twenty-four hours to reach the scene. They then told the villagers that, although their station is just two miles away, the complaint had to be lodged at another police station, which had jurisdiction over the particular village. The major efforts by the police are focused on the creation of new pickets in the affected areas. These pickets are insufficiently manned and their weapons are obsolete. During the massacres they either remain silent spectators or have even fled from the scene. During the attacks in March and May 1997, Ranvir Sena men were allegedly accompanied by members of the police force. Three days after the retaliatory Maoist attack, six communist extremist were killed by the police in a "fake encounter," i.e., after they had surrendered.

The state government has continually demanded the deployment of paramilitary forces by the central government. Five companies of the Central Reserve Police Force were sent to Bihar by the left-wing government in New Delhi after the Laxmanpur Bathe massacre in 1997, but they were withdrawn soon after the right-wing BJP government came to power.

After an incident on 13 February 1999 in Narayanpur, where twenty-one Dalits were massacred, the union government, rather than sending extra police forces to Bihar, dismissed the state government and imposed presidential rule, i.e., direct administration from New Delhi. However, a majority in the New Delhi parliament rejected the interference and the RJD government was reinstalled. The episode illustrated that party politics aimed at dislodging a state government were considered more important than a joint intervention against terrorist violence. Instead of helping to resolve the problem, the government of India has always condemned and criticized the state government for its failures. Massacres, and the reports of the "high-level" teams after visits to the area, have been misused in a partisan manner in order to increase the stranglehold of the union government on the state government.

The role of regional and international organizations in this issue is minimal. The regional organization South Asian Association of Regional Cooperation (SAARC) has no mandate to deal with these issues. India traditionally has been against any external involvement in its domestic issues. Besides, none of the other countries in the region or elsewhere has anything at stake in the ongoing violence perpetrated by the Ranvir Sena.

Multi-Track Diplomacy

The response from society and from nongovernmental organizations—domestic and international—to the caste violence is mixed. The role of NGOs in Bihar in creating awareness of the problem is commendable, but they have failed to make any impact on the government.

The caste/class conflicts in a polarized and backward society such as Bihar have set in motion a vicious circle of caste politics and caste consciousness, with various political parties stimulating the mobilization of caste for political purposes. Consequently there has been a tendency for the elite sections within each caste to set up their own *senas* to protect their socioeconomic and political interests. The Dalits were the last group to form their own *sena*. The Dalit Sena was the initiative of a right-wing politician, Ram Vilas Paswan, and was undertaken "in order to form a unit for the self defense of the Dalit community." By forming caste-based organizations, these leaders attempt to wean their electorate away from the more radical, class-based organizations in the state. The statements of some of these Yadav and Kurmi leaders with landed interests make this clear; the magazine *Frontline* (12 October 2001) reported "that in the matter of land the interests of the upper castes and the advanced sections among the backward classes converge."[2]

Political calculations and expediency have determined the response of the political parties to Ranvir Sena's activities. The ruling RJD has always blamed the Congress and the BJP (which has the support of the upper castes) for financing and guiding the Ranvir Sena to destabilize the RJD rule. In the aftermath of the massacres, political parties usually send a fact-finding team for an on-the-spot study of the massacre.

The right-wing opposition, especially the BJP, sees the growth of the Ranvir Sena as representing the failure of the Bihar government under Laloo Prasad Yadav and Rabri Devi. The killings are seen as the result of the encouragement of criminal gangs by a government that wants to remain in power rather than the manifestation of a caste war.

The CPI–M regards the nonimplementation of basic land reforms, nonpayment of minimum wages, and the nexus between the landlords, people, and criminals as the main reasons behind the vicious circle of violence. The CPI–M, like the other communist party, the CPI, is critical of both *sena* and the Maoist party organizations. The poor villagers "caught between the warring groups, spend sleepless nights," it says. The CPI–ML, the main opponent of the Ranvir Sena, has been more severe in its opposition. It organizes *bandhs* (strikes) both at state and national levels against its activities and the failure of the state and central governments to take any effective steps. Both parties see the *sena* more as a private army of the *bhupatis* (the haves) in a struggle with the have-nots, rather than as a Bhumihar caste party.

Gandhian organizations in the state have been active, working on relief projects and organizing communities in the tradition of nonviolence and tolerance. They, however, are not effective in the remote rural areas.

The People's Union for Democratic Rights (PUDR), like most political parties, has sent fact-finding teams to investigate the caste-based violence in Bihar, and has published various reports with recommendations. Also, the People's Union for Civil Liberties (PUCL) has published a couple of reports on violence in Bihar. Both the PUDR and the PUCL are ideologically aligned with the proponents of agrarian revolt and do not command any siginficant influence over the governments. Their championship of the Naxalite cause has weakened their position as a human-rights watchdog.

At the international level, Human Rights Watch (HRW) has been monitoring the problem for a long time and has made recommendations to the state and central governments. It has carried out a number of studies and investigations, and has approached the state government directly with a list of suggestions. These include the prosecution of senior officials found to be complicit in the attacks, the provision of full security to villagers, placing police pickets away from upper-caste areas, and creating independent commissions of investigation. It has been alleged by human-rights organizations that some politicians are members of the Ranvir Sena and that the police have sometimes accompanied the *sena* during their attacks or have conducted raids after attacks by the *senas*. The purpose of the raids is often to terrorize Dalits as a group, whether or not they are members of guerrilla organizations. *Sena* leaders and police officials have rarely been prosecuted for such killings and abuses.

There is, in this respect, a clear difference between the response of the state to militant activity by Naxalite groups and by the *senas*. Whereas a large number of Naxalites are killed in "encounters" with police, not a single Ranvir Sena member has suffered this fate. The administration is noticeably slow when it comes to tackling these armies. Evidence of police collusion with the Ranvir Sena has led to charges that the *sena* is being backed by the state administration and nonleftist political parties in order to check the growing leftist movement. Police have frequently operated as agents of the landed upper castes, conducting raids on Dalit villages and disguising killings as "encounters."

Prospects

The prospects of ending caste violence in general and of the Ranvir Sena in particular are gloomy. First, the land reforms, one of the main reasons for class conflicts in Bihar, have not been carried out effectively. In Bihar the caste war between the upper and lower castes has deep roots in the class war between the upper and lower classes.

Second, the ruling RJD, faced with challenges from within and outside the party, has been unable to govern competently. Many villages in Bihar are without basic amenities such as schools, health centers, roads, electricity, and water. The *sena* and the Maoist groups are symptoms of failed land reforms; the Ranvir Sena wants to stall changes in the agrarian structure.

Third, the police in Bihar are ineffective as a result of their inadequate strength, bad administration, and political interference. Lastly, many political parties are being supported by caste groups and they provide patronage to those who perpetuate violence. Upper castes such as the Rajputs and Bhumihars in Bihar support the BJP, Congress, and the Samata Party. Unless these political parties discontinue their political patronage of caste militias, caste-based violence in Bihar will continue.

Recommendations

To combat the caste violence and the growth of caste-based militias, efforts need to be made at both the macro and micro levels. Land reforms must be effectively implemented, the state police need to be modernized, developmental programs should be implemented, and political parties must function autonomously of caste influence.

The Minimum Wage Act, the land reform legislation, and the poverty alleviation programs have to be implemented urgently. The new government proposals to make sharecroppers the legal owners of land should be enacted as soon as possible, before sharecroppers are turned off the land and the question of landlessness and polarization is made even more intractable. The state administration should implement its own legislation. Lack of educational, health, transport, and communication facilities have precluded the participation of the impoverished masses in civil society. Although there have been various development packages devised in the past by the central and state governments, they have not sufficiently reached the target groups due to poor governance and widespread corruption. Only a better economic deal for landless labor and sharecroppers may turn the scales.

The restoration of democracy may lead to more transparency and influence from below. The holding of village council elections in June 2001, after a gap of twenty-four years, is a good first step in the restoration of democracy at the village level. The institutions, however, continue to be controlled by the village elite or their agents. Unless the poor people can free themselves from economic slavery, empowerment will remain difficult.

The Bihar police force needs to be urgently revamped to effectively handle the caste militia.

• The police force needs to be augmented in terms of numbers. Arming the police with better weapons would increase their prestige and morale and also instill fear in the private militias. The police also need to be provided with better transport and communications, enabling them to reach trouble spots more easily and quickly.

• Most importantly, steps need to be taken to recruit officers from the lowest ranks of society (Dalits and poor Muslims) into the police force. Caste is an important factor in the police and the administration of the state, particularly in some districts.

• The rules of conduct should be redefined. Care should also be taken that the police remain physically separate from the contending groups and do not accept upper-caste hospitality.

• A judicial body should be set up to investigate the role of the police in villages during and in the aftermath of massacres.

Peace committees, bringing together influential righteous citizens, Gandhian organizations, and other NGOs as well as the secular political parties, including the parties on opposing sides in the conflict, will have to be formed in order to maintain peace and restore sanity when conflicts have taken place. Such joint committees will also have an important function in overseeing the constitutional behavior of political parties, i.e., documenting and protesting against the political patronage of caste militias and caste organizations in general.

Resources

Newsletters and Periodicals
Economic and Political Weekly
"Ranveer Sena and Massacre Windows," by Arvind Sinha and Indu Sinha, 27 October 2001, pp. 4095–4099.
"State, Class and Sena Nexus," by Arvind Sinha and Indu Sinha, November 1996.

Reports
Human Rights Watch, *Broken People: Caste Violence Against India's Untouchables*, 1999: www.hrw.org/reports/1999/india/.
Institute of Peace and Conflict Studies, *Senas (Caste Armies) of Bihar*, by Alok Kumar Gupta: www.ipcs.org/nmt/milgroups/sena-india.html.
Institute for Human Development, *Semi-Feudalism Meets the Market: A Report from Purnea*, by Gerry Rodgers and Janine Rodgers, 2000.
People's Union for Civil Liberties
Report on Massacres in Jehanabad, 1999, Shankarbigha and Narainpur, 1999.
Killings at Rajebigha, Apsarh and Mianpur on June 3, 11 and 22, 2000, 2000.
People's Union for Democratic Rights
Agrarian Conflict in Bihar and the Ranbir Sena, October 1997.
A Time to Kill: A Report on Massacres in Jehanabad, August 1999.

Other Publications
The Republic of Bihar, by Arvind Das. New Delhi, Penguin, 1990.

Selected Internet Sites
www.cpiml.org/ (The parliamentary Maoist party, offering interesting party documents and journals)
www.dalitstan.org/sena/ (Web site of a sectarian political grouping of ex-untouchables)
www.ekta-parishad.org/ (Joint web site of the Gandhian organizations in Bihar, a useful source on local relief and peace initiatives)

Resource Contacts

Anand Chakravarty, A-1/4, Maurice Nagar, Delhi University, New Delhi, India
Alokh Sharma, Institute for Human Development, IAMR Building, Indraprashta Estate, New Delhi–10002, India
Dilip Simeon, Oxfam India Trust, e-mail: dilip@del2.vsnl.net.in

Organizations

Center for the Study of Developing Societies
29, Rajpur Road
Delhi, India 110054
Tel: +91-11-3951190
Fax: +91-11-2943450
E-mail: csds@del2.vsnl.net.in

Peoples Union for Civil Liberties (PUCL), Bihar State
201, Nilgiri Bhavan, Boring Canal Road
Patna, India

Data on the following organizations can be found in the Directory section:

Center for Policy Research
Institute of Peace and Conflict Studies
People's Union for Civil Liberties
People's Union for Democratic Rights

Suba Chandran is a research officer at the Institute of Peace and Conflict Studies, New Delhi. His areas of expertise include Afghanistan, Pakistan, Kashmir, religious fundamentalism, and terrorism. He has contributed to publications on these issues, and to the Landmine Monitor *2000 and 2001. Alok Kumar Gupta is working as lecturer in political science at the National Law University, Jodhpur (Rajasthan, India) and is working on his doctoral thesis. He has written a number of articles and chapters on issues related to South Asia in newspapers, journals, web sites, and books.*

Notes

1. Indrajit Bupta, XI Lok Sabha Debates Session II, 19 July 1996: http://alfa.nic.in/lsII/ses2/23190796.htm.

2. Kalyan Chaudhari, "Tension in the Air," *Frontline* 18(20), October 2001: http://www.flonnet.com/fl1820/18200470.htm.

7.8.8

Multiple Conflicts in Northeast India

Kristoffel Lieten

In Nagaland, separatist violence commenced in 1952. Since then, conflicts have proliferated in all Northeastern states in India, especially since the late 1970s. Every state in the region is currently affected by insurgent violence. Only Arunachal Pradesh, Meghalaya, and Mizoram lately have remained by and large peaceful, although some activities of the Naga and the Bru National Liberation Front (BNLF) in these areas have given recent cause for concern. While there have been several government initiatives, multi-track diplomacy and NGO peace activities are at an incipient stage. Governmental policies in this remote corner of India do not encourage international interventions—directly or indirectly—in any conflict-resolution process. The conflict is considered as a purely internal conflict in which no international organization should become involved. The government itself alternates between political pacification and development interventions on the one hand and military cleansing of the areas on the other hand.

India's Northeast comprises seven states: Assam, Arunachal Pradesh, Manipur, Meghalaya, Mizoram, Nagaland, and Tripura. The region is characterized by a pronounced ethnic, cultural, religious, and linguistic diversity. In addition to the nontribal population, which is dominant in Assam and Tripura, the region has more than 160 Scheduled Tribes (abbreviated as ST: the original inhabitants that have been recognized as such in a separate schedule of the government of India).

Northeastern India contains many natural resources (e.g., oil, wood, and hydropower potential). These resources are being exploited as national resources for the benefit of the entire country, but local sentiment has often referred to these activities as internal colonialism. It is also the case that many recent immigrants, or "nontribal" Indians, have been employed to run these industries and have been given good positions in the formal economy, for

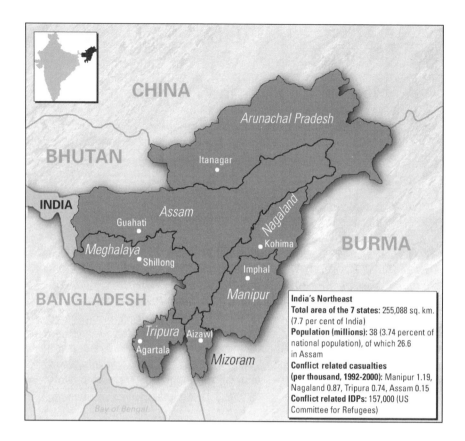

India's Northeast
Total area of the 7 states: 255,088 sq. km.
(7.7 per cent of India)
Population (millions): 38 (3.74 percent of national population), of which 26.6 in Assam
Conflict related casualties
(per thousand, 1992-2000): Manipur 1.19, Nagaland 0.87, Tripura 0.74, Assam 0.15
Conflict related IDPs: 157,000 (US Committee for Refugees)

example in state-run factories and institutions. It would be incorrect to state that the region is an impoverished and exploited corner of the country. The aggregate data suggest the opposite picture: with the exception of Tripura and Assam, all the states have a per capita income around, or substantially above, the national average. Literacy levels, with the exception of the remote state of Arunachal, also tend to be substantially higher than in the rest of India.

The northeastern region is connected with the rest of India through a narrow corridor, the "chicken's neck." At its narrowest, around Siliguri in North Bengal, separating Nepal and Bangladesh, it has an approximate width of 21 kilometers on the western side. Practically the entire boundary of the region is an international border: China to the north, Bangladesh to the southwest, Bhutan to the northwest, and Myanmar to the east.

The cultural diversity in northeastern India, with its various ethnic and linguistic groups, was made more complex as a result of the British policy of "importing" large numbers of administrators, tea plantation workers, and cultivators from other parts of India during colonial rule, which started with the submission of Assam in 1826. The prospect of integration with the local community was systematically undermined by the British policy of segregating the tribal populations into so-called nonregulated or excluded areas that were administered differently. Laws that prevailed in the rest of British India were thought to be unsuitable to the stage of development of the populations of the hill areas of the northeast. Also from the point of view of political expediency, given the emergence of the nationalist movement in the rest of British India, spatial integration with the rest of the subcontinent was deferred.

The "Inner Line" system prohibited access to these areas to all "outsiders," except those who obtained special permission from the government. It created a frontier within a frontier, accentuating the political and cultural schism between the tribal areas and the plains. The missionaries also added to the confusion by converting the hill tribals to Christianity. The conversion to various forms of Christianity is a good illustration of the simultaneous working of segregation (from the rest of India) and subordination within the system of colonialism. Many tribal clans, while rejecting the "alien cultural invasion" of mainstream Indians, thus more readily came to accept a modernizing influence from the West. This has contributed to the cultural cleavage in the region.

After independence, such isolationist policies persisted, partly because of the chicken's neck, which made the area marginal to the rest of India. The cumulative impact of these policies was a deepening of fissures between tribal and nontribal populations. Many areas were also excluded from the process of modernization that affected the rest of the country. Such exclusion was by and large unsustainable in a modernizing world to which the tribal elite (at least) was also attracted. Inevitably, with the progressive and natural erosion of the artificial barriers, the local populations were brought into increasing friction with migrant populations that were economically better adapted to the institutions and business opportunities of the modern world.

For much of the British period, economy and politics were largely dictated by the interests prevailing in Bengal. The partition of the colonial empire, cutting away East Pakistan (now Bangladesh), was particularly disastrous for the Northeast. The separation crippled crucial economic linkages between Calcutta and the northeastern regions. Inland water, road, and railway communications were abruptly terminated. Partition also brought with it waves of migration that disrupted, and continue to disturb, existing demographic equations. The enmity between India and Pakistan, and following the 1962 war with China, between India and China, sealed many of the previously porous borders and made the entire region into a tense security zone. In recent years, illegal migration of Bangladeshi (Muslim) nationals into India, which has a Hindu-chauvinist government, and the use of Bangladeshi and Bhutanese territory by insurgents operating in India's Northeast have added to the complex political imbroglio.

Whereas the two previous factors, the ethnic cauldron and the spatial isolation and marginalization, have been at the roots of the emerging conflict, political opportunism leading to an arrangement between various power elites and insurgents has fuelled the conflict in every affected state. The proliferation of armed groups based on various tribal and ethnic identities can also be explained as the result of the demonstration effect of the success of other such groups in the past. The advantages are not necessarily measured in terms of increase in political autonomy for the state and the ethnic group but, increasingly,

Figure 7.8.8.1   Insurgency-Related Casualties in Northeast India (1992–2000)

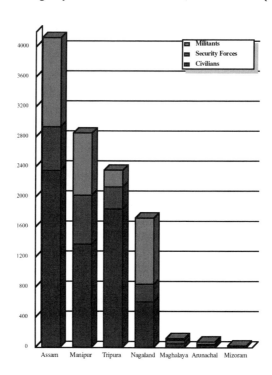

in terms of the financial gains through criminal operations that are undertaken by a number of militant groups, particularly in Tripura, Nagaland, and Mizoram.

In the meantime, the succession of insurgencies and movements seeking autonomy or independence or the assertion of an identity distinct from the rest of India has created a mental divide, with the rest of India now thinking of the areas beyond Assam as a remote, perpetually troubled corner.

The mobilization along tribal lines has become a basic feature in electoral politics and in the separatist and terrorist movements across the northeastern region. The conflicts in the various areas, as we shall see, alternate between intertribal conflicts, conflicts between tribes and nontribes, and between tribal groups and the (Indian) government.

There are a large number of NGOs in the northeastern states, although most of them are either dormant, or of dubious intent and affiliation. Manipur, for instance, has the largest number of NGOs registered with various ministries (333, as against 233 in Assam, which is by far the largest state in the region). This is certainly not an index of the developmental activities in the state, and the central government cut off all funding to NGOs in Manipur in December 2000, pending thorough checks on utilization, because of allegations of large-scale siphoning of funds to insurgents and to terrorist organizations. Most NGOs operate on government funding.

Assam

The insurgency in Assam began in 1979 with the Assamese middle-class movement against the immigrants from Bangladesh. After a period of escalating violence in its early days and an erosion of popular support in recent years, around four districts in the state are presently seriously afflicted by terrorist activities. Large numbers of cadres have surrendered, but as various groups operating from the underground have acquired a criminal character, disengaged from any consistent ideological objectives, acts of terror continue to inflict casualties. This is also the case with the second movement, which emerged in the late 1980s, namely the movement of the Bodo tribes against the Assamese majority. Many splinter groups have emerged and then disappeared after having been active for some time.

Conflict Dynamics
Insurgency in Assam emerged in July 1979 primarily out of a single issue: the illegal migrants from Bangladesh. Middle-class students in the All Assam Students Union (AASU) took the initiative. They were soon joined by the United Liberation Front of Asom (ULFA) under the leadership of Paresh Baruah, for whom the secession from India was the main objective . The ULFA operated in close coordination with the AASU until the agitation ended in August 1985. After the Assam Accord, which was signed with the union government in New Delhi and which agreed on the identification of illegal migrants, AASU leaders formed the Asom Gana Parishad (AGP) and rode to victory in the state assembly elections. The ULFA refused to submit to the new government and continued with its terrorist acts of arson and killings. When the AGP government was not in a position to maintain law and order, the state was brought under direct control of the union government (Presidents Rule) in November 1990. The Indian army, in between elections, conducted a series of military operations. The newly elected Indian National Congress government then suspended army operations and announced an amnesty for the militants. Within one year, some 4,000 ULFA militants surrendered to the authorities. Counterinsurgency operations forced the ULFA to go into exile in Bhutan and Bangladesh. The conflict in the 1980s and 1980s accordingly was on a smaller scale, and the solution was sought more in political conflict management than in large-scale military operations.

The second conflict in Assam emerged when the Bodos, a major tribe to the north of the Brahmaputra River, initiated a second insurgency on the issue of the dispossession of their tribal land by Bengali and Assamese settlers. They also disputed the neglect of the Bodo language and culture. Toward the latter half of the 1980s, the leadership of the All Bodo Students' Union (ABSU) started demanding a separate state within India and initiated a guerrilla war. The "Bodo Accord" with the Indian government in February 1993 paved the way for the establishment of the Bodoland Autonomous Council (BAC). However, since Bodo villages are not contiguous, the demarcation of the jurisdiction of the BAC remained a problem, and as of 2002 the BAC is

Baldev/Sygma/ABC

Bodies in the village of Ranglo, Assam province, India.
In February 1983, over 3,500 persons were massacred in clashes between
the residents of Assam and Bengalis, Muslim refugees who came from Bangladesh.

still to be demarcated properly. In the meantime, one Bodo section had repudiated the accord, and their organization, the Bodo Liberation Tigers (BLT), has continued its ethnic attacks. In an attempt to clean their prospective autonomous area from non-Bodo elements, large-scale attacks were carried out against other ethnic groups, displacing tens of thousands of people in distress migration.

The attacks on non-Bodos, not only on Bengali and Assamese settlers, provoked the emergence of other militant organizations along tribal, religious, and cultural fissures. The Mising, the Tiwa, and the Rabha have started agitations for an autonomous council and the government in 2002 was considering granting them. The Santhals and other non-Bodo communities have also begun to arm themselves and fight back. The Dimasi tribe have established militant wings around demands for an independent tribal homeland. This has, in turn, resulted in significant displacement of the Bodo population from areas where they are a minority. The Muslim United Liberation Front of Assam (one among a number of Muslim militant groups in the state) has raised the demand for a separate state comprising the five border districts in Assam, which have a Muslim majority.

Official Conflict Management
In 1991, a five-member ULFA team led by its general secretary, Golap Baruah, then in jail, was flown to New Delhi for peace talks. The prime minister agreed to call a cease-fire in counterterrorism operations, provided the ULFA abstained from violence. The ULFA team returned to Assam after the government officially released Baruah. Baruah, however, immediately went underground.

Thereafter, both the federal and the state governments have made various attempts to break the deadlock, but ULFA has placed three preconditions on a possible dialogue with New Delhi: talks outside India; talks under the supervision of the UN; and talks to be centered around their central demand of sovereignty. The initiative floundered and counterterrorism operations have continued at the same intensity.

In the meantime, AASU has continued with its agitation against Muslim immigrants from Bangladesh. It has started agitations for the withdrawal of the Illegal Migrants Act. Since the act came into force in the mid-1980s, less than 10,000 people have been identified as illegal and only 1,434 could be deported. AASU wants a repeal of the legislation and the introduction of more radical measures. It is supported by the Bharatiya Janata Party (BJP) but because a majority if the national parliament disagrees with the Hindu chauvinist stand on migrants, the stalemate continues.

In its peace initiatives with the Bodo groups in Assam, however, the government has made more headway. The BJP, the Hindu party dominating the union government in New Delhi, ruling fought the 1999 state assembly elections in alliance with the ABSU (and hence with the BLT) and the BLT has been engaged in a peace process on advantageous terms with the government of India since 1999. A cease-fire agreement was followed by tripartite talks between the BLT, the government of Assam, and the BJP-led union government in New Delhi. The discussion includes the extent of the BAC area. Since the victory of the Congress Party in the May 2001 assembly elections, the new state government and the BLT have again been engaged in violent clashes.

Assamese and Bodo nationalists have accused the government of India of internal colonization and exploitation. Yet the government has been forthcoming in developing various development initiatives to create a context conducive to peace. Various packages have been announced but the development and relief programs have been poorly implemented. Actual disbursement has been far short of the promises and funds have often disappeared in the pockets of corrupt middlemen. State government agencies, in their endeavor to implement development packages in the disturbed areas, are more often than not constrained by a corrupt and conniving administration. The development and rehabilitation schemes may even have given rise to the activities of strongly organized criminal groups of former militants in the state who, in collusion with bureaucrats and politicians, have taken hold of the state distribution systems.

Multi-Track Diplomacy

The state government during the 1990s followed a two-pronged strategy: to defeat the insurgents militarily and simultaneously to create a support basis among civil-society organizations. It urged influential groups such as the All Assam Students' Union, the Asom Sahitya Sabha, and the Bodo Sahitya Sabha (both literary associations) to take initiatives to construe a climate of dialogue and prepare grounds for talks. The organizations by and large rejected the initiative, declaring that it was the government's responsibility to make peace.

This case illustrates that NGO initiatives to resolve the conflict in Assam are limited. Yet, voluntary organizations together with the smaller political parties have taken some initiatives in mobilizing public opinion against indiscriminate killings and terrorist attacks. The cold-blooded killing of Hindi-speaking people in different parts of the state in the year 2000 brought thousands of ordinary people and several voluntary organizations right across the state into the streets.

While various organizations work in the field of development and welfare of different sections of the society, specific focus on conflict management and resolution has been absent. For example, the Tribal Welfare Society acts mainly on issues such as internal displacement, environmental degradation, and welfare and relief projects, targeting activities for the indigenous population. They have not worked on reconciliation and conflict resolution, however.

Some women's organizations have been active on specific issues of human-rights violations, but they have not sustained their efforts. More consistent has been the Bodo Women's Justice Forum, founded in 1993, which has organized various meetings around the issues of peace and human rights. Its weakness as a peacebuilder is its alignment with the political aims of Bodo independence.

Nagaland

Violence in Nagaland appears to be decreasing, but the peace process that was initiated in 1997 has dragged on inconclusively. A peace deal on the cessation of violence between the government of India with one group of the Naga rebels has come to naught because of opposition in the neighboring state of Manipur and the intense factionalism between the various Naga tribes.

The Nagas comprise nearly seventeen major tribes, among which are the Ao, Angami, Konyak, Tankhul, and Rengma. Each tribe and subtribe speaks a different language, belonging to the Tibeto-Burmese group of languages. Historically, different Naga tribes have lived in isolation for centuries, with only marginal contact with the people of the Brahmaputra Valley (part of present-day Assam) during the rule of the Ahom kings. The British, too, in their initial years of rule in Assam, successfully prevented the national movement from reaching the hills by keeping the Naga segregated. This policy was followed in all the princely states of British India and encouraged a sense of local independence separate from the unified India that the leaders of the nationalist movement were fighting for. In 1945, the colonial administration formed the Naga Hills District Council, which one year later became a political organization: the Naga Nationalist Council (NNC). A resolution seeking autonomy within Assam was adopted in a meeting at Wokha in June 1946. However, the subsequent rift among the Angamis and the Aos within the NNC led the Angamis to demand independence, while the Aos were largely in favor of autonomy within the Indian union.

The NCC, representing a minority of the Naga tribes, in 1947 signed a Nine-Points Agreement with the colonial administration, and on 14 August 1947, during the last days of the colonial administration, the legendary Angami Zapu Phizo declared the independence of Nagalim. The government of India, which came into existence three days later, swiftly moved to bring the Naga territories within the framework of the republic of India. By 1950, Phizo had assumed the presidency of the NNC and publicly resolved to establish Nagalim, the sovereign Naga state. In a plebiscite, which the chiefs of the traditional village councils of the NCC organized in some of the Naga areas in 1951, 99.9 percent were said to have supported independence for Nagalim. The government of India ignored the referendum and, moreover, suspected the Naga leadership of being manipulated by foreigners intent on breaking up the Indian union. Since then, both sides have been on collision course.

Conflict Dynamics
The NCC under the leadership of A. Z. Phizo in 1956 proclaimed the establishment of a government with its own constitution and a Naga army. Following the induction of the armed forces in the state in April 1956, a war of liberation was declared. In the bloody confrontation between insurgents and the Indian army 1,400 Naga and 160 soldiers of the army were killed. Phizo managed to flee to London, where the Naga cause attracted international sympathy. Divisions began to emerge within the Naga movement with the formation of the Naga People's Convention, which favored Indian statehood as an alternative to independence. The Delhi Agreement between this section of the Naga leadership and the government of India led to the formation of the state of Nagaland on 1 December 1963, which was by far the smallest state in India with only 350,000 inhabitants. The NCC rejected the agreement as a ploy to divide the Naga people. A peace mission by the government of India, which suspended the anti-insurgency operations, however, did not succeed in mollifying the leadership and the mission was dissolved in 1967. The NNC was progressively marginalized: moderate politicians opted for participation in the parliamentary system and counterinsurgency operations brought the situation under relative control, forcing the militants to the negotiating table. Under the Shillong Accord, signed between the central government of India and the representatives of the federal government of Nagaland on 11 November 1975 at the initiative of the Naga Peace Council and after the defeat of the depleted NCC forces, the Naga leadership accepted the Indian constitution and agreed to come overground and surrender their weapons. Phizo in London and the Chinese-influenced group led by Muivah in Burma repudiated the accord. This group formed a new underground organization, the National Socialist Council of Nagaland (NSCN). In the 1980s, Nagaland was at peace and when insurgency reemerged, all factions of the NSCN (and the NCC led by Adino, Phizo's daughter) were banned in 1991.

Divisions among the Naga tribes resulted in the split of the NSCN in 1988. The Konyak tribes formed the NSCN-K (Khaplang) under the leadership of Khole Konyak and S. S. Khaplang. The Tankhul faction, the NSCN-IM (Isak-Muivah), was led by Isak Swu and T. Muivah. The NCSN-IM claims to have nearly 3,000 armed cadres, fighting in parts of Nagaland and in districts of Arunachal Pradesh and Manipur; the NSCN-K is reported to have a strength of about 2,000 activists. There have been a number of clashes between the militants of both formations, the worst of which occurred in April 1988, when NSCN-K activists attacked the headquarters of the IM faction and killed over a hundred cadres. In August 1999, activists belonging to the IM faction killed Dally Mungro, general secretary of the Khaplang faction, in Kohima district. In the first three months of 2000, Tuensang district witnessed as many as ten fierce factional fights between the two groups and as many as seventy militants of both factions were reported to have been killed in clashes in the Mon district in the first week of May 2000. The internecine rivalry appears to have declined thereafter, but the internal fight for the control over the Naga cause continues to pose a serious threat to security and stability in Nagaland.

On the other hand, allegations of excesses by the security forces have also been noted. These include instances of custodial torture, molestation, and rape. Even though investigations have been made and the guilty were punished in many such cases, the generally slow nature of civil procedures remains a matter of intense discontent among the victims and their communities. These excesses and the failing judicial process help to sustain some sympathy for the armed underground factions.

Official Conflict Management

After church organizations had succeeded in convincing the Naga rebels to lay down arms, the government of India in 1973, after protracted negotiations, succeeded in clinching a deal with a breakaway faction of the rebels. Arms were surrendered and the constitution of India was accepted as the basis for further talks. This implied that at least one section of the Naga rebels rejected the idea of an independent Nagalim. The government of India subsequently made several efforts to involve more Naga rebels and the Shillong Accord (1975) between the government and the Naga leadership was the result of this process. For two decades thereafter, Nagaland did not witness any serious peace initiative.

A process of dialogue with the hard-liners commenced only in the mid-1990s. In June 1995, Prime Minister Narasimha Rao met both Isak and Muivah in Paris and later offered to hold unconditional talks with the Naga insurgent groups. In its response at the end of July 1996, the NSCN-IM set three preconditions for talks: a focus on sovereignty, to be held in a third country, and through a third-party mediator. Following these meetings, a cease-fire agreement was signed on 25 July 1997, during the period of the Janata government of I. K. Gujral. The agreement was restricted to the area within the state of Nagaland. Rao's successors, including the present government of Prime Minister Vajpayee, have had various meetings in foreign capitals and have extended the cease-fire agreement several times.

Ultimately, the government of India, in an agreement signed in Bangkok in June 2001, agreed to extend the area of cease-fire "without territorial limits," i.e., to all the Naga-dominated areas in the Northeast. The NSCN-IM leadership had insisted on normalization in all ancestral territories where Nagas live under a non-Naga administration. Widespread protests by other groups in those areas, particularly in Manipur where the assembly building was torched, made the federal government revoke its decision and restrict the cease-fire to Nagaland only. In practice, however, the cease-fire has been extended and the Naga leadership regards this as an recognition of its claims over parts of Manipur as well. In the 2002 state assembly elections in Manipur, the NSCN-IM entered the fray and gave protection to the Naga candidates in the hills of Manipur who had been made to sign a declaration of support to the Naga cause.

The government's parallel peace process with the NSCN-K resulted in a two months' cease-fire commencing in November 1998. In April 2000 the NSCN-K announced a formal cease-fire with the central government, and the security forces responded with a unilateral suspension of military operations. Although the cease-fire has yet to be formalized, violent incidents in the recent period have clearly been on the decline.

Multi-Track Diplomacy
The Baptist Church in Nagaland has been involved in the peace process since the beginning of the conflict, starting with the Peace Mission in 1963, which succeeded in securing a cease-fire and the temporary suspension of the armed conflict. In July 1997, the Baptist Church again was successful when it organized the Atlanta peace meeting at the end of which the NSCN leadership accepted initiatives to start a dialogue with the government of India.

The Naga People's Movement for Human Rights (NPMHR), an important human-rights organization in the state, has been leading the movement to highlight human-rights abuses by the security forces. Starting from the days of Operation Bluebird, during which some cases of human-rights violation were reported (involving Assam Rifles' personnel in and around Oinam village in Manipur's Senapati district in 1987), the NPMHR has been continuously drawing attention to such incidents. It has also initiated a People to People Dialogue by taking representatives of a number of Naga organizations to New Delhi and to other states in order to foster better understanding and respect between the Indian and Naga civil society. However, since they explicitly support the insurgents' cause and consider Nagaland as separate country, little service has been done to the broader cause of human rights and conflict resolution. The organization has a one-sided interest in human-rights violations and does not publicize or question the terrorist campaigns that some of the Naga groups resort to.

Lately, women's groups have also been involved in peace initiatives. Of particular importance is the Naga Mothers Association (NMA). The NMA has been active against alcoholism and drug abuse to which many of the unemployed youth have fallen victim. In recent years, the NMA has been closely associated with political issues. The NMA also collaborates with the leadership of the NSCN factions and other Naga organizations for a reduction in violence. It has organized various rallies and appeals to stop the "bloodbath." The campaign "Shed No More Blood" served as a channel of communication for various Naga groups and spread the message that peaceful conditions are the prerequisite for human development. The NMA coordinates with different churches in Nagaland to give momentum to the ongoing peace process between the union government and the NSCN-IM. It has also participated in meetings and conferences with the Naga Students' Federation (NSF), the Naga Hohos, and the NPMHR.

The Naga Hoho, the apex council of the Naga tribes, also has been active in efforts to bring about unity among the various militant factions and to find an acceptable solution. After the IM group joined the peace process, the Hoho, along with other organizations such as the NPMHR and the NSF, met the leaders of the Khaplang faction in Northern Myanmar and urged them to engage in mainstream politics. Later, in January 1999, the Naga Hoho president met the NSCN-IM leadership in Bangkok to discuss proposals for unity among the NSCN factions. After the incidents at the assembly in Manipur in June 2001, the Naga Hoho has undertaken a peace mission to Assam and to other places in order to convince Assamese and Meitheis that the cease-fire extension was no threat to their interests. The coordination committee of the Hoho has been active in trying to unite the various Naga tribes and to confront the government of India as a unified force rather than as opposing factions.

Activities of international NGOs and funding agencies have been primarily confined to the realm of monitoring human-rights issues and creating awareness abroad in support of the Naga struggle for independence. The Naga Vigil Human Rights Group, a UK-based NGO, founded in 1989 proposes to document the ongoing human-rights violations and make research material available to individuals and other NGOs. It has offices in the UK, Australia, Nepal, India, and Japan. It channels humanitarian aid such as medical goods to various relief projects such as the Rainbow Relief Project in eastern Nagaland. The Naga International Support Center (NISC), an Amsterdam-based NGO founded in May 2001, supports the Naga cause and seeks to generate a "free flow of information." The NISC and another Dutch NGO—the Netherlands Center for Indigenous Peoples—provide information and organize activities in support of the Naga movement.

Manipur

Most of Manipur is hilly area; the only exception is the narrow Imphal Valley. The Hindu Meitei, who comprise more than 50 percent of the population, and the Muslim Meitei-Pangals live in the valley. The hills are exclusively reserved for the tribals—mainly Naga and Kuki. Under the land tenure system of the state, the hill tribes are allowed to settle in the valley, but the Meitei and Meitei-Pangal are not allowed to buy land or settle in the hills. In addition, the tribals can avail of some benefits under various reservations schemes in government employment and educational institutions.

After the colonial power left India, Manipur became an independent kingdom, with its own constitution and, in 1948, an elected parliament with the *maharaja* (the king) as the constitutional head. Various secular and also communist organizations played a role in this transfer of power. Soon thereafter, without eliciting the opinion of his parliament, the maharaja in 1949 signed the Manipur

Merger Agreement with New Delhi. The circumstances under which he did so (or was coerced to do so) are still a matter of controversy. The insurgency in Manipur started in 1964. The primary conflict involved the fight for statehood. In the course of time, secondary conflicts have arisen out of tensions between various ethnic and tribal subgroups, often as a result of changes in patterns of land tenure and distribution. The number of insurgent groups in the state has been fluctuating; as many as eighteen are reported to be currently active.

In the assembly elections, the Indian National Congress Party usually had been the strongest party, with the Communist Party of India and the (socialist) Manipur People's Party as strong contenders. Politics in the state in the past had been characterized by its secular and composite character, not necessarily dominated by the majority Meiteis. Its first chief minister was a Muslim and two other chief ministers had a tribal background. In the last decade of the century, however, corrupt power politics in connivance with many of the thirty-five-odd underground militant outfits has transformed the structure of power in the state.

Conflict Dynamics
After the king of Manipur in 1949 had signed the agreement with the authorities in New Delhi, the local political leadership refused to accept the accession to India and rose in revolt. After many years of political turmoil and violence, Manipur was granted independent statehood (separate from Assam) only in 1972. The much smaller Nagaland had been granted statehood almost ten years earlier.

The beginnings of insurgency can be formally traced to the foundation of the United National Liberation Front (UNLF) on 24 November 1964, under the leadership of Samarendra Singh. In September 1978, radicalism went one step ahead with the emergence of the People's Liberation Army (PLA), an organization with a leftist ideology and allegedly trained in guerilla warfare in China. The PLA maintains that it wants to organize a revolutionary front covering the entire Northeast and uniting all ethnic groups, including the Meiteis, Nagas, and Kukis. Both these organizations as well as the PREPAK (People's Revolutionary Party of Kangleipak) are coordinating their activities in a common platform, the Manipur People's Liberation Front.

The period around 1980 witnessed an escalation in insurgent activities. The entire Imphal Valley was declared a disturbed area and various underground organizations were banned. A series of successful operations in the early 1980s reestablished peaceful conditions, but the insurgency reemerged toward the end of the 1980s.

The ethnic conflict with the Nagas has compounded the problem in the 1990s. Some of the tribes living in Manipur are Naga. Influential Naga leaders such as Muivah hail from this area, and so do many of his Tankhul tribesmen. A bitter struggle to control drug trafficking and contraband smuggling through the border town of Moreh resulted in a bloodbath between the Kukis and the Nagas when clashes erupted in 1992. Nearly a thousand people were killed and there was enormous destruction of property. After mass movements of populations between ethnically cleansed Kuki and Naga areas, peace returned to the border town.

Several organizations in the Indian Northeast have constituted a common platform called the United Liberation Front of Seven Sisters to oppose the demand for a "Greater Nagaland" (Nagalim). When the union government, on 14 June 2001, despite earlier warnings by the Manipur assembly, decided to extend the cease-fire with the Naga rebels led by Muivah to all Naga-dominated areas in the Northeast, violence erupted in Manipur: the state assembly building was burnt and thirteen protestors were killed on 18 June 2001. Civil-society organizations in Manipur were united in a mass movement against the decision and ultimately, the new cease-fire arrangements were revoked and restricted to Nagaland only. The Manipuri protestors see in the extension of a cease-fire to its own territories the portent of the future inclusion of some of its own territories in Nagalim. The Naga leaders who had signed the cease-fire did this in the understanding that the Indian army would no longer operate in the areas where they had established (or wanted to establish) control. An area much bigger than Nagaland itself lies outside Nagaland. NSCN-IM leaders have indeed argued that the impoverished Naga population in Manipur (and in other areas) is being exploited by the Meiti elite and that the Naga territory should extend to all the ancestral lands of the Naga. A cease-fire, apparently a positive departure, thus has generated a new conflict, because to the Manipuri it indicates that the Naga army could henceforth control parts of its own territory.

These events indicate that the latent tension between the various groups could at any time be converted into an overt conflict and several other tribes during the 1990s have actually established their own rebel groups. An estimated one thousand lives were lost in 1997–1998 in violent clashes between Kukis and the Paites, two groups who speak virtually the same language and share many customs and traditions. In addition, Meitei insurgents have also begun to agitate against *mayang* (outsiders) settled in Manipur. The People's Republic Army was set up in the early 1990s to target the Pangals (Manipuri Muslims), who constitute over 7 percent of the population and who are considered *mayang*. As a reaction, the Pangals set up their own militant groups.

Politics in Manipur appears to have shifted further in the direction of militant-backed extortion racket. A nexus has developed between the politicians who, in exchange for protection, election funds, and vote banks, commit themselves to let the underground organization control the public distribution system and corner the lucrative public-work contracts. In an interesting comment on the state assembly elections of February 2002, the magazine *Frontline* (29 March 2002) commented: "Politics in Manipur has less to do with ideology and agenda than with wars between private armies. It is turf war in a vast no man's land. In the hills, virtually each tribe has an underground outfit that offers protection to its politicians and extorts money from them."

Official Conflict Management

After insurgency emerged in a big way with the establishment of the PLA in 1978, the government declared the valley a disturbed area. Virtually the entire frontline leadership of the PLA was killed in counterinsurgency operations. The military measures successfully contained the insurgency until the latter half of the 1980s but, in the absence of a political solution, could not prevent the emergence of new outfits and violent conflicts between tribal groups in the early 1990s. Efforts to bring a negotiated peace to the region have been minimal. UNLF has put forward three conditions for talks with the center: the agenda should include sovereignty, India must first demilitarize the region, and a third country should monitor the talks.

Whereas in the 1980s, the security forces were the main instrument of dealing with the insurgence, recently there have been some efforts by successive state governments of Manipur to move toward a process of dialogue. The People's Front government headed by the Samajwadi (Socialist) Party offered a unilateral cease-fire to Manipur's seventeen separatist outfits, commencing 1 March 2001. Subsequently, a contact group was announced to liaise with insurgent groups in the state. The latter, however, rejected the cease-fire offer. A positive development was that an accord between the Kuki and Paite communities was signed in October 1998, soon after the violent clashes between both communities.

Multi-Track Diplomacy

The village councils and traditional tribal leadership from time to time have spoken out against violence, both by militants and by the state. These voices are, however, fragmented and their intervention is occasional and incident-specific.

There are also several civil-rights activists and women's groups in the state. The Nupi (Women's) Movement, has organized many demonstrations for peace and for the protection of human rights. The Manipur Chanura Leishem Marup is another leading women's organization, which has organized a series of human-rights workshops for women in Manipur since 1997. The activities of the organization primarily focus on empowering educated young women with the basic knowledge of human rights and on the protection of their communities against a range of evils such as drug abuse and alcoholism. The concerns have naturally tended to focus narrowly on civil liberties and the violation of rights, but at least some of these groups, for example, the Meira Paibies, tend to have ambivalent relationships with the militants and function as front organizations, coordinating actions and protests with militant demands and activities. Without taking a critical stand on the violence perpetrated by the insurgents, despite their commendable work against social ills, they have forfeited any potential role as mediators between the state and the community. This is also the case with the Naga Women's Movement, Manipur (NWUM), a powerful movement supportive of the wider Nagalim.

The threat of wider Nagalim, extending into Manipur, has reunited Meitei, Kuki, and Muslim civil-society organizations. The United Committee, Manipur (UCM), was formed to protest against the cease-fire extension with the Naga leadership. The massive demonstration on 18 June 2001 forced the government to reconsider the agreement.

Human Rights Alert (HRA) is an Imphal-based NGO consisting of human-rights activists, journalists, lawyers, academicians, and community workers. It works to highlight human-rights abuses by security forces. HRA coordinates its activities with Amnesty International, London; the International Service for Human Rights, Geneva; and the International Human Rights Internship Program, Washington, D.C. The Civil Liberties and Human Rights Organization (CLAHRO), founded in 1983, consists mainly of lawyers. It takes up cases involving human-rights violations in the law courts. The Committee on Human Rights, which consists of representatives of eighteen organizations, organizes rallies for the repeal of various acts governing the insurgency-affected states and it also has an important role in documenting incidents of human-rights violations.

As with other NGOs in the region, it is important to understand that many of these organizations closely coordinate their activities with extremist groups, and reflect deep ethnic biases in their projection of alleged human-rights abuses. The union government is reported to be contemplating suspension of all funds to NGOs based in Manipur, as several NGOs act in collusion with the underground organizations. The National Human Rights Commission has, however, maintained a relatively balanced perspective on human-rights violations throughout the country.

Tripura

Tripura has a 865-kilometer-long border with Bangladesh and insurgents and terrorists are using it to push arms into the state. Tripura, like Manipur, is one of the Indian states with a history of revolutionary peasant movements, and for much of the last quarter of the twentieth century had a communist state government. Insurgent groups have seriously disrupted attempts at land reforms and other progressive interventions. Particularly in Tripura, the dividing line between political insurgents and plain terrorists is blurred and many of the groups have transformed kidnapping into an industry.

Tripura is the only state in India's Northeast that has been transformed, in recent history, from a predominantly tribal to a predominantly nontribal state. In the early twentieth century, the tribal population, divided over nineteen tribes, accounted for close to 53 percent of the population. This equation remained relatively stable until the 1940s, when communal clashes in British-ruled East Bengal (now Bangladesh) followed by the partition provoked a steady migration of refugees into the princedom of Tripura and decreased the tribal population further to 37 percent. In 1991, the share in the population had come down to 31 percent.

Conflict Dynamics

Bengali migrants into Tripura have predominantly been cultivators practicing relatively advanced patterns of agriculture, compared to the *jhum* (shifting cultivation) of the indigenous people, and the tribes progressively lost control of their traditional lands. Their cause was taken up by Communist Party of India (CPI) and later by the Communist Party of India–Marxist (CPI–M). Leftist politics has always been strong in the state and several governments have been controlled by the CPI–M, which has a big following among tribals in their struggle for land. The Left Front governments were instrumental in creating the Tripura Tribal Areas where tribal culture and economic rights are protected from nontribal domination.

The strong showing of the CPI–M in elections coincided with the emergence of the Tripura Upajati Juba Samiti (TUJS) in June 1967, based on a brand of virulent ethnic politics. The TUJS raised the demand of autonomous district councils for tribals, the introduction of the local language (Kok Borok) as the medium of instruction for tribal students, and the restoration of alienated tribal lands. A Bengali communal organization, Amar Bangla (We Are Bengalis) came into being to counter the TUJS campaign. After the Tribal Areas Autonomous District Act of 1979 was passed by the CPI–M government, May 1979 and June 1980 saw two waves of vicious ethnic rioting. The rioting was instigated by the TNV (Tripura National Volunteers, established in 1978), with Amar Bangla activists retaliating. An estimated 1,800 people lost their lives and thousands of dwellings were burnt before the situation was brought under control after the army intervened in June 1980. This phase of the insurgency ended in August 1988, when Hrangkhawal, the TNV leader, signed a tripartite peace accord with the Union Home Ministry and the new Tripura government shortly after the defeat of the Left Front government. The Congress-TUJS coalition government had taken over after elections that were widely regarded as having been rigged. The apparent return to normalcy was short-lived. The next elections of 1993 and 1998, as well as the 2002 by-election to the national parliament, were again won by the CPI–M and the violent campaign reemerged.

There has been a substantial proliferation of terrorist factions in the state in the closing years of the twentieth century. Over thirty militant organizations are reported to be operating at various levels, and on a variety of "ideological" platforms, but most of them are just irregular criminal gangs, or are dormant. The National Liberation Front of Tripura (NLFT), with a strong Christian fundamentalist orientation, and the All Tripura Tiger Force (ATTF), a radical group controlled by leaders from the Debbarma tribe, are responsible for most militant activities. A critical development within the militant movement was the vertical split in the NLFT in September 2000 as a result of tribal rivalries between the Halams and the Debbarmas, and the emerging conflict between the Christians and the Hindus that led to a further breakup of the organization in 2001.

The spate of attacks on the tribal leaders belonging to the CPI–M in 2000 and 2001 were again clear signals that the NLFT continued with its terrorist campaign in order to dislodge the communists as entrenched protagonists of the tribal cause. The attacks were also seen as a desperate attempt, after the splits, to keep the control over its rank and file intact. It was also part of an attempt to eliminate the Left Front politically. In the run-up to the 2002 by-election, NLFT militants killed sixteen nontribal people in a crowded marketplace in Khowai as a warning against voting for the leftist candidate.

Abduction by these organizations has evolved into a well-organized criminal operation. A total of 555 incidents of abduction, including 481 by the NLFT and 41 by the ATTF, were reported in the state during the year 2000.

In Tripura, the civil population has been the main victim of terrorist activities (see Figure 7.8.8.1). Tribal radicals specifically target the nontribal population, whom they call "settler refugees." The level of violence is also heightened by the emergence of militant Bengali organization Amar Bangla.

Official Conflict Management

Official measures for conflict management have concentrated on a legal framework to defend the rights of the tribals and on persuasion to lay down arms. In 1979, the Left Front state government passed the Tripura Tribal Areas Autonomous District Council Act to help the tribal population to maintain their culture and protect their land rights. The impact on insurgency and the polarization of communities has, however, been negligible because extremist forces on both sides—the tribals and the Bengali settler community—around that time started their violent campaigns.

In the mid-1980s, Bijoy Hrangkhawal, the TNV leader, made it clear that unless the communists were out of power and were replaced by the Congress Party violence would continue. He intensified his offensive in the weeks preceding the elections to the state assembly, leading to the defeat of the Left Front, and the installation of a Congress-TUJS coalition government in 1988. The election victory of the Congress Party, the government party in New Delhi, meant a deal could be worked out. In June, the entire militant leadership was brought to Delhi for a peaceful settlement, which was signed on 10 August 1988, ending one chapter in the history of militancy in the state.

After the Left Front returned to power in 1993, the ATTF negotiated a bipartite settlement with the government, leading to the surrender of the bulk of its cadres, but the activities of other militant groups, particularly the NLFT and a section of the ATTF, have been on the increase. In the second half of the 1990s, the situation worsened and the communist-dominated government decided to request the federal government to promulgate the Disturbed Areas Act of 1988. By 1999, around half of the police districts had been declared disturbed areas under this act. Although a considerable number of militants have surrendered (more than 5,000 in the second half of the 1990s), it has had very limited impact on the scale of violence. Regarding the alleged existence of training camps in Bangladesh—the state government has handed over to the Union government maps with over concrete details on fifty-one hideouts and camps across the border—the government in New Delhi is still to pursue the issue with the government of Bangladesh.

Multi-Track Diplomacy

Peace initiatives have been taken by various organizations, but most of them are linked to political parties, particularly the CPI–M. Nonparty formations have been less active. One manifest exception is the peace movement initiated by the Jamatiya Hoda, the supreme council of the Jamatiya tribe, the third largest tribal group in Tripura. At their conference in December 2000, tribal leaders resolved not to pay any kind of "tax" to the militant groups and to support the government in its fight against insurgency. In addition to the Jamatiyas, the Reangs and Uchais are the other communities that have joined the larger antiterrorism campaign. Many of these are supporters of the leftist parties and their mass organizations, and they have been in the forefront of the struggle for peace and ethnic integration.

There is hardly any NGO movement in the state. The NGOs that exist operate as welfare and development organizations and have not made any attempt to initiate conflict-resolution activities. More powerful and enduring has been the work of the organizations linked to the Communist Party, mainly the Students Federation and the All-India Democratic Youth Federation. They have organized public opinion across ethnic lines.

The "Peaceful" Northeastern States

Meghalaya

After many years of peace, violence in Meghalaya has perceptibly increased over the past few years, with seventy-five persons killed between 1998 and 2000, as against twenty-two persons between 1992 and 1997. Intertribal rivalry and the common acrimony against the "outsiders" has led to the growth of a number of militant organizations constituted along exclusionary tribal identities. These include both organizations that represent the dominant tribal groupings in the state—such as the Khasi—and the smaller or minority groupings, such as the Naga and Gharo. While the violence of these organizations is directed against other ethnic groups, or is related to the increasing criminal and extortion activities that dominate their agenda, most of the militant groups operate under the camouflage of a variety of sectarian demands, including protection of the indigenous people against encroachment by outsiders and the creation of separate homelands along tribal lines.

Arunachal Pradesh

Arunachal Pradesh was long projected as an island of peace in the turbulent Northeast, and this is an impression that still persists, despite trends toward an overflow of the conflicts from its neighbors. In 2000, a total of thirty-four persons were killed in the state, including three security personnel, seven civilians, and twenty-four insurgents, as against three civilians and three insurgents in 1999. The overflow of violence from neighboring Nagaland affects the Naga-dominated Tirap and Changlang districts in particular. Insurgent groups such as the ULFA, NSCN-K, NSCN-IM, and Bodo militants are reportedly using sparsely populated Arunachal Pradesh territory to locate their hideouts and sporadic clashes between these groups have occurred. Extortion, which is one of the main sources of funding for the NSCN-IM, is widespread in the two districts, among others aimed at the staff of Oil India Limited, the oil-exploration agency. At least one indigenous insurgent group has begun to surface in the state: the East India Liberation Front, formed in 2001. Its purpose is to protect the Arunachali identity from the influx of outside settlers.

Mizoram

Mizoram has been relatively violence-free. During the year 2000, a total of four civilians, one militant, and seven security forces were killed in militancy-related violence. In 1999, two civilians and five security forces personnel lost their lives.

Peace had been restored to Mizoram in 1986 when a settlement was reached with Laldenga, the leader of the militant Mizo National Front. With that agreement Mizoram became a full-fledged state after an insurgency that had continued for twenty years. Since then, the state has remained, by and large, peaceful, although minority tribes such as the Bru (Reang), Hmar, and Lakher also allege neglect and discrimination and have started demanding concessions. The Bru Liberation Force has recently spearheaded much of the violence. The Bru leadership claims that they are oppressed by the majority Mizo, which is educationally and economically far better off. The Bru leadership is demanding a separate autonomous district council. Agitation around this demand sparked fierce ethnic violence between the Reang and the Mizo in October 1997, resulting in an exodus of the Reang to the adjoining North Tripura district. The Mizoram government is overtly against the district council and has made the surrender of the Bru militants a precondition for refugee repatriation. There are 30,000 Reang refugees now sheltered in Tripura.

Prospects

Although it appears that there has been a steady erosion of the popular base of many insurgent movements in the region, civil society initiatives have, at best, been sporadic and passive. A number of cease-fire agreements between militant groups and the government are already in place, and further negotiations are on to solve the other conflict. Unfortunately, where a multiplicity of insurgent organizations are operating, negotiations with some of the groups involved has tended to lead to escalation of violence by others.

Negotiations are usually in the form of secretive deals between Indian bureaucrats and leaders of one or the other insurgent organizations. Although some of the groups still insist on the intermediary role of a foreign party, the possibilities of any direct foreign intervention toward resolution is extremely limited since the government of India is absolutely opposed to all external involvement in internal conflicts. The fact that various conflict negotiations are taking place can be regarded as a positive sign for the future.

On the other hand, there are multiple reasons for the conflicts. The demographic destabilization as a result of immigration, both within the country and from Bangladesh, is often mentioned as the basic cause of the unrest. Migration, however, is not a new phenomenon and has not affected all the areas. Even in the areas where there has been considerable incoming migration, people of different ethnic origins have lived together peacefully until recently. The multiethnicity of the entire Northeast, which could be approached positively as a sign of integration and adjustment by many insurgent groups, has been attacked from a narrow ethnic position of identity politics. This attitude will make it difficult to reach a multicultural and multiethnic accommodation.

Other reasons are therefore at least as important as a cause for continuing conflicts. Such other reasons as middle-class unemployment, the feeling of neglect and marginalization within the Indian union, the criminalization of politics, the contraband trading networks (particularly of drugs), etc., can be addressed in a more civilized manner than is presently done in an attempt to fall back on ethnic identity. Ethnic cleansing apparently involves a shortcut to political expediency. The most significant obstacle to peace in the region apparently is the crisis of governance, with high levels of corruption and, despite a substantial investment of public resources, a dismal quality of government services. The problem is compounded by the lucrative criminal economy of terrorism that has now become entrenched in the region, the neighboring countries, or international organizations in tackling the problem jointly.

Recommendations

The solution to the various problems is political. Alienation, the result of a long-term process, needs to be assuaged by interventions at various levels. In order to scale down violence and ultimately establish peace, both sides in each conflict will have to accommodate some of the bottom-line positions of the other side. In exchange for regional autonomy, rather than separate statehood, which the government of India is not in a position to accept, the ethnic movements cannot escape accepting some basic principles of peaceful cohabitation.

Good Governance

The leakage of resources for development plans and infrastructure has been endemic. The increasing development expenditure and activities, absolutely essential as they are, have to concur with an overhaul of the government machinery so that unemployment can be taken on as the major battle against the root cause of the insurgency.

The restoration and strengthening of institutions of local self-governance could be looked at as an instrument of local development and local civil-society building, but care should be taken that the traditional tribal councils, who will be useful in monoethnic communities, do not divide multiethnic communities along tribal identities. Political mainstream parties who have done some commendable work in the past in terms of development and community building, as in Assam, Manipur, and Tripura, should be taken in as partners in a transparent local administration based on a popular vote.

The disruption of the lucrative regime of collusion between insurgents and various overground organizations, including government departments and political parties, should be taken on as a high-priority task. This should be a battle against criminal organizations and networks, clearly delinking it from the political intervention, which should be based on dialogue and persuasion, from both sides. The counterterrorism policy should first and foremost concentrate on elimination of the criminal circuit, particularly the drugs network, which keeps entire communities in its grip, either as victims or as profiteers.

The protection of tribal land and the positive discrimination (reservation) in education and in the civil service has helped to advance the position of tribal families and should be continued. The restoration of alienated lands to tribal populations has been a long-standing demand and should be looked at as land reform remains an important demand of poor and landless peasantry. Given the scale of alienation in certain areas and given the long-term entrenchment of the nontribal populations on those lands, it is not clear how practicable such efforts can be, and whether they will result in an abatement or escalation of violence. In Tripura, where land reforms were taken in hand, violence has actually followed in the wake of such restitution of land to the tribal population.

Border Management

Containment and regulation of migration have also been mentioned as a necessary step, and some movements have taken this as their only program. There have been several proposals, including the issue of identity cards and work permits, but their efficacy in stemming the tide of illegal immigrants into India and legal migrants between the states is questionable. Fencing off the border, as is currently being done, may help, but the enormous length of the border (98 percent of its borders are international borders) complicates this solution.

This situation could also be approached positively. If India were to make SAARC (the official South Asian Association for Regional Cooperation) into an effective structure, legal channels of trade would help to make the transborder operations more transparent between the countries involved (India, Bangladesh, Nepal and Bhutan) and reduce the involvement of terrorist groups in illegal cross-border trade. Borders can remain intact without hindrance to the movement of people.

National Integration

Peace campaigns involving all sections of civil society (traditional tribal structures, political parties, mass organizations, and some NGOs) as well as government organizations and business chambers will be difficult to organize, but will provide a sure and public sign that the majority of the people in the Northeast are on the side of peace, harmony, and stability.

For this to happen, transparency in the operations of the security forces (the army, the police, and the border security forces), which on various occasions have transgressed their legitimate role and have been accused of human-rights abuses, should be introduced. This would be one way of reclaiming trust in the Indian state.

An improved political say in national or regional affairs would help to assuage the feelings of alienation. The collective strength of the northeastern states in the federal Lok Sabha (Lower House) is 24 in a 543-member House, and this number cannot possibly be increased dramatically since it is based on the share in the population.

Helpful as a significant step would be the devolution of economic and financial affairs, which over the decades have increasingly become centralized. This step would add more residuary powers to the state governments. In the meantime, the accusations of "internal colonialism" should be addressed through independent studies. It will be helpful to know whether, and to what extent, the Indian state acts as a stepmother in its treatment of the states in the Northeast. That would constitute a sound basis for a further discussion on the degree of discrimination.

The government of India, rather than restrict the access to the area, would do well to organize the exchange of students and civil-society organizations for tours and study and to stimulate radio and TV to contribute to the dissemination of cultures and viewpoints across the regions of the subcontinent.

Resources

Newsletters and Periodicals

Eastern Panorama, news magazine of the Northeast, also online: www.eastpanorama. com/

Faultlines, Institute for Conflict Management

Grassroots Options, Shillong, Meghalaya, India. E-mail: rbtshillong@yahoo.com

NE Newsletter, Ministry of Home Affairs, Government of India. also online: www. mha.nic.in/

Northeast Sun, Sun Publications, New Delhi, India

Reports

All Bodo Students' Union, *Why Separate State of Bodoland (Demand and Justifications),* Kokrajhar, 1999.

Government of the Peoples Republic of Nagalim

Nagas in Revolution, by Rh. Raising, Oking, Oking Publicity and Information Service.

The Legal Status of Naga National Armed Resistance: Right to Self-Determination Under International Law & Why and How the Nagas Are Not Terrorists, Oking, Oking Publicity and Information Service, 2001.

International Centre for Peace Initiatives, *Assam Today: Can the Fires Be Put Out?* edited by Karan Sawhny, New Delhi, 1998.

Other Media Communications, *Naga Resistance and the Peace Process: A Dossier,* New Delhi, 2001.

South Asia Forum for Human Rights, *Peace Process in Nagaland and Chittagong Hill Tracts,* by Jehan Perera, Kathmandu, SAFHR paper series No. 5, 1999.

Other Publications

Frontier Travails: North East—The Politics of a Mess, by Subir Ghosh. New Delhi, Macmillan India, 2001.

India Against Itself: Assam and the Politics of Nationality, by Sanjib Baruah. Oxford University Press, New Delhi, 1999.

India's North East Resurgent: Ethnicity, Insurgency, Governance, Development, by B. G. Verghese. New Delhi, Konark Publishers, 1997.

Insurgents Crossfire: Northeast India, by Subir Bhaumik. Lancer Publishers, New Delhi, 1996.

Northeast India: The Ethnic Explosion, by Nirmal Nibedon. New Delhi, Lancers Publishers, 1981.

Politics of Identity and Nation Building in Northeast India, edited by N. C. Dutta. New Delhi, South Asian Press, 1997.

Strangers in the Mist, by Sanjoy Hazarika. Penguin Books, New Delhi, 1995.

Rites of Passage: Border Crossings, Imagined Homelands, by Sanjoy Hazarika. New Delhi, Penguin Books, 2000.

Uncivil Wars: Pathology of Terrorism in India, by Ved Marwah. New Delhi, Harper-Collins Publishers, 1999.

The Periphery Strikes Back, by Udayoon Mishra. Simla, IIAS, 2000.

Selected Internet Sites

mha.nic.in (Official web site of the Ministry of Home Affairs, Government of India; contains overview of conflicts in each state, annual reports of the MHA, and a weekly Northeast Newsletter)

nerdatabank.nic.in (Provides economic data of the Northeastern states)

www.angelfire.com/mo/Nagaland (Website of the National Socialist Council of Nagaland-Isak-Muivah, poorly maintained, occasional updates)

www.assam.org (Web site of the Guwahati-based *Northeast Daily Newspaper,* updated daily)

www.assamlive.com (Provides news and articles on Assam and neighboring states, updated daily)

www.assampolice.com (Official web site of the Assam state police, updated daily)

www.axom.faithweb.com (Compiles media reports on the Northeast and updated frequently)

www.geocities.com/CapitolHill/Congress/7434/ (Web site of the publicity department of the ULFA, poorly maintained and rather disorganized)

www.geocities.com/CapitolHill/Parliament/1533/ (Web site of the Manipur People's Liberation Front, occasional updates)

www.geocities.com/rpf_manipur/ (Web site of the Revolutionary People's Front [RPF] of Manipur, exhaustive material and well maintained)

www.kuknalim.net (Web site for Naga news, issues, and views)

www.northeastvigil.com (Compiles media reports on the entire Northeast and updated on a fortnightly basis)

www.satp.org (South Asia Terrorism Portal, web site of the Institute for Conflict Management, focuses on conflict and resolution in South Asia, with separate coverage for each of the major terrorism-affected states in India's Northeast)

Resource Contacts

Mukul Hazarika, Assam Watch, e-mail: assam.watch@virgin.net

Sanjoy Hazarika, Centre for North East Studies and Policy Research, e-mail: sanjoyha @rediffmail.com

Sushil Huidrom, Security Civil Liberties & Human Rights Organisation (CLAHRO), e-mail: sushilluidrom@Rediffmail.com

Babloo Loitongbam, Human Rights Alert, Manipur, e-mail: hralert@dte.vsnl.net.in

Luingam Luithui, Naga Peoples Movement for Peace, e-mail: luithui@hotmail.com

Frans Welman, Naga International Support Center, e-mail: f.welman@chello.nl

Organizations

All-India Democratic Youth Federation, Shillong, Meghalaya

Association of Voluntary Agencies for Rural Development—Northeast (AVARD NE), Guwahati, Assam

Arunachal Vikas Parishad,
Contact: Sri Dwarikacharya

P.O. Box 128, Itanagar 791111
Arunachal Pradesh, India
Tel: +91-360-3463

Bodo Women's Justice Forum
Contact: Anjali Daimari, c/o CPI(ML) office
R.G. Baruah Road
Sagarika Path, Guwahati 781 02, Assam
Tel: +91-361-561933
E-mail: neso@satyam.net.in

Borok People's Human Rights Organization
Contact: Hebal Koloy
Agartala, Tripura
E-mail: bphrotwipra@rediff.com

Committee for Human Rights, Manipur
Contact: C. C. Surjeet
E-mail: chongthamcha@yahoo.com

Humanity Protection Forum
West Tripura District, Tripura

Impulse NGO Network
Contact: Hasinah Kharbhih
Lower Lachumiere Near Horse Shoe Building, Temple Road
Shillong-793001, Meghalaya
Tel: +91-364-500587
Fax: +91-364-229939
E-mail: ingon@rediffmail.com

Janajati Vikas Samiti
Contact: Ramesh Babu
Room No. 101, Majestic Apartments
Circular Road, Dimapur-797112, Nagaland

Krishak Adhikar Sangram Committee
Sibsagar, Assam

Meghalaya People's Human Rights Council
Contact: Bino (DDG) Dympep
E-mail: mphrc@rediff.com

Nagaland Gandhi Ashram
Chuchengimlang Village, Mokokchung District, Nagaland

Naga International Support Center (NISC)
Tollenstraat 60
1054 RW Amsterdam, Netherlands
E-mail: f.welman@chello.com

Naga Mothers' Association
Kohima, Nagaland
Tel: +91-370-223319/ 240886
E-mail: nagamothers@yahoo.com

Nagaland Peace Centre
'D Block, Kohima-797001, Nagaland
Tel: +91-370-21392

Ramakrishna Mission
West Tripura District, Tripura
Tel: +91-381-230333/230222

Ramakrishna Sevashram
New Bongaigaon, Bongaigaon district, Guwahati, Assam

Shanti Sadhana Ashram
Basistha, Guwahati 781028, Assam
Tel: +91-361-563 873/565 887

Students Federation of India
Agartala, Tripura

The Other Media, K-14
1st floor, Green Park Extension
New Delhi 110 016, India
Tel: +91 -11-6163830/6196640
Fax: +91-11-6198042,
E-mail: admin@del3.vsnl.net.in

Tanyi Jagriti Foundation
P.O. Box No. 237
Neharlagun-791110, Arunachal Pradesh
Tel: +91-360-23234

Thongjao Women's Development Association
Thoubal District, Manipur

Tripura Adamjati Sevak Sangh
Contact: Chitta Ranjan Dev
Anukul Bhawan, No. 3, Joynagar 2nd Lane, Agartala, Pin-799001
South & West Tripura Districts, Tripura
Tel: +91-381-223988

Zogam Institute of Community Resources and Development
Imphal East District, Manipur

Zomi Mothers Association
Churachandpur District, Manipur

Data on the following organizations can be found in the Directory section:

Centre for North East Studies and Policy Research
Indian Confederation of Indigenous and Tribal People
Institute of Peace and Conflict Studies
International Centre for Peace Initiatives
North East Network
Naga Peoples Movement for Human Rights
Tribal Welfare Society

Kristoffel Lieten (born in Belgium, 1946) is an associate professor at the Amsterdam School of Social Sciences of the University of Amsterdam. Since his studies at the Jawaharlal Nehru University in New Delhi in the early 1970s, he has done extensive research on political and social developments in South Asia. He has worked as the South Asia correspondent of the Dutch and Belgium radio and has become a regular media commentator. He has cofounded the Dutch National India Committee and has written several books on various aspects of politics, history, and rural development in India.

7.9

Nepal:
Maoist Insurgency Against Lopsided Development

Kristoffel Lieten

The "People's War," an armed uprising by Maoist extremists, began in March 1996. By the end of 2001, the total number of deaths had reached two thousand and, following a series of dramatic attacks, the Nepalese government declared a state of emergency in November 2001. The immediate objective of the insurgents is to turn Nepal into a so-called New Democratic people's republic as a first step toward building a new socialist society. The Maoists have extended their activities throughout Nepal, but their stronghold lies in the hill districts in the western part of the country. The hilly terrain, with dense forests and few roads, is favorable for guerrilla warfare. It is a region that continues to be exploited in a feudal fashion by Hindu landowners who rule over the local Magars, a downtrodden ethnic group.

Landlocked Nepal has never been colonized but has remained in an impoverished and "semicolonized" feudal condition throughout the twentieth century. Despite a good deal of development aid and a sizeable income from tourism, it remains the poorest country in Asia, other than Afghanistan. Adult literacy in 2000 was only 40 percent and 42 percent of its 20 million people lived below the poverty line. The country has been ruled by the autocratic regime of the royal house and the so-called *panchayat* system, the traditional leadership appointed by the king. Political dissent has been summarily repressed while corruption and economic polarization have gone hand in hand. At the end of the 1980s, the opposition against the *panchayat* system came into the open. From 18 February 1990 onwards, a mass movement coordinated by the Nepali Congress Party (NCP) and the United Left Front (of communist parties) erupted. After massive public protest that lasted one-and-a-half months and left many dozens of people dead, multiparty democracy (after a short-lived existence in the late 1950s) was restored. Enthusiasm for the elections was great, particularly in the Kathmandu valley, but overall only around half of the electorate participated in the elections.

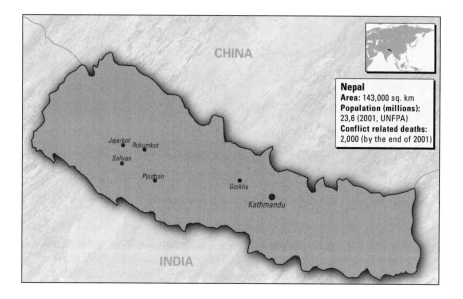

Following the promulgation of a new constitution, the NCP narrowly won the first general elections from the communists. The many communist factions, who had temporarily renounced their differences to operate as the United Marxist-Leninist Party (CPN-UML) were a force to be reckoned with. The next (midterm) elections (in 1994) were won by the UML. The UML appeared to offer a structural alternative with a policy that included land reforms and democratically elected village councils, but dissent in all parties, including the communist movement, soon destabilized the entire political system. In a period of ten years, more than a dozen majority, minority, and coalition governments collapsed and the country descended into a condition of political chaos and instability.

For a number of reasons, the hope that the majority had in the new democratic system was dashed. Members of the erstwhile *panchayat* government were brought in as an alternative to the power of the communists. With them, many politicians who had sustained the authoritarian regime, and had amassed wealth, were pardoned and even became policymakers under the new system.

Corruption continued as before and party leaders accumulated riches and wealth. The bureaucracy, which had been trained under the authoritarian *panchayat* system, continued in office.

By proclaiming Hinduism the state religion, the new constitution institutionalized religious discrimination. The representation in parliament of ethnic minorities, lower castes, and women is remarkably low. The high-ranking male Brahmins, who form only a small minority of the population, remain dominant. The discontent among the various ethnic groups and among the lower castes in the Hindu hierarchy, who de facto have been excluded from upward mobility, has created a wide divide between the ruling class in Nepal and the ethnically homogeneous underclasses.

The actual beneficiaries of development and of development aid were mainly the high-caste elites from towns and villages. What actually has happened is that development funding has become a major industry that was characterized by massive corruption, a complete lack of transparency, and inefficient implementation. The massive financial aid provided lucrative jobs for the Western-educated, Kathmandu-born employees and contractors, but local people hardly ever benefited. The polarization between the development-aided rich and the big majority of poor people thus generated resentment in the minds of the people. It is interesting to note that from 1956 onwards in the Rapti zone in the midwestern hills of Nepal, where the "People's War" movement is at its strongest, the United States had been active in aid projects meant to develop the region and to beat back the leftist influence. It was an area where feudalism was at its strongest and where rural discontent had brought the poor people onto the side of the communist crusade for equality and justice, which in fact meant land reform. The U.S. aid that was aimed at "attacking poverty and preventing a communist uprising," provided high salaries and imported life-styles to civil servants and traders but failed to bring development. It thus helped the common people build a critical consciousness toward such models of foreign-supported development that neither generated development nor justice. As soon as the development project, launched with a view to eliminating poverty and backwardness was phased out, the "People's War" erupted from the very heart of Rapti. The main international donor agencies, particularly India and the United States, are perceived as having contributed to the success of the Maoist movement by raising the expectations of rural people for the development of their region and by in fact creating a thin layer of wealthy beneficiaries, leaving the majority with a heightened sense of deprivation and inequality.

The Maoists thrive on this perception of economic and political imperialism by outside agencies. It was relatively easy for them to tap the discontent amongst the impoverished youth and hit back at those who are regarded as exploiters and profiteers. They could do this in regions where the communist movement had been traditionally strong.

An explanation of the rise of Maoism can be sought in these specific conditions in Nepal. The horse trading and jockeying for power in the elected parliaments have reinforced the conviction that radical change can only be achieved through an armed uprising, say the ideologues of the movement. The material environment, however, only provides the background to the galloping violence. The Maoist movement has also been assisted by the failure of mainstream politics to provide a coherent mass movement against poverty and injustice. Nepal is one of the countries where parliamentary communist parties have a substantial electoral following. They were respected for their stand on democracy, nationalism, antifeudalism, and antipoverty politics. However, they squandered their credit when they formed the government and succumbed to disunity and opportunism. The Maoists then could claim that they were taking on the mantle of righteous and radical resistance against the old system.

Conflict Dynamics

There is indeed another important side to the rise of the Maoist rebellion, namely pure power politics and opportunism. Maoism in Nepal is part of a long history of internal bickering within the communist movement. The first Maoist rebellion was known as the Jhapa Movement, after the southeastern district where it was centered, close to Naxalbari, just across the border in India where Maoists had also revolted. It was a "class-enemy annihilation campaign" carried out by the Coordination Centre in 1971. The embryonic organization later developed into the Communist Party of Nepal (Marxist-Leninist). The CPN(ML) merged in 1991 with the Communist Party of Nepal (Marxist) to become the CPN-UML.

Factionalism and splits around self-righteous leaders have characterized the communist movement in Nepal. One such leader, Prachananda, formed his own Maoist party in 1986. He did not join the United Left Front that in 1990 started the movement for the restoration of democracy and was very successful in the first parliamentary elections. As part of the rival United People's Front (UPF), Prachananda was less successful. His front gained nine seats. The Nepali Congress Party cornered 110 seats and the CPI-UML, 69 seats. By the time of the 1994 elections, Prachananda and Babu Ram Bhattarai, his close associate, split away from the UPF and approached the election commission for recognition. The recognition, however, was given to the main UPF group and Prachananda then called for a boycott of the elections, an action that at that time was perceived as a face-saving measure. In March 1995, his group was renamed the CPN (Maoist) and a decision was taken to start an armed rebellion. On 13 February 1996, less than one year later after the leaders had applied for recognition as an electoral party, the People's War was declared as the sole aim of the party.

In early February 1996, a charter with forty demands had been submitted to the government headed by Sher Bahadur Deuba. These demands called for the drafting of a new republican constitution by an elected constituent assembly, the abrogation of a number of treaties with India, the nationalization and redistribution of land and property, and the fulfillment of the social and economic needs of the people. It warned that it would take to the path of armed revolution unless the government discontinued oppression. Within two weeks, even before the deadline had expired, the Maoists struck in six districts. Observers have pointed out that the Maoist leaders have never been serious on negotiations and only believe in a nonnegotiable revolutionary takeover of the state. The demands function as mobilizing slogans rather than as concrete issues that can come up for political pressure on the government and negotiations with the government.

In the years thereafter, the Maoists have often been victims of violent attacks. The government has used local Nepali Congress Party cadres, police, and administration to suppress them. The worsening situation in the western hills around Rukum and Rolpa districts was due also to the narrow political aims of the Nepali Congress in its attempt to eliminate the communist movement.

Yako Cutting

Kathmandu: Women's Day protest against violence and rape

Particularly, Prime Minister Girja Prasad Koirala, with his strong antipathy for communists, has done little to control the harassment and terror by the local police and party activists. On the other hand, the Maoists have also engaged in indiscriminate killing. Political revenge marked by revenge killings of those involved on the government side became the standard answer of the Maoists and the area ultimately became embroiled in a cycle of ransacking, looting, and killing.

In the areas concerned, the mainstream communist parties had a strong following, and the Maoist terror campaign has also been directed against the communist cadres. In the Informal Sector Service Centre (INSEC) Yearbook (2000), the CPN (Masal), the mother organization to which the Maoists once belonged, accuses the Maoist groups of behaving in exactly the same way as their opponents, the government, feudal gangs, and hooligans. In sharp language, they are accused of threatening, robbing, kidnapping, and even killing ordinary people, especially if they belong to other political parties: "Such actions from Maoists are not appropriate steps in the People's War; these are cases of human rights violation. Their activities suggest that the Maoist party is gradually transforming itself into a fascist party and no longer has the character of a revolutionary party." Of all the people killed in the war, the Maoists have killed one-third. Only around 40 percent of the people killed by them were (low-ranking) police personnel; the rest were civilian victims.

Many gruesome incidents have taken place during the five years of the People's War. The most remarkable offensive took place in November 2001. On the night of 23 November, unilaterally breaking a cease-fire that had been in place since July, the Maoists staged simultaneous attacks in a number of places, using cooking-gas cylinders, pressure cookers, and pipes filled with dynamite, and inflicting large-scale human casualties and damages to the infrastructures. Two days later, about two thousand Maoists reportedly raided Salleri, the headquarters of the Solokhumbu district, and destroyed the Paphlu Airport tower and several police and government offices. They took control of the airport and then attacked police posts and unsuccessfully tried to occupy the army barracks. Solokhumbu is the main tourist area, the location of Mt. Everest, the tallest mountain peak in the world. The army rushed reinforcements to Salleri in helicopters and, in the ensuing battles, claim to have killed over two hundred Maoists. Following the Salleri incidents, the government of Prime Minister Deuba, after consultation with the king, decided to declare a state of emergency in all seventy-five districts of the country. The emergency was partially lifted in early April 2002. Journalists are still required to restrain their reports on the Maoist insurgency and political parties can again hold political meetings, albeit with the permission of local authorities.

In the weeks following the lifting of emergency, the Maoists struck heavily. In a single day, in the second week of April 2002, more than two hundred policemen and soldiers were reported to have been killed in a surprise attack in Dang district. Retaliatory action by the army caused heavy casualties on the Maoist side. Such surprise attacks and counterinsurgency operations occur regularly, and have claimed victims on all sides: Maoist guerrillas, police officers, alleged police informers, and innocent civilians. The combination of an inability to contain and address Maoist violence and the tendency of the police to violate human rights has done little to improve the standing of the authorities among the citizens.

Official Conflict Management

The state of emergency has resulted in more powers being given to the army and the curtailment of press and political freedom. The various legislative measures have given wide-ranging powers to the police, the army, and the intelligence agencies, which, because of Nepal's peculiar political arrangement, means ultimately more power has been given to the royal palace. Some commentators have suggested that some factions in the government and in the royal palace may be intent on keeping Maoism alive in the remote hill areas by continuing a crackdown on the grassroots cadres while giving free play to the top leadership.

The government has never been serious about tackling the three major issues that affect the people and that were raised by the UPF when the Maoists were still in parliament: inflation, poverty, and unemployment. Maoist violence has erupted each time the NCP have come to power, particularly when Girija P. Koirala became prime minister. During his first tenure (1992–1994), the police came down heavily on a general strike called by the UPF, killing sixteen people in Kathmandu. He also started the first police retaliation (Operation Romeo) against the Maoists in Rolpa district, inflicting serious damage on people and property. It was this conflict that was later to form the feeding ground for the People's War.

The first attempt by the government to come to grips with the Maoist activities was the formation of a working group by the coalition government of the National Democratic Party and the CPN-UML, headed by Bahadur Chand in April 1997. The working group highlighted the need for dealing with the problem through a national consensus. A commission of the UML itself (the Dhami Commission) refused to see the social and economic dimensions of the conflict and clearly spelled out that the Maoist insurgency was of a terrorist nature and that antiterrorist legislation was needed to deal with it. Before such legislation could be introduced, a new government headed by the royalist leader, Thapa, took over; this government was soon followed by a new NCP government headed by Koirala (April 1998). Koirala immediately gave orders for a major police offensive (the Kilo-Sera Two operation), during which more than forty people were killed. Like the earlier offensive in his first term as prime minister, the police action signaled the beginning of an intermittent series of clashes. The conflict escalated and peace talks were abandoned.

After the formation of the NCP government headed by Bhattarai in January 2000, a high-level Maoist problem-resolution committee (the Deuba Committee) held a series of informal meetings with the Maoists and collected suggestions from different political parties and civil-society groups. In the course of his work, Deuba held several rounds of discreet talks with the underground leaders. After the committee submitted its report in November of the same year, Home Minister Paudel officially met with a senior Maoist leader, Rabindra Shrestha. The talks were facilitated by a former minister and human-rights activist, Padma Ratna Tuladhar. The dialogue was followed by both sides blaming each other for killing the peace process and buying time while preparing for a new offensive.

During the new government period of Koirala, who succeeded Bhattarai, the Maoists refused to take part in any dialogue. In March 2001, the government complied with the long-standing Maoist demand that it reveal the whereabouts of their three hundred comrades in custody. A nongovernmental peace team headed by Padma Ratna Tuladhar then took initiatives to facilitate further talks. Such a dialogue was also advocated by the CPN-UML as the main opposition party in the parliament and the official National Human Rights Commission. Immediately afterwards, the Maoists again went on a rampage and killed several policemen in Rukumkot and Dailekh.

After the gruesome killing of practically the entire royal family by the king's son on 1 July, G. P. Koirala, under heavy pressure because of corruption scandals, was brought down and on 22 June his NCP government was replaced by an NCP government led by Deuba. After Deuba reemerged as the prime minister, peace initiatives were rekindled. On the day of Deuba's election, Maoists massacred seventeen policemen at a police post in Bajiura district. Nevertheless, within twenty-four hours Deuba declared a cease-fire and the peace initiative was quickly reciprocated by Prachananda. In November, however, Prachananda, the general secretary of the CPN, announced that the peace talks were suspended and that "there was no other alternative before the Nepalese people than to continue their struggle for nationalism, democracy and livelihood."

On several occasions, the government has attempted to get parliamentary approval for antiterrorist legislation and for the commissioning of the army. An armed police ordinance had been approved by the king, but it could not be endorsed by parliament. Until the declaration of the state of emergency, the Royal Nepal Army was, by and large, kept on the sidelines of the conflict.

The ousted prime minister, Koirala, is reported to be using the new spate of Maoist attacks to involve the king and the army in a new political arrangement.

Multi-Track Diplomacy

Concerns have been expressed on different occasions by Indian, European, and U.S. government officials, but no international initiatives to contain the conflict have been undertaken. India is particularly ill-placed to assist Nepal in restoring peace. The people in general and the Maoist supporters in particular regard India as an imperialist country intent on suffocating Nepal and restricting its access to the outside world. Requests for help from the government of Nepal have taken the form of appeals for more development aid and for more military hardware without involving any foreign country directly. Amnesty International has raised the issue of the need for a dialogue between the government and the Maoists and has issued three situation reports documenting the violations of human rights by both sides. In the latest of these—the report of April 2002—Amnesty International notes "a complete lack of accountability in relation to alleged unlawful killings, including extrajudicial executions and indeed in relation to many other forms of human right violations. . . . This lack of accountability has contributed to a prevailing sense of impunity." The International Red Cross has been mainly concerned with the conditions of detainees and the application of international humanitarian law standards.

Some international organizations and NGOs have organized discussion groups. The UNDP has held a workshop and now heads the Peace Support Group. The UN has sponsored the Harvard Online Conference. The Harvard Program on Humanitarian Policy and Conflict Research organized its first part of a web site, Online Conference in Nepal, from 25 January to 1 February 2001. The conference provided a broad platform to around eighty scholars, NGO activists, and officials to discuss conflict-related issues and suggest priorities for preventive action. The main aim of the conference was to exchange information for preventive action and to improve the understanding of the sources of social, political, and economic insecurity and their linkages. The Nepali and Western participants offered comprehensive and specific recommendations for the prevention of the current conflict and insecurity in Nepal.

A number of NGOs, such as the Rastriya Sarokar Samaj, a national network of movements and activists sympathetic to the Maoist cause, have been active in holding regular public forums as well as street meetings in Kathmandu. Many reports brought out by these like-minded NGOs have documented police involvement in cases of extrajudicial killings and the disappearance of individuals in their custody. The police have also been accused of concerted repression and discrimination against peasants and ethnic minorities.

These NGOs operate in isolation from the other organizations in civil society, including the political parties, and gloss over the reports of indiscriminatory violent attacks by Maoists on police officers, suspected informants, and even ordinary citizens. Various other NGOs, such as the South Asia Partnership–Nepal (SAP–Nepal), have organized a series of district, regional, and national-level consultation meetings and have suggested various short-term and long-term strategies. Its main objective has been to mobilize grassroots civil-society groups toward conflict resolution in the context of the social and economic development needs of the country.

The Washington-based Institute for Multi-Track Diplomacy and the Institute for International Mediation and Conflict Resolution held a workshop on "Conflict Resolution and Peacebuilding in Nepal" in June 2001. The workshop, organized in cooperation with the local South Asian Institute for Peace Studies, INSEC, and the Center for Economic and Social Development, provided training in conflict management and resolution skills for some local participants. The result of the workshop has been the start of a new campaign whereby all communities in Nepal are working together on peacebuilding. INSEC has done a particularly professional job, with a well-documented yearbook on human-rights violations and a comprehensive network for monitoring human-rights abuses.

The restoration of the multiparty system in 1990 has led to the mushrooming of Western-style NGOs, particularly in the field of human rights, democracy, and development. A handful of NGOs are genuinely active in peace and human-rights issues, but a weakness of all interventions is that trying to address the Maoist conflict without addressing the root causes will only have partial results in terms of conflict management. The initiatives are often in the form of, and limited to, conferences and discussions by professionals on aspects of human rights and the restoration of peace.

Yet these initiatives, taken together, after the advent of democracy, have increased the awareness of the people. Through election manifestos, political rallies, and interparty debates, people have become aware of the political and socioeconomic affairs around them. They have been able to distinguish between the potential contribution of parliamentary democracy and the actual factionalism and opportunism of most political parties. Following the restoration of democracy, civil society has played a key role in educating the people about the government's accountability to the people and about equality and exploitation. Similarly, development NGOs have involved people in piloting small schemes that aim at environmental protection, community health and sanitation, forest conservation, poverty elimination, and so on. These model projects have also helped them understand the dynamics of poverty and exploitation and the need for transparency.

Prospects

In the five years up to November 2001, some 2,000 people were killed in this civil war. There were another 2,000 deaths in the following five months, to the end of April 2002. That is a major escalation. The war is heating up tremendously, partly due to the fact that the army is now fully involved. There have been some talks between the government and the rebels, but the latter have doggedly persisted in mounting terrorist attacks. Peace talks usually appear to have been delaying tactics in preparation for new attacks and massacres. Both the government and the Maoists have declared themselves open to the possibility of dialogue, but these calls for "dialogue" may be a mere political slogan to which the main actors periodically pay lip service. The unwillingness of the government side to really come to effective negotiations is related to the fairly radical demands presented by the Maoists as prerequisites for dialogue. Yet, potentially, dialogue could bring about agreement on key issues such as the control of corruption and the commencement of a discussion on the development of concrete strategies to address fundamental economic, social, and ethnic problems.

A difficulty is that the Maoists claim exclusiveness on these issues. They see themselves as the only political movement fighting for social change. Any truce with mainstream political forces is considered impermissible revisionism and class betrayal. On the side of the forces of law and order, it is not always clear whether all actors involved are united on the issue of fighting Maoism. Some tacit support may exist. The royal house and the various factions of the NCP and the two republican (royalist) parties have often given the impression of being more interested in their own power politics. The "root cause" of the guerrilla warfare may have a hidden relationship to this wider political power game. As the conflict is also defined as the by-product of corruption and failed development of the past fifty years, movements of dissent can be expected to emerge again and again. The civil-society efforts are also weak in the sense that they are limited to small meetings and media publicity.

Recommendations

With a substantial increase in police expenditure and the declaration of the state of emergency in late 2001, the government seems to be equipped to tackle the Maoist conflict as a law-and-order problem. Given the peculiarly guerrilla-friendly terrain, and the many circumstances that have remained unchanged, Maoism, however, is not likely to be eliminated by military means. Suppressive measures will only have a temporary effect. Peace talks and political negotiations therefore remain the best option. This process should involve civil-society negotiators and left-wing parties as well as government representatives.

Nepal has a number of mainstream communist parties who, like the present-day Maoists, have been involved in armed revolution in the past. Prachananda and Baburam Bhattarai, the two main Maoist leaders, could be enticed to make a similar "safe landing" in the field of aboveground politics. This compromise solution may bring them greater rewards if they really have the support of the people. For such an escape route to materialize, the government of Nepal and the royal house should accept some changes in the constitution, which have already been requested by other left-wing parties.

Amnesty for all Maoists may become a difficult but necessary measure, but it may be a price worth paying while the demands that have been raised by the movement are taken seriously.

The two-pronged strategy will also require an economic package, including the bringing down of moneylending rates (the Maoists have brought down interest rates in some areas they control from over 50 percent to 18 percent). There is an urgent need for the extension of education, health care, food, housing, and social security for all, especially to the ethnic minorities whose neglect now forms the natural environment for the Maoists. Unless the stark polarization in Nepal is reduced and the state is seen to show concern for the majority of the rural poor, radical agrarian movements will erupt again and again. The Maoists have accused the government of buttressing social and ethnic hierarchies, and have come forward as defenders of victims of state discrimination. This fact in certain regions is reflected in a high level of support among the lower castes and the more disadvantaged ethnic groups. Consequently, economic and social development should be concentrated on the rights and needs of these groups. There should be a specific focus on the discrimination of women, who in present-day Nepal largely cannot inherit property (the 1990 Constitution provides equal rights for women to property inheritance, but there are no specific laws to enforce this).

Politics in Nepal has degenerated into a process of jockeying for power and money. The current need is for a national front of parties committed to pro-poor politics and honesty. Improvement in the legitimacy and credibility of politicians and bureaucracy, including investigation and punishment of past corruption to gain public confidence, is needed to restore the legitimacy of the political system. The organizations of civil society and the media may be expected to highlight these issues and gradually improve the democratic environment.

Resources

Newsletters and Periodicals
HIMAL magazine, Kathmandu

Reports
Amnesty International
  Nepal: Human Rights and Security, February 2000.
  Nepal: A Spiralling Human Rights Crisis, April 2002.
Centre for Nepal and Asian Studies, *Domestic Conflict and Crisis of Governability in Nepal,* edited by Dhurba Kumar, Kathmandu, 2000.
German Technical Cooperation (GTZ), *Nepal, Country Study on Conflict Transformation and Peace Building.* Eschborn, Germany, 2002.
Harvard School of Public Health, Program on Humanitarian Policy and Conflict Research, *Setting Priorities for Preventive Action in Nepal.* Final Report of the Web Conference, 25 January to 1 February 2001. (www.preventconflict.org/portal/nepal)
Informal Sector Service Centre, *Human Rights Yearbook 2001,* Kathmandu, 2001.
Ministry of Home Affairs, Nepal
  Dhami Report, Report of the Working Group on Maoist Activities and Appropriate Resolution, Kathmandu, August 1997.

Recommendations on the Resolution of Maoist Problems. Report of High Level
Committee on Recommendations for the Resolution of Maoist Problems, Kath-
mandu, November 2000.
South Asia Forum for Human Rights, *E-Briefs: People War in Nepal* 1(3), July 2000.
South Asia Partnership–Nepal, *The Features of "People's War" and the Peace Prospects and
Peace and Good Governance: Problems and Resolutions,* Kathmandu, February 2001.

Other Publications

Class, State and Struggle in Nepal, by Mikesell and Stephen Lawrence. New Delhi,
Manohar, 1999.
Foreign Aid and Foreign Policy: Major Powers and Nepal, by Khadka Narayan. New
Delhi, Vikas Publishing House, 1997.
Nepal in Crisis: Growth and Stagnation at the Periphery, by Blaikie Piers, John
Cameron, and David Seddon. Oxford, Oxford University Press, 1982.
People, Politics and Ideology: Democracy and Political Change in Nepal, by Martin
Hoftun et al. Kathmandu, Mandala, 1999.
"The Maoist Insurgence and Crisis of Governability in Nepal," by Panchan Maharjan.
In Dhurba Kumar (ed.), *Domestic Conflict and Crisis of Governability in Nepal,*
Kathmandu, Centre for Nepal and Asian Studies, 2000, pp. 163–196.
Women, Politico-Economic Rationale of People's War, by Baburam Bhattarai. Kath-
mandu, Utprerak Prakashan, 1998.
Women, War and Peace in South Asia, by Rita Manchanda. New Delhi, Sage, 2000.

Selected Internet Sites

http://nepalresearch.com/politics/background/maodem.htm (Nepal research web site;
has, for example, the Maoists 40 Point Demands)
www.himalmag.com/ (Direct access to the *HIMAL* fortnightly, which has good analytical pieces on the conflict)
www.hsph.ed/hpcr/cpi_portals_nepal.htm (A conflict-prevention initiative by Harvard
scholars with a detailed data base of summarized articles and links)
www.inhured.org (Inhured International—one of the NGOs working on human rights,
education, and development; a member of the Him-Rights association of human-
rights organizations; its web site also has the Maoist demands)
www.insec-nepal.com (Informal Sector Service Centre)
www.nepalhomepage.com/dir/politics/politics.php (Nepal home page; government and
politics directory)
www.nepalnews.com.np/ (Links to news resources and newspapers in Nepal)
www.rwor.org/home-e.htm (Revolutionary Worker Online)
www.safhr.org (South Asia Forum for Human Rights)
www.yomari.net/p-review/ (*People's Review*)

Resource Contacts

Shiva Hari Dahal, National Peace Campaign, e-mail: npcpeace@ntc.net.np
Daman Nath Dhunganga, former Speaker, House of Representatives, and member of
Peace Dialogue Facilitating Committee, Kathmandu. Tel: +977-1-430414
Dipak Gyawali, Interdisciplinary Analysts, e-mail: ida@wlink.com.np
Dhruba Kumar, Centre for Nepal and Asian Studies, Tribhuvan University, GPO Box
3757, Kathmandu, Nepal
Rita Manchanda, South Asian Forum for Human Rights, e-mail: south@safhr.wlink.
com.np
Pancha Maharjan, scholar at the Centre for Nepal and Asian Studies, Kathmandu
John McDonald, Institute for Multi-Track Diplomacy, e-mail: imtd@imtd.org
Gauri Pradhan, President CWIN, e-mail: cwin@mos.com.np
Chitra Tiwari, Nepalese professor, e-mail: cktiwari@erols.com

Padma Ratna Tuladhar, coordinator, Peace Dialogue Facilitating Committee, Kathmandu, Nepal. Tel: +977-1-411664

Organizations

National Human Rights Commission
Pulchowk, Lalitpur, Nepal
Tel: +977-1-547974

Nepal Bar Association–Human Rights and Public Concerns Committee
Bar Bhavan, Supreme Court Complex
Kathmandu, Nepal

Data on the following organizations can be found in the Directory section:

In Nepal
 Forum for Protection of Human Rights
 Group for International Solidarity
 Human Rights and Peace Campaign Nepal
 Human Rights and Peace Society
 Human Rights Organisation of Nepal
 Informal Sector Service Centre
 Institute of Human Rights Communication
 International Institute for Human Rights, Environment and Development
 National Peace Campaign
 South Asia Forum for Human Rights
 South Asia Human Development Forum Network
 South Asian Institute for Peace Studies
 South Asia Partnership–Nepal

In the United States
 Institute for Multi-Track Diplomacy

Kristoffel Lieten (Belgium, 1946) is an associate professor at the Amsterdam School of Social Sciences of the University of Amsterdam (lieten@pscw.uva.nl). Since his studies at the Jawaharlal Nehru University in New Delhi in the early 1970s, he has done extensive research on political and social developments in South Asia. He has worked as the South Asia correspondent of the Dutch and Belgian Radio and has become a regular media commentator. He has cofounded the Dutch National India Committee and has written several books on various aspects of politics, history, and rural development in India.

7.10

Pakistan

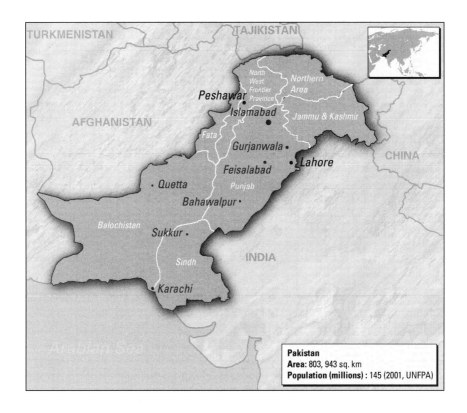

Pakistan
Area: 803, 943 sq. km
Population (millions) : 145 (2001, UNFPA)

7.10.1

An Introduction to Pakistan's Ethnic and Religious Conflicts

Farhan Hanif Siddiqi

Pakistan's political and social history provides an interesting case study of the dynamics of conflict formation as well as opportunities for researchers and academicians in the field of conflict resolution and conflict management. At the outset, Pakistan faces a myriad of ethnic and religious conflicts. The social environment plays an important role in shaping and reshaping as well as intensifying these conflicts. Included in the social environment are the very low literacy rates, a feudal agro-based economy, imbalanced economic development, the inequitable distribution of power and resources, and a pseudo-federal system.

The key factor in understanding conflict formation is the state structure. The dilemma of state building and nation building came naturally to the postcolonial state at the time of independence. A viable and effective state structure, in terms of the bureaucracy and the military, was necessary to sustain the new nation-state and its independence. However, the state structure came to manifest itself much more strongly over government and civil society, with the result that the military and political processes became synonymous with each other. Starting with the military regime of Ayub Khan, Pakistan has seen overt military rule in the 1980s during the time of Zia-ul-Haq and at present with Pervez Musharraf in power. The predominance of the bureaucratic-military nexus has resulted in an overcentralized state structure, a negation of democratic politics, a weak civil society, and religious and ethnic conflicts.

The state structure and the conflicts it generates can be explained with respect to three levels of analysis: the domestic, regional, and international. At the domestic level, the main debate includes the religious issue, the ethnic issue, and the crisis of governability. At the regional front, the enmity with India over the Kashmir issue provides an interesting case study of the legitimacy of the ruling establishment. At the international front, the relationship with the United States is the key variable for understanding the debate on democracy and dictatorship in Pakistan.

At the domestic level, an overcentralized state structure has tended to augment both religious and ethnic conflicts. As far as religion is concerned, Islam played an important role in the movement for Pakistan. Islam provided the ideological foundation for the two-nation theory, which claimed the distinctiveness of the Hindus and Muslims and called for a separate nation-state for the Muslims of the Indian subcontinent. It is interesting to note that soon after the Partition of 1947 the Islamic factor sailed into oblivion as the state managers acquired a secular tone. Pakistan's state structure since partition has remained secular, with Zia's period being the exception when the Islamic factor played an instrumental role. During Zia's rule, religion was used to provide legitimacy to an illegitimate government and also to mobilize Islamic parties in the *jihad* against the Soviet Union in Afghanistan. Zia's reliance on a Sunni version of Islam alienated the minority Shia community and one finds the prevalence of the Shia-Sunni conflict in Pakistan ever since. Moreover, with the success of the Iranian revolution, Pakistan became an important playground for the Sunni Gulf states and the Irani Shia state to play out their rivalries against each other through their support of Islamic parties in Pakistan.

On the other hand, the ethnic factor has played an important role in Pakistan's political history. Pakistan, being a multiethnic state, needed to evolve an adequate system of representation and a just and equitable distribution of power and resources in order to maintain ethnic peace and harmony. However, the dominance of the state structure, especially the bureaucracy and the military, by one or two ethnic groups, tended to augment ethnic tensions and violence. The most important in the context of Pakistan has been the Bengali ethnic movement, which led to the breakup of Pakistan and rise of a new state, Bangladesh, in 1971. The Bengalis nurtured serious grievances from the Pakistani state structure, as they were not given adequate representation at the state level. Moreover, since a working parliamentary form of government was nonexistent in Pakistan, the Bengalis found themselves alienated and exploited. These grievances led to a movement that called for federal autonomy. Later on, through grave violence that was inflicted on the Bengalis, a separate state emerged. The violence done to the Bengalis called into question the ideology of the two-nation theory, as one witnessed Muslims inflicting violence and oppression on Muslims themselves. After the secession of East Pakistan and its reinvention as the country of Bangladesh, other ethnic movements came to challenge the Pakistani establishment. These were the Baluch Movement in the 1970s, the Sindhu Desh Movement in the 1980s, and the Muhajir Qaumi Movement in the 1990s. The state used its force to brutally suppress all three movements with no room for accommodation and compromise. It seems as if there was no lesson learned from the separation of East Pakistan.

At the regional front, the enmity with India provides the causality for the justification of the state structure and huge defense budgets. The Kashmir issue, a legacy of the colonial period, has come to haunt relations between India and Pakistan. Three wars and a mini-war in Kargil have been fought between the two nations, but still the Kashmir issue remains unresolved. Pakistan insists on a just and fair resolution of the Kashmir issue through the implementation of the United Nations resolutions, but the issue itself has become instrumental in legitimating the incumbent regimes, whether military or nonmilitary. Although India and Pakistan are implementing and have implemented a regime of confidence-building measures (CBMs) to settle bilateral issues, the nonresolution of the issue points to the issue being a lifeline for the state structures of both the countries. In the case of Pakistan, when the host of social problems continue to plague the nation-state, the important question is to concentrate and solve the dispute first or to solve the immense amount of ethnic, religious, and class conflicts within the country. The state structure, however, sees the dispute in a traditional manner, which emphasizes the buildup of conventional and nuclear weapons as well as ballistic missiles to combat India. This comes at a tremendous cost as the defense expenditure helps to sustain an illiterate, malnourished, and underdeveloped society and a social environment that causes conflicts of various types.

At the international front, the relationship of Pakistan with the United States has served to perpetuate military rule and the strengthening of the state structure at the expense of democratic institutions and a strong civil society. Pakistan's year of independence coincided with the outbreak of the Cold War between the United States and the Soviet Union. The United States, sensing a threat to its interests in the Middle East and South Asia, immediately cultivated the friendship of Pakistan because of its geographical proximity to the Middle East and the Soviet Union. The military and financial aid provided to Pakistan by its foreign ally helped to sustain illegitimate and undemocratic regimes in power. During the 1960s and the Afghanistan-USSR war in the 1980s, the Pakistani military establishment played an important role in helping the United States to procure its interests in the region. At present, history is repeating itself as an undemocratic regime is being sustained as a result of the 11 September 2001 incident.

The present military regime—despite its undemocratic credentials—is following a liberal line. Countrywide, local elections have been held with the aim of devolving power to the common people and their representatives. Moreover, major constitutional changes have taken place and general elections are scheduled in October 2002. More importantly, after 11 September, the military regime's main initiative has been with regard to the eradication of the *jihadi* culture in Pakistan. This culture of Islamic fundamentalism was a direct result of the Afghanistan war in the 1980s and its momentum grew with the rise of the Taliban in 1994. President Musharraf has made it clear that *jihadi* groups will not be tolerated and their linkages within the state structure of Pakistan will be rooted out.

The Pakistan of today stands at a critical juncture. First of all, there is a fear of fallout of the Taliban in Pakistan. Second, the debt burden needs to be tackled for long-term economic development in the country. Third, the state structure needs to be reformed to guarantee adequate representation of all social groups within the society. Lastly, and most importantly, problems of the common people need to be solved so that a benevolent and peaceful social environment free of conflicts is established.

Farhan Hanif Siddiqi is a lecturer in the Department of International Relations at the University of Karachi. His specific area of interest is the state and politics of ethnicity in Pakistan.

7.10.2

The Sindhi-Mohajir Conflict

Moonis Ahmar[1]

Sindh is located in the southeastern part of Pakistan. This territory was called Sindomani by the Greeks, the Sundhudesha by ancient Hindus, Sindh by Arabic geographers, and Sindu by its occupants, who also used the name Sindu for the Indus River. The Partition of 1947 changed the demographic complexion of Sindh. While the Muslim Sindhis constituted a majority, a substantial number of Hindu Sindhis, Christians, and Parsis were also living in that territory, particularly in Karachi, which at the time of partition was a city of 300,000 inhabitants. After partition, more migrants from India settled in Sindh, mostly in Karachi. Sindh is the only province of Pakistan where ethnic polarization is serious because of the presence of large ethnic groups and their clashes of interests.

Before 1947, there was no record of conflict between Sindhi- and Urdu-speaking populations, while feelings of Sindhi nationalism were noticeable even before the emergence of Pakistan. When Sindh was a part of Bombay, Muslim Sindhis resented the manner in which their rights were usurped by the outsiders. In prepartition Sindh, nonlocals dominated business and administrative positions. Yet the Sindhi language and culture remained superior as compared to other languages of West Pakistan and Sindhis wanted to maintain their identity. The influx of millions of migrants from India after partition changed the demographic balance of the province. From 1947 to 1955, the Sindhi cities of Karachi, Hyderabad, Sukkar, and Mirpurkhas became strongholds of Urdu-speaking migrants, called Mohajirs (Mohajir in Urdu means "migrant") from India. The exodus of the Hindu population from Sindh to India and the influx of a new Muslim population from India to Sindh changed the dynamics of politics and economics of that area. The original Sindhi inhabitants came to resent the domination of the Urdu language and the culture of Muslim migrants from India and other parts of Pakistan.

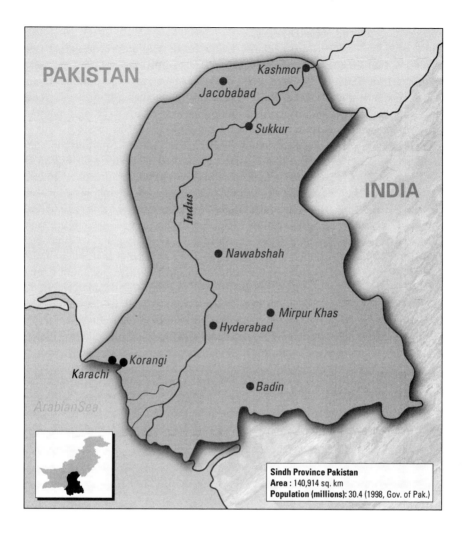

The Sindhi-speaking masses were faced with double jeopardy, first by the state and second by the feudal lords of their own ethnic background. Feelings of insecurity and paranoia began to deepen among native Sindhis because of the state policy to discourage local culture and impose the Urdu language as the medium of education. With the reemergence of the provinces in West Pakistan, Sindhi leaders began to hope for a better role in their province. The general elections of December 1970 clearly demonstrated the ethnic division of Sindh: the rural areas mainly voted for the Sindhi-dominated Pakistan Peoples Party (PPP) and the urban areas of the province voted for the Urdu-speaking candidates. The PPP and Jayae Sindh Movement managed to unite the Sindhi-speaking population of Sindh against the injustices perpetrated by the state forces led by the Mohajir-Punjabi elite.

Political, Cultural, and Social Dynamics

Politically, the Sindhi-Mohajir relations were influenced by several trends, one reversing the other. First, there was the influx of millions of Urdu-speaking migrants from India in the postpartition period. This created a political crisis in which the Sindhis felt that they were being reduced to a minority in their own land. Such fears and insecurities among native Sindhis gave legitimacy to the cause of Sindhi nationalism, which gave birth to the Jayae Sindh Movement. The PPP, which was founded by Zulfiqar Ali Bhutto, a Sindhi leader, despite adhering to the concept of a federal structure, also became a champion of the rights of Sindhi people. The feeling of insecurity and fear prevailed among native Sindhis that their political control over Sindh was being compromised because of the Mohajir clout in the national power setup. The Mohajir community, given their better educational background and pivotal role in the Pakistan separatist movement, possessed political power. Things began to change in 1958 with the military coup and the imposition of martial law in which the Punjabi-Pathan elite began to replace the Mohajir's political, economic, and administrative influence. The federal capital was shifted from Karachi to Rawalpindi in 1959 and Karachi was separated from Sindh in the mid-1960s. A feeling of marginalization emerged within the Mohajir community, first during the martial law regime of Ayub Khan and later on during the rule of Bhutto. The emergence of Mohajir nationalism paved the way for the formation of the Mohajir Qaumi Movement (MQM) in 1984. Because of its focus on protecting the political and economic rights of the Urdu-speaking migrant community, MQM emerged as a big political force in urban Sindh, capturing

Released bonded laborers in relief camp, Hyderabad

Piers Benatar/Panos

maximum seats at the provincial and national assembly elections held in 1988, 1990, 1993, and 1997.

Cultural and social dynamics. The Urdu-speaking migrants from India who settled in Punjab and North West Frontier Province (NWFP) were absorbed into the local cultural setup, but in Sindh the assimilation process, particularly in urban areas, did not take place. This was because of the small number of native Sindhis living in such areas. Since the Mohajir community assumed a dominant demographic status in the urban areas of Sindh, they did not feel the need to learn the Sindhi language or get an understanding of Sindhi culture. As a result, the cultural gap between the Mohajirs and Sindhis widened, resulting in growing social tension. The 1972 language riots in Sindh were an attempt of native Sindhis to assert their culture. While the Sindhi culture was close to rural and feudal traditions, the Mohajirs had an urban middle-class background and were against reverting to social orthodoxy. As a result, the two cultures were unable to reach a level of mutual coexistence.

Economic and administrative issues. The Mohajirs primarily belonged to business, trade, and other professional fields. Since they had an edge in education vis-à-vis native Sindhis, their role in administration was quite significant. Native Sindhis resented the manner in which Karachi, which was the economic and administrative center of Pakistan in its formative phase, was dominated by the Mohajirs. However, things began to change in the early 1970s when the regime of Zulfiqar Ali Bhutto formulated a policy based on 60 percent rural and 40 percent urban quota in state jobs and admissions in state-owned educational institutions. The purpose was to improve the socioeconomic standard of people living in rural areas. Since the majority of Sindhi-speaking people lived in rural areas, the objective of the quota system was to benefit their position. As a consequence to Zulfiqar Ali Bhutto's policy of promoting the interests of native Sindhis, the Mohajir community searched for its identity, resulting in the creation of the MQM. The Mojahir leaders legitimized their quest by asking why the rights of Urdu speakers to have a separate identity were not accepted by the state. The nationalization of banks, insurance companies, and various industries by the Bhutto regime in 1972 and his administrative measures to benefit native Sindhis in employment and in other areas led to the erosion of Mohajir influence in Sindh, resulting in a sense of deprivation in that community.

Conflict Dynamics

During the first twenty-four years after the creation of Pakistan, the Sindhi-Mohajir conflict remained low-key. After the establishment of the Pakistani nation in 1947, it became clear that the assimilation process, which could have developed basic understanding between Sindhis and Mohajirs, could not take place. Mohajirs remained committed to the "Two-Nation Theory" (the theory that Hindus and Muslims are separate nations) and possessed a hostile attitude toward ethnic nationalism. They pressed for the adoption of the Urdu language as a source of unity and identity. Sindhis viewed such an assertion as an attack on their culture and traditions. Steps taken to replace Sindhi with Urdu in educational institutions became a cause of insecurity among the Sindhis, and they developed hostility not only against the Urdu-speaking migrants from India but also against the state's power. When Urdu was introduced as a compulsory language for primary classes in 1962, the decision triggered a strike in November of that year.

There was a Mohajir-Punjabi nexus that was considered detrimental to the interests of the Sindhi. It was argued by the Sindhi leaders that those who had migrated to Sindh at the time of partition should assimilate in local culture instead of expressing cultural arrogance. Moreover, the Mohajirs enjoyed a monopoly in business, trade, and jobs, which created resentment among Sindhis.

Between 1972 and 1977 there were violent confrontations between the two communities, first in July 1972. The trigger was the passing of a language bill by the Sindh assembly in that month, recognizing Sindhi as the language of the province. The bill was passed despite the adoption of Urdu as the language by the provinces of Balochistan, NWFP, and Punjab. The Urdu-speaking population protested because it considered such an act a source of promoting Sindhi nationalism at the expense of the ideology of Pakistan. The language riots created bitterness and hostility between the Sindhi and Mohajir communities and divided the province along ethnic lines. The Sindhi-speaking population migrated to the rural areas that they dominated, while the Urdu-speaking population primarily migrated to urban areas. To calm matters, it was decided that the chief minister of the province would be Sindhi-speaking while the governor of the province would be Urdu-speaking. The gradual introduction of the Sindhi language in educational institutions and reserving the quota of 40 and 60 percent respectively for the urban and rural Sindh lessened tensions somewhat. But the 60 percent employment reservation given to rural areas became another source of conflict between the Sindhis and the Mohajirs.

With the dismissal of Bhutto's government and the imposition of martial law on 5 July 1977, the Sindhi-Mohajir conflict took a new turn. While the majority of native Sindhis were supporting Bhutto's PPP, the bulk of the Mohajir population voted against his party during the elections of March 1977. Agitation against the regime of Zulfiqar Ali Bhutto mostly concentrated in the Urdu-speaking cities of Karachi and Hyderabad. Ironically, Mohajirs didn't benefit during the martial law of General Zia-ul-Haq because the Zia regime did not try to resolve the issues, which were central to the Mohajir community.

Between 1986 and 1988 tensions between the two communities gradually diminished. With the influx of Pathans and Punjabis in Sindh and their connections with the regime of General Zia-ul-Haq, the traditional domination of the Mohajir community in the cities of Karachi and Hyderabad began to erode. The taking over of the transport system by the Pathan community and the business and jobs by the Punjabis created a sense of insecurity among the Mohajirs, who feared more marginalization of their role in Sindh.

In August 1986, in a huge public meeting in Karachi, Altaf Hussain, the leader of the Mohajir community, proclaimed the formal launching of the MQM. He accused the Punjabi-dominated establishment of hurting the rights of the Mohajir community. In view of the marginalization of Sindhis and Mohajirs because of Zia's martial law, proposals for Mohajir-Sindhi unity were also presented. For the first time in Sindh's politics, there were indications of Mohajir-Sindhi reconciliation against their common enemy.

The Sindhi-Mohajir honeymoon came to an end in late 1988 when ethnic tension between the Sindhi and Mohajir communities living in the city of Hyderabad escalated over the policies of the MQM-dominated municipal body of the city. On 31 October 1988 hundreds of people were killed as a result of sniper fire in Hyderabad, resulting in bloody ethnic riots between Sindhi and Mohajir communities.

The renewed tension between Mohajirs and Sindhis was one of the outcomes of the breakup of the alliance between the MQM and Benazir Bhutto's PPP. The MQM, which had joined the Bhutto government after the November 1988 elections, left in August 1989 because of the nonfulfillment of its demands by the PPP regime. These demands centered on the repatriation of stranded Pakistanis in Bangladesh, ending the quota system, and withdrawal of cases against MQM activists. With the rupture of the PPP-MQM alliance, ethnic violence in Sindh claimed hundreds of lives between May and June 1990. With the dismissal of Benazir Bhutto's government by the president on charges of corruption and mismanagement, the level of violence of Sindh was reduced.

During the October 1990 elections, the Sindhi-dominated PPP was defeated in general elections. The MQM retained its electoral upper hand in urban Sindh and joined the coalition government with the Punjabi-dominated Pakistan Muslim League of Prime Minister Nawaz Sharif, which had won the general elections. For the first time since its inception, the MQM became a strong partner in Sindh's government. But its role in the government, both in Sindh and at the federal level, was short-lived because the army—fearful of MQM's growing strength—decided to launch an operation against the group in June 1992. As a result, the MQM withdrew its support of the Pakistan Muslim League and went underground. It launched a campaign against the role of intelligence agencies in dividing the MQM and weakening its power. This situation continued until the government of Nawaz Sharif was dismissed by the president on charges of inefficiency and corruption in April 1993. Although his government was reinstated by the supreme court in May 1993, Nawaz Sharif decided to resign from the post of prime minister, paving the way for the holding of general elections in October 1993, which brought Benazir Bhutto's PPP back to power.

The MQM mobilized its cadre for agitation against the government in early 1994. The Sindhi-dominated PPP, meanwhile, blamed the MQM for engaging in antistate activities and seeking support from India for an independent homeland for the Mohajirs of Sindh, charges the MQM denied. Between November 1994 and September 1995, Karachi witnessed violent incidents claiming thousands of lives. Violence in urban Sindh continued, despite the government crackdown.

The defeat of the PPP in the February 1997 elections at the hands of Nawaz Sharif's Pakistan Muslim League and the retention of its vote bank in these elections by the MQM again created an MQM–Pakistan Muslim League alliance, which again was short-lived. Despite joining the Muslim League in a coalition in Sindh and in the federal cabinet, the MQM continued to complain about discriminatory policies. In October 1998, the MQM left the government and again became a target of state repression.

The present phase in the Sindhi-Mohajir conflict, following the military coup of 12 October 1999, is based on three important realities. First, high-profile tensions between Mohajirs and Sindhis have been replaced with "realistic coexistence." To the Sindhis and the Mohajirs, it has become clear that both communities cannot annihilate each other and both need to recognize and respect their interests. The MQM, which had violent confrontations with native Sindhis during 1988–1990, has also come to the conclusion that sustained conflict with them can only benefit the Punjabi-dominated military and bureaucracy. The creation of trust and confidence and the removal of paranoia between the Sindhi and Mohajir communities can help ensure political stability and peace in the province of Sindh.

Recently, one can notice some systematic effort on the part of MQM and Jayae Sindh Quami Mahaz (Sindhi National Front) to seek Sindhi-Mohajir alliances on important issues such as the fair distribution of water. For the first time in many years, one can see organized efforts by Sindhi- and Urdu-speaking leaders to remove mistrust and past cleavages so as to form a united front against the Punjabi elite.

External Factors

Before the formation and rise of the MQM, the struggle for the rights of the Urdu-speaking population in Sindh was not identified with any external hand. It was only in the course of the MQM drive for assertion and its demand for a

---

Casualties in Ethnic Riots in Sindh

Language riots of July-August 1972:
    Total number of people killed in these riots was 125.[2]

Incident of Pakka Qila in Hyderabad on 31 October 1988:
    215 people were killed in clashes in Hyderabad and Karachi. During 1988–1990 1,338 people were killed.[3]

In State-MQM confrontations:
    During 1992–1993, 340 people were killed. In 1994 1,105 people were killed. The highest ration of killings in the history of Karachi was in 1995 in which 2,284 people were killed.[4]

separate Mohajir identity that the establishment began to link instability in urban Sindh with the involvement of foreign forces. Unlike urban Sindh, the Sindhi nationalist movement was believed to have obtained support from external elements.

Several conspiracy theories linking foreign elements in Sindh's ethnic conflicts have been presented over a period of years. During the Cold War days, the role of the Soviet Union and India was mentioned. After the emergence of the MQM as a strong force in urban Sindh, it was alleged by the state that the United States and India were behind creating unrest in the Urdu-speaking community and that the slogan of a separate Mohajir state composed of Karachi and Hyderabad had the blessings of Washington and New Delhi. In 1992, when the state had launched a crackdown operation against the MQM, official sources revealed that the prime objective of Mohajir nationalists was to create "Jinnahpur," which would have sovereign status with the support of India. When Karachi was in the grip of severe violence in 1994, the government asked the Indian consulate to close its operations in the city because of its alleged involvement in MQM-sponsored terrorism.

Sindh is the most ethnically diversified province of Pakistan and the two major ethnic groups, i.e., Sindhis and Mohajirs, still lack basic understanding. The third ethnic force in Sindh, i.e., Punjabis and Pathans, form another bloc. The unresolved ethnic issues of Sindh provide an opportunity for foreign elements to exploit the situation for their own interests.

Official Conflict Management

When the language riots broke out in 1972, the then government of Z. A. Bhutto tried to defuse the situation by giving concessions to the Urdu-speaking population. Although Bhutto's government had a soft spot for the Sindhi-speaking population, it realized that continuous violence in Sindh, particularly in its capital, Karachi, could be disastrous for the economy of the country. Some confidence-building measures to promote ethnic harmony between Sindhis and Mohajirs were also taken by Bhutto's government, such as keeping the post of governor of the province for the Urdu-speaking community. During Zia's time and in the post-Zia period (after 1988), official conflict management remained low-key. It can be argued that the state itself was involved in widening the ethnic cleavage between the Sindhis and Mohajirs instead of managing the conflict.

Official conflict-management activities in the Sindhi-Mohajir conflict may be seen at two levels, federal and provincial. There exists a wide belief in Sindh that most of the sources of grievances among Sindhis and Mohajirs against each other could be removed by official administrative measures both by the Sindh and the federal governments. If the quota system, which is still a major source of irritation between Sindhis and Mohajirs, is handled to the satisfaction of both communities and economic steps providing adequate development funds in both rural and urban Sindh are given, the ethnic discord in Sindh could be gradually minimized. The government can also introduce social and educational reforms so that the level of intolerance between Sindhis and Mohajirs could be reduced.

Multi-Track Diplomacy

The role of civil society, state, and media in the Mohajir-Sindhi conflict is quite interesting because of their contradictory reactions. Civil society in Sindh remains weak and divided. There are a few reasons for this, but chief among them is the urban-rural divide. First, the rural population is overwhelmingly Sindhi (92 percent) while the urban population is half Urdu and one-quarter Sindhi (figures from the 1998 Provincial Census). Urban Sindh has high levels of literacy; rural Sindh has a poor educational standing. Urban Sindh is industrialized and politicized; rural Sindh lives in an oppressive and exploitative feudal structure. Urban Sindh has a strong middle class. The two faces of the province do not see eye to eye. These problems are exacerbated by a policy of divide and rule followed by the ruling elite and the absence of an assertive role of the intelligentsia and political parties of Sindh for democracy.

The state tried to deal with the issue of Mohajir nationalism by using force (particularly against MQM supporters), promoting division within the MQM, and encouraging Punjabi and Pathan settlers against the MQM. Since the state was not trying to deal with the problem of Mohajir or Sindhi nationalism in a political manner, the end result was more insecurity and ill will in Sindh against state policies.

None of the mainstream political parties that have dominated the state apparatus have done anything to reduce ethnic tensions. Quite the contrary, they have been a complicating factor. The PPP is a case in point. When it controlled the federal and Sindh governments, tensions between Sindhis and Mohajirs increased because support for Sindhi nationalists had remained a hallmark for the PPP leadership since the days of Z. A. Bhutto. During the tenure of Z. A. Bhutto (1972–1977) and his daughter Benazir Bhutto (1988–1990 and 1993–1996), Sindhi-Mohajir relations were marred with violence. Given the fact that the Bhutto family hails from rural Sindh, Urdu-speaking Mohajirs held the view that they had followed a policy of patronizing Sindhis at the expense of Mohajirs.

The media had a significantly negative impact on Sindh ethnic politics. The vernacular press printed stories and reports about Sindhi-Mohajir conflicts without proper investigation. The print media did not help much in creating reconciliation and goodwill between Sindhis and Mohajirs. A section of the print media was used by the establishment in order to promote a further rift between the two communities. The electronic media, which is under state control, did not help to create harmony and understanding between the two communities.

During the violent phases of the Sindhi-Mohajir conflicts, civil society generally failed to curb the level of violence and promote the process of peace between the two communities, although efforts at the community level by nonpartisan people proved to be useful in scaling down the level of violence in the two phases of active Sindhi-Mohajir conflicts.

Other segments of civil society, such as labor movements, student groups, and social organizations, tried to promote ethnic harmony between Sindhis and

Mohajirs but their scope was limited for two main reasons: (1) the absence of a political process during the long spell of martial law (1977–1985) and (2) the vested interests pursued by the military-bureaucratic establishment to promote ethnic division in Sindh so as to counter the role of national political parties. Because of illiteracy, backwardness, and other social ills, civil society could not play a cogent role in promoting a sense of ethnic tolerance in Sindh. A large section of the print media, particularly the vernacular press, acted in a totally irresponsible manner during spells of ethnic violence in Sindh and contributed to the ethnic divide.

The current absence of an active ethnic conflict between the two communities is not because of the positive role played by the civil society but because of a strong feeling among Sindhis and Mohajirs that as permanent residents of Sindh they should avoid the politics of hate and violence. Given the fact that only vested-interest groups benefit from violence, both Sindhis and Mohajirs are attempting to avoid direct confrontation with each other.

Prospects

Presently, the dynamics of the Sindhi-Mohajir conflict contain not only a potential for meaningful cooperation but also the resurgence of violence between the two communities. From 1990 onwards, the nature of Sindhi-Mohajir relations has changed from overt hostility to covert acceptability. The process of assimilation, which should be a reciprocal process, has not yielded positive results because both Sindhi and Mohajir communities still possess deep-rooted mistrust and suspicions. Cultural, political, and economic cleavages between Sindhis and Mohajirs tend to discourage initiatives for ethnic harmony and cooperation in Sindh. Both state and nonstate actors need to play an active role in the prevention and management of Sindhi-Mohajir conflict in short- and long-term ways. Particularly, if the role of state is positive for promoting ethnic harmony in Sindh, much can be done to resolve decades-old Sindhi-Mohajir conflicts.

The events unfolding after the terrorist attacks on New York and Washington on 11 September 2001 and the subsequent U.S. war on terrorism have launched a discussion in Sindh on its implications for the political dynamics of the province. Following the subsequent war in Afghanistan leading to the collapse of the Taliban regime in Kabul, the centrifugal forces in Sindh will gain ground. Steps for seeking better understanding between progressive forces of Mohajirs and Sindhis are being taken in order to deal with the threat of religious fanaticism in Sindh. If the state fails to control the backlash of events in Afghanistan on Pakistani society, there is a possibility that the nationalist forces of Sindh will rise in order to deal with religious extremist elements. In that scenario, there is also a possibility of a patch-up between Sindhis and Mohajirs because both are concerned about the rising influence of *jihadi* elements. In this scenario, a Sindhi-Mohajir alliance, instead of sustained confrontation, is a long-term possibility.

India can certainly intervene in a subtle manner in Sindh and support nationalist forces of the province if the *jihadi* elements create more problems for New Delhi in its controlled parts of Kashmir.

Recommendations

These may be divided into short-term and long-term recommendations because the nature of ethnic divide in Sindh is such that a step-by-step approach
will have to be followed in order to build trust and confidence. Given the fact
that the conflict is primarily internal, it has few chances of an external intervention at the state level or by foreign organizations such as the United Nations. Based on the passive nature of the conflict since 1990, it is expected that
it will not escalate and has bright prospects for resolution if short- and long-
term recommendations are taken into account by the community leaders and
both provincial and federal governments. They are the following.

Short-Term Recommendations

- Reduction of mistrust by encouraging social contacts and interaction
  between Sindhis and Mohajirs. This is possible by discouraging migration in Sindh along ethnic lines.
- Removal of the feeling among Sindhis that Mohajirs want to have a
  province at their expense. Reassurance given by Mohajir leaders that
  they are against the division of Sindh on ethnic grounds can help to reduce insecurity among the Sindhis. Similarly, an expression of tolerance by the Sindhi-speaking population vis-à-vis their Urdu-speaking
  counterparts is also potentially helpful.
- Reciprocal cultural exchange in order to bring the young generation of
  Sindhis and Mohajirs closer.

Long-Term Recommendations

The best prospects for peacemaking lie with effectively dealing with the ignorance and backwardness in rural Sindh that promotes feelings of ethno-nation-
alism and extremism. There is a need on the part of Sindhi and Mohajir groups
to target real issues such as water sharing, energy, and unemployment, instead
of confronting each other. Investment and education need to be promoted in
rural Sindh so that the sense of deprivation in that part of the province might be
reduced. The state needs to formulate policies that could bring Sindhis and
Mohajirs closer instead of doing nothing against those who promote hate and
paranoia between the two communities. Mohajirs need to understand that as
permanent residents of Sindh they should not have extraprovincial loyalties and
should seriously think of working with Sindhis for the betterment of the
province. This would require a proactive approach: building confidence between Sindhis and Mohajirs at the grassroots level so that the forces of intolerance from both sides are curbed. Most important, Sindhi-Mohajir relations
could be made cordial and tension-free only if there is a political process. In the
absence of democratic political processes, ethnic discord cannot be removed.

The media need to act in a responsible manner because the Urdu and
Sindhi press follow a totally different line while dealing with lingual and cultural

contradictions. The print media of Sindh can contribute a lot to encouraging the process of assimilation.

Resources

Newsletters and Periodicals
DAWN/The News International, Karachi
Naqeeb, a magazine published by the Muhtada Quami Movement (MQM)
Sindh Quarterly (stopped publishing since early 1990s)

Reports
United Nations Research Institute for Social Development (UNRISD), *Pakistan: Ethno-Politics and Contending Elites,* by Abbas Rashid and Farida Shaheed. Discussion Paper No. 45, June 1993, online: http://www.unrisd.org/engindex/publ/list/dp/dp45/toc.htm#TopOfPage.

Other Publications
Ethnicity and Politics in Pakistan, by Feroz Ahmed. Karachi, Oxford University Press, 1998.
Ethno National Movements of Pakistan: Domestic and International Factors, by Tahir Amin. Islamabad, Institute of Policy Studies, 1988.
Pakistan Society: Islam: Ethnicity and Leadership in South Asia, by Akbar S. Ahmed. Karachi, Oxford University Press, 1987.
State and Civil Society in Pakistan: Politics of Authority, Ideology and Ethnicity, by Iftikhar H. Malik. London, Macmillan, 1997.
The Sindh Story, by K. R. Malkani. Karachi, Allied Publishers Private Limited, 1984.

Selected Internet Sites
paknews.com/ (Pakistan news site)
sindh.net/ (Sindh Network)
www.bsos.umd.edu/cidcm/mar/cbwebpg.html (Minorities at Risk project, info on Sindh and Mohajir ethnic groups and their current concerns)
www.kawish.com/ (Daily newspaper only avaliable in Sindh, *Daily Kawish*)
www.mqm.org (MQM's official web site)
www.mqmuk.demon.co.uk/ (Site of MQM International Secretariat)
www.satp.org (Institute for Conflict Management)
www.sindh.gov.pk/index.shtml (Government of Sindh)
www.world-sindhi-congress.com (World Sindhi Congress–Sindhi Unity Forum)
yangtze.cs.uiuc.edu/~jamali/sindh/res/ (Web directory of information about Sindh and Sindhis)

Data on the following organizations can be found in the Directory section:
Human Rights Commission of Pakistan
Pakistan-India People's Forum for Peace and Democracy
Program on Peace Studies & Conflict Resolution
Sustainable Development Policy Institute

Moonis Ahmar is associate professor at the Department of International Relations, University of Karachi, Pakistan, and director of the Program on Peace Studies and Conflict Resolution. His field of specialization is confidence-building measures and conflict resolution in Central Asia, South Asia, and the Middle East. He is teaching courses in conflict resolution and crisis management at the International Relations Department, University of Karachi. Formerly he worked at the Arms Control Program, University of Illinois at Urbana-Champaign, United States. He was a visiting research associate with the Henry L. Stimson Center, Washington, D.C.; the Middle East Institute and the Center for Strategic and International Studies, Washington, D.C.; and with Kroc Institute for International Peace Studies, University of Notre Dame, Indiana. He has published extensively. Recently he has been awarded an Asia Fellowship to conduct research in Bangladesh on the theme "A Comparative Study of Pakistan and Bangladesh: Economic, Political and Cultural Dynamics."

Notes

1. The author is thankful to Ms. Nausheen Wasi, Mr. Farhan H. Siddiqi, Mr. Naeem Ahmed, and Mr. Fahim Raza for providing information and going through the earlier drafts of the survey.

2. Source: Khan Zafar Afghani, Taasub, Tashuddud Aur Tazad, *Fanaticism, Violence and Clashes,* vol. 1. Lahore, Al Mustafa publishing Systems, 1997, pp. 55–86.

3. Source: Ibid., pp. 268–495.

4. Source: Ibid., pp. 553–724, 870, 1601.

7.10.3

Fratricidal Conflict Between Pakistan's Shias and Sunnis

Karan R. Sawhny & Nidhi Narain

Internal and external factors have conspired to create and complicate one of Pakistan's most intractable problems: the conflict between the Sunni and Shia Muslims. The stop-start violence escalated in 1979, when the Iranian revolution ran its course and the Soviet Union invaded Afghanistan. With the proliferation of extremist Sunni religious and educational institutions in various parts of Pakistan and the Afghani cause a rallying point for disaffected young people, there was a real danger that this conflict could spin seriously out of control. To its credit, the new government of General Pervez Musharraf—even though it came to power in an illegitimate fashion—has put measures into place to curb the threat of further polarization and thus reduce the levels of violence.

Pakistan is the only state explicitly established in the name of Islam, yet fifty years after its independence, the role and place of Islam in the country remain unresolved. There is a basic divide regarding the relationship between religion and the state between those who see the existence of Pakistan as necessary to protect the social, political, and economic rights of Muslims and those who see it as an Islamic religious state.

A combination of domestic and international developments over the past two decades appears to be pushing Pakistan in the direction of a more explicitly religious state. Just in the last year, for example, the government of Pakistan has introduced strict *sharia* laws and some analysts have even begun to consider the prospect of a Talibanized Pakistan. The shift from liberalism to a more overt religious character for the country has been affected by developments in neighboring Iran, Afghanistan, India, and, of course, the aftermath of the 11 September 2001 attacks against the United States.

In the initial two decades after Pakistan's creation, religion rarely came in the way of state policies. This was largely because the state apparatus was dominated by a combination of feudal or Western-educated politicians and the

Boy and baby with Pakistani flags, celebrating Independence Day, Rawalpindi

civil servants who had been trained under the system run by the former British rulers of the subcontinent. This state apparatus had little interest in pushing a religious agenda. Moreover, the middle class, who in a country such as Pakistan tend to be conservative, was nonexistent, and the poorest of society had little representative voice.

The Iranian revolution had a particular impact on Pakistan. Historically, Shia-Sunni clashes occurred regularly in Muslim-majority pockets throughout South Asia. However the atmosphere of condoning violence became a serious problem in the early 1980s. Pakistan was becoming a staging ground for majoritarian Sunni assertiveness upon the Shia minority, which began after the Khomeni revolution in Iran. It was clear that the Sunni Arab states (Saudi Arabia, Bahrain, and United Arab Emirates) saw a dangerous security threat in the rise of revolutionary Iran. This led to the funding of a proxy war in Pakistan between Sunni extremists and the Shia minority. Over the last two decades, an endless cycle of tit-for-tat Shia-Sunni violence has claimed hundreds of lives.

The Shia and Sunni Sects

The Islamic Republic of Pakistan is predominantly an Islamic state. In the early days of Islam, there were no Sunni-Shia divisions. These emerged as a result of political differences regarding the caliphate (ruler) after the demise of the Prophet Muhammad. Almost all the Muslim countries throughout the world are predominantly Sunni and include Pakistan, Afghanistan, India, and the Arab world.

"Sunni" is derived from the Arab word *Sunna*, meaning "customary practice." *Sunna* refers to the words and deeds of Prophet Muhammad, as recorded in the Quran, the sayings of Prophet Muhammad (Hadith), and the *shariah* (Islamic law). The Shias comprise 15 percent of the Muslim population in Pakistan. The Shias revere Ali, Prophet Muhammad's cousin and son-in-law. The word *Shia* is derived from the Arabic word *Shi'ah,* which means "party" or "following." Iran is the only country in the world that has a majority Shia population.

Shias and Sunnis belong to all ethnicities and are to be found among all linguistic groups in Pakistan; no clear dividing line on the basis of ethnicity or language can be found between these two sects. In the North West Frontier Province (NWFP) and the "Northern Areas," tribal divisions can be made that are congruent also to the sectarian divides. And except for the Pushto-speaking tribes in Balochistan, no such clear division is possible in the other provinces of Pakistan.

Political Underpinnings of the Shia-Sunni Conflict
In recent years, Pakistan has been witness to a remarkable upsurge of sectarian violence between the Sunnis (who account for some 75 percent of its population) and the Shia minority, causing the deaths of hundreds of people. Several senior religious leaders have been killed and bombs have been detonated in mosques during prayers. The Pakistani authorities have to appear evenhanded in their approach toward the sectarian conflict. If any action is taken against a Shia or Sunni organization (terrorist or otherwise), the administration attempts to take equivalent action against a counterpart from the other sect.

The political underpinnings of the Shia-Sunni conflict cannot be underemphasized. For instance, there is no doubt that former military ruler Zia-ul-Haq followed a policy of Sunni sectarianism, which witnessed a dramatic mushrooming of *madrassas* (strict Islamic schools) all over Pakistan. But there were limits to the discrimination against Shias. Thus, in 1984 when the Saudi Arabian authorities demanded that the Pakistani army replace Shia soldiers in Pakistani army units based in Saudi Arabia with Sunni soldiers, General Zia-ul-Haq decided to withdraw the entire contingent of Pakistani troops in that country.

Zia came to power through a military coup that displaced the self-styled civilian regime of Zulfikar Ali Bhutto. Zia used the process of Islamization in part to provide an Islamic justification for the continuation of a military-dominated regime. His stance contradicted popular culture in which people are personally religious and not publicly religious. By relying on an Islamic-based policy, the regime fomented factionalism by legislating what Islam is and what it is not. As a result, it could no longer provide unity as it was now defined to exclude certain groups. Shia-Sunni disputes and ethnic disturbances between cultural groups can all be traced to Pakistan losing its ability to use Islam as a common moral vocabulary. Most importantly, an attempt was made to dictate a specific image of women that was largely antithetical to that existing in everyday life.

In this period a more serious conflict between the two main sects arose. This became apparent when Zia promulgated the Hadood ordinance in 1979, which incorporated Islamic punishments as conceived in the Sunni tradition.

The Shia community became restive and termed this ordinance an encroachment on its jurisprudence. The Zakat and Usher Ordinance of 1980 further offended Shia sentiments and led to sectarian violence. Shias, unlike the Sunnis, do not regard Zakat as a compulsory tax but the ordinance provided for the compulsory collection of this tax from certain kinds of assets, particularly bank accounts. The Shias condemned the ordinance as contrary to the teachings of their sect. This led to violent confrontations and the government was forced to amend it. In the process, the Shia community became increasingly politicized, inspired by Khomeini's revolution in Iran. The more the Zia government pursued its Islamization program, the more the Shias felt alienated. This was further exacerbated by the political assassination of their leader, Altaf Hussaini, and the activities of militant Sunni organizations.

The most aggressive stance toward the Shia minority in Pakistan was taken by the Deobandi organizations associated with head of the Jama'at-e-Ulema-e-Islam (JUI), Maulana Mufti Mahmud, which were publishing highly inflammatory writings against this sect. Much of this resentment is the result of the Shia demand for a separate quota of electoral seats and administrative positions. As long as Maulana Mufti Mahmud was the head of the JUI, he was able to contain the anti-Shia sentiment within his following. However, when the JUI split into the Fazlur Rehman (Mufti Mahmud's son) and the Sami-ul-Haq group, both factions started competing with each other to show which group was more anti-Shia.

In the last decade, the struggle, which essentially began between the Shia-Sunni groups as a result of Zia's drive for Islamization, has been transformed from a theological to a political battle. As sectarian parties entered into the fray to prevent the passage of any set laws that were adverse to them, major political parties were ready to forge alliances with them. By gaining respectability through their entry into politics, the extremist elements were strengthened.

Conflict Dynamics

Ethnic violence in Pakistan began in the Balochi uprising (1958) and went on into the late 1970s. It was followed by the horrific killings in the 1971 operations by the Pakistani army and the suppression of the movement for the restoration of democracy in the Sindh province (1984). This engendered an atmosphere of permissiveness toward the use of violence by the state in West Pakistan. The division of Pakistan along sectarian lines are as follows:

- Gilgit-Baltistan in the Northern Areas
- Parachina and Peshawar in the North West Frontier Province
- Lahore, Faislabad, Jhang, Multan, Mianwali, Sargodha, and Dera-Ghazi Khan in Punjab
- Karachi in Sindh. The ethnic clashes in Sindh between the Mohajir Quami Movement (MQM) and other communities were compounded by the violence that the state had first created by its repression of the

Balochi tribesmen and Bengali separatists. Recurrent acts of communal violence in Karachi are a common feature. The MQM articulated a separate "Mohajir" nationality as a political vehicle to advocate ways and means of addressing grievances.

External Factors

While the Sunni-Shia conflict is primarily a "homegrown" phenomenon, the role of external factors certainly comes into the equation. During the reign of Zia-ul-Haq, large sums of money and armaments had begun to pour into Pakistan from the United States, Saudi Arabia, and Iran. The money was used to set up Sunni *madrassas*, especially in Pakistan's most populous province, the Punjab. The funding from welfare organizations and charities from the oil-rich Arab states usually came through the *hawala* channel (it literally means "trust" or "reference") that leaves no trace, unlike banking transactions. Exporters, expatriates, and terrorists lined up to raise funds through this "efficient, cost-effective and private" illegal parallel banking system. This is the most effective method of money laundering that is part of the vast underground economy of Pakistan.

The *madrassas,* thus funded, preached a particularly puritanical Wahabi form of Islam that was fiercely opposed to the Shias as well as the Sufis. Saudi funding seems to have been principally motivated by a desire to counter the Iranian-style radicalism in the region. General Zia, for his part, attempted to cultivate a religious lobby through the *madrassas* in an attempt to build a strong ideological bloc against India. Not to be outdone, the Iranians began sponsoring Shia *madrassas* in various parts of the country. This led to increasing Sunni-Shia tensions.

Private donations were also sent in the name of the Afghan *jihad* against the Soviet invaders. Only a fraction of the aid actually reached the Afghans. A large part of it went into the hands of locals, triggering off a veritable gun culture, which first manifested itself in street fighting in Karachi, and then in the form of Sunni-Shia battles, particularly in the Punjab. The Afghan war bred large numbers of Pakistanis trained in the use of sophisticated weaponry. After the withdrawal of Soviet forces from Kabul, they headed for Bosnia, and later Chechnya, Tajikistan, Sin Kiang, and especially Kashmir. Yet others took up the gun to wage war against sectarian enemies within Pakistan in the name of establishing an Islamic system in the country. Many of these *jihadists* were the products of the *madrassas* that attracted students from poor families because they offered free education.

The Barelvi-oriented Jamat'at-e-Ulema-e-Pakistan (JUP) and Jamat'at-e-Ulema-e-Islam (JUI) have reportedly received a lot of cash from the Iraqi government to fight against the Iran-supported Shia-based organizations.

In assessing the role of external factors, "the hidden hand of the Indian intelligence agencies" cannot be ruled out. The pattern of violence, especially the indiscriminate throwing of bombs in mosques, is indicative of random terrorism intended to create a sense of panic and insecurity.

Internal Factors
The political explanation of the Sunni-Shia conflict today can be presented at different levels. First, the prolonged absence of channels for political participation during the years of the martial-law regime seem to have created a situation in which political unrest was expressed in ethnic and sectarian protests and demands. The restrictions on national political parties and the suspension of the normal political processes created a vacuum that was filled by the emergence of ethnic, sectarian, and *biradari* (kinship)-based organizations, each having their own agenda. Second, successive governments in Pakistan have used sectarian discord and conflict for short-term gains. Third, sectarian violence erupts in such a way that socioeconomic deprivations get translated into a cultural world view involving a feeling of isolation and hostility against the "other." Volunteers affiliated with religious-based political parties belong to the lower socioeconomic order in society and the semi-educated unemployed youth in urban centers have tended to take part in armed conflict.

Shia-Sunni Militant Outfits Involved in Sectarian Strife

Sipah-e-Sahaba. The origins of this outfit lie in the feudal setup of Pakistani Punjab and politico-religious developments of the 1970s and 1980s. Political and economic power in the Punjab was a privilege of large landowners who were mostly Shias, a minority as compared to the Sunni sect. Urban Punjab, in contrast, was a nonfeudalized middle-class society, largely from the Sunni sect.

The Sipah-e-Sahaba (SSP) is reported to be an offshoot of the Jamiat-e-Ulema-e-Islam (JUI). It was reportedly set up at the behest of the Zia-ul-Haq regime as part of efforts to build an Islamic counter to prodemocracy forces opposed to the military regime of the 1980s. It was established in September 1985 in an environment of sectarian hostility in Pakistani Punjab. In 1986 a violent anti-Shia riot broke out in Lahore. Following this there was a spate of assassinations of prominent Sunni leaders in 1987 and 1988. In February 1990, one of SSP's founders, Maulana Jhangvi, was killed. These assassinations deepened the spiral of sectarian violence, though the extent of SSP's involvement is not clear. Sunni violent organizations have suspected Iran of aiding Shia extremists, and in what is believed to be an act of retribution to Jhangvi's killing, Iran's counsel general in Lahore, Sadeq Ganji, was killed in December 1990.

The socioeconomic rationale for SSP's origin is explained largely from the economic profile of Jhang, the home base of SSP. Located in a region that divides central from southern Pakistani Punjab, Jhang still has a significantly high proportion of large landholdings, leaving feudalism relatively undisturbed. Most large landlords, who are Shias, dominate both society and politics in the region. But, over the years, the area has developed as an important *mandi* (market town), gradually increasing the power of traders, shopkeepers, and transport operators in the region; in short, there is an emerging middle class. Seeking a political voice and role, this class, largely from the Sunni community, has been challenging the traditional feudal hold. The most serious political challenge to the control of feudal interests has been articulated in the form of violent sectarianism, with the formation of the SSP. This has meant that the contest for access to resources and status and the competition for domination over the state apparatus is not framed in terms of class divisions, or modernization imperatives, but confrontationist sectarian identities. A sizeable proportion of traders and shopkeepers continue to fund the SSP in Jhang; however, most do not believe in the violence associated with the party—rather it is now a matter of buying security. Nevertheless, there is a decline in their support for the SSP over recent years as a result of the economic consequences of sectarian strife.

Within the Shia community, the strengthening of the *ulema* under the influence of the Iranian revolution as compared to the feudal *zakirin* and *khateebs,* has led to a relative decline in the power of Shia feudal lords. The Shia population looks toward the *ulema* for leadership, emerging as the new power center. This has affected the nature of Shia-Sunni relations in two ways: (1) the activism generated by the powerful role of the *ulema* with puritan emphasis is perceived as a threat by the Sunni population, and (2) the Shia feudal lords can no longer effectively play the role of crisis managers at the community levels.

Lashkar-e-Jhangvi. In 1996, protesting against what they termed as the moderating nature of the organizations, the more radical and extremist elements of the SSP walked out of the outfit to form the Lashkar-e-Jhangvi, a group that only involves itself in sectarian violence. By contrast, the SSP has always retained an explicit political profile too, contesting elections and having been a constituent of a Punjab coalition government. It has branches spread in all thirty-two districts of Pakistani Punjab and reportedly has over 100,000 workers.

The Lashkar-e-Jhangvi (LeJ) is one of the most violent terrorist groups operating within Pakistan. It uses terror tactics in its aim to force the Pakistani state into accepting its narrow interpretations of Sunni sectarian doctrines as official doctrines. The victims of its terror tactics have been leaders and workers of rival Shia outfits, bureaucrats, policemen, and worshippers of the "other" sect. Almost the entire leadership of the LeJ is made up of people who have fought in Afghanistan. Its command structure is not clear. Some reports attribute the ruthless success of the outfit to its multicellular structure, where the outfit is divided into small groups that are not in touch with each other all the time.

Tehrik-Nifaz-i-Fiqah-Jafria. The Tehrik Nifaz-i-Fiqah-I-Jafria (TNJF) came into being in 1979 at a convention of Shia Muslims in Punjab. Allama Mufti Syed Jaffer Hussain was the founder of this organization. This first exclusively Shia organization in Pakistan was formed at a time when many Muslims, especially Shias, the world over had become inspired by the victory of the Iranian revolution under the leadership of Ayatollah Khomeni. On 6 July 1987, the organization determined a political role for itself and was converted into a religious-political party.

The organization has committed itself, among other things, to bringing about a pure Islamic system in Pakistan and the protection of all social, political, and religious rights of the Shias. After the death of its leader in 1983, the TNJF split into two factions, the more radical and pro-Iranian transforming into a political party, the Tehrik Jafria Pakistan (TJP). In Karachi, the TJP collaborated with the Mohajir Quami Movement led by Sajid Ali Naqvi since 1988; the TJP reportedly still has close links with Iran.

Official Conflict Management

Domestic Reform Process Since 1999

In his first speech after the military coup of 12 October 1999, General Musharraf said, "Islam teaches tolerance, not hatred, universal brotherhood, not enmity, peace and not violence. I have great respect for the *ulama* and expect them to come forward and present Islam in the true light. I urge them to curb the elements, which are exploiting religion for vested interests and bringing a bad name to our faith."

In 2000, the government of Pakistan began interacting with the Taliban in Afghanistan and counseling them to inculcate tolerance and moderation in their ways. They were urged to send back those who had been involved in terrorist acts in Pakistan and who had sought refuge in Afghanistan. In addition the Pakistan-Afghanistan border was sealed. A directive was issued that no student of any *madrassa* would be allowed to travel to Afghanistan without the appropriate documents. On the occasion of the Seerat Conference (held on the birthday of the Prophet Muhammed in May 2001), General Musharraf addressed the *ulama* belonging to all schools of thought and spoke firmly against religious extremism.

"Roadmap to Democracy"

During his Independence Day speech on 14 August 2001, General Musharraf unveiled a "roadmap to democracy." Elections for the provincial and national assemblies and senate are slated for 1–11 October 2002. There is still the need to set up a comprehensive electoral infrastructure, including an election commission, delimitation of constituencies, and the drafting of constitutional amendments that implement "checks and balances." It is unclear how the process of amending the constitution will take place in the absence of an elected parliament or what "checks and balances" may include. Transfer of power will take place by November 2002.

While there remain numerous questions about Musharraf's "roadmap to democracy," the four-phase plan will blunt international criticism toward the military regime for two reasons. First, Musharraf seems to understand the relationship of democratic institutions and international pressure. If this is the case, chances are that the interests of Pakistan override the interests of the regime's survival. Second, Musharraf has laid out a very specific plan, with dates, by which he will be held accountable by Pakistan's political elites and by the international community. He plans to convene a national security council composed of key military and civilian officials to oversee civilian rule. The thinking behind the national security council is paradoxical: the military needs to have a role to prevent another military intervention. "He wants a kind of military-civilian partnership," says Rifaat Hussain, a political analyst at Islamabad's Quaid-i-Azam University.

Pakistan's political prospects are an important part of the regional security calculus. With the collapse of the Taliban movement and the move toward a broad-based moderate government in Kabul, attention is focusing on Islamabad, where there are fears that Islamic extremism may continue to fuel cross-border terrorism, especially in Kashmir. If Musharraf can quell the militants and at the same time put the country back on the road to stable civilian rule and accountability, it would greatly help restore security to the region.

This view's biggest doubters sit in neighboring India, where there is acute suspicion of Pakistan—especially the military. In a recent speech, Indian opposition leader Manmohan Singh cited "uncertainties about the political regime in Pakistan" and the "question mark" about ownership of the country's nuclear assets. Some Indian defense analysts even go so far as to describe Pakistan as a "failing state," with disintegration in the cards. With India urging the United States to spurn Pakistan and act against alleged terrorist activity there, Musharraf is under pressure to prove that his government's support for Islamic militants is over and that he can forge a reasonably democratic and stable government.

Disarmament

In the same Independence Day speech, General Musharraf's government banned new licenses for assault weapons and announced a drive against unlicensed weapons. The display of guns in public places (markets, mosques, and meetings) is now forbidden. This was undertaken to overcome the "Kalashnikov culture" of collecting and firing guns that has become a national tradition in Pakistan. By the new ordinance, no one will be allowed to display arms or force people to give donations for the purchases of weapons, even in the name of *jihad*. However, extremist Islamic groups vow to fight to keep their guns. The gun sellers argue that because the local police turn a blind eye whenever someone is shot, the gun culture endures. They assert that since there is no stable government the sale of weapons cannot be controlled. Moreover, the people will simply not allow the government to take the weapons—part of their tradition—away. Much of the weaponry in Pakistan is homemade, and in Sindh a weapon for a Pathan tribesman is part of his cultural heritage and his perception of personal security.

Moves Against Extremists

In an attempt to manage sectarian violence, the government of Pakistan banned the Lashkar-e-Jhangvi and the Sipah-e-Mohammadi on 14 August 2001. It also amended the antiterrorism law. The objective of the new ordinance was aimed at bringing back peace and restoring investor confidence. The state bank of Pakistan froze the accounts of the two outlawed militant groups. On 24 August 2001, the Pakistani police sealed the headquarters of the militant outfits and confiscated weapons and "offensive" literature. The police also arrested several leaders of sectarian groups blamed for the relentless religiously motivated attacks that have left many dead in Pakistan. The religious extremists regard the ban on the collection of funds as a crackdown on religious and sectarian militancy.

Ban on Collection of Funds in the Name of Jihad

On 14 August 2001 the government of Pakistan also banned fundraising in the name of *jihad* and ordered Islamic militant organizations to remove signboards from their offices. The official statement of the government noted with grave concern that *jihadi* organizations were displaying their signboards and collecting contributions by placing boxes on shops and roadsides. The *jihadi* organizations have condemned these moves, calling them un-Islamic acts, alleging that they were conducted under pressure from the United States as a means of appeasing them.

Reforming Madrassa Education

In his speech on 12 January 2002, General Musharraf addressed issues relating to education and religion. He announced new measures designed to regulate the activities of both Islamic educational institutions and places of worship. Consequently, the government promulgated an ordinance to establish the Pakistan Madrassa Education Board. Its primary objective is to develop a network of model *madrassas* and promote full-fledged, comprehensive, and specialized Islamic education in tandem with the general education system. The law will require registration, regulation, standardization, and uniformity of the curricula to be followed by the *madrassas*. There is a consensus among Pakistan watchers that the religious schools play an important role in imparting education to children where the government-run schools are unable to cope with the rush. This may be seen as an effort to regulate their functioning and bring them into the mainstream. A new *madrassa* ordinance would be issued shortly under which their functioning would be regulated and governed by the same rules and regulations applicable to other schools, colleges, and universities. All *madrassas* will be registered by 23 March 2002 and no new *madrassa* will be opened without permission of the government. If any *madrassa* is found indulging in extremism, subversion, militant activity, or possessing any type of weapons, it will be closed. In addition, all *madrassas* will have to adopt the new syllabi by the end of this year. To this end, the government has decided to provide financial assistance. The government will also help the *madrassas* in the training of their teachers. The Ministry of Education has been instructed to review courses of Islamic education in all schools and colleges with a view to improving them.

Rules have also been established for foreign students attending *madrassas*. Those who do not have proper documents would be required to comply with the formalities by 23 March 2002 or may otherwise face deportation. A foreigner wanting to attend *madrassas* in Pakistan will have to obtain the required documents form his/her native country and a no objection certificate from the government on the basis of which he or she would be admitted. The same rules would apply to foreign teachers.

Checks on Mosques/Places of Worship

General Musharraf further announced that checks would be kept on mosques to ascertain that they do not spread political and sectarian prejudices. This means in concrete terms that if the imam of a mosque fails to display responsibility, curbs would be placed on him. Second, all mosques will be registered and no new mosques will be built without permission. Further, the use of loudspeakers will be limited to call for prayers, the Friday Sermon, and Vaaz. Special permission has been given for Vaaz, but if misused, the permission will be canceled. And finally, if there is any political activity, inciting of sectarian hatred, or propagation of extremism in any mosque, the management would be held responsible and action would be taken in accordance with the law.

Multi-Track Diplomacy

Fratricidal conflict between the Shias and Sunnis is viewed as an internal problem by the government. The government of Pakistan considers third-party intervention to be out of the question. Still, several Islamic solidarity organizations have attempted to bring together the differences between the two sects, but to no avail.

Although the NGO movement spread rapidly in Pakistan, especially in the areas of sustainable development, environmental issues, gender rights, human rights, rural development, and so on, the Pakistani authorities and major political parties, particularly the religious parties, have been extremely suspicious of NGO activities. This is the case with organizations receiving financial support from foreign sources. As a consequence, no NGO is active in the issue of resolving the Shia-Sunni conflict. It is significant to note that Pakistani newspapers are highlighting the importance of the work of NGOs throughout the country. The media has been expressing the need for integrating development with government policies.

Since its foundation in 1986, the Human Rights Commission of Pakistan (HRCP) has become a broad-spectrum, countrywide human rights body. Nationally, the HRCP has established a leading role in providing a highly informed and independent voice in the struggle for human rights and democratic development in Pakistan—a role increasingly recognized as well internationally. It publishes a yearly report on the state of human rights. Its activities focus, among other issues, on:

- Mobilizing public opinion in favor of accepted international human-rights standards

- Taking appropriate action to prevent violations of human-rights and to provide legal aid and other assistance to victims of those violations and to individuals and groups striving to protect human rights
- Taking note of and investigating allegations of violations of human rights, recommending to appropriate authorities action for redress, and publishing reports and recommendations

Amidst fears of a possible takeover of religious elements in Pakistan by foreign governments, the International Committee of the Red Cross has attempted to engage politico-religious parties in Pakistan in the hope of instilling in them a greater regard for humanitarian law and the Geneva Conventions. Their way of operating was by constantly seeking references in the Quran and its teachings to remind them that human rights were not invented by the West and that greater respect for the adversary's right is, in fact, an Islamic trait.

A number of independent research organizations, of which there are very few, have engaged in research related to the sectarian conflict. Foremost among these is the Islamabad-based Sustainable Development Policy Institute (SDPI). The goal of SDPI's research program, mostly on governance and human development, is to provide support for informed decisionmaking and, thus, to catalyze the transition to sustainable development. The research is multidisciplinary in character. It is problem-oriented rather than discipline-oriented. SDPI conducts both independent and collaborative research.

The Aga Khan Rural Support Program
In the summer of 1999, before General Musharraf took over as chief executive of Pakistan, the threat of sectarian violence reared its head in the northern areas where one of Pakistan's most prominent NGOs, the Aga Khan Rural Support Program (AKRSP), has been carrying out rural development work for over two decades. By far the most extensive institution in northern Pakistan, as a noncommunal and nonprofit organization, the AKRSP has introduced simple financial mechanisms with built-in transparency and demonstrated a remarkable capacity to respond to local needs. The success of its projects has enhanced the credibility of the Aga Khan Foundation and attracted large amounts of funds from donors.

It is however true that the AKRSP's work was concentrated in Ismaili areas. Out of its total project aid of 139.35 million rupees for the six subdivisions of Chitral, an amount of 118.83 million rupees was allocated to two Ismaili-majority areas. This created some alarm among the Sunni population. The Sunni clergy in particular was not happy with the gradual empowerment of the Ismailis, formerly a submissive community that suffered regular conversions from its ranks to the Sunni sect. With the advent of the AKRSP, not only did conversions stop, but the Ismailis also switched to a more urban form of worship, converting their Sunni-like mosques into *khoja jamaatkhaans*. The AKRSP also brought with it symbols of prestige such as four-wheel-drive jeeps and helicopters, and relatively high-paid jobs, which created resentment within the Ismaili community itself, who perceived the predominantly Sunni employees of the organization with envy. These elements joined the Sunni clerics in deriding the AKRSP. The donors were aware of sectarian tensions in the areas covered by the program. In 1989, the British government (one of the donors) suggested that the AKRSP name be changed. While this was resisted initially, the organization succumbed to pressure by the World Bank to include non-lsmaili members on the AKRSP's board of directors. Three Sunni members were accepted on the fourteen-member board. As recently as July 1999, the annual review mission of the donors expressed concern over the "continuing concentration of benefits in Ismaili areas." Since then the district administration has been under pressure by the government and the Aga Khan Foundation to ensure the AKRSP's continuing work in the area so that the people's spirits and hopes can be once again restored.

Prospects

A statement presented by Dr. Mumtaz Ahmad provides some insight in terms of the future prospects, among other things.

> There have been some encouraging trends at the level of civil society that promise a better future for Pakistan. First, the emergence of a host of human rights organizations during the past decade and a half, specifically concerned with issues of rule of law and civil liberties. Second, the press in Pakistan has never been freer in its entire history than it is today and is likely to play an important role in promoting freedom and liberty. Third, a majority of Pakistani citizens are becoming wary of Islam being used as an instrument of politics. Fourth, the emergence of a liberal Islamic discourse that seeks to reaffirm the Islamic principles of tolerance, democracy, pluralism, civil liberties and rule of law from within the Islamic tradition. A new generation of Islamic thinkers is challenging the monopoly of the extremists on Islamic discourse. Finally, liberal Islamic thought of Muslim émigré intellectuals (primarily in the U.S.) is also contributing significantly towards the development of a progressive religious-intellectual discourse.
>
> In order to fortify democratic practices in Pakistan and deal effectively with the extremist groups indulging in sectarian violence, the state's economic base and institutional capacity to maintain law and order must be strengthened. In the final analysis, the most effective way to contain sectarian violence is not by censure, condemnation and sanctions but by constructive engagement involving all those party to the conflict. The search for a peaceful resolution of the fratricidal conflict must be part of a larger agenda and promoting democracy, pluralism, rule of law and civil liberties. Once these practices are institutionalized, religious freedom, without taking violent turns, is a natural outcome.[1]

Recommendations

Promotion of an Intrafaith and Interfaith Dialogue Process

General Musharraf's 12 January 2002 speech detailed the damage religious intolerance had inflicted on the country and argued the case for a "progressive, modern and dynamic nation." Islamic law has a built-in mechanism for responding to the needs of changing social contexts. It allows for creative effort or *itihad* within the parameters set by the basic sources of Islamic law—the Quran and the Hadith—to meet the requirements of new situations. The *ulama* could interact with Muslim scholars in different fields, be it in the fields of science, economics, and interreligious dialogue, to exercise this function of *itihad*. Explaining the teachings of one's own religion and understanding the beliefs of others is a central element of the dialogue process. At another level, there is the need for people of different religious sects to act together to attain desirable social goals. Thus, by cooperating with each other on issues of common concern, the Shias and the Sunnis can begin to live with each other, while recognizing their differences.

Program for Religious Tolerance

The annual report of the U.S. Commission on Religious Freedom on Pakistan (1 May 2001) recommended that the U.S. government should urge the Pakistani government to take steps to prevent sectarian violence and punish its perpetrators, including disarming militant groups and any religious schools that provide weapons training. It urged the government of Pakistan to establish and support mechanisms of interfaith dialogue that encompass all religious communities and facilitate widespread dissemination of the work and findings of this dialogue. In addition, the U.S. government should, through its own foreign assistance and in conjunction with other donors, support the following in Pakistan: (1) teacher training and other educational programs in religious tolerance; (2) judicial reform and law enforcement training; and (3) improvements in the public education system in order to promote the availability and quality of education for all Pakistanis. However directly, U.S aid for education should include support for programs designed to promote religious tolerance, conflict resolution, and greater awareness and understanding among religious communities.

Regional-Cooperation Option

The government of Pakistan has a proclivity for trumpeting its Islamist identity and its inevitable role in South Asia as the "guardian of the faith." The Pakistani leadership could in such a situation place the regional-cooperation option energetically, as it can address the problem of its external security head on by focusing directly on the regional military threat. Regional cooperation encourages the search for ways to reduce this threat. It could even eventuate in enhanced cooperation.

The Deeni Madrassas

The menacing growth of *deeni madrassas* in the educational landscape of Pakistan have helped cultivate intolerance and hate. Students have also been encouraged to be uncritical, submissive to authority, and treat education as a process simply of memorizing certain "facts." At the same time, it also encourages teachers to adopt the authoritarian attitude required for establishing the finality of their word and those in textbooks. The curriculum in the *madrassas* has enforced the distortion of historical facts in textbooks, encouraged religious chauvinism, and glorified militarism. It is hard to imagine a process of education less likely to contribute toward a strong commitment to increasing tolerance and democratization in society.

Clearly, the failure of the state to provide basic education and welfare produces unemployed and frustrated youth, who turn to the *madrassas* as a source of refuge, and who are turning in significant numbers toward militant sectarian and ethnic outfits based on primitive loyalties of *biradri* (group), clan, ethnicity, and sect, where instinctive bonding replaces that formed by rational choice.

The recent decision to regulate the *madrassas* is a welcome step taken by the government. It would help if the law regarding the registration of the *madrassas* would look into the sources of funding (the drug trade, among others) of these institutions before allowing for their registration. This would go a long way in the state being able to control the functioning of these institutions.

Religious Parties

Religious parties remain very relevant political and social organizations for the "wise men of Islam," the *mullahs* and the *ulama* who wield "great moral power." For decades the leaders of Pakistan have acquired power and sought legitimacy to rule through the support of the religious parties. Therefore, it is critical for the government of Pakistan to disassociate from them in the polity of the state—i.e., to demonstrate good governance by providing basic welfare and security to its citizens would definitely curtail acts of sectarian violence.

Prohibit Propaganda and Offensive Literature

The enforcement of a strict code of conduct and effective legal action should be taken against those who deliver objectionable speeches or publish such literature with the purpose of igniting sectarian rift. Peace committees could be established at all levels, especially the district level, to maintain sectarian harmony. In keeping with General Musharraf's decision to root out sectarian activities, local police teams have already begun removing sideboards, posters, banners, and flags from the offices of the Sipah-e-Sahaba and the Tehrik-e-Jafaria Pakistan. Local printing presses and computer-designing offices are being checked by police personnel to stop the publishing of offensive literature. The owners have been directed to inform the area police in case they are approached for getting pamphlets and handbills published. The holding of public meetings and rallies without the prior permission of the authorities has also been banned.

Human Rights

Many religious-freedom violations in Pakistan stem from abuses of law enforcement in the Pakistani legal system and the failure of that system to protect fundamental rights, including the right to religion, in a timely manner. The Report on Human Rights and Development in Pakistan by the International Centre for Human Rights and Development corroborates this point. Thus, improvements in the transparency, accountability, ethics, and independence of law enforcement and the judicial system will have significant derivative benefits from the protection of religious freedom.

As Hina Jilani of the International Centre for Human Rights and Democratic Development pointed out in the *Report on Human Rights and Development in Pakistan:*

> The rights to life, liberty, and security of person have remained vulnerable to violation in Pakistan, at the hands of both the state and non-state parties. While constitutional guarantees do exist for fundamental rights, the state has not honored these guarantees. It is generally agreed that the Islamic policies of the military government in the 1980s contributed to a major decline in religious tolerance. Sectarian divisions have become more pronounced since the legitimacy to rule became firmly linked to Islam, not in response to popular demand, but through the machinations of general Zia. How far legislative measures can succeed in the absence of any steps to deal with the larger issue of the politicization of religion, and with external interests supporting religious factionalism in Pakistan, remains to be seen.[2]

Peace Plan

The government of Pakistan could adapt a peace plan, which played an important role in bringing the MQM (Altaf group), the army, and the authorities to a political settlement in 1984. According to this plan, suggested by the former Inter-Service Intelligence chief, Lieutenant General Hamid Gul, a citizen's initiative could be adapted to bring the warring sects together into a conflict-resolution effort.

Resources

Newsletters and Periodicals

"A Farewell to Arms," by Ismail Khan, *Newsline* 3, Karachi, 2000, pp. 68–70.
"Development in Jeopardy," by Behroz Khan, *Newsline* 10, Karachi, 1999, pp. 43–44.
"Illegal Arms Recovery Move Expedited," by Farhat Abbas, *The Nation* 2(13), 2000.
"In Whose Interest?" by I. A. Rehman, *Newsline* 1, Karachi, 2000, pp. 58–59.
"Islamization and Legal Reform in Pakistan 1979–1989," by C. Kennedy, *Pacific Affairs,* 1990.
"Measures Should Be Taken to Empower People to Have Access to Information," by Shazia Malik, *The Nation* 2, 2000, p. 3.
"NGO Under Fire," by Ilyas Khan, *The Herald* 10, Karachi, 2000, pp. 41–42.
"The Business of Arms," by Ismail Khan, *Newsline* 3, Karachi, 1999, pp. 71–72.
"The Direction We Are Heading," by M. A. Niazi, *The Nation* 2, 2001, p. 8.
"There Should be a Difference Between Jehad and Terrorism," by Taimur Siddiqui, *Newsline* 2, Karachi, 2001, p. 26.
"The Shia-Sunni Conflict in Pakistan," by Yoginder Sikand, *The Weekend Observer,* 25 March 2000.

Reports

Amnesty International, *Pakistan: Crackdown on Sectarian Violence Must Not Jeopardize Rights,* London, 14 January 2002.

Initiative on Conflict Resolution and Ethnicity, "Conflict Within Islam: The Pakistan Experience," by Farrukh Sami Khan. In *The Ethnic Studies Network Bulletin,* No. 7, July 1994.

Institute of Policy Studies, *Ethno-National Movements of Pakistan,* by Dr. Tahir Amin, Islamabad, 1993.

International Centre for Human Rights and Democratic Development, *Report on Human Rights and Development in Pakistan,* by Hina Jalabi, online: http://www.ichrdd.ca/.

Regional Centre for Strategic Studies, *The Sectarian Conflict in Pakistan: A Case Study of Jhang,* by Mukhatar Ahmad Ali, Under the Kodikara Award, Colombo, October 1999.

U.S. Commission on Religious Freedom, *Annual Report on Pakistan,* 1 May 2001.

Other Publications

Deeni Madrassas: Government Report on Religious Institutions in Pakistan, prepared by the Zia-ul-Haq regime in 1979, Islamabad, 1999.

Islamic Reassertion in Islam, by A. Weiss. New York, Syracuse University Press, 1986.

Narcotics and Global Politics, by Musa Khan Jalalzai. Lahore, Frontier Post Publications, 1994.

"Pakistan in 1999," by Hasan-Askari Rizvi. In Ahmad Munawar (ed.), *Current Affairs Digest,* Lahore, A. H. Publisher, January 2000.

Pakistan 2000, edited by Craig Baxter and Charles H. Kennedy. Karachi, Oxford University Press, 2001.

"Pakistan and the Post Cold War Environment," by Rizvi, Hasan-Askari. In Craig Baxter and Charles H. Kennedy (eds.), *Pakistan 1997,* India, HarperCollins, 1998.

Pakistan, Islam & Economics: Failure of Modernity, by Izzud Pal. Karachi, Oxford University Press, 1999.

"Pakistan's Coup: Sowing the Seeds of Democracy?" by Ahmed Rashid. In Craig Baxter and Charles H. Kennedy (eds.), *Pakistan 1997,* India, Harper Collins, 1998.

"Revivalism, Islamization, Sectarianism, and Violence in Pakistan," by Mumtaz Ahmad. In Craig Baxter and Charles H. Kennedy (eds.), *Pakistan 1997,* India, Harper Collins, 1998.

Sectarian and Ethnic Violence in Pakistan, by Musa Khan Jalalzai. Karachi/Islamabad/Lahore, Izharsons Publications, 1996.

The Failure of Political Islam, by Oliver Roy. London, I. B. Tauris Publishers, 1994.

Resource Contacts

Moonis Ahmar, Department of International Relations, Karachi University, e-mail: amoonis@hotmail.com

Dipak Gupta, Institute for International Security and Conflict Resolution, e-mail: dgupta@mail.sdsu.edu

Ahmed Rashid, e-mail: review@brain.net.pk

I. A. Rehman, Human Rights Commission of Pakistan, e-mail: hrcp@hrcp.cjb.net

Farhan H. Siddiqi, Department of International Relations, Karachi University, e-mail: Farhan_74@hotmail.com

Selected Internet Sites

www.members.tripod.com/Pakistan (General information and selected reports on Pakistan)

www.musalman.com (Islamic Search Engine Portals for Muslims)

www.paknews.org/links.html (Pakistan News Service Links Directory)
www.pk.gov.pk (Official web site of the government of Pakistan)
www.pscr.kuird.org/ (Department of International Relations, oldest department in the field of international relations in Pakistan)
www.satp.org (Institute for Conflict Management)
www.shianews.com (Shia news from around the world)

Data on the following organizations can be found in the Directory section:

Aga Khan Development Network
Human Rights Commission of Pakistan
International Centre for Peace Initiatives
Pakistan-India People's Forum for Peace and Democracy
Program on Peace Studies and Conflict Resolution
Sustainable Development Policy Institute

Karan R. Sawhny is currently the director of the International Centre for Peace Initiatives, New Delhi, an NGO and think tank involved in capacity building for conflict resolution in South Asia. He is also the editor of the journal Peace Initiatives. *Nidhi Narain is the assistant editor of the journal* Peace Initiatives, *endorsed by the International Centre for Peace Initiatives. She is also the projects and coordination officer of the center. Most of the research work on all of the center's activities, particularly on security issues and conflict resolution, are undertaken by her.*

Notes

1. Statement of Dr. Mumtaz Ahmad (professor of political science, Hampton University, Virginia) to the United States Commission on International Religious Freedom, 18 September 2000.

2. International Centre for Human Rights and Democratic Development, *Report on Human Rights and Development in Pakistan,* by Hina Jalabi, online: http://www.ichrdd.ca/.

7.11

Sri Lanka:
Finding a Negotiated End to
Twenty-Five Years of Violence

Nick Lewer & Joe William

The island of Sri Lanka is situated in the Indian Ocean just twenty miles off the southeastern tip of India, with whom it has strong historical and cultural connections. For the last twenty years or so it has experienced a series of violent and bloody conflicts, which have mostly gone unnoticed by the international community. These include two uprisings by a Sinhalese group, the JVP, in 1971 and 1987–1989, and a war with the Liberation Tigers of Tamil Eelam. It is on the latter that we will concentrate in this chapter. The causes of the conflict are hotly contested, and it has been referred to variously as a terrorist problem, a war of secession, a protracted social conflict, an ethnic conflict, and a complex political emergency. But there is no doubt that the war has had a massively destructive impact on Sri Lanka's human, social, and economic capacities, and its infrastructure. There have been many attempts at official and unofficial levels to bring peace to the country.

Compared with other parts of the British colonial empire, the transition to independence for Ceylon in 1948 (in 1972 Ceylon became Sri Lanka) was comparatively peaceful. The type of democracy introduced by the British led to a majority system in which the Sinhalese would always control the country's parliament. Subsequent policies, especially with regard to language and access to education by successive Sri Lankan (Sinhalese-dominated) governments, and the reactions to these by the Tamil people, sowed the seeds of what has become a protracted and violent conflict that was particularly exacerbated by anti-Tamil riots in 1958, 1977–1978, and 1983.

The conflict, which has been raging at varying intensities since the 1983 attacks against the Tamil population, can be described as being between the largest, and now the most militarily effective Tamil militant group, the Liberation Tigers of Tamil Eelam (LTTE), and the Sinhalese government of Sri Lanka. The situation has been further inflamed by two violent insurrections

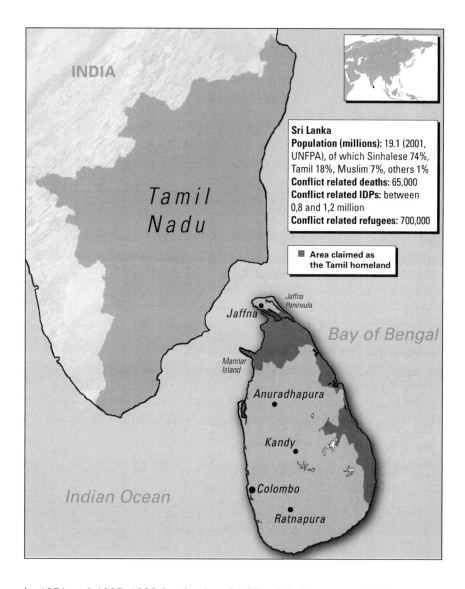

Sri Lanka
Population (millions): 19.1 (2001, UNFPA), of which Sinhalese 74%, Tamil 18%, Muslim 7%, others 1%
Conflict related deaths: 65,000
Conflict related IDPs: between 0,8 and 1,2 million
Conflict related refugees: 700,000

■ Area claimed as the Tamil homeland

in 1971 and 1987–1989 by the Janatha Vimukth Peramuna (JVP), a group made up mostly from disaffected Sinhalese youth, which combined a potent mixture of Marxism and nationalism. The second JVP insurrection was in part triggered by the arrival of an Indian Peace Keeping Force (IPKF) in 1987. The rebellion by the JVP during this time had an important influence on the course of events. How the war is understood and labeled by the various actors is important when considering peace interventions. For example, many Sinhalese talk in terms of a "terrorist problem," while supporters of the LTTE may see it as a war of secession—for Tamil Eelam. It also has the characteristics of a "complex political emergency" in that it is multidimensional with profound human suffering, has roots that are in part political, and there is a challenge to the state.

Sri Lanka has become a highly militarized society where the use of violence is widespread, not only in the war zones but also in the rest of the country where, for example, election violence has become endemic. Although many analysts describe the current situation as an "ethnic war," it is also a crisis of the state in that the LTTE and JVP conflicts are both symptomatic of broader issues concerning the identity, policies, and legitimacy of the state. The legitimacy of the state itself is questioned by some because of corruption and abuses of power, and the disputed and flawed nature of elections in past years.

Internationally, the key influence on Sri Lanka has been India, who has intervened through diplomatic and political initiatives (Indo-Lanka Accord), by sending an IPKF in 1987 and, during the late 1980s and early 1990s when Indian intelligence agencies trained and equipped Tamil militants. The southern Indian state of Tamil Nadu has played an important role in the conflict, especially after riots in 1983 when thousands of Sri Lankan Tamils fled there. This had two effects: first, it "internationalized" the conflict, and second, it raised strong emotions among the Tamils of Tamil Nadu, which put pressure both on Tamil Nadu and national politicians to do something on behalf of the Sri Lankan Tamils. The role of the Tamil diaspora has been influential in helping to raise large amounts of funding for the LTTE.

The LTTE, formed in 1976 from the Tamil New Tigers, consider themselves to be the sole representatives of Sri Lankan Tamils, with operational cadre strength of over 5,500. They are highly motivated and well organized, and have proven themselves to be extremely adaptable, having moved from guerrilla actions to conventional battles at different stages of the war. They also maintain a naval arm, the "Sea Tigers," and a suicide force, the "Black Tigers."

Characteristics of the LTTE

- The Liberation Tigers of Tamil Eelam is an armed group capable of sustainable guerrilla actions, terrorist attacks, and also fighting large conventional battles. It has a tight organizational structure (military and political) under the control of one person, and it is completely disciplined.
- It has systematically eliminated other Tamil militant groups, controls territory in the north and east of Sri Lanka, and runs a parallel government (with a police force, judicial system, and other structures).
- It is the only organization that has consistently stood for the right of national self-determination of the Tamil nation as defined in the Vaddukkodai Resolution (1976), and mandated by some 85 percent of the Tamil-speaking population in the 1977 general election.
- It has consistently demanded that the government offer an alternative to a separate state (based on the 1985 Thimpu Principles), which various administrations have failed to address. But, while it has secessionist

Tamil Tiger, Jaffna

ambitions and a political perspective, it has not specifically articulated
its own alternative to Tamil Eelam.
- It has extensive international linkages and has created a worldwide
  business empire. For example, the LTTE has extensive shipping interests that are used for the delivery of weapons to the LTTE in Sri Lanka.
- It has broad support from Tamil people living in Sri Lanka, and from
  the Tamil Diaspora. It has an effective publicity and propaganda program, which can rapidly mobilize political, economic, and financial
  support of the Tamil diaspora.
- It is proscribed as a terrorist organization in Sri Lanka, and by a few
  other countries.
- It has a culture of martyrdom symbolized through a cyanide capsule
  worn around the neck by LTTE fighters.

In 1948 the newly formed state did not give minorities, including Tamils,
real protection against majority Sinhalese rule. Later changes in the constitution
gave a preeminent position to Buddhism and the Sinhala language (the 1956
Official Languages Act—the "Sinhala-Only" Bill—of Prime Minister S. W.
Bandaranaike). This affected all areas of life including education, government
services, the security forces, and how Sri Lankan citizenship was defined.
Power was concentrated in the Sinhala-dominated legislature. In the view of
the Sinhalese, this was necessary because Tamils had been overrepresented in
professional occupations such as medicine, engineering, police, judiciary, and
in the universities in relation to their percentage of the total population. A new
republican constitution was adopted in May 1972, strengthening Sinhala-

Buddhist ideology. The constitution afforded Buddhism the "foremost place" in the state and confirmed Sinhala as the only official language. It further specified that Sinhala would be the language of the legislature, courts, and related institutions throughout the island. The new constitution also removed Article 29 of the previous constitution, which had provided at least minimal guarantees to minorities. Because of the electoral and representational system, the Tamils felt that they were excluded from having any real influence on political legislation and decisionmaking.

In response to the 1972 Constitution, the main Tamil opposition party at the time, the Tamil United Liberation Front, called for the self-determination of the Tamil people of Sri Lanka and their own "homeland" (Tamil Eelam) in the Vaddukkodai Resolution of 1976. It could be argued that this marked the end of attempts to create a multiethnic Sri Lankan state.

Several state instruments give the government considerable power during emergencies. The Sri Lankan constitution (Article 155) and the Public Security Ordinance (No. 25 of 1947) empower the president to declare a state of emergency, and in July 1979 the Prevention of Terrorism (Temporary Provisions) Act of 1979 (PTA) was enacted. This is still in force. The PTA has allowed successive Sri Lankan governments to arrest and detain people without proper judicial inquiries. Prisoners have been subjected to torture, inhuman and degrading treatment, and many have "disappeared," and some analysts argue that this PTA is the "engine of state terrorism." Similar stories are heard in relation to prisoners held by the LTTE. Perpetrators of human-rights abuses seemed to act with impunity, confident that no serious inquiries would follow. Denial of justice and abuse of police power in Sri Lanka is often justified by reference to the ongoing civil war, and in relation to human-rights abuses committed by the LTTE insurgents. It should be noted that human-rights cases against members of the security forces, including the police, rarely result in a successful prosecution. This climate of impunity encourages local politicians, members of the security forces, and other armed groups to pursue personal agendas and engage in corrupt practices. This connection between military and civil "war economy" interests contributes to the tensions in the conflict-affected areas of the island.

In analyzing the conflict, reference must also be made to the "double minority" factor—both Sinhalese and Tamil perceive themselves to be minority populations under threat, the former in relation to the Tamil population in South India, and the latter in relation to the Sinhalese majority in Sri Lanka. This sense of being an embattled minority has fuelled competing Sinhala and Tamil nationalist perceptions that have become entwined with religious and cultural discourses. Both draw on a mythical history, which emphasizes ancient enmities between the Sinhala and Tamil kingdoms. The political map is, however, far more complex than a simplistic division between competing Tamil and Sinhala nationalisms. For example, growing poverty in areas of the south, political and social exclusion, an inability of the state to deliver political and economic promises, and corruption are all factors that have fuelled the conflicts. Long-term structural stability in Sri Lanka depends on fundamental reforms of the state.

The land colonization policy of successive Sri Lankan governments has caused much resentment. It has been Sinhalese policy to establish "colonies" of Sinhalese settlers (mostly farmers) in the eastern province especially, an area traditionally viewed by Tamil nationalists as theirs. The role of foreign aid was instrumental in this, particularly through their support of the Mahaweli and Galoya irrigation schemes. The government explained that these was to populate uninhabited areas and relieve overpopulation in more crowded areas of the island. Tamils say that the real objective is to dominate, and change, the ethnic demography of Tamil areas.

Views differ over the importance religion has played in the conflict, and some say that historically there was not "religious" conflict per se. The religious element seen in the conflict today is influenced by a twentieth-century interpretation of Buddhism (as promulgated by Dharmapala), which began to explicitly link Sinhala nationalism and Buddhism.

The Muslim community in Sri Lanka has also been on the receiving end (and participated in) acts of violence. During the mid-1980s there were violent clashes between the LTTE and the Muslim communities in the north and east of Sri Lanka. The most serious of these included the massacre of 120 Muslim worshippers at a mosque in Batticaloa in August 1990, and the forced expulsion of the Muslim population by the LTTE from the Jaffna and Mannar districts in October 1990. A subsequent rise in Muslim activism and militancy, and tensions between the Muslim and Tamil communities in the east (with an associated demand for a separate Muslim administrative district) highlight another fault line in the Sri Lankan conflict map. One community that has been caught in the middle between the Sinhalese and Sri Lankan Tamils is the plantation Tamil community of Indian origin. This community, largely marginalized from mainstream government development projects, but maintaining a distinctly separate identity and culture from their Sri Lankan Tamil-speaking brethren, has often been at the receiving end of violence directed against Tamils in general—as was seen in 1958, 1977, 1981, 1983, and thereafter.

Conflict Dynamics

The demands of the Tamils are summarized in the four Thimbu Principles articulated by Tamil negotiators with the government at the Thimpu Talks of 1985.

- Recognition of the Tamils of Ceylon as a nation
- Recognition of the existence of an identified homeland for the Tamils in Ceylon
- Recognition of the right of self-determination of the Tamil nation
- Recognition of the right to citizenship and the fundamental rights of all Tamils in Ceylon

These demands were unacceptable to the government negotiators. While the LTTE position has now shifted and they are talking in terms of an alternative to a separate state on the basis of recognition of Tamil nationhood derived from a historic homeland, the Thimpu Principles have basically remained the core of Tamil demands. The first three of the four principles still remain divisive issues. On their side, the government is now willing to go as far as considering a devolution of power to regional councils. The failure to incorporate the interests and needs of the minority identity groups, systematic discrimination, and the attitude of chauvinistic elements within the majority community have been at the root of the Sri Lankan crisis since independence. The very fabric of society has been ripped apart by combustible factors of ethnic relations fuelled by language, religion, and negative historical memories, and fanned by political violence and brutal acts of terror. Political and criminal violence is common in much of Sri Lanka and the livelihoods of ordinary people are blighted by hardship, insecurity, and death. 1983 brought Sri Lanka to the crossroads of history. It brought out the truth about the complexity of its society along with a portentous message. Sinhalese and Tamils in Sri Lanka were fated by history and geography to coexist in close proximity and while this could have been cordial and amicable, as it often was, what has been witnessed is a vortex of rancor and violence that has made the restoration of harmony a persistently elusive goal.

Sri Lanka's ongoing ethnic conflict, and the separatist war it has given rise to, can be described as the country's most intractable and destructive problem. The war that has raged between the Sri Lankan state and the LTTE has caused nearly 65,000 deaths and incalculable damage to personal and public property. According to UNHCR, a total of 1.5 million persons have been uprooted and displaced internally within Sri Lanka or have taken refuge in Europe, North America, and Australia.

Parts of the northern and eastern provinces of the island are either under effective military rule or under the control of the LTTE. One feature of the Sri Lankan conflict is the shifting control over territory between the protagonists. What is common under the different security regimes of the government and the LTTE is a limited respect for human rights and humanitarian norms.

How Sri Lankans perceive peacefulness differs between the north, east, central, and southern parts of the country. The search for peace has taken many forms; from the government strategy of "War for Peace" and elimination of terrorism by the Sri Lankan military, to a war of liberation as espoused by the LTTE. The perception of the "other"—the Sinhalese of the Tamils, the Tamils of the Sinhalese, the Tamils and Sinhalese of the Muslims, further reinforced by religious differences—has contributed to suspicion and distrust between and among the different ethnic and religious communities. Polarization of communities continues with little contact with one another, beginning from preschool through to university education. Disparities in access to employment provide little scope for communities to come together. Grievances felt by all sides are heavily loaded by history and, it would seem, manipulated by ethnically motivated interests to keep these grievances alive and to maintain the polarized and vindictive narrative.

In 1994 the Peoples Alliance (PA) government under President Kumaratunga was elected on a peace platform, but despite early enthusiasm her position was undermined both by opposition from within her own government and from the United National Party (UNP) opposition. On the other hand, all but one of the Tamil political parties, despite their many differences, aligned themselves by accepting the leadership of the LTTE to negotiate on behalf of the Tamil people. While there was recognition that neither side could achieve a military victory, the concept of military dominance (by both sides) persisted. The war has generated an economy of its own and it is not certain that military expenditure will necessarily decline with the cessation of hostilities. The total strength of Sri Lanka's security forces (including the police) was approximately 235,000 in 1996, an increase of 400 percent over a ten-year period. Estimates of active members of the LTTE vary widely between five and twenty thousand people. The common feature of most of the combatants on both sides is that they are from economically poor rural backgrounds. With an end to the war, they have little to look forward to in terms of employment—their own homes are mostly in areas already suffering from high youth unemployment.

The LTTE made a unilateral declaration of a month-long cease-fire in December 2000, which was extended by them on three occasions. Given the poor track record of the LTTE in abrogating cease-fire agreements in the past, the government was reluctant to seize the opportunity offered by the LTTE. De-escalation leading to cease-fire is an indispensable component of any meaningful process that aims at a negotiated settlement. In December 2001, after general elections marred by extensive violence, a new government, the United National Front (consisting of the UNP, defecting Peoples Alliance MPs, and the Sri Lanka Muslim Congress) was elected to power. Prime Minister Ranil Wickramasinghe quickly initiated a new round of peace negotiations based around a reinvigorated Norwegian process.

Official Conflict Management

Over the past fifty years several political initiatives within Sri Lanka have attempted to address the root causes of Tamil discontent with legislative and constitutional processes within the contexts of attempts to reform the state. There have also been direct negotiations between the government and the LTTE. Over the years, Sinhalese-dominated governments have also included non-LTTE Tamil political parties in strategic alliances at different times. Other attempts at political accommodation include the Bandaranaike-Chelvanayakam Pact (1957) and the Senanayake-Chelvanayakam Pact (1965). These pacts tackled the issues of resettlement of Sinhalese on land that Tamils considered their traditional places, some devolution of power to Tamil-speaking regional councils, and recognition of Tamil as a national minority language. On both occasions, the agreements were ignored and not implemented by the government of the time, causing anger and increasing frustration amongst the Tamils, who responded with nonviolent campaigns of civil disobedience. There were also an increasing number of Tamil youths who, impatient with their elders, were turning to armed insurrection. However, progress was made with the proposal for the District Development Councils as described in the Annxure C Proposals to the constitution (1983). But, later in 1983, events took a turn again for the worse when the UNP government of the time added the Sixth Amendment to the constitution, which imposed a ban on all political parties and individuals that advocated separatism. Talks at Thimpu, the capital of Bhutan, in 1985 under the auspices of the Indian government, also failed. There was limited success of these talks in that the fourth demand (of granting citizenship to 96,000 Tamils of Indian origin) was met in January 1986. India continued to facilitate talks, and as a result of the Indo–Sri Lankan Accord (1987) an IPKF was dispatched to Sri Lanka with the objectives of: supervising a cease-fire between the LTTE and the Sri Lankan army; accepting the surrender of LTTE and other Tamil militants' weapons (and if they refused to do so, disarm them by force); and policing the northeast whilse an interim Tamil administration was established to prepare for elections for a North Eastern Provincial Council, which would enable some devolution of power from Colombo to the predominantly Tamil regions. Three years later the IPKF was forced to leave Sri Lanka after suffering military defeats by the LTTE, and also because the government of Sri Lanka no longer wanted their presence on the island. Talks between the UNP and the LTTE were held in Colombo toward the end of the IPKF presence. These continued after the departure of the IPKF but broke down, and war resumed.

The election of the PA, led by Chandrika Kumaratunga, in 1994 brought new hopes for a peace settlement. Three rounds of talks were held in Jaffna between October 1994 and April 1995. During the talks the four pillars of the government of Sri Lanka's strategy were (1) establishing rapport with the Tamil people; (2) a commitment to maintaining the "cessation of hostilities"; (3) implementing programs for rehabilitation and reconstruction; and (4) formulating a political package. There were problems from Sinhalese nationalists and LTTE hard-liners. The negotiations broke down after the LTTE withdrew, and the government pursued a twin-track strategy of political devolution (a plan that granted a degree of autonomy, but not a separate state, to the Tamils) and military operations (with the objective of bringing the LTTE to the negotiating table in a weak position). This was known as "War for Peace" (peace through war). Some commentators believed that the manner in which the devolution package was presented was deliberately intended by the PA to politically marginalize and isolate the LTTE even further. Toward the end of 2000, the LTTE announced a unilateral cease-fire, which was rejected by the government. More recently, the Norwegians (1999–2001) have been working to promote a peace process through their "shuttle" facilitator, Eric Solheim. While supported in principle by the PA, UNP, and the LTTE leaderships, there is considerable opposition to this process from Sinhalese political and religious chauvinistic groups. Solheim's role diminished (the government complaining about his too "public" approach and to what was perceived as his own agenda), and the Norwegian facilitation was upgraded to the direct involvement of the Norwegian foreign minister. As previously mentioned, the Norwegian peace process continued after the election of the UNF government, finally culminating in the signing of an "Agreement for a Cease-Fire" between the government and LTTE in February 2002. One of the elements of this agreement was the provision of international monitoring from Scandinavian countries.

A range of diplomatic initiatives is under way to bring the nation closer to sustaining peace. Internationally, the government and the LTTE are coming under increasing pressure for a permanent political settlement. As we have already mentioned, in all this, India's role as mediator/facilitator is critical. India's proximity to Sri Lanka and the language and cultural links between the two countries (especially that of Tamil Nadu) exacerbated the conflict at the initial stages. India banned the LTTE following the findings of the *Jain Report* on the assassination of Rajiv Gandhi. The official Indian line on Sri Lanka is that the Tamil-majority areas ought to have a large measure of autonomy in newly demarcated provinces. Following the military gains made by the LTTE in April–May 2000, some Tamil allies of the BJP government in Tamil Nadu openly supported secession, the creation of an independent Tamil Eelam, and military help for the LTTE. As for the government, after these serious military reverses, it approached India for help in May 2000. It was widely thought this request pertained to military assistance in the contingency that the Sri Lankan army had to be evacuated from Jaffna. India's publicly proffered "humanitarian aid," the offer of $2 million to meet urgent fiscal needs of the government of Sri Lanka, was of some consolation. India is aware that it has some influence with both the government and the LTTE, and can enable and facilitate third-country "intervention" or "mediation" without actually getting sucked into the conflict itself. India is also aware that sentiments of regional parties in Tamil Nadu must be taken into account. The sum and substance of policy statements from New Delhi may be categorized into four "Nos": no military intervention, no military assistance, no mediation unless both sides request it, and no to Tamil Eelam.

Some European governments have persistently promoted peacemaking initiatives. For example, Norway has a track record of brokering peace accords, the most notable one being the Oslo Process in the Middle East between Israel and Palestine. The arrival of Norway as facilitator in 1999 marked a major initiative. Norway's facilitation is acceptable to India because it is being kept informed at every stage, and it is also acceptable to both Colombo and the LTTE. Norway has proved hospitable to Sri Lankan Tamils, including refugees, and has built an excellent rapport with Tamils who have trusted lines of communication to the LTTE. Before the renewed outbreak of the fighting in April–May 2001, there was some optimism over the prospects of the Norway-brokered peace talks. Unfortunately, neither the government nor the LTTE were prepared to set aside conditionalities, as each sought to strengthen its military bargaining power before going to Oslo. Instead of agreeing to commence the dialogue immediately, both the PA government and the LTTE stipulated parallel preconditions. The PA government demanded a complete cessation of LTTE's operations, whereas the LTTE demanded the cessation of the Sri Lankan military offensive and the withdrawal of Sri Lankan forces from the north. Given the political and military orientations of both sides, it was obvious that these demands would not be met.

The highest proportion of the Sri Lankan diaspora lives in Commonwealth countries. Individually and collectively, these governments have been consistent in their call for a peaceful resolution of the conflict, and have made repeated offers of international mediation. The government of Sri Lanka favors "facilitation" rather than "mediation" and has rejected such offers.

Britain has had a long and close relationship with Sri Lanka for more than two hundred years, with bilateral links in many areas. In 1998 the Conservative government facilitated the signing of the Liam Fox Agreement to promote a bipartisan approach between the PA and the opposition UNP to help design a unified approach in negotiating with the LTTE, but neither the PA government nor the opposition UNP translated it into action. The Country Strategy of the UK Department for International Development (DFID) for Sri Lanka emphasizes that finding a lasting solution to the war is a major priority of eliminating poverty in Sri Lanka. While acknowledging that the path to peace will be difficult and complex, it states that a political solution offers the only prospect for a long-term resolution of the conflict.

Canada has been active in promoting peaceful solutions, and frequently raises issues in appropriate international settings. Canada regards dialogue, respect for human rights, and the condemnation of terrorist actions as central to furthering peace in Sri Lanka. The Canadian government, through the Canadian International Development Agency (CIDA), supports a range of activities to strengthen governance mechanisms and promote human rights, peace, and the empowerment of women in Sri Lanka. A Peace Fund created by CIDA in 1995 is designed to promote peace by supporting efforts at more broadly based dialogue and exchanges between the various ethnic and religious communities in Sri Lanka. Canada is also engaged in the Lysoen process of dialogue between the foreign ministers of various countries, including Canada, Norway, Switzerland, Thailand, and South Africa, as a conceptual framework for the inclusion of nonstate actors in multi-track diplomacy (especially representatives of armed belligerents), in examining human-security issues. The Lysoen process could provide the enabling environment in which state and parastate actors could engage with each other outside of a formal peace process.

India and the United States have the shared objective of preserving the unity and territorial integrity of Sri Lanka, with agreed respect for the rights of the Tamil minority. After an appeal made by the government of Sri Lanka, following the attack on the Temple of the Tooth in Kandy, the Clinton administration formally designated the LTTE as a terrorist organization in 1997. This prevents any official dialogue with representatives of the LTTE and fund-raising on behalf of the organization in the United States. According to media reports, the Clinton administration was fully aware of Indian sensitivities on Sri Lanka and the many complex considerations that drive India's policy toward it.

Some analysts in Sri Lanka would claim that the above picture paints a rather rosy picture of Western governments as a bunch of altruistic do-gooders intervening into Sri Lanka. While foreign governments have been calling for peace, they have also been providing weapons and other assistance to allow the government to pursue the war. A recent contextual interpretation notes a connection between a Western-style liberalized economy (promoted among others by the IMF in return for structural adjustment loans) linked into world capitalism, and the ongoing civil conflict. The authoritarian war climate has been used by the government to push through economic reforms, such as privatization, demanded by such donors. The argument continues that the resulting support from Western agencies and governments has helped the Sinhala elite to continue to fight the war.

The United Nations Development Program (UNDP) has consistently called on the Sri Lankan government to resolve the conflict by peaceful means. International donors, while remaining detached from the course of the armed conflict, put on intermittent pressure by linking peace and human-rights issues to their aid provision. UNICEF has promoted and organized cease-fires on "Days of Tranquility" during national polio immunization campaigns, and also promoted children as "Zones of Peace."

The European Parliament in May 2000 called for European members of the United Nations to introduce the issue of Sri Lanka for discussion before the Security Council of the UN. The European Union (EU) was reported to have reminded both the government and the LTTE of their responsibility to ensure the safety of the civilian population in conflict zones, particularly on the Jaffna peninsula. The EU joined the UN Secretary-General in urging both parties to cooperate with the Norwegian government in their endeavors to facilitate a negotiated settlement of the conflict, and expressed concern about the humanitarian consequences of the recent upsurge in fighting. The EU also sent a team of election monitors to observe the 2000 general elections. Also, Sri Lankan organizations such as the Centre for Monitoring Elections Violence was established at the Centre for Policy Alternatives, and Peoples' Forum for Free and Fair Elections was set up at the Marga Institute to record and observe the elections process.

The Sri Lanka Development Forum meets periodically in Paris under the auspices of the World Bank, when the government presents its polices to the donor community. At the meeting held in October 2000, President Kumaratunga defined the government's priorities as: (1) rebuilding democracy and democratic institutions; (2) rebuilding the economy and improving the quality of life; and (3) reestablishing peace. The key message from the donors was that development and economic growth could not happen with the war continuing, and that links between conflict and poverty were self-evident. The Japanese delegation emphasized that the time had come to go beyond rhetoric and to solve the conflict, and the Canadians stressed that it was time to translate good intentions into action plans.

The government is leading the effort to develop the Relief, Rehabilitation, Reconciliation (3Rs) Framework, whose objectives are to help strengthen Sri Lanka's capacity to: (1) ensure that basic needs of the people affected by conflict are met; (2) rebuild productive lives where feasible; and (3) facilitate reconciliation and partnership across ethnic lines. With the bulk of funding coming from the Dutch government and administered by UNDP, the 3Rs Framework process is a catalytic dialogue eliciting contributions from key stakeholders on how the government, civil society, and donors could work together in promoting peace and reconstruction. Within the 3Rs Framework, a series of district consultations were held with local NGOs, local government officials, and other civil-society elements. Also, a number of sectoral consultations were held including those concerning education, language, and religion. Findings from the district and sectoral consultations were fed back into four working groups (Aid Modalities, Institutional Building and Donor Coordination, Reconciliation and Peacebuilding, and Programmatic Priorities) of the 3R Framework whose task was to look at ways of operationalizing a wide range of recommendations. Following a joint meeting of the working groups, a further small group consisting of members drawn from each of the working groups is preparing a consolidated document of recommendations to be submitted to the government of Sri Lanka for early implementation. It is hoped that government acceptance of the 3Rs Framework recommendations will help eliminate policy and operational obstacles in relief, rehabilitation, and reconciliation and also help reduce constant tensions between humanitarian concerns and security concerns.

Multi-Track Diplomacy

While Sri Lanka has a diverse and articulate civil-society sector, it should not be assumed that all civil-society actors are benign and act as constructive forces for peace. Certain elements of civil society are promoters of the conflict. For example, nationalist groups such as the National Movement Against Terrorism (NMAT) and elements of the Buddhist Sangha could be said to have fuelled the conflict. Also, as elsewhere, it must be remembered that the NGO community in Sri Lanka is not a homogenous one, but fragmented and spanning a broad spectrum of interests. Coordination of NGOs has always been problematic, and to help promote this the Consortium of Humanitarian Agencies (CHA) was formed in 1997. The CHA sponsored other coordinating bodies, which included the Emergency Group (EG), the Northern Task Group (NTG), and the Eastern Forum. There are also smaller and more localized NGO fora (whose relationships are at times antagonistic to each other). The peace movement is constrained by internal debates and intergroup rivalries. But civil-society groups such as the Movement for Inter Racial Justice and Equality (MIRJE), INFORM—a human rights documentation centre based in Colombo—and the National Peace Council can be effective in mobilizing support for the peace process, as was the case in 1994.

During 2000 a group of civil-society leaders from leading peace organizations began meeting regularly under the name of the Peace Support Group. They have issued joint statements and placed media advertisements advocating pro-peace positions. For the past two years the business community has been increasingly active in the area of promoting peace. Initially, a group of business leaders made a highly publicized effort to get the government and the opposition parties to agree on a bipartisan approach to finding a political solution to the conflict. This was followed by the "Sri Lanka First Campaign," organized by another group of business leaders, who launched a major media campaign and also organized a mass "holding of hands for peace" campaign in September 2001. Political attempts to involve civil society have also been made by the government. After peace talks broke down in 1995, the PA government attempted to mobilize civil society in support of their peace initiatives through the Sudu Nellum ("White Lotus") Movement, an effort to "wage the battle for peace." Also, leaders of the Christian and Buddhist clergy traveled to the Vanni (an area controlled by the LTTE), under the auspices of the Inter-Religious Alliance for Peace, to meet leaders of the LTTE and local civil-society groups.

Within Sri Lanka, NGOs have had a long history of being involved in the broad spectrum of activities that fall under the aegis of peacebuilding and conflict resolution, including the promotion of dialogue and communication between the different groups. Much of this activity has been undertaken under the label of training by organizations such as International Alert (IA) and Quaker Peace and Service (QPS), and Sri Lankan NGOs such as the National Peace Council (NPC), Samadana/M, and Ahimsa. IA has also facilitated meetings for politicians from all parties at venues out of Sri Lanka, and has been involved in exchanges for professional groups, such as journalists, to other countries (such as Northern Ireland) who have experienced internal conflict.

Local NGOs and research organizations are playing an increasingly important part in catalyzing democratic discussion and debate. These have included the Marga Institute, the International Centre for Ethnic Studies (ICES), the Law and Society Trust (LST), Consortium of Humanitarian Agencies (CHA), Sarvodaya, Social and Economic Development Centre (SEDEC), Centre for Society and Religion (CSR), and Centre for Policy Alternatives (CPA). All these organizations have been active in trying to inform and educate people about elements that contribute to a strong civic society, and have been working to improve public awareness about civil, political, cultural and socioeconomic rights, and equal access to justice. Many NGOs have also begun to incorporate a peacebuilding and conflict-resolution focus to their activities. According to the CHA, "a widening rippling of peace constituency is observable," and there is a sense of war weariness and a yearning for peace and stability among the actors and the sufferers. Exchanges of workers, women, youth, and schoolchildren between the northeast and the south have been promoted by the government and NGOs to encourage better understanding and to remove prejudices.

One visible actor has been the NPC, established in February 1995 to co-ordinate nonviolent peace initiatives and be a catalytic body to facilitate peace and conflict resolution. The NPC's primary goal is to facilitate an attitudinal shift in selected constituencies of the population who are either opinion form-ers (media, local politicians), or stakeholders (disabled soldiers, Muslim refugees). Based upon this attitudinal shift, NPC seeks to empower and mobi-lize the democratic participation of citizens' groups and organizations, strengthen the building of a people's movement for peace and reconciliation, and promote respect for human rights. The programs NPC has undertaken range from multimedia campaigns opposing the war—for example, promot-ing the theme "Peace for Children"; advocacy campaigns based on the cost of war; building grassroots peace constituencies in strategic districts and sectoral groups (disabled soldiers, internally displaced persons); media and reporting on the conflict; peace rallies and conventions; and meetings between local Sin-halese and Tamil government officials from different districts. At a political level, NPC has brought together Sri Lankan members of parliament from dif-ferent political parties to meet parliamentarians and peace activists from South Africa, Northern Ireland, Philippines, and Bangladesh in order to help forge relationships across ethnic and political-party lines.

PRASANNI (Praja Sanwada Saha Sannivedana Kendraya, or Centre for Community Dialogue and Communication) is a Sri Lankan NGO working to mobilize grassroots rural constituencies and urban working-class sectors through a nationwide program called the "Citizens Initiative for Constitutional Change." PRASANNI's strategy was to mobilize a national peace constituency by bringing together all the major communities and sectors in Sri Lanka to build an "informed democratic consensus for a constitutional framework for a democratic and pluralist political settlement to the conflict." A national con-vention in 2000 was attended by 1,800 delegates from all over the country.

Interreligious groups, such as the Inter-Religious Peace Foundation (IRPF), led by clergy and laypersons from Buddhist, Hindu, Christian, and Is-lamic faiths, are an emerging force in the peacebuilding arena. In addition to dialogue among themselves, they spread messages of peace and harmony through the essential unity advocated by all religions.

At a South Asian regional level, the Kathmandu-based South Asia Forum for Human Rights (SAFHR) has supported the peaceful resolution of conflicts through a mechanism of people-to-people dialogue. These dialogues have be-come catalysts for generating networks of regional constituencies to address the challenges of militarization, within the context of intrastate and interstate conflicts. SAFHR's peace studies and peace audit program aims at exploring an alternative paradigm for peace that asserts people's absolute right to peace.

International NGOs have been involved in a myriad of initiatives associated with nonviolent conflict resolution, and in efforts to encourage communication, understanding, and collaboration between and within communities. International NGOs have provided key channels of communication between the conflict zones and the outside world, and prevented what could otherwise have become major humanitarian tragedies, while working within narrow humanitarian mandates. CARE International and Oxfam are among NGOs that have introduced attempts to mainstream relationship building as part of their programs in Sri Lanka. The ICRC continues to play its usual protection role in Sri Lanka, treating war victims, visiting prisoners, and promoting the Geneva Conventions. The International Working Group on Sri Lanka (IWG), an informal network of non-government agencies from Europe, North America, and Australia, promotes respect for human rights and humanitarian law as instruments of peacebuilding. Through high-level political and NGO contacts in their respective countries, IWG members are in a position to lobby governments, the UN, donor governments, and institutions on a range of issues concerning Sri Lanka.

Relations between the government and NGOs have been difficult at times, a relationship that has been described as one of "suspicious cooperation." It seems that some sections of the government and the general population have the view that international NGOs are pro-LTTE, that the LTTE exploits naive NGOs, and that the LTTE uses humanitarian aid to support their military efforts. This perception is supported by media often hostile toward NGOs. There is a continual tension between the NGOs' determination to keep their independence, and the government's requirement that they are accountable, operate within the prescribed guidelines, and work in areas indicated by the government.

NGOs, especially international NGOs, can themselves only be part of the overall process of creating a peaceful and just society. The bottom line is that the people and their government themselves must ultimately be responsible for sustainable peace and development.

Prospects

Several key questions remained unanswered. Would the LTTE really be prepared to settle for anything less than Tamil Eelam, after twenty-five years of violent struggle during which time thousands of cadres had been killed? A generation of Tamil fighters had grown up with this objective as their sole aim, and with no experience of contact or cooperation with the Sinhalese side. Can the government concede to the LTTE's demands, and survive politically? Also impacting on the peace process are southern politics and the capacity of the present government to carry through required reforms. The concept of the defense of the unitary state is still paramount, and the Sinhalese have also suffered many dead and injured in their battle against what most perceive as a terrorist organization. The degree of mistrust between both sides is deep and ingrained. Questions about a postconflict role for the LTTE have yet to be tackled. For example, what is the political role for the LTTE leadership? There will also be considerable problems of demobilization, demilitarization, and reconstruction within the constraints of a stretched and overdrawn budget. In this there will be a vital role for the international community to help Sri Lanka rebuild its social infrastructure.

What can be noted over the last five years are two qualitative changes in perception. First, there seems to be agreement sometimes wavering on the need for a consensus position between the PA and the UNP. Second, the government, the opposition UNP, and the LTTE have accepted the role of a third-party facilitator. In the final analysis, Sri Lanka needs a peace based on equal recognition and justice for all of Sri Lanka's ethnic groups as the moral basis for any resolution to this multilayered and factorially complex conflict.

Recommendations

While much energy has been put into bringing about peace, we would suggest that more planning is also required for a postconflict situation. This means preparing the people for peace, where a future means that deadly enemies will have to sit together and plan the future at local community and national levels. As in other postconflict situations, there will be terrible traumatic experiences and emotional hurt to come to terms with. The international community must help with the enormous cost of rebuilding all areas of Sri Lanka. Poverty, which has been exacerbated by the war, is deepening.

There are no easy prescriptions or formulas to propose. Making and building peace is complex and requires long-term patient processes, combined with complementary actions at timely moments. Some of the initiatives described in the previous sections should be encouraged, providing they have support from those most directly affected by the conflict. As for other countries affected by conflict, there needs to be more cooperation and integration between the many efforts at both official and unofficial levels. Care should be taken that interventions of good intent do not in fact do more harm than good. It is important that peacemaking and peacebuilding initiatives at all levels are linked, integrated, and coherent, and that young Sri Lankans can once again believe in a peaceful vision for Sri Lanka's future.

Resources

Newsletters and Periodicals
Newsletter, Regional Centre for Strategic Studies, Colombo
Sri Lanka Journal of Social Sciences (SLJSS), National Science Foundation of Sri Lanka, Colombo
Tamil Guardian, Tamil Guardian Limited, London

Reports
Centre for Policy Research and Analysis, Faculty of Law, University of Colombo, *Lost Opportunities: Past Attempts at Resolving Ethnic Conflict in Sri Lanka,* by K. Loganathan, 1996.
Conciliation Resources, *Demanding Sacrifice: War and Negotiation in Sri Lanka,* by J. Armon and L. Philipson, ACCORD Series, London, 1998.
Conflict Policy Research Project, Netherlands Institute of International Relations, *The Netherlands and Sri Lanka: Dutch Policies and Interventions with Regard to the Conflict in Sri Lanka,* by G. Frerks and M. van Leeuwen, The Hague, 2000.
Department for International Development, *Aid, Conflict and Peacebuilding in Sri Lanka,* by J. Goodhand, London, November 2000.
International Alert, *Negotiating Peace in Sri Lanka: Efforts, Failures and Lessons,* edited by K. Rupesinghe, London, 1998.
International Centre for Ethnic Studies

Pursuit of Peace in Sri Lanka: Past Failures and Future Prospects, edited by K. M. De Silva and G. H. Peiris, Kandy/Colombo, 2000.

Sri Lanka: The Devolution Debate. Colombo, 1996 and 1997.

Life and Peace Institute, *New Routes, A Journal on Peace Research and Action, Sri Lanka Sources and Resources of Conflict,* vol. 5, nos. 1-2, Uppsala, Sweden, 2000.

National Peace Council/Marga Institute, *Cost of the War. Economic, Social and Human Cost of the War in Sri Lanka,* Colombo, January 2001.

National Steering Committee, *National Framework for Relief, Rehabilitation and Reconciliation in Sri Lanka,* Colombo, November 2001.

South Asia Forum for Human Rights, *Peace Process in Sri Lanka,* Peace Audit Report 2, April 2001.

Other Publications

Creating Peace in Sri Lanka: Civil War and Reconciliation, edited by R. Rotberg. Washington, DC, Brookings Institution Press, 1999.

India, Sri Lanka and the Tamil Crisis 1976–1994, by A. Bullion. London, Pinter, 1995.

"NGO-Government Relations in Sri Lanka," by Koenraad van Brabant. In J. Bennet (ed.), *NGOs and Governments: A Review of Current Practice for Southern and Eastern NGOs,* Oxford, INTRAC/ICVA, 1997.

"Sri Lanka: Civil Society, The Nation and the State-Building Challenge," by P. Saravanamuttu. In A. Van Rooy (ed.), *Civil Society and the Aid Industry: The Politics and Promise,* London, Earthscan, 1998.

Sri Lanka: History and the Roots of Conflict, by J. Spencer. London, Routledge, 1991.

Selected Internet Sites

eelamweb.com/ (Eelam Web)
members.tripod.com/~fosus (Friends of Sri Lanka in the United States)
ourworld.compuserve.com/homepages/umberto/Tamil.htm (Eliminate LTTE terrorism)
tamilnet.com/ (Tamil Net)
www.apcjp.org/slforum/slforum.htm (U.S. NGO Forum on Sri Lanka)
www.eelam.com/ (Tamil Eelam home page)
www.icescmb.slt.lk (International Centre for Ethnic Studies)
www.incore.ulst.ac.uk/cds/countries/srilanka.html (INCORE Conflict Data Service)
www.inpact.org (Initiative for Political and Conflict Transformation)
www.lacnet.org/slnet/ (Sri Lanka Net)
www.lacnet.org/suntimes (Sunday *Times*)
www.lanka.net/lakehouse/ (Daily news)
www.lankaweb.com/ (LankaWeb)
www.priu.gov.lk/ (Official government site)
www.rcss.org (Regional Centre for Strategic Studies)
www.sinhaya.com/ (SINHAYA-UK)
www.slt.lk/news/ (Sri Lankan government information department)
www.spur.asn.au/ (Society for Peace, Unity, and Human Rights in Sri Lanka)
www.teedor.org/ (Tamil Eelam Economic Development Organization)
www.uthr.org (University Teachers for Human Rights—Jaffna, Sri Lanka)

Resource Contacts

Freddy de Alwis, Inter-Religious Peace Foundation, tel/fax: +94-1-811700
Sathivale Balakrishnan, Centre for Development Alternatives, e-mail: cadrights@ids.lk
Sunil Bastian, International Centre for Ethnic Studies, e-mail: bastian@sri.lanka.net
Tyrol Ferdinands, National Peace Council of Sri Lanka, e-mail: tyrol@sri.lanka.net
Oswald B. Firth, Centre for Society and Religion, e-mail: csrlibra@slt.lk
Kethesh Loganathan, Centre for Policy Alternatives, e-mail: cpa@sri.lanka.net

Joseph Montville, Center for Strategic and International Studies, e-mail: jmontvil@
 csis.org
Paikiasothy Saravanamuttu, Centre for Policy Alternatives, e-mail: cpa@sri.lanka.net
Teresita C. Schaffer, Center for Strategic and International Studies, e-mail: tscaffer@
 csis.org

Organizations

Centre for the Study of Human Rights
Faculty of Law, Reid Avenue, University of Colombo
Colombo 3, Sri Lanka

International Working Group on Sri Lanka
33 Islington High Street
London N1 9LH, U.K.

Movement for the Defence of Democratic Rights (MDDR)
1149 Kotte Road
Rajagiriya, Sri Lanka
E-mail: mddr@slt.lk

Prasanni-Praja Sanwada Saha Sannivedana Kendraya
P.O. Box 66
Nugegoda, Sri Lanka
E-mail: prasanni@eureka.lk

Social Scientists Association
425/15 Thimbirigasaya Road
Colombo 5, Sri Lanka

Suriya Women's Development Forum
20 Dias Lane
Batticaloa, Sri Lanka
Tel: +94-65-23 297
E-mail: suriyaw@slt.lk

University Teachers for Human Rights—Jaffna
E-mail: uthr-j@sltnet.lk.

Data on the following organizations can be found in the Directory section:

In Sri Lanka
   AHIMSA–Centre for Conflict Resolution and Peace
   Center for Community Dialogue and Communication
   Centre for Development Alternatives
   Centre for Policy Alternatives
   Centre for Policy Research and Analysis
   Centre for Society and Religion
   Consortium of Humanitarian Agencies
   INFORM
   International Centre for Ethnic Studies
   Inter-Religious Peace Foundation
   Marga Institute
   Movement for Inter-Racial Justice and Equality
   National Peace Council of Sri Lanka
   People's Peace Front

Regional Centre for Strategic Studies
SAMASEVAYA
Sewa Lanka Foundation

In Nepal
South Asia Forum for Human Rights

Joe William is an advisor attached to the Canadian High Commission and the Canadian International Development Agency in Sri Lanka. He is chair of the Management Committee of the Mine Action Resource Centre (MARC), a founding member of the National Peace Council of Sri Lanka, and a member of the Peace Support Group—a local think tank set up to support the peace process. He also holds a master's degree in peace studies from the University of Bradford. Nick Lewer is a senior lecturer and director of the Centre for Conflict Resolution at the Department of Peace Studies, University of Bradford, UK. He has experience working in Sri Lanka on community, training, and research projects with donors and NGOs.

PART 3

Directory

Introduction to the Directory

The directory that follows contains profiles and contact information for 187 organizations working in the fields of conflict prevention and peacebuilding across Central and South Asia. The prime focus is on key organizations—mainly nongovernmental—that are based and active in these regions. It also includes a selection of organizations from North America and Europe that are involved in relevant activities in Central and South Asia. Finally, relevant global and internationational organizations like the UN are also included.

Because organizations working in the field of development cooperation, humanitarian aid, or human rights have increasingly incorporated ideas of conflict prevention and peacebuilding into their prime mandate, we have also opted to include organizations that, at first sight, might not be perceived as conflict prevention organizations.

The shaded box that appears at the upper right of each profile presents the organization's main activities in conflict prevention and peacebuilding.

The countries/regions in which the organization's activities are focused are presented above the organization's name.

As far as possible, the given number of staff and budget relates to the organization's specific activities in the field of conflict prevention and peacebuilding.

Additional information on some organizations may be found in the survey chapters in Part 2 of this publication. Some of this information has been omitted here due to space limitations.

Asia

Monash Asia Institute

RESEARCH
EDUCATION

The Monash Asia Institute (MAI) was established by the Monash University, one of the world's leading research centers on Asia. Its role is to serve as an umbrella organization for six research centers on Asia within the university, including the National Centre of South Asian Studies. The Institute has organized conferences, dialogues, and policy-oriented research on Asian subjects dealing with a wide range of critical regional issues such as the nuclear confrontation in South Asia and relations between North and South Korea. The teaching program is providing postgraduate courses in Asian Studies and Development Studies. An Asian Studies Research Library is available for students and other researchers.

Monash Asia Institute
P.O. Box 11A
Monash University
Vic 3800
Australia

Tel: +61 (3) 9905 2124
Fax: +61 (3) 9905 5370
monash.asia.institute@adm.monash.edu.au
www.arts.monash.edu.au/mai

Contact: Marika Vicziany, Director
Publications: To Be Free: Stories from Asia's Struggle against Oppression, 1998; *Democratization in Taiwan,* 1998; *From Hope to Despair: Education, Development and the State in Cambodia Since UNTAC,* 1998.

South Asia

National Centre for South Asian Studies

RESEARCH
EDUCATION

The primary aim of the National Centre for South Asian Studies (NCSAS) is to provide information, expertise, and contacts with South Asia, including India, Pakistan, Sri Lanka, Bangladesh, and neighboring countries. One element of conflict resolution is to further security and disarmament through conferences in order to build stronger confidence. An annual event at NCAS is the Dialogue on Security and Disarmament in South Asia and the Asia Pacific. The Centre maintains various databanks, including a list of experts on South Asia. It publishes a bi-weekly electronic newsletter and hosts a virtual forum on South Asian security matters. In 2001, the Centre began to commission research reports on regional security including South Asia-Afghanistan relations.

Monash Asia Institute
P.O. Box 11A
Monash University
Vic 3800
Australia

Tel: +61 (3) 9905 2124
Fax: +61 (3) 9905 5370
monash.asia.institute@adm.monash.edu.au
www.arts.monash.edu.au/mai/ncsas

Contact: Marika Vicziany, Director
Publications: NCSAS bi-weekly electronic newsletter; *The Role of Non-Governmental Organisations in Rural Development: The Bangladesh Case, 1996.*

Asia Pacific

Research School
of Pacific and Asian Studies

The Research School of Pacific and Asian Studies (RSPAS) of the Australian National University is one of the largest research centers in the Asia-Pacific region. Its major disciplines include anthropology, international relations, political science, and strategic and defense studies. Research has been done on security matters in the region, Asia-Pacific economies, and Australia's relations with the Asia-Pacific region. The school has an active program of postgraduate training and fellowships. In 2001, the School established the Centre for Conflict and Post-Conflict Studies Asia-Pacific to examine causes of conflict and the processes of peacemaking and reconstruction in the region.

Australian National University
Canberra
ACT 0200
Australia

Tel: +61 (2) 6125 2183
Fax: +61 (2) 6257 1893
schlsec.rspas@anu.edu.au or
ron.may@anu.edu.au
rspas.anu.edu.au

Contact: Ron May, Head of the Centre for Conflict and Post Conflict Studies Asia Pacific

Number of staff: 15

Publications: RSPAS Print News Announcements, Political Crises in North East Asia: An Anatomy of the Taiwan and Korean Crises, 2001; *The Day the World Changed? Terrorism and World Order,* 2001; *Business as Usual? Local Conflicts and Global Challenges in Northern Australia,* 2001.

OSCE participating states

Organisation for Security and Co-operation in Europe

RESEARCH
EDUCATION
ACTION
ADVOCACY

Once a forum for talks between two highly polarized blocs, the intergovernmental Organisation for Security and Co-operation in Europe (OSCE) now aims to consolidate common values, build civil societies, prevent local conflicts, bring peace to war-torn areas, and promote a cooperative system of security. The OSCE embraces a region comprising Canada, the United States, all the countries of the former Soviet Union, and the whole of Europe. An important element of the OSCE's work is its long-term field missions to such countries as Turkmenistan, Uzbekistan, Kazakhstan, Kosovo, Georgia, and Estonia. In order to identify ethnic tensions and to promote their early resolution, the Organisation has created the Institution of High Commissioner on National Minorities.

OSCE Secretariat
Kärntner Ring 5-7
1010 Vienna
Austria

Tel: +43 (1) 5143 6180
Fax: +43 (1) 5143 6105
info@osce.org
www.osce.org

Contact: Keith Jinks, Public Information Officer
Number of staff: > 4,000 (including field staff)
Budget: > $1,000,000

Publications: The OSCE Handbook; The OSCE Newsletter; OSCE Human Dimension Commitments: a Reference Guide, 2001.

Bangladesh, South Asia

Bangladesh Institute of International and Strategic Studies

RESEARCH

Established in 1978 under administrative control of the Bangladesh Ministry of Foreign Affairs, the Bangladesh Institute of International and Strategic Studies (BIISS) promotes research and deliberation on international affairs, security, and developmental issues. One of its objectives is to study conflict and cooperation among nations in national and regional perspectives. The Institute's research activities include conflict studies, disarmament, and non-proliferation. It organizes many regional and international seminars and workshops, such as a recent training workshop, Conflict Prevention and Management, and a roundtable, Peace Building in the Chittagong Hill Tracts.

1/46 Old Elephant Road
Ramma 1000
Bangladesh

Tel: +880 (2) 934 7984/
+880 (2) 721 1618
Fax: +880 (2) 831 2625
dgbiiss@bdonline.com or dgbiiss@bd.drik.net
www.biiss.org

Contact: Abdur Rob Khan, Director
Number of staff: 30
Publications: BIISS quarterly journal; *Quarterly Bangladesh Foreign Policy Survey* (BFPS).

Bangladesh

Bangladesh Inter-religious Council for Peace and Justice

RESEARCH
EDUCATION

Bangladesh Inter-religious Council for Peace and Justice (BICPAJ) is a religious non-profit NGO that holds monthly discussion meetings on justice and peace issues. The Council also runs projects for youth and poor children. BICPAJ's peace education center consists of staff trained in conflict resolution, education, research, and basic training in conflict resolution. Training programs focus on young people, women, and ethnic tribal people of Bangladesh.

14/20 Iqbal Road, Mohammadpur
Dhaka 1207
Bangladesh
_____

Tel: +880 (2) 323 630
Fax: +880 (2) 812 2010
saffron@citechco.net

Contact: Brother Jarlath D'Souza
Number of staff: 2
Budget: <$25,000
Publications: Reports of local training/workshops.

South Asia

Centre for Alternatives

RESEARCH
EDUCATION
ACTION
ADVOCACY

The Centre for Alternatives is a forum for policy research that assists institutions or governments seeking alternatives in the area of international relations, security, refugee issues, development, and conflict management. The staff members are specialized in conflict resolution programs. For instance, the researchers conduct field studies of ethnic groups in Chittagong Hill Tracts. There, the Centre also undertakes monitoring in the post-accord situation. Another program aims to write an alternative history of the 1947 partition of India through interviewing people at the field level in Pakistan, India, and Bangladesh. The Centre is closely linked with four other South Asian research organizations.

431, Lecture Theatre
Faculty of Arts
University of Dhaka
1000 Dhaka
Bangladesh
_____

Tel: +880 (2) 966 1900-59
   Ext. 4550
Fax: +880 (2) 861 5583 or
   831 6769
calter@bangla.net

Contact: Imtiaz Ahmed, Director
Number of staff: 12
Budget: < $25,000
Publications: Alternatives (monthly) and *The Daily Star*, both found on the website www.dailystarnews.com; *Theoretical Perspectives,* annual journal of social sciences and arts; *South Asian Refugee Watch,* bi-annual journal published in association with five other regional institutes based in Delhi, Colombo, Islamabad, and Kathmandu.

India, Bangladesh, Pakistan, Nepal, Sri Lanka

Centre for Development Research

RESEARCH
EDUCATION
ACTION
ADVOCACY

The Centre for Development Research (CDRB) is engaged in independent study and research on contributing to efforts within and outside Bangladesh for regional and international development. Among its priority areas are socio-economic studies, regional and international cooperation, and human resources development. The Centre also carries out the Research on Conflict in Chittagong Hill Tracts program, aiming to understand the nature of the conflict and to help find ways of resolving it. The Centre's publications include a book on this subject, as well as articles and papers arising from the seminars it organizes.

55, Dhanmondi, Road #8-A
G.P.O. Box 4070
Dhaka 1209
Bangladesh

Tel: +880 (2) 811 5463/ 1877
Fax: +880 (2) 811 7277
cdrb@dhaka.agni.com

Contact: Mizanur Rahman Shelley

Number of staff: 4

Budget: <$25,000

Publications: Chittagong Hill Tracks of Bangladesh: The Untold Story, 1992; *Asian Affairs,* quarterly journal.

South Asia

Centre for Policy Dialogue

RESEARCH

The Centre for Policy Dialogue (CPD) services the growing demand of the emerging civil society of Bangladesh for a more participatory and accountable development process. It does so by conducting research, disseminating information, and influencing the policymaking process. The Centre has organized a series of major dialogues, bringing together ministers, NGOs, members of parliament, and other functional groups in a nonconfrontational environment. The CPD's Dialogue and Communication Division deals with conflict prevention and resolution by arranging workshops and conferences. By organizing policy appreciation workshops for policymakers the CPD also works on capacity building.

House No. 40/C
Rd. no 11 (New)
Dhanmondi R/A
G.P.O. Box 2129
Dhaka 1205
Bangladesh

Tel: +880 (2) 812 4770
Fax: +880 (2) 813 0951
cpd@bdonline.com
www.cpd-bangladesh.org

Contact: Rehman Sobhan, Chairman

Number of staff: 5–6

Budget: $25,000–$100,000

Publications: SAARC, Present and Future, 2000; *Gender, Land and Livelihood in South Asia*

Human Development in South Asia, 1999; *Cultural Cooperation in South Asia: The Search for Community,* 1999.

South Asia, Middle East, Global

Centre for the Study of Peace

The Centre for the Study of Peace is a non-profit organization that is mainly concerned with research and training in conflict resolution. The Centre focuses on individuals, communities, ethnic groups, and nations. The Centre provides short courses and programs to increase awareness and to teach conflict resolution. Other activities of the Centre include data collection, research, and fact finding.

Shaleha Villa, House No. – C/11,
  Block No. – G
Kamargari
Bogra 5800
Bangladesh

Contact: Shahidur Rahman, Director
Number of staff: 3

Fax: +880 (51) 72 419

Bangladesh

Coordinating Council for Human Rights in Bangladesh

The Coordination Council for Human Rights in Bangladesh (CCHRB) is a non-government and non-political organization that came into existence after the gathering of different human rights organizations and development NGOs in Bangladesh. Its objectives are to investigate and analyze the human rights situation in Bangladesh, to coordinate information on what various organizations are doing in the areas of human rights and social justice, to promote the role of human rights in integral development of the poor, and to offer legal education and legal aid. CCHRB holds regular forum meetings and publishes annually the State of Human Rights Report of Bangladesh.

113 Siddeswari Circular Road
Dhaka 1217
Bangladesh

Publications: State of Human Rights Report of Bangladesh, annual publication.

Tel: +880 (2) 912 5270
Fax: +880 (2) 912 5269
cchrb@bangla.net

Asia Pacific

Peace for All

RESEARCH
EDUCATION

The Bangladesh non-governmental organization, Peace for All, works in the areas of conflict prevention, development, and human rights by means of education, research, and training. It has a program called Peace—No Conflict, based on educating and motivating citizens with the aim of establishing peace in conflicts in Asia and the Pacific. In this program it cooperates with the organization Responding to Conflict in the United Kingdom.

127 Motijheel C/A
Room #2, 4th floor
G.P.O. Box 3448
Dhaka 1000
Bangladesh

Tel: +880 (2) 956 5907/805 266
Fax: +880 (2) 956 5498

Contact: Tohuruzzaman, Programme Coordinator
Budget: $25,000–$100,000
Publications: Peace News Line, newsletter.

Bangladesh

Society for Environment and Human Development

EDUCATION
ACTION
ADVOCACY

The work of the Society for Environment and Human Development (SEHD) includes researching, reporting, documenting, training, and advocacy on environment, human rights, ethnic issues, and development. Its mission is to research and report facts of life areas that get little or no attention. By doing this the SEHD seeks to minimize misinformation and manipulation in the media, and help people develop informed opinions. This will keep pressure on governments, bureaucrats, MDBs, and specialized agencies to shift attention toward people-centered development, not just growth-oriented development. One program in the field of conflict resolution focuses on documentation and policy research, targeting indigenous communities, commercial sex workers, victims of development projects, and human right abuses.

4/4/1 (B) (3rd floor),
  Block-A, Lalmatia
Dhaka 1207
Bangladesh

Tel: +880 (2) 912 1385
Fax: +880 (2) 912 5764
sehd@citechco.net

Contact: Philip Gain, Director
Number of staff: 5
Budget: < $25,000
Publications: The Chittagong Hill Tracts: Life and Nature at Risk; Sex Trade in Bangladesh: Livelihood at the Cost of Life; Bangladesh: Land, Forest and Forest People; Handbook on Election Reporting.

Bangladesh

South Asia Partnership—Bangladesh

EDUCATION
ACTION

South Asia Partnership—Bangladesh (SA—Bangladesh) is a networking organization active in the field of rural development. It works through capacity building of people, communities, and small NGOs. The primary intention of SAP—Bangladesh is to develop and build partnerships between and among community groups, local NGOs, and Canadian NGOs. After the peace agreement, SAP started working with the Chittagong Hill Tracts through its Integrated Rural Development Program. The organization also promotes the empowerment and socioeconomic advancement of women through training and workshops. SAP has branches all over Southern Asia and is a Canadian initiative.

House No. 63, Block "Ka"
Mohammadpur Housing,
    Pisciculture and Farming
    Cooperative Society Ltd.
G.P.O. Box 4182
Dhaka 1207
Bangladesh

Contact: Nurul Alam, Executive Director

Tel: +880 (2) 812 103, 814 697
Fax: +880 (2) 813 033
Sapbdesh@citechco.net

Bangladesh, India, Nepal, Sri Lanka, Pakistan, Myanmar

Technical Assistance for Rural Development

RESEARCH
EDUCATION
ACTION
ADVOCACY

Technical Assistance for Rural Development (TARD) is a non-profit NGO with the primary mandate of facilitating education and development in order to establish human rights, peace, and stability, and of creating an enabling environment for economic, social, and political freedom. The staff is involved in citizen diplomacy, advocacy, education, fact finding, and human rights promotion. TARD carries out a Peace Development Program that targets intergovernmental and civil society levels. This program aims to activate the actors for establishing social harmony, peace, and justice in Bangladesh and South Asia.

4/16 Humayun Road
Mohammadpur
Dhaka 1207
Bangladesh

Tel: +880 (2) 912 2191
Fax: +880 (2) 812 1154
tard@citechco.net

Contact: Mahpara Rahman, Programme Officer

Number of staff: 30 (total), 5 (conflict resolution)

Budget: $100,000–$500,000

Publications: Rohinga Refugees in Bangladesh; Directory of Human Rights in Bangladesh.

Asia, Balkans, Africa

International Crisis Group

RESEARCH
ADVOCACY

The work of the International Crisis Group (ICG) is grounded in field research. Teams of political analysts, based on the ground in countries at risk of conflict, gather information from a wide range of sources, assess local conditions, and produce regular analytical reports containing practical recommendations targeted at key international decisionmakers. ICG's reports are distributed widely to officials in foreign ministries and international organizations and made generally available at the same time via the organization's website. ICG works closely with governments and those who influence them, including the media, to highlight its crisis analysis and to generate support for its policy prescriptions. In Asia, ICG is present in Burma, Cambodia, Indonesia, and in Central Asia.

149 Avenue Louise, level 16
1050 Brussels
Belgium

Tel: +32 (2) 502 9038
Fax: +32 (2) 502 5038
icgbrussels@crisisweb.org
www.crisisweb.org

Contact: Gareth Evans, President and Chief Executive

Number of staff: 58

Budget: > $1,000,000

Publications: Central Asian Perspectives on 11 September and the Afghan Crisis, 2001; *Central Asia: Islamist Mobilization and Regional Security,* 2001; *Indonesia: Ending Repression in Irian Jaya,* 2001; *Burma/Myanmar: How Strong Is the Military Regime?* 2000; *Cambodia: The Elusive Peace Dividend,* 2000.

Global

Médecins Sans Frontières

ACTION
ADVOCACY

Médecins Sans Frontières (MSF) is an international humanitarian aid organization that provides emergency medical assistance to populations in danger in more than 80 countries. In carrying out humanitarian assistance, MSF is also mandated to raise awareness of crisis situations. MSF acts as a witness and will speak out, either in private or in public, about the plight of populations in danger for whom it works. MSF has headquarters for field operations in France, Switzerland, Luxembourg, Spain, the Netherlands, and Belgium. A further 14 sections, from Sweden to Australia, support operations in the form of representation, recruitment of field volunteers, fundraising, and information.

39, rue de la Tourelle
1040 Brussels
Belgium

tel: +32 (2) 280 1881
fax: +32 (2) 280 0173
intnl@brussels.msf.org
www.msf.org

Contact: Rafael Vila Sanjunder, Secretary General

Kashmir

Kashmiri-Canadian Council

ADVOCACY

The Kashmiri-Canadian Council (KCC) is dedicated to promoting the Kashmiri cause, both within Canada and internationally. In Canada, the non-profit KCC is working with NGOs, media, academics, students, and conscientious Canadians. It aims to raise awareness of the Kashmiri people's struggle for self-determination as enshrined in successive UN resolutions. The Council is also dedicated to supporting Kashmiri civilians in Canada.

44516-2376 Eglinton Avenue East
Scarborough, ON M1K 5K3
Canada

Tel: +1 (416) 282 6933/293 2608
Fax: +1 (416) 282 7488 293 1601
kcc@kashmiri-cc.ca
www.kashmiri-cc.ca

Publications: The Kashmir Quarterly,
news journal; *Kashmir Dispute:
A Nuclear Hot-Spot in South Asia;
Kashmir: An Unresolved Dispute.*

South Asia

South Asia Partnership—Canada

RESEARCH

South Asia Partnership—Canada (SAP Canada) is a forum of Canadian organizations that work together with South Asian organizations toward sustainable human development in South Asia. Through the SAP organizations in six South Asian countries (see separate entries), SAP Canada manages a number of development programs related to community action, strengthening civil society, peace, and human rights. Within Canada, SAP Canada serves as an information center for issues pertaining to South Asia. It organizes seminars and workshops, and maintains an email list service and a resource center on South Asian issues.

1 Nicholas Street, Suite 200
Ottawa, ON K1N 7B7
Canada

Tel: +1 (613) 241 1333
Fax: +1 (613) 241 1129
sap@web.net
www.sapcanada.org

Global

International Work Group for Indigenous Affairs

The International Work Group for Indigenous Affairs (IWGIA) works at local, regional, and international levels to further the understanding and knowledge of indigenous people. Its activities include publications, human rights work, networking, conferences, campaigns, and projects. The IWGIA collaborates with indigenous groups all over the world. In Asia, the group carries out projects in the Pacific region and in South and Southeast Asia, for example the Naga Women's Peace Building Project. The main priority of IWGIA has been providing assistance for empowerment and capacity building.

Classensgade 11 E
DK 2100 Copenhagen
Denmark

Tel: +45 (35) 270 500
Fax: +45 (35) 270 507
iwgia@iwgia.org
www.iwgia.org

Contact: Jens Dahl, Director

Publications: Quarterly Journal Indigenous Affairs; Land Rights of the Indigenous Peoples of the Chittagong Hill Tracts, Bangladesh, 2000; *"Life is not Ours": Land and Human Rights in the Chittagong Hill Tracts, Bangladesh,* 2000; *The Indigenous World* yearbook.

Global

UNESCO's Culture of Peace Program

UNESCO's Culture of Peace Program (CPP) is based on the principles established in the UN Charter and on respect for human rights, democracy, and tolerance, the promotion of development, education for peace, the free flow of information, and the wider participation of women as an integral approach to preventing violence and conflicts, and efforts aimed at the creation of conditions for peace and its consolidation. In working with a wide range of partners, UNESCO aims to advance a global movement for a culture of peace. This implies, for example, organization of regional or international seminars and the mobilization of projects. UNESCO has offices in Almaty, Dhaka, Islamabad, Kathmandu, New Delhi, and Tashkent.

7 Place de Fontenoy
75352 Paris 07 SP
France

Tel: +33 (1) 4568 1319
Fax: +33 (1) 4568 5521
cofpeace@unesco.org
www.unesco.org/cpp

Contact: Francoise Riviere, Director

Publications: Culture of Peace, newsletter; *Conflict Resolution: New Approaches and Methods,* 2000; *World Directory of Peace Research and Training Institutions,* 2000; *Human Rights of Women: A Collection of International and Regional Normative Instruments,* 1999.

Asia

Asian Human Rights Commission

RESEARCH
EDUCATION
ACTION
ADVOCACY

The Asian Human Rights Commission (ARHC) was founded in 1986 by a group of prominent jurists. The commission monitors, reports, and takes preventive actions on human rights violations. In the long term, the Commission strives to help bring about the implementation of human rights according to international humanitarian law in the national laws of all Asian countries. The ARHC publishes special reports for the UN Human Rights Commission. It has an Urgent Appeal Desk that operates around the clock. Educational, monitoring, and exchange programs are carried out, building on local contacts, for instance in Kashmir and China.

Unit D, 7th Floor,
  Mongkok Commercial Centre
16-16B Argyle Street
Kowloon
Hong Kong

Tel: +852 2698 6339
Fax: +852 2698 6367
ahrchk@ahrchk.org
www.ahrchk.net

Contact: Basil Fernando, Executive Director

Number of staff: 11

Publications: Religious Perspectives on Human Rights, weekly e-newsletter; *Hong Kong after 1997: The First 1000 Days,* 2000; *Sri Lanka: Disappearances and the Collapse of the Police System,* 1999; *Problems Facing the Cambodian Legal System,* 1998.

South Asia

Anuvrat Global Organisation

RESEARCH
EDUCATION

The Anuvrat Global Organisation (ANUVIBHA) is a non-profit, non-governmental organization that functions as an international center for peace and nonviolent action. The organization aims to popularize the Anuvrat Movement, seeking individual commitments to basic human values. Although ANUVIBHA is a spiritual organization, it stresses that its strategies to resolve conflicts are empirical and are an outcome of extensive research. Conflict prevention activities involve education, research, negotiation, and publishing. The organization maintains a peace palace and children camps where it organizes training in the culture of peace and nonviolence. Every two years the organization holds an international peace conference. The Anuvrat Global Organization aims to extend support to the United Nations and its agencies.

P.O. Box 1003
Jaipur 302015
India

Tel: +91 (141) 510 347
Fax: +91 (141) 510 118
anuvibha@datainfosys.net
www.anuvibha.com

Contact: S. L. Gandhi, Secretary General

Number of staff: 10

Budget: $25,000–$100,000

Publications: Ahimsa (Non violence), Peacemaking & Conflict Prevention & Management Conference report; *Anuvibha Reporter,* journal; *Anuvrat Movement: A Constructive Endeavor Towards a Multicultural Non-Violent Society; Many Facets of Non-Violence.*

Kashmir, Northeast India

Centre for Dialogue and Reconciliation

With its main focus on dialogue between the different castes, religions, and genders of India and Pakistan, the Centre for Dialogue and Reconciliation (CDR) wants to serve as a catalyst for peace and reconciliation. This non-profit, non-governmental organization holds conferences and discussions. The Centre initiates independent research and forms action plans for the conflict areas in the region. The main conflict prevention program, Dialogues of Understanding, deals with the conflict in Kashmir and Jammu. It aims to build deeper trust among all sections of Kashmiri society.

J-1346 Palam Vihar
Gurgaon
Haryana 122 017
India

Contact: Sushobha Barve, Executive Secretary

Tel: +91 (124) 646 0602
sushobha@vsnl.com or cdrec@vsnl.in

Northeast India, West Bengal, Bangladesh, Nepal, Bhutan

Centre for North East Studies and Policy Research

The Centre for North East Studies and Policy Research is a non-profit organization that aims to prevent conflicts in the Northeastern part of India. This isolated region lies in the midst of the countries of Nepal, Myanmar, Bangladesh, and Tibet/China and is only joined to the rest of India by a narrow strip of land. The Centre's main conflict prevention activities are aimed at getting small groups of influential community leaders to come together in a series of informal dialogues aimed at understanding each other's positions, perspectives, and history.

B/14, Press Enclave
Saket Street
New Delhi 110 017
India

Tel: +91 (11) 686 4120
Fax: +91(11) 696 4262
sanjoy@c-nes.org or
hazarika@c-nes.com

Contact: Sanjoy Hazarika, Managing Trustee
Number of staff: 1
Budget: < $25,000
Publications: Directory of Philanthropy in North East India, December 2000.

India

Centre for Policy Research

RESEARCH

The Centre for Policy Research (CPR) is an autonomous institution and think tank. The CPR was established with the objective of studying major policy issues before the nation and suggesting alternative policy options. The CPR conceives of its larger role as one of contributing to the clarification of the continuing national debate on the present and future development of the Indian society.

The CPR works in close cooperation with policymakers both political and administrative, academic policy researchers, and the media. It seeks to bring together on each issue the key policy actors, namely, politicians, policy thinkers, and administrators.

Dharma Marg, Chanakyapuri
New Delhi 110 021
India
――――――――

Tel: +91 (11) 611 5273
Fax: +91 (11) 687 2746
cprindia@vsnl.com
www.cprindia.org

Contact: Vapai Panandiker, President
Number of staff: 77
Budget: $100,000–$500,000
Publications: Newsletter.

India

Centre for
Study of Society and Secularism

RESEARCH
ADVOCACY

The Centre for Study of Society and Secularism is an organization that studies problems relating to communalism and secularism in Indian society. The Centre undertakes research projects in the field of religious, communal, and ethnic conflicts and comparative religions. It organizes interfaith discussions, conducts training programs, and publishes informational materials such as pamphlets, booklets, and posters on communal harmony. The library and documentation center of this organization is open to scholars, journalists, and students. The main documentation themes are the elections, communalism, bomb attacks, and secularism.

Irene Cottage, Second Floor
4th Road, Santa Cruz (E)
Mumbai 400 055
India
――――――――

Tel: +91 (22) 614 9668/615 3489
Fax: +91 (22) 617 3624
csss@vsnl.com

Contact: Asghar Ali Engineer, Chairman
Number of staff: 15
Budget: $25,000–$100,000
Publications: Secular Perspectives, a series of research studies.

South Asia

Coalition for
Action on South Asian Cooperation

RESEARCH

The Coalition for Action on South Asian Cooperation (CASAC) is an informal network of opinion and policymakers. The coalition aims to facilitate the process of regional cooperation in South Asia, in accordance with the decisions of SAARC Summits and recommendations of the Kathmandu Conference. CASAC activities include networking; organizing meetings and discussions; acting as an advocacy forum; preparing a compendium of institutions involved in regional cooperation; working to put regional cooperation into the spotlight of the media; and publication of papers to create a greater awareness of the benefits of regional cooperation. CASAC targets all levels of society, from NGOs and politicians to community-level contacts through exchanges.

C/o Friedrich-Ebert-Stiftung
K-70B, Hauz Khas Enclave
New Delhi 110 016
India

Contact: Nancy Jetly
*Publications: South Asia 2010:
Challenges and Opportunities,* 2001.

Tel: +91 (11) 656 1361
Fax: +91 (11) 656 4691
fes@fesindia.org

South Asia

Delhi Policy Group

RESEARCH
ACTION
ADVOCACY

The Delhi Policy Group (DPG) is an independent think tank supported by the corporate sector. The DPG argues for broadening the security debate in South Asia by raising the issue of non-military security. The endeavor of the Group has been to lay the foundation for fresh thinking on government policy and to influence the formulation and execution of the national policy through analysis, criticism, and interaction. The DPG facilitates interaction between planners, legislators, bureaucrats, and thinkers. It conducts seminars and workshops with national and international guests. It also initiates studies and research projects.

India Habitat Centre, Core 5-A, 1st Floor
Lodhi Road
New Delhi 110 003
India

Contact: K.S. Bajpai, Chairman
Number of staff: 3
Budget: < $25,000
Publications: Bulletin; *Myanmar &
North East India; Kashmir: An
Agenda for the Future.*

Tel: +91 (11) 464 9571/464 9844
Fax: +91 (11) 464 9572
dpgroup@vsnl.com
www.delhipolicygroup.org

South Asia, India

Fellowship of Reconciliation India

EDUCATION
ACTION
ADVOCACY

As a religious organization, the Fellowship of Reconciliation (FORI) has a history that dates back to 1950. FORI has since adopted conflict prevention, development, human rights, and training as its core functions. The Fellowships' program Training in Mediation and Conflict Management is intended for students, teachers, NGOs, GOs, and trainers. Its goal is to offer training and build support for women peacemakers, stimulate mediation for families and the political field, provide nonviolence education, and teach conflict management. FORI works with international partners like the International Fellowship of Reconciliation, the German Fellowship of Reconciliation, and the Swedish Ecumenical Council.

35/761 North Janatha Road
Palarivattom, Cochin-25
Kerala
India

Tel: +91 (484) 345 594/339 403
Fax: +91 (484) 339 403
Cap@kelnet07.xlweb.com

Contact: Beena Sebastian, Director
Number of staff: 15
Budget: $25,000–$100,000
Publications: Training manual in
regional languages.

India

Gandhi Peace Foundation

RESEARCH
EDUCATION
ACTION
ADVOCACY

The Gandhi Peace Foundation was established by eminent Indians to study and promote the relevance of the nonviolent alternative bequeathed by Mahatma Gandhi with respect to present-day problems. It publishes books linking Gandhian ideals to issue areas such as economics, pollution, disarmament, and social conflict. Promotion also takes place by means of fellowships, youth camps, training programs in non-violence and social change, and an international network with individuals and Gandhian groups. The Foundation has stimulated peace initiatives in Nagaland, Assam, Punjab, and Kashmir, and has intervened in the deeper causes of disturbances in some regions through relief and rehabilitation measures.

221-223, Deen Dayal Upadhyama Marg
New Delhi 110 002
India

Tel: +91 (11) 323 7491/323 7493
Fax: +91 (11) 323 6734
avard@del3.vsnl.net.in

Contact: Anupam Mishra, Joint
Secretary
Number of staff: 531
Budget: < $25,000
Publications: Ghandi Marg, quarterly
(English), monthly (Hindi);
research monographs.

India

Indian Confederation of Indigenous and Tribal People

RESEARCH
ACTION
ADVOCACY

The Indian Confederation of Indigenous and Tribal People (ICITP) is a network of more than 500 tribal organizations, run by a small staff and volunteers, working toward awareness, solidarity, and advocacy of human rights and democracy. Its central concern is with the threat to survival arising from the loss of life-supporting resources in the name of development. In 1997 the ICITP undertook peacebuilding in the northeast of India in an armed conflict for autonomy of Bodoland. The ICITP mediated in the intertribal conflict, stimulated a joint strategy by different tribal groups, and initiated a peace dialogue with the state and central authorities.

C-9/9555
Vasant Kunj
New Delhi 110 070
India

Contact: Ran Dayal Munda
Number of staff: Volunteers
Budget: $25,000–$100,000

Tel: +91 (11) 613 9586/613 9584
Fax: +91 (11) 613 9584
icitp@bol.net.in

South Asia, India

Indian Institute for Peace, Disarmament & Environmental Protection

RESEARCH
EDUCATION
ACTION
ADVOCACY

The Indian Institute for Peace, Disarmament & Environmental Protection (IIPDEP) combines research and raising awareness in its programs on the effects of specific weapons such as landmines and small arms upon social, regional, ethnic, or national conflicts. It also studies the underlying causes of these conflicts. Two peace museums, one based in Nagpur, another travelling through India, are devoted to nuclear disarmament in response to the threatening nuclear conflict between India and Pakistan. The IIPDEP organizes conferences, seminars, workshops, and international networking that address government institutions, as well as NGOs, women, and other groups.

537, Sakkardara Road
Nagpur 440 009
India

Contact: Balkrishna Kurvey, President
Number of staff: 3
Budget: $25,000–$100,000

Tel: +91 (712) 745 806
Fax: +91 (712) 743 664
iipdep@nagpur.dot.net.in

Publications: IIPDEP Newsletter; Ethnic Conflict and Its Peaceful Resolution.

India, Sri Lanka

Indian Social Institute

The Human Rights Department program for Legal Aid and Dalit Studies Unit of the Indian Social Institute (ISI) have conflict prevention as their main goal and are engaged in on-the-spot studies, advocacy, and the mobilization of mass support for the issues concerned. The non-profit Institute was founded in 1951 and is a center for research, training, and action for social and economic development. ISI sees itself as a national resource center for social activists. The Institute plans to develop a database on economic policy, globalization, debt relief, the IMF, the agrarian scene, and human rights.

10 Institutional Area
Lodi Road
New Delhi 110 003
India

Tel: +91 (11) 462 2379/462 5015
Fax: +91 (11) 469 0660
isi@unv.ernet.in or
prakash@unv.ernet.in

Contact: Prakash Louis, Executive Director

Number of staff: 68 (total), 9 (conflict prevention)

Budget: $100,000–$500,000

Publications: Subaltern, quarterly newsletter; *State of Human Rights in India,* 2000; *Women in Panchayati Raj; Indo-Naga Conflict: Problems and Resolution.*

Global

Indian Society of Human Rights

The Indian Society of Human Rights (ISHR) recently changed its charter to include conflict prevention and management in all aspects. The Society's staff consists of professionally qualified activists who are engaged in citizen diplomacy, data collecting, lobbying, mediation, negotiation, and research. In the area of conflict resolution the ISHR is currently involved in Tibet, where it is working toward a peaceful settlement of the Tibet freedom movement. In Kashmir, the ISHR aims to prevent war, to rehabilitate Kashmir refugees, and to lobby for a peaceful settlement. For many years it has been involved in East Timor, where it is currently striving to ensure that those who violated human rights are brought to justice and punished for their misdeeds.

34/26 Tashkent Marg
Civil Lines
Allahabad
Utar Pradesh 211 001
India

Tel: +91 (532) 602 353
Fax: +91 (532) 420 903/608 951
samchopra52@yahoo.co.in or
pionalld@nde.usul.net.in

Contact: Shambhu Chopra, Honorary Director

Number of staff: 10

Budget: < $25,000

Publications: Quarterly newsletter; annual report.

India

India Peace Centre

EDUCATION

The India Peace Centre (IPC) is a spiritual organization working at dialogue, inter-religious harmony, and communal peace. Its central activity is bringing peace education to young rural grassroots workers and urban youth. Basic assumptions are drawn from a blend of Christian doctrine and Gandhian philosophy. The IPC has provided workshops on conflict resolution, the Alternative to Violence Project, and a consultation on religious-cultural approaches to problems of violence and communalism. In addition to training courses, the IPC plans to take up work in potential conflict situations in the future.

C.K. Naidu Road, Civil Lines
Nagpur 440 001
Maharashtra
India
_____

Tel: +91 (712) 556 952
Fax: +91 (712) 520 554

Contact: Hansi De, Director

Budget: < $25,000

Publications: The Search for Peace: The Ghandian Techniques; Moral Foundations of the Indian Civilization.

India

Indira Ghandi Institute of Development Research

RESEARCH
EDUCATION

Carrying out research from a multidisciplinary view is the primary mandate of the Indira Ghandi Institute of Development Research (IGIDR). This advanced research institute was established by the Reserve Bank of India. Sponsored by agencies such as the UNDP and World Bank, the IGIDR's research projects cover a number of areas including energy, environment, trade, finance, agriculture, food security, and industry studies. The output of this research is disseminated through discussion papers, reports, books, and monographs. The IGIDR carries out training for advanced degrees and promotes cooperation and interaction between scholars and institutions in India and abroad.

Goregaon (E)
Mumbai 400 065
India
_____

Tel: +91 (22) 840 0919/20/21
Fax: +91 (22) 840 2752/2026
tvs@igidr.ac.in
www.igidr.ac.in

Contact: R. Radhakrishna, Director

Number of staff: 63

Budget: > $1,000,000

Publications: The Process of Liberalization in India, 1997; *Climate Change and North-South Cooperation,* 1997; *Policy Regimes and Industrial Competitiveness: A Comparative Study of East Asia and India,* forthcoming.

South Asia

Institute for Conflict Management

RESEARCH

The Institute for Conflict Management (ICM) is an autonomous, non-governmental, non-profit society engaged in the search for solutions to the widening sphere of conflict and violence in South Asia. The Institute's primary concerns are collective violence and internal security that threaten the fabric of civil society in the modern states, in particular, terrorism.

South Asia faces growing civil strife, ethnic conflicts, religious tensions, and trans-border terrorism that affect all countries in the region. Because the probabilities of large-scale conventional wars are diminished through the proliferation of nuclear weapons, non-traditional, irregular, and low-intensity wars have now become the prevalent form of inter-state conflicts.

ICM aims to explore, define, and implement concrete conflict solutions related to low-intensity conflicts. A key goal is to create an effective body of data, information, and analysis on terrorism and internal conflicts in the region, including small and internal wars, insurgencies, and protracted ethnic, communal, or sectarian strife.

A conspicuous activity of ICM is the maintenance of the South Asia Terrorism Portal (SATP) website, until now the largest website on terrorism and low level warfare in South Asia, currently with over 2000 pages. The SATP facility opens up the analytical context for research and analysis on extremist movements in the region.

Research activities of ICM focus on state responses in terrorist affected areas, such as administrative, juridical, legal, and security reforms. Another key focus for the future is the potential for, and defense against, information warfare, including a recent project on the uses of data mapping, simulation, and information analysis and technologies for counterterrorism.

ICM collaborates intensively with governmental agencies, academic institutions, and grassroots voluntary organizations. Target groups range from international and national policy makers to civil institutions and populations in Southeast Asia.

11, Talkatora Road
New Delhi 110 001
India

Tel: +91 (11) 371 5455/0374/0375
Fax: +91 (11) 373 6471
icm@del3.vsnl.net.in
www.satp.org

Contact: Ajai Sahni, Executive Director

Number of staff: 8

Budget: $25,000–$100,000

Publications: Faultlines, journal on security and conflict management in South Asia; *Kashmir Saga: A Bundle of Blunders,* 1999.

India

Institute for Development and Communication

RESEARCH
EDUCATION
ACTION

The Institute for Development and Communication (IDC), situated in northwest India, researches and evaluates development strategies and policy. It is actively involved in various facets of conflict resolution in South Asia such as research, early warning, and evolving strategies for rehabilitation. An important component is the education of different segments of the population in order to sensitize them to the culture of violence. The IDC also educates trainers, such as college teachers and local body representatives. Further, it organizes seminars and symposia on conflict management, handling subjects such as the Punjab, terrorism, and fundamentalism in South Asia.

SCO 1126-27 (First Floor), Sector 22 B
Chandigarh 160 022
Haryana, India

Tel: +91 (172) 707 942/720 654
Fax: +91 (172) 720 654
krpramod@ch1.vsnl.net.in

Contact: Pramod Kumar, Director

Number of staff: 35

Budget: $100,000–$500,000

Publications: Terrorism, Fundamentalism & Peace in South Asia; Identities in Conflict: A Case of Punjab; training manuals; booklets in Hindi and Punjabi.

Bangladesh, Bhutan, India, Maldives,
Nepal, Pakistan, Sri Lanka, China

RESEARCH
ADVOCACY

Institute of Peace and Conflict Studies

The Institute of Peace and Conflict Studies (IPCS), an autonomous research institute established in 1996 by the Centre for Study of Developing Societies, specializes in alternative policy studies and promotes alternative approaches to security issues relevant to India and the world.

The Institute publishes its research findings in several media, including, the Internet, books, papers, and national and international journals. Its strategies are to organize and participate in small-scale discussions and seminars in order to contribute to security issues of current interest to leading opinion makers. The IPCS edits a periodic newsletter and provides documentation and summarized debates on its website.

Recent projects include:

• An interactive home page devoted to national, regional, and international security issues with separate sections including a reference library providing daily abstracts from leading newspapers on selected security issues and a roundtable section with debates on strategic issues significant to India.
• The creation of an extensive online database, comprising country-specific chapters on military personnel, equipment, and armaments, and an overview of foreign policy and security issues.
• In 2001, the co-organization of the Regional Conference on Human Security in South Asia, with the objective of defining a theoretical framework for the alternative discourse on security in South Asia.
• Regular seminars under the auspices of the Friday Discussion group, engaging scholars, media personages, army officials, foreign services, and civilian services.

Key areas of IPCS address disarmament and arms control, comprehensive and cooperative security, non-military threats to security, confidence-building measures, China's security policies, and regional cooperation in South Asia.

The Institute has established a dialogue with similar institutions in other countries and offers interviews, programs, and seminars to foreign visitors, including academic bodies and military institutions.

197, Vasant Enclave
New Delhi 110 057
India

Tel: +91 (11) 615 3160
Fax: +91 (11) 615 2009
ipcs@del2.vsnl.net.in
mail@ipcs.org or
ipcs@vsnl.com
www.ipcs.org

Contact: P.R. Chari, Director

Number of staff: 7

Budget: $25,000–$100,000

Publications: IPCS Bulletin, newsletter; *Security and Governance in South Asia,* 2001; *Kargil: The Tables Turned,* 2001; *Letha; Comprehensive and Cooperative Security in South Asia,* 1998.

India
Inter-Community Peace Initiative

The aim of the Inter-Community Peace Initiative, or the Minorities Council, is to prevent and resolve communal conflicts between various religious communities in India, especially between the majority Hindu and Muslim/Christian minorities. The Peace Initiative is an independent civil society organization whose main activities are promoting human rights awareness, developing democracy, monitoring, and fact finding. The organization has a working relationship with the World Council of Muslims For Inter-Faith Relations in Chicago (USA).

20, Jaswant Apartments
Okhla, Jamia Nagar
New Delhi 110025
India

Tel: +91 (11) 632 4452
iqbalansari2001@hotmail.com

Contact: Iqbal A. Ansari, Secretary-General

Number of staff: 2

Budget: < $25,000

Publications: Human Right Today, (with the Institute of Objective Studies, New Delhi); *Communal Riots: Prevention & Control; From Conflict to Conciliation.*

South Asia

International Centre
for Peace Initiatives

The International Centre for Peace Initiatives (ICPI) aims to conceptualize, develop, and promote innovative approaches to peace at the global, regional, and national levels. It sees its role as a social entrepreneur at the leading edge of the world's and India's public policy agenda, addressing top governmental and political levels.

The ICPI works as a catalyst in partnership with leading constituencies and addresses the long term need for peace. Its work is organized in the form of initiatives on strategic issues. Such initiatives comprise policy research in the identified issue, behind-the-scenes consultations with relevant decision-makers and experts, consensus-building efforts in a confidential environment, seminars, and publications.

In the early 1990s the ICPI focused on advocating a global security regime free of nuclear weapons. In the mid-1990s the ICPI shifted its focus to the intractable conflicts in the South Asian region, especially Kashmir and Assam.

The ICPI has had an ongoing commitment to conflict resolution in the Kashmir Valley since its first fact-finding mission in 1995. It facilitated dialogue between Kashmiri and India's national leaders, coordinated the Kashmir Peace Appeal at the Hague Appeal for Peace, and organized a conference of Kashmiri leaders. In 2001 an ICPI team visited Kashmir with the aim of assessing the prospects of reconciliation and reconstruction.

Recently the ICPI started a joint research program on peace and security issues with experts from India and Pakistan addressing difficult issues of peace and security with a specific objective of identifying forward-looking solutions to conflicts. Another current initiative was launched in 1999 and seeks to engage owners and editors of indigenous-language media in confidence building between disputing countries. The ICTP publishes a bi-monthly journal, providing a forum for the discussion of innovative approaches to peace. The journal covers a broad spectrum of the humanities and the social and behavioral sciences.

C-306 Montana, Lokhandwala Complex
Andheri West
Mumbai 400 053
India
_____

Tel/fax: +81 (22) 631 8260
S-123 Panchshila Park
New Delhi 110 017
India
_____

Tel/fax: +91 (11) 687 6326
info@peaceinitiatives.org
karansawhny@bol.net.in

Contact: Karan Sawhny, Director

Number of staff: 10

Budget: $25,000–$100,000

Publications: Peace Initiative, journal; Pipelines and Powergrids for Peace, 2000; *The Beginning of The Future,* joint approach paper with the Institute of Regional Studies, Islamabad, 2000; *A Handbook for Conflict Resolution in South Asia,* 1996.

South Asia
International Centre for Peace Studies

The International Centre for Peace Studies is a non-governmental, non-profit organization whose activities include evolving frameworks to study conflict situations, conceptualizing the conflicts, and developing peace strategies. The Centre also has a focus on human rights with regard to peace and conflict. The primary mandate of the Centre lies within the realms of the academic, consultancy, research, and security. It focuses on the issue of autonomy in the Indian states of Jammu and Kashmir at present. The Centre is linking up with social-developmental organizations, operating at the grassroots level in conflict areas, and exploring the relationships between social, economic, and political development and peace.

A-39, First Floor,
    South Extension Part-I
New Delhi 110 049
India

Tel: +91 (11) 469 8886/464 9996
Fax: +91 (11) 464 9996
cpsnd@del2.vsnl.net.in

Contact: Riyaz Punjabi, President
Number of staff: 10
Budget: < $25,000
Publications: Newsletter; *Journal of Peace Studies,* bimonthly research journal; *Kashmir Trends,* weekly digest; *South Asia Watch,* bimonthly media survey.

Kashmir
Kashmir Foundation
for Peace and Development Studies

The Kashmir Foundation for Peace and Development Studies is a relatively new organization that seeks to provide a genuinely Kashmiri viewpoint. Syed Baba, a member of the ruling National Conference and a sitting member of the Jammu and Kashmir Legislative Council, set up the "valley-based" Foundation. The Foundation initiated an important peace conference in the summer of 2000 that has led to the formation of four working groups: Promoting a Political Dialogue, Ending Human Rights Abuses, Relief and Rehabilitation for Victims of Violence, and Encouraging Sustainable Development.

Gogjibagh, Srinagar
P.O. Box 1223
G.P.O. Box 1
Srinagar, Kashmir
India

Tel: +91 (194) 434 225
hopekashmir@rediffmail.com

India

Martin Luther King Centre for Democracy and Human Rights

EDUCATION
ACTION
ADVOCACY

The Martin Luther King Centre for Democracy and Human Rights is a professional, independent non-profit organization. The goal of the Centre is the advancement of democracy for international peace, political stability, and human progress through protection of human rights and the judicial system by nonviolent means. The Martin Luther King Centre for Democracy and Human Rights aims to accomplish this by development and rehabilitation, data collecting, education, fact finding, and lobbying.

G.P.O. Box 185
Bhubaneswar-751 001
Orissa
India

Contact: Shanti Ranjan Behera, Director
Number of staff: 10
Budget: <$25,000

Tel: +91 (674) 302 283/6792 57532
livelydemocracy@yahoo.com or
Shanti_ranjan@rediffmail.com

Nagaland

Naga Peoples Movement for Human Rights

ACTION
ADVOCACY

Nagaland is a region in the far east of India, close to the border of Myanmar. The Naga Peoples Movement for Human Rights aims to bring an end to the India-Naga conflict by encouraging a dialogue with the state of India on a people-to-people level. The Movement tries to mobilize Indian intellectuals, human rights groups, and civil and democratic rights groups to participate and contribute to the struggle for peace and justice in Nagaland. A delegation of various organizations from Nagaland is undertaking "A Journcy of Conscience" to different parts of the Indian subcontinent.

Opp. WWII Cemetery
Midland – 251
Kohima 797001
Nagaland
India

Tel: +91 (370) 223 231
npmhr1@usa.net

Northeast India

North East Network

RESEARCH
EDUCATION
ADVOCACY

The North East Network (NEN), a women activist's network, came into being during the mobilization process for the Beijng Conference. Its primary objective was to sustain the empowerment of rural women in the unstable northeast around such crucial issues as reproductive health and conflict resolution. NEN is engaged in the advocacy of regional peace initiatives at all levels in order to forge the involvement of women as decisionmakers in peace processes. The Women in Armed Conflict Situations Unit collaborates closely with local groups and peace forums. General activities like capacity building and training on gender are carried out at grassroots level in Assam, Meghalya, and Nagaland.

la Chaumiere
Shillongh 793001
Meghalja
India

Tel: +91 (364) 211 425/501 320
Fax: +91 (364) 501 320
roshmi@cal.vsnl.net.in.

Contact: Roshmi Koswami, Director
Number of staff: 4
Budget: <$25,000
Publications: Kindling a Light, newsletter.

Pakistan, India

Pakistan-India People Forum for Peace and Democracy

RESEARCH
EDUCATION
ADVOCACY

The Pakistan-India People Forum for Peace and Democracy is based in India. The key issue for this NGO network organization is the problematic relationship between the countries Pakistan and India. Consequently the situation in Kashmir and Jammu is another vital theme.

The Forum organizes meetings between Pakistani and Indian citizens, sometimes in India, sometimes in Pakistan. The first meeting was held in 1995. The goal of these symbolic meetings is to demonstrate that prior to the arrival of Islam in South Asia the two countries shared a common past. The Forum claims religion is not the most important divide between the two nations but that the core of the problem lies in the lack of democratic rights of the common people.

The Forum's activities are focused on conflict prevention and resolution by mediation, policy and advocacy work, research, citizen's diplomacy, early warning, education, lobbying, and publishing. The Forum also organizes conferences and workshops. It does not have a department that is exclusively responsible for conflict prevention but the Committee on Kashmir has conflict prevention and resolution as its main responsibility.

The Forum tries to influence the governments of India and Pakistan concerning nuclear weapons. According to the Forum a nuclear war between India and Pakistan will never be a rational solution. The Forum asks for a move toward regional disarmament, independent of the wishes of the nuclear weapon states.

The continuing strife in Kashmir is another focal point of the Forum, which asks the Indian government to stop the aggressive activities of the Indian army in Kashmir and at the same time demands that the Pakistan government stop assisting the militant forces in Kashmir.

Indian Chapter
B-14 (second floor) Gulmohar Park
New Delhi 110 049
India

Pakistan Chapter
4K Gulbarg 2
Lahore
Pakistan

Tel: +91 (11) 651 4847/656 1743
Fax: +91 (11) 651 1504
admin@del3.vsnl.net.in

Contact: Sushil Khanna, General Secretary
Number of staff: Voluntary
Budget: < $25,000

India

Peoples Union for Civil Liberties

The Peoples Union for Civil Liberties (PUCL) is a non-partisan and self-funded organization that was formed in 1980, after the demise of the People's Union for Civil Liberties and Democratic Rights. The organization monitors human rights throughout India. For example, in August 2001, PUCL filed a petition to the Indian Supreme Court regarding the incidents of starvation deaths while the Food Corporation of India had sufficient stocks. The PUCL also organizes the annual JP Memorial Lectures and the Journalism for Human Rights Award. At its research facility, the PUCL records articles from the main New Delhi newspapers relating to human rights (from 1996 onward).

81 Sahayoga apartments
Mayur Vihar - 1
New Delhi 110 0091
India

Tel: +91 (11) 249 2342
Fax: +91 (11) 225 0014/6931
national@pucl.org or
   puclnat@yahoo.com
www.pucl.org

Contact: Y. P. Chhibbar, General Secretary

Publications: PUCL Bulletin, a monthly bulletin; *JP Memorial Lectures Collection,* 2001; *Report on Police Firing in Mahendragarh, Haryana,* 1997.

India

PRASHANT

RESEARCH
EDUCATION
ACTION
ADVOCACY

PRASHANT, formerly known as St. Xavier's Social Service Society, was founded by Jesuits and originally focused on relief and development in three slum areas of Ahmedabad. Today, it also works on conflict prevention, communal harmony, peace, and justice in its current initiative called Shanti. Activities have included peacebuilding programs at the grassroots, children's programs, lectures and symposia, public interest litigation, filing law suits against communal discord and injustices, and uniting leaders of different faiths for dialogue and prayer. Notable activities in poor communities have been street plays in which slum dwellers themselves were involved, and "myth busting" information campaigns to counter inflammatory propaganda.

P.O. Box 4002
Navrangpura P.O.
Ahmedabad 380 009
Gujarat
India
_____

Tel: +91 (79) 744 9744/745 5913
Fax: +91 (79) 748 9018/630 162
cprakas@ad1.vsnl.net.in or sjprashant@icenet.net

Contact: Fr. Cedric Prakash sj, Director

Number of staff: 10

Budget: $25,000–$100,000

Publications: PRASHANT Notes, occasional newsletter.

South Asia

South Asia Human Rights Documentation Centre

RESEARCH
EDUCATION

Based in New Delhi, the South Asia Human Rights Documentation Centre (SAHRDC) is comprised of a small office and a network of individuals across the region. The documentation center collects information on human rights and documents violations of civil and political rights. It also distributes collected information through its electronic human rights features service and publishes investigative reports. Whenever necessary it initiates campaigns through "action alerts," to stop violations of human rights. The SAHRDC has also established various training programs on human rights issues.

B-6/6 Safdarjang
  Enclave Extension
New Delhi 110 029
India
_____

Tel: +91 (11) 619 1120/686 5736
Fax: +91 (11) 686 5736/619 1120
hrdc_online@hotmail.com
www.hri.ca/partners/sahrdc/index.htm

Number of staff: 7

Publications: Human Rights Features Service, electronic features; *Abandoned and Betrayed: Afghan Refugees under UNHCR Protection in New Delhi,* 1999; *The Bhutanese Political Crisis and Refugee Problem,* 1998; *National Human Rights Institutions in the Asia Pacific Region,* 1998.

South Asia

South Asia Network on Women in Politics

RESEARCH
EDUCATION
ADVOCACY

The mission statement of this women's network is to create an environment of peace in South Asia. The South Asia Network on Women in Politics (SANWP) has therefore started the South Asia Initiative for Peace in the Region, which organizes peace initiatives by women's groups and NGOs at a regional level. This has resulted in a bus journey to Pakistan and conferences in Dhaka and Delhi. Generally SANWP encourages training of women in leadership and advocates for gender equity in politics. The Network is further engaged in data collecting, research, and policy advice. Chapters of SANWP are in place in Nepal, Bangladesh, Sri Lanka, India, and Pakistan.

C/o Centre for Social Research
2 Institutional Area, C-1 Vasant Kunj
Nelson Mandela Road
New Delhi 110 070
India

Tel: +91 (11) 689 9998
Fax: +91 (11) 613 7823
csr@giasd101.vsnl.net.in

Contact: Ranjana Kumari, Coordinator
Number of staff: 2
Budget: $25,000–$100,000

India

South Asia Partnership—India

EDUCATION
ACTION

The South Asia Partnership—India (SAP—India) is a network of non-governmental organizations and other civil society groups in different parts of India. SAP—India has initiated a dialogue and debate on curbing the use of small arms and light weapons. It is also involved in capacity building for NGO's, training Panchayati Raj functionaries, empowering women through socio-economic development, and promoting self-help groups. SAP—India is part of the South Asia Partnership system, which has national organizations in Bangladesh, Nepal, Pakistan, Sri Lanka, and Canada.

B-5/174, Safdarjang Enclave
New Delhi 110 029
India

Tel: +91 (11) 619 5689, 616 6725
Fax: +91 (11) 610 0412
benedict@sap-india.org or
sapindia@bol.net.in
www.sap-india.org

Contact: Benedict A., Executive Director
Number of staff: 7
Publications: SAP India Annual Report, 2000–2001; *Small Arms Proliferation: Threat to Internal Security and World Peace,* report of the two-day seminar, February 2–3, 2001; *Human Security, Peacebuilding and Development: Threat from Small Arms and Light Weapons,* proceedings of the Hyderabad Seminar, March 23–24, 2001.

Northeast India

Tribal Welfare Society

EDUCATION
ACTION
ADVOCACY

The Tribal Welfare Society (TWS) is a non-profit organization engaged in peacebuilding and conflict resolution through socioeconomic development, awareness raising, legal education, and general community development. The ultimate goal is to bring peace and harmony to the troubled region of northeast India where many ethnic groups are settled. It carries out the Constitutional Awareness Program to create space for different groups to enter into dialogue by means of workshops and leadership training courses. Other conflict resolution activities include conferences, publication of training materials, and cultural exchange programs. The TWS maintains a large network with tribal, human rights, academic, and women organizations.

C/o ABAVP
No.1 West Kidwai Nagar
New Delhi 110023
India

Tel: +91 (11) 508 9856
Fax: +91 (11) 508 9856/54
mariatm@hotmail.com

Contact: Maria Mangte, General Secretary
Number of staff: 3
Budget: < $25,000

South Asia

Women in Security, Conflict Management and Peace

RESEARCH
EDUCATION
ADVOCACY

Initiated in 1999, Women in Security, Conflict Management and Peace (WISCOMP) is a project of the Foundation for Universal Responsibility of His Holiness The Dalai Lama. It provides a network of men and women committed to enhancing the professional efficacy and contribution of Asian women to international relations, conflict management, and peace.

WISCOMP strives to help women form networks and increase their participation so as to strengthen their role in multi-track diplomacy processes in the South Asian region. WISCOMP works to shift the balance to favor a more people-oriented and gender-sensitive approach. WISCOMP aims to achieve this goal through education, research, the organization of symposia, and through the facilitation of dialogue between parties in conflict.

WISCOMP awards annual Scholar of Peace Fellowships. These fellowships are open to academics, professionals, and media persons interested in conducting high-quality academic research, media projects, and special, innovative projects on a range of issues related to peace and security in South Asia. Financial support is provided for up to a year.

WISCOMP also organizes roundtable discussions on contemporary issues (for instance women and Kashmir) with a number of leading academics, journalists, and policy experts. Every year WISCOMP conducts an annual symposium for women and men in South Asia to share their experiences, build networks, and enhance their professional skills through a series of workshops. Furthermore the organization holds Conflict Transformation Interactions between students of Pakistan and India.

WISCOMP is part of a number of international networks including The Women's Initiative for Peace in South Asia (New Delhi), The South Asian Women's Network (online), The Hague Appeal for Peace (The Hague), the Women Building Peace Campaign (London), and Women in International Security (Washington).

UGF, Core 4 A, India Habitat Centre
Lodi Road
New Delhi 110 003
India

Tel: +91 (11) 464 8450/465 1606
Fax: +91 (11) 464 8451
wiscomp@vsnl.com
www.furhhdl.org

Contact: Meenakshi Gopinath, Director

Number of staff: 4

Budget: < $25,000

Publications: WISCOMP Update, newsletter; Women Reporting Conflict, 1999; *Summer Symposium on Human Security in the New Millennium,* 2000, conference report.

Kashmir

Women's Initiative
for Peace in South Asia

ACTION
ADVOCACY

This women's group visits conflict areas in an effort to create peace. Through these actions the Women's Initiative for Peace in South Asia (WIPSA) strives to broaden women's involvement in peace processes and to end the isolation of people in conflict areas. In 2000, Indian women made a bus journey to Pakistan, and Pakistani women made a return trip to India. Indian and Pakistani women also jointly visited Jammu and Kashmir. WIPSA published a report on Kashmir and sent recommendations to the Indian and Pakistani governments.

Gandhi Ashram
Kingsway Camp
Delhi 110 009
India

Contact: Nirmala Deshpande

Number of staff: 5

Publications: WIPSA report on Kashmir, 2000.

Tel/fax: +91 (11) 743 4514
nirmala@sansad.nic.in

East and Southeast Asia

Association for
Southeast Asian Nations

RESEARCH
EDUCATION
ACTION

Since 1967 the Association for Southeast Asian Nations (ASEAN) has stimulated social, economic, and cultural cooperation in Southeast Asia. In 1976 its members signed an important treaty to promote regional peace and stability through political and security dialogue. This treaty also provides a code of conduct for the peaceful settlement of disputes. A historical highlight for ASEAN was the settlement of the Cambodian conflict through mediation and diplomacy in early 1990s. A further step toward conflict prevention was the creation of the ASEAN Regional Forum. Since the admission of Cambodia in 1999, ASEAN represents all Southeast Asian states. There are connections with dialogue partners, including India.

70A, Jl. Sisingamangaraja
Jakarta 121 110
Indonesia

Publications: ASEAN annual reports; ASEAN Public Information Series; ASEAN briefing papers.

www.aseansec.org

East and Southeast Asia

Association for Southeast Asian Nations—Regional Forum

RESEARCH
ACTION

The Association for Southeast Asian Nations—Regional Forum (ARF) was established by the Association for Southeast Asian Nations (ASEAN) in 1994 with the purpose of promoting confidence among nations through security dialogues in the Asia-Pacific region. Currently, participants are the ten ASEAN members and eleven ASEAN dialogue and consultative partners from Asia and abroad. The forum process provides an annual ministerial meeting and several supporting bodies, such as Inter-sessional Meetings (CBM) and related Track-II Meetings. Recently an extended discussion on the concept of preventive diplomacy has emerged among the member states. The Forum publishes an Annual Security Outlook.

Secretariat ASEAN
70A, Jl. Sisingamangaraja
Jakarta 121 110
Indonesia

mcabad@aseansec.org or
termsak@aseansec.org
www.aseansec.org

Publications: Annual Security Outlook.

Global

Japan Center for Preventive Diplomacy

EDUCATION
ACTION
ADVOCACY

The Japanese Center for Preventive Diplomacy (JCPD) was established in 1999 to promote the role of Japanese civil society in the field of preventive diplomacy. The Center runs programs in Southwest and Southeast Asia and in the Middle East, with activities ranging from peace education and preventive diplomacy workshops to fact-finding missions. It also established a postgraduate program for preventive diplomacy. Together with the Japan Institute of International Affairs, the Center has published a directory of organizations working for conflict prevention in Asia and the Pacific. It also maintains the Dialogue Webpage for Conflicts Worldwide.

2-17-12-803 Akasaka
Minato-ku
Tokyo, 107 0052
Japan

Tel: +81 (3) 3584 7457
Fax: +81 (3) 3584 7528
jcpd@jfir.or.jp
www.jcpd.gr.jp

Contacts: Ito Kenichi, President; Asomura Kuniaki, Executive Director

Number of staff: 13

Budget: > $1,000,000

Publications: JCPD Newsletter, quarterly newsletter; *Directory of Organizations for Conflict Prevention in Asia and the Pacific,* 2000; *On Modern Preventive Diplomacy,* 2000; *An Introduction to Preventive Diplomacy,* 1999.

Asia Pacific

Japan Institute of International Affairs

RESEARCH
EDUCATION

The Japan Institute of International Affairs (JIIA) is an independent research organization dedicated to fostering studies of international relations through the exchange of research information within Japan and abroad. It organizes study groups and international meetings; conducts joint projects with other research organizations; and provides assistance to invited, foreign researchers. Recently the Institute organized an international symposium on the role of NGOs in conflict prevention. In 2001 there was a follow-up symposium on conflict prevention in Asia. One division of JIIA is totally committed to research on the Asia-Pacific region, covering themes such as security and confidence building.

11F Kasumigaseki Building
3-2-5 Kasumigaseki
Chiyoda-ku
Tokyo 100 6011
Japan

Tel: +81 (3) 3503 7261
Fax: +81 (3) 3503 7292
info@jiia.or.jp
www.jiia.or.jp

Contact: Hisashi Owada, President

Number of staff: 50

Budget: > $1,000,000

Publications: Japan Review of International Affairs, quarterly journal.

Kazakhstan, Central Asia, CIS countries

RESEARCH
EDUCATION
ADVOCACY

Center for Conflict Management

The Center for Conflict Management (CCM) is a non-governmental organization that aims to contribute to the prevention and resolution of violent conflicts in Kazakhstan and Central Asia, the development of civil society, and transformation of public consciousness.

The CCM operates with five main spheres of activity: educational programs; research and monitoring; promotion of nonviolent conflict resolution, peace, and tolerance; institutional development of NGOs; development of cooperation among NGOs working for conflict management and civic education; and practical activities in conflict management and prevention.

Since 1998 the CCM has organized annual Summer Schools on Conflict Management for practitioners from Central Asia and the Caucasus, in partnership with the UK-based NGO Responding to Conflict. In 2001 the CCM conducted a Summer University on Conflict Studies for university staff from Central Asia and the Caucasus with the aim of introducing conflict studies at the university level. CCM staff has facilitated training on conflict resolution and civic education in various countries of Central Asia.

The CCM is also involved in tolerance education and in addressing the issues of prejudice against ethnic minorities and refugees in Kazakhstan, which includes educational seminars for different target groups, publications, and awareness raising through the media.

In 1999 the CCM initiated the Central Asian Conflict Management Network, which unites around twenty active NGOs in the region. The network has been established in the framework of the CIS NGO Working Group on Conflict Management in which the CCM has served as a lead agency, together with International Alert (UK). The Working Group is supported by UNHCR.

The CCM is also active in the sphere of civic education. It is currently cooperating with the Ministry of Education in an effort to introduce civic education into the school curriculum.

The CCM is a co-founder of the Association of Conflict Researchers (Russia). It has produced a database on conflict management organizations in the CIS that is available online.

Office 301, 32a Manasa Street
Almaty 480 008
Kazakhstan

Tel/fax: +7 (3272) 539 384
ccm@online.ru
www.ccm.freenet.kz

Contact: Elena Sadovskaya, President

Number of staff: 12

Budget: $100,000–$500,000

Publications: First Steps (Amnesty International manual on Human Rights translated from English into Kazakh), 2001; *Manual on Civic Education for Teachers,* 2000; *Methods of Conflict Management and Prevention Seminar Report,* 1998; Kazakhstan: Social Conflicts—Expertise, Prognoses and Resolution Techniques, 1997.

Kazakhstan

Center for Social Research

The Center for Social Research (CSR) is a local NGO that aims to contribute to the development of democracy in Kazakhstan through the study and analysis of social processes, development of practical recommendations, conducting seminars and training, and conveying the transformation of public awareness through mass media. The CSR is implementing a program on the eradication of violence through monitoring, roundtables, newspaper publication, dissemination of booklets, and radio programs at the grassroots level. The CSR cooperates with a number of local NGOs.

Office 442, 18 Sovetskoi
  Konstitutsii Street,
Karaganda 470074
Kazakhstan

Tel: +7 (3212) 754 607/734 875
maltabar@hotmail.com

Contact: Valentina Nikolaevna Ukrainskaya, Director

Number of staff: 10

Budget: < $25,000

Kazakhstan

Center for the Support of Democracy

The Center for the Support of Democracy (CSD) is an NGO and a network whose mission is to provide information, consultancy, and research with the aim of strengthening constitutional democracy in Kazakhstan. The CSD is a member of the network of "democracy support centers" in Kazakhstan, financed by National Democratic Institute (USA). In 2000 the CSD conducted research on ethnic conflicts and national identity in Kazakhstan. The CSD is planning to work on refugee issues by providing advice to refugee organizations.

appt. 13, 2 Alalykina Street
Karaganda 470061
Kazakhstan

Tel: +7 (3212) 520 683
Fax: +7 (3212) 523 012/411 477
cad@nursat.kz

Contact: Marina Pavlovna Sabitova, Director

Number of staff: 5

Budget: < $25,000

Publications: Mass Political Consciousness, 2000.

Kazakhstan

Dialogue

Dialogue is an information and communication service that was established in August 1996 with the aim of contributing to the development of a multicultural society in Kazakhstan through research, educational, and peacemaking activities. Dialogue has conducted a number of monitoring and expert assessments, including evaluation of inter-ethnic relations for the Assembly of Peoples of Kazakhstan and OSCE. Currently it is focused on media and community campaigns, such as development of the media dialogue between the state authorities and society on the issues of ethno-cultural needs of the Diaspora. Dialogue is engaged in the development of democratic mechanisms of ethno-cultural self-assertion of the Uzbek Diaspora in South Kazakhstan.

Office 10, 12-G Patrice
  Lumumba Street
Shymkent 486011
Kazakhstan
———————
Tel/fax: +7 (3252) 537 028
savdial-shm@nursat.kz
savigsa@inbox.ru

Contact: Igor Savin, Director

Number of staff: 4

Budget: < $25,000

Publications: Dialogue, bi-monthly bulletin, available online at www.uko.nm.ru; "Multiculturalism and Prevention of Ethnic Conflict in Post-Soviet Kazakhstan," in *Humanitarian Dimension: Culture, Politics, Economics: Collection of Materials of International Scientific-Theoretical Conference* (25–26 May 2001), in Russian, 2001.

Kazakhstan

ZHARiA

ZHARiA (Women's Association of Development and Adaptation) works for the harmonization and adaptation of women to the undergoing reforms in the society and the defense of women's rights. ZHARiA runs the "Conflict: pro et contra" program, which aims at preventing inter-ethnic conflicts through education in the methods of conflict analysis and resolution. The project operates in the northern and central parts of Kazakhstan. In the framework of the project, six seminars have been organized. ZHARiA works in partnership with the Ministry of Culture, Information and Public Accord, as well as with ethno-cultural centers, schools, and universities in northern and central Kazakhstan.

Appt. 38, 13 mikrorayon 2
Astana 473000
Kazakhstan
———————
Tel/fax: +7 (3172) 366 634
zharia@kepter.kz

Contact: Nabieva Gulzi, Director

Number of staff: 8

Budget: < $25,000

Kyrgyzstan
Adult Training Center, Osh affiliation

EDUCATION
ACTION

The Adult Training Center (ATC) is an NGO with the mission to contribute to the process of democratization in Kyrgyzstan through adult education, including civic education, professional education, and raising awareness on legal issues and interpersonal relations. The ATC is also involved in research in the sphere of adult education. The ATC organizes practical training on conflict prevention and tolerance education for the grassroots activists in the Osh, Jalal-Abad, and Batken provinces of Kyrgyzstan. In 1997–1998 the ATC tested an approach to early prognosis of conflicts, identification of the causes of interethnic conflicts, and methods for their prevention.

205 Lenin Street, room 307
Osh 714000
Kyrgyzstan

Tel: +996 (3222) 55 780/55 621
Fax: +996 (3222) 55 780
atc-osh@mail.kg
www.atc.kg

Contact: Kambarbek Adyshev, Training Manager
Number of staff: 6
Budget: < $25,000
Publications: ATC Newsletter.

Central Asia

Bishkek Migration Management Center

RESEARCH
EDUCATION
ADVOCACY

The Bishkek Migration Management Center (BMMC) is an NGO and a network. The aim of the Center is to create the necessary conditions and potential for developing an effective migration management system in the Central Asian states.

The BMMC is currently undergoing re-registration and plans to change its name to the Regional Center on Migration and Refugee Issues.

The BMMC is involved in developing the international system for the protection of refugees in Central Asia, which implies improvement of the legislation and procedures for granting refugee status. The program includes organizing seminars and drafting laws and regulations. The Center is involved in subregional consultations on the problems of Afghan refugees in Central Asia.

The BMMC is also involved in setting up a regional information exchange on migration and refugee issues, through regular conferences such as the Regional Conference on Migration Problems in Central Asia (1998) and the International Conference on Migration Policy for Central Asia, Caucasus and Neighboring States (2000).

The BMMC is part of the network of the International Organisation for Migration's (IOM) Centre of Technical Co-operation and the International Labour Organization's (ILO) Labor Migration Division. It also closely cooperates with the OSCE Office for Democratic Institutions and Human Rights.

139 Toktogula Street
Bishkek 720001
Kyrgyzstan

Tel: +996 (312) 663 290/663 370
Fax: +996 (312) 664 714
bmmc@elcat.kg
freewww.elcat.kg/bmmc/

Contact: Talaybek Turgumbaevich Kydyrov, Director

Number of staff: 10

Budget: $100,000–$500,000

Publications: Information bulletin; *Refugees in the Kyrgyz Republic; Problems of Russian Speaking Population in the Kyrgyz Republic; Research on Internal Registration of Citizens in the Kyrgyz Republic.*

Kyrgyzstan, Ferghana Valley

Center for Social Research of the National Academy of Sciences of the Kyrgyz Republic

RESEARCH
EDUCATION

The Center for Social Research (CSR) is an academic organization that is involved in research and educational activities. The CSR provides information for the EAWARN and FAST conflict-monitoring projects, run correspondingly by the Institute of Ethnology and Anthropology of the Russian Academy of Sciences and Swiss Peace Foundation. The Center staff also publishes regularly in analytical bulletins.

265-A Chui Avenue
Bishkek 720071
Kyrgyzstan

Tel: +996 (312) 243 735
Fax: +996 (312) 218 522
nurbekcsr@freenet.kg or polra99@hotmail.com

Contact: Nurbek Ashimkanovich Omuraliev, Director

Number of staff: 4

Budget: < $25,000

Kyrgyzstan, Tajikistan, Uzbekistan

Foundation for Tolerance International

EDUCATION
ACTION
ADVOCACY

The Foundation for Tolerance International (FTI) is a non-profit, non-partisan, non-governmental organization with a mission to prevent interethnic conflicts. To achieve this, it aims to coordinate community-based activities and civil forums that promote peace, tolerance, and conflict resolution strategies, and to support locally initiated solutions to regional interethnic conflict.

The Foundation has grown up over the last two years. Beginning life as the Training Project in 1998, it now pursues several directions of activity, which include a variety of projects in the field of conflict prevention.

Among those, FTI has worked on the resolution of resource-related conflicts in the Batken oblast (province) of Kyrgyzstan. The project involved consensus-building activities, mediation, and negotiation for local communities. In many of its project, the FTI works in partnership with Tajik NGO Ittifok Centre for Youth Initiatives. Other partners have included a range of local NGOs in Batken oblast: Osh State University (Kyrgyzstan), Teachers Association (Kyrgyzstan), Swiss Co-ordination Office, Delaware University (USA), and UNOPS.

Appt. 8, 116 Orozbekova Street
Bishkek 720040
Kyrgyzstan

Tel: +996 (312) 222 233/223
  390/661 615
Fax: +996 (312) 222 233
fti@infotel.kg
www.fti.org.kg

Contact: Raya Kadyrova, Director

Number of staff: 32

Budget: $100,000–$500,000

Publications: Salam Asia Newsletter; training materials.

Ferghana Valley, Central Asia

Institute for Regional Studies

RESEARCH
EDUCATION
ADVOCACY

The Institute for Regional Studies (IFRS, previously Kyrgyz Peace Research Center) is an NGO founded in 1994. In order to provide a mechanism for effective changes in the society, a training program involving participants from the Central Asian countries is organized on the issues of conflict prevention and resolution. The Institute's activities are focused on facilitating a sense of citizenship among the people of the region, encouraging participation in public life, and providing broad access to relevant information on democracy. The IFRS seeks to maintain peace by making recommendations to governmental bodies, international organizations, and local NGOs.

appt.105, 77 Toktogul Street
P.O. Box 1880
Bishkek 720000
Kyrgyzstan

Tel: +996 (312) 281 771
Fax: +996 (312) 280 635
ifrs@elcat.kg
www.ifrs.elcat.kg

Contact: Anara Tabyshalieva, Director

Number of staff: 10

Budget: $25,000–$100,000

Publications: Central Asia: New Space for Cooperation, 2000; *Man in the State,* manual for schoolchildren, 2000; *Kyrgyzstan: Some Aspects of the Social Situation,* 2000; *The Challenge of Regional Cooperation in Central Asia: Preventing Ethnic Conflict in the Ferghana Valley,* together with the United States Institute of Peace, 1999; *Person and Law,* manual for schoolchildren, 1999.

Central Asia

International Crisis Group, Central Asia Project

RESEARCH
ADVOCACY

The Central Asia Project was initiated by the International Crisis Group (ICG) in October 2000. The ICG strives to provide high-quality advice and advocacy to help governments, international organizations, and the world community at large in preventing or containing deadly conflict. The Central Asia Project produces reports based on thorough field research on various aspects of the situation in Central Asia. The reports are available online.

7 Michurin Street
Osh 714000
Kyrgyzstan

Tel: +996 (3222) 20 470/20 370/55 055
Fax: +996 (3222) 21 218
icgosh@crisisweb.org
www.crisisweb.org

Contact: David Lewis, Director ICG - Central Asia Project

Number of staff: 6

Publications: Central Asia: Fault Lines in the New Security Map; *Incubators of Conflict: Central Asia's Localised Poverty and Social Unrest*; *Central Asia: Islamist Mobilization and Regional Stability*, 2001; *Central Asia: Crisis Conditions in Three States*, 2000; *Recent Violence in Central Asia: Causes and Consequences*, 2000; *Central Asia: Border Disputes and Conflict Potential Report*, 2002; *The IMU and the Hizb-at-Tahrir: Implications of the Afghanistan Campaign*, Briefing, 30 January 2002.

Kyrgyzstan

Osh Media Resource Center

ADVOCACY

The Osh Media Resource Center (OMRC) is a non-profit media development organization that aims to develop the independent media of southern Kyrgyzstan. The OMRC is a member of the Central Asian Media Support Project, which unites professional media associations from Uzbekistan, Tajikistan, and Kyrgyzstan. Through its primary mandate of working with journalists, the OMRC also addresses the issues of conflict. In May 2000 it organized the conference The Role of Mass Media in Post-Soviet Conflict Areas.

271 Kurmanjan Datka Street
Osh 714000
Kyrgyzstan

Tel: +996 (3222) 20 858
Fax: +996 (3222) 55 259
omrc2000@netmail.kg

Contact: Alisher Akhmadovich Khamidov, Director

Central Asia

Spravedlivost Regional Human Rights Organisation

RESEARCH
ACTION

The mission of the Spravedlivost Regional Human Rights Organisation is to form an open multi-ethnic and multi-confessional society, and to establish the rule of law. Besides human rights defense work, Spravedlivost (Justice) focuses on ethnic and confessional monitoring, and trust-building measures among local communities in the Kyrgyz-Uzbek border regions. It analyzes the conditions of the ethno-cultural groups, provides regular reports based upon the ethno-confessional monitoring, and drafts suggestions on early warning for the authorities. The Organization maintains a database on ethnic and cultural groups of the region, on non-customary confessions, and on the dynamics of dissemination of the radical Islam ideas.

27 Erkin-Too Street
Jalal-Abad 715612
Kyrgyzstan

Tel/fax: +996 (3722) 56 038
valery@elcat2.bishkek.su or
opzo@mail.ru
www.spravedlivost.bishkek.su

Contact: Valery Sergueevich Uleev, Director
Number of staff: 21
Budget: < $25,000
Publications: Rights for All, newsletter.

Kyrgyzstan

Youth Human Rights Group

RESEARCH
EDUCATION
ADVOCACY

The mission of the Youth Human Rights Group (YHRG) is to promote human rights and the rights of the children among Tajik and Afghan refugees in Kyrgyzstan. Its research into the situation, conducted in partnership with UNHCR and Save the Children (UK), provided a basis for future educational and practical work. The YHRG educational program for teachers includes a component of tolerance education and respect for diversity. The YHRG is also active in awareness-raising initiatives through dissemination of printed materials and production of radio programs, lobbying, and consulting on the existing legislation.

Appt. 8, 41-B Moskovskaya Street
Bishkek 720000
Kyrgyzstan

Tel: +996 (312) 681 370
Fax: +996 (312) 681 091
youth@elcat.kg
www.yhrg.elcat.kg

Contact: Maria Lisitsyna, Director
Number of staff: 8
Budget: < $25,000
Publications: Chaika (Seagull), quarterly bulletin; *The Covenant of the Rights of the Child in Drawings,* 2000; manuals on Teaching the Rights of the Child, 1999; *Refugee Children in Kyrgyzstan,* 1998

Asia Pacific

Council for Security Cooperation in the Asia Pacific

ACTION

The Council for Security Cooperation in the Asia Pacific (CSCAP) is a Track II security forum. It provides an informal place for scholars, officials, and others in their private capacities to discuss political and security issues. The staff organizes working groups in order to create space for specific themes and to provide policy recommendations to intergovernmental bodies. In a recent CSCAP workshop, a working definition and statement of principles on preventive diplomacy was shaped. This was thereafter presented at a large Asian forum. CSCAP has member committees in twenty countries in the region. It is also associated with the Department of Public Information of the United Nations.

Secretariat CSCAP
Institute of Strategic and
    International Studies Malaysia
1 Persiaran Sultan Salahuddin
P.O. Box 12424
50778 Kuala Lumpur
Malaysia

Tel: +60 (3) 293 9366
Fax: +60 (3) 293 9430
jawhar@isis.po.my or
cscap@isis.po.my
www.cscap.org

Contact: Mohamed Jawhar Hassan, Director General

Publications: CSCAP Newsletter; AUS-CSCAP Newsletter; Regional Maritime Management and Security, 1998; *No Better Alternative: Comprehensive and Cooperative Security in the Asia-Pacific,* 1997; *Asia Pacific Multilateral Nuclear Safety and Non-Proliferation: Exploring the Possibilities,* 1996.

Bhutan

Centre for Protection of Minorities and Against Racism and Discrimination in Bhutan

RESEARCH
EDUCATION
ADVOCACY

The Centre for Protection of Minorities and Against Racism and Discrimination in Bhutan (CEMARD—Bhutan) is a non-governmental human rights organization in exile. Its main aim is the elimination of all forms of racism and racial discrimination. Its activities include education in human rights, research, and lobbying. Through the promotion of human rights and justice for religious, ethnic, and linguistic minorities in Bhutan, CEMARD—Bhutan is working toward a sustainable peace in Bhutan.

Indrayeni Height, Sanepa
G.P.O. Box 3485
Kathmandu
Nepal

Tel: +977 (1) 529 106
Fax: +977 (1) 549 284
rakesh@bwco.wlink.com.np
www.geocities.com/cemardbhutan/

Contact: Rakesh Chhetri, Executive Director

Number of staff: 5

Budget: $25,000–$100,000

Nepal

Forum for
Protection of Human Rights

RESEARCH
ADVOCACY

The Forum for Protection of Human Rights (FOPHUR) is the oldest human rights activist organization in Nepal. It was founded by prominent personalities in such fields as politics, economics, academia, law, and journalism. The Forum aims for transformation toward a democratic state, amnesty for political prisoners, and freedom from police abuse. FOPHUR conducts fact finding on human rights and publishes this information. The organization has 52 district units throughout the country.

P.O. Box 5457
Maitighar, Kathmandu
Nepal
_____
Tel/fax: +977 (1) 257 637

Contact: B.K. Mainali, President

Budget: < $25,000

Publications: Human Rights Bulletin, in Nepali and English.

South Asia

Group for International Solidarity

EDUCATION
ACTION
ADVOCACY

The Group for International Solidarity (GRINSO-Nepal) is a non-profit, non-governmental human rights organization that has Special Consultative Status with the ECOSOC of the United Nations. GRINSO's traditional focus has been on women, street children, and marginalized indigenous people, but it has recently started a new project monitoring the refugee verification process in Jhapa. The Group is committed to achieving peaceful neighborhoods and an equitable social system. GRINSO believes strongly in group actions and therefore works with other organizations at the national, regional, and global levels.

P.O. Box 5690
Kathmandu
Nepal
_____
Tel: +977 (1) 420 904/427 650/ 419 894
Fax: +977 (1) 413 459
grinso@mos.com.np

Contact: Rajan Dahal, Director

Number of staff: 35

Nepal

Human Rights and Peace Campaign Nepal

RESEARCH
EDUCATION
ACTION
ADVOCACY

The Human Rights and Peace Campaign Nepal (HURPEC-Nepal) deals with a wide range of concerns, including the status of internal refugees, the prostitution problem in hotels and restaurants in Kathmandu, trafficking of girls, street children, the situation in Maoist territory, and the rights of laborers. Unfortunately a lot of the program of the Human Rights and Peace Campaign have been postponed after the Royal Massacre. HURPEC-Nepal is a non-profit, non-governmental networking organization that organizes conferences and carries out some monitoring activities. The Campaign has organized several cycling tours to promote awareness of human rights and peace.

Central Office
G.P.O. Box 21405
Gairidhara, Kathmandu
Nepal
_____

Tel/fax: +977 (1) 434 175
hurpec_nepal@hotmail.com
info@hurpec.org
www.hurpec.org

Contact: Milan Karki, President
Number of staff: 2
Budget: < $25,000
Publications: HURPEC Journal, newsletter.

Nepal

Human Rights and Peace Society

RESEARCH
EDUCATION
ADVOCACY

The Human Rights and Peace Society (HURPES) is a non-governmental, non-political, and independent organization. Its primary objectives are to run campaigns and programs to create a strong base for human rights culture through the presence of human rights communities. In the area of conflict prevention HURPES initiates peace processes and campaigns to discourage any tendency, custom, or tradition that sparks violence. Recently HURPES organized seminars in 42 districts of Nepal on the rights of children, focusing on children in armed conflicts. Among the participants were judges, members of parliament, lawyers, police officers, activists, representatives of ministries, and child rights NGOs. Last year, HURPES also organized peace conferences in 50 districts within Nepal, including conflict-prone areas.

KHA 2/13
P.O. Box 12790
Kalikasthan
Kathmandu
Nepal
_____

Tel: +977 (1) 420 712
Fax: +977 (1) 420 369
kpahadi@hurpes.wlink.com.np
www.peacesocietynepal.org

Contact: Krishna Pahadi, Executive Chair
Number of staff: 3 (15 regular volunteers who work for human rights and peace issues)
Budget: $25,000–$100,000
Publications: Peace Journal, newsletter; research reports.

Nepal

Human Rights Organisation of Nepal

RESEARCH
ACTION
ADVOCACY

In 2001 the Human Rights Organisation of Nepal (HURON) adopted conflict solution as its primary area of focus. HURON acted as a facilitator to bring the government and Maoists to the table for a meaningful dialogue. Its work is concentrated in the Peace Campaign, which aims to create a mass movement with the participation of civil society in favor of dialogue. Activities include marches, seminars, films, and providing services such as interactive talk programs and conflict management material. Previously HURON has worked on the restoration of the democratic process, which has involved closely monitoring human rights abuses and mobilizing public opinion against repressive policies.

Putlai Sadak, Ramshah Path
P.O. Box 5424
Kathmandu
Nepal
—————————
Tel: +977 (1) 411 033
Fax: +977 (1) 425 532
huron@wlink.com.np or
goss@mos.com.np
www.huron.org.np

Contact: Sudip Pathak, President
Number of staff: 10
Budget: < $25,000

Nepal

Informal Sector Service Centre (INSEC)

RESEARCH
EDUCATION
ADVOCACY

Founded in 1988, the Informal Sector Service Centre (INSEC) has grown into an NGO specializing in human rights monitoring, grassroots advocacy, and advocacy for marginalized issues and groups of people. It has been a catalyst for the liberation of bonded laborers and the Dalit minority from socioeconomic exploitation and injustice. Heavily focused on the rights of agricultural workers, INSEC conducted a campaign for a minimum wage and is launching a campaign for agrarian reform. INSEC also addresses women's and children's rights issues, and for the last eight years it has published the Human Rights Yearbook. Human rights education is its cornerstone program.

Syuchatar-4, Kalanki
P.O. Box 2726
Kathmandu
Nepal
—————————
Tel: +977 (1) 278 770
Fax: +977 (1) 270 551
insec@wlink.com.np
www.insec-nepal.com

Contact: Subodh Raj Pyakurel, General Secretary
Number of staff: 70 (total), (10 conflict prevention)
Budget: $25,000–$100,000
Publications: Informal, quarterly human rights journal; *Human Rights Yearbook,* annual.

Nepal

Institute of Human Rights Communication, Nepal

RESEARCH
EDUCATION
ADVOCACY

The Institute of Human Rights Communication, Nepal (IHRICON) is a human rights organization run by Nepalese journalists and women activists that aims to protect human rights through the media. To monitor human rights throughout the country, the Institute has formed a network of journalists monitoring human rights in their area. It also carries out continuous media monitoring. The results of both of these monitoring activities are published in IHRICON's Human Rights News Service, as well as other print and electronic media. In public hearings the Institute brings together journalists, victims of violations, and human rights activists to identify common issues and to generate new thinking. IHRICON provides training on human rights journalism to media workers and others.

G.P.O. Box 5188
Anmnanagar
Kathmandu
Nepal

Tel/fax: +977 (1) 231 079
ihricon@mos.com.np
www.ihricon.org

Contact: Shobha Gautam, President

Number of staff: 12

Publications: Health and Nutritional Feature, journal on public health issues; Human Rights News Service, online news service.

Nepal

International Institute for Human Rights, Environment and Development

RESEARCH
EDUCATION
ADVOCACY

With Special Consultative Status with the ECOSOC of the United Nations, the International Institute for Human Rights, Environment and Development (INHURED International) is a relatively old human rights organization whose history goes back to the times of the Panchayati dictatorship. Issues of concern for this non-governmental, non-profit organization are the monitoring of international instruments on human rights, gender justice, and environment, electoral observation, plus fact finding and documentation on national and regional human rights.

INHURED/HimRight House
G.P.O. Box 4690
Kathmandu
Nepal

Tel: +977 (1) 520 054/523
  805/520 042
Fax: +977 (1) 520 042/521
  180/435 791
info@inhured.wlink.com.np
www.inhured.org

Contact: Gopal Krishna Siwakoti, Executive Director

Publications: Violence Against Women— Challenges and Prospects: A Case Study of the Kingdom of Nepal, forthcoming; *Copenhagen + Five: Monitoring the UN Specialised Agencies for Social Development; Nepal: Beijing plus five review,* NGO Country Report, monitoring platform, pledge, and performance; *Statistics of Refugee Influx in South Asia: Developing a More Global Regime.*

Nepal

National Peace Campaign (NPC)

RESEARCH
EDUCATION
ADVOCACY

The National Peace Campaign (NPC), set up in 1999, is a non-governmental, non-profit organization whose primary purpose is to build a center for peace studies in order to conduct short-term and long-term courses on peace and conflict resolution. In addition it will also support activists, groups, and local and regional organizations on capacity building, training, and service delivery. In 2001 the NPC operated the Conflict Management and Peace Building in Nepal Program, calling on grassroots, government, and civil society involvement.

P.O. Box 10101
Kathmandu
Nepal

Tel: +977 (1) 632 054
Fax: +977 (1) 226 820
npcpeace@ntc.net.np

Contact: Shiva Hari Dahal, Director
Number of staff: 3
Budget: $25,000–$100,000

Bhutan

People's Forum for Human Rights

RESEARCH
EDUCATION

The People's Forum for Human Rights Bhutan (PFHRB) was established in exile in order to advocate for the recognition of human rights in the state of Bhutan. The Forum was founded by a refugee who was forced to flee Bhutan after protesting against the lack of freedom of the Hindi Nepali ethnic group in South Bhutan and Sharchops in the East. The PFHRB's mission is to document human rights violations committed by the Bhutanese government, to report on the condition of prisoners, to develop an international campaign for the release of all political prisoners, and to create awareness of the UN Universal Declaration of Human Rights in the Bhutanese community.

Anarmani 4
Birtamod
Jhapa
Nepal

Tel: +977 (2) 340 824
rizal_pfhrb@jhapa.info.com.np

Contact: D.P. Kafley, General Secretary
Number of staff: 3
Publications: Weekly update on the Bhutanese Refugee Joint Verification Process, together with the Bhutanese Refugee Representative Repatriation Committee; Country report on Bhutan.

Bhutan

Society for Human Rights and Education in Bhutan

EDUCATION
ADVOCACY

The Society for Human Rights and Education in Bhutan (SURE-Bhutan) is a Nepal-based organization for Bhutanese refugees presently in Nepal and India. SURE-Bhutan wants to improve the human rights situation in Bhutan. The Society also seeks to make it possible for Bhutanese refugees to return to Bhutan without problems. SURE-Bhutan's main activities are lobbying, education, training, early warning, and publishing.

Jawalakhel
P.O. Box 8975
EPC 1502
Kathmandu
Nepal

Contact: Narayan Katel, Director

Number of staff: 5

Budget: $25,000–$100,000

Tel: +977 (1) 153 0312
sure_bht@col.com.np

Nepal, Bangladesh, Pakistan, Bhutan, India, Sri Lanka

RESEARCH
EDUCATION
ADVOCACY

South Asia Forum for Human Rights

Human rights, peace, and democracy are the main areas of concern of the South Asia Forum for Human Rights. SAFHR, set up in 1990, is a regional public forum for the promotion of respect for the universal values of human rights, the interdependence of human rights, and the indivisibility of human rights.

In the strife-torn region of South Asia, SAFHR is a human rights organization with "peace as value" as its cornerstone. It sees peace as a space for the enjoyment of the rights of all peoples. Peace is not simply the absence of war or the management of crisis but a fundamental value to be integrated into programs for realizing peoples' security—that is, security of food, shelter, health, and livelihood in a non-hegemonic democratic regional order.

SAFHR's programs address some of the core concerns of the human rights agenda—displacement of indigenous peoples and minorities, refugees and migrants, impunity, inter-state and intra-state conflicts, peace accords, militarization, and the strengthening of peace constituencies in civil society. The aim is to link these issues in a framework of human rights, peace, tolerance, governance, and democracy.

In the last few years, the orientation of SAFHR's programs has shifted toward peacebuilding and conflict prevention, for instance the Human Rights and Peace Studies Orientation Course and regional dialogues around Media in Conflict, Peace Audits of Accords and Peace Processes, and Strengthening Women Building Peace. More recently SAFHR has also become more directly engaged with capacity building in civil society for peace activism, and with promoting the democratization of peace processes through advocacy campaigns on Civil Society Peace Activism in Kashmir and Northeast India, and a Peoples Peace Assembly in Nepal.

SAFHR works through a network of 35 partners comprising civil society organizations that are committed to human rights and peace.

3/23 Shree Darbar Tole
Patan Dhoka
G.P.O. Box 12855
Lalitpur/Kathmandu
Nepal

Tel: +977 (1) 541 026
Fax: +977 (1) 527 852
south@safhr.org
www.safhr.org

Contact: Tapan K. Bose, Secretary-General

Number of staff: 5

Budget: $100,000–$500,000

Publications: Refugee Watch; Shrinking Space: Minority Rights in South Asia; Reporting Conflict: A Radical Critique of the Mass Media by Indian & Pakistani Journalists, SAFHR paper series 9, 2001; *Peace Audit Report 2: Peace Process in Sri Lanka,* SAFHR paper series 8, 2001; *Protection of Refugees in South Asia: Need for a Legal Framework,* SAFHR paper series 6, 2000; *Ten Week War in Kargil from the News Files,* SAFHR paper series 7, 1999; *Peace Process in Nagaland and Chittagong Hill Tracts,* SAFHR paper series 5, 1999; *Living on the Edge: Essays on the Chittagong Hill Tracts,* 1997; *States, Citizens and Outsiders: The Uprooted People of South Asia,* 1997.

South Asia

South Asia Human Development Forum Network

The South Asia Human Development Forum Network (SAHDNet) was created in 2000 to strengthen regional dialogue on human development among organizations, civil society, and donors in South Asia. The Forum originated with an idea of SAP Canada and is still taking form. Its priority is to provide a platform for policy advocates with the mandate of bringing national agendas together. Thus the focus lies on issues related to government policies and the SAARC agenda. The Forum has founded national focal points in five South Asian countries. Those national offices have committed themselves to action, including in the areas of conflict, peace and justice, and democracy.

Regional secretariat at SAP Nepal
Babar Mahal
P.O. Box 3827
Kathmandu
Nepal

Tel:+977 (1) 223 230/258 782
Fax: +977 (1) 241 338
hdfnet@bellanet.org
www.hdfnet.org

Contact: Rohit Kumar Nepali, Executive Director SAP Nepal

Publications: Report of the South Asia Human Development Forum Kathmandu Meeting, April 2000; *Report of the First Meeting of Focal Points, South Asia Human Development Forum Network,* May 2001.

Nepal

South Asia Partnership—Nepal

The South Asia Partnership-Nepal (SAP—Nepal) was set up with Canadian support to strengthen the grassroots NGOs in Nepal. SAP—Nepal is a Nepalese NGO, operating through three regional offices, covering 62 of the 75 districts of Nepal. This way, SAP—Nepal provides support services to grassroots organizations in, for example, information, communications, and human resource development. An important current concern is with the Maoist insurgency in part of Nepal. SAP has organized a series of workshops in 25 districts about this problem, culminating in a two-day workshop in Kathmandu called Peace and Governance: People's Cry for Peace.

Babar Mahal
P.O. Box 3827
Kathmandu
Nepal

Tel: +977 (1) 223 230/258 782
Fax: +977 (1) 241 338
sap@ngdo.wlink.com.np
www.sapnepal.org

Contact: Rohit Kumar Nepali, Director

Number of staff: 65

Publications: A Civil Society Perspective for Good Governance in Nepal, workshop report in English and Nepalese; *Role of NGOs,* workshop report in English and Nepalese; *Management of People Based Development Training,* training manual; *NGOs Directory.*

South Asia

South Asian Association for Regional Cooperation

RESEARCH
ACTION

The South Asian Association for Regional Cooperation (SAARC) is an inter-governmental platform of Bangladesh, Bhutan, India, Maldives, Nepal, Pakistan, and Sri Lanka. From its establishment in 1985 through the early 1990s, its activities focused on conflict prevention, addressing poverty, human rights, and disadvantaged women. Today SAARC has limited activities, mainly on the economic level. Therefore it offers no direct solutions to regional conflicts and disputes. When a tense situation frustrates formal bilateral negotiations, the Association provides unofficial occasions for disputing countries to re-start talks. With changing international circumstances, it could assume a role in conflict prevention.

SAARC Secretariat
P.O. Box 4222
Kathmandu
Nepal

Contact: Nihal Rodrigo, Secretary-General
Publications: SAARC NEWS, newsletter.

Tel: +977 (1) 221 794/785
Fax: +977 (1) 227 033/223 991
saarc@saarc-sec.org
www.saarc-sec.org

South Asia

South Asian Institute for Peace Studies

EDUCATION

The South Asian Institute for Peace Studies (SAIPS), a new institute on peace studies in South Asia, held its first course in September 2001. The founders see a need for an action-oriented movement to promote peaceful communities, an equitable social system, and respect for life in the region. This new facility will carry out advanced training on peace and development studies and conflict management; it will establish a library and study center to promote information flow among peace organizations; and organize research and seminars. The board is also tasked with advocacy in the form of meetings and discussions among and between mid-level leadership, high-level leadership, officials, NGOs,and those in combat.

P.O. Box 5824
Kathmandu
Nepal

Contact: Kiran Basnet, Executive Director

Tel: +977 (1) 632 026/632 054
Fax: +977 (1) 242 390
saips@enet.com.np

Europe, Global

European Centre
for Conflict Prevention

RESEARCH
ADVOCACY

The European Centre for Conflict Prevention (ECCP) is an independent NGO based in the Netherlands. Its mission is to contribute to prevention and resolution of violent conflicts in the world. The Centre acts as the secretariat of the European Platform for Conflict Prevention and Transformation and initiates, coordinates, and implements the activities of the Platform. The Platform is an open network of about 170 organizations in Europe, the United States, Africa, and Asia working in the field of conflict prevention and peacebuilding. In addition, the Centre has specific networking and awareness-raising objectives focused on the Netherlands.

As an information clearinghouse, the Centre maintains one of the most comprehensive websites, with information available regarding organizations and activities in the field of conflict prevention. The ECCP's information center holds a large collection of material produced by other organizations, mainly NGOs, involved in the field.

The Searching for Peace Program, part of the clearinghouse function, is aimed at analyzing conflict prevention efforts in the main violent conflicts of the world. The results are published in a series of books as well as on the organization's website. A directory on the main local and international NGOs working in the field of conflict prevention and peacebuilding is included.

In line with ECCP's aim of raising awareness of the importance and possibilities of conflict prevention, People Building Peace is an ongoing project aimed at collecting and publishing inspiring stories of conflict prevention and peacebuilding, with special attention to the civil society. Media & Peacebuilding is a project aimed at developing an operational framework for peacebuilding activities of the media.

Another project, Lesson Learned in Peacebuilding, is an attempt to capture the failures and successes of conflict prevention and peacebuilding activities. The aim is not only to collect these but also to disseminate them in a way that other organizations and actors involved in violent and non-violent situations could learn about these lessons so in future failures could be less and successes could be prolonged.

P.O. Box 14069
3508 SC Utrecht
The Netherlands

Tel: +31 (30) 242 7776
Fax: +31 (30) 236 9268
info@conflict-prevention.net
www.conflict-prevention.net

Contact: Paul van Tongeren, Executive Director

Number of staff: 10

Budget: $100,000–$500,000

Publications: Conflict Prevention Newsletter, quarterly newsletter; *Searching for Peace in Europe & Eurasia: An Overview of Conflict Prevention and Peacebuilding Activities,* 2002; *Searching for Peace in Southeast & East Asia: An Overview of Conflict Prevention and Peacebuilding Activities,* forthcoming; *Towards Better Peacebuilding Practice,* 2002; *People Building Peace: 35 Inspiring Stories from Around the World,* 1999.

South Asia, Central America, Sub-Sahara Africa

Netherlands Institute of International Relations "Clingendael"

RESEARCH
EDUCATION
ADVOCACY

The overall objective of the Clingendael Institute is to promote a better understanding of international affairs among politicians, academics, civil servants and diplomats, the media, and the public at large. The Clingendael Conflict Research Unit (CRU) is part of Clingendael's research department and focuses on the study of intrastate conflict and conflict management, especially in the developing world. The CRU focuses in particular on the current gap between academic research and policy at a time when efforts to prevent and resolve violent conflicts are demanding new conceptual and analytical frameworks. The goal of CRU research is to develop innovative perspectives and policy approaches to intrastate conflict.

Clingendael 7
P.O. Box 93080
2509 AB The Hague
The Netherlands

Tel: +31 (70) 324 5384
Fax: +31 (70) 374 6667
tbouta@clingendael.nl
www.clingendael.nl/cru/

Contact: Georg E. Frerks, Head of Conflict Research Unit

Number of staff: 5

Budget: > $1,000,000

Publications: The Netherlands and Afghanistan: Dutch Policies and Interventions Regarding the Civil War in Afghanistan, 2000; The Netherlands and Sri Lanka: Dutch Policies and Interventions with Regard to the Conflict in Sri Lanka, 2000.

OSCE participating states

Office of the OSCE High Commissioner on National Minorities

RESEARCH
ACTION
ADVOCACY

The Office of the OSCE High Commissioner on National Minorities has been established to identify and seek early resolution of ethnic tensions that might endanger peace, stability, or friendly relations between the participating states of the Organization for Security and Co-operation in Europe (OSCE). Operating independently from all parties involved, the High Commissioner is empowered to conduct on-site missions and engage in preventative diplomacy at the earliest stage of tension. In addition to seeking first-hand information, the High Commissioner aims to promote dialogue, confidence, and cooperation. He has been involved in minority issues in OSCE participating states such as Kazakhstan and Kyrgyzstan.

P.O. Box 20062
2500 EB The Hague
The Netherlands

Tel: +31 (70) 312 5500
Fax: +31 (70) 363 5910
hcnm@hcnm.org
www.osce.org/hcnm

Contact: Walter Kemp, Senior Adviser

Publications: The Lund Recommendations on the Effective Participation of National Minorities in Public Life, 1999; The Hague Recommendations Regarding the Education Rights of National Minorities in Public Life, 1999; The Role of the High Commissioner on National Minorities in OSCE Conflict Prevention: An Introduction, 1997

Bangladesh

Organising Committee
Chittagong Hill Tracts Campaign

RESEARCH
ADVOCACY

The Organising Committee Chittagong Hill Tracts Campaign is a non-profit organization that seeks to mobilize international support for the right to self-determination of the indigenous Jumma peoples of the Chittagong Hill Tracts. The Committee aims to expose human rights violations and the violations of democratic rights of the Jumma peoples. The conflict prevention activities of the organization consist mainly of keeping in contact with the various groups and organizing conferences and workshops. The organization's main activities are fact-finding, lobbying, monitoring, publishing, and research. The Organizing Committee Chittagong Hill Tracts works in close cooperation with the International Work Group for Indigenous Affairs (IWGIA) in Copenhagen (see separate entry.)

P.O. Box 11699
1001 GR Amsterdam
The Netherlands

Tel: +31 (20) 6629 953
Fax: +31 (20) 6645 584
occhtc@xs4all.nl

Contact: Jenneke Arens
Number of staff: Volunteers
Budget: < $25,000

Global

Unrepresented Nations
and Peoples Organisation

EDUCATION
ACTION
ADVOCACY

One of the aims of the Unrepresented Nations and Peoples Organisation (UNPO) is to assist its 51 member nations, peoples, and minorities in preventing violent conflicts, or in resolving them through negotiations and political means. Through its Conflict Prevention Programme, UNPO provides training in diplomacy and conflict resolution, professional services, and advice relevant to these purposes. UNPO also encourages and facilitates dialogue between potential adversaries and carries out behind-the-scenes diplomacy.

P.O. Box 85878
2508 CN The Hague
The Netherlands

Tel: +31 (70) 360 3318
Fax: +31 (70) 360 3346
unponl@unpo.org
www.unpo.org

Contact: Cathy Shin, Conflict Prevention Programme Coordinator
Number of staff: 16 at HQ
Budget: $100,000–$300,000
Publications: UNPO News, quarterly newsletter; *Nonviolence and Conflict: Conditions for Effective Peaceful Change,* 1998; *UNPO Monitor of the United Nations Working Group on Indigenous Populations,* 1997.

Afghanistan

Afghan Development Association

ACTION

The Afghan Development Association (ADA) carries out multi-sectoral rehabilitation, development, and emergency programs in Afghanistan. The programs aim to create self-reliance and self-sufficiency for individuals and local communities. By improving socioeconomic conditions the Afghan Development Association wants to eradicate poverty in Afghanistan. The ADA also intends to fight all kinds of discrimination and to restore civil rights. The Human Resource Development Department conducts conflict management workshops for ADA staff as well as for the community. The ADA's programs are designed to help bring rival groups together by introducing projects that are beneficial to them.

House 17-F/A-1,
  Khusal Khan Khattak Road
U.P.O Box 922
University Town
Peshawar 922
Pakistan

Tel: +92 (91) 845 212/845 312
Fax: +92 (91) 45 296
afgdevas@brain.net.pk
www.pcpafg.org/Organizations/ADA/

Contact: Abdul Razique Samadi, Managing Director
Number of staff: 458 (total)
Budget: > $1,000,000

Afghanistan, Pakistan

Afghan NGO's Coordination Bureau

EDUCATION
ACTION

The Afghan NGO's Coordination Bureau (ANCB) is a non-political forum consisting of 140 Afghan member NGOs. Serving the Afghan community both in Afghanistan and Pakistan, it coordinates and facilitates humanitarian and development activities. One special program is dedicated to raising national consensus and to alleviating tension and crises throughout Afghanistan. The specialists involved are scholars, intellectuals, social figures, and political and religious leaders.

25 Chinar Road
University Town
U.P.O. Box 1041
Peshawar
Pakistan

Tel:+92 (91) 44 536
Fax: +92 (91) 43 476
ancb@pes.comsats.net.pk or
mail@ancb.pwr.sdnpk.undp.org

Contact: Mohammad Bashir Barekzai, Director
Number of staff: 22
Publications: Coordination (Hamahangi), newsletter; *Paiwastoon,* magazine in national languages; report of preparatory workshop for conducting peace seminar in Kabul.

Afghanistan

Agency Coordinating Body for Afghan Relief

RESEARCH

The Agency Coordinating Body for Afghan Relief (ACBAR) works as a contact channel of 154 Afghan and international NGOs, varying from health agencies to a "mine-dog" organization. Aiming to maximize the benefits of available resources for the Afghan people, the agency coordinates and assists their work. One important activity is to advocate on behalf of ACBAR members to the Pakistani and Afghan authorities. Another is organizing subcommittees on subjects, such as agriculture and women's affairs, on which UN agencies have participated. In the field of conflict prevention there are plans to establish a framework for conflict prevention training within the aid community.

2 Rehman Baba Road
U. P.O. Box 1084
Peshawar
Pakistan

Publications: Annual Directory of Humanitarian Agencies Working for Afghans.

Tel: +92 (91) 40839/44392/45316/45247
Fax: +92 (91) 840 471
acbaar@radio.psh.brain.net.pk
www.pcpafg.org/Organizations/acbar/

Pakistan, South Asia

Christian Study Centre

RESEARCH
EDUCATION
ACTION
ADVOCACY

The Christian Study Centre (CSC) is an ecumenical research center that helps the church in Pakistan to reflect its own position. The Centre also carries out research and education in the area of Islamization, its impact on the position of women and minorities, and Christian-Muslim relations. A conflict prevention element is the promotion of interfaith harmony and dialogue by means of training grassroots youth from different religions and supporting NGOs in carrying out interfaith dialogue activities. The CSC publishes books, articles, and a quarterly theological journal. It manages an extended research library and documentation service on the subjects of its concern.

126-B Murree Road
P.O. Box 529
Rawalpindi 4600
Pakistan

Tel: +92 (51) 556 7412/556 8567
Fax: +92 (51) 558 4594/558 6617
csc@shoa.net
cscpak@isb.comsats.net.pk

Contact: Mehboob Sada, Staff Member; Haroon Nasir, Research Assistant/Library Coordinator
Number of staff: 16
Budget: $25,000–$100,000
Publications: Al-Mushir, quarterly journal; *Laho ka rang aik hai* (The Colour of Blood is One): *Stories of Joyful Coexistence;* English-Urdu Dictionary of Christian Terminology.

Afghanistan

Co-operation Center for Afghanistan

EDUCATION
ACTION

Promoting and protecting human rights and alleviating poverty among the Afghan people are the core objectives of the Co-operation Center for Afghanistan (CCA). Since its foundation in 1990, the CCA has been educating the public on human rights. Its human rights activities include awareness raising, education and training, and human rights monitoring. In 2000 the CCA held a seminar on violence and violence eradication in Afghanistan. Held in Peshawar, the seminar participants called upon warring sides in Afghanistan to choose nonviolent means of solving their disputes.

4, P/1, Phase IV,
  Main Road Opposite PDA
Hayat Abad
G.P.O. Box 1378
Peshawar
Pakistan

Tel/fax: +92 (91) 816 386/815 647
hussaini@pes.comsats.net.pk
www.ccamata.com

Contact: Sarwar Hussaini, Executive Director

Number of staff: 70

Publications: CCA Newsletter, in English; Taavon, bimonthly journal in Dari and Pashtu languages; *Sadaf,* quarterly journal for women in Dari and Pashtu languages.

Afghanistan, Pakistan

Co-operation for Peace and Unity

RESEARCH
EDUCATION
ADVOCACY

The Co-operation for Peace and Unity (CPAU) is a network of Afghan individuals dedicated to the building of peace in Afghanistan. Founded in 1996, the CPAU aims to promote knowledge and awareness of peace, social justice, and human rights. The CPAU organizes conflict prevention training programs called Working with Conflict and Do No Harm.

The CPAU has two strategic aims. Firstly, to promote peacebuilding and social justice through strengthening the role of the aid community, civil society organizations, and the public sector. The CPAU supports the adoption of Do No Harm as a guiding principle by the aid community. Secondly, to develop and strengthen the human resources necessary for development and peacebuilding.

The CPAU's training courses, Working with Conflict and Do No Harm, focus on the processes by which conflict develops into violence. Training programs are attended by groups ranging from aid workers, community leaders, and schoolteachers to field staff and management of aid organizations. The CPAU stresses that its main intention is grassroots education aimed at building an inclusive civil society in Afghanistan.

23, Chinar Road
University Town
Peshawar NWFP 2500
Pakistan

Tel: +92 (91) 40 436
Fax: +92 (91) 840 471 (Attn: CPAU)
afahim@brain.net.pk or
sulnad@yahoo.com

Contact: Ahmad Fahim Hakim, Programme Coordinator; Muhammad Suleman, Management Coordinator

Number of staff: 12 resource persons

Budget: $25,000–$100,000

Publications: The Secret of Communication; Peace from the Islamic Perspective; poster on fire analogy and similarities between fire and conflict.

Pakistan, South Asia

Foundation for Research on International Environment, National Development and Security

RESEARCH

Friends, as the Foundation is commonly called, is a non-partisan research organization that aims to be apolitical. Research topics cover sustainable development and the security of Pakistan, but also on regional and global issues. Subjects include the culture of dialogue and tolerance, human rights, nuclear disarmament, and conventional arms control, good governance, and security to ensure national progress. The Foundation also undertakes projects with international organizations like UNESCO and think tank organizations of countries such as Iran, China, Germany, Bangladesh, and the Central Asian Republics.

88, Race Court Road, Street 3
Rawalpindi Cantt.
Pakistan
_____

Tel: +92 (51) 556 3309/551 0761
Fax: +92 (51) 556 4244
fr786pak@isb.comsats.net.pk
www.friends.org.pk

Contact: S.M. Rahman, Secretary General
Number of staff: 32
Budget: $25,000–$100,000

Publications: National Development and Security, quarterly journal; *FRIENDS Perspective,* monthly publication in English and Urdu; *The Culture of Peace in Central South Asia SAARC and the New Paradigm of Security.*

Pakistan

ACTION
ADVOCACY

Human Rights Commission of Pakistan

Since its founding in 1986, the Human Rights Commission of Pakistan (HRCP) has developed to become a broad-spectrum, countrywide human rights body. The HRCP aims to play a leading role in Pakistan as an independent voice in the struggle for human rights and democratic development of Pakistan. This non-profit, non-governmental organization works for the implementation of the Universal Declaration of Human Rights, it promotes studies in the field of human rights and tries to mobilize public opinion. The HRCP monitors the behavior of the police, visits refugee camps, and is setting up an electoral monitoring database.

Aiwan-i-Jahmoor
107 Tipu Block
New Garden Towm
Lahore 54600
Pakistan
_____

Tel: +92 (42) 583 8341/586
4994/588 3579
Fax: +92 (42) 588 3582
info@hrcp.cjb.net

Contact: I.A. Rehman, Director

Publications: State of Human Rights in Pakistan, annual report in English and Urdu; HRCP quarterly newsletter; *Jehd-i-Haq,* monthly human rights investigations, in Urdu.

South Asia, Iran, Afghanistan, China, Central Asia

RESEARCH
ADVOCACY

Institute of Regional Studies

"Know thy neighbor" is the theme of the Institute of Regional Studies, an independent, non-profit scholarly research center devoted to the objective study of the region in which Pakistan is situated. The Institute aims at broadening the mental horizon of the peoples inhabiting the region and wants to promote awareness of each other's problems and aspirations. The research organization covers a wide spectrum of research in foreign and internal affairs, economy, technology and industry, and sociocultural and security related issues. The Institute is in touch with similar research institutes the world over and exchanges material.

NAFDEC Complex 56-F,
  Blue Area, F6/1
Nazimuddin Road
Islamabad 44000
Pakistan

Tel: +92 (51) 920 3974
Fax: +92 (51) 920 4055
aziz@irspak.isb.sdnpk.org
www.irs.org.pk

Contact: Ambassador Khalid Mehmood,
Director

Number of staff: 7

Publications: Regional Studies, quarterly journal; *Rebuilding Sino-Indian Relations (1988–2000): Rocky Path, Uncertain Destination, 2000; Pakistan and Regional Economic Cooperation in SAARC—ECO.*

Afghanistan

ACTION

Islamic Coordination Council

In 1985 several Muslim NGOs from different countries came together to establish a platform for Islamic NGOs that was named the Islamic Coordination Council (ICC). The goal of the ICC was to help Afghan refugees, both outside Afghanistan and those internally displaced. The Council aimed to establish relationships with the governments of Pakistan and Afghanistan, the specialized UN agencies, and Western NGOs; to approach Muslim donors for fund raising; and to provide and facilitate an information-sharing system. The ICC coordinates various activities of its members to avoid overlapping.

Flat #409, 4th Floor
Gul Haji Plaza
Jamrud Road
University Town
Peshawar
Pakistan

Tel: +93 (91) 45342

Contact: Ahmad Elsanousi

Pakistan

Justice and Peace Commission

The Justice and Peace Commission is a Christian church-based organization that holds prayer services, seminars, workshops, and speech contests to help build peace and harmony to Pakistan society. The Commission's main conflict-prevention program is called Social Justice Sunday and is organized for NGOs, teachers, religious leaders, local communities, and women. Other activities of this non-governmental, non-profit organization are human rights promotion, lobbying, training, fact finding, and research. A recent publication deals with Pakistan minorities and their struggle for rights.

Nagshband Colony
G.P.O. Box 175
Multan 60000
Pakistan

Tel:+92 (61) 220 482
Fax: +92 (61) 220 580
nidda@brain.net.pk

Contact: Sr. Norris Nawab PBVM

Number of staff: 14

Budget: $25,000–$100,000

Publications: JP bi-annual newsletter; media watch service (monthly).

Pakistan, South Asia

National Commission for Justice and Peace

The National Commission for Justice and Peace (NCJP), a church-based human rights body, aims to raise human rights awareness, to study questions of human rights relating to the teaching of the church, to publish, and to actively respond to human rights issues through fact finding, monitoring, and legal intervention. One program of the NJCP provides training for volunteers at the grassroots level in fact finding and reporting human rights violations. The NJCP encourages people to respond to injustice through the Legal Aid Program and prepares its own annual Human Rights Monitor. The Commission has working relations with local NGOs, and Asian human rights and religious organizations.

E-64/A St. No.8
Officers Colony, Walton Road
Lahore
Pakistan

Tel: +92 (42) 666 8692
Fax: +92 (42) 665 5549
peterjac@shoa.net

Contact: Peter Jacob, Executive Secretary

Number of staff: 14

Budget: $25,000–$100,000

Publications: The Mirror, quarterly newsletter; Human Rights Monitor 2000, a report on the religious minorities in Pakistan.

Pakistan, India

Pakistan-India People Forum
for Peace and Democracy

RESEARCH
EDUCATION
ADVOCACY

The Pakistan-India People Forum for Peace and Democracy is based in India. The key issue for this NGO network organization is the problematic relationship between the countries of Pakistan and India. Consequently the situation in Kashmir and Jammu is another vital theme.

The Forum has organized meetings between Pakistani and Indian citizens, in India, and in Pakistan since 1995. The goal of these symbolic meetings is to demonstrate that, before the arrival of Islam in South-Asia, the two countries shared a common past. The Forum for Peace and Democracy claims religion is not the most important divide between the two nations but that the core of the problem lies in the lack of democratic rights of the common people.

The Forum's activities address conflict prevention and resolution through mediation, policy and advocacy work, research, citizen's diplomacy, early warning, education, lobbying and publishing conferences and workshops. It does not have a department that is exclusively responsible for conflict prevention but the Committee on Kashmir has conflict prevention and resolution as its main responsibility.

The Forum lobbies the governments of India and Pakistan concerning nuclear weapons emphasizing that a nuclear war between India and Pakistan will never be a rational solution. The Forum for Peace and Democracy asks for a move towards regional disarmament.

The continuing strife in Kashmir is another focal point of the Forum for Peace and Democracy. The Forum asks the Indian government to stop the aggressive activities of the Indian army in Kashmir and at the same time demands that the Pakistan government stop helping the militant forces in Kashmir.

Pakistan Chapter
4K Gulbarg 2
Lahore
Pakistan

Indian Chapter
B-14 (second floor) Gulmohar Park
New Delhi 110 049
India

Tel: +91 (11) 651 4847/656 1743
Fax: +91 (11) 651 1504
admin@del3.vsnl.net.in

Contact: Sushil Khanna, General Secretary, Indian Chapter
Number of staff: Voluntary
Budget: < $25,000

Pakistan

Pakistan Peace Coalition

ACTION
ADVOCACY

The Pakistan Peace Coalition (PPC) is a joint forum of the Action Committee Against the Arms Race, the Joint Action Committee for People's Rights, and the Citizen's Peace Committee. The forum was set up in the aftermath of the nuclear tests by India and Pakistan when peace groups felt the need for a collective struggle to mobilize public opinion against nuclear weapons. The PPC wants to bring pressure upon the Pakistani state to reduce defense spending and at the same time increase public access to information about peacebuilding and related issues.

141-D (Annexe), Block 2, PECHS
Karachi 75400
Pakistan

Contact: B.M. Kutty, Convener

Tel: +92 (21) 455 2170/455 7009
Fax: +92 (21) 454 8115
ppc@cyber.net.pk
www.mnet.fr/aiindex/PPC

Asia

Program on Peace Studies & Conflict Resolution

RESEARCH
EDUCATION

The initiators of this program launched in 2000—aimed to establish a full program of peace studies, confidence-building measures (CBM), and conflict resolution under the University of Karachi. The objectives for the future are to train, network and to exchange ideas with similar researchers, to publish, and to promote peace studies in local languages. Another aim is to initiate discussions. At this early stage two projects have been carried out, the most recent of which involves researching CBM in the post-nuclear South Asia.

Department of International Relations
University of Karachi
University Road
Karachi 75270
Pakistan

Tel: +92 (21) 924 313-7 Ext 2274
Fax: +92 (21) 497 2526
info@ppscr.org
www.ppscr.org/

Contact: Moonis Ahmar, Program Director

Publications: The Arab-Israeli Process: Lessons for India and Pakistan, 2001; *The Challenge of Confidence Building in South Asia,* 2001; *The CTBT Controversy: Different Perceptions,* 2000.

Afghanistan

Research and Advisory Council of Afghanistan

RESEARCH
EDUCATION
ACTION

The Research and Advisory Council of Afghanistan (RACA) is an independent training and consulting organization whose priority is raising awareness of conflict issues among Afghan refugees in Pakistan. Its main activity is a Conflict Transformation Program that provides workshops and training courses. This program aims to develop peacebuilding capacities, to empower women to take part in the peace process, and to promote nonviolent approaches in Afghan society. The participants are composed of refugees, teachers, NGO workers, and students. RACA has working relationships with the Afghan refugee schools and university located in Peshawar. It distributes training material, books, journals, and the (free) *Salaam Journal.*

P.O. Box 706
University Town
Peshawar
Pakistan

Tel: +92 (91) 823 627
pcsiua@psh.brain.net.pk

Contact: M. Naseerudin Akhunzada, Director
Number of staff: 12
Budget: $25,000–$100,000
Publications: SALAAM, quarterly journal.

Afghanistan

Revolutionary Association of the Women of Afghanistan

EDUCATION
ACTION

Established in Kabul, the Revolutionary Association of the Women of Afghanistan (RAWA) has been fighting for human rights and social justice in Afghanistan since 1977. From the outset RAWA has advocated democracy and secularism and has taken a principled anti-fundamentalist stand. RAWA's activities in Pakistan include data collection, education, and raising awareness of human rights issues in Afghanistan. The Association publishes and distributes *Payam-e-Zan* or "Women's Message," a tri-lingual magazine reporting human rights violations against women. Inside Afghanistan, RAWA's work consists mainly of support to female victims.

P.O. Box 374
Quetta
Pakistan

Tel:+92 (300) 855 1638
Fax: +1 (760) 281 9855 (USA)
rawa@rawa.org
www.rawa.org

Contact: Council of Leadership
Budget: < $25,000
Publications: Payam-e-Zan (Women's Message), tri-lingual magazine; *The Burst of the Islamic Government Bubble in Afghanistan,* in English.

Pakistan

South Asia Partnership—Pakistan

**EDUCATION
ACTION**

South Asia Partnership—Pakistan (SAP-PK) was founded by a group of leading Pakistani activists in 1987. SAP-PK's mission is to facilitate CBOs and groups working with the disadvantaged sections of society. The program Development Support Communications facilitates community partners and ethnic groups in understanding and dealing with problems, crises, and conflict at local, subregional, and national levels. Instruments for this conflict-prevention activity are the organization of dialogues, seminars, and forums. SAP-PK is part of a network of SAP organizations in Canada and five other South Asian countries.

Haseeb Memorial Trust Building
Nasirabad, Raiwind Road
Thokar Niza Beg
Lahore 53700
Pakistan

Tel: +92 (42) 542 6470-73
Fax: +92(42) 541 1637
sappk@syberwurx.com

Contact: Mohammed Tasheen, Executive Director

Number of staff: 62 (total), 7 (conflict prevention)

Budget: $100,000–$500,000

Publications: Gender Handbook, 1999; *Decentralization of State.*

Pakistan, South Asia

Sustainable Development Policy Institute

**RESEARCH
ADVOCACY**

The Sustainable Development Policy Institute (SDPI) is a non-government public interest think tank that provides advice to public, private, and voluntary organizations and undertakes policy-oriented research and advocacy. Though mainly involved in development and environment issues, the SDPI recently adopted peace and security as a separate area in the research program. It also carries out research on the experience of women in current conflicts and is developing a network of female researchers working on gender and peace in South Asia. The SDPI is part of several local, regional, and international networks, and for instance, operates within Pakistan on the secretariat of the Citizens' Peace Committee.

#3 UN Boulevard,
    Diplomatic Enclave 1, G-5
Islamabad 2342
Pakistan

Tel: +92 (51) 227 8134
Fax: +92 (51) 227 8135
main@sdpi.org
www.sdpi.org

Contact: Saba Gul Khattak, Deputy Director

Publications: SPDI Research and News Bulletin, bi-monthly bulletin; *Do IMF & World Bank Policies Work?* 1999; *Class, Conflict and Change: Profile of a Punjabi Village,* 2000.

Sri Lanka

AHIMSA—Centre for
Conflict Resolution & Peace

RESEARCH
EDUCATION

The AHIMSA organization is dedicated to promoting nonviolent conflict-resolution skills and attitudes among the Sri Lanka people. One of its major programs extends psycho-sociological support to the victims of violence and conflicts, together with the education departments of particular localities. Training, education, publishing, fact finding, and early warning are the prime activities of this non-governmental, non-profit network. The Centre works together with National Integration Program Unit under the Sri Lanka Ministry of National Integration and Ethnic Harmony.

36/8, Parakum Mawatha
Nawala Road
Nugegoda
Sri Lanka

Tel/fax: +94 (1) 856 526
ahimsa@sltnet.lk

Contact: Kassapa Diyabedanage and Monica Alfred, Program Coordinators

Number of staff: 5

Budget: < $25,000

Publications: Community Relations Development; Student Research Projects in Conflict Resolution and Peace; training materials.

Sri Lanka

Berghof Research Center for Constructive
Conflict Management—Sri Lanka Office

RESEARCH
EDUCATION
ACTION

The Berghof Research Center for Constructive Conflict Management aims to strengthen civilian capacities for conflict management. In July 2001 the German-based Center opened an office in Sri Lanka. Through educational and information sharing activities, the Sri Lanka Office aims to enhance capacities for constructive conflict management in Sri Lanka. The programs of the Office include the promotion and support for a post-graduate diploma course in Conflict Resolution and Peace Studies and the organization of the workshop Organizing Successful Interim Processes in Ethnopolitical Disputes: Lessons and Challenges.

53/2 Gregory Road
Colombo 7
Sri Lanka

Tel: +94 (1) 669 710/1
Fax: +94 (1) 669 712
berghof@sltnet.lk or
info@berghof-center.org
www.berghof-center.org

Contact: Norbert Ropers, Director

Number of staff: 7

Publications: Berghof Handbook for Conflict Transformation, 2002

Sri Lanka, South Asia

Center for Community Dialogue & Communication (PRASANNI)

RESEARCH
EDUCATION
ACTION
ADVOCACY

The program of the Center for Community Dialogue & Communication (PRASANNI) are entirely based on conflict resolution. With the help of citizens diplomacy, lobbying, training, research, and networking the Center seeks to settle the ethnic-based conflict in Sri Lanka. Another conflict theme is the promotion of the role of women to develop a culture of peace and equality. The organization is divided into district-based units, a women's unit, and a research unit. PRASANNI is a non-profit organization whose partners include the Inter-Religious Peace Foundation, Life and Peace (Sweden), and Accord (South Africa).

P.O. Box 66
Nugegoda
Sri Lanka

Tel: +94 (75) 522 415
Fax: +94 (1) 856 400
prasanni@eureka.lk

Contact: Padmi Liyanage, Director
Number of staff: 10 (fulltime), 7 (volunteers)
Budget: $100,000–$500,000

Publications: Resource pack on conflict resolution; *Citizens' Resolution for Constitutional Change; Globalisation and Issues of Peace.*

Sri Lanka

Centre for Development Alternatives

RESEARCH
EDUCATION
ADVOCACY

The aim of the Centre for Development Alternatives is to function as a social action forum for youth, students, and politicians. The Centre intervenes, short term and long term, on issues creating or promoting conflicts in order to prevent or to resolve them. The networking organization (both regional and internationally) runs a legal assistance program for poor people in order to restore their rights. The Centre also carries out coexistence work to safeguard the diversified identities and to strengthen the multi-ethnic and multi-religious nature of Sri Lankan society. Cooperation with other organizations is based on particular issues.

582/10, Peradeniya Road
Kandy 2000
Sri Lanka

Tel: +94 (8) 232 687/236 082
Fax: +94 (8) 236 082
cdaright@ids.lk

Contact: Sathivale Balakrishnan, Executive Director
Number of staff: 18
Budget: $25,000–$100,000

Sri Lanka

Centre for Policy Alternatives

The Centre was formed in the belief that there is an urgent need to strengthen institution- and capacity-building for good governance and conflict resolution in Sri Lanka and that non-partisan civil society groups have an important and constructive contribution to make to this process.

The primary role envisaged for the CPA in the field of public policy is one of pro-active intervention aimed at the dissemination and advocacy of policies of non-violent conflict resolution and democratic governance. Accordingly, the work of the Centre involves a major research component. Other activities are policy advice, publishing, citizen's diplomacy, lobbying, and data collecting. The Centre for Policy Alternatives also organizes conferences and workshops.

The Centre's main conflict prevention activity is a program called Peace Monitor. With this program the Centre aims to identify developments that are conducive as well as inimical to peacemaking in Sri Lanka. The program is focused on the maintenance of a database and publishing and is meant for civil society, politicians, the international community, peace activists, and policymakers.

The Conflict and Peace Analyses Programme was set up to develop and strengthen the CPA's engagement in the field of conflict resolution. The focus is the protracted ethnic conflict in Sri Lanka, its genesis, manifestations, present trends, and future trajectory. The program also seeks to intervene in processes relating to national reconciliation, national reconstruction, and the restitution of peace with justice in Sri Lanka.

The Centre for Policy Alternatives is part of the Centre for Monitoring Election Violence (CMEV), and is associated with the Free Media Movement (FFM) and the Coalition Against Political Violence. CMEV has monitored the incidence of election-related violence since the 1997 local government elections.

32/2 Flower Road
Colombo 7
Sri Lanka

Tel: + 94 (1) 565 304/6
Fax: +94 (74) 714 460
cpa@sri.lanka.net
www.cpalanka.org

Contact: Ketheshwaran Loganathan, Coordinator
Conflict & Peace Analysis Unit

Number of staff: 5

Budget: $25,000–$100,000

Publications: Media Monitor, newsletter; *Peace Monitor,* newsletter; Peace Analysis (Sama Vimarshi) series; *Ethnic Conflict and the Responsibility of Civil Society; The Peace Process and the Responsibility of the Minority Parties.*

Sri Lanka

Centre for Policy Research and Analysis

RESEARCH

The University of Colombo established the Centre for Policy Research and Analysis (CEPRA) in the Faculty of Law, with the objective of creating an institutional framework to facilitate research, the exchange of ideas, and advisory services in the areas of constitutional and legislative reform and conflict management and resolution. The Centre believes in close interaction between academic, professional and policymaking communities to strengthen the democratic process. In collaboration with International Alert, CEPRA conducts a postgraduate degree course on conflict management and resolution. CEPRA staff are also regular commentators in the national and international media.

University of Colombo
Colombo 03
Sri Lanka

Tel: +94 (1) 595 667
Fax: +94 (1) 7868 297/598 462
cepra@sri.lanka.net

Contact: Dr. Jayadeva and Rohan Edrisinha, Co-Directors

Publications: The People's Alliance Government and the Peace Process, 1996; *The CEPRA Oral History Transcripts,* 1996; *Swiss Federation: Lessons for Sri Lanka,* 1996.

Sri Lanka

Centre for Society and Religion

RESEARCH
EDUCATION
ACTION
ADVOCACY

The Centre for Society and Religion (CSR) works to encourage an alternative democratic society based on religious and cultural values. The Centre carries out conflict prevention programs, which facilitate encounters among rural groups with different ethnic backgrounds. The recent program, Tamil and Sinhala Youth—Building Bridges for Peace, combines awareness raising with practical exercises in communication and conflict management skills. Another equality program, People Living on the Plantations, offers Tamil plantation workers and Sinhala village people tools to work at more peaceful relations. The CRS is member of the Youth for Peace network. The Centre also maintains working relations with some European NGOs.

281, Deans Road
Colombo 10
Sri Lanka

Tel: +94 (1) 695 425/688
  690/677 233/789 089 (residence)
Fax: +94 (1) 682 064
obfirth@sltnet.lk
csrlibra@slt.lk

Contact: Oswald B. Firth, Director

Number of staff: Social Justice, monthly newsletter; *Women in the Face of Conflict,* in Sinhala; Articles on Sri Lanka's ethnic conflict, its causes and strategies for a sustainable peace.

Sri Lanka

RESEARCH

Consortium of Humanitarian Agencies

The Consortium of Humanitarian Agencies (CHA), an association of agencies working in areas affected by conflict, is concerned with improving the quality, effectiveness, professionalism, and transparency of its members. The CHA provides a forum for members to meet and interact with non-member stakeholders in conflict areas, facilitates strategic inter-agency initiatives, and also operates through the secretariat services of collective interest. In the field of conflict resolution the CHA is developing a framework for relief, reconciliation, and rehabilitation. Additional activities include a refugee studies program, symposia, and the establishment of humanitarian help desks with e-mail facilities in three districts of Sri Lanka.

No. 10, Kynsey Terrace
Colombo 8
Sri Lanka

Tel/fax: +94 (74) 610 943/4
cha_info@sri.lanka.net
www.humanitarian-srilanka.org

Contact: Jeevan Thiagarajah, Executive Director

Number of staff: 12

Publications: CHA Newsletter; yearbook; consortium directory of members/ observers; toolkit on the guiding principles on internal displacement.

Sri Lanka

RESEARCH
EDUCATION
ADVOCACY

INFORM

INFORM is a non-governmental human rights organization providing monitoring, documentation, and training services. Its primary mandate is advocacy to improve the human rights situation in the context of the ongoing ethnic conflict in Sri Lanka. To this end INFORM was actively involved in promoting constitutional reform, including an expanded chapter on fundamental rights, and in defending the human rights of civilians in the conflict zones. INFORM is also engaged in various networks that seek a negotiated political settlement to the conflict in Sri Lanka. Key activities are the formation of groups at community level, media releases, a monthly newsletter, and linking with national and regional networks.

5 Jayaratha Avenue
Colombo 5
Sri Lanka

Tel: +94 (1) 584 350/501 339
Fax: +94 (1) 580 721/584 350
     +94 (1) 591 314

Contact: Sunila Abeysekera, Executive Director

Number of staff: 10

Budget: $25,000–$100,000

Publications: Monthly newsletter.

South Asia

International Centre for Ethnic Studies

With areas of research ranging from domestic violence against women to the promotion of international peace, the International Centre for Ethnic Studies (ICES) is a multi-subject research organization. The non-profit, non-governmental Centre was established in 1982 and has a multi-ethnic staff reflecting its commitment to diversity and an international board of directors.

Intensive dialogues with political activists and thinkers in combination with detailed archival work has inspired the Centre to identify the four principal objectives that run as unifying themes throughout its work. These are: the advancement of human rights; engendering national cohesion; the promotion of international peace; and the creation of a more equitable development process.

ICES's work can be categorized into four areas: multiculturalism, structural arrangements, South Asian collaboration, and violence against women. These concerns have found expression in international projects involving the cooperation of scholars within Sri Lanka and abroad.

ICES has several programs of research aimed at promoting peace. Strengthening Democratic Governance in Conflict Torn Societies is a program carried out in collaboration with the Institute of Development Studies at the University of Sussex and the Sussex European Institute. It has also has held workshops on issues such as the Northern Ireland Agreement looking at how it is relevant to Sri Lanka.

The Centre's policy-oriented programs include Post-Settlement Peace Building in Sri Lanka, which reviews peace building failures in this country. ICES has also produced a report on the causes of conflict in developing societies which looks at individual country situations.

2 Kynsey Terrace
Colombo 08
Sri Lanka
_____

Tel: +94 (1) 679 745/685 085
Fax: +94 (1) 698 048
ices@icescolombo.org
www.icescolombo.org

Contact: Radhika Coomaraswamy, Director

Number of staff: 30

Budget: $100,000–$500,000

Publications: Nethra, quarterly journal; *Culture of Politics of Identity in Sri Lanka,* 1998; *Rediscovering a South Asian Community: Civil Society in Search of Its Future,* 1997; *Civil Society in Sri Lanka: A Symposium,* 1996.

Sri Lanka

Inter-Religious Peace Foundation

`EDUCATION`
`ACTION`

The Inter-Religious Peace Foundation (IRPF) draws together Buddhist, Christian, Hindu, and Islamic leaders in Sri Lanka. It seeks to offer an inter-religious platform from the lay to clergy level to address issues of peace, conflict, and human rights. One program of the Foundation conducts action research assessing the will of communities to start peacebuilding. Through consultations with representatives of various ethnic and religious organizations the program aims to mobilize grassroots groups and to support a peaceful dialogue. The goal is to encourage peace-minded people to forge mutual solidarity and to urge, in new alliances, the government to continue to solve the conflict politically.

Sri Isipathanaramaya
180/34 Grandpass Road
Colombo 14
Sri Lanka

Contact: Oswald B. Firth

Tel: +94 (1) 440 387
Fax: +94 (1) 446 672
obfirth@sltnet.lk
www.wcc-coe.org/wcc/what/interreligious

Sri Lanka

Marga Institute

`RESEARCH`
`EDUCATION`
`ADVOCACY`

The Sri Lanka Centre for Development Studies (Marga Institute) is a private non-profit center for development, research, and advocacy. The Institute intends to be a leader and coordinator of a network of NGOs and CBOs engaged in the prevention of conflict and violence arising from ethnic divisions and political rivalries in Sri Lanka. The Institute focuses on four areas: the history of ethnic conflict, the financial cost of war and recovery, the human cost of war, and the national campaign against political violence. The main conflict research program focuses on the underlying reasons for ethnic conflict.

93/10 Dutugamunu Street
Colombo – 06
Sri Lanka

Contact: Godfre Gunatilleke, Governor
Number of staff: 3
Budget: < $25,000

Tel:+94 (1) 828 544/828 545
Fax: +94 (1) 828 597
marga@sri.lanka.net
www.lanka.net/marga

Publications: Marga News, newsletter; *Marga Journal,* in Sinhala Tamil and English; *Reflections on Governance; The Impact of Labour Migration on Households: A Comparative Study in Seven Asian Countries.*

Sri Lanka

Movement for
Inter-racial Justice and Equality

RESEARCH
EDUCATION
ADVOCACY

The Movement for Inter-racial Justice and Equality (MIRJE) was founded in 1977 by a group of concerned individuals—academics, professionals, trade unionists, party activists, religious personnel, and community organizers in an attempt to foster harmony among ethnic communities. MIRJE believes in the founding of a federal state in which there is both regional autonomy and effective means of power sharing at the center. The voluntary Movement conducts programs on education, ideological construction, and networking. Important activities are fact-finding missions, the organization of festivals and campaigns, and the drafting of a federal constitution.

19/4, 1/1 Nawala Road
Nugegoda
Sri Lanka

Contact: Charles Abeysekara
Publications: YUKTHIYA, weekly newspaper; *Sarinihar,* fortnightly newspaper, in Tamil.

Tel/fax: +94 (1) 815 003/815 004
mirje@sri.lanka.net

Sri Lanka

National Peace Council of Sri Lanka

RESEARCH
EDUCATION
ACTION
ADVOCACY

The non-partisan peace organization National Peace Council of Sri Lanka (NPC) was founded in 1995. In the view of the NPC, the only way to end war in Sri Lanka is through political negotiations that include the opposition and that address the national aspirations of the Tamil people. The NPC is engaged in workshops and multimedia campaigns on issues related to the promotion of peace negotiations. The NPC also mobilizes people through large-scale peace events in cooperation with partner organizations. In addition the Council runs high-profile programs for politicians and opinion makers. For instance it has conducted workshops for parliamentarians coupled with an exposure visit to conflict situations abroad.

12/14 Purana Vihara Road
Colombo 6
Sri Lanka

Contact: Tyrol Ferdinands, General Secretary
Number of staff: 9
Publications: Sámá Yámaya, newsletter.

Tel: +94 (75) 818 344/819 064
Fax: +94 (75) 819 064
peace2@sri.lanka.net
www.peace-srilanka.org

Sri Lanka

ACTION

People's Peace Front

The People's Peace Front (PPF) seeks to raise a powerful peoples' voice advocating a negotiated conflict solution for the ethnic conflict. It has grown into a coalition of 107 peace, human rights, and other civil groups, varying from non-governmental organizations to small voluntary groups and peoples' organizations. So far the Front has been engaged such activities as massive poster and postcard campaigns and demonstrations. At crucial conflict moments the PPF has issued statements and letters, for instance on censorship and attacks aimed at groups or individuals. All activities of the Front are on a voluntary basis and are directed by collective leadership.

c/o National Peace Council
291/36A Havelock Gardens
Colombo 6
Sri Lanka

Contact: S.P. Nathan, Coordinator
Number of staff: 5

Tel: +94 (75) 529 696
Fax: +94 (75) 502 522
peace2@sri.lanka.net

South Asia

Regional Centre for Strategic Studies

RESEARCH
EDUCATION
ACTION
ADVOCACY

The Regional Centre for Strategic Studies (RCSS) is a non-profit and non-governmental organization for collaborative research, networking, and interaction on strategic and international issues pertaining to South Asia. Established in 1992, the Centre is a forum for studies, training, and multi-track dialogue and deliberation on issues of regional interest.

All activities of the RCSS are designed with a South Asia focus and usually involve experts from all South Asian countries. The Centre is envisaged as a forum for advancing the causes of cooperation, security, conflict resolution, confidence building, peace, and development in the countries of the South Asian region.

The RCSS serves its South Asian and international constituency by networking programs that promote interaction, communication, and exchange between institutions and individuals engaged in South Asian strategic studies. It also organizes regional workshops and seminars and sponsors and coordinates collaborative research. The Centre also disseminates output of their research through publications that include books, monographs, and a quarterly newsletter.

Another activity of the RCSS is the implementation of a project entitled the Regional International Affairs Program in Asia (RIAPA). The objective of the project is to assist interested funding organizations in developing new and innovative collaborative programming in the areas of international affairs, regional peace, security, and cooperation in Asia with a particular focus on non-traditional security issues.

2, Elibank Road
Colombo 5
Sri Lanka

Tel: +94 (1) 599 734-5
Fax: +94 (1) 599 993
edrcss@sri.lanka.net or
rcss@sri.lanka.net
www.rcss.org

Contact: Maj. Gen. (Ret.) Dipanker Banerjee
Number of staff: 8
Budget: $500,000–$1,000,000
Publications: RCSS newsletters and quarterly bulletin; RCSS Policy Studies, monograph series; *Directory of Individuals and Institutions Engaged in South Asian Strategic Studies*; *South Asia at Gun Point: Small Arms and Light Weapons Proliferation*, 2000; *Confidence Building Measures in South Asia*, 2000.

Sri Lanka

SAMASEVAYA

EDUCATION
ACTION
ADVOCACY

Under the slogan "Civil Society for Peace," Samasevaya organizes various projects such as peace education, the celebration of Human Rights Day, the peace rally Don't Wage War On My Behalf in the district of Anuradhapura, and the production of local radio programs to promote peace ideas. The main conflict prevention program of Samasevaya is called Mediation and focuses on people in conflict. It is set up in cooperation with the Sri Lankan Ministry of Justice. Samasevaya is a non-governmental, non-profit organization that works mainly in the fields of poverty alleviation, child development, election monitoring, and youth activities.

National Secretariat
Anuradhapura Road
Talawa 50230
Sri Lanka

Contact: Samson Jayasinghe, National Secretary

Number of staff: 10

Budget: < $25,000

Tel/fax: +94 (25) 76 266
afej@srilanka.net

Sri Lanka

Sewa Lanka Foundation

EDUCATION

The Sewa Lanka Foundation is a non-governmental, non-profit organization whose main goal is the integration of the affected communities in the north and east of Sri Lanka back into the main socioeconomic stream. The Foundation implements programs that are focused on all three ethnic groups, making sure that it provides ample space for different communities to interface and engage in reconciliation. The Relief Program fulfils the basic human requirements of displaced people, the Rehabilitation Program is aimed at rebuilding the economic and social infrastructure, and the Development program helps the people to become socioeconomically self-sustainable.

1D1, 128, 2nd Floor
High Level Road
Nugegoda
Sri Lanka

Contact: Lakshi Abeysekera, Director Special Projects Division

Number of staff: 30 (total), 6 (conflict prevention)

Budget: < $25,000

Tel: +94 (1) 821 018
Fax: +94 (1) 821 020
sewahq@sri.lanka.net
www.sewalanka.org

Central Asia, Caucasus

Central Asia and the Caucasus Information and Analytical Center

RESEARCH

Central Asia and the Caucasus Information and Analytical Center (IAC) is a private center engaged in research on a range of topics related to social and political development in Central Asia and the Caucasus. One area of study is inter-ethnic conflict, including strategies for early prevention and settlement. IAC publishes the results of its research in its periodical, Central Asia and the Caucasus, which is accessible online. The organization has branches in the countries of Central Asia and the Caucasus, and in the United States, Russia, United Kingdom, Germany, Israel, Turkey, Iran, and Ukraine.

Rödhakegränd 21
974 54 Luleå
Sweden

Tel/fax: +46 (920) 620 16
murad@communique.se or
murad@ca-c.org
www.ca-c.org

Contact: Murad Esenow, Director

Number of staff: 10

Budget: $100,000–$500,000

Publications: Central Asia and the Caucasus: Journal of Social and Political Studies, periodical in English and Russian.

Global

Department of Peace and Conflict Research, Uppsala University

RESEARCH
EDUCATION
ADVOCACY

The Department of Peace and Conflict Research at Uppsala University was established in 1971 to conduct research and offer courses in peace and conflict studies. Besides its educational activities, the Department runs interdisciplinary projects dealing with the origins and dynamics of conflicts, conflict resolution, and international security issues in a number of regions including West, Central, and Southeast Asia. The Department also runs a Conflict Data Project, which continuously collects data on armed conflicts and has published statistics on major armed conflicts in the SIPRI Yearbook since 1988. The Department also publishes an annual report of all armed conflicts.

Uppsala University
Box 514
751 20 Uppsala
Sweden

Tel: +46 (18) 471 0000
Fax: +46 (18) 695 102
info@pcr.uu.se
www.pcr.uu.se

Contact: Kjell-Åke Nordquist, Director

Number of staff: 33

Budget: > $1,000,000

Publications: States in Armed Conflict, annual publication; *A Century of Economic Sanctions: A Field Revisited,* 2000; *Gendering UN Peacekeeping: Mainstreaming a Gender Perspective in Multidimensional Peacekeeping Operations,* 1999; *Anarchy Within: The Security Dilemma between Ethnic Groups in Emerging Anarchy,* 1999.

Central Asia, Caucasus, Balkans

CIMERA

RESEARCH
EDUCATION
ACTION

CIMERA works on the development of civil society in the Caucasus, Central Asia, and the Balkans, combining projects on governance with research activities. CIMERA focuses on media development by enhancing the professional skills of journalists. It also organizes cross-border cooperation among journalists, politicians, and policy experts. By encouraging collaboration among professionals in areas with conflict potential, and simultaneously confronting participants with a variety of viewpoints, CIMERA works to increase understanding of the fears and hopes of all parties, and thereby to reduce the potential for conflict.

Rue de l'Athénée 28
P.O. Box 474
1211 Geneva 12
Switzerland

Tel: +41 (22) 347 5206
Fax: +41 (22) 346 6466

Contact: Britta Korth, Project Director for Central Asia

Number of staff: 10

Budget: $100,000–$500,000

Publications: Media Insight Central Asia, monthly electronic newsletter; *Report on the Media Situation in Tajikistan,* 2000.

Global

International Committee of the Red Cross

RESEARCH
EDUCATION
ACTION
ADVOCACY

The International Committee of the Red Cross (ICRC) is an impartial, neutral, and independent organization whose exclusively humanitarian mission is to protect the lives and dignity of victims of war and internal violence and to provide them with assistance. It also endeavors to prevent suffering by promoting and strengthening international humanitarian law and universal humanitarian principles. The ICRC's mandate has been conferred on it by the international community. It is enshrined in the Geneva Conventions of 1949 and their Additional Protocols of 1977. Since its origin, the ICRC has taken initiative on and has been closely associated with the development of these instruments of international humanitarian law.

19 Avenue de la Paix
1202 Geneva
Switzerland

Tel: +41 (22) 734 6001
Fax: +41 (22) 733 2057
webmaster.gva@icrc.org
www.icrc.org

Contact: Paul Grossrieder, Director General

Number of staff: 825 (HQ), 9,000 (field, for all activities)

Budget: > $1,000,000 (for all activities)

Publications: The International Review of the Red Cross, quarterly magazine; *Strengthening Protection in War: A Search for Professional Standards,* 2001; *The ICRC and Civil-Military Relations in Armed Conflict,* 2001; *War, Money and Survival,* 2000.

Global

Office for the
Coordination of Humanitarian Affairs

RESEARCH
ACTION
ADVOCACY

The UN Office for the Coordination of Humanitarian Affairs (OCHA) is mandated to coordinate UN assistance. It is also committed to conflict prevention through advocacy efforts and humanitarian policy development. OCHA discharges its coordination function primarily through the IASC, with the participation of humanitarian partners such as the Red Cross Movement and NGOs. At present, OCHA maintains 32 field offices in Africa, Asia, and Europe including the Integrated Regional Information Network (IRIN). Instrumental in implementing its conflict-prevention goal is its leading role in the UN Framework for Coordination Team, an inter-agency body that identifies countries at risk and promotes appropriate preventive and preparedness measures.

Palais des Nations
1211 Geneva 10
Switzerland

Tel: +41 (22) 917 1234
Fax: +41 (22) 917 0023
ochagva@un.org
www.reliefweb.int/ocha_ol

Contact: Ramesh Rajasingham, Humanitarian Affairs Officer

Publications: OCHA News; Guiding Principles on Internal Displacement, 1999; OCHA Orientation Handbook on Complex Emergencies, 1999.

Global

Swiss Peace Foundation

RESEARCH
EDUCATION
ACTION
ADVOCACY

The Swiss Peace Foundation (SPF) is an independent action-oriented peace research institute. The SFP hosts the Center for Peacebuilding (Kompetenzzentrum Friedensförderung—KOFF). This Center aims to support the constructive role of Switzerland in settling international conflicts. The SFP also runs the FAST early warning project, which prepares periodic risk analyses in Central and South Asia (Tajikistan, Uzbekistan, Kyrgyzstan, Kazakhstan, Afghanistan, Pakistan, India), among other regions. These aim to recognize potential crisis situations early enough and to provide decisionmakers with information and advise that have solid scientific backing.

Sonnenbergstrasse 17
P.O. Box
3000 Bern 7
Switzerland

Tel: +41 (31) 310 2727
Fax: +41 (31) 310 2728
info@swisspeace.ch

Contact: Laurent Goetschel, Executive Director

Number of staff: 20

Budget: > $1,000,000

Publications: Conflict Prevention and Power Politics: Central Asia as a Show Case, 2001, SPF Working Paper; Afghanistan: Reconstruction and Peacebuilding in a Regional Framework, 2001, KOFF Peacebuilding Report; FAST Country Risk Profiles.

Global

United Nations
High Commissioner for Refugees

ACTION

In recent years the United Nations High Commissioner for Refugees (UNHCR) has increased its emphasis on conflict prevention, although it has no special department exclusively responsible for this. The High Commissioner is mandated to take action in situations of severe human rights violations and is expected to alert governments and other agencies. The work of the Reintegration and Local Settlement Section is sometimes described in terms of peace building activities, such as ensuring the reintegration of returning refugees and displaced people. The focus of the organization changes from year to year, depending of the patterns of displacement.

94 rue de Montbrillant,
1202 Geneva
Switzerland

tel :+41 (22) 739 8111
fax: +41 (22) 739 7367
cdr@unhcr.ch
www.unhcr.ch

Contact: Niels Harild, Head of UNHCR reintegration and local settlement section

Publications: Refugees, quarterly magazine; *The State of the World's Refugees,* UNHCR global report

Global

United Nations
Institute for Disarmament Research

RESEARCH
ACTION
ADVOCACY

The United Nations Institute for Disarmament Research (UNIDIR) was established in 1980 for the purpose of undertaking independent research on disarmament and related problems, particularly international security issues. It aims to provide the international community with diversified and complete data, and to assist ongoing negotiations on disarmament, particularly on nuclear armaments, by means of factual studies and analyses. Among other activities, UNIDIR is currently running a project on peace-building and practical disarmament in Africa, and contributes to the monitoring and evaluation of mine action programs.

Palais des Nations
1211 Geneva 10
Switzerland

Tel: +41 (22) 917 3186
Fax: +41 (22) 917 0176
plewis@unorg.ch
www.unog.ch/unidir

Contact: Patricia Lewis, Director

Publications: Disarmament Forum, quarterly journal; *Illicit Trafficking in Firearms: Prevention and Combat in Rio de Janeiro Brazil,* 2001; *Peacekeeping in Africa: Capabilities and Culpabilities,* 2000; *Tactical Nuclear Weapons: Options for Control,* 2000; *The Small Arms Problem in Central Asia: Features and Implications,* 2000.

Tajikistan, Central Asia

Asia Plus

Asia Plus is an information agency that informs Tajik society and the international community about issues including politics, economics, defense, lawmaking, relevant to Tajikistan. The agency was established in 1995 and has since been involved in data collecting, fact finding, publishing, and research activities. It has provided information support for the peace process in Tajikistan, supplying information collected and disseminated at the grassroots level.

35/1 Bokhtar Street, 8th floor
Dushanbe 734002
Tajikistan

Tel: +992 (372) 217 863/217
    220/218 490
Fax: +992 (372) 510 136
info@asiaplus.tajik.net
www.asiaplus.tajnet.com

Contact: Umed Babakhanov
Number of staff: 25
Budget: $25,000–$100,000
Publications: Newsletter.

Tajikistan, Afghanistan, Central Asia

Center for Conflict Studies and Regional Research

The Center for Conflict Studies and Regional Research (CCSRR) is an NGO that deals with conflict prevention and resolution, as well as research in history, politics, conflicts, and related subjects. The CCSRR is currently implementing a program titled We Are the Tajik Citizens, together with the Center for Social Technologies (Tajikistan), which involves teaching students in conflict resolution skills, with the ultimate aim to contribute to sustainable peace in Tajikistan. Previously the Center conducted research on Tajik-Afghan borders and security issues in Central Asia and organized a conference on Afghan conflict and security issues in Tajikistan.

appt. 27, 35 Husseinzoda Street
Dushanbe 734025
Tajikistan

Tel: +992 (372) 234 390
iskandar@ac.tajik.net

Contact: Kosimsho Iskandarov, Director
Number of staff: 25
Budget: < $25,000

Tajikistan

Center for Social Technologies

The Center for Social Technologies (CST) is a local NGO that aims to develop and introduce progressive social technologies, including those on community-based conflict prevention and resolution. Currently the CST develops programs on education in conflict prevention for local communities in the border regions of Tajikistan. In partnership with the Center for Conflict Studies and Regional Research (Tajikistan) the CST is implementing the We Are the Tajik Citizens Program, which aims to develop conflict resolution skills among students from the cities of Dushanbe and Garm by means of organizing meetings and producing radio programs.

appt.36, 17/2 Navoii Street
Dushanbe 734026
Tajikistan

Tel: +992 (372) 373 057/231 497
cst@ac.tajik.net

Contact: Zilya Irekovna Shomakhmadova, Director

Number of staff: 4

Budget: < $25,000

Tajikistan, Kyrgyzstan

Center for Youth Initiatives

Ittifok, Center for Youth Initiatives (Markazi Tashabbusi Javonon) is an NGO in northern Tajikistan that aims to contribute to the development of civil society in the Republic of Tajikistan by means of efficient employment of youth potential through various educational and social programs.

Currently the Center's work focuses on two programs: Conflict Prevention between Tajikistan and Kyrgyzstan and Reconciliation and Community Development. The Conflict Prevention between Tajikistan and Kyrgyzstan Program aims to prevent interethnic conflicts in the border communities of Tajikistan and Kyrgyzstan through consensus- and trust-building activities; joint educational, cultural, and social programs; development of a network of local mediators; and increasing public awareness on non-violent conflict resolution. The program targets the grassroots population in five border regions of these two countries and is implemented in partnership with the Foundation for Tolerance International (Kyrgyzstan). The Reconciliation and Community Development program is implemented in partnership with a number of Tajik NGOs and aims at promoting reconciliation in Tajik society and providing assistance to communities in addressing various issues. The activities include problem identification, conflict resolution, and development of social partnership, family health, and family law. The program is implemented in ten Tajik communities.

appt. 35, 53 Lenin Street
Khujand 735700
Tajikistan
_____

Tel/fax: +992 (3422) 67 318
davron@cyi.khj.tajik.net

Contact: Kamol Kamilov, Chairperson

Number of staff: 15

Budget: $25,000–$100,000

Publications: Modules of the seminars for the community leaders and activists (including: "Conflict Introduction," "Monitoring and Conflict Assessment," "Process of Consensus Building," and "Mediation and Negotiation"), 2000; *ABC of Civil Education,* 1999; *Politics for People,* 1998.

Afghanistan, Tajikistan

Fidokor

EDUCATION
ACTION
ADVOCACY

Fidokor is a local NGO that provides social, legal, and humanitarian assistance to vulnerable groups, and assists local NGOs in addressing social problems through supplying them with information. Fidokor also provides psychological and social rehabilitation to returnees and other victims of the civil war, as well as addressing the issues of poverty, thus contributing to the development of the peace process in Tajikistan.

Currently the organization is involved in three programs: (1) Conflict Resolution and Tolerance Education, which aims to mitigate tension in the areas of mass return of refugees after the civil war; (2) The Coalition for Tolerance and Peace, which unites four local NGOs in their work on conflict resolution; and (3) Children are Our Future, which provides psychological and social rehabilitation to the returnees' children. In the framework of these programs Fidokor facilitates training seminars, produces publications and TV programs, and organizes sports, social, and cultural events. All three programs are implemented in the Khatlon region, the most volatile region in Tajikistan, and due to that the Fidokor head office has been recently moved to the city of Kurgan-Tube in the Khatlon region. Fidokor is working in partnership with the field offices of international organizations, such as Counterpart Consortium, UNHCR, and Mercy Corps International, as well as with a number of local NGOs.

Previously, Fidokor had also been active in the field of providing humanitarian assistance and rebuilding schools and hospitals after the civil war.

6 Lokhuti Street
Kurgan-Tube 735140
Tajikistan

Tel: +992 (3222) 24 191/25 664
shamsoro@vakhsh.tajik.net

Contact: Dilbar Muhammedovna Halilova, Director

Number of staff: 12

Budget: $25,000–$100,000

Publications: Conflict Resolution and Tolerance Education, teachers manual, 2000; *Conflict Resolution and Tolerance Education: Collection of Children's Essays,* 2000; monthly newspaper, in Tajik.

Tajikistan

Foundation to Support Civil Initiatives

EDUCATION
ACTION
ADVOCACY

The Foundation to Support Civil Initiatives (FSCI) is a local NGO established in June 1995. It provides assistance in the processes of democratic change and in the establishment of strong civil society in Tajikistan through the development of NGOs. Since 1996, the FSCI has been a member of the Public Council for National Peace and Accord, the process which is led by the Tajik president Emomali Rakhmonov. In the framework of the program, in 1999–2000 FSCI conducted 36 training seminars on conflict prevention for the local population in the volatile southern regions of Tajikistan.

office 19, 73-A Shotemura Street
Dushanbe 734002
Tajikistan
_____

Tel/fax: +992 (372) 215 857
root@tfsci.tajik.net or
muazama@yahoo.com

Contact: Muazama Burkhanova, Director
Number of Staff: 6
Budget: < $25,000
Publications: Civil Society, information bulletin; *Conflict Resolution at Grassroots Level in Tajikistan,* training module.

Tajikistan

Manizha Information and Education Centre

EDUCATION
ACTION

The Manizha Information and Education Centre was founded in March 1999. It provides training for those involved in conflict management and prevention activities in Tajikistan. Manizha's work is currently focused on conflict management at workplaces and within families, as well as prevention of interethnic conflicts. The latter involves peace and confidence building activities among different ethnic groups in Tajikistan. The program was implemented in partnership with local NGOs as well as with the Academy for Educational Development and CARE International. Manizha is a member of the Central Asian Network on Conflict Management and the Central Asian Network of Independent Media.

Appt. 5, 19/4 Nazarshoev Street
Dushanbe 734012
Tajikistan
_____

Tel: +992 (372) 213 711/217 558
Fax: +992 (372) 217 559
iec_manizha@tojikiston.com

Contact: Alisher Jamshedovich Rahmonberdiev, Director
Number of staff: 16
Budget: < $25,000
Publications: Sozvezdie (Constellation), newspaper.

Tajikistan

National Association of Political Scientists of Tajikistan

RESEARCH
ACTION

The mission of the National Association of Political Scientists of Tajikistan (NAPST) is to facilitate the development of political science, to enhance the political culture of society, and to develop the international links of Tajik researchers in the field. It was founded in July 1994 and since then has actively researched and publicized the current situation in Tajikistan. NAPST holds a political discussion club "The process of peace-building in Tajikistan: problems and ways to resolve them," which gathers together politicians, the military, economists, and conflict researchers with the aim of discussing the post-conflict revival of Tajikistan and ways of addressing current problems.

7 Gorky Street
Dushanbe 734025
Tajikistan
────────────
Tel: +992 (372) 213 396
Fax: +992 (372) 347 035
abdu@napst.td.silk.org

Contact: Abdugani Mamadazimov

Budget: < $25,000

Publications: Parties and Movements of Tajikistan, bulletin; materials from the conferences.

Tajikistan

Public Committee for the Promotion of Democratic Processes

RESEARCH
ACTION

The mission of the Public Committee for the Promotion of Democratic Processes is to develop a wide variety of initiatives aimed at the promotion and strengthening of democratic processes in Tajikistan. Since its establishment in 1999, the Public Committee has launched a three-year, four-track civic initiative in Tajikistan. The four tracks are: (1) A sustained dialogue process involving policymaking elites focusing on the relationship between state, religion, and society in Tajikistan; (2) A two-year educational program in collaboration with the Ministry of Education of Tajikistan to design and develop an undergraduate university curriculum in the field of conflict resolution and peacebuilding to be taught at eight universities around the country; (3) A regional economic development pilot program to test and promote a community-based participatory process around local economic development issues; and (4) A national Tajikistani Issues Forums Network to promote the practice of deliberative talk and discussions around public issues of concern to all Tajikistani citizens.

Rudaky Avenue 35, Apt#9
Dushanbe 734025
Tajikistan
────────────
Tel/fax: 992 (372) 213120
okpdv@tajik.net

Contact: Parviz Mullodjanov, Director of Programs

Number of staff: 2 (full-time), 3 (part-time)

Tajikistan, Afghanistan, Central Asia

Sharq Research and Analysis Center

The Sharq Research and Analysis Center was established with the mission of supporting democratic reforms, conducting basic and applied research, and establishing contacts with other researchers. Sharq has conducted research on Conflict and Society in Tajikistan (1996-1999), Political Parties and Elite in Tajikistan (1996-1999), Political Islam (1997-2000), and Migration in Tajikistan (1997-2000). The Center provides information for the EAWARN and FAST conflict monitoring projects, run respectively by the Institute of Ethnology and Anthropology of the Russian Academy of Sciences (Russia) and Swiss Peace Foundation (Switzerland). In 1997-2000, Sharq staff worked as independent experts in the Inter-Tajik Dialogue in the framework of the Dartmouth Conference.

Appt. 9, 7 Bofand Street
Dushanbe 734042
Tajikistan

Tel: +992 (372) 218 370/218 995
Fax: +992 (372) 218 995
sharq@tajik.net or
olimov@tajik.net

Contact: Muzaffar Abduvakkosovich Olimov, Director

Number of staff: < $25,000

Publications: Tajikistan on the Threshold of Changes, 1999; *Inter-Tajik Conflict: Pathway to Peace,* 1998.

Tajikistan

Silk Road—Road of Consolidation

The National Foundation, Silk Road—Road of Consolidation, was set up in August 1998 with the aim of consolidating the unity of the Tajiks and of facilitating the development of the newly independent state. The foundation strives to revive, develop, and enrich the national, historical, and cultural heritage of the Tajiks, and to reveal the importance of the Silk Road for people of the world. In July 1999 and 2000 the foundation together with the Presidential Cabinet organized the first and second Caravans of Peace and Consolidation.

7 Gorky Street
Dushanbe 734025
Tajikistan

Tel: +992 (372) 213 396
Fax: +992 (372) 344 973
silk@road.td.silk.org

Contact: Naimjon Yasinov, Director

Number of staff: 9

Publications: Road of Consolidation, magazine.

Tajikistan

Sudmand

Sudmand is a non-governmental organization with the mission to contribute to the processes of societal transformation through educational programs. Sudmand is currently working on the Ties of Friendship Project, which aims to decrease tension in the relations between conflicting regions of Tajikistan (Kuliab and Pamir provinces). The project targets youth and involves such types of activity as seminars on conflict resolution and tolerance education, meetings with military servants, and a festival of youth friendship. Within this project Sudmand co-operates with the government of Tajikistan (Youth Committee), USAID, and Counterpart Consortium.

16 S.Safarov Street
Kuliab 735360
Tajikistan
_____

Tel: +992 (3322) 34 988/22 692
Fax: +992 (3322) 34 988
sudmand@kulob.tajik.net

Contact: Dodarbek Saidaliev, Director
Number of staff: 9
Budget: < $25,000

Publications: Bo Rohi Vakhdat (Along the Road of Friendship), newsletter.

Tajikistan, Central Asia

Tajikistan Center
for Citizenship Education

The mission of the Tajikistan Center for Citizenship Education (TCCE) is to initiate and develop a wide system of citizenship education in Tajikistan and to ensure a more active participation of Tajik citizens in the most acute political, social, and economic problems. Since its establishment, the TCCE has organized regular "Civic Forums" aiming at promoting civic education. Following the Tajikistan peace process TCCE embarked on the issues of post-conflict settlement and development as well as peace education. The Center coauthored an issue of Accord Bulletin on "Politics of Compromise: The Tajikistan Peace Process" together with Conciliation Resources (UK).

Room 2, 7 Gorki Street
Dushanbe 734025
Tajikistan
_____

Tel/fax: +992 (372) 217 033
gula@nosirova.tajik.net or
abdullaevk@irex-tj.org

Contact: Gulchehra Nosirova, Director
Number of staff: 2
Budget: < $25,000

Publications: Regionalism and Unity of Nation,1998.

Tajikistan, Central Asia

Traditions and Modernity

Traditions and Modernity (T&M) is a women's NGO whose mission is to help create a gender balance in all spheres of Tajik society through implementation of research and educational projects. In 2001 T&M launched a program entitled Women, Conflict, Politics: Central Asia in cooperation with UK-based NGO Women in Societies in Transition. The program aims to explore the relationship between women, conflict, and politics in Central Asia and to identify and implement appropriate strategies to improve women's rights and interests in conflict situations. T&M is part of the Women in International Affairs in Asia (WIIAA) and Vital Voices Global Partnership (VVGP) networks.

appt. 18, 84/5 Popov Street
Dushanbe 734013
Tajikistan

Tel: +992 (372) 218 959/244 915
akuvatova@yahoo.com or
mnkhegai@yahoo.com

Contact: Margarita Khegai, Director

Number of staff: 3

Publications: Women's and Gender Studies in Tajikistan, 2000; *Gender and Culture,* manual, 1999.

Asia

Asian Cultural Forum on Development

Established in 1975, the Asian Cultural Forum on Development (ACFOD) now has members in some 30 countries in the Asia Pacific region. The Forum advocates for development and aims to promote peace, harmony, and human rights. ACFOD names human resource development as its main concern and also mobilizes action campaigns on concern issues. The Forum has initiated talks with the LTTE guerillas in Sri Lanka, the Separatist movements in Nepal as well as in Bangladesh and Burma. In the future ACFOD plans to be involved in training on conflict resolution, non-violence, and mediation.

494 Lardprao 101 Road, Soi 11
Klong Chan, Bangkapi
P.O. Box 26
Bungthonglang
Bangkok 10240
Thailand

Tel: +66 (2) 377 9357/370 2701
Fax: +66 (2) 374 0464
acfodbkk@ksc15.th.com
ksc11.th.com/acfodbkk/

Contact: Banton Ondam, Coordinator

Number of staff: 5

Budget: $25,000–$100,000

Balkans, Russia, Northern Ireland, East and
Central Africa, Middle East, South and Southeast Asia

EDUCATION
ACTION

Agenda for Reconciliation

Agenda for Reconciliation (AfR) is an international programme of Initiatives of Change (formerly the Moral Re-Armament network), which is devoted to conflict prevention and other peace-making initiatives within and between nations. Its work is based on the beliefs that durable peace depends on genuine processes of healing the past, and that reconciliation is only possible where trust has been built. An international Steering Committee with its secretariat in London co-ordinates this work.

24 Greencoat Place
London SW1P 1RD
United Kingdom

Tel: +44 (20) 7798 6000
Fax: +44 (20) 7798 6001
www.caux.ch/afr

Contact: Peter Riddell, Secretary of the International Steering Committee
Number of staff: 150 activists
Budget: $100,000–$500,000
Publications: For a Change, periodical; Forgiveness: *Breaking the Chain of Hate,* 1999; *Conflict and Resolution,* 1998; *The Forgiveness Factor,* 1996; *Religion, the Missing Dimension of Statecraft,* 1994.

Global

RESEARCH
EDUCATION
ACTION
ADVOCACY

Amnesty International

With national sections in over fifty countries, Amnesty International (AI) is one of the world's leading human rights organizations. In addition to focusing on individual cases of human rights abuse, it also reports on systematic violations, offers recommendations on how to prevent these, and pressures governments through public and lobby campaigns to heed them. For sudden escalations of human rights violations, such as are typical in violent conflicts, the organization has a special crisis response team. AI's human rights education work also contributes to the prevention of violent conflict.

99-119 Rosebery Avenue
London EC1R 4RE
United Kingdom

Tel: +44 (20) 7814 6200
Fax: +44 (20) 7833 1510
information@amnesty.org.uk
www.amnesty.org.uk

Contact: Campaigning and Crisis Response Programme
Number of staff: 320 at international HQ
Budget: > $1,000,000
Publications: More than 200 books, reports, and circulars in over a dozen languages annually.

Global

Bradford University
Department of Peace Studies

RESEARCH
EDUCATION
ADVOCACY

The Department of Peace Studies at Bradford University in England was established a quarter of a century ago and has grown to be the largest university center for peace studies in the world.

The Department has developed a large undergraduate program leading to a BA Honors degree in Peace Studies with nearly 200 full-time students, but has balanced this with the development of a substantial graduate school and a doctoral program with around 50 research students. Together with 20 lecturers and research fellows, they work primarily in the following areas: international politics and security studies, development and peace, regions in conflict (especially former Yugoslavia, the Middle East, Africa and Latin America), conflict resolution, politics and society; international politics, and the environment.

The Department has a large publishing program, including publication of its regular Newsletter three times a year and the Bradford Arms Register Studies (BARS) Project. The Strengthening of the Biological and Toxin Weapons Convention and Preventing Biological Warfare Project maintains a dedicated information service on Bradford University's website to more effectively disseminate information on the process of strengthening the Biological and Toxin Weapons Convention (BTWC) worldwide.

Further applied work in conflict resolution is conducted within the Department's Centre for Conflict Resolution. This Centre, an applied research unit within the Department, combines theoretical studies in peacekeeping, mediation, and conflict resolution with a range of practical programs, many of them concerned with training mediators and peacemakers in areas in conflict. Staff have worked in former Yugoslavia, Cyprus, Sri Lanka, and Uganda, and they have collaborated in mediation training for diplomats and a wide range of NGOs in Britain and overseas. The research and project work of the Centre is comprehensively described on its website at www.brad.ac.uk/confres. The Department has recently been recognized as a Rotary Centre for International Studies in Peace and Conflict Resolution.

Richmond Road
Bradford BD7 1DP
United Kingdom

Tel: +44 (12) 7423 5235
Fax: +44 (12) 7423 5240
n.lewer@bradford.ac.uk
www.brad.ac.uk/acad/peace

Contact: Dr. N. Lewer, Head of the Centre for Conflict Resolution

Number of staff: 20

Publications: Newsletter; *Confronting Ethnic Chauvinism in a Post-War Environment: NGOs and Peace Education in Bosnia,* 2000; *Women, Gender and Peacebuilding,* 2000; *International Non-government Organisations and Peacebuilding: Perspectives from Peace Studies and Conflict Resolution,* 1999.

Afghanistan
British Agencies Afghanistan Group

RESEARCH
EDUCATION
ACTION
ADVOCACY

The British Agencies Afghanistan Group provides a forum for a network of British agencies assisting Afghans both inside and outside Afghanistan, and facilitates communication and cooperation among these agencies. It provides its members with information by monitoring developments, analyzing information, producing position papers, and interacting with other networks and agencies. It encourages its members and other NGOs to integrate peacebuilding into their development and assistance programs, and to adopt long-term community-based approaches to programming in conflict areas. The Group also consults with governments and international organizations on the situation in Afghanistan.

Refugee Council
3-9 Bondway
London SW8 1SJ
United Kingdom
_____

Tel: +44 (20) 7820 3098
Fax: +44 (20) 7820 3107
peter.marsden@refugeecouncil.org.uk

Contact: Peter Marsden, Information Co-ordinator

Number of staff: 5 (total), 1 (conflict resolution)

Budget: < $25,000

Publications: Afghanistan: Monthly Review.

Tajikistan, Fiji, Sri Lanka, Cambodia,
Philippines, Caucasus, Angola, West Africa, Uganda
Conciliation Resources

RESEARCH
EDUCATION
ACTION
ADVOCACY

Conciliation Resources (CR) is a non-governmental international service for conflict prevention and resolution seeking to provide sustained assistance to partner organizations and their initiatives at community and national levels. The Accord Program has had projects on the peace processes in Tajikistan, Sri Lanka, Cambodia, and the Philippines. An education pack of training and discussion materials is produced to accompany the Accord publications. Other project activities in these countries have included policy seminars, briefing meetings, and other initiatives to encourage the development of strategies that will consolidate the peace processes in the respective countries.

173 Upper Street
London N1 1RG
United Kingdom
_____

Tel: +44 (20) 7359 7728
Fax: +44 (20) 7359 4081
conres@c-r.org
www.c-r.org

Contact: Catherine Barnes

Number of staff: 10 (UK), 5 (Sierra Leone)

Budget: > $1,000,000

Publications: "Accord: An International Review of Peace Initiatives," a book-length publication series; occasional papers.

Caucasus, Great Lakes Region of Africa,
West Africa, Central and Southeast Asia, Central America

FEWER

FEWER (Forum on Early Warning and Early Response) is an independent global network of organizations committed to preventing conflict by providing early warning and informing peacebuilding efforts. FEWER's activities are led by its members. The network is composed of NGOs, UN agencies, and academic institutions who work together to exchange knowledge and experience in the field of early warning, conflict prevention, and conflict resolution. FEWER's motivation is strictly humanitarian. The services provided by FEWER are oriented toward the promotion of human rights, sustainable development, and peace. FEWER provides local perspectives on the causes and dynamics of violent conflict and peace building to different policymaking communities.

Old Truman Brewery
91-95 Brick Lane
London E1 6QN
United Kingdom

Tel: +44 (20) 7247 7022
Fax: +44 (20) 7247 5290
secretariat@fewer.org
www.fewer.org

Contact: David Nyheim, Director
Number of staff: 8
Budget: $500,000–$1,000,000
Publications: Development in Conflict:
A Seven Step Tool for Planners (together
with International Alert and Saferworld) 2001;
Conflict Analysis and Response Definition:
Abridged Methodology (together with the West
Africa Network for Peacebuilding and the
Centre for Conflict Research) 2001; *Conflict*
Prevention in the Caucasus: Actors, Response
Capacities and Planning Processes (together
with the EastWest Institute) 2001; *Generating*
the Means to an End: Planning Integrated
Responses to Early Warning (together with
CIPDD, EastWest Institute, International Alert,
IEA-RAS-EAWARN and WANEP) 2000;
Thesaurus and Glossary of Early Warning and
Conflict Prevention Terms (together with
PIOOM) 2000.

Sri Lanka, Caucasus, Great Lakes Region, West Africa

International Alert

RESEARCH
EDUCATION
ACTION
ADVOCACY

International Alert (IA) was founded as an action-based, non-governmental organization to contribute to the prevention and resolution of violent internal conflict. Together with various organizations and individuals, IA has worked to peacefully resolve many of the world's most intractable disputes. IA seeks to strengthen the ability of people in conflict situations to make peace by facilitating dialogue at different levels of society in conflict and helping develop and enhance local capacities through funding or training. In Sri Lanka, International Alert has been active since 1993 in a range of activities aimed at ending the 20 years of war on the island. Activities within this program include encouraging dialogue, advocacy and awareness raising, and the support of seminars and workshops.

1 Glyn Street
London SE11 5HT
United Kingdom
—————————
Tel: +44 (20) 7793 8383
Fax: +44 (20) 7793 7975
general@international-alert.org
www.international-alert.org

Contact: Martin Honeywell, Associate Director
Number of staff: 40
Publications: Cost of the War: Economic, Sociopolitical and Human Costs of the War in Sri Lanka, 2001; *Conflict-Sensitive Approaches to Development: A Review of Practice,* 2001; *Negotiating Peace in Sri Lanka: Efforts, Failures & Lessons,* 1998.

Southeast Asia, Middle East, Northern Ireland,
Basque Country, West Africa, South Africa

International Conflict Research (INCORE)

RESEARCH
EDUCATION
ADVOCACY

A joint program of the United Nations University and the University of Ulster, the International Conflict Research (INCORE) aims to integrate research, training, practice, policy, and theory, and to provide an international focus on ethnic violence. INCORE's Policy and Evaluation Unit was established in 1998 to examine, research, and analyze the ways in which conflict management research and practical lessons from past practice are currently utilized by policymakers. INCORE's Conflict Data Service, available on its website, provides current and historical information on all major ongoing conflicts, theme sites on a variety of issues relevant to conflict, and information on conflict resolution institutions throughout the world.

Aberfoyle House
Northland Road
Derry/Londonderry BT48 7JA
Northern Ireland
United Kingdom
—————————
Tel: +44 (28) 7137 5500
Fax: +44 (28) 7137 5510
incore@incore.ulst.ac.uk
www.incore.ulst.ac.uk

Contact: Mari Fitzduff, Director
Number of staff: 10
Budget: $100,000–$500,000
Publications: Ethnic Conflict Research Digest, journal; *Ethnic Studies Network Bulletin; From Protagonist to Pragmatist: Political Leadership in Societies in Transition,* 2001; *Assessment of UN Research Needs,* 1999.

Kashmir

Kashmir Council for Human Rights/ Organisation for South Asian Peace

RESEARCH
ADVOCACY

The Kashmir Council for Human Rights (KCHR) and the Organisation for South Asian Peace (OSAP) are both London-based non-profit, non-governmental organizations. KCHR and OSAP are dedicated to working toward a peaceful settlement of the Kashmir dispute, in order to stop the violation of human rights and stimulate restoration of the civil liberties for the people of Kashmir. Activities include data collecting, lobbying, and human rights work.

142 Otley Road
Leeds LS 16 5JX
United Kingdom
──────────────
Tel/fax: +44 (1132) 368 5458
majidsirajuk@yahoo.com
hanif@gharib.demon.co.uk
www.ummah.nct/kashmir/kchr/

Contact: Majid Siraj, Chairman
Number of staff: 3
Budget: < $25,000

Publications: Voice of Kashmir, newsletter;
Towards Peace in Kashmir: Political Fragments & Subjectivity, forthcoming.

Global

Minority Rights Group International

RESEARCH
ACTION
ADVOCACY

Minority Rights Group International (MRG) is a non-governmental organization working to secure rights for ethnic, religious, and linguistic minorities worldwide, and to promote cooperation and understanding between communities. MRG has over 30 years of experience promoting the rights of marginalized, non-dominant groups within society. MRG has four main activities: researching and publishing; advocacy to secure the rights of minorities; educating children and teachers on minority issues; and cooperative efforts with other organizations and activists who share its aims to build alliances, discuss ideas, develop skills, and further minority rights worldwide.

379 Brixton Road
London SW9 7DE
United Kingdom
──────────────
Tel: +44 (20) 7978 9498
Fax: +44 (20) 7738 6265
minority.rights@mrgmail.org
www.minorityrights.org

Contact: Alan Phillips, Director
Number of staff: 26
Budget: > $1,000,000

Publications: Outsider, newsletter; *World Directory of Minorities,* 2001; *Muslim Women in India,* 1999; *Forests and Indigenous Peoples of Asia,* 1999.

Bosnia and Herzegovina, Croatia, Georgia,
Northern Ireland, Afghanistan, Sri Lanka, Guatemala

RESEARCH
EDUCATION

PRDU

The academic Post-War Reconstruction and Development Unit (PRDU) specializes in research, consultancy and training of professionals in issues of the management and planning of reconstruction after war, humanitarian intervention in complex political emergencies, and post-war recovery. The Unit developed a one year MA in Post-War Recovery Studies to provide accessible, professionally relevant, multi-disciplinary training specifically developed to cover these areas of concern. The PRDU is part of the Department of Politics of the University of York.

Derwent College
University of York
Heslington
York YO10 5DD
United Kingdom

Tel: +44 (1904) 432 640
Fax: +44 (1904) 432 641
www.york.ac.uk/depts/poli/prdu

Contact: Roger MacGinty, Lecturer

Number of Staff: 11

Publications: *Revival*, newsletter; *Institutional Development of Southern NGOs: What Role for Northern NGOs?* 2000; *From Rhetoric to Reality: The Role of Aid in Local Peacebuilding in Afghanistan*, 1998; *Urban Triumph or Urban Disaster?: Dilemmas of Contemporary Post-war Reconstruction*, 1998; *Water under Fire*, 1997.

Global

Responding to Conflict

RESEARCH
EDUCATION
ACTION
ADVOCACY

Since its foundation in 1991, Responding to Conflict (RTC) has sought ways to support and extend the efforts of people engaged in resolving or ameliorating the situations of political and social conflict in which they live.

RTC therefore works with local and international NGOs and increasingly also with UN agencies, diplomats, government officials, and public service institutions. Using French, Spanish and Russian as well as English, RTC provides a range of practical opportunities for individuals and organizations to reassess and redirect their programs, and facilitates the sharing of insights and experience across cultures and continents.

RTC's regular courses are "Working with Conflict," for practitioners in development, human rights, emergencies and peace-building; and a workshop called Strengthening Practice and Policy, for staff of international agencies with advisory or direct management responsibility for relief, development, rights, and peace-building programs.

In addition to the open program of courses, RTC staff are frequently invited by both local and international organizations to accompany them in working on situations of actual and potential conflict in different parts of the world. Wherever possible they share this work with colleagues in the region.

For a few years RTC and the Coalition for Peace in Africa (COPA) have been engaged in a joint project, "Linking Practice to Policy: a multi-level approach to peace-building." This project aims primarily to influence policy-makers of international agencies and governments. Initially, the project is concerned with documenting case studies of African peace-making initiatives using video, sound, and photography as well as written material.

Responding to Conflict currently has a new three year international program called Action for Conflict Transformation (ACTION) which focuses on capacity-building in conflict-affected areas. ACTION will bring together experienced practitioners who are catalysts for conflict transformation and peace-building in their own conflict-affected areas of the world. They work and learn together as an international team.

1046 Bristol Road
Birmingham B29 6LJ
United Kingdom

Tel: +44 (121) 415 5641
Fax: +44 (121) 415 4119
enquiries@respond.org
www.respond.org

Contact: Simon Fisher, Director

Number of Staff: 8

Publications: Working with Conflict: Skills and Strategies for Action, 2000.

Afghanistan

Afghanistan—America Foundation

ACTION
ADVOCACY

Based in Washington, D.C., the Afghanistan Foundation seeks to foster public and governmental understanding of Afghanistan and its people. The Foundation works to reduce confrontation and enhance the prospects for peace and stability in the region. It has held educational and policymakers' forums on Capitol Hill since 1996, convening prominent Afghan and U.S. policymakers. The Foundation's main focus following the overthrow of the Taliban has been facilitating reconstruction and development.

209 Pennsylvania Avenue, SE
Suite 700
Washington DC 20003
United States

Contact: Don Ritter, Chairman
Publications: US Policy in Afghanistan: Challenges and Solutions, 1999.

Tel: +1 (202) 543 1177
Fax: +1 (202) 543 7931
afghan@att.net
www.afghanistanfoundation.org

Afghanistan

Afghanistan Peace Association

ACTION
ADVOCACY

The Afghanistan Peace Association (APA) was formed in 1989 after a number of Afghans came together with the common goal of permanent peace and national unity. According to the constitution of this independent and neutral assembly, the association aims to reach its goal "through discussion, comprehension and exchange of views, in order to ban war and disarm individuals, factions, ethnic groups and tribes." So far the APA has stated its goals of demilitarizing the country and establishing free and democratic elections through its website and the publication, Voice of Peace.

P.O. Box 540 926
Flushing, NY 11354-0926
United States

Contact: Ahmad Dawer Nadi, Chairman
Publications: Voice of Peace.

Tel: +1 (718) 461 6799
Fax: +1 (718) 866 8616
AfghanPeace@hotmail.com
www.afghan-web.com/apa/

Global

Applied Conflict Resolution
Organizations Network

The Applied Conflict Resolution Organizations Network (ACRON) is a network of over 22 organizations actively engaged in peacebuilding activities around the world. As an organization, ACRON seeks to enhance the effectiveness of international conflict resolution and peacebuilding activities by: promoting communication, coordination, and collaboration among applied conflict resolution organizations; increasing awareness of and funding for the field; and building bridges to other applied and academic organizations in related fields. ACRON members are mostly—but not exclusively—non-governmental US-based non-profit organizations. All have significant experience in the field of applied conflict resolution and peacebuilding.

c/o The Institute of World Affairs   *Contact:* Neil Laslett, the Institute of World
1321 Pennsylvania Ave., SE   Affairs
Washington, DC 20003
United States

Tel: +1 (202) 544 4141
nlaslett@iwa.org
www.acron.iwa.org

Asia

Asia Foundation

The Asia Foundation consists of a widespread network that stretches throughout Asia Pacific and the United States. The Foundation has focused on issues ranging from effective law, governance, and citizenship to the equal participation of women, and peace, and stability in the region. The government and law program includes programs on conflict resolution, elections, and non-governmental organization support. In this connection, the Foundation has supported a study of how the structures and procedures of alternative dispute resolution may be institutionalized in Indonesia. The Foundation also offers an inter-faith and inter-ethnic conflict resolution program.

465 California Street 14th Floor   *Contact:* William P. Fuller, President
San Francisco, CA 94104
United States   *Publications: Democratic Transitions and
                                    the Role of Islam in Asia,* Asian Perspective
                                    Series, 2000; *Approaches to Human Rights
Tel: +1 (415) 982 4640   in Southeast Asia,* Asian Perspective Series,
Fax: +1 (415) 392 8863   2000; *Focus on Pakistan,* Asian Perspective
info@asiafound.org   Series, 2000; *Funding Civil Society in
www.asiafoundation.org   Asia: Philanthropy and Public-Private
                                    Partnerships,* 1997.

Asia Pacific

Asia Pacific Center
for Justice and Peace

RESEARCH
EDUCATION
ADVOCACY

The Asia Pacific Center for Justice and Peace (APCJP), based in the United States, works with organizations in the Asia and Pacific region to strive for political, social, cultural, and economic justice. The organization's Program on Peace, Human Rights and Democracy focuses on key areas of ethnic and political conflict that are under-reported or misreported in the United States. Its goal is to provide a link between grassroots organizations in the Asia Pacific and policymakers in Washington. The Center functions as a host of the U.S. NGO Forum on Sri Lanka, bringing together Tamil and Singhalese participants.

110, Maryland Avenue, NE
Suite 504
Washington, DC 20002
United States
_____

Tel: +1 (202) 543 1094
Fax: +1 (202) 546 5103
apcjp@igc.org
www.apcjp.org

Contact: Miriam Young, Executive Director

Number of staff: 6

Publications: The Asia Pacific Advocate, quarterly newsletter; *Philippine News Survey,* monthly news selection; *Sri Lanka Forum News,* monthly news summary.

South Asia

Association for
Communal Harmony in Asia

EDUCATION
ADVOCACY

The U.S.-based Association for Communal Harmony in Asia (ACHA) is a voluntary organization of South Asians who seek to promote respect and harmonious contacts among South Asians, regardless of where they live. To this end it runs a service center for the local South Asian population in Portland that provides cultural courses and links people to appropriate translation services. A "yellow pages" directory of South Asian professionals, compiled by the ACHA, helps people reach out to others across national-origin barriers. On the Internet, the ACHA publishes information on peace processes in South Asia, including an e-bulletin, to highlight peace activities in the original home areas.

4410 Verda Lane NE
Keizer, OR 97303
United States
_____

Tel: +1 (503) 393 6944 or
     +1 (503) 251 0070
pritamr@open.org
www.asiapeace.org

Contact: Pritam K. Rohila, President

Number of staff: Volunteers only

Budget: < $25,000

Publications: ACHA Peace Bulletin, newsletter; South Asian directory of local resources.

Global

ADVOCACY

Collaborative for Development Action

Incorporated in 1985, Collaborative for Development Action (CDA) has worked in over seventy-five countries to support local economic and social development. Current projects include the Local Capacities for Peace Project (LCPP) and the Reflecting on Peace Practice Project (RPP). The LCPP seeks to identify ways in which assistance given in conflict settings may be provided so that it contributes to peacebuilding. In the RPP, many types of agencies collaborate in gathering experiences from their recent conflict-focused programs and identify what works and what does not work. Both projects are rooted in field-based case studies of work in different areas of the world, including Sri Lanka, India, Afghanistan, and Tajikistan.

26 Walker Street
Cambridge, MA 02138
United States

Tel: +1 (617) 661 6310
Fax: +1 (617) 661 3805
mail@cdainc.com
www.cdainc.com

Contact: Wolfgang Heinrich, Project Co-ordinator
Number of staff: 6
Publications: Do No Harm: How Aid Can Support Peace—Or War, 1999; *Rising from the Ashes: Development Strategies in Times of Disaster,* 1998.

Global

RESEARCH
ACTION
ADVOCACY

DPKO Lessons Learned Unit

The Lessons Learned Unit of the Department of Peacekeeping Operations (DPKO) was set up in April 1995 in order to develop structural mechanisms to collect and analyze information on the various missions being fielded by the United Nations and to recommend ways of improving their effectiveness. The unit seeks to avoid duplicating similar work being done within the UN or elsewhere. Instead it attempts to bring these separate initiatives together. A resource center gives access to books, documents, and other material. The DPKO is active in Kashmir, Tajikistan, and Afghanistan.

UN Department of Peace Keeping Operations
One United Nations Plaza
Room S-927
New York, NY 10017
United States

Tel: +1 (212) 963 3745
Fax: +1 (212) 963 1813
peace-keeping-lessons@un.org
www.un.org/depts/dpko/lessons

Central Asia, Central and Eastern Europe, Russia

EastWest Institute

RESEARCH
EDUCATION
ACTION
ADVOCACY

The EastWest Institute (EWI), founded in 1981, has aimed to defuse tensions and conflicts that threaten geopolitical stability in Eastern Europe. In the past the Institute has served as a security think tank and has supported the development of democracy, free enterprise, and European integration. In the future the Institute wants to serve as a long-term strategic partner facilitating stability, economic development, and democracy, focusing special attention on Russia, Trans-Caucasus, and Central Asia. The EWI provides information about economic and business developments, advises governments on reforms, and organizes conferences. EWI has offices in Brussels, Kiev, Prague, Moscow, and New York.

700 Broadway, 2nd floor
New York, NY 10003
United States
_____

Tel: +1 (212) 824 4100
Fax: +1 (212) 824 4149
iews@iews.org
www.iews.org

Contact: John Edwin Mroz, President

Number of staff: 65

Budget: > $1,000,000

Publications: EWInsights, quarterly bulletin; *Russian Regional Report,* weekly survey.

Global

Human Rights Watch

RESEARCH
ACTION
ADVOCACY

Human Rights Watch (HRW) is the largest human rights organization based in the United States. Its researchers conduct fact-finding investigations into human rights abuses in all regions of the world. In Asia, HRW closely monitors the countries suffering from major conflict, such as Afghanistan, Sri Lanka, Indonesia, and Burma. HWR publishes dozens of reports every year, all of which can be found on their website. Other recent actions in regard to Asia are the Landmine Monitor Report 2000 (which also covers the Asia Pacific region), policy recommendations to governments, and current campaigns such as The Campaign to Ban Landmines and Stop The Use Of Child Soldiers.

350 Fifth Avenue, 34th floor
New York, NY 10118 3299
United States
_____

Tel: +1 (212) 290 4700
Fax: +1 (212) 736 1300
hrwnyc@hrw.org
www.hrw.org

Contact: Kenneth Roth, Executive Director

Publications: Human Rights Watch World Report 2001; news releases; Crisis of Impunity: The Role of Pakistan, Russia and Iran in Fueling the Civil War in Afghanistan, 2001; Indonesia: Violence and Political Impasse in Papua, 2001; *Behind the Kashmir Conflict: Abuses by Indian Security Forces and Militant Groups Continue,* 1999.

Global

Institute for
Conflict Analysis and Resolution

RESEARCH
ACTION
ADVOCACY

The Institute for Conflict Analysis and Resolution (ICAR) aims to advance the understanding and resolution of significant and persistent human conflicts among individuals, groups, communities, identity groups, and nations.

The ICAR community has close ties with a number of affiliated organizations, which play an important role in the field of conflict resolution, locally, nationally, and internationally. At the heart of the Institute's work is the systematic and ongoing analysis of the nature, origins, and types of social conflict and of the processes and conditions required for the co-operative resolution of conflicts.

The Institute pursues its mission through four major components. It offers M.Sc. and Ph.D. degrees in conflict analysis and resolution, as well as training and short courses for general and specialized audiences.

Enhancing the degree programs are three additional components: research and publication, a clinical and consultancy program, and public education. The research and publication component focuses on exploration of conditions which attract parties to the negotiation table, the role of third parties in dispute resolution, and the testing of a variety of conflict intervention methods.

A clinical program is offered to students through the Applied Practice and Theory Program and through consultant work with individual faculties, associates and affiliate organizations.

Community outreach is accomplished through the publication of books and articles, public lectures, conferences, seminars, and special briefings on the theory and practice of conflict resolution. In all, ICAR can be considered one of the major institutes when it comes to linking theory and practice of conflict management.

George Mason University
Fairfax, VA 22030-4444
United States

Tel: +1 (703) 993 1300
Fax: +1 (703) 993 1302
icarinfo@osf1.gmu.edu
www.gmu/edu/departments/icar

Publications: Culture and Conflict Resolution, 2000; *The New Agenda for Peace Research,* 2000; *Conflict Resolution: Dynamics, Process and Structure,* 2000.

South Asia, Balkans, Cyprus, Africa

Institute for Multi-Track Diplomacy

EDUCATION
ACTION

The mission of the Institute for Multi-Track Diplomacy (IMTD) is to promote a systems approach to peacebuilding and to facilitate the transformation of deep-rooted social conflicts. The Institute seeks to integrate different approaches in any given case of conflict transformation. An example of one of the activities is the India-Pakistan Business and Conflict Resolution Program, which aims to increase awareness and to engage the business community in concrete peacebuilding initiatives. Another example is the Inter-Kashmir Dialogue and Negotiation Skills Workshop, a project that brings together concerned citizens from both sides of the Line of Control (LoC) in Kashmir. IMTD is also active in Nepal, where it co-organized a workshop on conflict resolution and peacebuilding in June 2001.

1819 H Street NW Suite 1200
Washington, DC 20006
United States

Tel: +1 (202) 466 4605
Fax: +1(202) 466 4607
imtd@imtd.org
www.imtd.org

Contact: Chris Bjornestad, Program Associate
Number of staff: 5
Budget: $500,000–$1,000,000
Publications: PeaceBuilder, newsletter; *The Need for Multi-Track Diplomacy; Multi-Track Diplomacy: A Systems Approach to Peace;* occasional paper series.

Central Asia, Central and
Eastern Europe, Balkans, CIS countries

Open Society Institute

ACTION

The Open Society Institute (OSI) promotes the development and maintenance of open societies around the world. OSI does this by supporting an array of activities dealing with educational, social, legal, and health-care reform and by encouraging alternative approaches to complex and controversial issues. It has a special program to help young people, a program for small-business entrepreneurs, a program in English language,and an Information Program. The Constitutional and Legal Policy Institute program supports legal reform, basic rights, and democratic institutions in Central Asia, Mongolia, and Central and Eastern Europe.

400 West 59th Street
New York, NY 10019
United States

Tel: +1 (212) 584 0600
Fax: +1 (212) 548 4679
www.soros.org/osi

Publications: Open Society News.

Global

United Nations Department of Political Affairs

RESEARCH
ACTION

The United Nations Department of Political Affairs (DPA) provides advice and support on all political matters to the Secretary-General relating to the maintenance and restoration of peace and security. DPA monitors, analyzes, and assesses political developments throughout the world; identifies potential or actual conflicts in whose control and resolution the United Nations could play a useful role; recommends to the Secretary-General appropriate actions in such cases and executes the approved policy; and assists the Secretary-General in carrying out political activities decided by him and/or mandated by the General Assembly and the Security Council in the areas of preventive diplomacy, peace-making, peace-keeping and post-conflict peace-building.

UN Plaza
DPA Policy Planning Unit
Room S-3780
New York, NY 10017
United States

Contact: Tapio Kanninen, Chief Policy
Planning Unit

Tel: +1 (212) 963 5118
Fax: +1 (212) 963 5065
commond@un.org
www.un.org/depts/dpa

Global

United Nations Development Programme

EDUCATION
ACTION
ADVOCACY

Over the past several years the United Nations Development Programme (UNDP) has come to place greater emphasis on conflict prevention. The Emergency Response Division sees poor governance as a major factor in the development of man-made crises, so it works on capacity building for good governance nationally and internationally by means of preventive development and training. Among other things, the Programme provides electoral assistance, support for judiciaries, and public sector management. UNDP's core goal of supporting sustainable human development is in itself a strong foundation for the prevention of conflict in the long term.

304 E. 45th St.
New York, NY 10017
United States

Contact: Robert Piper, Deputy Director
Emergency Response Division

Tel: +1 (212) 906 5324
Fax: +1 (212) 906 5364
aboutundp@undp.org
www.undp.org

Global

United States Institute of Peace

RESEARCH
EDUCATION
ACTION

The United States Institute of Peace (USIP) is a federal institution created and funded by Congress to strengthen U.S. capacity to promote the peaceful resolution of international conflict. The Institute meets its congressional mandate through an array of programs, including grants, conferences, and educational activities. It seeks to support policymakers by providing independent and creative assessments of how to deal with international conflict situations by political means. In Asia, the Research and Studies Program conducts frequent working group meetings directed toward building confidence on the Korean Peninsula.

1200 17th Street NW
Suite 200
Washington, DC 20036 3011
United States
_____

Tel: +1 (202) 457 1700
Fax: +1 (202) 429 6063
usip_requests@usip.org
www.usip.org

Contact: Richard H. Solomon, President
Publications: Peace Watch Newsletter; Guide to IGO's, NGO's and the Military in Peace and Relief Operations, 2001; *US Leadership of the Cambodia Settlement & Normalization with Vietnam,* 2000; *Peaceworks;* special reports.

Afghanistan

Women's Alliance for
Peace and Human Rights in Afghanistan

RESEARCH
EDUCATION
ADVOCACY

The Women's Alliance for Peace and Human Rights in Afghanistan (WAPHA) promotes awareness of human rights violations in Afghanistan and advocates for the social, political, economic, and civil rights of Afghan women and girls. The Alliance has educated the UN, the United States, and other countries on the Afghan conflict and ways of solving it. It has presented various papers on this subject. WAPHA mobilizes NGOs and people at the grassroots level through lobbying and awareness, research, and advocacy activities. The Alliance also organizes workshops and conferences and publishes newsletters, an electronic news list, and training materials.

P.O. Box 77057
Washington, DC 20013-7057
United States
_____

Tel: +1 (202) 882 1432
Fax: +1 (202) 882 8125
zieba@aol.com or
info@wapha.org
www.wapha.org

Contact: Zieba Shorish-Shamley, Director
Number of staff: 3
Budget: < $25,000
Publications: Urgent Action Alert, appeals.

Uzbekistan, Central Asia

Association of Uzbekistan for Sustainable Water Resources Development

EDUCATION
ADVOCACY

The mission of the Association of Uzbekistan for Sustainable Water Resources Development (AUSWRD) is to bring together water resource specialists to discuss the issues of water consumption and conflict in Central Asia. In 1996 the Association contributed to the establishment of a group of independent experts from the six countries of the Aral Sea basin for discussing the conflict-related issues of the region. The Association also provides training to local community leaders in the border regions of Uzbekistan on addressing the issues of water consumption and conflict.

Office 208a, 39-G Kari-Niyazova Street
Tashkent 700 000
Uzbekistan

Tel/fax: +998 (71) 137 4665
auswrd@yahoo.com
abdullaev.freeyellow.com/
    AUSWRD.html

Contact: Iskander Abdullaev,
Executive Director
Number of staff: 6

Publications: Quarterly newsletter;
General Strategies in Prevention of Aral Sea Problems, 1996.

Uzbekistan, Central Asia

Union for Defence of the Aral Sea and the Amudarya

RESEARCH
ACTION
ADVOCACY

The Union for Defence of the Aral Sea and the Amudarya (UDASA) is a union of people who strive to protect the sea and the rivers that nourish it with the aim of improving environmental conditions and fostering stability in the region. One of the oldest NGOs in the region, UDASA considers the issues of water consumption an important aspect of conflict prevention in Central Asia. UDASA has a wide network of contacts among environmental NGOs in Central Asia and worldwide.

8th floor, 41 Berdakh Avenue
Nukus 742000
Karakalpakstan
Uzbekistan

Tel/fax: +998 (61) 217 7229
udasa@nukus.freenet.uz
www.cango.net.kg/homepages/uz/udasa/

Contact: Yusup Kamalov
Number of staff: 3

Internet Resources

In compiling this list of web-based resources on conflicts and conflict prevention in Asia, and in Central and South Asia more specifically, we have tried to select those that will provide links and directions to the most important sources available. Along with resources directly related to the conflicts in South and Central Asia, we have also included some more general sources. Of course this list is by no means exhaustive, and the inclusion or exclusion of a website does not necessarily imply a value-based assessment. If you know of any websites that you think should be added in a later edition of this book, and on the links section of our own website, please let us know.

AccessAsia
www.accessasia.org
The website AccessAsia is a large clearinghouse for information on contemporary Asian affairs and policy-related issues. It includes databases of Asia specialists, Asia research organizations, and a conference kiosk. The site also provides a great number of links to Asian news sources in its news links section. Sources include general Asian news, as well as the main news sources of all of the countries in Asia.

Akhbar, a window on South Asia
www.indowindow.com/akhbar
Akhbar is a South Asian information portal maintained by scholars, social activists, and volunteers. Its main feature is a regular magazine with articles on a current topic. Akhbar also provides access to South Asia resources in its South Asia Documents Documentation Centre.

AlertNet
www.alertnet.org
This site was developed by Reuters in order to provide quick and easily accessible information to disaster relief organizations. It includes the latest news as well as news from the field, which are compiled in a clear overview by country. The country profiles and relief resources guides on topics and regions are also useful.

Asia Foundation
www.asiafoundation.org
On its website, the Asia Foundation provides news about the Asian region from a variety of sources, as well as links to a number of its partner organizations in Asia. There is also an explanation of the grant-making procedures of this large donor organization.

Asian Development Bank
www.adb.org
Although focused primarily on development in the Asian region, this website offers a large amount of information on related topics such as governance, involuntary resettlement, law, and policy reform. The site offers direct access to information on countries, topics, field offices, and resources, and also contains a database of Asian NGOs.

Asian Studies WWW Virtual Library
coombs.anu.edu.au/WWWVL-AsianStudies.html
The Asian Studies WWW Virtual Library is part of the WorldWide Web Virtual Library Project published by the Research School of Pacific and Asian Studies at the Australian National University in Canberra. The library is divided into global, regional, and national resources. It also includes an Asian Studies WWW Monitor, which presents a daily digest of new Asian-focus online resources.

Asia Source
www.asiasource.org
This is an online resource developed by the Asia Society, a U.S. institution that aims to enhance the understanding of Asian cultures. It includes up-to-date information on cultural, political, social, economic, and historical issues in Asia. It offers sections on world press and special reports on current topics.

Asiaweek
www.asiaweek.com
Asiaweek is a newsmagazine on Asian affairs in general. It offers links to other Asian news sites such as Time Asia and CNN Asia.

British Association for South Asian Studies
www.staff.brad.ac.uk/akundu/basas/index.html
The British Association for South Asian Studies offers a great number of links on South Asian issues, as well as tips on how to search for South Asia material on the Internet. The South Asia links list includes search engines and indexes, news sites, and other media and resources. In addition, there are a number of country-specific sites listed.

Canada Asia Pacific Resource Network
www.caprn.bc.ca
This website offers a large directory of NGOs and trade unions in the Asia-Pacific region. The NGO section of this database is organized according to various topics, such as human and democratic rights, women's rights, and development and sustainability.

Carnegie Commission for Preventing Deadly Conflict
www.ccpdc.org
This website is valuable for its many online documents, including the extensive Final Report, published in December 1997, that presents the findings of the commission's work over three years, the causes of conflict, and methods of preventing deadly conflict.

Carter Center
www.cartercenter.org
An important part of the Carter Center's activities are its Peace Programs. These include conflict resolution programs and human rights monitoring in various countries in the world. Descriptions of these programs can be found in the section on international activities. Also, various speeches, news releases, election reports, and reports of Carter's visits ("trip reports") are easily accessible through this site.

Central Asia-Caucasus Analyst
www.cacianalyst.org
The Central Asia-Caucasus Analyst of the Central Asia-Caucasus Institute, an independent research and policy institution affiliated with Johns Hopkins University, is a biweekly briefing on important events in the region. It can be downloaded in pdf format. The site also includes field reports and news bites.

Center for World Studies Indigenous Studies Virtual Library
www.cwis.org/wwwvl/indig-vl.html
The Center for World Studies Indigenous Studies Virtual Library provides links to a number of resources on indigenous peoples, like important documents sorted by region, UN documents, and related treaties.

Conciliation Resources
www.c-r.org
The website of Conciliation Resources contains large sections of the Accord Series— excellent international reviews of peace initiatives in specific countries and regions. The series includes, for example, reviews of Tajikistan, Cambodia, Sri Lanka, Fiji, and the Philippines. A collection of occasional papers can also be viewed online.

Council for Security Cooperation in the Asia Pacific
www.cscap.org
The website of the Council for Security Cooperation in the Asia Pacific offers a number of links to other directories and organizations related to security cooperation in the Asia Pacific region.

CRInfo
www.crinfo.org
The Conflict Resolution Information Source is set up as a cooperation of various participants, sponsored by the William and Flora Hewlett Foundation. The site contains a wealth of information on conflict resolution and related topics, as well as on education and training, organizations, and networking. There are various search engines and listings of subjects, and for easy reference it is possible to browse by topic or keyword. Especially valuable is the Today's News section in which the latest news is assembled from various sources and arranged by subject.

Derechos Human Rights in South Asia
www.derechos.org/saran
This website offers links to websites, NGOs, international organizations, reports, and articles related to human rights in South Asia. It can be searched by topic or by country. For each of the South Asian countries, it offers links to news sites, NGOs, and human rights reports. It also has a special section on women.

Digital South Asia Library
dsal.uchicago.edu/
The Digital South Asia Library is a project of the Center for Research Libraries in Chicago. The library contains links to images, maps, statistics, electronic books, journals, and more. It also contains a link to the South Asia Resource Access on the Internet.

Eurasianet
www.eurasianet.org
This is a comprehensive site focusing on the latest news and analyses of current affairs, and political and social developments. Additional features include newsmaker interviews with leading experts, book reviews, a discussion forum, and special sections on

human rights, the environment, and election watch. Excellent resource pages by country are also presented. This site is operated by the Central Eurasia Project of the Open Society Institute.

European Centre for Conflict Prevention
www.conflict-prevention.net
This website offers a host of valuable information on conflict prevention and peacebuilding. All of the organization's publications appear online, most importantly the surveys on conflict prevention and peacebuilding in Africa, Europe, the Caucasus, and Central and South Asia (with more regions to follow). These surveys—with regional as well as thematic focuses—provide comprehensive background information on the causes of a conflict and on the prevention and transformation activities that take place in relation to it, as well as on organizations working in the field. With profiles of about 800 organizations worldwide, this site offers the most comprehensive directory of organizations available on the internet.

Forum on Early Warning and Early Response
www.fewer.org
This site offers comprehensive early warning reports on various regions in the world, including Central Asia, Southeast Asia, and the Caucasus, and lists links to other valuable information and documents available on the internet. There is also a focus on documents on methodology development, most successful conflict prevention practice, and small arms flows.

Global Beat
www.nyu.edu/globalbeat/
The Global Beat website, developed and maintained by the Center for War, Peace, and the News Media at New York University, is a web-based resource on international issues for journalists, editors, and other interested people. The site collects articles and opinions from researchers, research institutes, and journals on topics such as East and South Asian Security, Nuclear Weapons & Proliferation, the Middle East, and the Balkan Conflicts.

Harvard University Program on Humanitarian Policy and Conflict Research
www.preventconflict.org/portal/centralasia
This site serves as a portal to specifically crafted information and analysis on human security issues in Central Asia necessary for informed debate and policymaking. The site provides a searchable database of links to critical reference materials, maps, and regional and international news sources on the region, as well as easy access to information on organizations and specialists active in the field.

Heidelberg Institute of International Conflict Research
www.hiik.de
Two unique projects set up by the Department of Political Science of the University of Heidelberg can be found at this site. First, there is the Conflict Barometer, which gives a concise annual update of the status of conflicts around the world. Second, there is the KOSIMO database, which contains 693 political conflicts since 1945. In a short overview, it describes these conflicts by using 28 variables such as the background of a conflict, international diplomacy, and transformation efforts.

Himal
www.himalmag.com
Himal is a South Asian review magazine that serves as a platform for information and debate on current South Asian issues. It offers the latest news from many South Asian newspapers, as well as opinions and essays on various topics.

Human Rights Watch Asia
www.hrw.org/asia/
The Asia section of the website of Human Rights Watch offers an overview of and on-line access to the Human Rights Watch reports, press releases, and letters related to Asian countries. The site can be searched by topic, such as women's rights and refu-gees, and by country.

INCORE
www.incore.ulst.ac.uk
The website of the Initiative on Conflict Resolution & Ethnicity contains a compre-hensive collection of quality links and documents. The host of information is subdi-vided along various lines. First are regularly updated country guides, which provide a list of news sources, discussion groups, academic links, and NGOs by country. Then there is a list of peace agreements, an ethnic conflict research digest with bibliogra-phies of recently published documents, and a list of thematic guides on subjects such as media and conflict and women and conflict. Further, there is an information bank for quick reference on subjects such as academic and training programs, organizations, and bibliographic databases. A more thorough search can be done in the researcher database.

India Development Information Network
www.indev.org
This website was set up by the British Council to provide access to development in-formation on India. It contains four databases on organizations, projects, key docu-ments, and statistics. There are links to over 2,500 development organizations in India.

Institute for War and Peace Reporting
www.iwpr.net
A professional collaboration of international and local journalists provides weekly in-depth analyses of global events and issues and those specific to Central Asia and Af-ghanistan on this site. It also contains valuable special reports and a comprehensive list of links to local media.

Institute of Peace and Conflict Studies, New Delhi
www.ipcs.org
The homepage of the Institute of Peace and Conflict Studies contains a substantial number of articles and news reports, organized by country and topics relevant to the South Asian region. It is updated daily.

Interactive Central Asia Resource Project
www.icarp.org
This site offers an excellent portal to information on countries in Central Asia. It provides biographies and quick facts on the countries, as well as a list of links to institutions, experts, bibliographies, and news sources. The site also contains a valuable list of publications.

International Alert
www.international-alert.org
This site focuses on the projects run by International Alert (IA), including those in Sri Lanka, as well as an extensive list of links and a collection of IA publications, which can be downloaded in full-text versions. The site is a gateway to the international cam-paign to promote the role of women in peacebuilding.

International Crisis Group
www.intl-crisis-group.org
This website is one the most resourceful and accurate sites about conflicts and conflict prevention. The site is subdivided along the lines of International Crisis Group's (ICG)

projects in Africa, Asia, and the Balkans. ICG's Asia Program is currently centered around projects in Central Asia, Cambodia, Indonesia, and Burma/Myanmar. All ICG's policy reports (country specific and issue reports) are easily accessible and regularly updated. Interesting, too, is the special section on news and reports on the EU and conflict prevention. A useful feature is the capability to customize the home page according to the country or subject of one's interest.

International Security Network (ISN)
www.isn.ethz.ch
The International Security Network (ISN) site is maintained by the Centre for Security Studies and Conflict Research in Switzerland. The website is valuable for its links library and databases. The extensive ISN Links Library offers full-text publications by (inter-) governmental organizations, NGOs, and the media. These documents can be browsed by countries/regions, subjects, and directories. Equally useful is the FIRST (Facts on International Relations and Security Trends) Reference Database. This joint project with the Stockholm International Peace Research Institute offers documents from research institutes around the world in the field of international relations and security. The site also contains a daily updated Security Watch section in cooperation with Reuters.

Japanese Center for Preventive Diplomacy
www.jcpd.gr.jp
Together with the Japan Institute of International Affairs, the Japanese Center for Preventive Diplomacy maintains an online directory of organizations for conflict prevention in Asia and the Pacific. This website also holds a dialogue area for conflicts. On this interactive forum, many different practitioners of conflict resolution participate in discussions on different conflicts in the world, with a focus on Asia.

Nira's World Directory of Think Tanks
www.nira.go.jp/ice/tt-info/nwdtt99/id-asi.html
This URL connects to the Asia section of this comprehensive resource of think tanks. Asian think tanks are listed by country.

Organisation for Security and Cooperation in Europe
www.osce.org
This valuable website offers not only general information on the Organisation for Security and Cooperation in Europe's (OSCE) activities, but also the latest news, press releases, statements, a comprehensive calendar of events, and in-depth stories in the section In Focus. The home page of the Forum for Security Co-operation offers a large number of documents on the military aspects of security. Country-specific information is accessible through the sites of the mission headquarters.

Program on Peace Studies and Conflict Resolution,
Karachi University Department of International Relations
www.ppscr.org
Besides information on the research and teaching activities of the Program on Peace Studies and Conflict Resolution, this website offers a great number of links to organizations and research institutes in the field of conflict resolution and peace studies.

Project Ploughshares
www.ploughshares.ca/content/ACR/acr.html
The website of Project Ploughshares offers a large number of resources related to peace and conflict worldwide. The annual Armed Conflicts Reports offer updates of conflicts around the world, as well as maps on Armed Conflict, Peacekeeper/Observer/Enforcement Missions, Nuclear Weapons, and Nuclear-Weapon-Free Zones.

ProPoor InfoTech Centre
www.propoor.org
This website was established by the Indian NGO ProPoor InfoTech Centre and serves as a portal site to South Asian NGOs. It includes links to many NGOs in South Asia, persons, projects, news, and employment opportunities.

Red Cross
www.icrc.org
Apart from weekly ICRC news and an overview of regional operations, this site offers information and articles on various topics, including women and war, children and war, and humanitarian action in armed conflicts. There is a large and informative section on international humanitarian law.

Regional Centre for Strategic Studies
www.rcss.org
The website of the Regional Centre for Strategic Studies provides access to an extensive directory of individuals and institutions engaged in South Asian Strategic Studies. It is based on a survey conducted in 1995-1996 and arranged by country and city.

Relief Web
www.reliefweb.int
This site promotes itself as serving the information needs of the humanitarian relief community. It is indeed a valuable news source on complex emergencies and natural disasters around the world. For each county, an additional and comprehensive list of links provides a diverse range of subjects including country profiles, development, disaster, history, politics, defense, refugees, and media links. The site also features a large map center and the IRIN (Integral Regional Information Networks) news service that also covers Central Asia.

South Asia Citizens Web
www.mnet.fr/aiindex/
The South Asia Citizens Web promotes dialogue and the exchange of information on South Asian citizen initiatives. It also offers a daily mailing list with the latest South Asian civil society initiatives and commentary.

South Asia Human Rights Documentation Centre
www.hri.ca/partners/sahrdc/index.htm
The website presents resources on human rights in South Asia. The South Asia Human Rights Documentation Centre also offers a news feature called Human Rights Features. This monthly online feature provides information on human rights, democracy, and good governance.

South Asia in Review
www.southasia-inreview.com
South Asia in Review is an online quarterly journal of the United States Institute of Strategic Studies for South Asia.

South Asian Community Center for Education, Research and Action
www.saccer.org
The website of this organization offers links to the Green Party of India, Movement against Nuclear Power, and India-Pakistan Reconciliation School. The latter was set up by the South Asian Community Center and provides for online lessons on reconciliation for Pakistani and Indian youth. The school is also run by correspondence.

South Asia Net
www.arts.monash.edu.au/mai/southasianet/resources.htm
This website provides a number of resources for South Asia scholars, including publications and a resources database on South Asia. It also offers a large database of websites on South Asia that can be searched by keyword.

South Asia Resource Access on the Internet
www.columbia.edu/cu/lweb/indiv/southasia/cuvl/
SARAI was set up by the Department of South & Southeast Asian Studies at Columbia University in New York. It includes internet resources arranged by country, topic, and organization, including academic jobs and postings, conferences and events, and an international directory of South Asia scholars. It is a part of the Asian Studies WWW Virtual Library.

South Asia Watch
www.zmag.org/southasia/
This website is an activist-oriented resource on South Asian politics, economics, and development. There are links to activist groups, magazines, and readings on South Asia. Other link topics include the politics of development, caste and indigenous peoples, intercommunalism, and anti-nuclear sites.

Swedish South Asian Studies Network
www.sasnet.lu.se
Swedish South Asian Studies Network is an international network for research, education, and information about South Asia, based at Lund University, Sweden. It provides a vast amount of information on conferences, journals, training, education, research institutes, individual researchers, and more, related to South Asia.

The Times of Central Asia
www.times.kg
This site offers daily news from the region and also has country guides and links. Access to full text articles and news is available after registering.

UN Department of Peacekeeping Operations
www.un.org/Depts/dpko/dpko/cu_mission/body.htm
This site presents an overview of and in-depth information on past and current peacekeeping operations of the United Nations.

United Nations Development Programme
www.undp.org
The country office websites offer news, documents, and publications on the development situation in a specific country and give an overview of development cooperation projects and United Nations Development Programme (UNDP) programs. Many country office sites provide details of peacebuilding activities. The home page offers a section on conflict and security and is also a portal for the sites of the UNDP offices around the world.

United States Department of States—Bureau of South Asian Affairs
www.state.gov/www/regions/sa/index.html
The home page of the Bureau of South Asian Affairs provides information on the South Asian countries, fact sheets, human rights reports, and travel advice for the region. There are also links to some other main, related U.S. information sources, such as the Library of Congress, the Peace Corps, and the Central Intelligence Agency.

United States Institute for Peace
www.usip.org
This website is invaluable for the large amount of reports and documents that can be accessed online. The United States Institute for Peace Digital Library in International Conflict Management is being expanded, and currently includes a digital collection of peace agreements and truth commissions. Furthermore, special reports, the Peace Watch Newsletter, and the Peaceworks series of reports on special subjects can all be found in full-text version. The site further hosts an overview of events in the peace (research) field, often including webcasts, and the On the Wire section, which contains interviews with experts.

World Bank
www.worldbank.org
The website of the World Bank offers valuable information on related subjects such as legal and judicial reform and poverty reduction. The frequently updated country statistics provide a useful source of information. The site also provides regional overviews of World Bank strategies and projects, including those of the South Asian region.

Selected Bibliography

Abdullaev, Kamoludin, and Catherine Barnes. *Politics of Compromise: The Tajikistan Peace Process.* London: Conciliation Resources, 2001.

ACHA Peace Bulletin, Association for Communal Harmony in Asia, Oregon, United States.

ACR Newsletter, Association for Conflict Resolution, Washington, DC, United States.

Afghan Development Association (ADA). *Strengthening Peace in Afghanistan Through Sustainable Human Development.* Peshawar: ADA, 1997.

Afghanistan Monthly Review, British Agencies Afghanistan Group, London, United Kingdom.

Ahmar, Moonis. *The Challenge of Confidence Building in South Asia.* New Delhi: Har Anand, 2001.

———, *Chronology of Conflict and Cooperation in South Asia 1947–2001.* Karachi: PPSCR; KUIRD, 2001.

———, and Farhan H. Siddiqi.*The Challenges of Conflict Resolution and Security in 21st Century: Problems and Prospects.* Karachi: University of Karachi, Program on Peace Studies & Conflict Resolution, [s.a.].

———, (ed.). *The Arab-Israeli Peace Process: Lessons for India and Pakistan.* London: Oxford University Press, 2001.

Ahmed, Imtiaz and Meghna Guhathakurta, (eds.). *SAARC: Beyond State-Centric Cooperation.* Dhaka: Center for Social Studies, 1992.

Ahmed, Ishtiaq. *State, Nation and Ethnicity in Contemporary South Asia.* London: Pinter, 1998.

Ahmed, Mehtabuddin, and Prosenjit Chowdury, (eds.). *The Turbulent North East.* New Delhi, 1996.

Akiner, Shirin. *Central Asia: Conflict or Stability and Development?* London: Minority Rights Group International (MRG), 1996.

Ali, S. Mahmud. *The Fearful State: Power, People and Internal War in South Asia.* London: Zed Press, 1993.

Alistair Lamb. *Kashmir: A Disputed Legacy 1846–1990.* Herfordshire: Roxford Books, 1991.

All Bodo Students' Union (ABSU). *Why Seperate State of Bodoland: Demand and Justification).* Kokrajhar: ABSU, [1999].

Allison, Roy, and Lena Jonson (eds.). *Central Asia Security: The New International Context.* London: RIIA, 2001.

Anderson, Mary B. *Do No Harm: How Aid Can Support Peace—Or War.* Boulder, CO: Lynne Rienner, 1999.

Armon, Jeremy and Liz Philipson (eds.). *Demanding Sacrifice: War and Negotiation in Sri Lanka.* London: Conciliation Resources, 1998.

629

Asia Foundation. *Focus on Human Rights.* San Franscisco: The Asia Foundation, 1998.
———, *Governance Reform and Lessons from the Economic Crisis in Asia.* San Fransisco: The Asia Foundation, 1999.
———, *Strengthening Democracy through Women's Political Participation.* San Fransisco: The Asia Foundation, 1999.
Asia Pacific Advocate, Asia Pacific Center for Justice and Peace, Washington, DC, United States.
Asia Pacific Human Rights NGOs. *Asia Pacific NGO Human Rights Congress: New Delhi, December 1996.* Bangkok: Asia Pacific Human Rights NGOs, 1996.
Asia Survey, Institute of East Asian Studies, University of California, Berkely, United States.
Asian Affairs, Royal Society for Asian Affairs, Surrey, United Kingdom.
Asian Strategic Review, Institute for Defence Studies and Analyses, New Delhi, India.
Banerjee, Dipankar, *CBM's in South Asia: Potential and Possibilities.* Colombo: Regional Centre for Strategic Studies (RCSS), 2000.
———, *Comprehensive and Cooperative Security in South Asia.* Institute of Peace and Conflict Studies, 1998.
———, *Confidence Building Measures in South Asia.* Colombo: Regional Centre for Strategic Studies (RCSS), 1999.
———, *South Asia at Gun Point: Small Arms and Light Weapons Proliferation in South Asia.* Colombo: RCSS, 2000.
———, and Joseph A., Mallika. *Anti-personnel Landmines: A South Asian Regional Survey.* [s.l.]: [s.n.], 1999.
———, (ed). *Security Studies in South Asia: Change and Challenges.* New Delhi: Manohar Publishers & Distributors, 2000.
Banerjee, Sumanta, (ed.). *Shrinking Space: Minority Right in South Asia.* Kathmandu: South Asia Forum for Human Rights, [s.a.].
Barakat, Sultan, Mohammed Ehsan, and Arne Strand. NGOs and Peace-Building in Afghanistan: workshop report 3–7 April 1994. York: University of York, 1994.
Baruah, Sanjib. *India Against Itself: Assam and the Politics of Nationality.* New Delhi: Oxford University Press, 1999.
Basrur, Rajesh M. (ed). *Security in the New Millennium: Views from Asia.* New Delhi: India Research Press, 2001.
Bastian, Sunil. *The Failure of State Formation, Identity Conflict and Civil Society Responses: The Case of Sri Lanka.* Bradford: University of Bradford, Department of Peace Studies, Centre for Conflict Resolution, 1999.
Beersmans, Paul. *Jammu en Kasjmir: het omstreden paradijs.* Deurne: Continental Publishing, 1999.
Behera, Navnita Chadha, *State, Identity and Violence: Jammu, Kashmir and Ladakh.* New Delhi: Manohar Publishers, Centre for Policy Research, 2000.
———, Paul M. Evans, and Gowher Rizvi. *Beyond Boundaries: A Report on the State of Non-Official Dialogues on Peace, Security & Cooperation in South Asia.* Toronto: Joint Centre for Asia Pacific Studies, 1997.
———, et al. *People-to-People Contacts in South Asia.* New Delhi: Manohar, 2000.
———, and V.A. Pai Panandikar (eds.). *Perspectives on South Asia.* New Delhi: Konark, 2000.
Behuria, Ashok K. *Accession of Kashmir to the Indian Dominion: An Historical Study.* New Delhi: South Asian Centre for Strategic Studies, 1999.
Berghof Research Centre for Constructive Conflict Management. *Berghof Handbook for Conflict Transformation.* Berlin: The Berghof Research Centre for Constructive Conflict Management, 2002.
Bertocci, Peter J. "Resource Development and Ethnic Conflict in Bangladesh: The Case of Chakmas in the Chittagong Hill Tracts," in Dhirendra Vajpeyi and Yogendra K. Malik (eds.), *Religious and Ethnic Minority Politics in South Asia, New Delhi,* 1989, pp. 160-161.

Bhattarai, Teeka, et al. *Forests and Indigenous Peoples of Asia*. London: Minority Rights Group International (MRG), 1999.

Bhaumik, Subir, *Insurgents Crossfire: Northeast India*. New Delhi: Lancer Publishers, 1996.

———, Meghna Guhathakurta, and Sabyasachi Basu Ray Chaudhury (eds.). *Living on the Edge: Essays on the Chittatong Hill Tracts*. Kathmandu: South Asia Forum for Human Rights, 1997.

Bhengra, Ratnaker, C.R. Bijoy, and Shimreichnon Luithui. *The Adivasis of India*. London: Minority Rights Group International (MRG), 1998 .

BIISS Quarterly, Bangladesh International Institute for Strategic Studies, Dhaka, Bangladesh.

BICC Bulletin, Bonn International Centre for Conversion, Bonn, Germany.

Bose, Nayana, and Adnan Rehmat (eds). *Cross Currents*. Colombo: RCSS, 2001.

Bose, Sumantra. *The Challenge in Kashmir: Democracy, Self-Determination and a Just Peace*. New Delhi/London: Sage Publications, 1997.

Bose, Tapan K. *Protection of Refugees in South Asia: Need for a Legal Framework*. Kathmandu: SAFHR, 2000. (SAFHR paper series No. 6).

———, and Rita Manchanda (eds.). *States, Citizens and Outsiders: The Uprooted Peoples of South Asia*. Kathmandu: South Asia Forum for Human Rights, 1997.

Bosu Mullick, S., Edwin Jaydas, Anto Akkara, and Anita Jaydas. Indian Confederation of Indigenous and Tribal Peoples (ICITP). *Indigenous Identity: Crisis and Reawakening*. New Delhi: Navdin Prakashan Kendra, 1993.

Carter Center News, Carter Center, Atlanta, United States.

CCA Newsletter, Co-operation Center for Afghanistan, Peshawar, Pakistan.

Central Asia and the Caucasus: Journal of Social and Political Studies, Central Asia and the Caucasus Information and Analytical Center, Luleå, Sweden.

Central Asia-Caucasus Analyst, The Central Asia-Caucasus Institute of the Johns Hopkins University/The Nitze School of Advanced International Studies, Washington, DC, United States.

Central Asian Survey, Taylor & Francis Group, Carfax Publisher, London, United Kingdom.

Chandran, Suba, et al. *Next Steps in Jammu & Kashmir: Give Peace a Change*. New Delhi: Peace Publications, 2000.

Chari, P.R., *Security and Governance in South Asia*. New Delhi: Manohar, 2001.

———, and Pervaiz Iqbal Cheema. *Simla Agreement of 1972*. New Delhi: Manohar Publishers, 2001.

———, Pervaiz Iqbal Cheema, and Iftekharuzzaman (eds.). *Nuclear Non-proliferation in India and Pakistan: Suth Asian Perspective*. New Delhi: Manohar Publishers, 1996.

———, (ed.). *Perspectives on National Security in South Asia*. New Delhi: Manohar Publishers, 1999.

Chaudhury, Sabyasachi Basu, and Shahid Fiaz. *Ten Week War in Kargil: from the News Files*. Kathmandu: SAFHR, 1999. (SAFHR paper series No. 7).

CODEP Newsletter, Conflict, Development and Peace Network, London, United Kingdom.

Coexistence Noticeboard, Coexistence Initiative, New York, United States.

Cohen, J. *Conflict Prevention in the OSCE: An Assessment of Capacities*. The Hague: Netherlands Institute of International Relations Clingendael, 1999.

Committee for Initiative on Kashmir. *Kashmir War: Proxy War: A Report*. New Delhi: Committee for Initiative on Kashmir, 1993.

Communalism Combat, Sabrang Communications, Mumbai, India.

Conflict Prevention Newsletter, European Centre for Conflict Prevention, Utrecht, the Netherlands.

Consortium of Humanitarian Agencies. *Compendium of Humanitarian Agencies & Donors (Northern Province—Sri Lanka)*. Colombo: Consortium of Humanitarian

Agencies, 1999.

———, *Directory of the Consortium of Humanitarian Agencies.* Colombo: Consortium of Humanitarian Agencies, 1999.

Contemporary South Asia, Taylor & Francis Group, Carfax Publisher, London, United Kingdom.

Critical Asian Studies, Communication for a Sustainable Future, Cedar, MI, United States.

Crocker, Chester A. *Herding Cats: Multiparty Mediation in a Complex World.* Washington, DC: United States Institute of Peace Press (USIP), 1999.

Current History, Current History Inc, Philadelphia, United States.

Das, Veena (ed.). *Mirrors of Violence: Communities, Riots and Survivors in South Asia.* Delhi: OUP, 1990.

DasGupta, Sumona. *Breaking the Silence: Women and Kashmir.* New Delhi: Foundation for Universal Responsibility, 2000.

Dawisha, Karen, and Bruce Parrot (eds.). *Conflict, Cleavage and Change in Central Asia and the Caucasus.* Cambridge: CUP, 1997.

Diamond, Louise, and John McDonald. *Multi-track Diplomacy: A Systems Approach to Peace.* West Hartford, CT: Kumarian Press, 1996.

Dutta, N.D. (ed.). *Politics of Identity and Nation Building in Northeast India.* New Delhi: South Asian Press, 1997.

Ebel, Robert, and Rajan Menon (eds.). *Energy and Conflict in Central Asia and the Caucasus.* Boston: Rowman & Littlefield, 2001.

Economic and Political Weekly, Sameeksha Trust, Mumbai, India.

Eisenhower, Susan, and Roald Sagdeev (eds.). *Islam and Central Asia.* Washington, DC: Center for Political and Strategic Studies, 2000.

Ethnic Conflict Research Digest, INCORE, Londonderry, Northern Ireland.

Ethnic Studies Network Bulletin, INCORE, Londonderry, Northern Ireland.

European Centre for Conflict Prevention (ECCP), IFOR, and Coexistence Initiative of the State of the World Forum. *People Building Peace: 35 Inspiring Stories from Around the World.* Utrecht: ECCP, 1999.

———, PIOOM, and Berghof Research Institute for Constructive Conflict Management. *Prevention and Management of Violent Conflicts: An International Directory.* Utrecht: EPCP, 1998.

EWInsights, East West Institute, New York, United States.

Far Eastern Economic Review, Review Publishing Company Limited, Hong Kong.

Faultlines, Institute for Conflict Management, New Delhi, India.

Fisher, Simon, et al. *Working with Conflict: Skills and Strategies for Action.* London: Zed; Birmingham: Responding to Conflict, 2000.

Footpaths, Eastern Mennonite University, Harrisonburg, PA, United States.

Frontline, The Hindu, Chennai, India.

Galama, Anneke, and Paul van Tongeren (eds.). *Towards Better Peace Building Practice: Working Document for International Conference, October 24th–26th, 2001, Soesterberg, the Netherlands.* Utrecht: The European Centre for Conflict Prevention (ECCP); Kontakt der Kontinenten (KdK), 2001.

Gandhi Peace Foundation. *Jammu and Kashmir: The Way Out.* New Delhi: The Gandhi Peace Foundation, 1996.

Gandhi, Rajmohan. *Revenge and Reconciliation.* New Delhi: Penguin, 1999.

Ganguly, Sumit. *The Crisis in Kashmir: Portents of War, Hopes of Peace.* Cambridge: Cambridge University Press, 1977.

Ghosal, Baladash, (ed.). *Diplomacy and Domestic Politics in South Asia.* New Delhi: Konark Publishers, 1996.

Ghosh, Partha S. *Migrants and Refugees in South Asia: Political and Security Dimensions.* Shillong: North-Eastern Hill University Publications, 2001.

Ghosh, Subir. *Frontier Travails: North East: The Politics of a Mess.* New Delhi: Macmillan India, 2001.

Goodhand, Jonathan, and David Hulme. *NGO's and Peace Building in Complex Political Emergencies: A Study of Afghanistan.* Manchester: Institute for Development Policy and Management, 1999.

Government of the Peoples Republic of Nagalim. *The Legal Status of Naga National Armed Resistance: Right to Self-determination underIinternational Law & Why and How the Nagas Are Not Terrorists.* Oking: Government of the People's Republic of Nagalim, Oking Publicity and Information Service, 2001.

Grovers, Dennis (ed.). *Talibanisation: Extremism and Regional Instability in South and Central Asia.* Brussels: SWP-CPN, 2001

Gunatilleke, Godfrey. *Cost of the War: The Economic, Socio-political and Human Cost of the War of Sri Lanka.* Colombo: The National Peace Council of Sri Lanka (NPC), 2001.

Gurr, Ted Robert. *Peoples Versus States: Minorities at Risk in the New Century.* Washington: United States Institute of Peace Press (USIP), 2000.

Harris, Peter, and Ben Reilly (eds.). *Democracy and Deep-rooted Conflict: Options for Negotiators.* Stockholm: International Institute for Democracy and Electoral Assistance (IDEA), 1998.

Hazarika, Sanjoy. *Rites of Passage: Border Crossings, Imagined Homelands.* New Delhi: Penguin, 2000.

———, *Strangers of the Mist: Tales of War and Peace from India's Northeast.* New Delhi: Penguin Books India, 1995.

Herald, Dawn Newspapers, Karachi, Pakistan.

Himal South Asia, Himalmedia, Kathmandu, Nepal.

HRCP Quarterly Newsletter, Human Rights Commission of Pakistan, Lahore, Pakistan.

Human Rights Bulletin, Forum for Protection of Human Rights, Kathmandu, Nepal.

Hyat, Kamila, and Human Rights Commission of Pakistan. *State of Human Rights in 2000.* Lahore: HRCP, 2001.

IANSA Newsletter, International Action Network on Small Arms, London, United Kingdom.

Iftekharuzzaman (ed.). *Ethnicity and Constitutional Reforms in South Asia.* New Delhi: Manohar, 1998.

———, *Regional Economic Trends and South Asian Security.* New Delhi: Manohar Publishers, 1997.

IIAS Newsletter, International Institute for Asian Studies, Leiden University, Leiden, the Netherlands.

Indigenous Affairs, International Workgroup for Indigenous Affairs, Copenhagen, Denmark.

INSEC. *Human Rights Yearbook 2001.* Kathmandu: INSEC, 2001.

Institute for Development and Communication (IDC). *Terrorism, Fundamentalism & Peace in South Asia.* Chandigarh: IDC, [s.a.].

Institute for Regional Studies (IFRS). *Central Asia: New Space for Cooperation.* Bishkek: IFRS, 2000.

Interdependent, European Centre for Global Interdependence and Solidarity, Lisbon, Portugal.

International Alert (IA). *Negotiating Peace in Sri Lanka: Efforts, Failures & Lessons.* IA, 1998.

International Crisis Group (ICG). *Afghanistan and Central Asia: Priorities for Reconstruction and Development.* Osh: ICG, 2001 .

———, *Central Asia: Border Disputes and Conflict Potential.* Osh: ICG, 2002.

———, *Central Asia: Crisis Conditions in Three States.* Brussels: ICG, 2000.

———, *Central Asia: Drugs and Conflict.* Osh: ICG, 2001.

———, *Central Asia: Faultlines in the New Security Map.* Osh: ICG, 2001.

————, *Central Asia: Islamist Mobilisation and Regional Security.* Osh: ICG, 2001.

————, *Central Asia: Water and Conflict.* Osh: ICG, 2002.

————, *The IMU and the Hizb-ut-Tahrir: Implication of the Afghanistan Campaign.* Osh: ICG, 2002.

————, *Kyrgyzstan at Ten: Trouble in the "Island of Democracy."* Osh: ICG, 2001.

————, *The Loya Jirga: One Small Step Forward?* Osh: ICG, 2002.

————, *Pakistan: The Dangers of Conventional Wisdom.* Osh: ICG, 2002.

————, *Securing Afghanistan: The Need for More International Action.* Osh: ICG, 2002.

————, *Tajikistan: An Uncertain Peace.* Osh: ICG, 2001.

————, *Uzbekistan at Ten: Repression and Instability.* Brussels: ICG, 2001.

International Institute for Democracy and Electoral Assistance (IDEA). *Consolidating Democracy in Nepal: Assessment Mission Report.* Stockholm: International IDEA, 1997.

International Migration, International Organisation for Migration, Geneva, Switzerland.

International Negotiation, Kluwer Law International, Cambridge, MA, United States.

International Review of the Red Cross, International Committee of the Red Cross, Geneva, Switzerland.

International Studies Quarterly, International Studies Association, London, United Kingdom.

International Work Group for Indigenous Affairs (IWGA). *Land Rights of the Indigenous Peoples of the Chittagong Hill Tracts.* IWGA: Bangladesh, 2000.

————, *Life Is Not Ours: Land and Human Rights in the Chittagong Hill Tracts.* IWGA: Bangladesh, 2000.

IPCS Bulletin, Institute of Peace and Conflict Studies, New Delhi, India

IPRA Newsletter, International Peace Research Association, Mie, Japan.

Jammu and Kashmir Media File (ed.). *Kashmir Trends: A Digest of News Views and Trends.* New Delhi: India National Press on Kashmir, 1999.

Japan Review of International Affairs, Japan Institute for International Affairs, Tokyo, Japan.

Jayaram, N., and Satish Saberwal. *Social Conflict.* Delhi: OUP, 1996.

Jentleson, Bruce W. (ed.). *Opportunities Missed, Opportunities Seized: Preventive Diplomacy in the Post-Cold War World.* New York: Carnegie Commission on Preventing Deadly Conflict, 2000.

Journal for Strategic Studies, Frank Cass Publishers, London, United Kingdom.

Journal of Central Asian Studies, Association for the Advancement of Central Asian Research, Stillwater, OK, United States.

Journal of Conflict Resolution, Peace Science Society (International), London, United Kingdom.

Journal of Conflict, Security and Development, Centre for Defence Studies, London, United Kingdom.

Journal of Peace Research, Peace Research Institute, Oslo, Norway.

Journal of Peace Studies, International Centre for Peace Studies, New Delhi, India.

Juan, Chee Soon. *To Be Free: Stories from Asia's Struggle against Oppression.* Melbourne: Monash University, 1998. (MAI Publication)

Junghare, Indira Y., N. Ram, and S.P. Udayakumar. *Indo-Pakistan Relations: What Lies Ahead?: Symposium: University of Minnesota April 15 and 16, 1999.* East Bank: University of Minnesota, South Asian Languages and Cultures, 2000.

Kabir, Mohammad Humayun. "The Problems of Tribal Separatism and Constitutional Reform in Bangladesh," in Iftekharuzzaman (ed.), *Ethnicity and Constitutional Reform in South Asia,* Manohar, New Delhi, 1998, p. 18.

Kanti Bajpai, et al. *Jammu and Kashmir: An Agenda For The Future.* New Delhi: Delhi Policy Group, 1999.

Kartha, Tara, and Ayesha Siddiqua Agha. *Curbing the Weapons of Civilian Destruction in South Asia.* Mumbai: International Centre for Peace Initiatives, 1999.

Kashmir Quarterly, Kashmiri-Canadian Council, Scarborough, ON, Canada.

Kashmir Study Group. *1947–1997: The Kashmir Dispute at Fifty: Charting Paths to Peace: Report on the Visit of an Independent Study Team to India and Pakistan Sponsored by the Kashmir Study Group.* New York: Kashmir Study Group, 1997.

———, *Kashmir: A Way Forward.* New York: Kashmir Study Group, 2000.

Khan, Abdur Rob (ed.). *Globalization and Non-Traditional Security in South Asia.* Dhaka: Academic Press and Publisher Limited, 2001.

Krishna, Maj Gen Ashok, and P.R. Chari (eds.). *Kargil: The Tables Turned.* New Delhi: Manohar Publishers, 2001.

Krummenacher, Heinz. *Conflict prevention and power politics: Central Asia as a show case.* Bern: Schweizerische Friedensstiftung: Institut für Konfliktlösung (SFS), 2001.

Lederach, John Paul. *Preparing for peace: conflict transformation across cultures.* Syracuse: SU, Syracuse University, 1995.

Lund, Michael S. *Preventing violent conflicts: a strategy for preventive diplomacy.* Washington, DC: United States Institute of Peace Press (USIP), 1996.

Maclean, Matthew. *Small NGO power: LTDP Program at work.* Dhaka: South Asia Partnership-Bangladesh, 1999.

Maley, W. (ed.). *Fundamentalism reborn? Afghanistan and the Taliban,* London: Hurst & Company, 1998.

Manchanda, Rita. *Reporting Conflict: A Radical Critique of the Mass Media by Indian & Pakistani Journalists.* Kathmandu: SAFHR, 2001. (SAFHR paper series No. 9).

Marsden, Peter. *Afghanistan: Minorities, Conflict, and the Search for Peace.* London: Minorities Rights Group International (MRG), 2001.

Mathews, Dylan. *War Prevention Works: 50 Stories of People Resolving Conflict.* London: Oxford Research Group, 2001.

Media Insight Central Asia, CIMERA, Geneva, Switzerland.

Media Monitor, Centre for Policy Alternatives, Colombo, Sri Lanka.

Mekenkamp, Monique, Paul van Tongeren, and Hans van de Veen (eds.). *Searching for Peace in Central and South Asia: An Overview of Conflict Prevention and Peacebuilding Activities.* Boulder, CO: Lynne Rienner (in association with the European Centre for Conflict Prevention), 2002.

Miall, Hugh, Oliver Ramsbotham, and Tom Woodhouse. *Contemporary Conflict Resolution.* Cambridge: Polity Press, 1999.

Minority Rights Group International (MRG). *World Directory of Minorities.* London: MRG, 1997.

Mitsuru Donowaki. *An Introduction to Preventive Diplomacy.* [s.l.]: Mitsuru Donowaki, 1999.

Modern Asian Studies, University of Cambridge, Cambridge, United Kingdom.

Mohsin, Amena. *The Politics of Nationalism: The Case of the Chittagong Hill Tracts.* Dhaka: University Press Limited, 1997.

Molbech, Anette (ed.). *The Indigenous World 2000–2001.* Copenhagen: The International Work Group for Indigenous Affairs (IWGIA), 2001.

Muivah, Th. *A Rejoinder to the Indian Propaganda Stunt: "Does Violence Get a Mandate?"* Oking: Government of the People's Republic of Nagalim, Oking Publicity and Information Service, 1994.

Multiple Action Research Group (MARG). *Within the Four Walls: A Profile of Domestic Violence.* New Delhi: MARG, 1998.

Muni, S.D., and Lokraj Baral (eds). *Refugees and Regional Security in South Asia.* New Delhi: Konark Publishers, 1996.

National Commission for Justice and Peace Catholic Bishops' Conference in Pakistan. *Human Rights Monitor 2000: A Report on the Situation of Religious Minorities in Pakistan.* Lahore Cantt.: National Commission for Justice and Peace, 2000.

National Peace Council of Sri Lanka. *The Cost of War: Sri Lanka.* Colombo: The National Peace Council of Sri Lanka, 1998.

Nelson, Jane. *The Business of Peace: The Private Sector as a Partner in Conflict Prevention.* London: International Alert (IA); New York: Council on Economic Priorities (CEP); London: The Prince of Wales Business Leaders Forum (PWBLF), 2000.

Nethra, International Centre for Ethnic Studies, Colombo, Sri Lanka.

New Routes, Life & Peace Institute, Uppsala, Sweden.

North South Security Porgramma of King's College, et al. *The Colombo Statement: Workshop on the Indigenous and Regional Press from India, Pakistan and Sri Lanka: Perspectives on the New Millenium (Colombo, June 28–30, 1999).* London: North South Security Program of King's College, 1999.

ODIHR Newsletter, OSCE Office for Democratic Institutions and Human Rights, Warsaw, Poland.

Organization for Security and Co-operation in Europe (OSCE). *OSCE Handbook*/3d ed. Vienna: OSCE, 2000.

OSCE Newsletter, Organization for Security and Co-operation in Europe, Vienna, Austria.

Other Media Communications. *Naga Resistance and the Peace Process: A Dossier.* New Delhi: Other Media Publications, 2001.

Outsider, Minority Rights Group, London, United Kingdom.

Pakem, B. *Nationality, Ethnicity and Cultural Identity in North-East India.* New Delhi: Omsons, 1990.

Pakistan—India Peoples' Forum for Peace and Democracy. *Proceedings, Recommendations and Declaration of the Third Joint Convention, Calcutta 28–31, 1996.* New Delhi: Pakistan—India Peoples' Forum for Peace and Democracy, 1996.

Parliamentarians for Global Action (PGA). *Asian Regional Forum on Economic Revitalization: May 30–31, 1997, Manila, Philippines.* New York: PGA, 1997.

PeaceBuilder, Institute for Multi-Track Diplomacy, Washington, DC, United States.

Peace Initiative, International Centre for Peace Initiatives, New Delhi, India.

Peace Monitor, Centre for Policy Alternatives, Colombo, Sri Lanka.

Peace News for Nonviolent Revolution—Peace News Limited, London, United Kingdom.

Peace Watch Newsletter, United States Institute of Peace, Washington, DC, United States.

Perera, Jehan. *Peace Process in Nagaland and Chittagong Hill Tracts.* Kathmandu: SAFHR, 1999. (SAFHR paper series No. 5).

Phadnis, Urmila. *Ethnicity and Nation-building in South Asia.* New Delhi: Sage, 1990.

Philippine News Survey, Asia Pacific Center for Justice and Peace, Washington, DC, United States.

PUCL Bulletin, People's Union for Civil Liberties, New Delhi, India.

Radhakrishnan, N. *Gurudev Tulsi: Some Reminiscences.* Kerala: G. Ramachandran Institute of Nonviolence, 1998.

Raising, Rh. *Nagas in Revolution.* Oking: Government of the People's Republic of Nagalim, Oking Publicity and Information Service, [s.a.].

Raja Devasish Roy, et al. *The Chittagong Hill Tracts: Life and Nature at Risk.* Dhaka: Society for Environment and Human Development (SEHD) .

Rashid, Ahmed. *Taliban: Islam, Oil and the Great Game in Central Asia.* London: Tauris, 2000.

———, *The Resurgence of Central Asia: Islam or Nationalism?* Karachi: Oxford University Press; London: Zed Books, 1994.

Ravi Nanda. *Kashmir and Indo-Pakistan Relations.* New Delhi: Lancer Books, 2001

RCSS Newsletter, Regional Centre for Strategic Studies, Colombo, Sri Lanka.

Regional Centre for Strategic Studies (RCSS). *Directory of Individuals and Institutions Engaged in South Asian Strategic Studies.* Colombo: RCSS, 1998.

Regional Studies, Institute of Regional Studies, Islamabad, Pakistan.

Reporting Central Asia, Institute for War and Peace Reporting, London, United Kingdom.

Revival, Post-war Reconstruction and Development Unit, University of York, United Kingdom.

Reychler, Luc, and Thania Paffenholz (eds.). *Peacebuilding: A Field Guide.* Boulder, CO: Lynne Rienner, 2001.

Rotberg, Robert. I., The World Peace Foundation, and The Belfer Center for Science and International Affairs. *Creating Peace in Sri Lanka: Civil War and Reconciliation.* Washington: Brookings Institute Press, 1999.

Roy, Olivier. *The New Central Asia: The Creation of Nations.* New York: University Press, 1999.

SAARC NEWS, South Asian Association for regional Cooperation, Kathmandu, Nepal.

Salam Asia Newsletter, Foundation for Tolerance International, Bishkek, Kyrgyzstan.

Samaddar, Ranabir. *"Those Accords": A Bunch of Documents.* Kathmandu: South Asia Forum for Human Rights (SAFHR), 1999.

————, and Shahid Fiaz. *Peace Audit Report 2: Peace Process in Sri Lanka.* Kathmandu: SAFHR, 2001. (SAFHR paper series No. 8).

Sawhny, Karan R. (ed.). *Assam Today: Can the Fires Be Put Out?* New Delhi: International Centre for Peace Initiatives (ICPI), 1998.

Schofield, Victoria. *Kashmir in Conflict: India, Pakistan and the Unfinished War.* London: I.B.Tauris, 2000.

Search for Common Ground Newsletter, Search for Common Ground, Washington, DC, United States.

Secular Perspectives, Centre for Study of Society and Secularism, Mumbai, India.

Security Dialogue, Peace Research Institute, Oslo, Norway.

Shelley, Mizanur Rahman. *Emergence of a New Nation in a Multi-Polar World: Bangladesh.* Dhaka: Academic Press and Publishers Limited, 2000.

————, *The Chittagong Hill Tracs of Bangladesh: The Untold Story.* Dhaka: Centre for Development Research Bangladesh (CDRB), 1992.

Sobhan, Rehman. *Rediscovering a South Asian Community: Civil Society in Search of Its Future.* Colombo: International Center of Ethnic Studies, 1998.

Sollenberg, Margareta (ed.). *States in Armed Conflict 1999.* Uppsala: Uppsala University, Department of Peace and Conflict Research, 2000.

South Asia Human Rights Documentation Centre (SAHRDC). *Report of the Alternate NGO Consultation on the Second Asia—Pacific Regional Workshop on National Human Rights Institutions.* New Delhi: SAHRDC, 1998.

————, *Return of the Maoists: Midnight Knocks and Extra-Judicial Killings in Nepal.* New Delhi: SAHRDC, 199?.

————, *The Bhutanese Political Crisis and Refugee Problem.* New Delhi: SAHRDC, 1998.

South Asia in Review, United States Institute for Peace, Washington, DC, United States.

South Asian Survey, Indian Council for South Asian Cooperation, New Delhi, India.

South Asia Partnership-Bangladesh (SAP-Bangladesh). *Directory and Bibliography of Training and Policy Advocacy on Women's Participation in Local Political Process.* Dhaka: SAP-Bangladesh, [s.a.].

Sri Lanka Forum News, Asia Pacific Center for Justice and Peace, Washington, DC, United States.

Strategic Analysis, Institute for Defence Studies and Analyses, New Delhi, India.

Survival, International Institute for Strategic Studies, London, United Kingdom.

Tabyshalieva, Anara. *The Challenge of Regional Cooperation in Central Asia: Preventing Ethnic Conflict in the Ferghana Valley.* Washington: United States Institute of Peace (USIP), 1999.

Tamil Guardian, Tamil Guardian International, London, United Kingdom.

Tehranian, Majid (ed.). *Asian Peace: Security and Governance in the Asia-Pacific Region.* London: I.B. Tauris, 1999.

The Week, Malayala Manorama Group, Kerala, India.

Transnational Institute (TNI) et al. *Linking Arms: Asia-Europe Cooperation on Alternative Security Strategies.* [s.l.]: Focus on the Global South, 1999.

———, Institute for Policy Studies (IPS). *Testing the Limits: The India-Pakistan Nuclear Gambit.* Amsterdam: TNI; Washington: IPS, 1998.

Tribunal Update, Institute for War and Peace Reporting, London, United Kingdom.

UNPO News, Unrepresented Nations and Peoples Organisation, the Hague, the Netherlands.

Van Tongeren, Paul, Hans van de Veen, and Juliette Verhoeven (eds.). *Searching for Peace in Europe and Eurasia: An Overview of Conflict Prevention and Peacebuilding Activities.* Boulder, CO: Lynne Rienner Publishers (in association with the European Centre for Conflict Prevention), 2002.

Verghese, B.G. *India's North East Resurgent: Ethnicity, Insurgency, Governance, Development.* New Delhi: Konark Publishers, 1997.

Waslekar, Sundeep (ed.). *Kashmir: Fact-Finding Mission.* New Delhi: International Centre for Peace Initiatives (ICPI), 1995.

———, *Political Leaders and Track Two Diplomacy in South Asia.* New Delhi: International Centre for Peace Initiatives (ICPI), 1995.

———, *Visions of the Future.* New Delhi: International Centre for Peace Initiatives (ICPI), 1996.

———, *A Handbook for Conflict Resolution in South Asia.* New Delhi: Konark Publishers, 1996.

Zia, Mohammed Ehsan. *Peacebuilding in Afghanistan: International Rhetoric Local Reality: The Strengthening of Local Capacities for Peace.* York: The University of York, Post-War Reconstruction and Development Unit, 2000.

Subject Index

Abdullah, Farooq, 368, 372
Abdullah, Sheikh, 364–366
Abdullajanov, Abdumalik, 173
Accountability as a peacebuilding principle, 130
Afghanistan: border conflicts/regional disputes, 250, 253–254; civil society, development of, 125–127; conflict dynamics, 112–116; drug trafficking, 89–90, 114, 183; Durand Line, 254; elders, 125–126; General Agreement on the Establishment of Peace and National Accord in Tajikistan, 176; global/regional level, conflict dynamics at the, 113; governance, promotion of good, 131–132; health issues, 132; history behind, 109; Inter-Tajik Dialogue on national reconciliation, 175; Islamic Movement of Uzbekistan, 90–91; Jirga institution, 125–127; Kashmir, relations with, 368–369; local level, conflict dynamics at the, 114–115, 132; long-term challenges, 131–132; mapping conflicts/human rights violations, 19–22; mujahedeen, 71–72, 104, 110–111, 367–368; multi-track diplomacy, 119–127; national level, conflict dynamics at the, 114; 1970s and emergence of socialist/Islamist movements, 109–110; nongovernmental organizations, 121–125, 127; official conflict management, 116–119; "Operation Enduring Freedom," 19–22, 111–112; opium, 20; Pakistan, relations with, 104; peacebuilding principles, 129–132; People's Democratic Party, 109–110; Principled Common Programming, 120; prospects for peace, 127–128; recommendations for effective conflict prevention, 128–132; refugees, 77, 254; regional introduction to Central Asia, 67; regional networks/cooperation, 21; religion and conflict, 90–91, 97–98; resources, informational, 115, 132–136; resources and conflicts, 87–88, 114, 115, 132; Revolutionary Association of the Women of Afghanistan, 44–45; short-term challenges, 130–131; Strategic Framework, 119–120, 129–130; Support Group, 119; Tajikistan, relations with, 172–173; war (1979-post-Taliban), 110–112; Western aid/interventions, 119–120, 128–132, 182–183; women, 44–45, 115. See also Taliban regime
Africa, resources and conflicts in, 85
Aga Kahn, Karim, 178
Agha, Gul, 21
Agriculture and caste violence/class war in Bihar, 395–396
Agriculture in Ferghana Valley, 147, 152–153
Aid, humanitarian. See Western aid/interventions
AIDS (acquired immune deficiency syndrome), 184
Akaev, Askar, 73, 152
Aksai-chin-Xinjiang Highway and India-China border dispute, 258
AKUF database for conflict survey, 25–27
Alash Orda, 99
Albright, Madeleine, 200
Alliances and people-to-people relationships, 12
Al-Qaida organization, 19–22, 91, 104, 105, 107, 111–112, 182
Ambedkar, B. R., 328
Amnesty International, 196, 314, 367, 422, 440
Amsterdam Treaty, 268
Amu-Darya River, 151, 188
Andhra Pradesh state in India, 384–385, 391
Angami people of Nagaland state in India, 414

Annan, Kofi, 17
Anti-Slavery Society, 314
Ao people of Nagaland state in India, 414
Arab funding and Shia-Sunni conflict in
   Pakistan, 469
Arafat, Yasser, 52
Armenian earthquake, 171
Arunachal Pradesh state in India, 347,
   425–426
Arvari River, 287
Asian Development Bank, 309, 314
Aslonov, Kadreddin, 171
Assam state in India, 23–24, 41–42, 299–300,
   411–414
Australia, 309
Autocracies in Central Asia, 24
Autonomy demands in India: Akali Dal, 348;
   All Assam Students' Union, 348; analysis,
   355–356; Arunachal Pradesh, 347;
   background on, 346–348; Bharatiya Janata
   Party, 348; Bodoland, 352–353;
   Bundelkhand, 351–352; Chhatisgarh, 347,
   349; classical autonomy vs., 345–346;
   Congress Party, 348; Coorg, 350; Gorkhaland, 352; Harit Desh, 351;
   integrationist and disintegrationist models
   of autonomy, 346, 353; Jharkhand, 347,
   348–349; Kamtapur, 352; Kashmir,
   354–355, 366, 372–373; Kosala, 347;
   linguistic reorganization, 346; Nagaland,
   347; new states, three, 348–349; northeast
   region, 346–347; Purvanchal, 351; response
   of state to threats of secession, 353–355;
   States Reorganisation Committee of 1953,
   346; Telengana, 347; upcoming demands
   for autonomy/statehood, 349–353;
   Uttaranchal/Uttarakhand, 347, 349;
   Vidarbha, 349–350; Vindhya Pradesh, 350
Awami League in Bangladesh, 214, 301, 309,
   310
Azhar, Maulana M., 369

Badal, Parkash S., 299
Bahauddin, Mohammad, 99
Baluchistan, 250
Bandaranaike, S. W., 486
Bangladesh: border conflicts/regional
   disputes, 252, 259–261, 284; Center for
   Advanced Studies, 221; confidence-
   building measures, 241–242; Farakka
   Barrage dispute, 213–214, 218, 241–242;
   labor inflow and border management,
   272–274; National Party, 301; nonofficial
   dialogues, 213–214, 217–218, 230;
   population statistics, 292;
   refugees/migrations, 252, 261, 272–274,
   411, 413; religion and conflict, 300–301;
   water conflicts/issues, 214, 263, 279–281.
   See also Chittagong Hill Tracts (CHT),
   indigenous struggle in the

Barak, Ehud, 52
Baruah, Golap, 412–413
Baruah, Paresh, 23–24, 411
Basmachi Muslim rebels in Ferghana Valley,
   142, 169
Basu, Jyoti, 214
Bengali ethnic movement, 450. See also
   Bangladesh
Bharatiya Janata Party (BJP) in India, 294,
   331, 342, 348, 359–360, 368
Bhat, Abdul G., 374
Bhattarai, Baburam, 442
Bhave, Vinoba, 328
Bhindranwale, Jarnail S., 299
Bhutan, 23–24, 241, 251–252, 259, 269
Bhutto, Benazir, 116, 371, 457, 460
Bhutto, Zulfiqar A., 244, 254, 454–456, 459,
   460, 467
Bihar state in India, 384, 385. See also Caste
   violence and class war in Bihar
bin Laden, Osama, 20, 21, 105, 107, 112
Blueprints for conflict prevention, lack of,
   49–50
Bodo people and Bodoland region in India,
   352–353, 411, 412
Bonn process, Afghanistan and the, 118, 126,
   129
Bookkeeping argument for conflict
   prevention, 59
Border conflicts/regional disputes in South
   Asia: Afghanistan, 250; Afghanistan-Iran,
   253–254; Afghanistan-Pakistan, 254;
   Bangladesh, 252; Bangladesh-India,
   259–261, 284; Bangladesh-Myanmar, 261;
   Bhutan, 251–252, 259; China, 250,
   257–259; ethnic tensions, 249; India,
   250–251; India, northeast, 428; India-
   Bangladesh, 259–261; India-China,
   257–258; India-Myanmar, 258–259;
   Kalapani border area, 259; labor inflow and
   border management, 272–274; Maldives,
   253; Nepal, 251, 259; 9-11 attacks on
   America, 10, 11–13; overview, 250–253;
   Pakistan, 250–251; Pakistan-India,
   254–257, 278–279; prospects for peace,
   262–263; recommendations for effective
   conflict prevention, 263; refugees, 249;
   resources, informational, 264–265; Sri
   Lanka, 252–253; Sri Lanka-India, 261–262
Bottom-up approach to peacebuilding, 127
Brahimi, Lakdar, 118
Brasstacks Exercise (1987) and Indo-Pak
   tensions, 241
Bretton Woods Institution, 83
Britain and Sri Lanka, 493
British colonial rule: Bangladesh, 304, 305;
   India, northeast, 408; Kashmir, 362, 364;
   Nagaland state in India, 414–415; Pakistan,
   465–466; Sri Lanka, 483
Broad approach to conflict resolution, 29–34,

131
Bru (Reang) people in northeast India, 426
Buddhism, 300–301, 486. *See also* Religion
    and conflict in South Asia
Bukhara, People's Republic of, 168
Bundela, Raja, 352
Bundelkhand region in India, 351–352
Burundi, 55
Bush, George W., 21

Canada and Sri Lanka, 493
Caspian subregion, policy recommendations
    for, 82
Caste violence and class war in Bihar:
    Bhoomi Sena, 398; communism, 396, 403;
    conflict dynamics, 398–400; Dalit Sena,
    402; feudal rigidity in the agrarian
    structure, 395–396; human rights/abuses,
    399–400, 403; judicial area, 401; Minimum
    Wage Act, 404; multi-track diplomacy,
    402–403; official conflict management,
    400–402; peace committees, 405; People's
    Union for Civil Liberties, 403; People's
    Union for Democratic Rights, 403; police
    officers, 400, 401, 404–405;
    politics/political issues, 396–398, 401–403;
    prospects for peace, 403–404; Rashtravadi
    Kisan Mahasabha, 398; Rashtriya Janata
    Dal, 396, 404; recommendations for
    effective conflict prevention, 404–405;
    resources, informational, 405–406; senas in
    Bihar, three reasons for emergence of,
    397–398; state interventions, lack of
    effective, 395; Sunlight Sena, 398. *See also*
    Naxalite movement
Caucasus region, 67
Cauvery River, 277–278
Central Asia. *See* Ferghana Valley; Policy
    recommendations for Central Asia;
    Regional introduction to Central Asia;
    Religion and conflict in Central Asia;
    Resources and conflicts in Central Asia;
    individual countries
Central Intelligence Agency (CIA), 21, 369
Chaliha, B. P., 42
Chand, Bahadur, 439
Chandrashekar, 371
Chhatisgarh state in India, 347, 349
China: border conflicts/regional disputes, 250,
    257–259; Kazakhstan, relations with, 88;
    Kyrgyzstan, relations with, 88; Nepal,
    relations with, 251; regional introduction to
    Central Asia, 67; resources and conflicts,
    87–88; Shanghai Cooperation Organization,
    154, 155; Shanghai Five cooperation
    organization, 105; Uyghur nationalist
    insurgency, 87–88; Uzbekistan, relations
    with, 199
Chittagong Hill Tracts (CHT), indigenous
    struggle in the: Bangladesh Nationalist

Party, 304; civil society in Bangladesh,
    312–314; conflict dynamics, 307–309;
    geographic/population statistics, 306;
    history behind, 304–307; multi-track
    diplomacy, 311–316; National
    Implementation Committee, 318;
    nongovernmental organizations, 314–316,
    319; official conflict management,
    310–311; Pakistan, 304; Parbatya
    Chottogram Jana Samhati, 307, 308, 310,
    311, 316–317; prospects for peace,
    316–317; recommendations for effective
    conflict prevention, 318–319;
    refugees/migrations, 308, 316–318;
    rehabilitation measures, 309; resources,
    informational, 319–322; United Peoples
    Democratic Front, 309, 314, 316
Christianity, 343–344, 409
CIDCM database for conflict survey, 25–27
Civil groups/institutions and conflict
    resolution/reconciliation, 2–3. See also
    Local people/internal parties;
    Nongovernmental organizations;
    Nonofficial dialogues in South Asia;
    Regional networks/cooperation
Civil society, Central Asia and development
    of: Afghanistan, 125–127; Ferghana Valley,
    160, 162–163; Kazakhstan, 69; Kyrgyzstan,
    69; policy recommendations for Central
    Asia, 78–79; regional introduction to
    Central Asia, 69; Tajikistan, 181;
    Turkmenistan, 70
Civil society, South Asia and development of:
    Chittagong Hill Tracts, indigenous struggle
    in the, 312–314; India, 358; Kashmir, 375;
    Manipur, 420–422; Sindhi-Mohajir conflict
    in Pakistan, 460–461; Sri Lanka, 495–497
Clements, Kevin, 50, 51, 53, 55, 56
Clinton, Bill, 21, 493
Coca-Cola, 385
Cold War, 29, 116, 268, 450
Commonwealth of Independent States (CIS),
    172, 174
Communalism, India and, 336–337, 340–344
Communication counterterroist measures, 22
Communism: caste violence/class war in
    Bihar, 396, 403; India, northeast, 419, 423,
    425; Islamic Renaissance Party, 100;
    Kamtapur region in India, 352; Kashmir,
    374; Manipur, 419; Naxalite movement,
    383–388; Nepal, 251; Tajikistan, 72, 101,
    169, 171, 172, 180, 181; Tripura region in
    India, 423–425. See also Maoist insurgency
    in Nepal
Comprehensive approach as a peacebuilding
    principle, 129–130
Confidence-building measures in South Asia
    (CBMs): Brasstacks Exercise (1987), 241;
    case for and against, 239–241;
    conclusions/chapter summary, 245–246;

defining terms, 237; evolutionary step-by-step approach, 244; "Graduated Reduction in Tensions" strategy, 245; India-Bangladesh Agreement (1997), 241, 242; India-Bhutanese Agreement (1974), 241; India-Nepal Agreement (1996), 241; lessons and recommendations, 243–245; nonmilitary, greater emphasis on, 244; nuclear weapons, 239–240, 245; overview, 237–238; paradoxes, 241–243; secret vs. open diplomacy, 243–244; security situations, 238–239; Simla Agreements (1972), 241, 243, 244, 256, 364–365, 372; Sri Lanka Agreement (1998), 241; state structure and conflict formation, 450; Tashkent Agreement (1966), 241, 243, 372; win-win situation, insuring a, 243
Confidentiality, 48
Conflict dynamics, 52. *See also under individual subject headings*
Congo, 55
Coorg region in India, 350
Corruption: discontented populations, 87; Ferghana Valley, 161, 162; Kazakhstan, 74; Kyrgyzstan, 73; Maoist insurgency in Nepal, 433, 434, 439, 443; regional introduction to Central Asia, 75; Sri Lanka, 487; Tajikistan, 183
Cost analysis arguments for conflict prevention, 59
Council for Security Cooperation in Asia Pacific, 213
Council on Foreign Relations in U.S., 227
Crime, criminal activities and organized: Afghanistan, 114; children and women, cross-border trafficking in, 212; Chittagong Hill Tracts, indigenous struggle in the, 317; Ferghana Valley, 149–150; India, 360; India, northeast, 427; Naxalite movement, 387, 392–393; trade, illegal, 95. *See also* Corruption; Drug trafficking
Cultural understanding and conflict prevention, 54
Cyprus, 48
Cyrillic alphabet, 141

Delhi Agreement (1953) between Kashmir and India, 364, 415
Democracy/democratic institutions: autonomy demands in India, 355; caste violence/class war in Bihar, 404; Chittagong Hill Tracts, indigenous struggle in the, 318; India, 327, 342; Kashmir, 366–367, 370; Kazakhstan, 24; Kyrgyzstan, 24; Maoist insurgency in Nepal, 433–434; Organization for Security and Cooperation in Europe, 82; Pakistan, 450; regional introduction to Central Asia, 69; Shias and Sunnis, conflict between Pakistan's, 472–473; Tajikistan, 24, 184; Turkmenistan, 24; Uzbekistan, 24

Deuba, Sher B., 23, 436, 438–440
Dev, Narendra, 328
Development and peacebuilding programs, coordination between, 58
Development vs. sustainability and water conflicts/issues, 288
Devi, Rabri, 396
Dimasi people in northeast India, 412
Dostiev, Abdulmajid, 173
Dostum, Rashid, 21
DPCR database for conflict survey, 25–27
Drug trafficking: Afghanistan, 89–90, 114, 183; Ferghana Valley, 81, 149–150, 160, 164; overview, 95; Pakistan, 114; policy recommendations for Central Asia, 81; Russia, 90; Tajikistan, 89–90, 181–182, 184–185; Taliban regime (Afghanistan), 114; Uzbekistan, 197
Dublin Convention, 268
Durand Line and Afghanistan-Pakistan relations, 254
Dysfunctional societies as root cause of terrorism, 22

Economic conditions/issues: Afghanistan, 125, 250; autonomy demands in India, 355; development and peacebuilding programs, coordination between, 58; Ferghana Valley, 147–148, 150–151, 160, 161, 164, 183; generalizing about role of economic resources in conflict, 95–96; India, northeast, 407–409; Kazakhstan, 70; Kyrgyzstan, 73; Lessons Learned in Conflict Interventions and Peacebuilding, 57–58; Maoist insurgency in Nepal, 433–435, 438–439, 443; market reforms, 70, 73; Naxalite movement, 389–393; nonofficial dialogues in South Asia, 211; Pakistan, 296; policy recommendations for Central Asia, 80; regional introduction to Central Asia, 70; Sindhi-Mohajir conflict in Pakistan, 455, 459, 461; Tajikistan, 182–184; terrorism, root cause of, 22; themes, pervasive, 94–96; Turkmenistan, 70; unemployment, 94, 147–148, 164, 183, 438; Uzbekistan, 70, 95, 190, 196–198, 202–203. See also Caste violence and class war in Bihar; Naxalite movement; Poverty; Resources and conflicts in Central Asia
Education: Afghanistan, 132; Ferghana Valley, 164; Islamic Renaissance Party, 100–101; Kashmir, 375; Manipur, 421; multiculturalism in India, 334; regional introduction to Central Asia, 69; Shias and Sunnis, conflict between Pakistan's, 474–475, 478–479; Sindhi-Mohajir conflict in Pakistan, 459–460; Sri Lanka, 496–497; terrorism and counterterroist measures, 22; Uzbekistan, 205
Ego in check, conflict prevention and keeping,

60
Eminent domain and water conflicts/issues,
    287
Energy issues, 152, 162, 199, 219
Ershad, Hossain M., 308, 310
Escudero, Stanley T., 178
Ethnic tensions: Afghanistan, 115; border
    conflicts/regional disputes in South Asia,
    249; Ferghana Valley, 141–145, 149, 151,
    160, 161, 163; Kazakhstan, 86; Kyrgyzstan,
    67–68, 74; Pakistan, 296, 449; Tajikistan,
    170; Uzbekistan, 86, 190. See also
    Chittagong Hill Tracts, indigenous struggle
    in the; India, multiple conflicts in northeast;
    Sindhi-Mohajir conflict in Pakistan; Sri
    Lanka
Europe: Charter of the Fundamental Rights of
    the European Union, 268; European Centre
    for Conflict Prevention, 3, 4, 47; European
    Platform for Conflict Prevention and
    Transformation, 3; refugees/migrations,
    268; regional groupings, increasing power
    of, 211; Sri Lanka, 494; Uzbekistan,
    200–201. See also Lessons Learned in
    Conflict Interventions and Peacebuilding;
    Organization for Security and Cooperation
    in Europe
Evaluation/reflection and conflict prevention,
    59–60

Failed states as root cause of terrorism, 22
Farakka Barrage dispute between
    India/Bangladesh, 213–214, 218, 241–242
Ferghana Valley: agriculture, 147, 152–153;
    borders drawn, 145–146; Center for
    Preventive Action project, 156–157; civil
    society, development of, 160, 162–163;
    conflict dynamics, 145–150; conflicts in the
    last thirteen years, review of, 143–145;
    corruption, 161, 162; criminal cluster,
    149–150; Cross-Border Conflict Prevention
    Project, 157; drug trafficking, 81, 149–150,
    160, 164; economic conditions/issues,
    147–148, 150–151, 160, 161, 164, 183;
    ethnic tensions, 141–145, 149, 151, 160,
    161, 163; Foundation for Tolerance
    International, 157; Goodwill Ambassadors
    Networks project, 157–158; history behind,
    141–142; infrastructure project, 158;
    International Crisis Group, 158–159;
    Islamic Movement of Uzbekistan, 104–105;
    Ittifok, 157; judicial systems, 162; media,
    the, 158, 163–164; multi-track diplomacy,
    155–159; official conflict management,
    150–155; Organization for Security and
    Cooperation in Europe, 159; Peace
    Promotion Program for Bordering Regions,
    157; policy recommendations for Central
    Asia, 78, 79; population issues, 146–147;
    preventive development program in south

Kyrgyzstan, 158; prospects for peace,
    159–161; recommendations for effective
    conflict prevention, 161–164;
    refugees/migrations, 146–147, 160; religion
    and conflict, 104–105, 142–146, 148–149,
    153–154; resources, informational,
    164–166; resources and conflicts, 91,
    151–152, 162, 163; travel restrictions and
    border controls, 161–162; unemployment,
    147–148; United Nations, 155–156; water
    issues, 147, 151–152, 162, 163; Western
    aid/interventions, 161, 162, 203
Firth, Oswald, 40

Gandhi, Indira, 299, 330, 340–342, 368
Gandhi, Mohandas K., 288, 293, 294
Gandhi, Rajiv, 348, 359, 371, 492
Ganges River, 214, 263, 279–280
Ganji, Sadeq, 470
Gas pipeline, Turkmenistan-Pakistan, 114
Gem trade, 114
Germany, 20, 217
Gharmi group in Tajikistan, 72, 101
Gharo people in northeast India, 425
Ghising, Subhas, 348
Gorbachev, Mikhail, 71
Gorkhaland region in India, 352
"Graduated Reduction in Tensions" (GRIT)
    strategy, 245
Green revolution and caste violence/class war
    in Bihar, 397
Gujral, I. K., 214, 217, 218, 371, 416

Haider, Salman, 214
Harit Desh region in India, 351
Harmon Doctrine, 282
Hasina, Sheikh, 214, 309, 310
Helsinki Final Act (1975), 239, 282–283
High-intensity conflicts on PIOOM list, 18,
    19
HIIK database for conflict survey, 25–27
Himmatzadeh, Mullah, 100, 101
Hindoustani, Mawlawi Q., 101
Hinduism. See Religion and conflict in South
    Asia
Holistic approach to conflict prevention,
    56–57
Hrangkhawal, Bijoy, 424
Humanitarian aid. See Western
    aid/interventions
Humanity, challenge of finding our way back
    to, 12–13
Human rights/abuses: caste violence/class war
    in Bihar, 399–400, 403; Chittagong Hill
    Tracts, indigenous struggle in the, 307–309,
    313, 314; Kashmir, 367, 377; Manipur, 422;
    Maoist insurgency in Nepal, 437–440;
    Nagaland, 417; Naxalite movement, 388,
    391; Organization for Security and
    Cooperation in Europe, 31;

refugees/migrations, 275; Shias and Sunnis, conflict between Pakistan's, 475–476, 479–480; South Asia Forum for Human Rights, 222; South Asia Human-Rights Documentation Center, 219–220; terrorism, downplaying abuses because of war on, 200; Uzbekistan, 159, 191, 196, 200, 202. See also Mapping conflicts/human rights violations
Hussain, Allama M. S. J., 471
Hussain, Altaf, 457

Identity cards and refugees/migrations, 273
Illegal activities. See Corruption; Crime, criminal activities and organized; Drug trafficking
India: "Agreement on Advance Notice of Military Exercises, Manoeuvres and Troop Movements," 239; All India Progressive Women's Organization, 43; Assam's hill people, 23–24, 41–42; Bharatiya Janata Party, 342, 359–360; Bhivandi-Jalgaon riots, 341; Bombay riots, 343; border conflicts/regional disputes, 250–251, 255–262, 278–279; Centre for Study of Society and Secularism, 344; Chittagong Hill Tracts, indigenous struggle in the, 305–306; Christian minority, new front against, 343–344; communalism, 336–337, 340–344; Communalism Combat, 344; democracy/democratic institutions, 327, 342; Farakka Barrage dispute, 213–214, 218, 241–242; Indian National Congress, 358–359; Indo-Lanka Accord, 485; Janata Party, 244, 341; Jan Sangh group, 341, 342; Krishna Commission Report, 333; labor inflow and border management, 272–274; local people/internal parties, 288; low-intensity conflicts on PIOOM list, 19; Mahakali Treaty (1996), 280–281; Mandal Commission Report (1990), 332, 338, 342; Nepal, relations with, 251, 284; nonofficial dialogues, 38–39, 213–214, 216–218, 225; nuclear weapons/issues, 225; Pakistan-India People's Forum for Peace and Democracy, 38–39; Partition of 1947, 339–340, 449; population statistics, 292; Ramjanambhoomi movement, 342–343; Rashtriya Sevak Sangh, 337–339, 344; refugees/migrations, 261, 272–274; religion and conflict, 293–295, 298–300, 336–344; Russia-Iran-Uzbekistan-Tajikistan-India axis, 113; Sangh Parivar, 344; secularism, 328, 331, 336–337; Shiv Sena, 341, 343; size of, relationships with neighbors and, 284; Sri Lanka, relations with, 484, 485, 491, 492; United Liberation Front of Assam, 23–24; untouchables, 43–44; violent conflicts, background to, 357–361; water conflicts/issues, 214, 241, 243, 244,

256, 263, 278–281, 284–286, 288; women, 43–44. See also Autonomy demands in India; Caste violence and class war in Bihar; Confidence-building measures in South Asia; Kashmir; Multiculturalism in India; Naxalite movement
India, multiple conflicts in northeast: All Assam Students Union, 411–413; All Tripura Tiger Force, 423, 424; Amar Bangla, 423; Arunachal Pradesh, 425–426; Asom Gana Parishad, 412; Asom Sahitya Sabha, 413; Assam, 411–414; Assam Accord, 411–412; autonomy demands, 346–347; Baptist Church in Nagaland, 417; Bodoland Autonomous Council, 412; Bodo Sahitya Sabha, 413; Bodo Women's Justice Forum, 414; border management, 428; British colonial rule, 408; Bru Liberation Force, 426; Center for Indigenous Peoples, 418; Civil Liberties and Human Rights Organization, 422; Communist Party of India/Marxist, 419, 423, 425; Congress Party, 424; Delhi Agreement (1953) between Kashmir and India, 365, 415; East India Liberation Front in Arunachal Pradesh, 426; economic conditions/issues, 407–409; geographical statistics, 408; history of, 408–409; Indian National Congress Party, 419; integration, national, 428–429; Manipur, 418–422; Manipur Chanura Leishem, 421; Manipur Merger Agreement with New Delhi, 419; Meghalaya, 425; Meira Paibies, 421; Mizo National Front, 426; Mizoram, 426; Muslim United Liberation Front of Assam, 411; Naga Hoho, The, 418; Nagaland, 414–418; Naga People's Movement for Human Rights, 417, 418; Naga Socialist Council of Nagaland, 300; Naga Vigil Human Rights Group, 418; Nationalist Socialist Council of Nagaland-K/IM, 415–418, 425; National Liberation Front of Tripura, 423, 424; nongovernmental organizations, 410–411; Nupi (Women's) Movement in Manipur, 421; peaceful states, 425–426; People's Liberation Army in Manipur, 419, 421; politics/political issues, 409–410, 427; prospects for peace, 426–427; recommendations for effective conflict prevention, 427–429; refugees/migrations, 407–409; religion and conflict, 299–300; resources, informational, 429–432; Tripura, 422–425; Tripura Tribal Areas Autonomous District Council Act, 424; Tripura Upajati Juba Samiti, 423; United Committee in Manipur, 421–422; United Liberation Front of Assam, 411–413; United Liberation Front of Seven Sisters in Manipur, 420; United National Liberation Front, 419, 421
Indian National Congress (INC), 293, 328,

331, 358–359, 419
India People's Party. *See* Bharatiya Janata
Party in India
Indigenous peacemakers, 32–33. *See also*
Local people/internal parties
Indonesia, 60
Indus River, 241, 243, 244, 256, 278–279
Infrastructure project in Ferghana Valley, 158
Interculturalism. *See* Multiculturalism in India
Interdependence defined differently after
events of Sept. 11, 10, 11–13
International Monetary Fund (IMF), 205
International Security Assistance Force
(ISAF), 20, 131
Iran: border conflicts/regional disputes, 250,
253–254; Central Asia and, comparisons
between, 74–75; General Agreement on the
Establishment of Peace and National
Accord in Tajikistan, 176; Inter-Tajik
Dialogue on national reconciliation, 175;
Pakistan influenced by revolution in, 466;
Russia-Iran-Uzbekistan-Tajikistan-India
axis, 113; Shias and Sunnis, conflict
between Pakistan's, 466, 469
Iraq and Shia-Sunni conflict in Pakistan, 469
Ireland, Northern, 51, 58
Irish Republic Army (IRA), 51
Irrational factors, importance of, 55–56
Iskandarov, Akbarsho, 172
Islam and campaigns against unofficial Islam,
71. *See also* Religion listings, Shias and
Sunnis, conflict between Pakistan's
Islamic Conference Organization, 371
Islamic Movement of Turkestan. *See* Islamic
Movement of Uzbekistan
Islamic Movement of Uzbekistan (IMU):
Afghanistan, 90–91; factionalism, regional,
98–99, 107; Ferghana Valley, 144–146, 148,
153–154; human-rights abuses, 196;
Kyrgyzstan, 104–105, 193–194, 198; name
change to Islamic Movement of Turkestan,
97, 105; 9-11 attacks on America, 106;
origins of, 193; regional introduction to
Central Asia, 71; repressive measures aimed
at, 190–191; Taliban regime (Afghanistan),
111
Israel, 52, 58, 106
Ivory Coast, 60

Jagmohan, Shri, 367
Jain Report in India, 492
Japan, 20, 494–495
Jhangvi, Maulana, 470
Jharkhand state in India, 347, 348–349, 384
Jhelum River, 256
Jinnah, Muhammad A., 293, 297
Jordan, 106
Joshi, P. C., 328

Kabiri, Mohiddin, 103

Kamtapur region in India, 352
Karateginis group in Tajikistan, 172
Kargil War, 368, 372
Karimov, Islam, 70–71, 105, 154–155,
170–171, 174, 190, 191, 195, 203
Karimov, Jamshed, 173
Karzai, Hamid, 20, 112
Kashkadar clan in Uzbekistan, 195
Kashmir: Afghanistan, relations with,
368–369; All Jammu and Kashmir National
Conference, 364; All Party Hurriyat
Conference, 374; anti-Indian sentiment,
297; Association of the Parents of
Disappeared Persons, 375; autonomy
demands, 354–355, 366, 372–373;
Bharatiya Janata Party, 368; British colonial
rule, 362, 364; Communist Party of India,
374; confidence-building measures in South
Asia, 241, 242; conflict dynamics,
365–370; Delhi Agreement (1953), 365;
geographical/population statistics, 298;
Harkat-ul Mujahedeen, 369, 374; history of,
297, 362, 364–365; Indo-Pak summit
(2001), 298; Islamic Conference
Organization, 371; Jaish-I-Mohammadi,
369, 374; Jammu and Kashmir Liberation
Front, 366, 369, 375, 377; Kargil War, 368,
372; Lahore Declaration, 372–372;
Lashkar-e-Toiba, 369, 374; Line of Control,
255, 365, 376; multi-track diplomacy,
373–375; National Conference, 372, 374; 9-
11 attacks on America, 22–23; nuclear
issues, 238–239, 262; official conflict
management, 370–373; Pakistani secret
service, 369; Panun Kashmir, 375; People's
Democratic Party, 374; population statistics,
363; prospects for peace, 376;
recommendations for effective conflict
prevention, 376–377; religion and conflict,
297–298; resources, informational,
377–381; Simla Agreements (1972),
364–365; Society for Human Welfare
and Education, 375; "State Autonomy
Report," 372–373; state structure and
conflict formation, 449–450; Tashkent
Declaration, 373; Treaty of Amritsar, 362
Kazakhstan: China, relations with, 88; civil
society, development of, 69; democracy, 24;
economic conditions, 70; ethnic tensions,
86; General Agreement on the
Establishment of Peace and National
Accord in Tajikistan, 176; Inter-Tajik
Dialogue on national reconciliation, 175;
Islamic Renaissance Party, 99; regional
introduction to Central Asia, 69–70, 74;
religion and conflict, 99; resources and
conflicts, 69–70, 74, 93–94; Shanghai
Cooperation Organization, 154; Shanghai
Five cooperation organization, 105
Kebedov, Abbas, 99

Kenya, 21
Khan, A. Moyeen, 213
Khan, Amanullah, 375
Khan, Ayub, 448, 454
Khan, Mohammed Daoud, 254
Khan, Genghis, 188
Khan, Ismail, 21
Khan, Liaquat A., 366
Khan, M. Morshed, 213
Khaplang, S. S., 415
Khasi people in northeast India, 425
Khodaberdaiev, Mahmud, 102
Khomeni, Ayatollah, 472
Khudonazarov, Davlat, 101, 171–172
Khujandis group in Tajikistan, 169, 170, 172, 173
Kibria, S.A.M.S., 214
Kittani, Ismat, 174
Knowledge creation and nonofficial dialogues in South Asia, 214–215
Koirala, Girja P., 437–439
Kokand Khanate in Ferghana Valley, 141
Kölabi group in Central Asia, 72, 73, 101, 170, 172, 173
Konyak, Khole, 415
Korea, North, 251
Kosala region in India, 347
Kukis people in northeast India, 420
Kumaratunga, Chandrika B., 23, 490, 491
Kyrgyzstan: China, relations with, 88; civil society, development of, 69; democracy, 24; ethnic tensions, 67–68, 74; Hizb ut-Tahrir, 106; Inter-Tajik Dialogue on national reconciliation, 175; Islamic Movement of Uzbekistan, 104–105, 193–194, 198; regional introduction to Central Asia, 67–68, 73–74; religion and conflict, 104–105, 193–194, 198; resources and conflicts, 69, 92–93; Shanghai Cooperation Organization, 154; Shanghai Five cooperation organization, 105; trade, illegal, 95; Uzbekistan, relations with, 105. See also Ferghana Valley

Lahore Declaration (1999) and Indo-Pak tensions, 239, 371–372
La' li Badakhshon group in Tajikistan, 88–89, 170
Land colonization policy in Sri Lanka, 488
Land privatization in Ferghana Valley, 150–151
Larma, Jyotirindra B., 308
Larma, Manobendra N., 306, 308, 312, 316
Learning as a peacebuilding principle, 130
Leninabadis group in Tajikistan, 101
Lessons Learned in Conflict Interventions and Peacebuilding: blueprints, there are no, 49–50; conflict dynamics, 52; cultural understanding, 54; development and peacebuilding programs, coordination

between, 58; economic help/valuable gains, rewarding moves toward peace with, 57–58; ego in check, keeping, 60; evaluation and reflection, 59–60; holistic approach suits best, 56–57; inactivity, avoid becoming a pretext for, 50–51; irrational factors, acknowledge importance of, 55–56; limitations of conflict prevention, be aware of, 51; local actors, mobilize the, 55; long-term commitment, 52; media, the, 58; networking, 57; 911 attacks on America, 49; overview, 47–49; peace, look actively for chances for, 57; public relations, 58–59; regional scope in mind, keep the, 54–55; resources, informational, 60–61; theory, build a, 53; time management, 52; viable strategy, conflict prevention is a, 50
Liberation Tigers of Tamil Eelam (LTTE), 23, 40, 252–253, 301. See also Sri Lanka
Literacy levels, 69
Local people/internal parties: Afghanistan, 114–115, 132; broad approach to conflict resolution, 32–33; Chittagong Hill Tracts, indigenous struggle in the, 314, 319; Ferghana Valley, 157, 163; India, 288; Indonesia, 60; Ivory Coast, 60; Lessons Learned in Conflict Interventions and Peacebuilding, 55; Manipur, 421; Pakistan, 115; policy recommendations for Central Asia, 78; Sri Lanka, 495–497; Tajikistan, 178–180, 184; Uzbekistan, 179, 202, 205; water conflicts/issues, 286–288; Yugoslavia, 60. See also Civil society, Central Asia and development of; Nonofficial dialogues in South Asia; Regional networks/cooperation
Lone, Abdul G., 366–367
Long-term commitment to conflict prevention, 52
Low-intensity conflicts on PIOOM list, 18, 19
Lysoen process of dialogue between foreign ministers, 493

Macartney-MacDonald Line and India-China border dispute, 258
Macedonia, 59
MacMohan Line and India-China border dispute, 258
Madrassas network in Afghanistan, 116, 296, 369
Madrassas network in Pakistan, 469, 474–475, 478–479
Mahakali River, 280–281
Mahalla councils in Tajikistan/Uzbekistan, 179, 202, 205
Mahkamov, Qahhar, 72, 171
Mahmud, Maulana M., 468
Maldives, 253
Malik, Yasin, 370, 375
Mandal Commission Report (1990), 332, 338, 342

Manipur region in India, 410–411, 418–422
Maoist insurgency in Nepal: Center for
   Economic and Social Development, 441;
   conditions contributing to, 435–436;
   conflict dynamics, 436–438; corruption,
   433, 434, 439, 443; democracy/democratic
   institutions, 433–434; Dhami Commission,
   439; Informal Sector Service Centre, 437;
   Jhapa Movement, 436; multi-track
   diplomacy, 440–441; National Democratic
   Party, 439; Nepali Congress Party,
   433–434, 436, 439; official conflict
   management, 438–440; overview, 23, 433;
   police, 441; prospects for peace, 442;
   Rastriya Sarokar Samaj, 440;
   recommendations for effective conflict
   prevention, 442–443; religion and conflict,
   434–435; resources, informational,
   443–445; underclasses and ruling class,
   wide divide between, 434–435; United
   Marxist-Leninist Party, 434, 436, 439;
   United People's Front, 436; Western
   aid/interventions, 435
Mapping conflicts/human rights violations:
   Afghanistan and "Operation Enduring
   Freedom," 19–22; autocracies/state
   economies in Central Asia, 24; comparison
   between seven data projects, 24–27;
   Interdisciplinary Research Programme on
   Causes of Human Rights Violations, 17–18;
   9-11 attacks on America, 22–24; overview
   of conflicts in Central and South Asia, 19;
   stage of conflict with crises thresholds, 18
Market reforms, 70, 73. See also Economic
   conditions/issues
Masoud, Ahmad S., 102, 103, 105, 111, 182
Mazumdar, Charu, 384
Mechanism for Conflict Prevention,
   Management and Resolution (MCPMR), 31
Media, the: Ferghana Valley, 158, 163–164;
   Lessons Learned in Conflict Interventions
   and Peacebuilding, 58; multiculturalism in
   India, 330–331; nonofficial dialogues in
   South Asia, 230–231; Sindhi-Mohajir
   conflict in Pakistan, 462–463; South Asian
   Media Association, 221; Tajikistan, 184;
   Uzbekistan, 191, 201–202, 205–206
Meghalaya state in India, 425
Meitei/Meitei-Pangal people in northeast
   India, 300, 418
Menon, Rashed K., 313
Merrem, Gerd, 177
Meskhetian Turks in Uzbekistan, 67, 94, 190
Middle East, 52, 58, 106. See also individual
   countries
Migration issues. See Refugees/migrations
Mishra, Brajesh, 213
Mishra, R. K., 226
Missing people in northeast India, 411
Mizoram state in India, 347, 426

Mohaijrs in Pakistan, 452. See also Sindhi-
   Mohajir conflict in Pakistan
Mookerjee, Shyama P., 328
Moral Re-Armament (MRA) in Assam state,
   41–42
Muhammad, Prophet, 466–467
Muivah, T., 416, 419, 420
Mujahedeen groups in Afghanistan, 71–72,
   104, 110–111, 368, 369
Mullah Omar, 20, 112, 114
Multiculturalism in India: All-Parties
   Conference in 1928, 326; Bharatiya Janata
   Party, 331; concept centering around three
   basic ideas, 325–326; conclusions/chapter
   summary, 333–338; constitutional
   protections, 329, 332; contemporary India,
   331–333; court cases, 330; defining terms,
   325; deinstitutionalization, 331–333;
   education, 334; founding fathers, foresight
   of the, 327–329; Indian National Congress,
   328, 331; Krishna Commission Report, 333;
   languages, diverse, 329–330; leadership
   quality, 332; Mandal Commission Report
   (1990), 332; media, the, 330–331; National
   Commission for Minorities, 330; National
   Commission for Scheduled Castes and
   Scheduled Tribes, 330; National Human
   Rights Commission, 330; Nehru Report,
   327; police, 333; politicization, the process
   of, 330, 333; reverse movement and process
   of othering at work, 331; secularism, 328,
   331; Western societies, India compared to,
   327; women, 334
Musharraf, Pervez: democracy/democratic
   institutions, 472–473; five year term, 376;
   military rule, 448; 911 attacks on America,
   23; nuclear weapons/issues, 229;
   propaganda and offensive literature, 479;
   religious tolerance, 477; terrorism, the war
   on, 112, 370, 450; Vajpayee, meetings with,
   368
Muslim. See Religion listings
Muslim Brethren, Egyptian, 100, 106, 107
Muslim League, 293–294, 297
Myanmar, 20, 252, 258–259, 261

Nabhani, Sheikh, 106
Nabiev, Rahman, 72, 101, 171
Nachappa, N. U., 350
Nagaland state in India, 41, 347, 414–418
Naidu, Chandrababu, 389–390
Naik, Niaz, 217, 226
Najibullah, Mohammad, 110, 369
Namangani, Joma K., 104, 105, 154
Naqvi, Sajid A., 472
Narayan, Jayaprakash, 328, 396
Narcotics. See Drug trafficking
Narmada River, 284–286
National Security Council (NSC), 21
Naxalite movement: Andhra Pradesh,

384–385; Association for the Protection of Democratic Rights, 391; Bihar, 386; Civil Liberties Committee, 392; Committee of Concerned Citizens, 392; communism, 383–388; conflict dynamics, 384–388; conflict management, 388–390; Indian People's Front, 386; MCC, 386–388; multi-track diplomacy, 390–391; peasant uprisings, India's long history of, 382–383; People's Revolutionary Front, 391; People's Union for Civil Liberties, 391; People's Union for Democratic Rights, 390; prospects for peace, 391–392; recommendations for effective conflict prevention, 392–393; resources, informational, 393–394; Telegu Desam Party, 389–390; United Struggle Against Fake Encounters, 391. See also Caste violence and class war in Bihar

Nazarbaev, Nursultan A., 74

Nehru, Jawaharlal, 294, 328, 331, 365, 366

Nepal: border conflicts/regional disputes, 251, 259; China, relations with, 251; confidence-building measures, 241; "Conflict Resolution and Peacebuilding in Nepal," 441; India, relations with, 251, 284; Mahakali Treaty (1996), 280–281; Nepal-China Border Agreement (1961), 251; Nepal Water Conservation Foundation in Kathmandu, 215, 223; population statistics, 292; refugees/migrations, 251, 252; royal family, killing of the, 23, 295; Sino-Nepal Border Protocols (1963), 251; water conflicts/issues, 215, 223, 280–281. See also Maoist insurgency in Nepal

Netherlands, 418

Nichols-Roy, Stanley, 41–42

9-11 attacks on America: Asia impacted by military responses to, 2, 22–24, 77; Islamic Movement of Uzbekistan, 106; Lessons Learned in Conflict Interventions and Peacebuilding, 49; myths under exploration, 9–16; "Operation Enduring Freedom," 19–22; repressive measures against Islamic groups, 159; Sindhi-Mohajir conflict in Pakistan, 461

Niyazov, Saparmurat, 70

Nongovernmental organizations (NGOs): Afghanistan, 121–125, 127; Assam state in India, 414; blueprints for conflict prevention, lack of, 50; broad approach to conflict resolution, 31–32; caste violence/class war in Bihar, 401; Chittagong Hill Tracts, indigenous struggle in the, 314–316, 319; cultural understanding, 54; Ferghana Valley, 157; flexibility and adaptability, 31–32; holistic approaches, 57; inactivity, avoid becoming a pretext for, 50–51; India, 343; India, northeast, 410–411; Inter-Tajik Dialogue on

national reconciliation, 177–178; Kyrgyzstan, 73; long-term commitment, 52; Manipur, 422; Maoist insurgency in Nepal, 440; Naxalite movement, 390–391; peacebuilding principles, 130; regional introduction to Central Asia, 69; Searching for Peace program, 4; Shias and Sunnis, conflict between Pakistan's, 475–477; Sri Lanka, 495–498; Sweden, 50; Tajikistan, 42, 178–180, 184; Tripura, 425; Uzbekistan, 201–203, 206. See also Nonofficial dialogues in South Asia; individual organizations

Nonofficial dialogues in South Asia: Action Committee Against Arms Race, 224–225; Association of SAARC Speakers and Parliamentarians, 230; Association of South East Asian Nations Regional Forum, 213; Center for Alternatives, Dhaka, 215, 223; Center for Policy Research, New Delhi, 214, 222; Center for Science and Environment, 221; Center for the Study of Developing Societies, New Delhi, 215, 223; Center of Policy Dialogue, Dhaka, 222; changing character of the dialogue process, 212–216; Citizen's Commission for South Asia, 223; Citizens Media Commission, Karachi, 230–231; civil society, interactions between government and, 228; Climate Asia Network South Asia, 221; Coalition for Action on South Asian Cooperation, 213, 220, 225; Coalition for Nuclear Disarmament and Peace, 225; Committee on Studies for Cooperation and Development, 215; Confederation of Indian Industries, 223; defining terms, 212–213; Disaster Institute and Center for Science and Environment in India, 222; Doon School Old Boys Society, 224; Duryog Nivaran, 222–223; erroneous assumptions about players/sites/policymaking, 227; evaluation, critical, 226–231; Farakka Barrage dispute, 213–214, 218; Fellowships in South Asian Alternatives, 215, 223; Forum on Women in Security and International Affairs in Bangladesh, 230; Friedrich Ebert Stiftung, 225; Friedrich Naumann Stiftung, 219; funding the dialogues, 225; governmental resistance to, 229; HIMAL, 220; Independent Group for South Asian Cooperation, 215, 218; Independent Human Rights Organization of Uzbekistan, 202; India-Bangladesh Dialogues, 213–214, 217–218; India-Bangladesh Joint Chambers of Commerce and Industry, 217; Indian Council for Research on International Economic Relations, 218; India-Pakistan Friendship Society, 217; India-Pakistan Joint Chambers of Commerce and Industry, 218; India-

Pakistan Peoples Forum for Peace and Democracy, 216; India-Pakistan Soldiers Initiative for Peace, 213, 216; India-Sri Lanka Joint Business Council, 216; Institute for Policy Studies and Marga Institute in Colombo, 222; Institute of Integrated Development Studies, Kathmandu, 222; Intermediate Technology, Nepal/Sri Lanka/Bangladesh, 222; International Center for Peace Initiatives, Mumbai, 230; Internet, the, 231; Jang, 217; knowledge creation, 214–215; Lahore Chamber of Commerce, 223; Lahore University of Management Sciences, 222; levels of the dialogue process, 216; media, indigenous/regional language, 230–231; Movement in India for Nuclear Disarmament, 225; multilateral dialogues, 218–223; nascent stage, 229; Neemrana dialogue between India and Pakistan, 213, 216, 217; Network of South Asian Writers, 215, 220, 223; nuclear weapons/issues, 225; objectives and strategies, 213–215; outreach, 223–224; overview, 211; Pakistan-India Peoples Forum for Peace and Democracy, 223–224; Pakistan-India People's Solidarity Conference, 225; parliamentarians, involvement of the, 230; People's of Asia Forum, 218; PHD Chambers of Commerce and Industry India-Pakistan Desk, 216–217; Regional Center for Strategic Studies, Colombo, 215, 220, 223; regionalism vs. nation-state ideology, 210; resources, informational, 231–236; Royal Military College, 216; SAARC Association of Speakers and Parliamentarians, 221; SAARC Chambers of Commerce and Industry, 219; SAARC LAW, 221–222; South Asia Center for Policy Studies, 215, 222; South Asia Citizens Web, 231; South Asia Forum for Human Rights, 222, 497; South Asia Human-Rights Documentation Center, 219–220; South Asia Labour Forum, 219; South Asian Dialogue, 215; South Asia Network of Economic Institutes, 215, 218; South Asia Media Association, 221, 230; South Asia Regional Initiative/Energy, 219; Sri Lanka, 40–41, 216; successes, 35–40; supportive mechanisms and processes, 211–212; Sustainable Development Policy Institute, Islamabad, 215, 221, 223; Tata Energy Research Institute at New Delhi, 221; women, 224–225, 229–230; Women's Initiative for Peace in South Asia, 224; younger Asians, 230

North American Free Trade Agreement (NAFTA), 211

North Atlantic Treaty Organization (NATO), 59, 201

Northern vs. Southern approach and refugees/migrations, 270–271

Norway, 23, 252–253, 491–493

Nosiri Khusraw group in Tajikistan, 170

Nuclear weapons/issues: "Agreement on Measures to Reduce Risk of Outbreak of Nuclear War," 239; confidence-building measures in South Asia, 239–240, 245; Kashmir, 238–239, 262; Movement in India for Nuclear Disarmament, 225; Musharraf, Pervez, 229; nonofficial dialogues in South Asia, 225; testing by both Pakistan and India, 251

Nuri, Mullah, 100, 101, 104

Omar, Mullah Mohammed, 20, 112, 114

One-size-fits-all approach to conflict prevention, 83

Opium, 20. See also Drug trafficking

Osama bin Laden, 20, 21, 105, 107, 112

Osman, Dawlat, 99

Padmanabhan, Sundarajan, 213

Paites people in northeast India, 420

Pakistan: Afghanistan, relations with, 104; "Agreement on Advance Notice of Military Exercises, Manoeuvres and Troop Movements," 239; Ajoka Theater Group, 39–40; Baluch Movement, 449; border conflicts/regional disputes, 250–251, 254–257, 278–279; British colonial rule, 465–466; Chittagong Hill Tracts, indigenous struggle in the, 304; democracy/democratic institutions, 450; drug trafficking, 114; economic conditions/issues, 296; ethnic tensions, 296, 449; General Agreement on the Establishment of Peace and National Accord in Tajikistan, 176; history, social and political, 448; Human Rights Commission, 475–476; Inter-Tajik Dialogue on national reconciliation, 175; Islam, unresolved nature of, 465; Jama' at-i Islami, 100; local people/internal parties, 115; Muhajir Qaumi Movement, 449; nonofficial dialogues, 38–40, 213, 216–218, 223–225; "Operation Enduring Freedom," 20–21; Pakistan-India People's Forum for Peace and Democracy, 38–39; Partition of 1947, 339–340, 449; population statistics, 292; religion and conflict, 100, 295–296, 449; resources and conflicts, 114; Russia-Iran-Uzbekistan-Tajikistan-India axis, 113; Sindhu Desh Movement, 449; state structure and understanding conflict formation, 448–451; Taliban regime (Afghanistan) influencing, 296; water conflicts/issues, 241, 243, 244, 255–257, 278–279, 305; Western aid/interventions, 450. See also Confidence-building

measures in South Asia; Kashmir; Shias and Sunnis, conflict between Pakistan's; Sindhi-Mohajir conflict in Pakistan
Palestinian-Israeli conflict, 52, 58, 106
Pamiris group in Tajikistan, 72, 101, 172
Panj River, 173
Parliamentarians for Global Action, 230
Partnership Cooperation Agreement (PCA), 200–201
Paswan, Ram V., 402
Patel, Sardar V., 328
Pathan people in Pakistan, 456, 459. See also Sindhi-Mohajir conflict in Pakistan
Paudel, Bishnu P., 439
People's Republic of Bukhara, 168
Perera, Rienzi, 40
Peru, 251
Phizo, A. Z., 415
Pirez-Ballon, Ramiro, 174
Policy recommendations for Central Asia: Caspian subregion, 82; civil society, development of, 78–79; drug trafficking, 81; environmental issues, 80; overview, 76–77; poverty, 79; regional cooperation, 79–80; religion and conflict, 77–78, 80; Tajikistan, 79, 81–82; Western aid/interventions, 78, 82–84
Politics/political issues: Afghanistan, 128; autonomy demands in India, 355; broad approach to conflict resolution, 34; caste violence/class war in Bihar, 396–398, 401–403; communalism in India, 340–344; elite politics, regional, 87; Ferghana Valley, 160, 162–163; Hindus/Muslims, divisions among, 337–339; India, 329, 358–360; India, northeast, 409–410, 427; Manipur, 420; multiculturalism in India, 330, 333; Naxalite movement, 389–390; 9-11 attacks on America and political marginalization, 11; Shias and Sunnis, conflict between Pakistan's, 466–468, 479; Sindhi-Mohajir conflict in Pakistan, 454–455, 461; Tajikistan, 172, 182, 184; Tripura region in India, 424; Uzbekistan, 190, 191–192, 197–198, 205–206; water conflicts/issues, 283. See also Policy recommendations for Central Asia; individual countries/subject headings
Population movements. See Refugees/migrations
Population statistics for South Asian countries, 292–293
Poverty: confidence-building measures in South Asia, 239; Ferghana Valley, 149, 160; globalization of economics unresponsive to human need, 12; Maoist insurgency in Nepal, 438, 443; 9-11 attacks on America, 11; policy recommendations for Central Asia, 79; Sri Lanka, 487; stratification, 94; Uzbekistan, 203, 205. See also Caste violence and class war in Bihar; Economic

conditions/issues; Naxalite movement; Resources and conflicts in Central Asia
Prabhakaran, Velupillai, 23
Prachananda, Shrestha, 436, 440, 442
Prasad, Rajendra, 328
Privatization process in Ferghana Valley, 150–151
Protection as precondition for viable peacebuilding process, 131
Psychological changes and broad approach to conflict resolution, 34
Psychological counterterroist measures, 22
Public relations, 58–59
Punjabi people in Pakistan, 456, 459. See also Sindhi-Mohajir conflict in Pakistan
Purvanchal region in India, 351

Qadir, Haji A., 21
Qaida, Al-, 19–22, 91, 104, 105, 107, 111–112, 182

Rabha people in northeast India, 412
Radcliffe Award, 260
Radhakrishnan, Sarvepalli, 328
Rahman, Shamsur, 313
Rahman, Sheikh M., 306–307
Rahman, Ziaur, 301, 307
Rahmanov, Emamali, 72, 73, 102
Rai, Lala L., 294
Rajagopalachari, Chakravarti, 328
Rakhmonov, Imomali, 144, 172, 173, 180
Ranvir Sena. See Caste violence and class war in Bihar
Rao, Narasimha, 389, 416
Rashadov, Sharif, 190
Red Cross, International Committee of the (ICRC), 31, 178, 476, 498
Reflection/evaluation and conflict prevention, 59–60
Refugees/migrations: Afghanistan, 254; Armenian earthquake, 171; Assam state in India, 411–413; Bangladesh, 252, 261, 272–274, 411, 413; Bhutan, 251, 269; border conflicts/regional disputes, 249; Chittagong Hill Tracts, indigenous struggle in the, 308, 316–318; Convention Relating to the Status of Refugees (1951), 268; Ferghana Valley, 146–147, 160; human rights, 275; India, 261, 272–274; India, northeast, 407–409; labor inflow and border management, 272–274; mixed situations and need for mixed responses, 274–275; Myanmar, 252, 261; Nepal, 251, 252; non-entrée regimes, 268–271; Northern vs. Southern approach, 270–271; observatory, migration, 271–272; overview, 267–268; policies toward, differing, 77; responsibility, the norm of, 270; Sri Lanka, 270, 489; state boundaries, flaws of carving, 212; Tripura region in India, 422–425. See also Sindhi-Mohajir conflict

in Pakistan
Regional introduction to Central Asia: civil
  society, 69; Kazakhstan, 69–70, 74;
  Kyrgyzstan, 67–68, 73–74; leadership,
  failure in, 68; prospects for peace, 74–75;
  resources, economic, 69–70; Soviet Union,
  demise of the, 66–67; Tajikistan, 67, 72–73;
  tensions/conflicts, aspects of
  postindependence fostering, 68–69;
  Turkmenistan, 69–70; Uzbekistan, 67–68,
  70–72; Western aid/interventions, 75;
  women, 69
Regional networks/cooperation: Afghanistan,
  21; broad approach to conflict resolution,
  31; caste violence/class war in Bihar, 401;
  Lessons Learned in Conflict Interventions
  and Peacebuilding, 54–55; Naxalite
  movement, 389; peacebuilding principles,
  129; policy recommendations for Central
  Asia, 79–80; power of, increasing, 211;
  Searching for Peace Program, 4; Shias and
  Sunnis, conflict between Pakistan's, 478;
  Sri Lanka, 497; water conflicts/issues, 282.
  See also Civil society listings; Local
  people/internal parties; Nonofficial
  dialogues in South Asia
Religion and conflict in Central Asia:
  Afghanistan, 90–91, 97–98; factionalism,
  regional, 98–99; Ferghana Valley, 104–105,
  142–146, 148–149, 153–154;
  fundamentalism, emergence of, 2; historical
  examples, 97–98; Hizb ut-Tahrir in
  Uzbekistan, 71, 92, 106–107, 148, 154,
  182, 183, 194–196; ideological dimension
  of Islamic opposition, 99–101;
  interreligious dialogue, 40–42; Islamic
  credentials of postindependence regimes
  contested, 98; Islamic Renaissance Party,
  97–103, 107, 170, 180; Kazakhstan, 99;
  Kyrgyzstan, 73, 104–105, 193–194, 198;
  policy recommendations for Central Asia,
  77–78; Russian attempts at stopping rise of
  militant Islam, 183; Shanghai Cooperation
  Organization, 183; Tajikistan, 90, 97,
  99–103, 170, 180; underground Islamist
  movements, 86; Uzbekistan, 71, 90–92,
  99–100, 103–107, 190–195, 198. See also
  Islamic Movement of Uzbekistan
Religion and conflict in South Asia:
  Bangladesh, 300–301; Christianity,
  343–344, 409; communal violence in India,
  340–344; conclusions/chapter summary,
  302–303; fundamentalism, the emergence
  of, 2; India's Hindu-Muslim conflict,
  293–295, 336–344; Kashmir and India-
  Pakistan Wars, 297–298; Maoist insurgency
  in Nepal, 434–435; Musharraf, Pervez, 477;
  Northeast, the, 299–300; overview,
  291–292; Pakistan, 100, 295–296, 449, 465;
  Sharia laws in Pakistan, 465; Sikhs in
  Punjab and elsewhere, 298–299, 348, 354,

368; Sri Lanka, 301–302, 488. See also
  Shias and Sunnis, conflict between
  Pakistan's
Rengma people of Nagaland state in India,
  414
Resources and conflicts in Central Asia:
  Afghanistan, 87–88, 114, 115, 132; Caspian
  subregion, 82; China, 87–88; Ferghana
  Valley, 91, 151–152, 162, 163; generalizing
  about role of economic resources in
  conflict, 95–96; Kazakhstan, 69–70, 74,
  93–94; Kyrgyzstan, 69, 92–93; overview,
  85–86; policy recommendations for Central
  Asia, 77–78, 80; regional introduction to
  Central Asia, 69–70; Tajikistan, 69, 85–90;
  themes, pervasive, 94–96;
  unemployment/poverty/stratification, 94;
  Uzbekistan, 90–94, 196–199. See also Drug
  trafficking
Responsibility, refugees/migrations and the
  norm of, 271
Riparian perspective and water
  conflicts/issues in South Asia, 281
Rome process, Afghanistan and the, 118
Roy, Arundhati, 16, 291
Roy, Atul, 352
Roy, Tridiv, 306
Rumsfeld, Donald, 182
Russia: Afghan war, former Soviet Union and
  the, 110–112; Central Asia, reasserting
  power in, 183; drug trafficking, 90;
  Ferghana Valley, 141–142, 145–146;
  General Agreement on the Establishment of
  Peace and National Accord in Tajikistan,
  176; Inter-Tajik Dialogue on national
  reconciliation, 175; Islam, attempts at
  stopping rise of militant, 183; Kazakhstan,
  relations with, 74; Russia-Iran-Uzbekistan-
  Tajikistan-India axis, 113; Shanghai
  Cooperation Organization, 154, 155;
  Shanghai Five cooperation organization,
  105; Soviet Union, demise of the, 66–67;
  Tajikistan, relations with, 72, 170, 172, 173,
  180; Tajikistan and former Soviet Union,
  168–170; Uzbekistan, relations with, 199;
  Uzbekistan and the former Soviet Union,
  189–190; Western aid/interventions as a test
  for, 78
Russian Commonwealth of Independent States
  Security Pact, 199
Rustamov, Hajji M., 101

Salih, Mohammed, 191
Samadov, Abdujalil, 173
Samarkand-Bukhara clan in Uzbekistan, 195
Sanginov, Habib, 150
Satellite technology and communications
  revolution, 211
Saudi Arabia, 116
Savarkar, Vinayak D., 294
Sayeed, Mufti M., 374

Secularism, India and, 328, 331, 336–337
Security and events of Sept. 11, 10
Security as precondition for viable peacebuilding process, 131
Senas, 341, 343. *See also* Caste violence and class war in Bihar
Sensitivity as a peacebuilding principle, 130
Serbia, 59
Setalvad, Teesta, 43
Sharia laws, 465
Sharif, Nawaz, 371, 457
Shias and Sunnis, conflict between Pakistan's: Aga Khan Rural Support Program, 476–477; Balochi uprising, 468–469; conflict dynamics, 468–472; defining terms, 466–467; democracy/democratic institutions, 472–473; disarmament, 473; education, 474–475, 478–479; extremists, moves against, 473–474; funding, external, 469; Hadood Ordinance in 1979, 467; human rights, 475–476, 479–480; intrafaith/interfaith dialogue process, 477–478; Iran, 466, 469; Jama' at-e-Ulema-e-Islam/Pakistan, 468, 469; jihad, ban on collection of funds in name of, 474; Lashkar-e-Jhangvi, 471, 473; madrasas network, 474–475, 478–479; Mohajir Quami Movement, 472, 480; multi-track diplomacy, 475–477; official conflict management, 472–475; overview, 296, 298; peace plans, 480; politics/political issues, 466–468, 479; propaganda and offensive literature, 479; prospects for peace, 477; recommendations for effective conflict prevention, 477–478; regional-cooperation option, 478; resources, informational, 480–482; Sipah-e-Mohammadi, 473; Sipah-e-Sahaba, 470–471; Tehrik Jafria Pakistan, 472; Tehrik-Nifaz-i-Fiqah-Jafria, 471–472; tolerance, program for religious, 478; worship, checks on mosques/places of, 475; Zakat and Usher Ordinance in 1980, 468
Shrestha, Rabindra, 439
Shura institution in Afghanistan, 125–127
Sierra Leone, 59
Sikhs, 298–299, 348, 354, 368
Silk Road, the Great, 141
Simla Agreements (1972) and Indo-Pak tensions, 241, 243, 244, 256, 364–365, 372
Sindhi-Mohajir conflict in Pakistan: conflict dynamics, 455–459; economic and administrative issues, 455, 459, 461; Jayae Sindh Movement, 453, 454, 458; language bill recognizing Sindhi as official language, 456; Mohajir Quami Movement, 454, 455, 457–460; multi-track diplomacy, 460–461; 9-11 attacks on America, 461; official conflict management, 459–460; overview, 452–453; Pakistan Peoples Party, 453, 454, 456, 457–458; political/cultural/social

dynamics, 454–455, 461; prospects for peace, 461; recommendations for effective conflict prevention, 462–463; resources, informational, 463–464; Two-Nation Theory, 455–456; urban-rural divide, 460
Singh, Ajit, 351
Singh, Bharmeshwar, 398
Singh, Hari, 297
Singh, Jaswant, 213
Singh, Maharaja, 362, 364
Singh, S. N., 384, 419
Sinhalese people. See Sri Lanka
SIPRI database for conflict survey, 25–27
Sir Creek, 256–257
Social conditions/issues: Afghanistan, 250; broad approach to conflict resolution, 34; Maoist insurgency in Nepal, 434–435, 439; Naxalite movement, 389, 390, 392, 393; Pakistan, 296; policy recommendations for Central Asia, 80; Shias and Sunnis, conflict between Pakistan's, 470; Sindhi-Mohajir conflict in Pakistan, 459–460; Sri Lanka, 487; terrorism, root cause of, 22; Uzbekistan, 196–198, 205. *See also* Caste violence and class war in Bihar; Civil listings; Naxalite movement
Somalia, 55
South Asia. *See* Border conflicts/regional disputes in South Asia; Confidence-building measures in South Asia; Nonofficial dialogues in South Asia; Refugees/migrations; Religion and conflict in South Asia; Water conflicts/issues; individual countries
Soviet Union, demise of, 66–67. *See also* Russia
SOWAP database for conflict survey, 25–27
Soz, Saifuddin, 374
Sri Lanka: Ahimsa, 496; Bandaranaike-Chelvanayakam Pact (1957), 490; border conflicts/regional disputes, 252–253, 261–262; British colonial rule, 483; Centre for Policy Alternatives, 496; Centre for Society and Religion, 496; confidence-building measures, 241; conflict dynamics, 488–490; Consortium of Humanitarian Agencies, 495, 496; constitution strengthening Sinhala-Buddhist ideology, 486–487; Development Forum, 494; District Development Councils, 491; double minority factor, 487; emergencies, state instruments giving government power during, 487; Indian Peace Keeping Force, 484, 485, 491; Indo-Lanka Accord, 485; INFORM, 495; International Centre for Ethnic Studies, 496; International Working Group on, 498; Inter-Religious Peace Foundation, 40–41, 497; Jain Report, 492; Janatha Vimukth Peramuna, 483–484; land colonization policy, 488; Law and Society

Trust, 496; legitimacy of the state, identity/policies and, 485; Liberation Tigers of Tamil Eelam, characteristics of, 485–486; local people/internal parties, 495–497; Marga Institute, 496; Movement for Inter Racial Justice and Equality, 495; multi-track diplomacy, 495–498; National Movement Against Terrorism, 495; National Peace Council, 495–396; 911 attacks on America, 23; nongovernmental organizations, 495–498; nonofficial dialogues, 40–41, 216; Norway-brokered peace talks, 491–493; official conflict management, 490–495; Official Languages Act (1956), 486; Peoples Alliance, 490, 491, 496, 497, 499; population statistics, 293; PRASANNI, 497; prospects for peace, 498–499; recommendations for effective conflict prevention, 499; refugees/migrations, 270, 489; religion and conflict, 301–302, 488; resources, informational, 499–502; Samadana/M, 496; Senanayake-Chelvanayakam Pact (1965), 490; Social and Economic Development Centre, 496; Sri Lanka Agreement (1998), 241; Sudu Nellum Movement, 496; terrorist problem vs. war of secession, 484; United National Party, 490, 499; Vaddukkodai Resolution Act of 1976, 487; Western aid/interventions, 493–495

Stalin, Joseph, 145–146

State economies in Central Asia, 24

Stevenson, Adlai, 366

Stockholm Accord (1986), 239

Successes, large and small: Ajoka Theater Group, 39–40; India, 41–42; interreligious dialogue, 40–42; Lessons Learned in Conflict Interventions and Peacebuilding, 50; nonofficial dialogues, 35–40; Pakistan-India People's Forum for Peace and Democracy, 38–39; Sri Lanka, 40–41; Tajikistan, 35–38; women working for peace/justice, 42–45

Sunni Muslims, 100, 296, 298. *See also* Shias and Sunnis, conflict between Pakistan's

Sustainability vs. development and water conflicts/issues, 288

Sweden, 50, 309

Syr-Darya River, 147, 151, 188

Tajikistan: Afghanistan, relations with, 172–173; Aga Khan Foundation, 178; Amnesty Law, 176; civil society, development of, 181; civil war, 88–90, 168, 172–174; Commission on National Reconciliation, 175, 177, 180; communism, 72, 101, 169, 171, 180, 181; conflict dynamics, 171–174; corruption, 183; democracy, 184, 24; Democratic Party, 170,
171, 174; drug trafficking, 89–90, 181–182, 184–185; ethnic tensions, 170; General Agreement on the Establishment of Peace and National Accord, 175–177; history behind, 168–170; Hizb ut-Tahrir, 106; international nongovernmental organizations, 178; Inter-Tajik Dialogue on national reconciliation, 175, 176–180; Islamic Movement of Uzbekistan, 90; Islamic Renaissance Party, 99–103, 170; Lali Badakhshan movement, 88–89, 170; local people/internal parties, 178–180, 184; multi-track diplomacy, 176–180; National Revival Movement, 173; nongovernmental organizations, 42, 178–180, 184; nonofficial dialogues, 35–38; official conflict management, 174–176; "Operation Enduring Freedom," 21; policy recommendations for Central Asia, 79, 81–82; politics/political issues, 172, 182, 184; prospects for peace, 180–182; Rastokhez Popular Movement, 171; recommendations for effective conflict prevention, 183–185; Red Cross, International Committee of the, 178; refugees/migrations, 171; regional introduction to Central Asia, 67, 72–73; religion and conflict, 90, 97, 99–103, 170, 180; resources, informational, 185–187; resources and conflicts, 69, 85–90; Russia, relations with, 72, 170, 172, 173, 180; Russia-Iran-Uzbekistan-Tajikistan-India axis, 113; Shanghai Cooperation Organization, 154, 155; Shanghai Five cooperation organization, 105; Soviet Union, the former, 168–170; trade, illegal, 95; Traditions and Modernity, 42; unemployment, 94; United States Institute of Peace, 178; United Tajik Opposition, 174, 175–177, 180, 181; Uzbekistan, relations with, 68, 168, 170, 172; women, 42–43. *See also* Ferghana Valley

Taliban regime (Afghanistan): defining terms, 115; drug trafficking, 114; Hizb ut-Tahrir, 107; Islamic Movement of Uzbekistan, 90–91, 104, 149; Islamic Renaissance Party, 102; "Operation Enduring Freedom," 20–21, 111–112; Pakistan influenced by, 296; power hierarchies/social identities, reworking, 115; regional introduction to Central Asia, 67; Revolutionary Association of the Women of Afghanistan, 45; rise and fall of, 115–116; Talibanization, 111, 115–116; United Nations, 117; Uzbekistan, relations with, 77; women, 45, 115

Talpatty Island/New Moore Island dispute between Bangladesh/India, 252, 260–261

Tamil Tigers in Sri Lanka, 23, 40, 252–253, 301. *See also* Sri Lanka

Tankhul people of Nagaland state in India, 414
Tanzania, 21
Tashkent clan in Uzbekistan, 195
Tashkent Declaration and Indo-Pak tensions, 241, 243, 373
Telengana region in India, 347, 384
Terrorism, the war on: Asia impacted by military responses to 9-11 attacks on America, 2, 22–24, 77; counterterroist measures, 21–22; Ferghana Valley, 160; human-rights abuses downplayed as a result of, 200; Islamic Movement of Uzbekistan, 106; Liberation Tigers of Tamil Eelam, 493–494; Musharraf, Pervez, 112, 370, 450; "Operation Enduring Freedom," 19–22, 111–112; Sri Lanka, 495
Thailand, 20
Thalweg Doctrine, 256
Theory building and conflict prevention, 53
Thero, Pandit M. A., 40
Time management and conflict prevention, 52
Timurid empire, 141
Timur the Lame, 188
Tiwa people in northeast India, 411
Track One paradigm of peacemaking activities in South Asia, 212
Track Two paradigm of peacemaking activities in South Asia, 212–214, 216–218, 226–228
Track Three paradigm of peacemaking activities in South Asia, 212, 224–225
Trade, illegal, 95. See also Corruption; Crime, criminal activities and organized; Drug trafficking
Tripura region in India, 422–425
Truman, Harry, 366
Turajanzade, Qazi A., 101–103, 174
Turkestan, 168
Turkmenistan: civil society, development of, 70; democracy, 24; economic conditions, 70; General Agreement on the Establishment of Peace and National Accord in Tajikistan, 176; Inter-Tajik Dialogue on national reconciliation, 175; neutrality policy, 70; refugees, 77; regional introduction to Central Asia, 69–70; resources and conflicts, 69–70, 114; Uzbekistan, relations with, 70

Unemployment, 94, 147–148, 164, 183, 438. See also Economic conditions/issues
United Arab Emirates, 116
United Nations: Afghanistan, 20, 112, 116–118; Agenda for Peace, 31; Chittagong Hill Tracts, indigenous struggle in the, 309, 310; Commission for India and Pakistan (UNCIP), 364, 365, 370–371; Convention of the Law of the Seas, 257; Convention on the Non-Navigational Uses of International Water Courses, 283; Development Program (UNDP), 112, 146, 158, 181, 200, 203, 309, 494; Ferghana Valley, 146, 155–156, 158; High Commissioner for Refugees (UNHCR), 268; Human Rights Commission, 310; International Convention on the Protection of the Rights of all Migrant Workers and Members of Their Families, 275; Kashmir, 364, 365, 370–371; Maoist insurgency in Nepal, 440; Military Observers Group in India, 370; Office for Project Services (UNOPS), 158; Office for the Coordination of Humanitarian Affairs, 117; peacebuilding principles, 130; policy recommendations for Central Asia, 83; refugees/migrations, 275; Sri Lanka, 494; Sub-Commission on Prevention of Discrimination and Protection of Minorities, 310; success and failures, 31; Tajikistan, 36, 37, 173, 174–176, 181, 182; Taliban, 117; track three dialogues, 224–225; UNHCR Handbook on Procedures and Criteria on Determining Refugee Status, 268; UNICEF (United Nations Children Fund), 309, 494; Uzbekistan, 200, 203; water conflicts/issues, 283; Working Group on Indigenous Populations, 310
United States Information Services (USIS), 217
Urdu language. See Sindhi-Mohajir conflict in Pakistan
U.S. Commission on Religious Freedom on Pakistan (2001), 478
Utaev, Abdullah, 103
Uttaranchal/Uttarakhand state in India, 347, 349
Uyghur population in China, 67, 87–88
Uzbekistan: Association of Businesswomen in Uzbekistan, 202–203; authoritarian rule, 191–192; China, relations with, 199; clan networks, 195–196; conflict dynamics, 191–199; democracy, 24; drug trafficking, 197; economic conditions/issues, 70, 95, 190, 196–198, 202–203; environmental issues, 203; ethnic tensions, 86, 190; Ferghana clan, 195; General Agreement on the Establishment of Peace and National Accord in Tajikistan, 176; health issues, 203, 205; history behind, 188–190; Hizb ut-Tahrir, 71, 92, 106–107, 148, 154, 182, 183, 194–196; human rights/abuses, 159, 191, 196, 200, 202; Human Rights Society, 202; Independent Human Rights Organization, 202; Internet, the, 201; interstate relations, 198–199; Inter-Tajik Dialogue on national reconciliation, 175; Islamic Renaissance Party, 99–100, 103; Islam Lashkari militias, 104; Kyrgyzstan, relations with, 105; local people/internal parties, 179, 202, 203, 205;

multi-track diplomacy, 201–203; 911 attacks on America, 159; nongovernmental organizations, 201–203, 206; official conflict management, 199–201; "Operation Enduring Freedom," 21; People's Democratic Party, 192; prospects for peace, 203–204; recommendations for effective conflict prevention, 204–206; refugees, 77; regional introduction to Central Asia, 67–68, 70–72; religion and conflict, 71, 90–92, 99–100, 103–107, 190–195, 198; resources, informational, 206–208; resources and conflicts, 90–94, 196–199; Russia, relations with, 199; Russia-Iran-Uzbekistan-Tajikistan-India axis, 113; Shanghai Cooperation Organization, 154; social conditions/issues, 196–198; Soviet Union, the former, 188–190; Tajikistan, relations with, 68, 168, 170, 172; terrorism, the war on, 77; trade, illegal, 95; Turkmenistan, relations with, 70; Washington-Tashkent alliance, 78. See also Ferghana Valley; Islamic Movement of Uzbekistan

Vajpayee, Atal B., 213, 229, 295, 368, 371, 372
Vali, Sheykh A., 103
Verghese, B. G., 218
Vermani, Vineet, 217
Vidarbha region in India, 349–350
Vienna Agreements (1990 and 1992), 239
Vindhya Pradesh region in India, 350
Visas and refugees/migrations, 273

Al Wahdat, 99
Wajed, Sheikh H., 301
Warsaw Pact, 239
Washington-Tashkent alliance, 78
Water conflicts/issues: Afghanistan-Iran border conflict, 253; Bangladesh, 214, 263, 279–281; basin approach, 282; Cauvery River, 277–278; development vs. sustainability, 288; evolution of water conflicts, 281–284; Ferghana Valley, 147, 151–152, 162, 163; Ganges Water Treaty, 214, 263, 279–280; India, 214, 241, 243, 244, 256, 259, 263, 278–281, 284–286; Indus Waters Treaty (1960), 241, 243, 244, 256, 278–279, 281; Kaptai Dam, 304; Mahakali Treaty (1996), 280–281; Morse Commission and Narmada (Sardar Sarovar) water project in India, 284; Narmada (Sardar Sarovar) project, 284–286; Nepal, 215, 223, 280–281; Pakistan, 241, 243, 244, 255–257, 278–279, 304; people, project-affected, 286–287; policy recommendations for Central Asia, 80; politics/political issues, 283; regional networks/cooperation, 282; resources, informational, 288–290; riparian perspective, 281; state boundaries,

flaws in carving, 212; traditions, reviving old, 287–288
Weapon systems and events of Sept. 11, 10
Western aid/interventions: Afghanistan, 119–120, 128–132, 182–183; Chittagong Hill Tracts, indigenous struggle in the, 309; confidence-building measures, 243; Ferghana Valley, 161, 162, 203; Maldives, 253; Maoist insurgency in Nepal, 435; nonofficial dialogues in South Asia, 225; Pakistan, 450; past conflict resolution situations too narrowly Western, 33; policy recommendations for Central Asia, 78, 82–84; regional introduction to Central Asia, 75; Russia, 78; South Asia Regional Initiative/Energy, 219; Sri Lanka, 493–495; Uzbekistan, 205; Washington-Tashkent alliance, 78. See also World Bank
Wickremesinghe, Ranil, 23, 490
Women: Afghanistan, 44–45, 115; All India Progressive Women's Organization, 43; Assam state in India, 414; Chittagong Hill Tracts, indigenous struggle in the, 313; emotions/inspiration and working for peace, 56; Forum on Women in Security and International Affairs in Bangladesh, 230; India, 43–44; Manipur, 421; Maoist insurgency in Nepal, 443; multiculturalism in India, 334; Nagaland, 417–418; nonofficial dialogues in South Asia, 224, 225, 229–230; policy recommendations for Central Asia, 79; refugees/migrations, 268; regional introduction to Central Asia, 69; Revolutionary Association of the Women of Afghanistan, 44–45, Sri Lanka, 493; Tajikistan, 42–43; Taliban regime (Afghanistan), 45, 115; trafficking in, cross-border, 212; Uzbekistan, 202–203
Work permits and refugees/migrations, 273–274
World Bank: Afghanistan, 112, 114; Indus Treaty (1960), 243, 278, 281; Narmada (Sardar Sarovar) water project in India, 284; Sri Lanka, 494; Uzbekistan, 205
World Commission on Dams (WCD), 287
Wular Lake, 256

Yadav, Laloo P., 396, 400
Yamuna River, 352
Yoldashev, Tahir, 104
Young Asians and nonofficial dialogues in South Asia, 230
Yugoslavia, 60
Yussuf, Mohammad, 104

Zahir, Mohammad, 118
Zia, Begum K., 301
Zia, Khaleda, 309, 310
Zia-ul-Haq, 448, 449, 456, 459, 469
Ziayev, Mirza, 103

Index of Organizations

Page numbers presented in bold type indicate an entry in the Directory.

Action Committee Against Arms Race
  (ACAAR), 224–225, 229
Adult Training Center, Osh Affiliation (ATC),
  546
Afghan Development Association (ADA),
  565
Afghanistan Peace Association (APA), **608**
Afghanistan—America Foundation, **608**
Afghan NGO's Coordination Bureau (ANCB),
  565
Aga Khan Foundation, 178, 476–477
Agency Coordinating Body for Afghan Relief
  (ACBAR), **566**
Agenda for Peace, 31
Agenda for Reconciliation (AfR), **600**
AHIMSA—Centre for Conflict Resolution &
  Peace, **576**
Ajoka Theater Group, 39–40
All India Progressive Women's Organization,
  43
Amnesty International (AI), 196, 314, 367,
  422, 440, **600**
Anti-Slavery Society, 314
Anuvrat Global Organisation (ANUVIBHA),
  518
Applied Conflict Resolution Organizations
  Network (ACRON), **609**
Asia Foundation, **609**
Asia Pacific Center for Justice and Peace
  (APCJP), **610**
Asia Pacific Economic Commission (APEC),
  211
Asia Plus, **591**
Asian Cultural Forum on Development, **599**
Asian Human Rights Commission (ARHC),
  518
Association for Communal Harmony in Asia
  (ACHA), **610**
Association of Businesswomen in Uzbekistan,
  202–203
Association of SAARC Speakers and

Parliamentarians, 230
Association of Southeast Asian Nations
  (ASEAN), **540**
Association of Southeast Asian Nations—
  Regional Forum (ARF), 213, **541**
Association of the Parents of Disappeared
  Persons, 375
Association of Uzbekistan for Sustainable
  Water Resources Development (AUSWRD),
  617
Australian National University, **508**

Bangladesh Institute of International and
  Strategic Studies (BIISS), **509**
Bangladesh Inter-religious Council for Peace
  and Justice (BICPAJ), **510**
Berghof Research Center for Constuctive
  Conflict Management—SRI Lanka, **576**
Bishkek Migration Management Center
  (BMMC), **547**
Bradford University Department of Peace
  Studies, **601**
British Agency Afghanistan Group, **602**
Brookings Institution, 227

Canadian International Development Agency
  (CIDA), 225, 493
CARE International, 498
Center. See also Centre
Center for Community Dialogue &
  Communication (PRASANNI), **577**
Center for Conflict Management (CCM), **543**
Center for Conflict Studies and Regional
  Research (CCSRR), **591**
Center for Policy Research, 214, 222
Center for Science and Environment, 221
Center for Social Research, **544**
Center for Social Research of the National
  Academy of Science of the Kyrgyz
  Republic (CSR), **548**
Center for Social Technologies (CST), **592**

Center for the Study of Developing Societies, 215, 223
Center for the Support of Democracy (CSD), **544**
Center for Youth Initiatives, **593**
Center of Policy Dialogue, Dhaka, 222
Central Asia and the Caucasus Information and Analytical Center (IAC), **587**
Centre. *See also* Center
Centre for Alternatives, 215, 223, **510**
Centre for Development Alternatives, **577**
Centre for Development Research (CDRB), **511**
Centre for Dialogue and Reconciliation (CDR), **519**
Centre for North East Studies and Policy Research, **519**
Centre for Policy Alternatives, 496, **578**
Centre for Policy Dialogue (CDP), **511**
Centre for Policy Research (CPR), **520**
Centre for Policy Research and Analysis (CEPRA), **579**
Centre for Protection of Minorities and Against Racism and Discrimination in Bhutan, **552**
Centre for Society and Religion (CSR), 496, **579**
Centre for Study of Society and Secularism, 344, **520**
Centre for the Study of Peace, **512**
Christian Study Centre (CSC), **566**
CIMERA, 158, 202, **588**
Citizen's Commission for South Asia, 223
Citizens Media Commission, 230–231
Climate Asia Network South Asia, 221
Coalition for Action on South Asian Cooperation (CASAC), 225, 521
Collaborative for Development Action (CDA), **611**
Committee on Studies for Cooperation and Development, 215
Conciliation Resources (CR), **602**
Confederation of Indian Industries, 223
Consortium of Humanitarian Agencies (CHA), **580**
Co-operation Center for Afghanistan (CCA), **567**
Co-operation for Peace and Unity (CPAU), **568**
Coordinating Council for Human Rights in Bangladesh (CCHRB), **512**
Council for Security Cooperation in the Asia Pacific (CSCAP), **552**

Delhi Policy Group (DPG), **521**
Department of Peace and Conflict Research, Uppsala University, **587**
Dialogue, **545**
Disaster Institute and Center for Science and Environment in India, 222

Doon School Old Boys Society, 224
DPKO Lessons Learned Unit, **611**

EastWest Institute (EWI), **612**
European Centre for Conflict Prevention (ECCP), 3, 4, 47, **562**

Fellowship of Reconciliation India (FORI), **522**
Fellowships in South Asian Alternatives, 215, 223
FEWER, **603**
Fidokor, **594**
Ford Foundation, 217, 218, 225
Forum for Protection of Human Rights (FOPHUR), **553**
Forum on Early Warning and Early Response (FEWER), **603**
Forum on Women in Security and International Affairs in Bangladesh, 230
Foundation for Research on International Environment, National Development and Security, **569**
Foundation to Support Civil Initiatives (FSCI), **595**
Freedom House, 24

Gandhi Peace Foundation, 522
Goodwill Ambassadors Networks project, 157–158
Group for International Solidarity (GRINSO), **553**

Harvard Program on Humanitarian Policy and Conflict Research, 440
Human Rights Alert (HRA), 421
Human Rights and Peace Campaign Nepal (HURPEC), **554**
Human Rights and Peace Society (HURPES), **554**
Human Rights Commission of Pakistan (HRCP), **569**
Human Rights Organisation of Nepal (HURON), **555**
Human Rights Society, 202
Human Rights Watch (HRW), 367, 391, 403, **612**

Independent Group for South Asian Cooperation, 215, 218
Independent Human Rights Organization of Uzbekistan, 202
India-Bangladesh Dialogues, 213–214, 217–218
India-Bangladesh Joint Chambers of Commerce and Industry, 217
Indian Confederation of Indigenous and Tribal People, **523**
Indian Council for Research on International

Economic Relations, 218
Indian Institute for Peace, Disarmament &
Environmental Protection (IIDEP), **523**
Indian Social Institute (ISI), **524**
Indian Society of Human Rights (ISHR), **524**
India-Pakistan Friendship Society, 217
India-Pakistan Joint Chambers of Commerce
and Industry, 218
India-Pakistan Peoples Forum for Peace and
Democracy, 216
India-Pakistan Soldiers Initiative for Peace,
213, 216
India Peace Centre (IPC), **525**
India-Sri Lanka Joint Business Council, 216
Indira Ghandi Institute of Development
Research (IGIDR), **525**
INFORM, 495, **580**
Informal Sector Service Centre (INSEC), 441,
555
Institute for Conflict Analysis and Resolution
(ICAR), **613**
Institute for Conflict Management (ICM), **526**
Institute for Development and Communication
(IDC), **527**
Institute for International Mediation and
Conflict Resolution, 441
Institute for Multi-Track Diplomacy (IMTD),
48, 441, **614**
Institute for Policy Studies and Marga
Institute in Colombo, 222
Institute for Regional Studies (IFRS), **549**
Institute of Human Rights Communication,
Nepal, (IHRICON), **556**
Institute of Integrated Development Studies,
222
Institute of Peace and Conflict Studies (IPCS),
528
Institute of Regional Studies, 570
Inter-Community Peace Initiative, **529**
Interdisciplinary Research Programme on
Causes of Human Rights Violations
(PIOOM), 17–18, 24–27.
International Alert (IA), 496, **604**
International Center for Peace Initiatives,
230
International Centre for Ethnic Studies
(ICES), 496, **581**
International Centre for Human Rights
Development, 480
International Centre for Peace Initiatives
(ICPI), **530**
International Centre for Peace Studies, **531**
International Committee of the Red
Cross(ICRC), 31, 178, 476, 498, **588**
International Conflict Research (INCORE),
604
International Crisis Group (ICG), 143,
158–159, 202, **515**
International Crisis Group, Central Asia
Project, **550**

International Human Rights Internship
Program, 422
International Institute for Human Rights,
Environment and Development
(INHURED), **556**
International Labour Organization (ILO), 146,
310
International Monetary Fund (IMF), 205
International Peace Academy, 230
International Service for Human Rights, 422
International Studies of the Institute of
Oriental Studies in Moscow, 176
International Work Group for Indigenous
Affairs (IWGIA), 314, **517**
Internews, 201–202, 206
Inter-Religious Peace Foundation (IRPF),
40–41, 497, **582**
Inter-Tajik Dialogue on National
Reconciliation, 175, 176–180
Islamic Coordination Council (ICC), **570**
Ittifok, 157, **593**

Jammu and Kashmir Hussaini Relief
Committee, 375
Japan Center for Preventive Diplomacy
(JCPD), **541**
Japan Foundation, 225
Japan Institute of International Affairs (JIIA),
542
Justice and Peace Commission, **571**

Kashmir Council for Human Rights (KCHR),
605
Kashmir Foundation for Peace and
Development Studies, 375, **531**
Kashmiri-Canadian Council (KCC), **516**
Kettering Foundation, 176

Lebanon Conflict Resolution Network, 52
Lutheran World Federation in Guatemala, 52

Manizha Information and Education Centre,
595
Marga Institute, 222, 496, **582**
Martin Luther King Centre for Democracy
and Human Rights, **532**
Médicins Sans Frontières (MSF), 203, **515**
Minority Rights Group International (MRG),
314, **605**
Monash Asia Institute (MAI), **507**
Mothers of the Plaza del Mayo, 56
Movement for Inter-racial Justice and
Equality (MIRJE), 495, **583**

Naga International Support Center, 418
Naga Peoples Movement for Human Rights,
532
National Association of Political Scientists of
Tajikistan (NAPST), **596**
National Centre for South Asian Studies

(NCSAS), **507**
National Commission for Justice and Peace (NCJP), **571**
National Peace Campaign (NPC), **557**
National Peace Council of Sri Lanka (NPC), **583**
Netherlands Institute of International Relations "Clingendael," **563**
Network of South Asian Writers, 215, 220, 223
North East Network (NEN), **533**
North South Security program of King's College, London, 230

Office for the Coordination of Humanitarian Affairs (OCHA), **589**
Office of the OSCE High Commissioner on National Minorities, **563**
Open Society Institute (OSI), **614**
Organisation for Security and Co-operation in Europe (OSCE), 31, 82, 83, 159, 174, 179, 200, 206, **509**
Organisation for South Asian Peace (OSAP), **605**
Organising Committee Chittagong Hill Tracts Campaign, **564**
Osh Media Resource Center (OMRC), 158, **550**
Oxford Research Group, 56, 59

Pakistan Peace Coalition (PPC), **573**
Pakistan-India People's Forum for Peace and Democracy, 38–39, 223–224, **534, 572**
Pakistan-India People's Solidarity Conference, 225
Parliamentarians for Global Action, 230
Peace for All, **513**
People's Forum for Human Rights (PFHRB), **557**
People's of Asia Forum, 218
People's Peace Front (PPF), **584**
People's Union for Civil Liberties (PUCL), **535**
PIOOM (Interdisciplinary Research Programme on Causes of Human Rights Violations), 17–18, 24–27.
Post-War Reconstruction and Development Unit (PRDU), **606**
PRASHANT, **536**
PRDU, **606**
Program on Peace Studies & Conflict Resolution, **573**
Public Committee for the Promotion of Democratic Processes, **596**

Quaker Peace and Service (QPS), 496

Rajiv Gandhi Foundation, 221
Rand Corporation, 227
Red Cross. See International Committee of the Red Cross
Regional Centre for Strategic Studies (RCSS), 215, 220, 223, 585
Research and Advisory Council of Afghanistan (RACA), **574**
Research School of Pacific and Asian Studies (RSPAS), **508**
Responding to Conflict (RTC), **607**
Revolutionary Association of the Women of Afghanistan (RAWA), **574**
Rockefeller Foundation, 225
Russia Center for Strategic Research, 176

SAMASEVAYA, **586**
SAWNET, 231
Search for Common Ground, 49, 59
Sewa Lanka Foundation, **586**
Shanghai Cooperation Organization (SCO), 154–155, 183, 199
Shanghai Five cooperation organization, 105, 154, 183
Sharq Research and Analysis Center, **597**
Silk Road—Road of Consolidation, **597**
Social and Economic Development Centre, 496
Society for Environment and Human Development (SEHD), **513**
Society for Human Rights and Education in Bhutan (SURE), **558**
Soros Foundation, 201
South Asia Center for Policy Studies, 215, 222
South Asia Citizens Web, 231
South Asia Forum for Human Rights (SAFHR), 222, 497, **559**
South Asia Human Development Forum Network (SAHDNet), **560**
South Asia Human Rights Documentation Centre (SAHRDC), 219–220, **536**
South Asia Labour Forum, 219
South Asia Network of Economic Institutes, 215, 218
South Asia Network on Women in Politics (SANWP), **537**
South Asia Partnership(SAP)—Bangladesh, **514**
South Asia Partnership(SAP)—Canada, **516**
South Asia Partnership(SAP)—India, **537**
South Asia Partnership(SAP)—Nepal, **560**
South Asia Partnership(SAP)—Pakistan, **575**
South Asia Regional Initiative/Energy, 219
South Asian Association for Regional Cooperation (SAARC), 211, 215, 218–223, 230, 371, 390, 402, 428, **561**
South Asian Dialogue, 215
South Asian Institute for Peace Studies (SAIPS), 441, **561**
South Asian Media Association, 221, 230
Spravedlivost Regional Human Rights Organisation, **551**

Sudmand, 598
Survival International, 314
Sustainable Development Policy Institute
  (SDPI), 215, 221, 223, 476, **575**
Swiss Agency for Development and
  Cooperation, 157
Swiss Peace Foundation (SPF), **589**

Tajikistan Center for Citizenship Education
  (TCCE), **598**
Tata Energy Research Institute at New Delhi,
  221
Technical Assistance for Rural Development
  (TARD), **514**
Traditions and Modernity (T&M), **599**
Tribal Welfare Society (TWS), **538**

UN Commission for India and Pakistan
  (UNCIP), 364, 365, 370–371
UN Department of Political Affairs (DPA),
  615
UN Development Programme (UNDP), 112,
  146, 158, 181, 200, 203, 309, 494, **615**
UN High Commissioner for Refugees
  (UNHCR), 268, **590**
UN Institute for Disarmament Research
  (UNIDIR), **590**
UN Office for Project Services (UNOPS), 158
UN Office for the Coordination of

Humanitarian Affairs, 117
UNESCO's Culture of Peace Program (CPP),
  517
UNICEF (United Nations Children Fund),
  309, 494
Union for Defence of the Aral Sea and the
  Amadarya (UDASA), **617**
United States Institute of Peace (USIP), 178,
  616
University of Colombo, **579**
Unrepresented Nations and Peoples
  Organisation (UNPO), **564**
U.S. Agency for International Development
  (USAID), 155, 162, 203, 205, 219, 225

Wajir Peace Group, 56
W. Alton Jones Foundation, 225
West African Network for Peacebuilding
  (WANEP), 12–13, 54
Women in Security, Conflict Management and
  Peace (WISCOMP), 230, **539**
Women's Alliance for Peace and Human
  Rights in Afghanistan (WAPHA), **616**
Women's Initiative for Peace in South Asia
  (WIPSA), 224, 225, 230, **540**

Youth Human Rights Group (YHRG), **551**

ZHARiA, **545**

About the
Searching for Peace Program

The Searching for Peace Program of the European Centre for Conflict Prevention (ECCP) consists of several regional projects. The ultimate aim of these projects is to contributue to a peaceful transformation of violent conflicts around the world by filling the gaps in information, communication, and coordination that exist in the fields of conflict prevention and peacebuilding. The Searching for Peace publication series is the result of an ongoing process involving research and regional seminars, as well as collaboration with local partners, practitioners, and prominent international scholars.

Searching for Peace in Central and South Asia is the third book in the series, following *Searching for Peace in Europe and Eurasia* (2001) and *Searching for Peace in Africa* (1999). Subsequent volumes will cover Southeast and East Asia, the Middle East and North Africa, and Latin America and the Caribbean.

About the Book

Continuing a widely acclaimed series, *Searching for Peace in Central and South Asia* provides critical background information, up-to-date surveys of the violent conflicts in Afghanistan, Bangladesh, the Ferghana Valley, India, Nepal, Pakistan, Sri Lanka, Tajikistan, and Uzbekistan, and a directory of 187 organizations working in their field of conflict prevention and peacebuilding in the region. The authors include detailed, objective descriptions of ongoing activities, as well as asessments of future prospects for conflict resolution, focusing on efforts to make civil society an integral part of any peace process.

Monique Mekenkamp is coordinator of the Asia Program of the European Centre for Conflict Prevention (ECCP), based in Utrecht, The Netherlands. **Paul van Tongeren** is founder and executive director of the ECCP. **Hans van de Veen** is senior journalist and coordinator of an independent network of journalists, Environment and Development Productions, based in Amsterdam.

European Centre for Conflict Prevention
PO Box 14069
3508 SC Utrecht
The Netherlands

Tel: +31 30 242 7777
Fax: +31 30 236 9268
info@conflict-prevention.net
www.conflict-prevention.net